FROMMER'S
DOLLARWISE GUIDE™ TO AUSTRIA & HUNGARY

by Darwin Porter

Assisted by Danforth Prince

D0882410

1987-88 Edition

Published by Prentice Hall Press
A Division of Simon & Schuster, Inc.
Gulf + Western Building
One Gulf + Western Plaza
New York, New York 10023

ISBN 0–671–62057–6

Manufactured in the United States of America

*Although every effort was made to ensure the accuracy
of price information appearing in this book,
it should be kept in mind that prices
can and do fluctuate in the course of time.*

CONTENTS

MAPS

ACKNOWLEDGMENT

The author wishes to express his appreciation to Margaret Foresman for her enormous contributions in the preparation of this guide.

INFLATION ALERT: We don't have to tell you that inflation has hit Austria and Hungary as it has everywhere else. In researching this book we have made every effort to obtain up-to-the-minute prices, but even the most conscientious researcher cannot keep up with the current pace of inflation. As we go to press, we believe we have obtained the most reliable data possible. Nonetheless, in the lifetime of this edition— particularly its second year (1988)—the wise traveler will add 15% to 20% to the prices quoted throughout these pages.

A DISCLAIMER: Although every effort was made to ensure the accuracy of the prices and travel information appearing in this book, it should be kept in mind that prices do fluctuate in the course of time, and that information does change under the impact of the varied and volatile factors that affect the travel industry.

Readers should also note that the establishments described under Readers' Selections or Suggestions have not in many cases been inspected by the author and that the opinions expressed there are those of the individual reader(s) only. They do not in any way represent the opinions of the publisher or author of this guide.

Introduction

A DOLLARWISE GUIDE TO AUSTRIA AND HUNGARY

1. The Reason Why
2. Dollarwise—What It Means
3. About This Book
4. A Word About Cost
5. The $25-a-Day Travel Club

THIS BOOK IS about two small countries in Central Europe that were once the seat of a great empire. The territories and lands of both countries have been reduced by a roller-coaster ride from the heights to the depths. Austria, for example, only regained its full sovereignty as late as July 27, 1955; whereas Hungary, unsuccessful in its attempt at revolution in 1956, is still a Soviet-bloc land, having lost much of its territory, including Transylvania, to neighboring countries (in this case Romania).

1. The Reason Why

Even after the loss of its former colonies, Austria was left with a land of scenic grandeur and soaring alpine peaks. There are those (and perhaps I join them) who say that, when taken as a whole, Austria is the most beautiful country on earth.

A great world power in the 18th and 19th centuries, Austria still preserves reminders of its past in its epic monuments and grandiose baroque buildings.

The Federal Republic of Austria consists of nine fairly autonomous provinces, called Bundesländer: Vienna (of course), Upper Austria, Lower Austria, Salzburg, Tyrol, Vorarlberg, Styria, Carinthia, and tiny Burgenland. Each of these provinces contains great geographical and cultural differences, and it is the lucky visitor who gets to see all of Austria, which, though small, takes many weeks to visit in its entirety (and even then you'll have only skimmed the surface).

Austria is a sports-oriented country (and not just for skiers). It's also rich in music and drama, in art, museums, galleries, churches, and cathedrals.

West Germany (with which it once had an ill-fated alliance in the 1930s and early 1940s) lies to the north. On the northeast is Czechoslovakia, on the east is Hungary, and on the southeast lies Yugoslavia, three countries which Austria used to dominate in part. Of course Italy is to the south, and on its west is Switzerland, with which it often fought battles until that even tinier country fully gained its independence from Habsburg domination.

Austria is peaceful today, and if it thinks of empire, it is only nostalgically (I've talked to many Viennese who remember the last parade in their city of the Austro-Hungarian Empire). Nowadays its German-speaking populace (English is virtually a second language) are among the most hospitable and friendly in Europe.

Austria, like Switzerland, no longer sends its soldiers marching across other frontiers but is itself invaded in both summer and winter. Austria is a true biseasonal country, enjoying both a huge summer and winter tourist industry. The new invaders are tourists, and they come to seek out the grandeur of "the roof of Europe." About 75% of Austria is mountainous. Austria today has about 7.5 million in population, a people associated with gemütlichkeit, a warm, contented, friendly feeling generated by those who appreciate the good life.

This is best summed up by a popular saying in the country: "In Britain everything is allowed that is not expressly forbidden, in Germany everything is verboten that is not expressly permitted, and in Austria everything is permitted that is not expressly forbidden!"

A comparable amount of freedom and permissiveness doesn't exist in the Hungary of today, yet perhaps more than in any other country in Eastern Europe, Hungary is welcoming visitors as never before. It has made border crossings easier (visas are now granted at the frontier), and it is sprucing up its monuments and building better hotels and finer restaurants to receive the millions who cross its borders annually.

Austria itself is one of the least expensive countries of Western Europe, but Hungary is so cheap that the Austrians themselves visit it sometimes just to get their hair done.

These two countries which once formed the heart of the Austro-Hungarian Empire have long been separated by the tides of history—Austria now neutral, Hungary a part of the Warsaw Pact Nations. But—and only for the purposes of this guidebook—we will join them for a reunion once more. Vienna, now more than ever as in olden days, is the gateway to Budapest.

FROM THE ALPS TO THE DANUBE: The scenery of Austria is more varied than that of Switzerland, combining rich agricultural plains along the Danube, alpine peaks and lakes, and castles (often in ruins) that evoke the Middle Ages. All that, combined with acres and acres of vineyards, has made Austria a tourist mecca since the 19th century.

The name Austria, or Österreich, means "Eastern Empire," a designation given to the far eastern sector of the lands conquered by Charlemagne. But from prehistoric times, the part of Europe centering around present-day Austria has been a crossroads, with the Danube Valley allowing traverse both by land and water.

During the "twilight of the Habsburgs," culminating in 1918, Austria, poised between the West and the East, lost much of its territory and since then has faced international humiliation.

Memories of Hitler—who turned their country into a virtual colony of the Third Reich, in spite of the sentiment of many Austrians at the time who wanted to "amalgamate" with Nazi Germany—and of the succeeding partial Soviet occupation are still strong in the minds of many Austrians. However, despite reverses which may well be credited to the *hubris* of their rulers, Austria has recovered its spirit admirably.

This country, once reaching from czarist Russia to the Adriatic, now smaller than the state of Maine, is still a land of music. Its festivals, such as the one at Salzburg which is famous the world over, its skiing, and those monumental baroque edifices referred to hold an appeal that I, along with thousands of others, find irresistible.

Vienna is the most distinguished capital city in the German-speaking world, but although they share a common language, Austria and Germany are two very different countries. A visit to one will hardly be like a visit to the other.

Austria has one of the lowest inflation rates in Europe, and among the trio of big skiing countries, it's cheaper than either Switzerland or France.

As fat as this book is—probably the single biggest guide ever published on the hotels and restaurants of Austria—you should know that it represents only a fraction of the actual facilities available. What I'm sharing with you are my favorites. Perhaps, using the book as your seed core, you'll find dozens more on your own.

Likewise, this is the first major guide in English to describe in any detail the hotels, restaurants, shops, and nightclubs of Hungary, along with the country's many tourist attractions. And not only those found in Budapest but also in its colorful provinces, which take in the famed Danube Bend, Lake Balaton, and the Great Hungarian Plain.

THE BEST OF AUSTRIA AND HUNGARY: I have set for myself the formidable task of seeking out Austria and Hungary at their finest and condensing them between the covers of a book. The best towns, villages, cities, and sightseeing attractions are documented, as well as the best hotels, restaurants, bars, cafés, shops, and nightspots.

But the best need not be the most expensive. My ultimate aim—beyond that of familiarizing you with the offerings of Austria and Hungary—is to stretch your dollar power . . . to reveal to you that you need not pay scalper's prices for charm, top-grade comfort, and gourmet-level food.

In this guide I'll devote a lot of attention to those old tourist meccas—Vienna, Salzburg, Innsbruck, Budapest—focusing on both their obvious and their hidden treasures. But they are not the full "reason why" of this book. Important as they are, they simply do not reflect fully the widely diverse and scenic countryside of Austria and Hungary. To discover that, you must venture deep into the Tyrolean country or perhaps to the romantic windswept puszta of the Great Hungarian Plain.

2. Dollarwise—What It Means

In brief, this is a guidebook giving specific details—including prices—about Austrian and Hungarian hotels, restaurants, bars, cafés, sightseeing attractions, nightlife, and tours. Establishments in many price ranges have been documented and described, although I am constantly searching for bargains. Along with the deluxe citadels, I am more interested in the family-run *gasthof*-type place where you can often bask in gemütlich warmth but at low prices. In all cases, deluxe or budget, each establishment was measured by a strict yardstick of value. If they measured up—meaning if they were the best in their category—they were included.

Now, more than ever, one needs an accurate guidebook including tips for saving money. By careful planning and selecting from my listings, you'll find the true Austrian or Hungarian experience while remaining within a reasonable budget. This applies to independent travelers as well as those who visit Austria or Hungary on a tour. If you're one of the latter, and have already obtained your flight ticket and hotel, you'll still need a guide to direct you to restaurants, nightlife, and sightseeing attractions rarely covered on a package tour. If you're given a car, then you'll be in the market for suggestions of where to go in the country once you leave either Vienna or Salzburg, whichever is your "gateway" city.

SOME WORDS OF EXPLANATION: No restaurant, inn, hotel, nightclub, shop, or café paid to be mentioned in this book. What you read are entirely personal recommendations; in many cases the proprietors never knew their establishments were being visited or investigated for inclusion in a travel guide.

Unfortunately, although I have made every effort to be as accurate as possible, prices change, and they rarely go downward.

When checking into a hotel, always inquire about the rate and agree on it. That policy can save much embarrassment and disappointment when it comes time to settle the tab. If the prices quoted are not the same as those mentioned in this book, remember that my prices reflect those in effect at the time this edition was researched.

This guide is revised cover to cover every other year. But even in a book that appears with such frequency, it may happen that that cozy little wine tavern of a year ago has changed its stripes, blossoming out with cut-velvet walls, crystal chandeliers, and dining tabs that include the decorator's fee and the owner's new villa. It may further develop that some of the people or settings I've described are no longer there or have changed in this fast-moving world.

All that leads up to the next major point—

AN INVITATION TO READERS: Like all the books in the "Dollarwise" series, the *Dollarwise Guide to Austria and Hungary* hopes to maintain a continuing dialogue between its author and its readers. All of us share a common aim, I'm sure, and that is to travel as widely and as well as possible, at the lowest possible cost. In achieving that goal, your comments and suggestions can be of aid to other readers.

Therefore if you come across a particularly appealing hotel, restaurant, shop, or bargain, please don't keep it to yourself.

Comments about existing listings are always helpful. The fact that a hotel or restaurant (or any other establishment) appears in this edition doesn't mean that it will necessarily appear in future editions if readers report that its service has slipped or that its prices have not only risen drastically but unfairly.

Even if you like a place I've recommended, your comments are especially welcome, and have been known to brighten many a gray day.

Send your comments or finds—and, yes, those inevitable complaints that always arise—to Darwin Porter, c/o Frommer Books, Prentice Hall Press, 15th Floor, One Gulf & Western Plaza, New York, NY 10023.

3. About This Book

Here's how the *Dollarwise Guide to Austria and Hungary* sets forth its information:

In Part One, Chapter I explores the methods of "getting to" and "getting around" Austria. The most obvious means of reaching it would be by air from America, or perhaps you'll go by car after your exploration of Germany, Italy, or Switzerland. But my coverage of transportation within Austria will focus mainly on the railway lines and bargain passes.

Chapter II provides a general discussion of the country and a brief historical survey, along with a description of its people, customs, hotels, and cuisine. Winter and summer sports and practical facts about the country conclude this chapter.

Chapter III wings in on Vienna, one of the great tourist attractions of Europe, and covers all categories of hotel—deluxe, first class, middle bracket, inexpensive—and a large number of pensions (boarding houses). Restaurants, coffeehouses, and cafés are also surveyed.

Chapter IV continues the exploration of Vienna, focusing on sightseeing attractions, shops, and nightlife.

Crisscrossed by the Danube, Lower Austria, covered in Chapter V, is a land of castles and vineyards. Hotels are generally inexpensive, of the gasthaus type, but many first-class resorts exist in such spots as Baden. The chapter explores the Wienerwald (Vienna Woods), along with the wine villages. An itinerary, with sights, food, and inns along the "Wine Road," is presented. The major winter sports and mountain-air resorts in the high peaks of Semmering and Schneeberg are described. This chapter also explores another wine district, Weinviertel, north of Vienna, lying between the Danube and Czechoslovakia. Although the chapter deals with trips on Danube paddleboat steamers, the most space is devoted to castles and abbeys in the area—some in ruins, some turned into hotels, others into sightseeing attractions. Chief among these is the Benedictine abbey at Melk, the largest in Lower Austria.

Burgenland, described in Chapter VI, is known for its gardens, castles, and fortresses. We'll visit the mysterious Neusiedler See, a shallow, saltwater lake. This chapter adds a little paprika to the book, because it is much like Hungary. Spa and castle hotels will be surveyed, along with more modest guest houses. Burgenland is one of the great bargain areas of Austria and is rich in sights.

Chapter VII, on Salzburg, takes in the "city of Mozart." The annual Mozart Festival is described, along with both "Left Bank" and "Right Bank" tour notes. A full range of hotels, from deluxe to inexpensive, is surveyed, including some special ones in the environs. Likewise, restaurants range from inexpensive brewery-operated establishments to first-class selections serving an international cuisine. Special restaurants in the environs, including some with terraces and belvederes overlooking the Alps, are covered. Attractions range from Mozart's birthplace to the Fortress Hohensalzburg, along with details of how to get about, including by aerial cable railway. Nightlife takes in the casino, and there's also a sports section, as the Gaisberg mountain lies on the outskirts of the city.

Chapter VIII, Land Salzburg, covers that area of sports and spas—famous the world over—which lie within easy reach of Salzburg. Our selection of hotels ranges from the deluxe ones at Badgastein to modest mountain lodges. The great High Alpine Highway, the Grossglockner Road, is described, with peaks at 12,000 feet and views at 8,000-foot levels. A full range of towns includes hotels near Radstädter Tauern Pass, one of the most prestigious ski areas in Land Salzburg, and such famous resorts as Zell am See.

Chapter IX goes into Upper Austria, which is crossed in part by the Danube. Here the Salzkammergut, the lake country, is the most popular area with visitors. Major attention is devoted to Linz, the capital of Upper Austria, and its many sights nearby. The baroque Augustinian abbey of St. Florian, with its Bruckner organ and lavishly decorated imperial rooms, is one of the chief sights of the country. The highlights of this province emphasize attractions along the Danube. Little-known places are spotlighted, including Enns, the oldest town in Austria. The outstanding castles and abbeys of the area include Kremsmünster Abbey, founded in A.D. 777. A special section is devoted to

Bad Ischl, the fashionable spa and winter sports center where Franz Joseph held summer court in the heyday of Imperial Austria.

Chapter X turns to Innsbruck and Tyrol, the favorite part of Austria for nearly all visiting Americans. The obvious attention goes to the capital, baroque-style Innsbruck, acclaimed by many as one of the loveliest towns of Europe. Innsbruck's sights, hotels, restaurants, shops, and nightlife are followed by such sights in the environs as the winter-sports center at Igls. The Stubai Valley is previewed, both as a summer center and a winter ski mecca, with its glacier and mountains. A section includes one of the Tyrol's most exciting events, an excursion along the Karwendel railway, traveling by electric train along the Austrian-Bavarian border. Winter sports centers such as Seefeld are surveyed. Lienz, called by many "the prettiest little city in Europe," is given a special bouquet, and Kitzbühel, one of the best-known towns in Austria, is cited for exceptional ski facilities. The chapter includes information on the famous Zugspitze, from which at nearly 10,000 feet one can see the Swiss Alps and part of Bavaria. The valleys of the Tyrol, including Achen, Tuxer, and Ziller, are surveyed, along with a full range of Tyrolean hotels and restaurants, plus shopping for such specialties as dirndls, lederhosen, woodcarvings, and those famous Tyrolean hats.

Austria's westernmost province, Vorarlberg, unfolds in Chapter XI. It's much like Switzerland. Here we'll center mainly at Bregenz, a little town on the Bodensee (Lake Constance), and we'll explore the Bregenz Forest, a land of lovely woods, alpine meadows, and highlights. For the most part, hotels and restaurants in the area are small, family-type operations. Stübe taverns and restaurants—some of them centuries old—are presented.

Carinthia, in Chapter XII, is the southernmost part of Austria, bordering Italy. Framed by high mountains, it's a land of lakes and narrow valleys. Its best-known summer resorts lie around Wörthersee, and the most fashionable spot on the lake, Velden, has first-class hotels and boarding houses, including one of the finest in Austria, the baroque Schloss Velder. Winter sports resorts, such as Kanzelhöhe, known for its "perfect snow" and sunshine, are covered as well. There is a heavy emphasis on sports: boat races, waterskiing, swimming, and sailing.

The "green state," Styria, covered in Chapter XIII, in the southeastern part of the country, has Graz as its capital. The Styrian gray-and-green hunting suits are known all over the world. It is the Styrian version of the dirndl that is most popular. Its skiing terrains, publicized by the Alpine World Skiing Championships, are also covered. Old Graz is cited as one of the best bargain areas of Austria, in both restaurants and hotels. Other towns include Bad Aussee, an important spa and winter sports center, and the summer resort of Altausee, in the Styrian sector of the Salzkammergut. The province has many well-known hotels along with the relatively undocumented colorful old inns. Weinstüben are also very important here, along with cafés and pastry shops. A small number of museums are previewed, including the old buildings of the Landesmuseum Joanneum and the Styrian Folklore Museum.

Chapter XIV takes us into Hungary, introducing you to its history, people, food, drink, art, culture, and sports.

Chapter XV visits one of the most exciting tourist destinations in Europe—the lively capital of Hungary, Budapest, which is 1,000 years old. You'll be introduced to its many attractions, ranging from the beauty of its six bridges spanning the Danube to goulash parties. Hotels, restaurants, shopping, and day- and nighttime entertainment will be suggested.

The main sightseeing targets of the country outside Budapest are visited in

Chapter XVI, ranging from the Danube Bend to Lake Balaton to the Great Plain and puszta region, where horseback riding is the way to go. Great spas, a paprika factory, and vineyards from which come the famous wines of the country will be explored.

In Appendix I, Austrian (German) words and phrases for basic vocabulary use are listed, as well as menu listings you will find helpful.

Appendix II lists Hungarian vocabulary and menu terms.

4. A Word About Cost

Austria has had a low inflation rate when compared to some of the other countries of Western Europe. This has made the country one of the better buys in Europe.

Vienna and Salzburg are the two most expensive cities, with Innsbruck a runner-up. But one of the reasons for that is that these are the three cities the typical American visitor has heard of and therefore heads for. So I have a suggestion. If you have only a few days for Austria, don't just spend all your time in these high-priced tourist meccas, but head instead for a night or two in such old and historic cities as Graz and Linz where the hoteliers and the restaurateurs are not as tab-happy.

As for restaurants, the main meal of the day in Austria is taken at noon. That's when most restaurants, wanting to attract local business (not just the tourist), offer a fixed-price menu, often at an incredibly modest price. So when in Austria, do as the Austrians do and enjoy a most filling and reasonably priced lunch, perhaps ordering a much lighter dinner or supper when the tabs are likely to be much higher.

Sometimes, particularly if you're planning to tour a province such as the Tyrolean country, it's better to anchor into just one place in the countryside and take day trips. Chances are, you'll get a much better rate, especially on half-board arrangements, than you would by hotel-hopping, and because Austria is a small country, you can still explore everything that a province has to offer.

Whenever possible, try to book into a country inn on the half-board plan, which can mean amazing discounts for you. Half board means one main meal a day, along with breakfast. You're free to have lunch outside, and if you've planned your itinerary well, you can easily be back at your hotel for dinner in the evening.

If you'd like to see a part of Austria—any part, since all of them are fascinating—and economy is a major concern in your case, then there are some spots of Austria that are extremely reasonable, allowing you to keep costs bone-trimmed. Chief among these is Burgenland (see Chapter VI), a province much sought out and known to Europeans, but little known to most North Americans. Isolated, remote, almost forgotten (but not abandoned), East Tyrol is another such spot, as are certain sections of Styria and Carinthia.

Of course, if you can adjust your schedule, off-season travel can be quite a bargain in Austria. Sometimes hotel prices are lowered as much as 30%.

Costs have been rising greatly in Hungary, but after a trip through Western Europe it will come as a great relief to your pocketbook. As a quick rule of thumb, if you've traveled "second class" in most of the nations of Western Europe, you'll find that you can afford "first class" or deluxe (which exists mainly in Budapest) once you cross the border. Budapest, naturally, is the most expensive destination, and once you're out of that city into the countryside of Hungary, you'll encounter prices you haven't seen in the last decade or so.

TIME OUT FOR A COMMERCIAL: On your tour of Austria or Hungary, you will come close to many major attractions in other countries which you may want to explore. Since I had to set some limitation on the number of pages in this book, it was impossible to devote separate chapters to neighboring attractions.

I'll cite only an example or two to prove my point. For example, when you visit southern Austria you're close to the many attractions of Italy, including Venice. At Salzburg you're on the doorstep of exciting Bavaria. In Vorarlberg you're next door to Switzerland and Liechtenstein, that tiny principality left over from the Habsburg Empire.

Because of the geography of Austria and, again, depending on which sections of that country you plan to travel in, you may want to take along some of our sister guides as traveling companions.

Specific ones that might appeal to you include:
Dollarwise Guide to Switzerland, plus Liechtenstein
Dollarwise Guide to Germany
Dollarwise Guide to Italy
Eastern Europe on $25 a Day

5. The $25-a-Day Travel Club—How to Save Money on All Your Travels

In this book we'll be looking at how to get your money's worth in Austria and Hungary, but there is a "device" for saving money and determining value on *all* your trips. It's the popular, international $25-a-Day Travel Club, now in its 24th successful year of operation. The Club was formed at the urging of numerous readers of the $$$-a-Day and Dollarwise Guides, who felt that such an organization could provide continuing travel information and a sense of community to value-minded travelers in all parts of the world. And so it does!

In keeping with the budget concept, the annual membership fee is low and is immediately exceeded by the value of your benefits. Upon receipt of $18 (U.S. residents), or $20 U.S. by check drawn on a U.S. bank or via international postal money order in U.S. funds (Canadian, Mexican, and other foreign residents) to cover one year's membership, we will send all new members the following items:

(1) *Any two* of the following books

Please designate in your letter which two you wish to receive:

Europe on $25 a Day
Australia on $25 a Day
England on $35 a Day
Eastern Europe on $25 a Day
Greece including Istanbul and Turkey's Aegean Coast on $25 a Day
Hawaii on $35 a Day
India on $15 & $25 a Day
Ireland on $25 a Day
Israel on $30 & $35 a Day
Mexico on $20 a Day
New York on $45 a Day
New Zealand on $25 a Day
Scandinavia on $35 a Day
Scotland and Wales on $35 a Day
South America on $25 a Day
Spain and Morocco (plus the Canary Is.) on $35 a Day

Turkey on $25 a Day
Washington, D.C., on $40 a Day

Dollarwise Guide to Alaska
Dollarwise Guide to Austria and Hungary
Dollarwise Guide to Benelux
Dollarwise Guide to Bermuda and The Bahamas
Dollarwise Guide to Canada
Dollarwise Guide to the Caribbean
Dollarwise Guide to Egypt
Dollarwise Guide to England and Scotland
Dollarwise Guide to France
Dollarwise Guide to Germany
Dollarwise Guide to Italy
Dollarwise Guide to Japan and Hong Kong
Dollarwise Guide to Portugal, Madeira, and the Azores
Dollarwise Guide to Switzerland and Liechtenstein
Dollarwise Guide to California and Las Vegas
Dollarwise Guide to Florida
Dollarwise Guide to New England
Dollarwise Guide to New York State
Dollarwise Guide to the Northwest
Dollarwise Guide to Skiing USA—East
Dollarwise Guide to Skiing USA—West
Dollarwise Guide to the Southeast and New Orleans
Dollarwise Guide to the Southwest
Dollarwise Guide to Texas
(Dollarwise Guides discuss accommodations and facilities in all price ranges, with emphasis on the medium-priced.)

A Guide for the Disabled Traveler
(A guide to the best destinations for wheelchair travelers and other disabled vacationers in Europe, the United States, and Canada by an experienced wheelchair traveler. Includes detailed information about accommodations, restaurants, sights, transportation, and their accessibility.)

A Shopper's Guide to Best Buys in England, Scotland, and Wales
(Describes in detail hundreds of places to shop—department stores, factory outlets, street markets, and craft centers—for great quality British bargains.)

A Shopper's Guide to the Caribbean
(A guide to the best shopping in the islands. Includes full descriptions of what to look for and where to find it.)

Bed & Breakfast—North America
(This guide contains a directory of over 150 organizations that offer bed & breakfast referrals and reservations throughout North America. The scenic attractions, businesses, and major schools and universities near the homes of each are also listed.)

Dollarwise Guide to Cruises
(This complete guide covers all the basics of cruising—ports of call, costs, fly-cruise package bargains, cabin selection booking, embarkation and debarkation, and describes in detail over 60 or so ships cruising the waters of Alaska, the Caribbean, Mexico, Hawaii, Panama, Canada, and the United States.)

Dollarwise Guide to Skiing Europe
(Describes top ski resorts in Austria, France, Italy, and Switzerland. Illustrated with maps of each resort area plus full-color trail maps.)

Travel Diary and Record Book
(A 96-page diary for personal travel notes plus a section for such vital data as passport and traveler's check numbers, itinerary, postcard list, special people and places to visit, and a reference section with temperature and conversion charts, and world maps with distance zones.)

How to Beat the High Cost of Travel
(This practical guide details how to save money on absolutely all travel items—accommodations, transportation, dining, sightseeing, shopping, taxes, and more. Includes special budget information for seniors, students, singles, and families.)

Marilyn Wood's Wonderful Weekends
(This very selective guide covers the best mini-vacation destinations within a 175-mile radius of New York City. It describes special country inns and other accommodations, restaurants, picnic spots, sights, and activities—all the information needed for a two- or three-day stay.)

Museums in New York
(A complete guide to all the museums, historic houses, gardens, zoos, and more in the five boroughs. Illustrated with over 200 photographs.)

Swap and Go—Home Exchanging Made Easy
(Two veteran home exchangers explain in detail all the money-saving benefits of a home exchange, and then describe precisely how to do it. Also includes information on home rentals and many tips on low-cost travel.)

The Fast 'n' Easy Phrase Book
(French, German, Spanish, and Italian—all in one convenient, easy-to-use phrase guide.)

Motorist's Phrase Book
(A practical phrase book in French, German, and Spanish designed specifically for the English-speaking motorist touring abroad.)

The New York Urban Athlete
(The ultimate guide to all the sports facilities in New York City for jocks and novices.)

Where to Stay USA
(By the Council on International Educational Exchange, this extraordinary guide is the first to list accommodations in all 50 states that cost anywhere from $3 to $30 per night.)

(2) A one-year subscription to *The Wonderful World of Budget Travel*

This quarterly eight-page tabloid newspaper keeps you up to date on fast-breaking developments in low-cost travel in all parts of the world bringing you the latest money-saving information—the kind of information you'd have to pay $25 a year to obtain elsewhere. This consumer-conscious publication also features columns of special interest to readers: **Hospitality Exchange** (members all over the world who are willing to provide hospitality to other members as they pass through their home cities); **Share-a-Trip** (offers and requests from members for travel companions who can share costs and help avoid the burdensome single supplement); and **Readers Ask . . . Readers Reply** (travel questions from members to which other members reply with authentic firsthand information).

(3) A copy of *Arthur Frommer's Guide to New York*

This is a pocket-size guide to hotels, restaurants, nightspots, and sightseeing attractions in all price ranges throughout the New York area.

(4) Your personal membership card

Membership entitles you to purchase through the Club all Arthur Frommer publications for a third to a half off their regular retail prices during the term of your membership.

So why not join this hardy band of international budgeteers and participate in its exchange of travel information and hospitality? Simply send your name and address, together with your annual membership fee of $18 (U.S. residents) or $20 U.S. (Canadian, Mexican, and other foreign residents), by check drawn on a U.S. bank or via international postal money order in U.S. funds to: $25-A-Day Travel Club, Inc., Frommer Books, Prentice Hall Press, Gulf & Western Building, One Gulf & Western Plaza, New York, NY 10023. And please remember to specify which *two* of the books in section (1) above you wish to receive in your initial package of members' benefits. Or, if you prefer, use the last page of this book, simply checking off the two books you select and enclosing $18 or $20 in U.S. currency.

Once you are a member, there is no obligation to buy additional books. No books will be mailed to you without your specific order.

Part One

AUSTRIA

Chapter I

GETTING TO AND AROUND AUSTRIA

1. Traveling to Austria
2. Traveling Within Austria
3. The Grand Tour of Austria

DEEP IN THE HEART of Central Europe, Austria is not as remote as it may seem at first. It can easily be reached by plane from North America, and for many vacationers it's becoming a travel destination in its own right in both winter and summer. The time is long past when Austria was given only a quick stopover on a whirlwind visit to Europe.

1. Traveling to Austria

Although Vienna is accessible by a number of airlines, perhaps the easiest way to get from points throughout North America to Vienna is via an airline you might not have automatically thought of. It is **Alia, the Royal Jordanian Airline,** the national carrier of the Hashemite Kingdom of Jordan, whose deluxe 747s make five weekly nonstop flights to Vienna from New York, with daily flights scheduled by mid-1986. Alia is the only major scheduled airline flying nonstop from both Chicago and New York to Vienna.

The L-1011s of Alia also make twice-weekly flights to Vienna from Los Angeles, increasing to three times a week in summer, stopping in Chicago en route. Total travel time from Los Angeles to Vienna is 14 hours.

THE LESS EXPENSIVE FARES: Currently, your cheapest direct flight options on Alia as well as many other airlines fall into two general categories.

APEX Fares

APEX stands for "advance purchase excursion," and such fares are the most popular for transatlantic passengers. Alia, like practically every other airline, divides its flying seasons into low, shoulder, and peak. The airline requires that an APEX sojourn in Vienna last for between seven days and three months, with full payment, ticket issuance, and reservations made for travel in both directions at least 21 days in advance.

Once passengers have left the United States, any alteration in their advance reservation requires an additional fee of $100, payable at the time of the ticket change. The only drawback to this most economical of tickets is the requirement that a passenger plan travel dates far in advance, which you may or may not be willing to do, depending on your circumstances. (You'll find, howev-

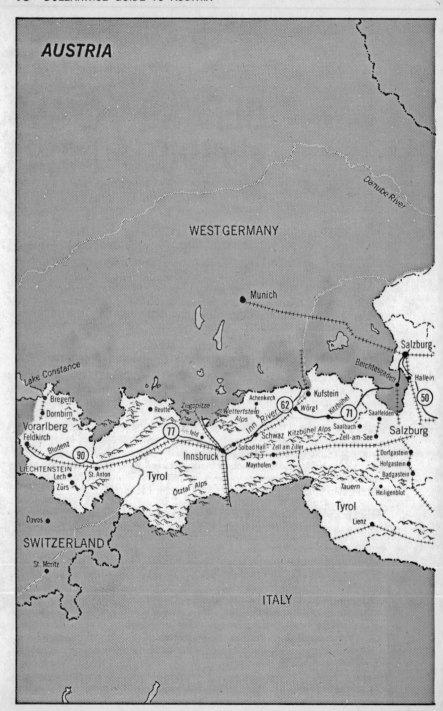

er, that if you change your return date once you arrive in Vienna, the APEX ticket plus the $100 penalty will still be the cheapest type of noncharter flight to Vienna.)

Alia offers an additional discount to passengers who are able to fly both eastbound and westbound on a Monday, Tuesday, Wednesday, or Thursday. Called **"midweek fares,"** these are $60 cheaper than fares for flights on weekends, which are defined as Friday, Saturday, or Sunday in either direction. Passengers traveling midweek in one direction but weekend in another will save $30.

The following chart indicates Alia's round-trip APEX fares to Vienna at the time of printing. *However, these fares are presented only for general guidance and are subject to change.*

Season	from Los Angeles	from Chicago	from New York
Low, midweek	$ 889	$ 805	$659
Low, weekend	949	865	719
Shoulder, midweek	949	865	719
Shoulder, weekend	1,009	925	779
Peak, midweek	1,089	965	819
Peak, weekend	1,149	1,025	879

Low season is defined as between November 1 and December 7 and from December 25 until April 30. Shoulder season is the entire month of May, plus the period between September 15 and October 31 and from December 8 until December 24. Peak season is the summer period when most North Americans go to Europe, lasting from June 1 until September 14.

Excursion Fares

Excursion fares differ from APEX in that no advance purchase or reservation is necessary. To qualify, a passenger must spend at least ten days outside the U.S. Excursion tickets are valid for one year. There are only two seasons on this type of ticket, as opposed to three seasons for APEX passengers. Peak season for this excursion fare applies to departures from the U.S. It is good between May 15 and September 14; low season fills in the calendar days for the rest of the year.

Excursion fares on Alia to Vienna are listed below.

Season	from Los Angeles	from Chicago	from New York
Low season	$1,286	$1,175	$1,029
High season	1,469	1,385	1,239

Economy Fares

Passengers who don't qualify for APEX or excursion fares can purchase normal economy fare tickets. Alia's one-way economy-class fare from Los Angeles to Vienna is $1,144; from Chicago, $839; from New York, $710. In economy, first, and business classes, round-trip tickets are double the price of a one-way ticket.

First and Business Classes

Alia offers special amenities to first- and business-class travelers, including helicopter service from points downtown in cities to airports, first-class airport lounges, plush sleeperettes in first class, and spacious seating in business class, gourmet dining, and the "Ya Hala" welcome service in the Jordanian tradition of hospitality. Business-class one-way tickets sell for $1,367 from Los Angeles, $1,108 from Chicago, and $905 from New York. Alia's first-class one-way fares from Los Angeles, Chicago, and New York are $2,341, $2,036, and $1,689, respectively.

For Information

The friendly personnel at the Alia sales offices will be happy to help you with flight information and reservations, and will also inform you of any price changes or fare adjustments that may have occurred since the printing of this guide.

Sales offices are in 11 different North American cities: Atlanta, Chicago, Dallas, Detroit, Houston, Los Angeles, Montreal, New York, San Francisco, Toronto, and Washington, D.C. You can also call toll free 800/223-0470 nationwide for passenger reservations (212/949-0050 in New York City).

ALTERNATIVE FARES TO AUSTRIA: There are several other budget options:

Charter Flights

Charters are often—but not always—the most affordable way to get to Europe from the U.S. The best way to learn about what's available and to compare prices between chartered and scheduled service is to consult **Jax Fax Travel Marketing Magazine,** a monthly travel industry publication available by subscription to travel agents. Ask your travel agent if you can peruse a copy. Jax Fax's address is 280 Tokeneke Rd., Darien, CT 06820.

The Austrian Tourist Information Office lists **Sunbeam Travel,** 274 Madison Ave., Suite 904, New York, NY 10016 (tel. 212/725-8835, toll free 800/247-6659) for New York–Vienna year-round charter flights. Sunbeam's fares range from $489 to $499, depending upon the season, seat availability, and duration of your stay. There's no advance purchase requirement, but make sure to check with them for updated schedules, restrictions, and price changes before finalizing plans. Travel is usually on Tarom Romanian Air Transport or Alia.

Do It Yourself Fares

You may also put together your own combination tickets to Vienna by flying to another European destination—London or Amsterdam, for example—and then flying from there to Vienna. This *can* save dollars, but not always.

As one of the air "crossroads" of Europe, Vienna is easily reached by air from nearly all the major capitals of Europe. Its national carrier, Austrian Airlines, offers the most frequent flights to Vienna but the national carriers of several major capitals of Europe also fly directly to Vienna. These include London, Paris, Frankfurt, and Zurich.

You can, for example, book a **People Express** (tel. 201/596-6000) no-frills Newark–London flight for around $400 round trip, then add on an **Austrian Airlines** London–Vienna round-trip flight for $250 off-season or $280 in peak season. Although your waiting time in airports might be considerably increased, you will have achieved a less expensive air fare of $650 or $680, depending on the season, and perhaps gain a sojourn in London as well. You can also fly into Brussels via People Express and continue from there.

Another possibility is to fly from New York to Munich. A low-season APEX flight on **Lufthansa,** costing around $538 round trip, can possibly be combined with an economical but rigidly restricted Austrian Airlines flight from Munich to Vienna for around $125. Skiers usually find that the mountains of western Austria are easily reached by overland transportation from Munich, making this an attractive option. Also, as of 1985, Lufthansa has regular service to Salzburg from Frankfurt.

For the first leg of your flight, shop around for the best airfare bargains through your newspaper or travel agent, and for the second leg, contact Austrian Airlines, 608 Fifth Ave., New York, NY 10020 (tel. 212/265-6350, or outside New York State, toll free, 800/872-4282), whose extensive service from most major European cities to Vienna is described in more detail in the "Traveling Within Austria—By Air" section of this chapter.

All fares and restrictions are subject to change, of course, so please double check with your airline before making final plans.

2. Traveling Within Austria

BY CAR: All main roads in Austria are hard surfaced. Between Salzburg and Vienna there is a four-lane autobahn (two lanes in either direction), and between Vienna and Edlitz the autobahn is six lanes. Part of the highway system includes mountain roads, and in the alpine region drivers face gradients of 6% to 15%.

In summer, driving conditions are good, but in winter, from December to March, motorists must reckon with snow on roads and passes at higher altitudes. Roads at altitudes of up to 5,580 feet are kept open in winter, although they may be temporarily closed because of heavy snowfall or avalanche danger. If you're planning to drive in Austria in winter, snow tires or chains will be needed.

Don't take chances. Ask about road conditions before you start on a trip. This is available in English seven days a week from 6 a.m. to 8 p.m. from the Austrian Automobile Club (tel. 72-99-7 in Vienna, 0222/72-99-7 elsewhere in Austria).

Traffic regulations are similar to those in other European countries where you drive on the right. The speed limit is 50 kilometers per hour (31 mph) in built-up areas within the city limits unless otherwise specified. Out of town, the limit is 130 kilometers per hour (80 mph) on motorways, 100 kilometers per hour (62 mph) on all other roads.

Driving under the influence of alcohol is severely punished. The permissible alcohol content of the blood is very low—two beers or eight ounces of wine can put you over the mark. The *minimum* fine is 5,000 AS ($266) and loss of driver's license.

The minimum driving age in Austria is 18. If you're over 18 and have a valid United States driver's license, you're not required to have an International Driver's License. However, you should inquire at your travel agency, an Austrian consulate, or an Austrian National Tourist Office (addresses in the U.S. and Canada are listed in "The ABCs of Austria," Chapter II) as to official validation of your home driver's license for use in Austria.

Use of seatbelts is compulsory, and children under 12 may not sit in the front passenger seat unless a child's seatbelt or a special seat has been installed.

If you are involved in or witness an accident resulting in bodily injury, you must report it immediately. If only property damage is involved, you may exchange identification with the other person, or if you can't find the owner of a vehicle you may have damaged, report the incident to the police. Otherwise you might be considered a hit-and-run driver.

Motor Fuel

At the present rate of exchange, fuel prices in Austria per U.S. gallon are: regular-grade unleaded gas, $2.23; premium-grade gas, $2.33; and diesel fuel,

$2.13. Regular-grade unleaded motor fuel is now generally available in Austria. Premium-grade gasoline is still leaded, but with smaller quantities of that environmentally suspect metal. This means that you can now take an American car to Austria without modification to the catalytic converter/exhaust system. Motor oil costs between $2.50 and $7 per quart, depending on the grade.

Austrian service stations do not accept U.S. oil company or general-purpose credit cards, although you will find stations with names familiar at home: Exxon, Mobil, Shell, and Texaco.

Parking

A number of Austrian cities and towns have restricted parking zones, where you can park for 90 minutes in specially marked "blue zones," so called because of blue lines on the road.

In Vienna, Graz, Linz, Klagenfurt, and Innsbruck, you must use a parking voucher to stop in limited-parking zones. You must purchase a voucher and when you park, write in the time you arrived and display it on the dashboard inside the windshield. You can buy vouchers at banks, gas stations, or tobacconists.

Parked vehicles that are obstructing traffic are towed away in a very short time, at the owner's or driver's expense.

Automobile Clubs

ÖAMTC (Österreichischer Automobil-, Motorrad- und Touringclub), 3 Schubertring, Vienna (tel. 72-99-0).

ARBÖ (Auto-, Motor- und Radfahrerbund Österreichs), 180 Mariahilfer Strasse, Vienna (tel. 85-35-355).

Motorcycles

The same requirements as for operating cars in Austria hold for operating motorcycles.

Both drivers and passengers of motorcycles must wear crash helmets. Lights must be kept on when the vehicle is being driven.

Car Rentals

Many visitors to Austria say that the only thorough way to see the landscape is with a car, and in a country where the most scenic valleys are sometimes inaccessible by train, you'll find that renting a car is usually the best way to travel once you get there.

If you're a skier, you needn't worry about driving in Austria even in winter. Access to the mountain ski resorts is so important to the nation's economy that Austria maintains some of the best snow-removal equipment in the world. Of course, you should exercise increased caution and slower speeds on alpine roads, but the truth is that most of the major highways are surprisingly free of snow even in the dead of winter.

Renting a car is easy. All drivers in Austria must have been in possession of a valid driver's license for at least one year prior to the rental of the vehicle. They must also present a valid passport at the time of signing the rental agreement. Drivers not in possession of a major credit card must pay a minimum deposit, plus the estimated cost of the rental and the estimated tax in advance.

Budget Rent-a-Car is, in my experience, one of the best and generally least expensive major car-rental companies and has more than 20 locations throughout Austria. These include all of the country's major airports, such as Vienna and Salzburg, as well as convenient locations within the major cities such as Innsbruck, Klagenfurt, and Linz. The cheapest car available at press time is a four-door VW Golf, with manual transmission and room for up to four passengers. If a car is reserved at least two business days in advance, the rate is $121 per week with unlimited mileage, plus 21% tax. This price does not take into account the season price reductions often publicized for the summer months, which may be in effect at the time of your trip.

If you want to travel in slightly better circumstances, choose a medium-size car such as a four-door Opel Ascona or Ford Sierra with manual transmission and considerably more room for $151 per week with unlimited mileage, plus 21% tax. An Opel Cadet, which is somewhat smaller than either the Ascona or the Sierra, offers four doors and automatic transmission for the same rental fee. Finally, if comfort and superbly crafted engineering are part of your alpine motoring fantasy, a sleekly beautiful Mercedes 190 is available with unlimited mileage for $39.95 per day, with a minimum rental of seven days, plus 21% tax. For more information, contact Budget by calling their 24-hour toll-free number, 800/527-0700, and ask for the international department.

Budget is not the only car-rental company represented in Austria. The familiar **Hertz** maintains 13 offices there, offering attractive rates roughly similar to those of its major competitors. To qualify for the cheapest rates, clients must book a car in advance. For up-to-date tariffs and more information, call toll free within the U.S.: 800/654-2211, or 800/268-1311 from within Canada (in Toronto, dial 245-2211).

Avis has about 15 locations in Austria, as well as a toll-free reservations number for U.S. residents: 800/331-2112. Its rates are also competitive. From British Columbia, dial 112/800/268-2310. From Toronto, call 622-0770. For the rest of Canada, dial toll free 800/268-2310.

National, through its affiliate Europcar, offers 11 Austrian locations, many of them at airports. If given enough advance notice, they'll make arrangements to have cars delivered to reasonable locations within Austria. National has a well-serviced fleet of Austria-based cars, although it doesn't offer some of the less expensive cars provided by its larger competitors. For information and reservations throughout the U.S. and Canada, call toll free 800/328-4567.

BY TRAIN: Rail travel is great in Austria, with fast, clean trains taking you through scenic regions. If you don't have a car, this is the preferred way to travel, as trains will take you to nearly all places in Austria, except for remote hamlets tucked away in almost inaccessible mountain districts. Many other services tie in with railroad travel, among them car or bicycle rental at many stations, bus transportation links, and package tours, including boat trips and cable-car rides.

On the 3,600-mile railroad system linking Austria with all of Europe, fares are based on mileage, with the ticket tariff being different for local and express trains. Main lines are electrified and mainly, except in rough mountain areas, double track. Branch lines are diesel powered on single tracks. Some private short lines and narrow-gauge railroads still use steam power. Most trains have both first- and second-class seating arrangements, first-class travel costing about 50% more than second. Seats can be reserved in advance for a cost of about 30 AS ($1.60) per person.

If you travel by train in Austria, chances are you'll take an Inter-City Express Train which connects Vienna with all major cities in the country, including Salzburg, Klagenfurt, Graz, and Linz. A train trip from Salzburg to Vienna takes about three hours.

Eurailpass

Austria is part of the Eurail system, and Eurailpass is good for unlimited trips on all routes of the Austrian Federal Railways and on Danube boats. For many years travelers to Europe have been taking advantage of Eurailpass, one of the continent's great travel bargains. The ticket entitles bona fide North American residents to unlimited first-class travel over the 100,000-mile national railroad networks of Western European countries, except Great Britain. Passes may be purchased for as short a period as 15 days or for as long as three months.

The pass cannot be purchased in Europe, but you can buy yours before you go from travel agents in all towns and from railway agents in major cities such as New York, Montréal, Los Angeles, and Chicago. The Eurailpass is also available at the offices of CIT Tours Corp., the Swiss National Railways, the German Federal Railroads, and the French National Railroads, all of which have offices in major U.S. cities.

Vacationers planning a trip can secure the pass for $260 for 15 days, $330 for 21 days, $410 for one month, $560 for two months, or $680 for three months. Children under 4 years of age travel free if they don't occupy a seat. Otherwise, for them as for other children under 12, a half-fare ticket must be purchased.

Fifteen-day or one-month tourists have to estimate the rail distance to determine if such a pass is to their benefit. To obtain full advantage of the ticket for the shorter periods, you'd have to spend a great deal of time on the train. Obviously, the two- or three-month traveler gets the greatest economic benefits, making the Eurailpass ideal for extensive trips.

The advantages are tempting: no tickets, no supplements—simply show the pass to the ticket collector, then settle back to enjoy the scenery. Seat reservations are required on some trains. Many of them have couchettes (sleeping cars), for which an additional fee is charged.

Eurail Youthpass is a single, convenient card designed for people under 26 years of age, entitling the holder to unlimited second-class rail travel, paid for in advance. The Youthpass is available for one month at $290, for two months at $370. This pass is valid wherever Eurailpass is honored.

Eurail Saverpass is a money-saving ticket offered for three or more people traveling together. It is good for 15 consecutive days of unlimited first-class rail travel in the same countries and with the same privileges as Eurailpass. All it requires is that your group remain together throughout the trip. The price of the 15-day saver is $199 per person.

Nationwide Network Pass (Bundesnetzkarte)

An Austria Ticket, formerly offered for trips of 9 or 16 days with no age requirements, has been done away with. Instead, travelers who are more than 26 years of age and wish to cover considerable miles in Austria can obtain a Nationwide Network Pass.

First-class rail travel costs 1,950 AS ($103.74) on this pass for 9 days, 2,640 AS ($140.45) for 16 days, and 4,200 AS ($223.44) for one month. In second class, the fares are 1,300 AS ($69.16) for 9 days, 1,760 AS ($93.63) for 16 days, and 2,800 AS ($148.96) for one month.

Austria Ticket

An Austria Ticket is available only for second-class train travel and only to persons under 26 years of age. The cost is 950 AS ($50.54) for 9 days, 1,350 AS ($71.82) for 16 days.

This ticket is good on all lines of the Austrian railroad network, domestic buses of both the Federal Railways and the Postal Service, the Austrian Federal Railways ships on the Wolfgangsee, Vienna's Schnellbahn (Rapid Transit), the Federal Railways cog railways on the Schneeberg and the Schafberg, and scheduled lines on the Danube operated by the Austrian Steamship Company

(DDSG). The ticket also entitles the holder to fare reductions on certain ship-lines on Lake Constance (Bodensee) and on many cable-car lines.

The Austria Ticket for young people can be bought at all Austrian railroad stations and from German Federal Railroads, 747 Third Ave., New York, NY 10017 (tel. 212/308-3100).

Senior Citizens' Discount

In Austria, women 60 years of age and over and men 65 and over, regardless of nationality, can travel on half-fare passes valid on the Austrian Federal Railways and on the bus systems of the Federal Railways and the Postal Service. The reduction is not applicable on municipal transit lines such as subways, streetcars, or buses, even in towns where the Postal Service operates the local bus service.

To purchase a half-fare ticket, a **Railway Senior Citizen's Identification** must be obtained in advance. This is issued at all railroad stations, at certain major post offices, and at the central railroad stations (Hauptbahnhof) in Frankfurt and Munich, Germany, as a service to foreign visitors using these cities as their air-travel gateways who wish to continue their trip to Austria by rail. In Zurich, Switzerland, both the Senior Citizen's and the Austrian Network passes are available at the rail station at the Zurich airport. At the main rail station, Zurich Hauptbahnhof, you can purchase only the Senior Citizen's pass. This makes it possible to take a train into Austria without having to break your trip at the border.

The price of the identification is 160 AS ($8.51), and it is valid from January 1 to December 31. A passport photo is required, and you must present your passport to prove your age. With this Senior Citizen's Identification, not available in the United States, you can buy tickets for your half-fare travel in Austria. The reduction is also granted for express trains, first-class tickets, and for checked luggage. If a TEE (Trans European Express) train is used, any supplement must be paid in full.

You can obtain the senior identification by mail from Austria by sending a photostat of the page of your passport which has your picture on it and states your age, plus one passport photo and a $10 (U.S.) traveler's check, to ÖeBB, Verkaufsdirektion, Abt. IV/4, 2-4 Gauermanngasse, Vienna. You can also get an old pass extended by sending it and the $10 to that address.

Other Railway Data

For information on short-distance round-trip tickets, cross-country passes, and passes for all lines in the individual provinces, as well as piggy-back transportation for your car through the Tauern Tunnel, check with the Austrian National Tourist Office, Austrian Federal Railways, 500 Fifth Ave., New York, NY 10110 (tel. 212/944-6880 or toll free 800/223-0284).

Bicycle Rental

From the beginning of April to the beginning of November, you can rent a bicycle at the following Austrian railroad stations:

Admont, Altmünster/Traunsee, Amstetten, Bad Goisern, Bad Hall, Bad Ischl, Bad Schallerbach-Wallern, Berndorf Stadt, Bruck-Fusch, Doersberg, Eisenstadt, Faak am See, Feldbach, Frohnleiten, Fürstenfeld, Gänserndorf, Gleisdorf, Gmünd NÖe., Gmunden, Gratwein-Gratkorn, Grein-Bad Kruezen, Hainfeld, Hallein, Hall in Tyrol, Hermagor, Hinterstoder, Hohenems, Hollabrunn, Horn, Kammer-Schörfling, Kirchberg a.d. Pielach, Klagenfurt, Klaus, Kötschach-Mauthen, Krems a.d. Donau, Kremsmünster, Langenzersdorf,

Launsdorf Hochosterwitz, Leibnitz, Lienz, Lochau-Hörbranz, Lunz/See, Melk, Mödling, Neumarkt-Köstendorf, Neunkirchen NÖe., Neusiedl/See, Oberdrauburg, Ossiach-Bodensdorf, Petronell-Carnuntum, Piesting, Pöchlarn, Pregarten, Puchberg/Schneeberg, Puerbach-Schrems, Reutte/Tyrol, Ried/Innkreis, Saalfelden, Salzburg, St. Aegyd/Neuwald, St. Johann/Pongau, St. Pölten, St. Valentin, Schärding, Scheibbs, Schladming, Seekirchen/Wallersee, Spitz/Donau, Stockerau, Traismauer, Türnitz, Tulin, Velden, Wörthersee, VölkermarktKuehnsdorf, Waidhofen/Thaya, Waidhofen/Ybbs, Werndorf, Wiener Neustadt, Wieselburg/Erlauf, Windischgarsten, Ubbs/Donau, and Ybbsitz.

A photo identification must be presented at the time of rental. The charge is 60 AS ($3.19) per day, which is reduced to 30 AS ($1.60) if a railroad ticket to the point of rental is held. You can reserve a bicycle in advance. The vehicle can be returned to where it was rented or to any other Austrian railroad station during business hours.

BY BUS: This is the third major means of getting about in Austria, although it is perhaps less desirable than traveling by car or train. Nevertheless, the country has adequate bus or motor-coach services run by federal and local authorities as well as by private companies. There are about 1,800 scheduled lines, including charter trips and excursions originating in tourist centers. The buses of Austria have an enviable safety record.

The motor-coach system of the **Austrian Postal Service** will take you into remote mountain hamlets. On a nearly 19,000-mile network of lines, the 1,500 Postal Buses go almost everywhere. Whether you're going to a ski resort at the height of the winter season or in the busy summer, I advise you to make reservations for Postal Bus travel. Information about Postal Service motor-coach travel is given in the Austrian Motor Coach Schedule (Kursbuch), or you may ask at Postal Travel Agencies in Vienna, Linz, and Graz; post offices in tourist areas; or the Austrian Federal Railways.

Bus travel will take longer to reach your destination than do the trains, but this has advantages, giving you the chance to sit back and see some of the most beautiful scenery in Europe passing before your eyes. Routes, timetables, and prices are to be found in the Austrian Bus Guide.

The **European Railways** offer Europabus services, with excursions to Budapest and other places. Information on Europabus is available at Generaldirektion der Österreichischen Bundesbahnen, Kraftwagendirektion, 4 Gauermanngasse, Vienna (tel. 56-50, extension 53-40); and at Austropa, Austrian Travel Agency Inc., 3-5 Opernring, Vienna (tel. 56-00, extension 233).

BY AIR: The flag carrier of Austria, **Austrian Airlines** (AUA) (Österreichische Luftverkehrs AG) no longer flies directly from New York to Vienna as it used to do, the run having proved unprofitable. However, the line has a fleet of DC-9s which hook up Vienna with nearly all the major capitals of both Eastern and Western Europe as well as providing connections to the Middle East. The airline's planes are named for famous composers.

In Austria, you can fly AUA to such cities as Salzburg, Linz, and Graz. Linz to Frankfurt, Germany, is a convenient run if, for instance, you have a return ticket on a line such as Lufthansa from Frankfurt to New York. Important addresses for Austrian Airlines offices you may need to know include:

Budapest—u. 5 V. Regiposta (tel. 171-550).
Frankfurt—1 Münchener Strasse (tel. 23-09-91).
Graz—16 Herrengasse (Lindhaus) (tel. 79-6-41).

Innsbruck—7a Adamgasse/Raika Passage (tel. 22-9-58).
Klagenfurt—17 8.-Mai-Strasse/Domgasse (tel. 56-6-47).
Linz—1 Schubertstrasse/Am Hessenplatz (tel. 27-00-55).
Munich (München)—9 Promenadeplatz (tel. 22-66-66).
Salzburg—9 Makartplatz (tel. 75-5-44).
Vienna—19 Kärntner Ring (tel. 65-57-57).
Zurich—66 Talstrasse (tel. 211-58-90).

If you want information on Austrian Airlines before you leave home, check with the office at 608 Fifth Ave., Suite 507, New York, NY 10017 (tel. 212/265-6350; outside New York State, toll free 800/872-4282).

Austrian Air Services (A.A.S.) has daily scheduled domestic flights connecting Vienna with several capitals of federal provinces: Graz, Klagenfurt, Linz, and Salzburg. The timetable for these flights is adjusted to the schedule of international flights. Austrian Airlines is the general representative for A.A.S.

Tyrolean Airways' regular flight network consists of up to four services per day between Innsbruck and Vienna and daily flights between Innsbruck and Frankfurt and Innsbruck and Zurich, as well as four flights per week between Innsbruck and Graz. Tyrolean services are included in computerized reservation systems. Therefore, reservations are accepted in travel agencies as well as by Austrian Airlines, Lufthansa, Swissair, and other IATA-Airlines and at the Tyrolean offices at Innsbruck Airport (tel. 05222/81777/77) and Tyrolean Vienna town office, 1010 Vienna, 1 Opernring (tel. 0222/56-36-74). All published IATA through fares to and from Innsbruck are applicable on Tyrolean Airways services. Tyrolean's Frankfurt, Zurich, and Vienna service provides ideal international connections with those gateways.

BY BOAT: Why not take a boat trip on the Danube or on one of Austria's beautiful lakes?

Passenger boats are operated by the **First Danube Shipping Co.** (Erste Donau-Dampfschiffahrts-Gesellschaft or DDSG), with main offices at 265 Handelskai, Vienna (tel. 26-65-36). Regular trips are made on a daily schedule from April to October. Special excursions are also available.

A 20% reduction in fare is yours if you purchase a round-trip ticket. Children under 6 ride free, and those from 6 to 15 go for half fare. International railroad tickets are valid on the Danube River boats, but with a supplement added. You must present your rail ticket at the DDSG ticket counter before embarking. Holders of Austria Tickets enjoy a 50% reduction in the fare. These boats do not transport cars.

There are also scheduled trips between Vienna and Budapest, Hungary, but you must have a valid passport and a visa.

Austrian Federal Railways has scheduled boat service, usually operating between May and September, on the following Austrian lakes: Wörther See, Ossiacher See, Millstätter See, Traunsee, Mondsee, Hallstätter See, Grundlsee, Attersee, Zeller See, Achensee, Plansee, and Bodensee (Lake Constance).

The Lake Constance boats visit the most popular tourist destinations daily from May to October A special ticket, *Bodenseepass*, is valid for 15 days. On 7 of the 15 days, you can go on excursions on any scheduled boat. Also, during the time the pass is valid, the holder can purchase tickets at reduced fares for any railroad, bus, and cable-car trips in the Lake Constance area.

Information on the Lake Constance offerings is available at Bodenseeschiffahrt, Bundesbahndirektion Innsbruck, 2 Claudiastrasse, Innsbruck (tel. 33-6-33-0).

On Lake Wolfgang in the Salzkammergut lake district, Austrian Federal

Railways boats connect interesting villages around the lake. A one-day pass permits repeated trips in any direction.

3. The Grand Tour of Austria

If your time is severely limited and you can only skim the surface of the attractions of this alpine country, you may want to take a Grand Tour of its highlights. Our trip begins with the assumption that you're coming from either Germany or Switzerland, perhaps having already traveled with our companion guides, *Dollarwise Guide to Germany* and *Dollarwise Guide to Switzerland & Liechtenstein.* Allow 15 days for this tour and be prepared for some fast traveling.

Day 1: We begin at Bregenz on Lake Constance, with city sightseeing, exploring the old quarter, and taking in the medieval gates and walls. In the afternoon, take an excursion to Pfaender by cable car for a view of the lake or else take a boat trip on Lake Constance. Remember that the Bregenz Festival is from mid-July to mid-August.

Day 2: Still based in Bregenz, you have a choice of three different excursions. You can go on a full-day bus ride to Schröcken or take a circular bus trip to the Bregenz Forests, the Flexen Pass, Bludenz, and Feldkirch. Another possibility is to take a circular bus trip to Partenen, the Silvretta mountains, Landeck, and the Arlberg.

Day 3: Take the morning train to Innsbruck, passing through some of Europe's most magnificent alpine scenery. Spend the afternoon sightseeing in Innsbruck, exploring the medieval city at the foot of the majestic Nordkette mountain range. Visit the Hofkirche with its impressive tomb of Emperor Maximilian I, the Imperial Palace, the Old Quarter, the Goldenes Dachl, the Ferdinandeum Museum, the Tyrolean Folk Art Museum (housing the best collection of this kind in the world), and Ambras Castle. In the evening, see a folklore performance.

Day 4: Still based in Innsbruck, take the morning cable car to Hafelekar at 7,400 feet for a panoramic view of the Tyrolean Alps. In the afternoon, go from nearby Igls by cable car to Patscherkofel at 7,370 feet, or else take a half-day excursion to the Alps: the Ziller Valley, the Gschnitz Valley, perhaps the Stubai Valley or Achensee.

Day 5: In the morning, take the train from Innsbruck to Salzburg, the four-hour trip taking you past green valleys and beautiful Austrian villages. Spend the afternoon sightseeing in one of the most colorful cities of Europe, where Mozart was born in a building which is among the featured attractions. In addition, see the cathedral, the Abbey of St. Peter with its fourth-century catacombs, the impressive Renaissance and baroque churches, the Festival Halls, the Mirabell Palace with its verdant gardens. If possible, attend the Salzburg Festival which runs from late July until the end of August. Or you can see a show of the marionettes, perhaps attend a concert or a folkloric program in the evening.

Day 6: In the morning, while still based in Salzburg, visit the Hohensalzburg Fortress, the huge fortified castle that dominates the skyline, and walk through the numerous courtyards and arcades. Take a guided tour through the attractive collections in the state rooms (45 minutes). In the afternoon, visit Hellbrunn Palace on the outskirts of the city, a magnificent baroque structure with formal gardens and trick fountains; or take a half-day excursion to one of the following areas: Gaisberg, the Salzkammergut Lake District, or the salt mine of Dürrnberg near Hallein.

Day 7: In the morning, take an express train from Salzburg to Linz on the Danube (1½ hours). See the center of this interesting, lively city, and later, still in the morning, take the riverboat down to Vienna (a 10-hour trip). The Danube Steamship Company operates this service from May to September; in other seasons, take the train from Linz to Vienna (3 hours). Along the Danube, you'll see magnificent abbeys, ancient towns, and historic ruins.

Day 8: Spend the morning sightseeing in Vienna, visiting such landmarks as St. Stephen's Cathedral, the Hofburg Imperial Palace, the Church of the Capuchin Monastery (housing the burial vault of the Habsburg emperors), and the Museum of Fine Art, one of the world's four ranking collections of paintings and archeological treasures. In the afternoon, stroll through the old streets of the Inner City, having a close look at the churches and palaces, and go to Belvedere Palace and walk through its sprawling gardens. Treat yourself to a relaxed hour in that singularly Viennese institution—a coffee house where you can sample a delicious pastry and have a cup of coffee with a top hat of whipped cream. In the evening, go to the opera or attend a theater performance, perhaps a concert. Note that the Vienna Festival is from late May to late June.

Day 9: In the morning, while still in Vienna, pay a visit to the summer residence of the Habsburg emperors with its splendid state rooms and its beautiful gardens, or attend the morning practice of the white Lippizaner stallions at the Spanish Riding School. In the afternoon, make a half-day excursion into the lovely surroundings of Vienna, stopping over at the ancient Cistercian Abbey of Heiligenkreuz and the convent of Mayerling, the site of the tragic death of Crown Prince Rudolph. Continue through romantic Helenental to the pleasant spa and holiday resort of Baden before returning to Vienna. In the evening, go to a heurigen in Grinzing, where fun-loving people eat, drink, and sing along with Schrammel musicians.

Day 10: Take a full-day excursion—on your own or else arranged by one of the various travel agencies. The most interesting for the immediate environs is a bus trip through the Wachau. You can visit the old town of Melk and its splendid Benedictine abbey. This is the world's largest monastic edifice, with a church, library, and elegant state rooms. You can go by boat down the Danube to Dürnstein, the ancient town between the river and the vineyards, with the ruins of a historic fortress high up on a hill, and then take the bus to Göttweig, the superb abbey with its fine architecture and rich collections. Have dinner in a vaulted restaurant before returning to Vienna.

Day 11: In the morning, take a train from Vienna to Graz, a journey of 3½ hours, going via the Semmering Pass, the oldest mountain railroad line in Europe. In the afternoon, take a walk through the center of Graz to see the old main streets and the major square. Go up to Schlossberg by funicular and see the Clock Tower and the old fortifications. Stroll by the Landhaus with its arcaded Renaissance courtyard and past Emperor Ferdinand II's mausoleum, then ride out to Eggenberg Palace and visit the Huntsman's Museum and the game preserve in the palace grounds.

Day 12: In Graz in the morning, visit the Joanneum Museum of the Province of Styria, with its prehistoric collection, and the Armory, the richest of its kind in the world. In the early afternoon, take a train to Villach, passing through the forests and mountains of Styria, which is called the green province. The ride takes 5 hours.

Day 13: In the morning, stroll through the old quarter of Villach, seeing the Town Hall and Paracelsus House. In the afternoon, take an excursion to Kanzelhöhe and Ossiacher See or visit the mountain resort of Mallnitz.

Day 14: In the morning, take the train from Villach to Lienz (3 hours), going through the lovely valley of the Drau River. In the afternoon, walk through the old streets of town, shop for souvenirs, and visit the museum of Castle Bruck. Go by chairlift to Hochstein or by cable car to Zettersfeld.

MILEAGE BETWEEN AUSTRIA'S MAJOR CITIES
Distance in Miles

	Arlberg	Bregenz	Brenner	Eisenstadt	Graz	Innsbruck	Kitzbühel	Klagenfurt	Linz	Salzburg	VIENNA	Zell am See
Arlberg		58	93	394	369	71	130	283	262	189	365	161
Badgastein	193	251	143	272	168	123	63	81	139	63	243	32
Bad Ischl	224	282	174	194	143	154	86	139	62	35	165	87
Bregenz	58		151	452	404	128	188	340	319	247	423	223
Brenner	93	151		344	297	23	80	233	212	127	315	115
Eisenstadt	394	452	344		109	321	253	183	145	206	31	254
Feldkirch	34	23	128	429	387	105	164	317	296	224	399	199
Graz	369	404	297	109		276	217	87	150	178	123	186
Innsbruck	71	128	23	321	276		59	212	191	119	294	94
Kitzbühel	130	188	80	253	217	59		153	124	51	227	35
Klagenfurt	283	340	233	183	87	212	153		168	158	195	131
Krems	339	397	289	88	141	269	201	207	90	154	47	202
Linz	262	319	212	145	150	191	124	168		77	116	137
Salzburg	189	247	127	206	178	119	51	158	77		186	52
Spielfeld	399	435	328	131	31	299	248	88	181	209	144	200
Villach	259	316	209	200	111	188	129	24	185	120	219	89
VIENNA	365	423	315	31	123	294	227	195	116	186		228
Zell am See	161	223	115	254	186	94	35	131	137	52	228	

Day 15: Take one of the most rewarding full-day excursions in Austria by exploring the Grossglockner, that high alpine road to Heiligenblut, one of the most scenic villages in all the Alps. Then go on to Franz-Josefs-Höhe at the flank of the country's highest mountains (12,470 feet).

Day 16: Armed with our companion guide, *Dollarwise Guide to Italy,* head for the sunny south and such resorts as Cortina d'Ampezzo or such major art cities as Venice.

Know that you have only skimmed the surface of the attractions of Austria, but surely there will be a second trip and perhaps even a third.

Chapter II

SETTLING INTO AUSTRIA

1. The Austrians
2. Food and Drink
3. Sports, Summer and Winter
4. Austria for Children
5. The ABCs of Austria

AUSTRIA HAS ALMOST A split personality. One side it has turned to the world—and perhaps the best known—is the glittering life of Vienna in its heyday, a world of romance and gaiety, the city of the Blue Danube (which isn't always so blue), of the waltz and the operetta. No person perhaps evokes this nostalgia for 19th-century Vienna more than Johann Strauss the Younger (1825–1899), whose best-known work is, naturally, "The Blue Danube Waltz."

But there's quite a different side to Austria, far removed from the life that revolved around the imperial court in Vienna's heyday. That is the spirit of the mountains, especially in Tyrol, a land of rugged individuality and independence, where man and woman in days gone by had to confront a harsh nature and control it in order to survive.

To understand Austria is to know the baroque. In this sense baroque isn't a mere architectural style: it defines the people as they lived. It suggests the condition of their soul at the time. Just as the architecture is flamboyant and theatrical, so were the people of Vienna. Much of that same style lives on today.

The theater has always been an important part of the life of Vienna since the 18th century. Even with electricity shortages in those dark and dim days of foreign occupation following their defeat in World War II, the Viennese still considered the lights of the theater essential, some ranking this as important as providing power to hospitals.

The Austrians have worked hard to rebuild their country in the aftermath of war and occupation. In some ways they are becoming as efficient as the Swiss. And how unlike their legendary character!

While Germans (except in southern Germany) greet you by saying "guten morgen" or "guten tag," in Austria the traditional greeting is "Grüss Gott," which translates more or less as "May God greet you." It's used by everyone—religious or not.

Nearly all Austrians worthy of the name still maintain part of their traditional dress. Some of these designs have not changed for centuries. You'll still see men in loden jackets (most often Styrian gray with green lapels) and shorts made of stout leather and called lederhosen. Felt hats are adorned with a feather or, more macho, a tuft of chamois hair. Women are known for their celebrated dirndl, a style that long ago came to America. Austrians view their national dress as part of their inheritance, to be passed on from one generation to the next.

They wisely have come to blend a respect for their proud traditions and former greatness with a kind of benign tolerance for the realities the present world has brought to them.

Today, like Switzerland, Austria is a neutral country, and maybe for that very reason the people can be more relaxed, friendly, and hospitable to strangers, knowing as they do that their hour has come and gone upon the world stage. From Vienna to remote East Tyrol, the Austrian is now prepared to enjoy life on his or her own terms, without some emperor or dictator determining the course of the land.

1. The Austrians

HISTORY: Austrian history seems to have been preordained by the country's geographical location centering along the Danube, which made it a crossroads and a battleground even in prehistoric times and the meeting point of three cultures—Romanic, Germanic, and Slav. Archeological finds have shown that even before the Iron Age numerous tribes passed through this territory, and about 1000 B.C. the Indo-European Illyrians of the Hallstatt Culture established a high level of barbarian civilization in the upper regions of what is now Austria, followed by the Celts who moved into the lower alpine areas about 400 B.C. and founded the kingdom of Noricum, with other tribes settling the west in regions now divided between Austria and Switzerland.

The Romans wrested the region from the Celts and other tribal settlers in about 15 B.C., establishing military garrisons and settlements at such strategic locations as Vindobona (Vienna), Juvavum (Salzburg), and Lentia (Linz), with resultant rapid economic and cultural development of the alpine and Danube regions. Roads were built, vineyards and wine making introduced, and Roman law instituted. The spread of Christianity began in about A.D. 300.

The decline of Roman power, culminating in removal of settlers in the fifth century, was speeded by the entrance into the region of Germanic tribes. The mass migration of the Romans left empty lands which were the target of repeated invasions as Teuton rule gave way to that of Huns, Avars, and then Magyars, until the region was taken over by the Bavarians from the northwest, under Frankish leadership. When Charlemagne became king of the Franks in A.D. 768, he established peace with his sword and achieved a more civilized culture.

After Charlemagne's death, the region again became a battleground, with a staggering number of claimants, ranging from Moravian to Magyar (ancestors of today's Hungarians). Finally the first Austrian dynasty, the Babenbergs, gained control. It was this royal family who fastened onto the fact that territory could better be gained by treaty, inheritance, marriage, and politics than through war, so that the population of the region they controlled grew, with farming, trade, and cities thriving. The aristocracy built their castles at strategic points, and by the end of the tenth century the region was already being mentioned as Ostarrichi, later replaced by the German name, Österreich (Austria).

Following the dying out of the Babenberg dynasty, with the resultant political and military maneuvering by hopeful successors, the Habsburgs moved into the picture, inaugurating an era that lasted more than 600 years after the crowning of Rudolph I in 1273. The Habsburgs too suffered the vicissitudes of rulerdom, but during their long reign, although their power was concentrated in Austria, they were to be Holy Roman Emperors and rulers of Austria, Hungary, Germany, Bohemia, Italy, Belgium, Spain, the Netherlands, and other nations and territories in Europe and the New World. The sphere of control of the Habsburgs waxed and waned, while their troops were involved in every conflict that erupted in Europe, with other nations being sometimes ally, sometimes adversary. During their dynastic supremacy the Habsburgs ruled over a wide diversity of ethnic groups as well as geographical areas. Under their umbrella came, at various times, the Slavs, Germans, Magyars, Romanians, Czechs, Poles, Ruthenes, Slovenes, Croats, and Serbs, plus other smaller cultural entities.

During the years of rule by the Habsburg House of Austria, there were 20 emperors and kings, and there was a time, at the height of their dynastic influence, when the sun never set on the Habsburg empire. Through the family's Spanish line, territories of the New World had been added in the 16th century, thus extending Habsburg possessions despite a breakaway from the dynasty's hegemony by the Swiss in the 14th and 15th centuries. Later, of course, Spain and the Netherlands were to be governed by a different branch of the Habsburg line, separating those countries from Austrian control.

The defeat of the Turks, who moved westward and even laid unsuccessful siege to Vienna in the late 17th century but were finally driven out of Central Europe in 1697, saw Austria begin to emerge as a major European power.

During the reign of Maria Theresa moderate and durable reforms were carried out, and her son, Joseph II, continued her work but with a more radical approach. However, two significant changes were his: the abolition of serfdom and the introduction of complete freedom of religion.

Napoleon, of course, played his part on the stage of Austrian history: French victories brought about the loss of Lombardy, Tuscany, provinces on the Rhine, Italian provinces, Bavaria, Baden, and Württemberg, the last three losses meaning that Germany was withdrawn from the Habsburg empire. The decimation of Austrian holdings led to the renunciation by Franz II of the title Holy Roman Emperor in 1806, which was just as well, since loss of Salzburg, Inviertel, Galicia, and the Slav lands soon followed.

Under the leadership of Prince von Metternich as foreign minister, and later chancellor, of Austria, after the abdication of Napoleon, many of the Polish and Italian territories lost during this tumultuous era were regained at the Congress of Vienna in 1814-1815, and Austria regained its niche as a world power, only to lose it, perhaps irrevocably, through backing the wrong side in World War I and being grabbed by Hitler in the dark days before World War II.

In the mid-19th century national revolutions tore the Austrian Empire asunder, and many dominions were lost—among them those in Italy and Germany—and Hungary almost went too. But a form of government was declared in 1867 under which Emperor Franz Joseph became ruler of a "Dual Monarchy," Austria and Hungary. This dualism saw Hungary become a constitutional monarchy of which Franz Joseph was king, while Austria remained a full monarchy of which he was emperor. This situation held until 1918, although the rumbles of dissatisfaction among minority national groups within the Dual Monarchy became ever louder. It was not until after the collapse of the Central Powers—Austria, Germany, Turkey, and Bulgaria—in World War I that the last Habsburg abdicated the throne on November 11, 1918, the monarchy was dissolved, and Austria and Hungary became separate republics.

From this review you may have gained the impression that the history of Austria has been somewhat muddled—and you're right. Many historians, in describing the Holy Roman Empire, have said that it wasn't holy, it wasn't

Roman, and it wasn't an empire. But it was in accord with the love of color, pageantry, titles, and the "follow the leader" nature of the Austrian people.

Since World War II and re-establishment of the Austrian republic, withdrawal of occupation forces in 1955 marked the beginning of coalition governments which have led to a stable economy, with return of property seized as German assets in 1945 and administered for ten years by the Soviet Union. On the withdrawal of the Soviets in 1955, Austria was given back major industrial plants, oilfields and installations, and the assets of the Danube Steamship Company, in return for money and goods as reparations to the Russians.

In the peace treaty of 1955, the Austrian State Treaty, signed by the United States, Great Britain, France, and Soviet Russia, Austria was recognized as a sovereign, independent, and democratic state, with the four powers declaring they would respect its independence and territorial integrity. The pre-1938 frontiers were guaranteed, political or economic union with Germany was prohibited, human rights and the rights of the Slovene and Croat minorities and of democratic institutions were pledged, and all National Socialist and Fascist organizations were dissolved. The Allied powers guaranteed Austrian neutrality, but this was not mentioned in the treaty.

However, the Austrian federal government passed a constitutional law declaring the country's permanent neutrality and stating that Austria would never in the future accede to any military alliances nor permit the establishment of military bases by foreign states on her territory.

Austria has seen days of glory and of tragedy, and today its people live in the peaceful, neutral, forward-looking remnant of an area chopped out of a once far-flung domain. But you won't find the Austrians mourning the lost empire. The fascinating mélange of nationalities, each of which has infused its racial characteristics and behavior patterns into the rich tapestry of Austria, gives this country an important place in the world of the 1980s.

RELIGION: In a country rife with conflicts of various sorts, it would be odd if there had been no dissension on religious beliefs, and of course there were in Austria. The Protestant Reformation began during the reign of Charles V in the 16th century and spread rapidly during the early years, being accepted by many German princes. Charles wasn't in favor of abandoning Catholicism, but he was too busy with other wars to check the spread of reform. Under Ferdinand I, Austria became a leader in the Catholic Counter-Reformation, a religious conflict which led to the Thirty Years' War (1618–1648) involving Europe's Catholic and Protestant rulers. Although the Treaty of Westphalia which ended the war recognized the right to existence of Protestant states and also the rights of Protestants in Catholic states, this latter guarantee did not include the Austrian Protestants.

Catholicism is still the dominant faith in Austria, although Joseph II, son of Maria Theresa, introduced religious freedom in the closing days of the 18th century.

The Jewish population of Austria was 200,000 in 1934, but those figures had shrunk to 11,000 in 1951. Most Jewish Austrians live in Vienna, as do most of the country's Protestants, the latter once estimated at only 6.2% of the population. Today religious freedom is practiced throughout the country.

GOVERNMENT: The country is a parliamentary democracy, and the head of the Austrian state is the federal president. The country's main legislative bodies are the houses of the Nationalrat and the Bundesrat. They form what is known as the federal assembly. The federal government is headed by a chancellor who, along with cabinet members, conducts any government affairs which are not the responsibility of the president.

In today's government, personal liberty is guaranteed, and the federal constitution prohibits discrimination on the grounds of sex, birth, class, religion, race, status, or language.

The political scene is dominated by the Socialist party and the People's party, each of which has achieved varying majorities.

LANGUAGE: The sole official language of the country is, of course, German. But, surprisingly, not everybody speaks it.

Austrians also speak Slovene, Croatian, Czech, or Hungarian. The largest group is the Croatian minority, who live for the most part in Burgenland. The second sizable group is the Slovenes, concentrated generally in southern Carinthia. Thousands of Hungarians live in Burgenland, and the smallest group of all, the Czechs, reside primarily in Vienna.

The difference in dialects between one part of Austria and another is considerable. Sometimes people who live "just across the valley" from each other find it hard to understand one another. The Viennese accent is known for its soft lilt (often satirized by Prussian Germans). Many Austrians have what is called a Bavarian accent.

THE PEOPLE: Ethnically, it is estimated that some 98% of the country's population is German. But there has been such a mixture of blood that pure representatives of a single race would be rare exceptions. Taken as a whole, the country is a mixture of Nordic and Dinaric (to a much smaller degree, Mediterranean and Baltic types).

Over the centuries each Austrian province from Burgenland to Tyrol has developed an ethnic and cultural identity. A lot of this had to do with geography. There's a vast difference between life in the alpine regions in the west and in the vineyards that flourish along Austria's eastern border with its former satellite, Hungary. The widely different range in climate and vegetation led to different ways of life, as well as customs and regional apparel.

MUSIC: In music, Austria has had a great history. In the heyday of baroque splendor in the 17th century, the imperial court at Vienna was a flourishing center of musical culture. Even the emperors themselves composed music! It was the most fruitful period of the Habsburg dynasty.

Opera, crossing the Alps from Italy, became an important part of the Viennese court. Vienna quickly established itself as the center of opera in the German-speaking world.

In the final years of the 18th century Vienna became the rendezvous point for the great composers of orchestral music: Wolfgang Amadeus Mozart, Joseph Haydn, Ludwig van Beethoven. Franz Schubert, the fourth of these great composers, was actually a native of Vienna and has been called the most Viennese of composers. In time they would be followed by Anton Bruckner (1824–1896), Johannes Brahms, and Hugo Wolf, along with Gustav Mahler (a pupil of Bruckner), and Franz Schmidt.

The operetta, introduced in the second half of the 19th century, was to become something pointedly Viennese in the history of the musical theater. Thus began what was known as the Golden Age of Operetta. The so-called silver age began around 1900, a movement led by Franz Lehar, a Hungarian who is known chiefly for his *The Merry Widow*.

Today such events as the Festival of Vienna, the Salzburg Festival, and the Bregenz Festival continue to make Austria a center of world culture.

ART AND ARCHITECTURE: The artistic heritage of Austria, reflecting German, Mediterranean, and Eastern European influences, can be traced from prehistoric times through the Roman era, the Middle Ages, the Renaissance, and up to modern times. Art objects from the late Bronze and early Iron Ages have been found, as well as such examples of Roman art as mosaics and murals from the second to the fourth centuries A.D. The coming of Christianity to the country led to the flourishing of ecclesiastic art, the earliest samples extant being illuminated manuscripts which show Scottish-Irish influence.

Stylized figures in the Byzantine style (eighth century) gave way to Romanesque stone and wood sculptures carved to decorate the abbeys and churches which flourished in medieval Austria. Frescoes in centers of worship can be seen throughout the country, with richly carved and painted altarpieces, panel paintings, and Gothic-style illuminated manuscripts. The influence of the Italian Renaissance is seen in both art and architecture of the later Middle Ages. Tombs of the royalty and nobility became increasingly ornate, as did art in all forms created for the glorification of abbeys and palaces. Trinity columns, statuettes, and busts joined the parade of artistic output during the 16th, 17th, and 18th centuries.

Painting was not of great merit in Austria in the 19th century, but some great art has originated in the country since the dawn of the present century. Such painters as Kokoschka, Klimt, and Schiele are recognized as among the best, with many promising followers springing up in modern times.

In the realm of architecture, when the Turks retreated, failing to capture Vienna, the flowering of the baroque burst across Austria, beginning in Salzburg. The architect Johann Bernhard Fischer von Erlach (1656–1723) brought this style to its zenith. He designed part of the Hofburg, the imperial palace of Vienna. He was rivaled by Lukas von Hildebrandt (1668–1745), who designed the summer palace of Prince Eugene, the Belvedere, which marked the peak of the baroque and rococo in Austria.

During the reign of Maria Theresa (1740–1780), the late baroque Theresian style came into its own, and seemingly everybody in the country painted new buildings in Maria Theresa ochre, a color which remains popular to this day.

In time baroque and rococo gave way to neoclassicism, and the time between the 1814-1815 Congress of Vienna and the March revolution of 1848 was the Biedermeier period (called the Vormärz).

In the heyday of Franz Joseph I, the famous Ringstrasse or "The Vienna Ring" was developed as a symbol of the wealth and national pride of the Austro-Hungarian Empire.

In spite of war damage, many of the great buildings of Vienna, and Austria in general, remain to delight the generations of today. One glory of the Ringstrasse, the famed Opera House, was hit by bombs and burned down on the night of March 13, 1945, in the closing days of World War II. It has subsequently been rebuilt.

LITERATURE: Neither the poetry and prose nor the dramatic work of Austrian writers has made much impact on the English-speaking world, perhaps primarily for the very reason that the literary productions of Austria do not translate into our language with the power of the original writing. From the minnesingers of the 12th to the 15th centuries came the great German epic, the *Niebelungen-*

lied, but even in Austria, such works based on the period of chivalry were little known among the common people. Many later literary efforts are so political in flavor as to preclude wide acceptance outside their own country.

Theater flourishes in Vienna, with the dramatic work of Austrian playwrights being popular even in the festival periods when many foreigners are likely to be in the audiences, striving to understand the German language.

2. Food and Drink

Cooking has never been ruled by treaties or dates. With the empire gone and the country today a small, neutral republic in Central Europe, Austrian cuisine has survived as one of the last remnants of a vanished empire. The culinary arts not only of Austria but also of Hungary, Yugoslavia, and Czechoslovakia have influenced the cookery you'll eat today.

In the heyday of the empire, the "love thy neighbor" policy was in vogue, perhaps overdone by some Austrian women. Many preferred to take as husband—or as lover—a handsome Hungarian, Yugoslav, or Czech. Perhaps the stunning uniform, especially that of the Hussars, had something to do with the choice. When the women of Vienna started to cook for their men, and the lovers requested dishes like mama made back in Budapest or Prague, the cuisine of the empire was born. Today Austria has one of the world's most lavish, lighthearted (but not light in calories!), and enthusiastic cuisines.

It's pointless to argue whether a dish is of Hungarian, Czech, Austrian, or even Serbian origin. Sometimes it's virtually impossible to tell which chef stole from the other. Personally, I've always been more interested in my palate's response to the taste than in the province in which a dish originated. And my palate responds well to *Wiener kuche* (Viennese cooking), which is the result of centuries of borrowing from foreigners combined with home concoctions.

Paprika and gulasch came from Hungary; dumplings, a mainstay of Viennese cookery today, originated in Bohemia, as did several sauerkraut dishes; wienerschnitzel may have first pleased diners in Milan. Each province of Austria, from Tyrol to Carinthia, has its own specialties. For example, the Styrians are fond of corn cake and chicken. In Tyrol you'll have the chance to sample one of the area's most popular dishes, *groestl* (minced veal with onions and potatoes).

Meals in this country are big and hearty, and the Austrians like to eat, taking as many as six meals or snacks a day. These include not only breakfast, with milk, butter, jam, and coffee, but also a *gabelfrühstück* (fork breakfast) at ten o'clock, which usually includes meat, perhaps little finger sausages. Lunch at midday is normally a big, filling repast, and the afternoon *jause* consists of coffee, open-faced sandwiches, and the luscious cakes which Austrian cooks make so well. Dinner may be a large meal, although many Austrians prefer a light repast then. The nightlife crowd often takes supper—perhaps *après théâtre*—before retiring. In other words, Austria is not a dieter's delight.

Austrians eat mainly meat dishes, except for fresh fish from the lakes and rivers. Among these, my personal favorite is the salmon trout of the Salzkammergut lake district.

Wienerschnitzel (breaded veal cutlets) is Vienna's most famous meat dish outside Austria. The most authentic local recipes insist that the schnitzel be fried in lard; others prefer butter or at least a combination of the two. On one point everybody agrees: the schnitzel should have the golden-brown color of a Stradivari violin.

The main meat specialty in Austria is boiled beef, or **tafelspitz**, said to reflect "the soul of the empire." It is the *specialité de la nation.* In fact, you won't find a single discriminating Viennese who hasn't, at least once in his or her life, eaten this celebrated dish. Try it at Sacher's in Vienna, or if the price there is too high, then the boiled beef can be ordered at a much cheaper *beisel,* the cousin of a French bistro. Of course, the tafelspitz at Sacher's will probably be served to you at a table graced by a silver candelabrum; at a beisel, the decorative note is likely to be an empty wine bottle holding a candle.

Boiled beef originated during the reign of Franz Joseph I who liked it for his midday meal. The rest of the kingdom followed his example, and before World War II the most celebrated people of Vienna ordered boiled beef at Meissl and Schadn's, the best known beef restaurant in Austria in the pre-Nazi era. There, one could choose from two dozen different cuts of beef. It became a ritual to order your favorite cut, and you had really arrived in status if the waiter knew your preference without having to ask. Alas! Meissl and Schadn's—that venerated landmark where the Austrian composer Gustav Mahler used to dine in 1897 when he was chief conductor of the Vienna State Opera—is no more. It was destroyed by Allied bombs during World War II.

Roast goose is served in Austria on festive occasions such as Christmas, but at any time of the year you can order *eine gute fettgans,* a good fat goose. After such a rich dinner, you may want to relax over some wonderful, strong coffee, followed by *schnapps.*

Soups are usually good in Austria and quite inexpensive. Among the favorites are *gulyassuppe* (a gulasch soup of—you guessed it—Hungarian origin) and *leberknödlsuppe* (meat broth with round dumplings containing chicken liver). There are infinite varieties of **gulasches,** both Austrian and Hungarian. These are usually stews of beef or pork, spiced with paprika. The Austrian version, *Wiener gulasch,* is usually less highly seasoned with paprika than the Hungarian.

Austrian **bread,** especially that baked in the ovens of Vienna, is considered among the best in the world. It comes in all shapes, sizes, and colors, made with many different grains and flours. Strudels too come in all shapes, sizes, and flavors. I often enjoy a poppyseed yeast strudel. In the baking line, the Lily Langtry of Vienna, Katharine Schratt, an actress at the Burgtheatre, was reported to make a special old Vienna coffee cake, *alt Wiener gugelhupf,* which was so good that the Emperor Franz Joseph I fell in love with her!

Austrians generally are exceedingly fond of **desserts,** and all over the country you will have the chance to sample *Salzburger nockerln,* a taste-tempting, frothy soufflé. Viennese pastries are also renowned, including chocolate saddle of venison cake, a delightful chocolate-almond concoction.

Even if you're not addicted to eating sweets, there's a gustatory experience you mustn't miss in the city of its origin: you must have **Sacher torte** in Vienna. This dessert is known all over the world, and many gourmets claim to have the original recipe for the "king of tortes," *die echte.* Master pastry baker, Franz Sacher, created the Sacher torte for Prince von Metternich, and tourists would often ask Madame Sacher for the recipe but she never gave it to them. Where else but in Vienna would a cake lead to a lawsuit? Demel's sued the Sacher Hotel, each insisting that it had the authentic recipe. The suit became a *cause célèbre.* But the hotel and Demel's still make Sacher torte today and ship it all over the world. You decide for yourself which does it better.

Madame Sacher helped cultivate the legend of Vienna as a citadel of gourmet cuisine. In Robert E. Sherwood's play *Reunion in Vienna,* this fabulous, cigar-smoking hostess was played by Helen Westley. The spirit of Madame Sacher lives on in Vienna and in the hotel she made famous.

Beer and Wine

Austria imposes few restrictions on the sale of alcohol, so except in alcohol-free places, you should be able to order beer or wine with your meal—even if it's

9 in the morning, or earlier, when many Austrians have their first strong drink of the morning, some preferring beer to coffee as a bracer to get them trucking.

In general, Austrian wines are served when new. Most of them are consumed where they are produced and are not known outside the region where they are grown. I generally prefer the white wine to the red, and perhaps you will too.

More than 99% of all Austrian wine is produced in vineyards in eastern Austria, principally Vienna, Lower Austria, Styria, and the youngest province of the country, Burgenland.

The most famous Austrian wine, **Gumpoldskirchen,** comes from Lower Austria, not only the largest province but the biggest wine producer. The center of the Baden wine district—called in Austria the Südbahnstrecke—is the village of Gumpoldskirchen, which gives the wine its name. This white wine is heady and rich, and just a little sweet.

An outer district of Vienna, **Klosterneuburg,** an ancient abbey on the right bank of the Danube, produces what is—arguably—the finest white wine in Austria. Monks have been making wine at this Augustinian monastery for centuries.

The ancient town of Krems, on the left bank of the Danube, produces very popular table wines, including **Kremser Sandgrube.**

The Wachau district, lying to the west of Vienna, also produces some fine wines known for their delicate bouquet, including **Loibner Kaiserwein** and **Duernsteiner Katzensprung.** These wines are fragrant and fruity.

By far the best red wine, and on this there is little disagreement, is **Vöslauer** from Vöslau. It's strong but, even though red, not quite as powerful as Gumpoldskirchen and Klosterneuburger.

From Styria comes Austria's best known rosé, the **Schilcher,** which is slightly dry, fruity, and sparkling.

Because many Viennese visiting the heurigen outside their capital didn't want to get too drunk, they started diluting the new wine with club soda or mineral water. Thus the **spritzer** was born, a drink that has now swept Europe and North America as well. The mix is best with a very dry wine. If you use a sweetish wine, you're likely to get what Marlene Dietrich once called "weak lemonade."

In all except the most deluxe places it is possible to order a carafe of wine (called *offener wein),* which will be much less expensive in price.

Austrian beers are relatively inexpensive and quite good, and they are sold throughout the land. **Gösser,** produced in Styria, is one of the most favored brews. It comes in both light and dark. In Salzburg, the **Augustiner Bräu** is famous, and in Innsbruck, **Adambräu.** The country brews most of its own beer (Vienna is a major production center, and **Schwechater** is the finest beer made in the city.)

Two of the most famous liqueurs—beloved by the Austrians—include **slivovitz** (a plum brandy which originated in Croatia) and **barack** (made from apricots, of Hungarian origin).

Imported whisky and bourbon are likely to be lethal in price. When in Austria, it's a good rule of thumb to drink the "spirit of the land." In this case that means wine and beer. It'll be far easier on your budget than Chivas Regal or whatever it is you drink back home.

The most festive drink, in my opinion, is **bowle** (pronounced bole). Austrians, especially the Viennese, often serve this at a party. It was first made for me by the great chanteuse Greta Keller, and I've been a devotee of it ever since. She preferred the lethal method of soaking berries and sliced peaches overnight in brandy. She would then pour three bottles of dry white wine over the fruit and let it stand for another two to three hours. Before serving, she'd pour a bottle of champagne over it! In her words, "You can drink it as a cocktail, during and after dinner, and on . . . and on . . . and on!"

The Heurigen

In 1784 Joseph II decreed that each vintner in the suburbs of Vienna could sell his own wine right on his doorstep to paying guests. And thus a tradition was born which has continued to this day.

Heurig means new wines or, more literally, "of this year." These taverns lie on the outskirts of Vienna, mainly in Grinzing but also in Nussdorf and Sievering. The latter two make a wine so full bodied that the legend is "one has to bite them!" Most of the heurigen are in a rustic style, with wooden benches and tables. Much of the drinking, however, takes place in vine-covered gardens in fair weather. A green branch hanging above the doorway usually designates a heurige. In some of the more old-fashioned places, on a nippy night there's a crackling fire in a colorful, often flower-bordered ceramic stove.

Schmaltzy Viennese songs are often featured. Naturally, there's likely to be not only a gypsy violin but perhaps an accordion or even a zither (remember the movie *The Third Man?*).

Many heurigen today are in fact quite elaborate restaurants; others are still simple, and it's quite acceptable in these to bring your own snacks or else drink the "new wine" with cheese and sausage you buy on the premises.

The wine is surprisingly potent, in spite of its innocent taste.

Once the Viennese came out to the wine districts just after the harvest. Nowadays the heurigen are year-round institutions.

The Ritual of Coffee Drinking

Although it may sound heretical, Turkey is credited with establishing the tradition of the famous Viennese coffeehouse. The Imperial City was successful in fending off two Turkish invasions, one in 1529 and another in 1683. The Turks, in their hasty retreat, left behind bags of coffee, and a legend was born.

It is said that the first coffeehouse opened in Vienna in the mid-17th century. The proprietor of this inaugural *Wiener kaffeehaus* was Frantz Kolschitzky, a notorious rogue.

In the heyday of Vienna, the literati gathered at the Café Central. There you might have encountered Karl Kraus, an ugly little man, almost a hunchback, who was as aggressive as his writings. Or perhaps Stefan Zweig, the man who became known throughout the world for his psychological tales such as *Amok* and *Kaleidoscope*.

In Vienna, *jause* is a 4 p.m. coffee-and-pastry ritual. Naturally, you select your favorite cake or pastry and, of course, one must not drink Viennese coffee in a café that doesn't evoke memories of Schubert, Mozart, Suppé, Lehar, Strauss, or Beethoven.

On your second visit to a Viennese coffeehouse, the *herr ober* should know at once which table you prefer (your *stammtisch)*, and how you like your coffee!

You can order your coffee several ways—everything from almost milk-pale *(verkehrt)*, which is one part coffee to four parts milk, to mocha (ebony-black coffee served in a delicate demi-tasse). *Kaffee mit schlagobers* is the easiest, simplest, and most traditional method of preparing coffee in Vienna. Whipped cream is served with it. You might even order *doppelschlag* (double whipped cream).

Turkish coffee is also brewed authentically in Vienna.

3. Sports, Summer and Winter

For information about sports to watch or to participate in, contact the **Austrian National Tourist Office,** 1 Margaretenstrasse, Vienna (tel. 57-57-14). They can put you in touch with the right persons or organizations to help you plan your vacation if you tell them what sport or sports you are interested in.

SUMMER: The mountains and lakes provide plenty of opportunities for all kinds of sports and pastimes.

Mountaineering

With more than 70% of Austria's total area taken up by mountains of all shapes and sizes, it's no wonder that outdoor-oriented visitors find the Alps to be a paradise for walking, hiking, and mountain climbing. Paths and trails are marked and secured, guides and maps are available, and there's an outstanding system of huts to shelter you. Austria has more than 450 chair lifts or cable cars to open up the mountains for visitors.

Certain precautions are essential, foremost being to inform your innkeeper or host of the route you plan to take. Also, suitable hiking or climbing shoes and protective clothing are imperative. Camping out overnight is strongly discouraged here because of the rapidly changing mountain weather and the established system of keeping track of hikers and climbers in the mountains. More than 700 alpine huts—many of which are really full-service lodges with restaurant facilities, rooms, and dormitories—are fixed points spaced about four to five hours apart, so that you can make rest and lunch stops. Hikers are required to sign into and out of the huts and to give the destination of the day before setting off in the morning. If you don't show up at a hut as planned, search parties go into action.

If you're advised that your chosen route has difficulties, be wise. Hire a mountain guide or get expert advice from some qualified local person before braving the unknown. Certified hiking and climbing guides are based in all Austrian mountain villages and can be found by looking for their signs or by asking at the local tourist office.

Above all, *obey signs.* Even in summer, if there's still snow on the ground you could be in an area threatened by avalanches. There are other important rules to follow for your own safety if you're going walking, hiking, or mountaineering. You can obtain these from the Austrian National Tourist Offices, from bookstores in Austrian cities, at the branches of various alpine clubs, or at local tourist offices in villages throughout the Alps.

Schools of mountaineering are found in 36 resorts, in all Austrian provinces except Burgenland, with regular courses, mountain tours, and camps for all ages. Distinction is made between summer and winter mountaineering, of course.

Camping

Austria has some 400 camping sites placed in its most beautiful areas. If you want to park away from a public campground, you must have the consent of the property owner. Also, you can't park your camp trailer on or beside a public highway unless you have a traction vehicle and obey parking regulations. Some mountain roads are either closed to or not recommended for campers. For details on camping opportunities and the cost at various campsites, ask for the camping list available at the National Tourist Office.

Water Sports

Austria has no sea coast, but from Lake Constance (Bodensee) in the west to the Neusiedl See in the east, the country is rich in lakes and boasts some 150 rivers and streams.

Swimming is, of course, possible year round if you wish to use an indoor pool or to swim at one of the many health clubs in winter. Recent major developments of swimming facilities at summer resorts, especially those on the warm waters of Carinthia, where you can swim from May to October, and in the Salzkammergut lake district between Upper Austria and Salzburg province, have seen this sport increase greatly in popularity.

The beauty of Austria underwater is attested to by those who have tried **diving** in the lakes. Most outstanding, I am told, are the diving and underwater exploration possibilities in the Salzkammergut lake district and in the Weissen See in Carinthia. You can receive instruction and obtain necessary equipment at both places.

If you prefer to stay on top of the water, you can go sailing, windsurfing, or canoeing on the lakes and rivers.

The **sailing** (yachting) season lasts from May to October, with activity centered on the Attersee in the Salzkammergut district, on Lake Constance out of Bregenz, and on Lake Neusiedler, a large shallow lake in the east. Winds on the Austrian lakes can be treacherous, but a warning system and rescue services are alert. For information on sailing, get in touch with the **Austrian Sailing Association** (ÖSV), 8 Grosse Neugasse, Vienna (tel. 57-86-88). A recognized sailing license, required for Lake Constance, can be acquired upon examinations through the Chief District Office in Bregenz.

Most resorts on lakes or rivers where **windsurfing** can be safely enjoyed have equipment and instruction available. This sport is increasing in popularity and has been added to the curriculum of several sailing schools, especially in the area of the Wörthersee in Carinthia, warmest of the alpine lakes.

If you're interested in shooting the rapids of a swift mountain stream or just paddling around on a placid lake, don't miss the chance to go **canoeing** in Austria. Possibilities vary from slow-flowing lowland rivers such as the Inn or Mur to the wild waters of glacier-fed mountain streams suitable only for experts. Special schools for fast-water paddling operate from May to September at the village of Klaus on the Steyr River in Upper Austria, at Opponitz in Lower Austria on the Ybbs River, and at Abtenau in Salzburg province.

Austria is a **fishing** paradise, offering as it does many clear, unpolluted streams, deep rivers, and lakes. You can angle for trout, char, pike, sheat-fish (monster catfish), and pike-perch in well-stocked mountain streams. In the right-hand tributaries of the Danube, you might catch huck, a land-locked salmon which is an excellent fighter and a culinary delight, usually fished for in late fall. The waters of Wörthersee in Carinthia sometimes yield the North American big-mouth black bass with which an owner of Velden Castle once stocked the lake by accident. Intended for a pond on his estate, one barrel fell into the lake and burst, introducing the immigrants from America to a new happy home.

A Sports Potpourri

Hunters find game of all sorts both in the mountains and the lowlands of Austria. If you're a passable shot, you may want to try your skill as a Nimrod here. Who knows? You might bag a roebuck, a marmot, or a chamois in season. For wild boar, foxes, polecats, wild rabbits, and weasel, it's open season all year, but you can't hunt without a license. For the latest information on whether you can bring your sporting guns and ammunition into the country, or where you can secure such equipment, plus facts about where and how to get a hunting license, check with the National Tourist Office.

Golfing, once a pursuit only of a privileged few, has become a sport for everybody who takes the time to learn. One of the country's most outstanding 18-hole courses is at the Murhof in Styria, near Frohnleiten. Others are the Igls/ Rinn near Innsbruck, Seefeld-Wildmoos, Dallach on the shores of the Wörthersee in Carinthia, Enzefeld and Wiener Neustadt-Foehrenwald in Lower Austria, and the oldest of them all, Vienna-Freudenau, founded in 1901. There are numerous nine-hole courses throughout the country. The season generally extends from April to October or November.

Tennis courts are to be found at most resort hotels and at sports centers.

Ask at a local office of tourist information, at a railroad station, or at your resort hotel if you'd like to rent a bicycle. **Cycling** tracks and paths are laid out so that you can ride across the country untroubled by vehicular traffic.

For a change from land and water sports, why not take to the air? **Gliding,** for which Austria is well suited, can be arranged at many airfields, and instruction is available at Spitzerberg, some 30 miles east of Vienna; at Zell am See in Salzburg province; at Niedr-Oblarn and Graz in Styria; and at Wiener-Neustadt.

Hang-gliding has gained in popularity recently. Facilities for this dare-devil sport are spread across the country.

Hot-air **ballooning** is available at Puch near Weiz in Styria.

Personally, I'll stick to **horseback riding,** for which you can rent a mount for one ride or spend your holiday on an Austrian-style ranch.

Besides all these sports in which you can participate, Austria has a wealth of spectator sports, ranging from auto racing to soccer to boat racing to horse racing, plus much more.

Also in the world of sports to be enjoyed in summer, there's **grass skiing,** which doesn't require snow and can be practiced by those who don't care to go high into the Alps to ski on snow. Ask at the Tourist Information Office for a list of resorts providing this sport, as well as for details about centers offering summer snow skiing. As for winter snow sports, read on.

WINTER: The winter sports scene in Austria is snow-white, with the towering peaks of the Alps, snow-blanketed pastures and forests, and smooth ice on lakes providing such attractions as downhill and cross-country skiing, hot-dogging, ice skating, tobogganing, curling, bobsledding, sleigh riding, and mountaineering for the sturdy hiker.

Skiing

It may have lost world-power status with the death of the empire, but Austria today has world renown for its uphill transportation which whisks skiers to the snow slopes for their downhill ski runs. Some 3,500 facilities transport passengers on rides of scenic splendor to the sites where they can begin their enjoyment of the approximately 12,500 miles of marked runs. Intricate networks cover whole mountainsides so that you don't have to take a step uphill on your own. Ski "circuses" allow skiers to move from mountain to mountain, and a ski "swing" opening up opposite sides of the same mountain ties villages in different valleys into one big ski region.

Shuttle buses, usually free for those with a valid lift ticket, take you to valley points where you board funiculars, gondolas, aerial trains, or chair lifts. Higher up, you may leave the larger conveyance and continue by another chair lift or, even higher up, by surface lift, probably by T-bar.

Austria made its way into winter sports history through the selection of Innsbruck twice for the site of the Winter Olympics. But skiing here is not the monopoly of stars. It's a popular leisure activity of young and old, mainly because of the climate and topography. Compare the vast ski area transportation network today with that of 1945, when the country had only 12 cableways, eight mountain railways, and six ski lifts.

The Austrian Ski School is noted for its fine instruction and practice techniques, available in many places: Arlberg; the posh villages of Zürs and Lech/Arlberg where jet-setters gather; the Silvretta mountains; and Hochgurgl, Obergurgl, Hochsölden, and Sölden in the Tyrolean Ötztal, to name a few. Year-round skiing is possible in the little villages of the Stubaital, through use of a cableway on the Stubai glacier, more than 10,000 feet above sea level. Known to all top skiers in the world is Kitzbühel, another lure to the jet set, as is Seefeld.

Skiing is a family sport in Europe, and ski centers usually have gentle slopes and instruction for youngsters, plus babysitting services for the very small. Many places have something extra to offer, since Austria's ski resorts have been working villages for centuries, while skiing facilities are relative newcomers. The Valley of Gastein was known for its medicinal thermal springs long before it became a ski center. The people of Schladming, in the Dachstein mountains, wore their local costumes and lodens before the first cross-country skier came to the high plateau of the little, unspoiled village of Ramsau.

Among the most attractive large-scale skiing areas are the Radstädter Tauern region and Saalbach/Hinterglemm in Salzburg province. Here, as in most of the winter sports areas, you'll find ski huts with crackling fires in the grates and hot spiced wine or perhaps *Jägertee*, hot tea heavily laced with rum.

Hot-dogging is an American import to Austria and is a special kind of skiing involving acrobatics, trick skiing, artistic skiing, and ski "ballet." Organized hot-dogger activities usually occur early in the season in such places as Bad Kleinkirchheim, Badgastein, the Kitzsteinhorn near Zell am See, or the Stubai glacier.

Cross-country skiing is popular among those who want to enjoy the winter beauty in quiet. Many miles of tracks are marked for this sport, and special instructors are available.

Other Winter Sports

Tobogganing, called the *luge* in the Winter Olympics, requires no special skills and is a thrill sport for amateurs. Many towns have special runs, and some mountain roads are closed to allow sledding.

Eisschiessen is the alpine form of **curling.** Instead of stones, "sticks" are used, weighted wooden disks with handles.

You can ride horseback in the snow, but it's more romantic to go in a one- or two-horse open **sleigh** to huts in the winter forest for a mug of hot spiced wine.

Whether you wish to indulge in any of these activities in the bracing alpine air or not, at most resorts you can enjoy swimming in an indoor pool, basking in a sauna, playing tennis or ninepins, trying your skill on a rifle range, or working out in the exercise room or gymnasium.

And there's always après-ski festivity, the main drawing card for some winter vacationers.

For the spectator, there are many competitive winter sports events held at the resorts and elsewhere.

4. Austria for Children

If you're undecided as to whether to take your children with you on a visit to Austria, hesitate no longer. Of all the countries I have visited, I recommend

Austria as at or near the top of the list of ideal vacation places to share with the young—even the *very* young. The pleasures available for children (which most adults enjoy just as fully) range from seeing the magnificent Lippizaner stallions go through their "airs above the ground" paces at the Spanish Riding School in Vienna, to exciting cable car and chairlift rides (to ski or not to ski), boat trips on the Danube, zoos and castles, fortresses and dungeons.

In Vienna, besides the wonders of the Spanish Riding School (which you and your children may have seen in the Disney movie, *The Miracle of the White Stallions)*, an outstanding attraction is the Prater amusement park, with its giant ferris wheel, roller coasters, merry-go-rounds, games arcades, and tiny railroad. Even if your kids aren't very interested in the state chambers of palaces, take them to Schönbrunn, where the coach collection and the zoo will surely be enjoyed. In summer, beaches along the Alte Donau (Danube arm) are suitable for swimming. And there's always the lure of the konditorei, those shops where scrumptious Viennese pastries are sold.

Salzburg's Hohensalzburg fortress complete with dungeon vies with the trick fountains and zoo at the palace of Hellbrunn on the outskirts as a pleasurable experience for the young. Folklore evenings and performances of the marionettes at the Marionettentheater hold their own fascination. A children's grotto railway with dwarf and fairytale scenes at Linz, a visit to a salt mine or to ice caves, excursions to the Salzkammergut lakes, yodelers and an alpine zoo at Innsbruck are just a few of the fun things for persons of all ages.

These are rivaled if not topped by Minimundus on the outskirts of Klagenfurt at Wörthersee in Carinthia. This "small world," set on a broad stretch of land, has more than 100 miniature models of the most well-known buildings of the world, ranging from the Suleiman Mosque in Istanbul to the famous Moulin Rouge nightclub in Paris to the Taj Mahal. Minimundus lets you go around the world in 80 minutes, more or less.

Everywhere in Austria are facilities for summer sports—swimming, boating, minigolf, hiking—what have you. Perhaps most outstanding, however, are the winter programs for children at ski resorts. At Austria's ski schools former world champions and other racing celebrities take time for the younger pupils, helping them become used to snow, first through play and then through learning to ski. In many winter resorts, ski kindergartens take children from the age of three up. The charge for ski instruction, supervision, and food (lunch) comes to from 1,000 AS ($53.20) to 2,500 AS ($133) per week.

Information on children's ski activities is available from travel agencies and from representatives of the Austrian National Tourist Office (see "Information Before You Go" in the ABCs of Austria below). Nurseries and play areas are available so you don't have to worry about your child being kept hard at work on skis the entire day. Most schools have equipment to rent.

Babysitting services are available through most hotel desks or by applying at the Tourist Information Office in the town where you are staying. Many hotels have children's game rooms and playgrounds.

5. The ABCs of Austria

BANKING: Foreign and Austrian money can be brought into Austria without any restrictions, and there is no restriction on taking foreign money out of the country. However, Austrian schillings can only be taken out up to a limit of 15,000 AS ($798). To export more than that, you must have a special permit from the Austrian National Bank. Foreign currency and travelers checks can be exchanged at all banks, savings banks, and exchange counters at airports and railroad stations at the official exchange rate of the day as given out by the Austrian National Bank.

BANKING HOURS: In the federal provinces, banking hours vary according to the region. The exchange counters at airports and railroad stations are generally open from the first to the last plane or train, usually from 8 a.m. to 8 p.m. every day. For banking hours in Vienna, see "The ABCs of Vienna," coming up in Chapter IV.

CLIMATE: At the center of Europe, the temperature in Austria varies greatly depending on the location. The national average ranged from a low of 9°F in January to a high of 68°F in July. However, in Vienna the January average is 32°F, while for July it's 66°F. A New Yorker who lived in Austria for eight years told me the four seasons were "about the same." In a sub-alpine climate it's neither very, very hot nor, on the other hand, is it Siberian cold. Snow falls in the mountainous sectors by mid-November. Road conditions in winter can be very dangerous in many parts of the country. The winter air is usually crisp and clear, with many sunny days. The winter snow cover lasts from late December through March in the valleys, from November through May at about 6,000 feet, and all year at above 8,500 feet. The ideal times for visiting Vienna are spring and fall, which have mild, sunny days. "Summer" season generally means from Easter until about mid-October.

CLOTHING: In spring and fall, a few warm pieces and a topcoat or raincoat are advisable. In winter you'll need a sweater and an all-purpose raincoat, as evenings are cool, especially in the mountain areas. You'll be wise to plan your wardrobe according to where you'll be staying. Vienna is fairly dressy, especially in the evening. Mountain country demands some woollies and sturdy walking shoes, and if you get into alpine activities you'd better have a heavy sweater and a down parka. Don't forget to have boots or shoes with slip-proof soles for winter walking.

CONSULATES AND EMBASSIES: The **U.S. Embassy** is at 16 Boltzmanngasse (9th District) (tel. 31-55-11) in Vienna. However, for such matters as a lost passport (anything considered nonpolitical), go to the **U.S. Consulate** at 2 Friedrich Schmidt Platz (tel. 31-55-11, ext. 2506), Vienna. The **Canadian Embassy** is at 10 Dr.-Karl-Lueger-Ring (tel. 63-36-91), also in Vienna.

CRIME: No particular caution is needed, other than what a discreet person would maintain anywhere. Compared to the rest of the world, Austria is a very safe country in which to travel.

CURRENCY: The basic unit of currency is the Austrian **schilling** (AS), which contains 100 **groschen.** There are coins with denominations of 2, 5, 10, and 50 groschen and 1, 5, 10, and 20 schillings, and banknotes with denominations of 20, 50, 100, 500, and 1,000 schillings. As a general guideline the price conversions in this book have been computed at the rate of 18.8 AS equals $1 U.S. (1 AS equals $.0532). As for all European countries, the international exchanges are far from stable, and this ratio might be old hat when you go to Austria. As a guide, however, I'm including the following exchanges at the rates given above.

Schilling	U.S.$	Schilling	U.S.$
1	.05	500	26.60
5	.26	600	31.92
10	.53	700	37.24
25	1.33	800	42.56
50	2.66	900	47.88
100	5.32	1,000	53.20
150	7.98	1,100	58.52
200	10.64	1,200	63.84
250	13.30	1,300	69.16
300	15.96	1,400	74.48
400	21.28	1,500	79.80

CUSTOMS: Austrian officials are fairly lenient (and the most tolerant people in the world if you're just arriving from one of the Communist countries where they really check your luggage!). The duty-free limit is 400 cigarettes or 80 cigars or a pound of tobacco, if you're over 17 and you come from a non-European country. However, if you fly to Austria from the continent, the limit is reduced to 200 cigarettes or 50 cigars or 250 grams of tobacco. You can also bring in two liters of wine and a liter of liquor (but only .75 liter from a country in Europe). Likewise, you're allowed ten ounces of cologne and two ounces of perfume, along with $100 worth of souvenirs. Most items such as cameras, tape recorders, portable typewriters, sports equipment, or whatever, intended for your personal use, are allowable.

Upon leaving Austria, you're allowed to bring back $400 worth of merchandise into the U.S. without paying additional tax. The duty-free limit on gifts sent home from abroad has been raised to $50.

ELECTRIC CURRENT: Austria operates on 220 volts AC, with the European 50-cycle circuit. That means that U.S.-made appliances will need an adapter-converter. Many Austrian hotels stock adapter plugs but not power converters. Electric clocks, record players, and tape recorders, however, will not work well even on converters.

GAMBLING: Casinos are found in ten locations in Austria: Vienna, Velden am Wörther See in Carinthia, Baden near Vienna, Badgastein in Salzburg province, Salzburg, Seefeld and Kitzbühel in Tyrol, Linz, and Bregenzaand Riezlern/Kleinwalsertal in Vorarlberg. Each has its own style, giving the opportunity to try your luck in a historic downtown palace, a nostalgic spa pavilion, or a rustic alpine mansion as well as in modern settings.

GUIDES: In the federal provinces, guides are available through the Provincial Tourist Boards or the various city tourist offices.

HOLIDAYS: Bank holidays in Austria are as follows: January 1, January 6 (Epiphany), Easter Monday, May 1, Ascension Day, Whitmonday, Corpus Christi Day, August 15, October 26 (Nationalfeiertag), November 1 and 26, and December 25 and 26.

INFORMATION: The **Austrian National Tourist Office,** 1 Margaretenstrasse (tel. 58866-0) in Vienna dispenses information about the entire country. It cannot, however, make reservations for you. As you travel throughout the towns and villages of Austria, you'll see signs indicating a fat "i." Most often that will stand for "information," and you'll be directed to a local tourist office where, chances are, you can obtain maps of the area and might even be assisted in finding a hotel should you arrive without a reservation.

INFORMATION (BEFORE YOU GO): Your travel agent can supply you with the information you wish, or get in touch with the **Austrian National Tourist Office,** whose U.S. representatives are at: 500 Fifth Ave., New York, NY 10110 (tel. 212/944-6880); 500 North Michigan Ave., Suite 544, Chicago, IL 60611 (tel. 312/644-5556); 4800 San Felipe St., Suite 500, Houston, TX 77056 (tel. 713/850-9999); and 3440 Wilshire Blvd., Suite 906, Los Angeles, CA 90010 (tel. 213/380-3309; toll free 800/421-8281 on the West Coast, 800/252-0468 in California only). In Canada: 1010 Sherbrooke St. West, Suite 1410, Montréal, PQ H3A 2R7 (tel. 514/489-3709); 2 Bloor St. East, Suite 3330, Toronto, ON M4W 1A8 (tel. 416/967-3381); and Suite 1220-1223, Vancouver Block, 736 Granville St., Vancouver, BC V6Z 1J2 (tel. 604/683-5808 or 683-5809).

LANGUAGE: German is the official language of Austria, but since English is taught in the high schools, it is commonly spoken throughout the country, especially in tourist regions. Certain Austrian minorities speak Slavic languages, and Hungarian is commonly spoken in Burgenland.

PASSPORTS AND VISAS: Citizens of the U.S. or Canada need only a valid passport to enter Austria. No visa is required.

PHOTOGRAPHY: You'll want to take lots and lots of pictures in Austria, as it's one of the most beautiful countries on earth. However, take along as much film as you can, because film sold in Austria, although readily available, carries a 32% tax!

RADIO: The Austrian Radio network (ÖRF) has English news broadcasts at 8:05 a.m. daily. "Blue Danube Radio" broadcasts daily in English from 7 to 9 a.m., noon to 2 p.m., and 6 to 7:30 p.m. only in the Vienna area. The Voice of America broadcasts have news, music, and feature programs on AM (middle wave here) from 7 a.m. to 1 p.m. and in the middle of the afternoon and early evening. It is at 1197 on the dial.

STAYING IN A PRIVATE HOME: If you want to meet the Austrian people at home, sleep in comfortable rooms at moderate rates, and travel without a set itinerary, look for signs that say *Zimmer Frei* attached to the front of a house or to a short post at the front yard gate or driveway. This means the proprietors rent rooms on a bed-and-breakfast basis to travelers. You'll encounter these signs along Austria's highways, and even more so, along some of the most scenic byways.

Such accommodations in a farmhouse or in the home of a craftsman or worker are invariably spotlessly clean and quite pleasant. Almost all of them have hot and cold running water in the bedrooms, although private bath and toilet facilities are rare. (There's usually a toilet on every floor and one bathroom in the house). A continental breakfast is served. These B&B houses are often new and have modern furniture, although you can still find comfort in, say, an old farmhouse.

Rates for such rooms vary considerably, depending on the type of accommodation provided, but on the average, the charge is $5 (U.S.) to $10 for a single with breakfast, $8 to $15 for a double. Few such homes accept advance reservations, so you just stop in and inquire. When the rooms are filled, the sign is taken down or covered. You can find help in securing accommodations of this kind through the local tourist office.

You may need a few words of basic German, as only a few such proprietors speak a little English. If you're staying for only one night, you may be asked to pay your bill in advance, and it must be paid in Austrian schillings.

Whole families or traveling parties can have the experience of staying on a farm, renting several rooms or even a wing of the house, but generally a stay of at least a week is required and advance reservation through a local tourist office or regional tourist board is necessary. The correct form of address for the local offices is *Verkehrsverein,* then the name of the town near which you wish to stay, and the name of the country, Austria. Regional boards should be addressed by writing to *Landesfremdenverkehrsamt,* followed by the name of the capital of the respective Austrian province, and the name of the country. Your reservation will be confirmed upon receipt of a deposit.

I highly recommend that you seek out such accommodations if you really want to get to know the people of the country and how they live at home. Any language barriers can be overcome sufficiently to allow you to be directed to good country inns for dining and to interesting sights in an area.

SHOPPING: A large variety of quality items is available to the shopper in Austria. You'll find jewelry, including costume jewelry, leather goods, needlepoint articles, traditional-costume-inspired fashions, knitwear, sports wear and equipment, novelties, and hunting rifles, among the many Austrian-made goods offered.

SHOPPING HOURS: In most Austrian stores, hours on weekdays are 8 a.m. to 6 p.m., 8 a.m. to noon on Saturday. Many stores close for two hours during the middle of the day.

TAXES: A 20% or 32% value added tax (VAT) is included in the list price of items sold in Austria. Tourists must pay this VAT at the time of purchase, but can obtain a tax refund on purchases totaling more than 1,000 AS ($53.20) or more per store if the merchandise is taken out of the country unused. Your bill will show the VAT *(MWSt)* as a separate item or will say that the tax is part of the total price. In order to get the refund, you must fill out a form, U-34, which is available at most stores patronized by tourists. A sign will say "Tax-free Shopping." Get one for ÖAMTC quick refund if you plan to use the option of getting your money at the border. Check whether the store gives refunds itself or uses a service. Sales personnel will help you fill out the form and will affix the store identification stamp. Keep your U-34 forms handy when you leave the country and have them validated by the Austrian Customs officer at your point of departure. You may have to prove that the merchandise is unused before Customs will validate your forms.

After returning home, mail the validated U-34 form or forms to the store where you bought the merchandise, keeping a copy of each form. The store will mail to your home address a check, bank draft, or international money order covering the amount of VAT refund due you. It sounds complicated, but if you work it right, you may get up to 24.24% of your shopping expenditure refunded. Information and help in expediting some steps of this process are available at the Austrian Automobile and Touring Club (ÖAMTC), which has instituted methods of speeding up your receipt of the refund. Ask at its offices at major highway checkpoints or at a bank or travel agency handling its arrangements. Check with the Austrian National Tourist Office at one of its North American offices before you go. Ask for the ÖAMTC brochure "Tax-free Shopping in Austria."

TAXIS: In the large Austrian cities, taxis are equipped with officially sealed taximeters which show the cost of your trip in schillings. If a rate change has recently been instituted, there may be a surcharge added to the amount shown on the meter, pending adjustment of the taximeter. Surcharges will be posted in the cab. A supplement is charged for luggage carried in the vehicle's trunk. Zone charges or set charges for standard trips are the rule in most resort areas. Tip the driver 10% of the fare.

TIPPING: A service charge of 10% to 15% is included on hotel and restaurant bills, but it's a good policy to leave an additional 5% to 7% for waiters and 15 AS (80¢) per day for your hotel maid.

Railroad station, airport, and hotel porters get 10 AS (53¢) per piece of luggage, plus a 5-AS (26¢) tip. Your hairdresser should be tipped 10% of the bill, and the shampoo girl will be thankful for a 10-AS (53¢) gratuity. Hat-check women and toilet attendants are usually given about 5 AS (26¢).

TIME: Austria operates on Central European Time, which makes it six hours later than U.S. Eastern Standard Time. It advances its clocks one hour in summer, however.

TOBACCO: Tobacco is a state monopoly in Austria and sale is through shops and kiosks marked *Austria Tabak* as well as by vending machines, and in hotels, restaurants, cafés, and inns. A number of specialty tobacconist shops sell foreign tobacco products. Hobby, Milde Sorte, Memphis Light, Dames, and Falk are some of the most popular Austrian cigarette brands. In 1784 Joseph II founded the Österreichische Tabakregie, the oldest tobacco-processing concern in Europe.

YOUTH HOSTELS: Austria has about 100 youth hostels distributed throughout the provinces. Rates for bed and breakfast range from 80 AS ($4.26) to 130 AS ($6.92) per person. Accommodation and three meals a day range from 160 AS ($8.51) to 220 AS ($11.70), plus taxes (except in some exempt areas). Some hostels lock their doors between 10 p.m. and 6 a.m. to discourage late arrivals. Dormitories must be empty between 10 a.m. and 5 p.m. You must have an International Youth Hostel Federation membership card for use of Austria's youth hostels, and advance reservations are recommended.

In Austria, you can get information regarding the hostels from **Österreichischer Jugendherbergsverband,** 28 Schottenring, Vienna (tel. 63-53-53). A detailed brochure is also available at the Austrian National Tourist Office (see "Information," above) and its representatives abroad.

Chapter III

VIENNA

1. Getting Around in Vienna
2. Practical Facts
3. Where to Stay
4. Where to Dine
5. Coffeehouses, Tea Rooms, and Cafés

CITY OF MUSIC, cafés, waltzes, parks, pastries, and gemütlichkeit—that's Vienna. The capital city of Austria has long held an enchantment for visitors, gaining much of its charm even during times of great upheaval in the long reign of the Habsburgs and retaining it in the dark days of World Wars I and II, a charm which is present today.

Vienna is a true cosmopolitan city, with a blend throughout its history of tribes, races, and nationalities all becoming assimilated through the centuries, with countless, constant additions of foreigners of all backgrounds fusing their customs, ideas, and culture to become the witty, charming, and cynical Viennese.

From the time the Romans selected the site of a Celtic settlement for location of one of its most important Central European forts, Vindobona, the city which grew up in the Vienna Basin of the Danube has played a vital role in European history. Austria grew up around the city and developed into a mighty empire, but the Viennese character formed during the long history of the country can only be said to be a rich amalgam of the blending of cultures that have made Vienna what it still is today: a city whose people devote themselves to enjoyment of the good life.

Music, art, literature, theater, architecture, education, food, and drink (perhaps wine from the slopes where the Romans had vineyards in the first century A.D.)—all are a part of the gemütlichkeit of Vienna.

The splendor and brilliance of Habsburg Vienna was seen in the court panoply, where uniforms, decorations, gems, and precious metals made a dazzling, if sometimes tiring, show. Before some of the city's brilliance was dimmed by the fall of the empire, it was described as a "royal palace amidst surrounding suburbs."

The roster of renowned Viennese, either born in the city or spending much of their creative lives there, is endless—endless, that is, in that more names are added constantly as more Viennese make their appearance on the stage of cultural and professional life and become world renowned.

Whenever I watch the boat traffic flow past on the Danube (not as beautiful and blue as Johann Strauss described it but still an important, navigable Central European waterway), I am always a little awed at the thought of the immortal music and musical dramas which had their inception here. Mozart, Lehar, Schubert, Beethoven, the Strausses (all of them), Suppé, Gluck, Mahler, Brahms, Liszt, Hoffmann, Lanner, Haydn, Weber, Schönberg—in the music world alone these are some of the outstanding names which were known during the days of empire.

Another name familiar in Vienna toward the latter days of the Habsburgs is Biedermeier, but this is not the name of a real person but of a character in a book, and is the appellation used for a period and a style to describe avant-garde artists. The name Freud, however, is that of a real Viennese.

But I am not nostalgic for that era, because I know that talent, even genius, still burgeons in this beautiful country. Many personalities, especially theatrical, have come out of Vienna in recent decades and gone on to world acclaim: Erich von Stroheim, Hedy Lamarr, Curt Jurgens, Oskar Werner, Magda Schneider, Josef von Sternberg, Fritz Lang, G. W. Pabst, Maria Schell, Paula Wessely, and Greta Keller, to name a few.

The Viennese have always been hospitable to foreigners, but there was a time at the end of the 18th century when the emperor felt that tourists might spread pernicious ideas, and all non-Austrians were limited to a one-week stay in the capital. This of course is no longer so, nor has it been for nearly 200 years. Now you can laugh, play, feast, sightsee—enjoy all the offerings of the city to the fullest with the smiles of the Viennese welcoming you to gemütlich Vienna.

The face of the city has been altered by many occurrences—war, siege, victory, defeat, death of an empire, birth of a republic, bombing, occupation, and the passage of time—but Vienna is still the happy, cosmopolitan "Queen of the Danube."

AN ORIENTATION: First, you'll need a very good and detailed map to explore Vienna, as it covers more than 158 square miles and has some 1,500 miles of streets (many of them only narrow alleyways).

Most visitors will spend all their time in the **Inner City** or Innere Stadt of Vienna, its First District. This is that famed section encircled by the Ringstrasse and the Danube Canal. Most of the city's best-known churches, baroque palaces, galleries, historic monuments, hotels, and museums lie within this much-frequented district.

The **Ringstrasse** runs along the line of the old city walls for about 2½ miles. My suggestion is that you take a tram along the Ring before you do any actual exploring. That way, you'll get a feel for monumental Vienna before taking it on block by block.

The Ringstrasse on your map will come under a number of different names: sometimes it's called the Opernring, or the Schottenring, or else the Burgring or the Dr. Karl-Lueger-Ring. After an interruption by the Danube Canal, the Ringstrasse resumes with such names as the Stubenring, the Parkring, the Schubertring, and the Kärntnerring.

The **Graben,** once the southwestern frontier of Vienna, is hardly that now. Absorbed by the city, it is today a major shopping artery. But if Vienna has a "main" street, it is surely the **Kärntnerstrasse,** which is jampacked with pedestrians during the day. It extends as far as the **Karlsplatz.** Along the way, you'll find some of Vienna's best known hotels and cafés.

Beyond the Danube Canal is the Second District, with the famous amusement park, the **Prater.** In the Third District, you'll find the **Belvedere Palace,** and in the Eighth District, **Schönbrunn Palace.**

Note: The area code for Vienna is 0222.

1. Getting Around in Vienna

Whatever means of transportation you may select for your visit to the Austrian capital and its environs, these basic suggestions may help make your visit a happy one.

AIRPORT: Vienna's international airport is **Wien Schwechat,** about 12 miles from the city center, which can be reached either by bus or by train. There is a regular bus service between the airport and the City Air Terminal (Wien Mitte), at the Hotel Hilton. Buses run every 30 minutes from 6 to 8 a.m. and every 20 minutes from 8 a.m. to 7:20 p.m., and to accommodate flights arriving after 7:20 p.m. The one-way fare is 55 AS ($2.93). There's also a service between the airport and the railroad stations, Westbahnhof and Südbahnhof, leaving Westbahnhof every 30 minutes between 6 a.m. and 7 p.m. (reaching Südbahnhof 15 minutes later) and starting from the airport every 30 minutes between 7 a.m. and 7 p.m. A train service runs between the airport and the City Air Terminal and Wien Nord (Praterstern) from 7:30 a.m. to 8:30 p.m. Trains run about every hour. A minibus service will shuttle you between the airport and your hotel. Seats may be reserved at the airport, at your hotel, or with your airline. A one-way taxi ride from the airport into the inner city is likely to cost from 260 AS ($13.83) to 400 AS ($21.28). Therefore it's better to take the bus. An official Tourist Information Office in the arrival hall of the airport is open October to May daily from 9 a.m. to 10 p.m., June to September from 9 a.m. to 11 p.m.

RAILROAD STATIONS: Vienna has two main railway stations, the **Südbahnhof** and the **Westbahnhof.** The Südbahnhof, Südtirolerplatz, 1100 Vienna (tel. 222-1553 for train information), services all trains heading south, which includes parts of eastern Italy, all of Yugoslavia, and the southern provinces of Styria, Carinthia, Burgenland, and Wiener Neustadt. The Westbahnhof, Europaplatz, 1150 Vienna (for train information, telephone 222-1552), services all trains heading west, including those to Salzburg, Innsbruck, all of Germany, and any connections to Italy that are made through Salzburg via the Brenner Pass. Train information for both stations will be given if you call 222-7200.

PUBLIC TRANSPORTATION: Whether you want to visit historical buildings or the Vienna Woods, museums, theaters, the Prater, or the heurigen, the **Vienna Transport** (Wiener Verkehrsbetriebe), with its network of facilities covering hundreds of miles, can take you there—by U-Bahn (underground), Stadtbahn (metropolitan), streetcar, or bus.

Vienna has a uniform rate, allowing the same tickets to be used on all these means of transportation as well as on the Schnellbahn (Rapid Transit) of the Austrian Federal Railways and on some connecting private bus lines.

There are no conductors on most buses and streetcars, which means you must have the correct change, 19 AS ($1.01), when you get your ticket at a vending machine at the station or aboard the vehicle you choose. A ticket from the machine will be stamped with the date and time of purchase. It's wiser to buy your tickets in advance at a Tabak-Trafik (tobacconist shop) or at an advance-sales office. Here you can get reduced-fare tickets in blocks of five, costing 13 AS (69¢) per ticket. Tickets purchased in advance must be stamped before you start your ride by the machine on conductorless streetcars or at the platform barriers of the underground or Stadtbahn. Once a ticket is stamped, it may be used for any one trip in one direction, including changes.

You can ride directly into the inner city on the underground U-1 or on city bus 1-A, 2-A, or 3-A. The underground runs from 6 a.m. to midnight seven

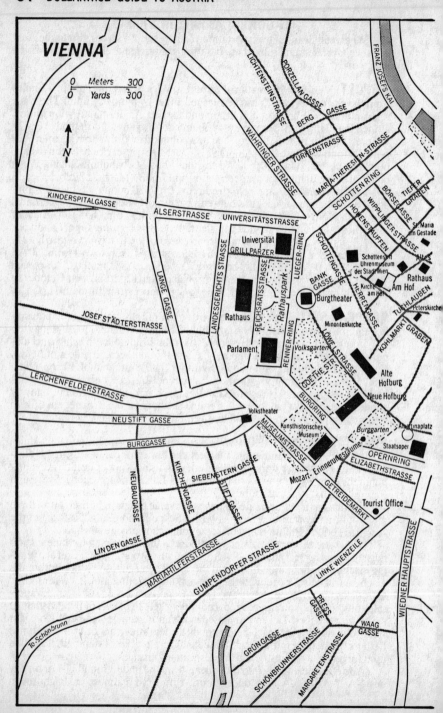

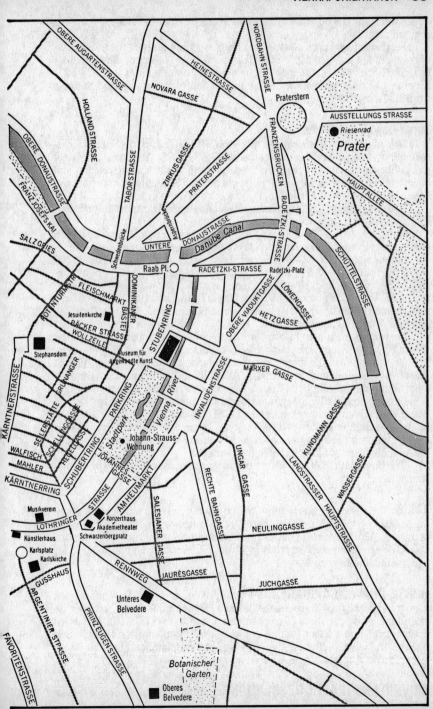

days a week and the buses from 7 a.m. to 8 p.m. Monday to Friday, 7 a.m. to 3 p.m. on Saturday.

Further information, all types of tickets, and free maps of the transportation system are available at Vienna Transport's main offices at the Karlsplatz (tel. 57-31-86) or at St. Stephen's Square underground stations (tel. 52-42-27) Monday to Friday from 8 a.m. to 6 p.m., on Saturday, Sunday, and holidays from 8:30 a.m. to 4 p.m.

Three-Day Vienna Ticket

One of the city's best deals for tourists is Vienna Transport's Special Sightseeing Pass, a three-day rover ticket costing 93 AS ($4.95). You can use not only the public transportation network (underground, Stadtbahn, streetcars, and buses), which covers hundreds of miles, but also the Schnellbahn in the Vienna area and buses carrying the letter "B," for as many rides as you like.

The three-day ticket is available at Vienna Public Transport Information Centers at the following locations:

Karlsplatz (tel. 57-31-86), open Monday through Friday from 8 a.m. to 6 p.m., on Saturday, Sunday, and holidays from 8:30 a.m. to 4 p.m.

Stephansplatz (tel. 52-42-27), open the same days and hours as Karlsplatz.

Praterstern (tel. 24-93-02) and Kagran Center (tel. 23-23-97), open Monday through Friday from 10 a.m. to 6 p.m.

All advance-sales offices of Vienna Public Transport, open Monday from 6 a.m. to noon, Tuesday and Wednesday from 6:30 a.m. to 12:30 p.m., Thursday and Friday from 12:30 to 6:30 p.m.

Opernpassage Tourist Information (in the pedestrian underpass next to the Opera/Kärntner Ring/Karlsplatz) daily from 9 a.m. to 7 p.m.

You can also get the three-day ticket at tourist information offices: Vienna West (on the Autobahn from Salzburg, Autobahnstation Wien-Auhof) and Vienna South (on the Autobahn from Graz, exit Zentrum, 149 Triester Strasse).

Other places selling the tickets are at the airport in the arrival hall next to where you pick up your baggage; at the DDSG landing pier, Reichsbrücke; and at the information offices of the Austrian Travel Agency (Österreichisches Verkehrburo) at the main railway stations. The one at Westbahnhof is found in the upper hall and at Südbahnhof in the lower hall.

The three-day ticket is valid on three consecutive days including the day it is stamped.

TAXIS: Taxi stands are marked by signs, or you can call for a radio cab by phoning 31-30, 43-69, 62-82, or 91-01. Fares are indicated on an officially calibrated taxi meter. The fare for trips outside the Vienna area, for instance to the airport, should be agreed on with the driver in advance. Count on spending about $5 for a trip within the city center.

HORSE-DRAWN CARRIAGES: Vienna's *fiakers*, or horse-drawn carriages, have transported people around the inner city for some 300 years. You can clip-clop along in one for about 20 minutes at a cost of 500 AS ($26.60). In the first district you'll find a fiaker for hire at the following sites: north side of St. Stephen's, on Heldenplatz near the Hofburg, on Josefplatz, and in front of the Albertina on Augustinerstrasse.

DRIVING AND TRAFFIC REGULATIONS: In general, Austria's traffic regulations do not differ much from those of other countries where you drive on the right. In Vienna the speed limit is 50 kilometers, about 30 miles per hour. Honking car horns is forbidden everywhere in the city. From December 15 to March 30, between 8 p.m. and 5 a.m., parking is prohibited on all streets where streetcars run. You are allowed a maximum stop of ten minutes even though parking is forbidden. In limited-parking areas you may park on weekdays between 8 a.m. and 6 p.m. only if you have a valid ticket, allowing parking for up to 1½ hours. The parking tickets may be obtained from the ticket offices of the Vienna Public Transport, from many gasoline stations, from tobacconists, and from most bank branches. The tickets are canceled by having marked on them the year, month, date, and time of day. *Warning:* The "No Parking" signs with the additional sign "Kurzparkzone" (limited-parking zone) are only displayed at the beginning and end of the zones. Special maps indicating location of hotels, one-way streets, and parking facilities in the first district are available at the official tourist offices. If you have car trouble, 24-hour service is offered by ARBÖ (tel. 78-25-25) and ÖAMTC (tel. 95-40).

2. Practical Facts

AMERICAN EXPRESS: You'll find the Vienna American Express office at 21-23 Kärntnerstrasse (tel. 52-05-44-0).

BABYSITTING: Phone 95-11-35 or 65-28-93 for information about babysitters (most of whom speak English). Call only Monday to Friday from 8 a.m. to 2:30 p.m.

BANKS AND EXCHANGE OFFICES: The open hours of Vienna banks and savings banks are 8 a.m. to 3 p.m. on Monday, Tuesday, Wednesday, and Friday, to 5:30 p.m. on Thursday (branch offices are closed from 12:30 to 1:30 p.m.). Monday through Saturday you can change money in many travel agencies, and daily in the exchange offices of the Westbahnhof from 7 a.m. to 10 p.m., and the Südbahnhof from 6:30 a.m. to 10 p.m. At the airport the exchange windows are open from 6:30 a.m. to 11 p.m.; in the City Air Terminal (Wien Mitte) from 8 a.m. to 12:30 p.m. and from 2 to 6 p.m.; and in the Tourist Information Office in the Opernpassage from 8 a.m. to 7 p.m.

CHURCH SERVICES: For information on services held by the religious group of your choice, call the following numbers: Roman Catholic (tel. 53-25-61); Evangelist (tel. 52-83-92 or 52-83-93); Jewish, with a temple at 4 Seitenstättengasse (tel. 63-45-16); Anglican, 17-19 Jaurèsgasse (tel. 73-15-75); or Methodist (tel. 37-72-45).

CLOTHING: For concerts and theaters, dark suits and cocktail dresses are recommended. For specially festive occasions such as opera premières, receptions, and balls, tails and dinner jackets are the preferred dress for men and evening dresses for women. You can rent men's evening wear, as well as carnival costumes, from several places in Vienna, which you will find in the telephone directory classified section (the yellow pages in the U.S.) under "Kleiderleihanstalten." I've learned that it's a good idea to take a light topcoat when I go out in the evening, even in summer, and I advise my women companions to carry or wear a stole or some other wrap.

DRUGSTORES: Chemist's shops are open Monday through Friday from 8 a.m. to noon and 2 to 6 p.m., and on Saturday from 8 a.m. to noon. At night and on Sunday you'll find the names of shops whose turn it is to be open at those times listed on a sign outside every shop.

EMERGENCIES: If you're faced with an emergency in Vienna, help is available. Depending on the nature of the situation, you may call: fire brigade (tel. 122), police (tel. 133), or ambulance (tel. 144).

HEALTH CLUB: Tu Was, Wien Hilton (tel. 75-41-81). Even if you're not registered at the Hilton, you are welcome to use the very popular health club on the third floor of this deluxe hotel. After registering at the desk, you'll be given a locker key, a towel, and access to the sauna, cold baths, and showers of this club where men and women easily mix together. After a sauna, guests relax, draped in towels, beside the TV of the clubroom. Entrance fees for a single visit are 200 AS ($10.64). The club is open daily between 10 a.m. and 10:30 p.m. Women who prefer to have their sauna alone are directed to a private room. Tu Was, translated from an Austrian dialect, means "Move!"

INFORMATION: The official **Tourist Information Office,** in the Opernpassage, the pedestrian underpass next to the opera (tel. 43-16-08), is open daily from 9 a.m. till 7 p.m. The **Austrian Information Office,** 1 Margaretenstrasse, corner of Wiedner Hauptstrasse (tel. 57-57-14), is open Monday through Friday from 9 a.m. to 5:30 p.m.

LOST PROPERTY: A lost property office is maintained at 22 Wasagasse (tel. 31-66-11-0), open Monday through Friday from 8 a.m. to 1 p.m. Items found on trains are taken to the central lost property office at Westbahnhof. Items left on buses and streetcars are passed on to the Wasagasse office after three days. If you miss something as soon as you get off the bus, you can pick it up at the Wiener Stadtwerke (Verkehrsbetriebe) (tel. 65-9-30-0) without waiting the three days.

MEDICAL SERVICE: A list of doctors can be found in the telephone directory under "Ärzte." All emergency calls for a physician on weekends from 7 p.m. Friday to 7 a.m. Monday and on holidays should be made to Ärztlicher Notdienst (tel. 56-35-11). Of course, your hotel or embassy can give you the name of an English-speaking doctor or dentist. For emergencies, telephone 55-00.

POST AND TELEGRAPH OFFICES: Addresses for both these facilities can be found in the telephone directory under "Post." Post offices are generally open Monday through Friday from 8 a.m. to 6 p.m. The central post office, 19 Fleischmarkt, and all railroad station post offices are open at night and on Sunday. Postage stamps are available at all post offices and at tobacco shops, and there are stamp vending machines outside most post offices. For information, phone 512-76-81. The central telegraph office is at 1 Börseplatz.

3. Where to Stay

Finding a room in Vienna, in spite of its great number of hotels, can be a problem, especially in August and September (the latter the time of the Vienna Fair), if you should arrive without a reservation. Vienna has some of the greatest hotels in Europe, more than 300 recommendable ones. If you arrive without a reservation in the peak visiting months, you may have to stay on the outskirts of Vienna, in the Grinzing or the Schönbrunn district, for example, and commute to the inner city by streetcar, bus, or underground.

In Vienna a five-star hotel such as the Imperial is decidedly luxurious and expensive. A four-star hotel is first class. Two- and three-star hotels are in the middle bracket, and a little one-star is the lowest of the lot, often no more than a boarding house (but often comfortable and quite clean).

THE DELUXE HOTELS: Hotel Imperial, 16 Kärntner Ring (tel. 65-17-65), is the grandest hotel in Vienna, evoking memories of the Austro-Hungarian Empire and Strauss waltzes in practically everyone who visits it. Luminaries from around the world use this as their headquarters, especially musical stars who prefer the location two blocks from the State Opera and one block from the Musikverein. Wagner stayed here with his family for a few months in 1875 (some scholars claim that he worked out key sections of both *Tannhäuser* and *Lohengrin* during that period). Other artists who have soothed their opening-night jitters in one of the rooms include Domingo, Caballé, Carreras, Fonteyn, Ormandy, Fürtwangler, and Karajan, along with the thousands of music lovers who travel to Austria to see and hear them.

The 165-room hotel was built in 1869 as the private residence of the Duke of Württemberg. The Italian architect Zanotti designed the facade like an almost overwhelmingly massive governmental building with a heroic frieze carved into the triangular pediment below the roofline. It was converted into a private hotel in 1873. The Nazis commandeered it as their headquarters during World War II, and the Russians requisitioned it in 1945, turning it into a shadowy ghost of its former self. Since Austria regained its independence, massive expenditures have returned it to the glory of its former beauty.

On the staircase leading up from the glittering salons you'll see archways supported by statues of gods and goddesses, along with two Winterhalter portraits of Emperor Franz Joseph and his wife Elizabeth. Everything is outlined against a background of polished red, yellow, and black marble, crystal chandeliers, Gobelin tapestries, and fine rugs. For many, the favorite rooms are the salons whose arched ceilings are painted with intricately designed garlands of fruit, ornate urns, griffins, and the smiling faces of sphinxes. Some of the royal suites are palatial, but all the rooms today are soundproof and air-conditioned, contain private bath, and are generally spacious. A café downstairs plays Viennese music, while the bar is an intimate rendezvous point.

Room rates include a 15% service charge and run from 2,500 AS ($133) to 3,200 AS ($170.24) in a single, from 2,800 AS ($148.96) to 5,000 AS ($266) in a double.

Hotel Bristol, Kärntner Ring (tel. 51516). You probably won't notice that this Vienna landmark looks any different from many other anonymously grand buildings in town from the outside. But connoisseurs of Austrian hotels maintain that this is a superb choice, with a decor evoking the full power of the Habsburg Empire. The hotel was constructed in 1894 next to the State Opera, in the ultimate of luxury, and it's been updated to give its clients the benefit of black tile baths and modern conveniences. Many of the architectural embellishments rank as objets d'art in their own right, from the black carved marble fireplaces and the oil paintings in the salons to the corkscrew baroque columns of rare marble in the Bristol restaurant, the Korso, which is, by the way, one of the best in Vienna. Even the chairs are crafted in a style that, depending on your mood, can be identified as either shield-back or heart-back Hepplewhite. Also the modern Rôtisserie Sirk and the elegant Café Sirk are meeting places for gourmets.

The *après-théâtre* ambience is a Viennese legend. The hotel's music room has a resident pianist who fills the ground floor with waltz-like melodies on the Grand Boesendorfer. On your way to the sumptuously appointed bedrooms, you'll see grandfather clocks in the corridors, most of them giving accurate time. The new executive floor offers luxurious comfort, enhanced by period furnishings in the style of the hotel's *fin-de-siècle* architecture. Its clubroom, in the tower, has comfortable wing chairs, an open fireplace, a self-service bar, library, TV, video recorder, stereo deck, and sauna. Each guest accommodation consists of a bedroom with a living room area and a small balcony providing a rooftop view of the Vienna Opera House and the Ringstrasse.

Prices include a 15% service charge. Singles cost from 2,100 AS ($111.72) to 2,900 AS ($154.28), while doubles go from 2,800 AS ($148.96) to 4,000 AS ($212.80). An extra bed can be set up in any room for an additional 450 AS ($23.94).

The **Wien Hilton,** Am Stadtpark (tel. 75-26-52), is one of this international chain's most handsome European properties, offering the plush accommodations and the predictably good service for which Hilton is known. Its modern design, soaring atrium lobby, and nighttime activity might come as a relief after "Olde World" Vienna. In fact, the updated art nouveau interior of this establishment has become a popular destination for the Viennese, who usually occupy as many tables in the excellent in-house restaurants and the convivial bar as hotel residents. The health club on the third floor, Tu Was, is filled with youthful members of the outside community, and the hotel's desirable location on the Stadtpark, a ten-minute walk from Vienna's cathedral, guarantees the establishment's popularity with business persons and sightseers alike.

The Hilton is attached to the City Air Terminal, which is the dropoff point for buses coming in at frequent intervals from the airport. The hotel offers 622 air-conditioned and comfortably upholstered rooms in styles ranging from modern to baroque, from Biedermeier to art nouveau. Single rooms rent for anywhere from 2,000 AS ($106.40) to 3,500 AS ($186.20), while doubles range from 2,400 AS ($127.68) to 4,500 AS ($239.40). The hotel has converted 42 guestrooms and one suite to provide extra comfort and facilities to guests on an exclusive new executive floor. The extra amenities, tailored to the needs of business persons, include hairdryers, toiletries, bathrobes, and additional phones. There is also an executive lounge on this floor offering continental breakfasts, afternoon coffee, snacks, and cocktails on a complimentary basis. This floor also provides special assistance by the staff as well as a no-stop checkout system.

The adjacent Stadtpark is connected to the hotel by a bridge, which strollers and joggers use during their excursions into the landscaped, bird-dotted expanses of the most famous park of Vienna. Even the glass-lined exterior is filled with bronze and aluminum balustrades, designed in a style reminiscent of art nouveau pioneer Gustav Klimt, whose other designs fill large expanses of the hotel's interior.

The Prinz Eugen restaurant (see dining section) is a gourmet bastion of fine food, acclaimed by many as the finest in Vienna. Since the Hilton towers over the city skyline, it affords very good views from the top floors. The Café am Park has a large open terrace where, in summer, you'll want to enjoy a Viennese coffee. An additional restaurant, the Vindobona Keller, offers a rustically appealing decor, an array of Austrian wines, excellent food, and heartthrobbingly romantic Austro-Hungarian music.

Hotel Sacher, 4 Philharmonikerstrasse (tel. 51-45-6). When the Sacher was built in 1876, Vienna, the empire, and the world were all very different places from what they are today. Nevertheless, much of the glory of the Habsburgs is still evoked during a walk through the public salons. The façade is appropriately grand, with enough neoclassical detailing to make a Roman feel at home, a striped awning over the sidewalk café, and flags from seven friendly nations displayed near the caryatids on the second floor. You might sense an undercurrent of espionage here. Enough novelists have used it in settings for their spy stories to evoke that image, yet despite that, both the crowned heads of Europe and the deposed heads (especially those of Eastern European countries) have dined and lived here.

In addition to intrigue, the Sacher has produced culinary creations that still bear its name. Franz Sacher, the celebrated chef, left the world a fabulously caloric chocolate cake called the Sacher torte, which has appealed to virtually everybody over the years.

The Sacher, especially its elegant coffeehouse, is the logical music-lover's choice in Vienna. You'll hear some kind of lilting classical music there in the afternoon, just as you had probably fantasized. All of the interior is a rococo splendor. The concierge, for a fee, can probably produce "unobtainable" theater and opera tickets.

Room rates include breakfast, service, and tax. The cost of a single without bath starts at 800 AS ($42.56), climbing to anywhere from 1,400 AS ($74.48) to 1,800 AS ($95.76) with private bath. Doubles with bath begin at a low of 2,100 AS ($111.72), rising to 3,500 AS ($186.30). Demi-suites and chambers with drawing rooms are more expensive. Half- or full-board terms can be arranged. The reception desk is fairly flexible about making arrangements for salons, apartments, or joining two rooms together, if it is possible to do so.

Im Palais Schwarzenberg, 9 Schwarzenbergplatz (tel. 78-45-15), is the only hostelry of Vienna with the status of having been named *Relais de Campagne*. Set in a 19-acre private park right in the center of town, the hotel is unique and historical. A walk around the gardens affords landscaped vistas accented with baroque staircases, balustrades ornamenting paths which stretch far away from the castle, and laughing cherubs who cavort with nymphs below arching beeches. The hotel occupies one wing of a baroque palace still owned by Prince Schwarzenberg.

It offers 43 rooms, each with period furniture, some of them with views over the garden, all of them with private bath and telephone. The palace was gutted during the Nazi era but was completely reconstructed after the Soviet occupation of Vienna. Today the same ambience of high ceilings with striated marble, crystal chandeliers, mythical beasts, oval mirrors, and gilt—lots of it— fill the public rooms between painted murals of festive deities. Guests enjoy the two-level bar and the restaurant.

The tastefully furnished rooms—some of them large and spacious, others quite small with very few amenities—are well maintained. Singles cost from 2,000 AS ($106.40) to 2,800 AS ($148.96), while doubles range from 3,600 AS ($191.52) to 4,500 AS ($239.40).

Hotel Ambassador, Kärntnerstrasse 22 (tel. 52-75-11). This renowned hotel sits on the square facing the Donner Fountain, with the shop-lined Kärntnerstrasse on the other side. Mark Twain stayed here, as have a host of diplomats and celebrities, including Theodore Roosevelt. The trademark of the hotel has alsway been the color red, either in the silk wall coverings, the bed-spreads, the upholstery, or the long carpet which is sometimes unrolled to the waiting limousine of some person known in world headlines. The wall-to-wall carpeting is, as you guessed, scarlet, relieved often by a discreet pattern of forest foliage. The public rooms have many, many chandeliers, which, in contrast to the vivid colors of everything else, appear sometimes as the most prominent furnishings. The Ambassador couldn't be better located: it's between the Opera House and St. Stephen's Cathedral.

High-season rates are in effect from April 1 to November 15 and from December 28 to January 2. At that time singles cost from 1,150 AS ($61.18) to 1,400 AS ($74.48), and doubles range from 2,200 AS ($117.04) to 2,600 AS ($138.32). The rest of the year, singles rent for 950 AS ($50.54) to 1,150 AS ($61.18), doubles from 1,850 AS ($98.42) to 2,400 AS ($127.68). Sumptuous accommodations include TV, radio, air conditioning, and breakfast. This hotel is an ideal choice for devotees of rococo *fin-de-siècle* decor.

Hotel Intercontinental, 28 Johannesgasse (tel. 7505). Glamorously redecorated, this hotel is considered the "grande dame" of Vienna's modern palaces, offering a sophisticated oasis of luxuriously inviting comfort. It lies at the northern edge of the centrally located Stadtpark, a few steps from the statue of an exuberant Johann Strauss playing his waltzes. After you register in the richly paneled lobby, you might head for a drink in the club-style Intermezzo Bar.

Upstairs, the elegantly decorated bedrooms have handcrafted cove moldings and all the modern comforts, along with a pleasingly conservative decor reminiscent in many cases of a townhouse in Britain. The wide-screen color TVs offer in-house movies, and other facilities include radio, mini-bar, and air conditioning, along with tile bath. Each room also has its own safety deposit box. Singles range from 1,850 AS ($98.42) to 2,800 AS ($148.96), while doubles go from 3,000 AS ($159.60) to 3,500 AS ($186.20). A sauna, exercise room, and solarium allow you to unwind after a long day of touring.

The lobby-level Brasserie, outfitted with lattices and a garden-style decor, serves one of the most popular luncheon buffets in the neighborhood, as well as temptingly prepared suppers and arrays of pastries worthy of the best coffee-houses in Vienna. In the more formal Vier Jahreszeiten (Four Seasons), grilled specialties are served by an intuitive crew of superbly polite waiters, eager to provide a memorable lunch or dinner. John Edmaier and his associate, Peter Martin, are the best managers the place has ever had, making the hotel sparkle.

The **Marriott,** 12a Parkring (tel. 53-36-11), is one of the newest hotels in Vienna and also one of the most dramatically designed. Its fan-windowed Mississippi riverboat facade displays expanses of tinted glass broken into glistening rectangles in the exterior of finely wrought enameled steel.

When it was originally built on the site of a covered garage, its designers allocated a third of the building for offices of the American Consulate and a few private apartments. The remainder contains 304 comfortably modern bedrooms, some of which are larger than those in the other contemporary palaces of Vienna. Singles range from 1,700 AS ($90.44) to 2,700 AS ($143.64), while doubles go from between 2,300 AS ($122.36) and 3,300 AS ($175.56).

The public rooms are elegant, and on my last visit one of the rooms was the site of a reception for the most prominent socialites of Vienna. The hotel's lobby culminates in a stunning stairway whose curved sides frame a splashing waterfall and masses of plants. Two of the trio of in-house bars offer live entertainment at cocktail hour, while a pair of top-quality restaurants feature appetizing and well-prepared Viennese and international specialties. In the gourmet restaurant, the Symphonika, an array of plushly pastel-colored banquettes clusters around a magnificent copy of a Hoffman-designed art nouveau chandelier. Exercise buffs appreciate the basement-level swimming pool, sauna, and Jacuzzi.

Hotel Modul, 78 Peter-Jordan-Strasse (tel. 47-15-84). The architecture for this modern hotel is striking, particularly since it sits at the edge of one of Vienna's green areas, the Türkenschanzpark. The facade looks almost like a row of organ pipes in a gigantic cathedral. Different tiers of vertical lines rise parallel to one another in a series of glass, steel, and concrete angles, all of which shimmer under the Austrian sun.

The hotel has 42 rooms, a trio of apartments, and a staff which does much to make a stay pleasant. Singles rent for 1,400 AS ($74.48) to 1,800 AS ($95.76), and doubles go for 2,000 AS ($106.40) to 2,600 AS ($138.32), with breakfast included in all tariffs.

The Modul, which lies in the suburb of Heurigen, has a bar and a restaurant, both tranquil and popular.

THE UPPER BRACKET: The **Parkhotel Schönbrunn,** 10-20 Hietzinger Hauptstrasse (tel. 82-26-76), is called by its owners "the guest house of the kaisers," which is completely true. Emperor Franz Joseph I constructed this edifice in 1907 as a guest house for his diplomatic visitors. Today it's a modern and updated hotel: the original core is still being used as public rooms, but modern wings and annexes house many of today's guests. Inside you'll find a coffeehouse furnished almost entirely in Biedermeier tables and chairs, along with a series of trendy public rooms. The Jagerstübl is traditionally outfitted in forest colors and white napery. A pool on the premises allows guests to release any leftover tensions from the day of sightseeing. The establishment lies 1½ miles from the West Station, and three miles from the city air terminal.

Singles rent for between 850 AS ($45.22) and 1,700 AS ($90.44), while doubles cost from 1,600 AS ($85.12) to 2,800 AS ($148.96), depending on the season. An extra bed is provided for an additional 450 AS ($23.94).

Hotel Romischer Kaiser, 16 Annagasse (tel. 52-77-51), is housed in a baroque national trust building which has seen its share of transformations. It was constructed in 1684 as the private palace of the imperial chancellor but has served both as a military academy and as a *fin-de-siècle* hotel. You'll find slightly more than two dozen romantically decorated rooms (my favorite piece has red satin upholstery over a chaise longue and white and gold paint with plenty of curlicues). In Vienna this is not only acceptable but perfectly charming. A small café on the ground floor will give you an idea of what Vienna must have been like as an imperial capital.

A single room rents for 1,100 AS ($58.52) to 1,300 AS ($69.16) in season, for 980 AS ($52.14) to 1,080 AS ($57.46) off-season. Doubles cost 825 AS ($43.89) to 1,000 AS ($53.20) per person in season, 750 AS ($39.90) to 940 AS ($50.01) per person off-season. Every room includes breakfast, bathroom, radio, phone, mini-bar, and color TV.

SAS Palais Hotel, 32 Heihburggasse at the Parkring (tel. 53-26-31), is one of Vienna's grandest renovations, an unused neoclassical palace converted into an extravagantly decorated hotel in 1985. Owned by SAS, the Scandinavian airlines, it has a cream-colored facade lavishly adorned with cast-iron railings, reclining nymphs, red banners, and elaborate cornices. In its imaginatively decorated lobby you'll find arching palms, a soaring ceiling, plushly upholstered chairs, and a cubbyhole bar with music.

An elegant basement-level restaurant decked out with peach-colored upholstery and a white ceramic stove offers beautifully presented food. Exercise buffs sometimes jog in the adjacent City Park before relaxing in the hotel's sauna and whirlpool. The hotel contains 165 compact but cozy rooms, each efficiently organized and comfortably furnished, with lots of alluring extras. Small singles on the top floor, under the mansard roof, cost from 1,800 AS ($95.76), with larger singles going for 2,400 AS ($127.68) to 3,000 AS ($159.60). Doubles range between 2,750 AS ($146.30) and 3,400 AS ($180.88), depending on their size and accessories.

Hotel König von Ungarn, 10 Schulerstrasse (tel. 52-65-20), is on a narrow street near the cathedral, a choice site. The building is a massive former private residence, painted yellow, with an angled roofline supporting three tiers of tiled gables. The walls date from the 16th century, and a hotel has been on the premises since 1815, with renovations completed in 1977. The interior is filled with interesting architectural details, such as marble columns supporting the arched ceiling of the King of Hungary restaurant, one of the finest in the city, a high-ceilinged mirrored solarium/bar area with a glass roof over the atrium, and a live tree growing out of an opening in the pavement. There are comfortable chairs, Venetian mirrors, and an atmosphere of old Vienna in the tall hinged windows overlooking the old town. Everywhere you'll find low-key luxury, old tradition, and modern convenience.

The hotel charges from 1,200 AS ($63.84) to 1,400 AS ($74.48) for a single, from 1,600 AS ($85.12) to 1,800 AS ($95.76) for a double, including breakfast.

Hotel Kaiserpark-Schönbrunn, 11 Grunbergstrasse (tel. 83-86-10). Not everyone can walk out his or her front door and stare immediately at Schönbrunn Palace, but if you stay here that's precisely what will happen. This elegant hotel is outfitted with lots of dark paneling and red velvet. The 45 bedrooms are as comfortable as you'd expect from an establishment of this quality. Each of them has a private bath, phone, TV, and radio. A public swimming pool in Schönbrunn Park is only a short walk away. K. Dietrich (no relation to Marlene), the manager, charges from 1,150 AS ($61.18) for a single, from 1,800 AS ($95.76) for a double. A buffet breakfast is included in the tariffs.

Hotel Tyrol, 15 Mariahilfer Strasse (tel. 56-41-34), is a privately owned hotel which is conveniently located in the center of town near the Imperial Palace. The interior is decorated with a combination of newly installed upholstered chairs and couches with a few select pieces of antique furniture. Each of the up-to-date rooms offers a bath, phone, radio, and TV, and there's a garage in the immediate vicinity. Rates in the soundproof rooms are from 750 AS ($39.90) to 950 AS ($50.54) for a single, from 980 AS ($52.14) to 1,400 AS ($74.48) for a double.

Hotel Europa, 3 Neuer Markt (tel. 52115-94). The welcoming parapet of this glass-and-steel hotel extends over the sidewalk almost to the edge of the street. You'll find it midway between the State Opera and the main cathedral, St. Stephen's. It offers 102 comfortable rooms, a Viennese café, and a first-class restaurant, Zum Donnerbrunnen, with evening zither music. The Europa Bar is elegant, dark, and glamorous, particularly since the lighting makes the many vertical lines look almost like the architecture inside a cathedral. Bedrooms are spacious and colorful, with lots of light coming in from the large windows, baths, and air conditioning. Josef Kvasnicka, the manager, charges from 1,400 AS ($74.48) for a single, from 2,000 AS ($106.40) for a double, depending on the season. Half board is available for an additional 320 AS ($17.02) per person per day. Breakfast is included in the price.

Hotel Amadeus, 5 Wildpretmarkt (tel. 63-87-38), is only two minutes away from the cathedral and within walking distance of practically everything else of musical or historical note within the city. Christa Wittenberger, the manager, maintains the 47 beds and the red-carpeted public rooms in tip-top shape. Some of the walls in the reception area are papered over with enlargements of old engravings of the Vienna of young Amadeus Mozart's era. The bedrooms offer peaceful nights, baths, phones, radios, refrigerators, and TV hookups. Singles rent for 1,100 AS ($58.52) to 1,500 AS ($79.80), and doubles cost 1,200 AS ($63.84) per person, including breakfast.

Hotel Prinz Eugen, 14 Wiedner Gürtel (tel. 65-17-41), displays a facade of identical soundproof windows with balconies facing toward a residential section of Vienna favored by diplomats. The hotel is immediately opposite Belvedere Palace and the railroad station of Vienna South. Subways will carry you quickly to the downtown section, and there are good highway connections. Inside you'll find a restaurant, a warmly paneled bar, and a series of conference rooms and salons that are often in demand by the local business community. The decor inside is a mixture of traditional pieces, a few antiques, some Oriental rugs, and a few glitzy touches such as glass walls with brass trim, adaptations of crystal chandeliers, and blowups of 18th-century illustrations of everyday life in Austria. Singles rent for 1,000 AS ($53.20) to 1,400 AS ($74.48), while doubles cost from 1,650 AS ($87.78) to 2,200 AS, breakfast included. An extra bed can be set up in any room for an additional 400 AS ($21.80).

Hotel Bellevue, 5 Althanstrasse (tel. 34-56-31-0). The sandstone facade of this five-story hotel reminds me a little of the Flatiron Building in Manhattan, as it's set on the acute angle of a street corner one block away from the Franz-Josefs Bahnhof. The Italianate embellishments seem to converge at a point on the fifth floor where the statues of two demigods support the corner of the roofline. Inside, the many renovations have stripped the former detailing, leaving a clean series of lines, often with high ceilings, amid wood paneling and a limited number of antiques. Bedrooms are functionally furnished with low beds, utilitarian desks and chairs, and a few padded armchairs. In high season (the Christmas holidays and from April to the end of October) singles rent for 1,300 AS ($69.16), and doubles cost 1,000 AS ($53.20) per person. During the rest of the year singles cost 1,000 AS ($53.20); doubles, 650 AS ($34.58) per person. A sauna inside is for the use of the guests.

Hotel am Schubertring, 11 Schubertring (tel. 72-15-51), is in a historical building on the Ringstrasse between the Vienna Opera House and the Stadtpark. It is near the Musikverein and the Konzerthaus, yet it provides quiet accommodation in a residential area. The highly ornamented facade conceals an updated interior decorated in pleasing shades of autumn colors, with soft muted tones in the bedrooms. The units, which look out over the rooftops of Vienna, have luxurious period furniture, accompanied by such modern comforts as air conditioning, direct-dial phones, mini-bars, radios, TV, and private bathrooms. Singles rent for 1,150 AS ($61.18) to 1,350 AS ($71.82) and doubles for 1,550 AS ($82.46) to 1,750 AS ($93.10). Breakfast is included in the tariffs. The hotel has a parking garage nearby.

Hotel Erzherzog Rainer, 27-29 Widner Hauptstrasse (tel. 65-46-46), is housed in an old-fashioned building with rows of gently curved bay windows rippling across the facade. It's only five minutes on foot to the Opera House and the Kärntnerstrasse, with a subway stop only a few steps away. The hotel is a well-run family business. Peter Nedomansky, the managing director, supervises the polite staff in their duties throughout the 84 well-decorated rooms. You'll find color TV, radio, and phone, and a private bath in all rooms. A booking service for opera and theater tickets operates out of the lobby, while Austrian specialties are served in the attractive restaurant, Chez Rainer. A cozy bar is modishly decorated in accents of black and brass. Other services offered include ten-hour cleaning on weekdays.

High-season rates are in effect during New Year's and from April to October, inclusive, when singles cost from 850 AS ($45.22) to 1,500 AS ($79.80), and doubles range between 1,600 AS ($85.12) and 2,000 AS ($106.40).

Hotel am Parkring, 12 Parkring (tel. 52-65-24), is a luxurious hotel in the top three floors of a massive, modern construction on the edge of Vienna's best known city park. From many of the windows you'll have views of St. Stephen's Cathedral less than a block away and have much of the rest of Vienna laid out at your feet. All of the air-conditioned units have direct-dial phones, mini-bars, and color TVs. The Himmelstube restaurant and the Coffee-Bar give an ambience that's unmistakably Viennese, particularly with the skyline so spread out before you. You'll take an elevator from the streetside private entrance directly to your floor. E. Stockringer is the director of this up-to-date establishment.

Singles cost from 1,400 AS ($74.48) to 1,500 AS ($79.80) during high season (from April to October, inclusive), while doubles range from 1,900 AS ($101.08) to 1,500 AS ($79.80). Rates are lowered in low season.

Hotel Maté, 34-36 Ottakringer Strasse (tel. 43-61-33). Many of the ceilings of this modern hotel are fashioned of handcrafted hardwood planks fastened together for an effect of visual interest. In one of the conference rooms the ceiling looks like an inverted topographical map of some Austrian mountain range, finished in natural wood grains. The rest of the public rooms are fitted with marble floors, comfortable upholstery, and in the case of the bar area, a combination of natural woods which frame magenta and red panels on the walls and ceilings. An indoor swimming pool has been built under a roofline that is shaped into a continuous barrel vault, with cutouts of Polynesian-style fish, potted palms, and rattan furniture. The outside of this hotel has decorative geometric designs on the streamlined facade, and there's a protective parapet. Singles cost from 990 AS ($52.67) to 1,170 AS ($62.24), while doubles range from 1,250 AS ($66.50) to 1,600 AS ($85.12).

Hotel Kummer, 71A Mariahilferstrasse (tel. 57-36-95), looks as highly ornamented as any public monument constructed during the height of the empire. Delightfully baroque, painted yellow with white trim, the facade is embellished richly, from Corinthian capitals with what look like acanthus-leaf bases to balustrades shaped like urns to four deities staring down from under the eaves. The public rooms inside, unfortunately, are not as well preserved as the exterior. Someone has replaced the old style with a modern interior which, while not as delightful as the street side, is comfortable and satisfactory in every way. The 110 rooms, within walking distance of the Vienna West train station, are all equipped with bath and soundproof windows. The carpeted restaurant and the bar area are attractive places.

Singles rent for 1,050 AS ($55.86) to 1,250 AS ($66.50), while doubles range from 1,500 AS ($79.80) to 2,200 AS ($117.04), with breakfast included.

Hotel President, 23 Wallgasse (tel. 59-990), was designed with enough angles in the facade to allow each of the bedrooms to have an irregular shape, usually with two windows in each unit, both facing toward different skylines. The facade is white and bronze, and there's a rooftop terrace where many guests sit sipping drinks for hours in summertime, separated from the buildings of old Vienna by an eight-story dropoff and a barrier of luxuriant green plants. Aside from the views, each of the bedrooms has a complete bath, comfortable furnishings, phone, radio, TV, air conditioning, mini-bar, and mini-safe. The Restaurant Casserole serves Viennese and international cuisine in a pleasingly informal setting every night till 11. S. Seyrling, the manager, charges 1,400 AS ($74.48) for a single and 1,900 AS ($101.08) for a double, breakfast included. Apartments for two persons are available for 2,300 AS ($122.36).

Hotel Royal, 3 Singerstrasse (tel. 52-46-31), is on one of the more prestigious streets of the old city. The outside presents a restrained dignity to the older buildings around it. The hotel lies less than a block from St. Stephen's Cathedral, on a pedestrian walkway which assures quiet evenings. Each of the 81 rooms is differently furnished, with some good reproductions of antiques and even an occasional original. The entire facility was built in 1960 and rebuilt in 1982. All units today have private bath, radio, TV, and room service if you want it. Singles rent for 950 AS ($50.54) to 1,300 AS ($69.16), and doubles cost 1,200 AS ($63.84) to 1,800 AS ($95.76). A buffet breakfast service, and taxes are included.

THE MODERATE RANGE: Hotel Kaiserin Elisabeth, 3 Weihburggasse (tel. 52-26-26), is perfectly located, a few blocks from the cathedral. The first thing you might notice about the interior is the surprising number of beautiful Oriental rugs, lying on top of well-maintained marble or wood floors. The main salon has a pale-blue skylight suspended above it, with mirrors and half-columns in natural wood. If you should select one of the hotel's rooms, you'll be interested to know that Richard Wagner, Franz Liszt, and Edvard Grieg all spent at least one night here. The rooms have been considerably updated since then, and although some parts of the building date from the 14th century, what you're likely to see in your private space is an up-to-date decor of polished wood, clean linen, and perhaps another Oriental rug. In the breakfast room you'll see a portrait of the Empress Maria Theresa above the fireplace. Singles rent for 500 AS ($26.60) to 650 AS ($34.58) without private bath. With private bath they cost from 950 AS ($50.54) to 1,200 AS ($63.84), and doubles with bath cost from 1,300 AS ($69.16) to 1,800 AS ($95.76), including breakfast, tax, and service.

Ring Hotel, 1 Maria am Gestade (tel. 63-77-01). You'll notice this 15th-century structure on the Concordiaplatz, at the bottom of a flight of steps leading up to one of Vienna's older churches. In summer many of the hinged windows will be opened outward toward the square, which becomes restfully quiet every night. This hotel is a real discovery, offering rooms with bath and attractive and unusual furnishings in high season, April to October, for 900 AS ($47.88) to 950 AS ($50.54) in a single and 1,200 AS ($63.84) to 1,300 AS ($69.16) in a double. In low season, singles rent for 680 AS ($36.18) to 750 AS ($39.90), while doubles range from 970 AS ($51.60) to 1,000 AS ($53.20). Breakfast is included in the price. There are many features about this place that you'd love to take home with you, including the wrought-iron lighting fixtures in the breakfast room and many of the decorative objects hanging on the walls. This is one of the best establishments in its category for value.

Fürst Metternich Hotel, 33 Esterhazygasse (tel. 57-82-60). Sienna-colored paint and ornate stone window trim identify this solidly built hotel which began life as an opulent private house. While many of the building's grander architectural elements were retained, including a pair of red stone columns in the entrance vestibule, as well as an old-fashioned staircase guarded with griffins, the high-ceilinged bedrooms were given a conservatively neutral decor during renovations completed in 1985.

Over morning coffee, your view will encompass colorful lithographs from the changing exhibition of pop art hanging in the breakfast room. One of the neighborhood's most stylish bars, the Offiziers Casino, is accessible from the lobby. The location is near the Mariahilferstrasse, about a 20-minute walk from the cathedral.

With breakfast included, the 57 bedrooms rent for 720 AS ($38.30) in a single and from 1,100 AS ($58.52) in a double in winter, rising to 1,200 AS ($63.84) in a single and to 1,700 AS ($90.44) in a double in summer. Each unit contains a tile bath, color TV, radio, and phone.

K & K Palais Hotel, 11 Rudolfsplatz (tel. 63-13-53). When its severely dignified facade was built in 1890, it sheltered the affair of Emperor Franz Joseph and his celebrated mistress, Katherina Schratt. Occupying a desirable position near the river, it remained unused for two decades until members of the Best Western chain renovated it in 1981.

Today, vestiges of its imperial past remain, in spite of the warmly contemporary decor which fills the airy lobby and the lattice-covered bar and coffeeshop. The public rooms are painted a shade of Austrian Imperial yellow, and one of Ms. Schratt's antique secretaries occupies a niche near a white-sided tile stove. Otherwise, the 66 bedrooms are comfortably outfitted with contemporary furniture, TV, radio, mini-bar, and private bath. In high season, singles go for 1,300 AS ($69.16), with doubles costing 1,800 AS ($95.76). In low season, singles rent for 870 AS ($46.28), with doubles renting for 1,200 AS ($63.84), with breakfast included. An extra bed can be set up in any double unit for another 300 AS ($15.96) per person.

K & K Hotel Maria Theresia, 6-8 Kirchberggasse (5 Breitegasse) (tel. 631-35-30). The initials of its name stand as a reminder of the dual monarchy (Kaiserlich und Königlich—"by appointment to the Emperor of Austria and King of Hungary"). Even the surrounding neighborhood, near the major museums and the center of the city, reminds its guests of the days of Maria Theresa. The location is within the romantic artists' colony of Spittelberg, within walking distance of the Winter Palace gardens, the Volkstheater, and the famous shopping street, Mariahilferstrasse.

The hotel offers 124 comfortably contemporary rooms, each with private bath, phone, radio, and TV. Depending on the season, rooms range from between 780 AS ($41.50) and 1,200 AS ($63.84) in a single and from between 1,100 AS ($58.52) and 1,600 AS ($85.12) in a double, with a breakfast buffet included. An extra bed costs another 300 AS ($15.96) per person. There are also in-house parking facilities.

Hotel am Stephansplatz, 9 Stephansplatz (tel. 63-56-05). You'll walk out of your door and face the front entrance to Vienna's cathedral if you stay in this comfortable 62-room hotel, with its unadorned facade. The public rooms are done in a mixture of modern and traditional, and some of the bedrooms contain painted reproductions of rococo furniture and red-flocked wallpaper. All the units have bath or shower and toilet, direct-dial phone, color TV, radio, and mini-bar. Maria Engelmann, the proprietor, charges from 1,050 AS ($55.86) to 1,200 AS ($63.84) in a single and from 1,400 AS ($74.48) to 2,100 AS ($111.72) in a double. Breakfast is included in all the tariffs. An extra bed will be provided for 400 AS ($21.80). A typical Viennese coffee shop, Dom Café, on the first floor is a well-known rendezvous spot.

Hotel Opernring, 11 Opernring (tel. 587-55-18), is a European branch of the Best Western hotel chain. It sits on the Ringstrasse, directly opposite the State Opera House. The hotel is comfortably furnished, with up-to-date furniture, such as reclining upholstered armchairs on chrome bases, wall-to-wall carpeting, and subtly patterned draperies. Aside from the decor, however, you'll quickly find that the efforts of the owner, Mrs. Susie S. Riedl, more than justify this as a choice for your stay in Vienna. If you write to her far enough in advance, she will forward the schedule for both of the Vienna Opera companies, and even arrange for ticket purchases for guests who live in foreign countries.

Doubles cost from 1,880 AS ($100.02) to 2,300 AS ($122.36), while triples are tabbed at 2,400 AS ($127.68) to 2,800 AS ($148.96). Singles are not available in summer but can be rented in the off-season for 1,100 AS ($58.52) to 1,300 AS ($69.16). All rates include breakfast.

Hotel Albatros, 89 Liechtensteinstrasse (tel. 34-35-08), lies close to the U.S. Embassy and the Franz-Josefs Bahnhof, some distance to the north of the Rathaus. If any reader associates an albatross with bad luck, you'll need to change your thinking about this one. The clean and comfortable bedrooms are cheerfully decorated, clean, and well furnished. Singles rent for 950 AS ($50.54), doubles for 1,200 AS ($63.84) to 1,500 AS ($79.80), with breakfast included.

Hotel Austria, 3 Wolfengasse (tel. 52-74-39). The staff of this friendly hotel always seems willing to tell you where to go in the neighborhood for a good meal or a glass of wine, and often distributes carefully typed sheets explaining the medieval origins of this part of Vienna. This unpretentious family-owned establishment (Karl and Amalie Korger are the owners) sits on a small street whose name will probably be unfamiliar to many taxi drivers, although a corner building on the adjoining street, 20 Fleischmarkt, is the point where you'll turn into the narrow lane. The staff maintains the comfortable furnishings in the lobby and in the chandeliered breakfast room in tip-top condition.

Single rooms without bath cost from 580 AS ($30.87) to 680 AS ($36.18), and singles with bath range from 790 AS ($42.03) to 960 AS ($51.07). Doubles cost from 810 AS ($43.09) to 930 AS ($49.48) without bath, from 1,150 AS ($61.18) to 1,380 AS ($73.42) with bath, breakfast included. To reach this hotel from the Westbahnhof, take the Stadtbahn, getting off at the Schwedenplatz. If you're coming from the Südbahnhof, take tram D from the Ring, then change to tram no. 1 or no. 2, and again get off at the Schwedenplatz.

Hotel Wandl, 9 Petersplatz (tel. 63-63-17). Stepping into this hotel is like stepping into a piece of another family's history since it's been in the same ownership for generations. The establishment lies quietly in the inner city and offers views of the steeple of St. Stephen's Cathedral from many of its windows, which often open onto small balconies with railings. The breakfast room is a high-ceilinged two-toned room with hanging chandeliers and lots of ornamented plaster, while the bedrooms usually offer the kind of spacious dimensions that went out of style 60 years ago. The hotel faces St. Peter's Church. Bathless singles cost 400 AS ($21.28), while singles with bath range from 600 AS ($31.92) to 720 AS ($38.30). Doubles cost 700 AS ($37.24) without bath, from 1,050 AS ($55.86) to 1,200 AS ($63.84) with bath. Breakfast is included. Some apartments for longer stays are offered.

Hotel Wimberger, 34-36 Neubaugürtel (tel. 93-76-36). The decorator of this century-old hotel had both a good sense of color and a good sense of humor. The bedrooms are decorated in a tastefully lighthearted combination of colors that is never garish and usually a lot of fun, from the pink-tile bathrooms to the panoply of colors and designs in the well-appointed bedrooms. Even the dining room, while more subdued than the rest of the hotel, is tasteful and makes a positive statement in pure white, cream, and blue-gray. This palatial 19th-century property stands across the street from the Westbahnhof. On the premises you'll find an old-fashioned coffeeshop and a restaurant whose marble floor is arranged in rectangles of black and white reflecting the light from the oversize windows. Without bath, singles cost 580 AS ($30.87); doubles, 800 AS ($42.56). With private bath, singles rent for 700 AS ($37.24) and doubles for 1,000 AS ($53.20).

Hotel Stephanie, 12 Taborstrasse (tel. 24-24-12), is an updated hotel across the Danube Canal from the cathedral, in an area easily accessible to the rest of the city. The interior is decorated in part with beautifully finished wall paneling in geometric designs and gilded wall sconces. Although upon closer examination much of the decor is reproduction, the hotel still gives a hint of the rococo splendor of 19th-century Vienna. A bar area is filled with black leather armchairs on chrome swivel bases and concealed lighting that throws an azure glow over the artfully displayed rows of bottles. All rooms have baths. During high season, April through October, singles cost from 1,050 AS ($55.86) to 1,300 AS ($69.16), and doubles from 1,500 AS ($79.80) to 1,800 AS ($95.76).

Hotel Post, 24 Fleischmarkt (tel. 52-66-87), lies in what was the slaughterhouse district in the Middle Ages and what is today an interesting section full of hotels and restaurants. The front of this hotel is constructed with a restrained dignity of gray stone with a facade of black marble covering the street level. The manager is quick to tell you that both Mozart and Haydn frequently stayed in a former inn at this address. Those composers would probably be amused to hear recordings of their music played in the coffeehouse/restaurant attached to the hotel. About half of the 105 rooms have private baths.

During high season, April through October, singles cost 840 AS ($44.69) with private bath, from 520 AS ($27.66) to 580 AS ($30.87) without bath. Bathless doubles range from 470 AS ($25) to 500 AS ($26.60) per person, and doubles with bath go for 620 AS ($32.98) to 690 AS ($36.71) per person. In low season, singles cost 690 AS ($36.71) with bath, from 440 AS ($23.41) to 490 AS ($26.07) without. Doubles rent for 550 AS ($29.26) to 600 AS ($31.92) per person with bath, from 450 AS ($23.94) to 490 AS ($26.07) per person without private bath. Breakfast is included in all rates.

Hotel Kärntnerhof, 4 Grashofgasse (tel. 52-19-23), advertises itself as a gutbürgerlich family-oriented hotel, which, depending on your tastes, might suit you perfectly. The decor of the public rooms is tastefully arranged around red and blue Oriental rugs, well-upholstered chairs and couches with cabriole legs, and an occasional 19th-century portrait. The bedrooms are more up-to-date, usually with the original parquet floors and striped or patterned wallpaper set off by geometrically colored curtains. Many of the private baths glisten with tiled walls and floors. The owner of this pleasant hotel supervises the maintenance of the 42 rooms and does what he can to be helpful, directing guests to the post office and other nearby Vienna landmarks.

Singles cost 560 AS ($29.79) without bath, 780 AS ($41.50) with bath. Doubles begin at 790 AS ($42.03) without bath and go up to 1,300 AS ($69.16) with complete facilities. The cathedral is only a four-minute walk from here.

Hotel Graben, 3 Dorotheergasse (tel. 52-15-31). Elegant is the only word I'd use to describe the facade of this inner-city hotel which housed, among other great names, Franz Kafka. The establishment lies on the Graben, which leads into the St. Stephansplatz, in a district loaded with antique dealers and on a street which insists on "pedestrians only" during most of the day. The hotel is graced with such architectural ornaments as carved marble fireplaces, Oriental rugs, and gilded chandeliers. In addition to the period antiques, you'll find a lot of art nouveau gracefully decorating the 46 bedrooms, all equipped with bath, radio, telephone, and mini-bar. The rate in a single is 850 AS ($45.22) to 1,350 AS ($71.82), with doubles ranging from 1,500 AS ($79.80) to 1,800 AS ($95.76). Many of these doubles are decorated in an art nouveau style or else with reproduction period antiques. Tariffs include a buffet breakfast, taxes, and service.

Hotel Regina, 15 Rooseveltplatz (tel. 42-76-81), was established in 1896 in a format which every Viennese would instantly recognize, the "Ringstrasse" style. The facade is appropriately grand for its neighborhood, close to the Votive Church, and looks a lot like a Renaissance French palace. The tree-lined street is usually calm and quiet, especially at night. It's an old-world hotel with red salons and interminable corridors. Singles with bath and shower cost from 1,000 AS ($53.20) to 1,400 AS ($74.48) per day, while doubles go for 1,200 AS ($63.84) to 2,200 AS ($117.04), these tariffs including a buffet breakfast, service, and taxes.

Hotel Savoy, 12 Lindengasse (tel. 93-46-46). You'll find a hotel called "the Savoy" in many European capitals, and this one is worthy of bearing that illustrious name. Built within walking distance of the Ringstrasse, the hotel is centered in one of Vienna's principal shopping districts known both for wholesale and retail purchases. Each of the 45 rooms is tastefully decorated in a low-key ambience guaranteed to make you feel at home, using such cosmetic touches as ruffled bedspreads, along with big-windowed views of the city. Each bedroom has its own private bath, as well as radio and TV. Singles cost 900 AS ($47.88), and doubles rent for 1,500 AS ($79.80), including breakfast. Garages and streetcar and bus stops are all to be found in the immediate vicinity.

Hotel Zur Rossmühle, 12 Hauptplatz (tel. 2411), in the Vienna suburb of Tulln an der Donau, is housed in a yellow building with white trim, standing on the central square of this quiet and historic village 30 minutes from the heart of Vienna. The entrance is under a rounded arch protected with a wrought-iron gate. The interior is an attractive combination of antique furniture and crystal chandeliers in a setting which has been modernized into a well-maintained series of white stucco walls and dramatically structured floor space. The 56 bedrooms are decorated in a streamlined baroque style, with simple furniture occasionally highlighted with accents of gilt and white. Singles cost 650 AS ($34.58), while doubles rent for 550 AS ($29.26) per person daily. Half board is available for another 150 AS ($7.98) per person daily.

Hotel Cottage, 12 Hasenauerstrasse (tel. 31-25-71), is in a residential part of Vienna, near the Türkenschanzpark, about a 20-minute tram ride from the heart of Vienna (take tram no. 38). This establishment charges from 1,000 AS ($53.20) for a single and 1,600 AS ($85.12) for a double, breakfast included. All bedrooms have bath or shower. If being in Vienna inspires you to practice your music, you'll find a grand piano in the tiny dining room.

SOME BUDGET HOTELS: Hotel Goldene Spinne, 1a Linke Bahngasse (tel. 72-44-86), is a low-key hostelry near the city air terminal, managed by a friendly, English-speaking staff who indicate to clients where most of the monuments are within the vicinity of this central location. Of its 42 units, only about a dozen contain private baths, which is not really a hardship considering the convenient placement of facilities in the halls near most of the rooms. Theophil Böck, the manager, maintains the corner building with charm. Some rooms are bathless, others have either a tub or shower, while still others contain complete bathrooms with toilets. Rates for singles, depending on the plumbing, are 420 AS ($22.34), 490 AS ($26.07), and 520 AS ($27.66), with doubles going for 660 AS ($35.11), 750 AS ($39.90), and 780 AS ($41.50). Triples, ideal for families, rent for 910 AS ($48.41) bathless and 1,000 AS ($53.20) with a complete bathroom. Four-bedded rooms with full baths cost 1,400 AS ($74.48). Breakfast is included in the tariffs.

Zur Wiener Staatsoper, 11 Krugerstrasse (tel. 52-12-74). You'll probably stop to admire the elaborately baroque facade of this family-run hotel even if you don't plan on staying inside, but after meeting Johann Ungersböck, the pleasant manager, you'll probably choose to make this your headquarters in Vienna. You'll find clean and comfortable rooms and an elevator, and you'll discover that the Staatsoper is convenient to most of the inner-city monuments. All rooms have private bath or shower, and rent for 900 AS ($47.88) in a double, for 650 AS ($34.58) in a single, breakfast included.

Hotel Graf Stadion, 5 Buchfeldgasse (tel. 42-52-84), is a moderately priced hotel immediately behind the Rathaus, within a ten-minute walk from most of the downtown monuments. The facade gives a hint at this building's early 19th-century elegance, particularly with the triangular or half-round ornamentation above many of the windows. All rooms have been redecorated and refurnished, each having a private bathroom. Singles cost 710 AS ($37.77), doubles from 1,100 AS ($58.52), and triples from 1,400 AS ($74.48). All rates include breakfast.

Hotel Rathaus, 13 Lange Gasse (tel. 43-43-02). You'll enter the Rathaus through a wrought-iron gate. The corridors are attractively tiled and decorated in a functional style, as are the bedrooms. Half of these have private bath or toilet. Without bath, singles rent for 480 AS ($25.54), doubles for 700 AS ($37.24). With shower and toilet, singles cost 580 AS ($30.87); doubles, 850 AS ($45.22). An additional bed can transform any double into a triple for an extra 250 AS ($13.30). Breakfast is included. You'll find this to be basically a no-frills, no-nonsense type of establishment, but because it's so well-situated near the university and the Parliament, and because its prices are so reasonable, I feel it's a worthy choice.

Hotel Wolf, 10 Strossigasse (tel. 42-23-20), represents what I think is a very good hotel bargain not far from the Parliament house. You'll be only a five- to ten-minute walk from the inner city, with tram and bus stops on the street corner near the front door. The hotel charges 300 AS ($15.96) per person per day in rooms without private bath, breakfast included. The showers in the hallways are free.

Hotel Schweiger, 4 Schikanedergasse (tel. 56-42-15), is a four-minute walk south from the southern edge of the Ring, in an imposingly proportioned stone building with garlands of what look like laurel leaves carved into the facade. The bedrooms are clean, often with parquet floors, and contain functional furniture and private bath. Singles cost from 500 AS ($26.60) per day, while doubles rent for 850 AS ($45.22) per day, breakfast included.

Hotel-Pension Museum, 3 Museumstrasse (tel. 93-44-26). The exquisite facade of this art nouveau hotel must have been the ultimate in Viennese chic when it was first constructed across from the Imperial Museums. Enough palaces, museums, and monuments are within a five-minute walk to keep any visitor occupied for several days of sightseeing. You'll appreciate the spacious proportions inside many of the bedrooms, some of which echo they're so big—especially the ones in front on the lower floors. All rooms have private baths, and you can have TV if you wish. The price in a single is 780 AS ($41.50), rising to 1,100 AS ($58.52) in a double, with taxes, service, and a substantial breakfast included in the rates.

Hotel Schneider, 5 Getreidemarkt (tel. 57-76-04), sits at the corner of a well-known street, the Lehargasse. The hotel is a recently constructed five-story building with panoramic windows on the ground floor and a red-tile roof; the facade is painted a baroque yellow with vertical white stripes. The interior is warmly decorated with well-polished 19th-century antiques and comfortably upholstered chairs, many of them chosen by the owner, who seems especially willing to welcome musicians from around the world. This is one of Vienna's better small hotels, situated near the flower market. Singles with private bath rent for 780 AS ($41.50) to 1,020 AS ($54.62); doubles with private bath cost 1,100 AS ($58.52) to 1,500 AS ($79.80). Breakfast is included.

A Summer Budget Hotel Chain

Academia Hotels, with headquarters at 3a Pfeilgasse (tel. 42-25-34, ext. 77), is a chain of budget accommodations all of which are reserved for university students during the term and operated as fully licensed and categorized hotels every summer between July 1 and September 30, offering comfortable rooms for tourists at reasonable rates. These hotels are among the best bargains in town, especially since all of them are within walking distance from the city center, only a few minutes by streetcar J or underground no. 2 from the opera. They are mainly group hotels but offer good value for individual travelers, as well. The chain also has hostelries in Graz and Salzburg.

Rates at the Academia accommodations all include a continental breakfast.

Hotel Academia, 3a Pfeilgasse (tel. 42-25-34), has 368 bedrooms, all with complete bath. Singles rent for 680 AS ($36.18), twin-bedded units for 470 AS ($25) per person, and triples for 400 AS ($21.80) per person. Full or half board is available for 370 AS ($19.68) and 210 AS ($11.17), respectively.

Hotel Atlas, 1-3 Lerchenfelderstrasse (tel. 93-45-48), is a 181-room establishment, with complete baths in all rooms. The charges are 730 AS ($38.84) in a single, 510 AS ($27.13) per person in a twin, and 455 AS ($24.21) per person in a room with three beds. Full- and half-board rates are the same as those for the Hotel Academia above.

Hotel Avis, 4 Pfeilgasse (tel. 42-63-74), offers 72 rooms, all with private bath, with half-board available for 210 AS ($11.17) and full board for 370 AS ($19.68). A single unit rents for 575 AS ($30.59), a twin-bedded room for 420 AS ($22.34) per person, and a triple accommodation for 360 AS ($19.15) per person.

The fourth in the quartet of hotels is the Hotel Aquila, 1a Pfeilgasse (tel. 42-52-35), which receives summer guests in its 72 bedrooms, each equipped with a shower. The price of a single is 540 AS ($28.73). Each occupant of a twin-bedded room pays 390 AS ($20.75), while persons staying in one of the three-bedded units pay 330 AS ($17.56) each. As at the other three hotels, and for the same prices, half and full board are available.

The Academia concern also has a youth hostel (Jugendgästehaus), the Haus Pfeilgasse, 4-6 Pfeilgasse, which contains 90 rooms. None of the units has private plumbing facilities, but there are spacious public restrooms on each floor. There is also a self-service restaurant on the premises. The charges are 285 AS ($15.16) in a single, 260 AS ($13.83) per person in a twin or triple.

THE BEST OF THE PENSIONS: Hotel-Pension Elite, 32 Wipplingerstrasse (tel. 63-25-18), is housed in a magnificent corner building next to the Vienna stock exchange. The neighborhood is appropriately grand for this edifice which looks like a former private palace. You'll be near the university, the Burg-theater, and the cathedral. The public rooms are tastefully furnished with a mixture of antiques and modern pieces, crystal chandeliers, lots of well-oiled paneling, green-tile fireplaces, and Oriental rugs. The establishment lives up to its name and deserves a high recommendation for good service in a refined framework. Without private shower or bath, singles cost from 510 AS ($27.13) to 765 AS ($40.70); doubles range from 760 AS ($40.43) to 1,200 AS ($63.84). Breakfast, which is included in the rates, is served in the elegantly upholstered and carpeted dining room.

Hotel-Pension Arenberg, 2 Stubenring (tel. 52-52-91), is an old-world pension in the most prestigious section of downtown Vienna, on the Ringstrasse near all the museums and palaces, three minutes away from the air terminal and close to the canal. Rooms are soundproof and often contain Oriental rugs, interesting art, and good furniture. The entire establishment boasts only 25 rooms, with room service available during the dinner hour only. A restaurant and a disco are housed in the same building. All units have bath or shower. In high season, April through October and during the Christmas holidays, the charges are 720 AS ($38.30) to 860 AS ($45.75) in a single, 1,200 AS ($63.84) to 1,400 AS ($74.48) in a double.

Pension Sacher, 1 Rotenturmstrasse (tel. 63-32-38 between 8 a.m. and 1 p.m., 46-97-693 after 4 p.m.), is an extremely well-run hostelry whose regular clients return year after year, partially because the pension's location on the Stephansplatz is a choice one. Although it is not now connected to the famous hotel with the same name, the Pension Sacher is owned by the great-grandson of the man who invented the Sacher torte in 1832. Carl Sacher's ancestor was the cook for Prince Metternich when the luscious dessert was first introduced to Viennese palates. His son, Edward, founded the Hotel Sacher, and his grand-son, father of the owner of the pension, also named Carl, founded Hotel Sacher in Baden near Vienna in 1881. The present Carl and his three sons, the only male descendants of the line, still have an interest in the Baden hotel and in an apartment facility in Baden.

The pension consists of eight apartments, each with a kitchenette, bathroom, and direct-dial phone. There is no staff other than a maid who comes in on workdays from 8 a.m. to 2 p.m. to tidy the rooms. The prices per day for a stay of from two to nine days are 670 AS ($35.64) to 715 AS ($38.04) in a single, 785 AS ($41.76) to 820 AS ($43.62) in a double, and 930 AS ($49.48) to 1,050 AS ($55.86) for a double with a sitting room. Heating is included in the rates given. The pension is on the seventh floor of the building. It is wise to write ahead for a reservation at this popular place. The pension is managed by the owner's daughter, Claudia Racek-Sacher.

Pension Wiener, 16 Seilergasse (tel. 52-48-160). Mr. and Mrs. Thau-Ohg sold their Hotel de France a few years ago to open this tiny pension, which is in an office building in a downtown section two blocks from the cathedral. You're made to feel like a guest in a private home at this friendly, tranquil oasis with plenty of up-to-date conveniences and old-fashioned hospitality. The 30 beds are in units with private bath, radio, color TV, phone, and refrigerator. From April till October a single rents for 980 AS ($52.14) to 1,020 AS ($54.26), while doubles cost 1,400 AS ($74.48), with breakfast served in your room.

Hotel Goldenes Einhorn, 5 Am Hundsturm (tel. 55-47-55). Much of the flavor of old Austria can be gleaned from a visit to this family-run guest house in a residential area between the cathedral and Schönbrunn Palace. The staff speaks four languages (including English), and welcomes visitors into a kind of old Vienna ambience they work hard to sustain. The reasonably priced rooms are highly recommended as a good and safe location in downtown Vienna. A bathless single goes for 330 AS ($17.56), and a double costs 560 AS ($29.79) with shower, 505 AS ($26.87) to 530 AS ($28.20) without. Breakfast is not included in the price, although guests will be directed to a nearby inexpensive coffeeshop where good Viennese morning meals are served.

Pension Reimer, 18 Kirchengasse (tel. 93-61-62), is reached by walking from the Opernring up Mariahilferstrasse, one of the two main shopping streets of the city. You will be welcomed by friendly, English-speaking Mrs. Margarete Mattis. The pension is quiet despite being in a central location. Rooms are large and clean, with modern furniture, and most of them are equipped with shower. The price charged for a single in the comfortable accommodations is 260 AS ($13.83). Doubles cost from 440 AS ($23.41) to 520 AS ($27.66), and triples rent for 700 AS ($37.24), with a room with four beds going for 950 AS ($50.54). Breakfast is extra, but service is included in the room rates. You can arrange for babysitting whenever necessary. The pension is open year-round.

Pension Nossek, 17 Graben (tel. 52-45-91). Mozart lived on the third floor of this centrally located building in 1781 and 1782, writing the *Haffner* Symphony and the *Abduction from the Seraglio*. In 1908, the building was converted into a guesthouse by the present owner's grandfather, and has been accepting travelers ever since into its comfortable interior. The pension occupies three floors of a thick-walled building, and has a tiny elevator. Dr. Renato Cremona, the charming owner, lived in Florida for several years before returning to Vienna. Most of the 33 rooms have been renovated, and all but a few contain a private bath or shower (however, only about 60% have a private toilet). The establishment lies a few blocks from the cathedral and is a good bet for a clean but unfrilly accommodation. With breakfast included, singles cost between 330 AS ($17.56) and 450 AS ($23.94), with doubles going for between 770 AS ($40.96) and 900 AS ($47.88). The higher price gets you a most spacious room.

Pension Neuer Markt, 9 Seilergasse (tel. 52-23-16), is housed in a white baroque building with an interesting elliptical facade facing a square with an ornate fountain, near the cathedral. The carpeted rooms are clean and well maintained in an updated motif of white walls and vibrant color accents. Some of the beds are set into niches, and many of the windows are bigger than you'd expect. All units have baths, phones, and central heating. Singles peak at 640 AS ($34.05), and doubles cost a maximum of 1,000 AS ($53.20).

Kellner's Altwienerhof, 6 Herklotzgasse (tel. 83-71-45). On foggy winter nights the amber carriage lights on the facade of this corner building almost seem to call out to the guests who eventually discover the old-world charm served here by the carload. The same family has managed this establishment for many years, welcoming visitors to the high-ceilinged reception area with the polished wood detailing and the wrought-iron space dividers. The rooms are comfortably furnished, each one different, usually with padded chairs and vibrant colors. Singles with bath cost 490 AS ($26.07) per day, while doubles with bath rent for 750 AS ($39.90), breakfast included.

Pension Dr. Geissler, 14 Postgasse (tel. 63-28-03), is an attractively informal guest house offering unpretentious lodgings at reasonable prices to visitors who will find themselves near the well-known Schwedenplatz at the edge of the Danube Canal. The bedrooms are attractively furnished with simple blond headboards, colorful draperies, and a few chairs. Singles with bath rent for 550 AS ($29.26). A double with bath ranges from 960 AS ($51.07) to 1,080 AS ($57.46). These prices include breakfast.

Pension Zipser, 49 Lange Gasse (tel. 42-02-28), is attractively situated within a five-minute walk of the Rathaus. It offers 50 rooms—many overlooking a private garden—which are reached by the elevator. They have phone, wall-to-wall carpeting, and central heating, and are efficiently managed by the Austerer family. The facade is ornamented with carved shell motifs above the third floor. Much of the renovated interior is tastefully adorned with wood detailing. Without bath, singles cost 480 AS ($25.54); doubles, 700 AS ($37.24). With bath, singles go for 580 AS ($30.87); doubles, 940 AS ($50.01), and triples, 1,080 AS ($57.46). Breakfast is included in all the tariffs.

Pension Bellaria, 41 Kirchengasse (tel. 93-63-81). Constructed around 1910, this small pension offers comfortable single, double, and triple rooms to guests who appreciate its central location. Without private bath, singles rent for 350 AS ($18.62) and doubles for 280 AS ($14.90) per person.

Hotel-Pension Barich, 3 Barichgasse (tel. 72-12-73), might be the choice for guests who prefer quiet residential surroundings. Northeast of the Südbahnhof, behind an unpretentious facade, is a small, well-furnished quiet hotel. The proprietors, who manage the establishment, speak fluent English. All of the 16 bedrooms are soundproof and have private shower or bath, toilet, direct-dial phone, radio, color TV with in-house video, mini-bar, and safe. Singles rent for 720 AS ($38.30) to 850 AS ($45.22), with doubles ranging from 1,150 AS ($61.18) to 1,300 AS ($69.16), and rates include breakfast and all taxes. Garage space is available on request.

4. Where to Dine

What you'll find in Vienna are restaurants of all types, serving not only the Austrian cuisine, but that of Yugoslavia, Hungary, and Czechoslovakia as well, along with Chinese, Italian, Russian, or whatever.

There are also many classic dishes of the *Wiene, kuche* (Viennese kitchen) that you'll want to try. Before dining out, refer to the notes on Austrian cookery in Chapter II under "Food and Drink."

THE UPPER BRACKET: Prinz Eugen Rôtisserie, Hilton Hotel, 2 Landstrasser Hauptstrasse (tel. 75-26-52), is one of the finest restaurants of Vienna. The setting is like that of an operetta version of a baronial château, filled with every comfort imaginable and certain to impress with its overlay of charm. There are three rooms, each one embellished in the style of the Belvedere Palace, itself dating from the 18th century. You might dine in a salon all in muted beige and gold, honoring the musical heritage of the Austrian capital. A second salon is the Baronial Hall, a grill, with scenes from the prince's battles adorning the walls, furniture, and oak paneling. The waiters serve international specialties from the open grill. The final room is the Belvedere Library, the bookshelves holding hundreds of antique volumes. It has dark-wood paneling.

Werner Matt, from Tyrol, is one of the founders of nouvelle cuisine Viennoise. As such, he is one of the leading chefs of Austria. Each day he creates a special gourmet menu based on the freshest ingredients available in the market, many of which he has had brought to Vienna for the purpose, supervising his staff of 75 persons in preparation and service, which is superb. Try his "variations of sweets" which look like works of art. Each dish is prepared for a discriminating palate. This place is an exclusive Viennese haunt, drawing both locals and foreign patronage, each group of which seems to appreciate its excellent wine cellar. You can order from the international menu from noon to 3 p.m. and from 6 to 11 p.m., paying from 450 AS ($23.94) to 1,200 AS ($63.84) for a set meal or from 500 AS ($26.60) to 750 AS ($39.90) on the à la carte. A business lunch of varying prices is offered Monday through Friday.

Restaurant Mattes, 8 Schönlaterngasse (tel. 52-62-75), located in a vaulted room, concealed behind an unprepossessing facade in the historic quarter of Vienna, is one of the most glamorous culinary citadels of Austria. Since it opened in 1981, it has hosted celebrities ranging from the President of Austria to the most distinguished gastronomes of Europe. Some of them often reserve one of the establishment's eight tables weeks in advance.

You'll be greeted at the door by one of the most intuitive maître d'hôtels in Vienna, Cologne-born Thomas Huen, who quickly establishes a feeling of dining amid friends in an elegant private home. The primroses on each table set off the gleaming crystal, silver, and the arrays of Austrian and international wines which chef Rudolf Schmölz has so carefully selected. With a pair of kitchen assistants, he personally prepares each dish, devoting the accumulated skill of his training at some of the best restaurants of Munich.

Mattes is considered expensive by neighborhood residents, but an amazingly good value by visiting gourmets. Set menus range from 650 AS ($34.58) to 1,000 AS ($53.20), while à la carte averages around 850 AS ($45.22). The menu changes frequently, depending on the ingredients available in local markets. The neatly typed menu includes impeccably prepared delicacies such as a terrine of vegetables and foie gras in aspic, potato cream soup with white Italian truffles, gratinée of river-bred crayfish with kohlrabi, tender chunks of seasonal venison in a port wine sauce, medallions of veal with truffled eggs, filet of sole with a chive sauce, and white chocolate mousse with cocoa sauce and strawberries. Reservations are strongly suggested for meals which most diners consider to be exquisite. Open for dinner only, closed Sunday.

Gottfried Restaurant, 45 Untere Viaduktgasse at 3 Marxergasse (tel. 73-82-56), one of the best new restaurants, was established in 1985 on a commercial street near the City Air Terminal. It revels in the kind of decor that many less successful restaurants would like to emulate, combining a perfectly controlled ambience with superb food. The pure white walls and lace-covered windows are flatteringly offset with ruby-colored Oriental carpets, pink napery, and unglazed terracotta floors. Add to this about a dozen polite and uniformed waiters, verdant plants, and comfortably contemporary armchairs covered in pastel-tinted upholstery, and you get an idea of what Gottfried is all about.

Considering the quality of the cuisine, the set menus are reasonably priced bargains at 420 AS ($22.34) at lunchtime and 940 AS ($50.01) at dinner, with à la carte meals costing from 800 AS ($42.56). Your meal might begin with potato soup with truffles or include carpaccio, a salad of lobster with fresh asparagus, a salad of wild duck, and a Provençale fish soup so rich it could almost be considered a relish.

Carinthian-born Josef Fadinger is the well-rehearsed chef whose meals are worth both the effort and the expense. The establishment is open for lunch and dinner Monday through Friday, for dinner only on Saturday. It is closed Sunday and for the last two weeks of August. Reservations are necessary.

Zu den 3 Husaren, 4 Weihburggasse (tel. 52-11-92), is an enduring favorite among Viennese restaurants. Some consider it as much an institution as St. Stephen's Cathedral. Few social or business leaders would consider a trip to Vienna without a dinner here. Over the years, it has entertained the famous (the Duke and Duchess of Windsor) and the infamous. Just off the Kärntnerstrasse, it has a large plate-glass window with plaster mannequins of the Hungarian officers who established the place after World War I. An interior view reveals Gobelin tapestries, valuable antiques, fine rugs, and masses of flowers.

The establishment is very expensive and very select, with a delectable cuisine that has been rated by practically everyone as the best traditional food in Vienna: To the background music of gypsy melodies, you dine on such dishes as lobster cream soup with tarragon, stewed rumpsteak with white cabbage and noodles, freshwater salmon with pike soufflé, breast of guinea fowl, and an array of sole dishes. The chef specializes in veal, including his deliciously flavored kalbsbrücken Metternich. The place is celebrated for its repertoire of more than 40 hors d'oeuvres, served from a trolley rolled through its elegant precincts. A dessert specialty is the Husaren pfannkuchen (Hussar's pancake), as well as a form of cheese-filled crêpe which, as if that weren't enough, has a chocolate sauce poured over it (the recipe is known only to the chef). The restaurant serves dinner nightly from 6. It's often closed for a month in parts of July and August, and also shuts down on Sunday. À la carte meals range from 750 AS ($39.90) to 1,200 AS ($63.84).

Sacher Hotel Restaurant, 4 Philharmonikerstrasse (tel. 52-55-75), is a famous, famous restaurant, serving the epitome of Viennese cookery. Long an enduring favorite—either before or after the opera—it has many detractors, but I'm not one of them. Seemingly all celebrities who come to Vienna eventually are seen in the red dining room, where they're likely to order the restaurant's most famous dish, tafelspitz, the Viennese boiled beef platter that was fit for an emperor. The chef serves it with a savory, herb-flavored sauce. Of course that emperor was not Franz Joseph I. Madame Sacher annoyed him by encouraging liaisons between archdukes and the attractive young members of the Vienna Opera Ballet.

Wear your finest for dinner here, and make sure you show up before 11 p.m. Count on spending from 600 AS ($31.92) up for a sumptuous meal. Waiters will often suggest various Austrian wines to accompany your dinner. For dessert, the Sacher torte enjoys world renown. Some people claim that the torte was invented by the cigar-smoking owner of the hotel, Frau Anna Sacher. However, it is also said to have been created in 1832 by Franz Sacher, while he served as Prince Metternich's chef. The Sacher torte is the most famous pastry in Vienna. It's primarily a chocolate sponge mixture. After it's baked, it's sliced in half and filled with apricot jam. Open for lunch and dinner every day.

Palais Schwarzenberg Restaurant, 9 Schwarzenbergplatz (tel. 78-43-15), has one of the most elegant backgrounds of any restaurant in the city. It lies in a famous hotel (see the previous recommendation). The owner is Prince Karl Johannes von Schwarzenberg, scion of one of the country's most aristocratic families. Take your time over an apéritif in the deluxe cocktail lounge, where the waiter will most likely recite the daily specialties of the chef. In summer you can dine on a terrace. Dining in such an imperial setting might cause you to imagine you are a Habsburg. The cuisine is refined, with many French dishes, and the service is first class and very old world. The wine cellar is superb, and the chef is a man of many talents. He seasonally adjusts his menu and therefore has many specialties, including medallions of veal with crabmeat and pearl onions. Dinner rangers from 500 AS ($26.60) to 1,000 AS ($53.20), and reservations are suggested. The restaurant is open all year.

Korso bei der Oper, 2 Mahlerstrasse (tel. 52-16-42). Dining guests walk across Aubusson carpets and past the antiques of the Hotel Bristol lobby before entering this citadel of gastronomic chic. Expensive paneling, scarlet-colored carpeting, fountain-shaped crystal chandeliers, Sheraton shield-backed armchairs, and lushly baroque corkscrew-shaped columns flanking a pink marble fireplace create an opulent atmosphere.

Chef Reinhard Gerer prepares an alluring mixture of both traditional and nouvelle cuisine for a discriminating clientele. Your meal might include tafelspitz as Franz Joseph liked it, roast chicken with a Calvados apple sauce, a rack of lamb with aromatic spices, medallions of beef with a shallot-flavored butter sauce and roquefort-flavored noodles. Your first course might include oysters, accompanied by one of the selections from an extensive wine list. Full meals cost from 700 AS ($37.24), and reservations are important. The restaurant is open for both lunch and dinner daily except Saturday when only dinner is served.

König von Ungarn (King of Hungary), 10 Schulerstrasse (tel. 52-53-19), is a beautifully decorated restaurant inside the famous inner-city hotel of the same name. The service here is superb, with a masterful assistance added by the owner, Don Pedro, who's usually on hand to guide you through the menu. If you're in doubt about what to order and Don Pedro isn't around, try the tafelspitz, the savory boiled beef dish which we've already sampled at the Sacher Hotel. It's elegantly dispensed from a trolley which makes the rounds through the richly decorated place. Other menu choices, which change frequently according to what is seasonal, include a ragoût of seafish with fresh mushrooms, tournedos with a mustard and horseradish sauce, and a stunning collection of appetizers that might include scampi in a caviar sauce. The restaurant is open daily except Saturday from 11:30 a.m. to 3 p.m. and from 6:15 p.m. until midnight. À la carte dinners average from 350 AS ($18.62) to 500 AS ($26.60), and considering what you get, that's not an overpriced check.

Zur Frommen Helene, 16 Breitegasse (tel. 93-46-82). If you want fish, veal, or pork, you should go elsewhere. But if you want a steak, this is the finest place to come to in Vienna. It's in an ochre-colored, turn-of-the-century house, with an art nouveau decor that offers plenty of visual distraction. It encompasses two different rooms on two different floors, both with late-19th-century memorabilia. In some cases the lamps look like jeweled tiaras hanging from chains. Part of the evening's amusement will be the unexpected flashes of flambé pans going off to different parts of the restaurant. The staff, in spite of the flames, has everything under control. In addition to steaks, they also provide a wide range of fresh salads and tempting desserts. French wine is sold by the carafe, and you may want to end your meal with an Irish coffee. Complete dinners range from 450 AS ($23.94) to 750 AS ($39.90), and are served from 6 p.m. until midnight every day of the week. Reservations are suggested, and the restaurant shuts down in August for vacation.

Steirereck, 2 Rasumofskygasse (tel. 73-31-68), means "corner of Styria," which is exactly what Heinz and Grete Reitbauer have tried to create in the rustic decor of this friendly and intimate restaurant, one of the finest in the city, lying on the Danube Canal. They do the cooking themselves, turning out such specialties as traditional Viennese dishes and nouvelle cuisine selections. For example, tafelspitz might be served in the old-fashioned way or else in a more trendy manner, with a warm cranberry sauce. Other dishes are likely to include veal with Calvados and wild rice, rack of lamb Styrian style, and soufflé of trout with sorrel noodles. The menu is wisely limited and well prepared, and it usually costs from 450 AS ($23.94) for a typical meal. The restaurant is closed on weekends and holidays, but open otherwise from 11 a.m. to midnight Monday to Friday.

Zum Weisser Schwan, 59 Nussdorferstrasse (tel. 34-16-50), is the most celebrated game restaurant in Vienna. Unlike most restaurants in the country, game is available here year round except when the restaurant is closed, which is on Saturday and Sunday but also from mid-July to mid-August and for part of December until January 10. It's imperative to book a table for dinner. The location is in a mellow old Viennese house with a historic courtyard more than 250 years old. The Pilsener beer here comes straight from a barrel, while the cuisine is straightforward, authentic, and without unnecessary frills. An average meal will cost 560 AS ($29.79) and could include woodcock "grandmother's style," filet of young deer with lentils, mushrooms, and bacon, or guinea fowl in a cream sauce. Other specialties include the classic partridge with red cabbage, pheasant wrapped in bacon, and young wild boar. There's also a well-stocked list of fish dishes, including perch, fogosch (a form of whitefish), and sole. A staff member will hand you a list of specialties which include virtually anything made from a goose, ranging from soup to a terrine to a well-seasoned breast.

Leupold's Kupferdachl, 7 Schottengasse (tel. 63-93-81), has been directed by the Leupold family for the past 30 years. Today it specializes in the Austrian equivalent of nouvelle cuisine, but the chef also prepares more conservatively traditional dishes. The rustically elegant interior has lots of paneling, a scattering of Oriental rugs, and a cozy ambience of powder-blue banquettes and elegantly detailed straight-backed chairs. Lunch averages around 350 AS ($18.62) to 450 AS ($23.94), while dinner costs from 450 AS ($23.94) to 600 AS ($31.92). The restaurant is open Monday to Friday from noon to 3 p.m. and from 6 p.m. to midnight. On Saturday it's open only for dinner, and is closed from late July until sometime in August.

At **Kervansaray & Hummer Bar,** 9 Mahlerstrasse (tel. 52-88-43), you get a sense of the historic link between the Habsburgs and their 19th-century neighbor, the Ottoman Empire. The place actually contains three different restaurants on the same premises (the deli is reviewed separately). The two remaining restaurants occupy two different floors, but each is committed to serving an array of delectable seafood flown in frequently from the North Sea or from the Bosphorus.

On the ground floor, in the Kervansaray, a team of polite waiters, many from Turkey, announce a changing array of daily specials. They also serve tempting salads from an hors d'oeuvres table. Perhaps the true visual treat of the evening is upstairs in the Lobster Bar where, in a spacious series of interconnected rooms dotted with Oriental carpets, guests enjoy the bounties of the sea.

A meal in either section of the restaurant often begins with a champagne cocktail and is followed by one of many appetizers, including a lobster and salmon caviar cocktail. Main courses include a short list of meat dishes, including filet steak with roquefort sauce, but they mainly consist of seafood, such as grilled filet of sole with fresh asparagus, bouillabaisse, a Norwegian salmon with horseradish and champagne sauce, and, most definitely, lobster. Full meals cost from 800 AS ($42.56) if you stick to the standard fare. But if shellfish is your weakness, a tab could run much higher. The restaurants are open daily except Sunday.

Restaurant Mitsukoshi, 2 Albertinaplatz (tel. 53-30-48). Upstairs, the Café Mozart is a model of baroque elegance, but in the basement diners experience a cross-cultural shock in discovering the most elegant and sophisticated Japanese restaurant in Austria. It was established in 1985 when one of Tokyo's best known department stores, Mitsukoshi, upgraded the decor of the café and opened the basement restaurant. Opalized marble, Japanese cypress, carefully arranged lighting, and Noh masks were incorporated into what is a showplace of Mitsukoshi design and style.

First, visitors enjoy a cup of Japanese tea or sake in a restrained lounge where the severe angles of a black granite fountain are softened with carefully arranged flowers, and then a kimono-clad waitress from Japan escorts visitors down a flight of steps to the alluringly simple dining room. There you can order an à la carte Japanese meal for 550 AS ($29.26) or a fixed price menu, ranging from between 400 AS ($21.28) and 900 AS ($47.88). Sushi, imported from Italy or Turkey, is followed by a full-service meal in a ritualized format of lacquer dishes and fresh vegetables.

The establishment is closed Sunday. Between Monday and Saturday, meals are served from noon to 2 p.m. and from 7 p.m. to midnight. Reservations are suggested. The main entrance to this establishment is around the corner from the Albertinaplatz on the Maysedergasse.

Landhaus Winter, 262 Simmeringer Lände (tel. 76-23-17), is a century-old country house surrounded with flowers in summer and decorated inside with powder-blue napery and rustic artifacts. It sits at the edge of the Danube Canal, providing a pleasant refuge for those Viennese who wish to escape the congestion of their city. The terrace is particularly pleasant on a summer day, although the interior is cozily paneled and elegant. Well-prepared fish is one of the specialties here, and a selection might include perch or eel, both cooked in a number of ways, or Greenland salmon, French oysters, Portuguese mussels, and a young brook trout from local waters. Meat dishes might include medallions of roebuck, tournedos with mushrooms, lamb steak with fennel, and filet of beef in a cabbage cream sauce. Reservations are suggested, and the restaurant is closed on Sunday evening and all day Monday. Meals range from 350 AS ($18.62) to 750 AS ($39.90).

Steinerne Eule (Stony Owl), 30 Halbgasse (tel. 93-22-50), is the exclusive haunt of some of the most prestigious gourmets of Vienna. With the prices it charges—between 300 AS ($15.96) and 700 AS ($37.24) for a fixed-price meal —you can see why. À la carte dinners cost less, from 200 AS ($10.64) to 500 AS ($26.60). The chef has learned to blend an attractive synthesis of nouvelle Austrian cuisine with traditional Viennese recipes. The menu changes according to the season and the market availability. Therefore, depending on this, you might get venison terrine with fresh goose liver, cream of asparagus soup, zucchini filled with goose liver pâté, or veal delicacies sometimes served with spinach noodles. For an innovative dessert, the chef occasionally features an avocado mousse with fresh strawberries or perhaps an apple parfait with kiwi fruit. Service is daily until midnight, except on Sunday and Monday.

Hauswirth, 20 Otto-Bauer-Gasse (tel. 57-12-61). The imposing entrance to this restaurant is under a rectangular corridor with a well-polished fan window at the far end. You'll push open the leaded-glass door to enter this art nouveau enclave which has become a stamping ground of well-dressed habitués. The summertime gardens are lovely, but in winter you'll probably eat in a paneled ambience of dark wood and crystal chandeliers. The chef adheres to *neue Wiener küche.* He seasonally adjusts his menu, which might include quail, venison, asparagus, lots of fresh berries, goose liver, sweetbreads, well-prepared steaks, and suckling lambs, along with a tempting array of homemade pastries. His place is open daily except Sunday and holidays from 11:30 a.m. to 3 p.m. and from 5:30 p.m. to midnight. À la carte meals range from 350 AS ($18.62) to 600 AS ($31.92). The cellar holds a large variety of the best of Austrian wines plus a well-chosen assortment from some of the best European vineyards.

Restaurant Fischerhaus, an der Höhenstrasse (tel. 44-13-20), in the Vienna Woods, is popular with members of Vienna's diplomatic community and the city's business elite. Former Austrian chancellor Bruno Kreisky is a regular client, and other celebrities have included Arnold Schwarzenegger, Happy Rockefeller, Robert Mitchum, and Elizabeth Taylor. The cellars read like an international directory of fine wines, especially those from the Napa Valley of California. The establishment is housed in a century-old farmhouse surrounded by greenery, with an outdoor terrace and an interior with a blazing wintertime fireplace and an intriguing collection of antique firearms and hunting memorabilia. Prices range between 350 AS ($18.62) and 900 AS ($47.88) for fixed-price meals, and from 500 AS ($26.60) for an à la carte dinner. Reservations are strongly suggested before heading here. The restaurant is closed from the first of November until the end of February. On Sunday it closes at 5 p.m.

Kellner's Altwienerhof, 6 Herklotzgasse (tel. 83-71-45), near Schönbrunn Palace, is a ground-floor room behind wrought-iron doors which is now one of the leading restaurants in the city, with a menu featuring an Austrian version of nouvelle cuisine. The chef also turns out a satisfying range of well-prepared traditional favorites. In a paneled room with trompe-l'oeil landscapes covering much of the wall space, you can dine on such delicacies as cold cucumber soup with shrimp, pike soufflé with crab sauce, gratinée of mussels with Riesling sauce and seaweed, a traditional tafelspitz, veal steak in a basil and tomato sauce with fresh zucchini, and fresh turbot with leafy spinach and red wine butter. The menu changes frequently. The restaurant is open Monday to Saturday from 11:15 a.m. to 3 p.m. and from 6 p.m. to midnight, and is usually closed for the last days of January and the first two weeks of February. Fixed-price lunches begin at 280 AS ($14.90), while set evening meals range from 650 AS ($34.58) to 700 AS ($37.24). À la carte meals begin at around 275 AS ($14.63) but could go as high as 750 AS ($39.90), depending on what you order.

THE MEDIUM-PRICED RANGE: **Restaurant Stiebitz** (Zum Schwarzen Kameel), 5 Bognergasse (tel. 63-81-25), dates from 1618 and has remained in the same family. A delicatessen against one of the walls of this popular place sells wine, liquor, and specialty meat items, although most of the action takes place among the chicly dressed clientele in the café. On a Saturday morning the café section is packed with weekend Viennese recovering from a late night out with massive doses of caffeine. Everyone stands here, drinking the beverages that the friendly uniformed waiters bring on trays, and selecting open-face sandwiches from the trays on the black countertops.

While you're here, be sure to glance through the door to the restaurant, where you'll see a perfectly preserved art deco room. Jeweled copper chandeliers hang from beaded strings, with discreet illumination beaming through their etched-glass globes. The walls are a combination of polished paneling, yellowed ceramic tiles, and an attractively dusky plaster ceiling frieze of grape leaves. The vine theme is repeated in the machine-age marquetry in several kinds of hardwoods, which graces many of the room dividers. The restaurant contains only 11 tables, and it might be a perfect place for a nostalgic lunch or dinner in Vienna. The international cuisine features specialties such as herring filet Oslo, potato soup, Valencian paella, Roman saltimbocca, and a host of daily specials. Meals range from 300 AS ($15.96).

Hotel Astoria, 32 Kärntnerstrasse (entrance is at 1 Führichgasse) (tel. 52-

65-85). The first-floor restaurant inside this hotel is one of the finest in Vienna. The foyer is filled with theatrical portraits of opera stars, and the decor inside is appropriately grand. The service is superb, and the clientele is often elegant and well-heeled. An opera menu is offered either before or after the performances at the nearby state-run institution. It costs 380 AS ($20.22), and could include prats on eggplant slices, cold cream of avocado soup, or pork filet with soy sauce, followed by a dessert of kiwi salad. More expensive à la carte items could include a parsleyed filet of sole with almonds, veal, beef, and game dishes. The typically Austrian dishes include tafelspitz and kaiserschnitzel, the latter with caper sauce and buttered rice. Dessert could be a concoction of truffled ice cream or a cranberry parfait. A la carte meals cost from 500 AS ($26.60). Lunch is served from noon to 3 p.m. and dinner from 6 to 11:30 p.m. every day, and reservations are suggested.

Franz Zimmer Schubertstüberln, 4 Schreyvogelgasse (tel. 63-71-87). Brown-and-white striped awnings cover the pink and white café chairs set onto a raised platform above the pink begonias and cobblestones of the quiet street near the Burgtheater. From looking at it, you'd never guess that the inside is as big as it is, but once you pass through the small garden entrance you'll see a series of rooms that have been elevated to a high pitch of the modern decorator's art. You'll find a room here for practically every taste, from the plushly modern bar with horseshoe-shaped banquettes to a rustically informal eatery. My favorite rooms are the two salons in pastel-colored high-ceilinged elegance, with immaculate linens and lots of light. Look carefully before you select an ambience here. If the first one isn't to your liking, you'll eventually find something that is. The distinguished chef has prepared several menus, allowing clients to spend very little money or quite a lot, depending on their tastes. A bistro menu, priced from 90 AS ($4.79), offers daily specials with three courses, including soup, a meat dish, and dessert, while more expensive dinners range from 300 AS ($15.96). The restaurant is open from 9 a.m. to midnight every day except Sunday, and reservations are suggested.

Abend-Restaurant Fuervogel, 21 Alserbachstrasse (tel. 34-10-392). For more than 75 years this has been a Viennese landmark, bringing Russian cuisine to a location across the street from the palace of the Prince of Liechtenstein. You'll eat in romantically Slavic surroundings with gypsy violins playing Russian and Viennese music in the background. Specialties include chicken Kiev, beef Stroganoff, veal Dolgoruki, borscht, and many other dishes that taste as if they came right off the steppes. Your hors d'oeuvres might be sakkuska, a variety platter popular in Russia. For dessert you might select a Russian ice cream called plombier. The restaurant is open every day except Sunday from 6 p.m. to 1 a.m. It's closed from mid-July until after the first week of August. An average meal will range between 225 AS ($11.97) and 500 AS ($26.60).

Ming Court, 32-34 Kärntnerstrasse (tel. 52-17-15), serves genuine Chinese food in a far eastern setting near the Vienna State Opera. The location is at the Hotel Astoria. Its entrance is around the corner at 1 Fürichgasse. An average meal costs around 400 AS ($21.28), and Korean barbecues are a specialty. The restaurant is open from 11:30 a.m. to 3 p.m. and from 5:30 p.m. to 1 a.m. every day of the year.

Rôtisserie Sirk, 53 Kärntnerstrasse (tel. 52-16-42), is a plushly modern restaurant conveniently near the Opera on the second floor of a building adjacent to the Hotel Bristol. The kitchen prepares conservative but flavorful meals with flair and gusto, and the Sirk represents good value, especially when compared to the higher-priced citadels around it.

On the lower street level is a glistening art nouveau café, complete with rich pastries, beveled glass, and big windows. Most diners, however, head immediately for the stairwell leading up to the second floor. Every night a traditional three-course Opera supper with a varied choice of components is offered for 350 AS ($18.62). Otherwise a full à la carte meal will cost around 400 AS ($21.28). Specialties include "3 Kleine Filets" (beef, pork, and veal) served with mushrooms, spinach, and a pepper cream sauce, roast duck crisp from the oven with red cabbage and bread dumplings, medallions of venison in a gooseliver sauce, or else saddle of veal with morels.

Meals are served between noon and 3 p.m. and between 7 p.m. and midnight. The café downstairs is open between 10 a.m. and midnight.

The pine-paneled **Marco Polo,** 9 Wehrgasse (tel. 57-83-65)—owned by an Italian/Austrian team, Edgardo (Edy) Marco de Polo and his delightful wife, Olga Schmid—is one of the warmest refuges in an otherwise nondescript neighborhood. With its immaculate napery, tiny bar, and simply decorated rooms, the place is a modest trattoria, yet it attracts such stars as Raf Vallone.

The real star of the place, however, is English-speaking Olga. The food is superb, especially the homemade ravioli which is worth a culinary award. The homemade pesto is always available, and meats, flavored with garlic and Italian herbs, are grilled to perfection. Other recommendable courses include gnocchi with gorgonzola, risotto ai frutto di mare, generous portions of carpaccio, green tagliatelle with salmon, spaghetti carbonara, saltimbocca, scaloppini marsala, and, for dessert, zabaglione with marsala. Each dish is freshly prepared with sensitivity.

Full meals cost from 360 AS ($19.15), and because the restaurant is small, reservations are important. It is closed on Monday throughout the year and on Sunday and Monday between June and November.

Restaurant Bukarest, 7 Bräunerstrasse (tel. 52-37-63), serves Balkan—mainly Romanian—specialties in a tunnel-like room with old vaulting, an exposed charcoal grill, and soulful gypsy music to accompany your meal. A café in front offers sidewalk tables for guests who prefer to be outdoors. Specialties include Serbian bean soup, salami, grilled sirloin steak stuffed with chopped meat, and a Jamaican pepper and garlic dish. Another dish of which the chef is proud is his mixed grill, and his baklava is outstanding. Expect to spend from 280 AS ($14.90) per person. The restaurant serves from 11:30 a.m. to 2:30 p.m. and from 6 p.m. to midnight every day of the week except Monday.

Sailer, 14 Gersthoferstrasse (tel. 47-21-21), near the Türkenschanzpark, is tastefully decorated in an old Vienna style, with wood paneling, Biedermeier portraits, and in one of the cellar rooms, antique chairs, each hand-carved in a different design. The art nouveau exterior is lit with spots at night, revealing an interior where clients are seated on two different levels, according to their choice. Specialties of the house include deer and elk, wild boar, pheasant, and partridge, each prepared according to classic and time-honored Viennese recipes, along with a tempting collection of tortes and pastries. The third-generation owners acquiesce to the demands of an updated light cuisine with daily specials which depend on the availability of produce in the marketplace. They serve weekdays from 11:30 a.m. to 2:30 p.m. and from 6 until 11 p.m. The restaurant closes on Sunday and holidays. Meals average 225 AS ($11.97) for lunch, going up to around 400 AS ($21.28) for dinner.

Restaurant Zauberlehrling, 2 Lazaristengasse (tel. 34-51-35), in Währing. Before you finish your meal in this charming and intimate restaurant it's likely that the chef will come out of the kitchen to welcome you personally. Translated, the name of the restaurant means sorcerer's apprentice, although from the quality of the Viennese and international specialties served here, it's obvious there's no neophyte back there rattling those pots and pans. Specialties include cream of snail soup with chives, appetizers with shrimp variations, medallions of veal in sherry sauce, and a series of seasonal menus featuring fish, game, and fresh vegetables. Dessert might be the Zauberlehrling Hausbombe or some equally rich concoction. An average meal will cost from 400 AS ($21.28). They're open Monday through Saturday from 6 p.m. to midnight (the kitchen closes at 11 p.m.), with an annual vacation taken from mid-July to mid-August and from the day before Christmas until January 1.

Niky's Kuchlmasterei, 6 Obere Weissgerberstrasse (tel. 72-44-18). The bill, when it comes after a long and pleasant meal, will arrive in an elaborate box suitable for jewels, along with an amusing message in German (if you can read it) which offers a tongue-in-cheek apology for cashing your check. The restaurant has a decor of old stonework with modern innovations both in the architecture and the cuisine. The large menu, the well-prepared food, the welcoming, friendly ambience, and the lively crowd of loyal habitués, make it a good choice for an evening meal. Its summer terrace is among the most exclusive in Vienna. Three courses average around 400 AS ($21.28). The restaurant is open Monday to Saturday from 10 a.m. to midnight.

Chez Rainer, 27 Wiedner Hauptstrasse (tel. 65-46-46), is an intimately elegant dining room attached to the attractive Hotel Erzherzog Rainer. The building was constructed in 1912, and has been renovated twice since then into the clean and inviting place it is today. The well-run service includes food items such as tafelspitz with applesauce, horseradish, chives, and sauteed potatoes, a tender Wiener schnitzel, and grilled fogasch with anchovy butter. Many of their specialties are based on the produce of the season, which is likely to include fresh strawberries or raspberries and, inevitably, summer vegetables. In the autumn they feature hare, deer, venison, and wild boar. Dessert might be shredded pancakes with stewed plums or a Salzburg-style soufflé. Fixed-price meals range from 300 AS ($15.96) to 475 AS ($25.27), with à la carte dinners costing from 200 AS ($10.64) to 400 AS ($21.28). A less expensive brasserie on the premises serves food until 1 a.m., offering an inexpensive quick lunch with beer on tap and tempting pastries.

Griechenbeisl, 11 Fleischmarkt (tel. 63-19-77), was established in 1450 and today is still one of the leading restaurants of Vienna. It has a labyrinthine collection of at least seven different eating areas on three different floors, all of them with low vaulted ceilings, smoky paneling, wrought-iron chandeliers, and green-vested waiters who scurry around with large trays of food. This is a long-enduring favorite with the Viennese and especially the foreign colony, who appreciate its mellow antique atmosphere and its dozens of charming touches. As you enter from the street, look down at the grate below your feet for an illuminated view of a pirate counting his gold. As you go in, be sure to see the so-called inner sanctum, with the signatures of former patrons ranging from Liszt to Mozart, from Beethoven to Molnar, from Mark Twain to Strauss.

The Pilsen beer is well chilled, and the food is bürgerlich (hearty, ample, and solidly bourgeois). The restaurant features nighttime accordion and zither music. Menu items include apricot quenelles, crêpes with poppyseed, both Hungarian and Viennese gulasch, sauerkraut garni, and braised leg of venison. À la carte meals range from 350 AS ($18.62), and they're served from 10 a.m. to 12:30 a.m.

THE BUDGET RESTAURANTS: Ofenloch, 8 Kurrentgasse (tel. 63-88-44), is a well-reputed eating house of old Vienna in the medieval section of town. The waitresses wear Biedermeier costumes and will give you a menu that looks more like a magazine. Some of the mock medieval illustrations inside are funny, and when you get around to reading the food items you'll be prepared for the gutbürgerlich aspect of many of them. Specialties include "Vanillerostbraten," two kinds of schnitzel, pork, noodle, and hearty soup dishes, as well as salads and cheese platters. For smaller appetites, there's a page devoted to wurst salads and one-dish meals, any of which would go well with the wine and beer consumed in quantities here. It's open daily except Sunday and holidays from 10 a.m. to midnight. A robust three-course meal will cost around 250 AS ($13.30).

Restaurant Kardos, 8 Dominikaner Bastei (tel. 52-69-49), serves Hungarian and mixed-grill specialties. However, the menu is adjusted seasonally so that the chef can turn out well-prepared foods using the freshest ingredients available to him. Regional recipes familiar to many Eastern Europeans are featured. Barack, an apéritif made from apricots, is offered, as well as piquant little rolls known as grammel. They're seasoned with pork and hot spices. The decor is brightly Hungarian, with contrasting sunny colors, elaborate pine detailing cut into country baroque patterns, and a cellar locale with gypsy music in wintertime. An average meal ranges from 200 AS ($10.64) to 250 AS ($13.30). The restaurant is open Tuesday through Saturday from noon to 2 p.m. and 6 p.m. to midnight. On Sunday, it is open only from noon to 3 p.m.; closed Monday. Stefan and Rozika, the hard-working owners, prepare some of the most elaborate food displays in Vienna. They are assisted in this by four of their five children.

Zwölf-Apostelkeller, 3 Sonnenfelsgasse (tel. 52-67-77), is an old wine tavern, parts of its walls predating the year 1561. You'll find rows of wooden tables under the vaulted ceilings, with illumination provided partially by the streetlights that have been set into the masonry floor. This place is popular with students, partly because of its reasonable prices and partly because of its proximity to St. Stephen's. It's so deep you feel you're entering a dungeon. The tavern is open every day from 4:30 p.m. to midnight. In addition to beer and wine, which sells for between 24 AS ($1.28) and 30 AS ($1.60) for a small carafe, the establishment serves light meals and snacks. These include a roast beef platter with tartar sauce, roast pork with horseradish, and several generous salads with wurst and cheese. Plates of food range from 75 AS ($3.99) to 125 AS ($6.65).

The sophisticated delicatessen, **DO & Company,** 3 Akademiestrasse (tel. 52-64-74), is to Vienna what Fauchon is to Paris. Depending on the season, the asparagus might have been flown in from Paris or Argentina, while the shellfish may have come from either the North Sea or the Bosphorus. Regardless of the origin, the rich display of food fills sprawling rows of glass cases laden with pâtés, seafood salads, and Viennese pastries. The establishment is connected by a corridor to the already recommended Kervansaray and Hummer Bar.

Visitors can carry their purchases away with them or move to one of the tiny, somewhat cramped tables scattered near the entrance. You can order a simple salad or else a portion of Norwegian lobster thermidor, one of three shrimp platters, salmon quiche, or filet of turbot. The place is likely to be packed, especially at lunchtime with young and demanding gastronomes willing to sacrifice space and ambience for a slice of the good life. You can spend anywhere from 80 AS ($4.26) to 350 AS ($18.62) for an elegant snack or a full meal, depending on your appetite and budget. The establishment is open from 9 a.m. to 7 p.m. every day.

Restaurant Siddhartha, 16 Fleischmarkt (tel. 53-11-97), is at the end of a covered arcade in the old city, in a crowded, clean ambience of white stucco, candlelight, fresh flowers, and vaulted ceilings. This restaurant serves only vegetarian food. It's very popular, and you'll be fortunate to get a seat on weekends during peak serving hours. Menu specialties include ratatouille, quiche Lorraine, a Siddhartha plate for two persons (mixed specialties), many curry dishes, roquefort crêpes, piccata milanese (with imitation veal), french onion soup, avocados in a cognac dressing, mushrooms Romanoff, and mangos in port. The restaurant is closed on Sunday. Fixed-price meals are available at lunchtime only, ranging from 75 AS ($3.99) to 85 AS ($4.52), while à la carte dinners cost around 300 AS ($15.96).

Alte Backstube, 34 Lange Gasse (tel. 43-11-01), is worth visiting just to admire the baroque sculptures which crown the top of the doorway leading into what was originally built as a private home in 1697. Four years later, it was transformed into a bakery, with wood-burning stoves installed in various parts of the ground floor. For more than 2½ centuries the establishment served the baking needs of the neighborhood, and then, in 1963, the Schwartzmann family added a dining room, a pleasant, dainty front room for drinking beer and tea, and a collection of baking-related artifacts. This, plus a cooperative staff, turned the historic building into one of the most pleasant restaurants of its kind in Vienna. The passageway leading into the cozily vaulted dining room is lined with documents, antique troughs, and tools related to baking, as well as baroque sculptures.

Once seated, you can order wholesome, robust Teutonic specialties such as braised pork with cabbage, veal tips in a sour cream sauce, Viennese-style gulasch, and roast venison with cranberry sauce and bread dumplings. There's an English-language menu if you need it. Try the house special dessert of cream cheese strudel with hot vanilla sauce. Full meals cost from around 300 AS ($15.96). The charming staff serves meals every day except Monday. From Tuesday through Saturday, the restaurant is open between noon and midnight. On Sunday and holidays, hours are from 3 p.m. to midnight.

Restaurant Anatol, 12 Würthgasse (tel. 36-11-81), offers good Viennese cookery, always with an emphasis on the light-textured creations of *die neuen Küchen* in an art nouveau ambience. It looks like a turn-of-the-century Austrian coffeehouse, serving well-prepared French, Italian, and Austrian food in a large central room and in a smaller salon off to the side. Fixed-price meals range from 65 AS ($3.46), while à la carte dinners go from 130 AS ($6.92) to 275 AS ($14.63). Reservations are suggested. The restaurant is open from noon to 2 p.m. and from 6 p.m. until midnight every day but Tuesday.

Dubrovnik, 3 am Heumarkt (tel. 73-27-55), is a Balkan restaurant where much of the menu is in Serbo-Croatian and where the staff wears the regional garb of different provinces of Yugoslavia. It's set up in two rooms on either side of a central vestibule filled with busy waiters rushing in and out of the kitchen, which you can see through an open door at the far end. In a decor of red carpeting and two decorative fish tanks, the efficient maître d' directs things to the music of a pianist and violinist in the other room, playing mostly Austrian and gypsy music, with some international selections. The menu lists many Yugoslav dishes, including Serbian bean soup, as well as specialties from the grill, including pork kidney and liver as well as a mixed grill. Among the fish dishes, the most exotic is the Serbian fogosch (a kind of whitefish), served with potatoes and garlic. Dessert could be baklava and both Bulgarian and Serbian cheese. The restaurant is open every day from 11:30 a.m. to 2:30 p.m. and from 6 p.m. to midnight. Meals average about 175 AS ($9.31) per person.

Figlmüller, 5 Wollzeile (tel. 52-61-77), in the inner city, is considered one of the most famous beisels in Vienna. The passageway down which it's located leads to a site which is about 500 years old. Inside, the relaxed ambience is one of good and simple Viennese cookery, with a Wiener schnitzel which is by now legendary. It sprawls across (and off) your plate, it's so big. You'll also find an excellent selection of Viennese sausages, along with tafelspitz and about ten fresh salads. Daily specials are written on a blackboard, and are served between 8 a.m. and 11 p.m. Monday to Friday and from 8 a.m. to 3 p.m. on Saturday.

The wines are excellent, and the restaurant is usually packed at the peak serving hours. Meals cost from 125 AS ($6.65) to 275 AS ($14.63).

Gösser Bierklinik, 4 Steindlgasse (tel. 63-33-36), which is also known as the Güldene Drache (golden dragon), serves what is reportedly the finest beer in the city. It's brewed in Styria. This is an ancient rustic institution in a building which, according to tradition, dates from Roman times. An inn was opened here in the early 16th century, way back during the reign of Maximilian I. With such a tradition, naturally the decor seems strictly from the Middle Ages, and the cuisine is quintessentially Viennese. The waitresses always seem to be carrying ample mugs of Gösser beer, and are often rushed and harassed. When you finally get their attention, you can order such hearty fare as veal chops with dumplings, plus a wide variety of gutbürgerlich ribstickers. You will likely spend from 200 AS ($10.64) for a full meal. The restaurant serves from 9 a.m. to 11:30 p.m. daily except Sunday and holidays.

Thomaskeller, 2 Postgasse (tel. 52-74-46), lies just off the Wollzeile, in the cellars of a Dominican monastery. It's one of the finest wine taverns in Vienna, with a casual atmosphere, friendly service, and carafes of excellent wine from Haugsdorf. Gutbürgerlich food is served in a gutbürgerlich setting under a tall vaulted ceiling of dark-red brick. Flags from the different parts of "the Empire" hang above the wrought-iron wall sconces and the two antique streetlights set into the brick floor. No one puts on airs. The waiters seem to have a sense of humor, and the daily specials are written on a blackboard. You'll find bargain dining in an authentic setting. A fixed-price evening meal will cost about 100 AS ($5.32), and might include Schweinebraten with sauerkraut and good apple strudel. Service is from 5 p.m. till midnight. You might prefer the lower section at the far end of the restaurant. This room is usually more popular with the locals and gives you a closer look at the drinkers and diners, both male and female, who make this their preferred hangout in the neighborhood.

Zum Weissen Rauchfangkehrer, 4 Weihburggasse (tel. 52-34-71), is 125 years old, the former guildhall of Vienna's chimney sweeps. In fact the name of the place, translated as the "white chimney sweep," comes from a blackened wretch who terrified his neighbor, the city baker, by falling into a drunken sleep in a kneading trough and emerging the next day like a ghost covered with flour. The interior is rustic, with pine banquettes that look vaguely like church pews, deer antlers, fancifully crafted chandeliers, and red and blue tablecloths. Stained glass is set into the dividers separating the many niches and cubbyholes, while big street-level windows let in lots of light. A piano in one of the inner rooms provides nighttime music. The menu offers such specialties as Viennese fried chicken, both a Tyrolean and a paprika schnitzel, veal gulasch, wild game specialties, bratwurst, tafelspitz, and several kinds of strudel. You should reserve a table, and you'll certainly want to finish with the house specialty, a fabulously rich chocolate cream puff whose long German name I won't give for reasons of space. You can dine here for 350 AS ($18.62). It's open daily from noon to 3 p.m. and from 6 p.m. to 1 a.m.

Toni Wagner's Glacisbeisel, Messepalast (tel. 96-16-58), is housed inside the walls of what were once the imperial stables. The location is near the English Theater, inside a maze of palatial buildings whose entrances lie on Museumstrasse. Toni Wagner renovated this historic building in 1976, and has done a thriving business ever since. The restaurant serves one of the best Wiener schnitzels I've ever tasted, as well as Viennese specialties such as tafelspitz (boiled beef with potato rösti), plus a milk and cream strudel with vanilla sauce. In summer the restaurant seats more than 300 diners on an open-air terrace constructed right into the ramparts in what used to be a vineyard. The restaurant is open from May 1 until September 30 Monday to Friday from 11 a.m. to midnight. From October 1 to December 31, hours are from 6 p.m. to midnight Monday to Saturday. It offers a relatively low-cost and filling meal at a cost ranging upward from 225 AS ($11.97).

De Alte Schmiede, 9 Schönlaterngasse (tel. 52-34-95). Before you descend the winding metal stairway leading to this basement restaurant, you'll be rewarded with a view of the old smithy for which it is named through the plateglass window separating it from the inside stairwell. The walls of this ancient forge look like something from a Louise Nevelson sculpture, with more than 1,000 antique metal-working tools hanging in orderly rows from the aged masonry walls. You might want to make a daytime excursion just for the sight of the occasional artist who still has access to the shop.

Upstairs in this building you'll find a Libresso open from 10 a.m. to 7 p.m. There the friendly management serves coffee and snacks, and newspapers in many languages, including English, are available. The works of young artists are displayed. Under the high vaulted ceilings of the brick-lined cellar restaurant, Viennese specialties "in the style of grandmother" are served. These might include tafelspitz, paprika braten, venison, wild pork cutlets, two kinds of strudel, seven kinds of soup, an occasional fish dish, and good Turkish coffee. A candlelit dinner costs from 350 AS ($18.62) and is served from 5 p.m. to 1 a.m. daily except Sunday. The café is also closed on Sunday.

Augustinerkeller, 1 Augustinerstrasse (tel. 52-34-83), lies in the basement of a palace that shelters the Albertina collection in the Hofburg complex. It has a lively group of patrons from all walks of life, and sometimes they get boisterous, especially when the Schrammel music goes on late into the night. This place offers one of the best values for wine-tasting in Vienna. The ground-floor lobby lists in big letters the prices of vintage local wines by the glass. A quiet crowd of drinkers take a taste from the hundreds of bottles near the stand-up stainless-steel counter.

You enter a vaulted brick room with a worn pine-board floor and wooden banquettes painted in horizontal stripes of black and lime green. This long and narrow room is usually packed with people and atmosphere, and often it features strolling accordion players. An upstairs room looks much the same as the one below, although it's less crowded, much quieter, and usually doesn't have music. Aside from the wine and beer, the establishment serves food from 10 a.m. to 11 p.m. The cooking is simple, including half a roast chicken on a spit at 60 AS ($3.19) as well as schnitzels from 50 AS ($2.66). A glass of wine (which is defined as one-eighth of a liter) begins at 12 AS (64¢) and usually costs a few more schillings at night.

Antiquitäten-Keller, 32 Magdalenenstrasse (tel. 56-69-533), offers a well-prepared but limited menu in an antique cadre of local beerhall style with nightly classical music. It's open from 6 p.m. to 1 a.m. seven days a week, with an annual closing sometime in August. Drinks cost from 25 AS ($1.33) to 30 AS ($1.60), while a main course of typical Viennese food goes for around 150 AS ($7.98) to 180 AS ($9.58). There are three rooms inside, so feel free to walk around a bit before selecting a place to sit. It can be reached from the Vienna State Opera on the U4 in about five minutes.

Restaurant Gösser Bierhaus, 2 Stubenbastei/Wollzeile (tel. 52-48-39), is an unpretentious and plainly decorated beer restaurant midway between the Vienna Hilton and St. Stephen's. All the brew served is on tap, and is usually accompanied by simple and tasty Viennese dishes, costing between 110 AS ($5.32) to 200 AS ($10.64). Servings are most generous. Hilda Koranda, the owner, is usually on the premises, opening her restaurant from 9 a.m. to 11:30 p.m. Tuesday to Saturday. Monday hours are from 9 a.m. to 3 p.m. She closes on Sunday. A summertime beer garden allows clients to take their meals outside.

Rathauskeller, 1 Rathausplatz (tel. 42-12-19), is decorated like a mammoth baroque beer barrel, with massively arched ceilings and stained-glass chandeliers. In the center of Vienna, in the basement of the City Hall, it serves robust, gutbürgerlich fare such as crayfish soup, Hungarian gulasch soup, Serbian bean soup, grilled pike-perch, special "City Hall gulasch," and veal paprika. If you have a hearty appetite, try the bauernschmaus, which is a farmer's banquet with pork chops, sauerkraut, bread dumplings, grilled sausages, and potatoes. This establishment has four separate settings, all of them ideal for consuming massive quantities of beer which on a rowdy night seems to be the intention of many a client. If you go to the big Grinzingerkeller you can hear Viennese music after 7 p.m. The cellar is open every day except Sunday from noon to 3 p.m. and from 6 p.m. to midnight. An average three-course meal will cost about 250 AS ($13.30).

St. Urbani-Keller, 12 am Hof (tel. 63-91-02), named after the patron saint of wine-making, is one of the most historic and one of the deepest cellars in Vienna. Carl Hipfinger renovated the cellar as a public gathering place in 1906. Many of the artifacts inside, from the paneling in the German Romantic style to the fanciful wrought-iron lighting fixtures, were designed by one of Austria's most famous architects, Walcher von Molthein, who rebuilt Vienna's Kreuzenstein Castle at the beginning of the century. The cellar has brick vaulting dating from the 13th century, and sections of solid Roman walls which you can admire while listening to the folkloric music at night.

The most popular room is the one on the lowest level, so be sure to continue your descent down the steep stairs until you reach the room with the thick oak tables at the bottom. There you'll find enough art, including numerous crucifixes and a Renaissance chandelier of St. Lucretia, to keep anyone interested. Many kinds of wine are served, but the featured vintage comes from the vineyards of the owner's family. That wine has been offered as gifts to everybody from the famous General Rommel (the so-called desert fox) to the president of Austria.

The establishment is open from 6 p.m. to 1 a.m., with hot food served until midnight seven days a week. Food items include filet steak "les gourmets," entrecôte with lyonnaise potatoes, swiebelrostbraten, tafelspitz, trout meunière, veal medallions Monte Carlo, and many kinds of soup, including cream of salmon. That fare is backed up by a wide selection of cheese and crêpes for dessert. Meals cost from 350 AS ($18.62), and if you've already eaten, no one will mind if you drop in just for a drink. Watch your step on the way up or down.

Buffet Trześniewski, 1 Dorotheergasse (tel. 43-15-68). Everyone in Vienna knows about this place, from the most hurried office worker to the city's most elite hostesses. Franz Kafka lived next door and used to come here for sandwiches and beer. It's unlike any buffet you may have seen, with a crowded format of six or seven cramped tables and a rapidly moving queue of clients who jostle for space next to the glass countertops. You'll indicate to the waitress the kind of sandwich you want, and if you can't read German signs, you just point.

Most people come here for at least six or seven of the delicious finger sandwiches, which include 18 combinations of cream cheese, egg and onion, salami, mushroom, herring, green and red peppers, tomatoes, lobster, and many more. You might also want to order small glasses of fruit juice, beer, or wine with your snack. If you want something to drink, the cashier will give you a rubber token which you'll present to the woman at the far end of the counter (again, you'll jostle your way through the crowd). Each of the sandwiches costs 7 AS (37¢), while drinks range from 6 AS (32¢) to 18 AS (96¢) apiece.

The buffet is open Monday to Friday from 9 a.m. to 7:30 p.m., from 9 a.m. to 1 p.m. on Saturday.

Piaristenkeller, 45 Piaristengasse (tel. 42-91-52), is a wine tavern where Erich Emberger has successfully renovated and reassembled the centuries-old vaulted ceilings into a beautiful and vast cellar room. This is a worthwhile establishment to visit to try all the traditional culinary specialties created from original recipes in the kitchen which once served the cloisters of which the cellar was a part. Meals cost from 200 AS ($10.64). Zither music accompanies the consumption of beer, wine, and food during the hours the cellar is open—6 p.m. to midnight.

5. Coffeehouses, Tea Rooms, and Cafés

The café has been called the most traditional Viennese institution. Today they come in all shapes and sizes. Many, frankly, are modern, while others have clung more to their traditional past. Some Viennese still use the café as their living room, where they meet and entertain their friends, especially if their apartments are too small. Others, however, have deserted the café completely, preferring to stay home these days and watch television.

In theory at least you're never rushed, even if you occupy a table for hours and order only one cup of coffee. Your coffee is always brought with a glass of water on the side. Most Viennese order a pastry to go with their coffee. Even though service is included in your tab, it is customary to leave an extra tip.

It's also possible to order simple meals in most of these establishments recommended. You can almost always get a hearty bowl of gulasch soup, and if not that, certainly sausage and hard-boiled eggs, along with good bread and cheese.

Café Demel, 14 Kohlmarkt (tel. 66-17-17). The windows of this much-venerated establishment are filled with fanciful spun-sugar creations of characters from folk legends. When I was last there, Lady Godiva's five-foot tresses sheltered a miniature village of Viennese dancers. Inside you'll find a splendidly baroque Viennese landmark of black marble tables, cream-colored embellished plaster walls, elaborate half paneling, and crystal chandeliers covered with white milk-glass globes. Dozens of different pastries are offered every day, including pralinentorte, Giselatorte, sandtorte, Neopolitanertorte, Nelsontorte, as well as cream-filled horns (kugelhupfs), plus a mammoth variety of elegantly salty small sandwiches made of smoked salmon, egg salad, caviar, or shrimp, among other ingredients.

You'll select what you want from the glass cases before going in to seat yourself on one of the bentwood chairs or paisley-covered loveseats. The counterwoman will give you a ticket which you'll keep. Another waitress will bring the confection to your table, along with whatever beverage you select. At the end of your visit you'll pay the waitress for the bill she'll calculate from the ticket stubs you've accumulated from the counterwoman. If you want to be traditional, ask for an Einspanner, which is a glass of espresso with a "hat" of frothy whipped cream. Coffee goes for 38 AS ($2.02), and pastries begin at 30 AS ($1.60).

Café Central, 14 Herrengasse (tel. 66-41-76). In spite of the modern dress of the clientele, this grandly proportioned café offers as good an insight into 19th-century café life as any coffeehouse in Vienna. A double staircase rises, in art nouveau/Romanesque grandeur, above the cluster of bentwood chairs, round-topped tables, and a vaguely Turkish bath decor. Lenin, under an assumed name, is said to have plotted the Russian Revolution with his cronies here. Then, as today, you can order a snack, a salad, or a light meal. A generous platter of food is priced from 80 AS ($4.26), and coffee and pastry cost from 50 AS ($2.66). It is open daily except Sunday and holidays from 9 a.m. to 7 p.m. The café is contained within the Ferstel Palace, near the Opera and the Hofburg.

Café Landtmann, 4 Dr. Karl-Lueger-Ring (tel. 63-06-21), is one of the great cafés of the Ringstrasse, with a history that goes back more than 110 years and a view overlooking the Burgtheater. It has traditionally drawn a colorful mixture of politicians, journalists, and actors, and was recently renovated at the cost of half a million dollars (some of the funds came from an urban-renewal kitty). The original chandeliers and the prewar chairs have been refurbished, and you can read Austrian and foreign newspapers in a spot which some VIP probably just vacated. An hour here, where you'll be charged around 105 AS ($5.59) for two coffees and a pastry, might be an attractive way to spend part of a day in Vienna. Full meals are served if you want them. The café is open every day from 8 a.m. to midnight.

Café Hawelka, 1 Dorotheergasse (tel. 52-82-30), just off the Graben, is one of the most famous rendezvous points in Vienna for poets, artists, and the literati. In fact if you yearn for a view of the kind of café where someone plotted a revolution in the 19th century, this is it. Trotsky used to meet here with radical cronies for long cups of coffee, and from the decor of marble-topped tables and bentwood chairs, you could easily imagine that the secretive conversations going on around you would be good material for a spy story. The setting is unmistakably Middle European, with smoke-stained places between the dark paneling and unusual artistic statements in mismatched black and gold frames.

Waiters in formal dress or in shirt sleeves and suspenders scurry from the well-stocked bar area with drinks on small silver trays. If the service is slow (which it usually is) you can amuse yourself by reading the bulletin board at the far end of the room, listing nearly every underground artistic event going on in Vienna.

On some nights you're likely to see Frau Hawelka herself, a small, gray-haired lady who usually leaves at midnight. She'll ask you if you'd like a tiny glass of her pear brandy and one of her homemade dumplings, buchteln. How could you possibly say no? The café is open daily except Tuesday until 2 a.m.

Café Imperial, 16 Kärntner Ring (tel. 65-17-65), is associated with the glittering hotel covered earlier in this guide. "Imperial Toast" is a very good snack here, and if you want a main meal you can always order tafelspitz, which the Emperor Joseph preferred to all other dishes. Meals begin at 250 AS ($13.30), which you can enjoy under the kind of ornate crystal chandeliers that Vienna has made famous.

Café Mozart, 2 Albertin Platz (tel. 52-27-07). There are at least five Mozart cafés in Vienna, but this one is the most famous of all of them. It attracts affluent members of the business community, along with opera singers and university professors. There's been a café named Mozart on this spot since 1794, although the current establishment was founded in 1840. Japanese interests renovated it into the plushly streamlined format you see today, which is certainly elegant but without the baroque detailing you might have hoped for. Fourteen different coffees are served, with prices starting at 30 AS ($1.60), and you can also order a Wiener schnitzel with salad for 130 AS ($6.92). The menu is in English. Scenes from *The Third Man,* that thriller starring Orson Welles and Joseph Cotton, were shot here.

Café/Restaurant Prückel, 24 Stubenring (tel. 52-61-15), was built around the turn of the century, and in 1955 when Austria had just gained its independence from foreign domination, it was completely remodeled. Open from 9 a.m. until 10 p.m., the café offers stacks of the most current international newspapers, comfortable chairs, and friendly waiters who serve snacks, desserts, beverages, or else full meals. A large bridge room accommodates card players who sometimes spend the day here. The owner, Christl Sedlar, offers 20 different kinds of coffee, including my favorite, kaffee Maria Theresia, which is a large black coffee with orange liqueur and whipped cream.

Café Tirolerhof, 8 Tegetthoffstrasse (tel. 52-78-33), is convenient after you've viewed the Albertina collection or been to the Spanish Riding School. Under management by the same family for the past 60 years, it's open Monday to Saturday from 7 a.m. to 9 p.m. and from 9:30 a.m. to 8 p.m. on Sunday. They offer very good apple strudel here, costing from 24 AS ($1.28), and coffee at 31 AS ($1.65) a cup.

Café/Restaurant Arabia, 5 Kohlmarkt (tel. 52-83-15), serves specialties such as asparagus in season, venison, fresh strawberries, and delectable Viennese pastries. Centrally located, the café is open from 7 a.m. to 8 p.m. every day of the year. An average meal costs between 100 AS ($5.32) and 130 AS ($6.92).

Restaurant-Café Carrousel, 3 Krugerstrasse (tel. 52-73-97), in the middle of the city, a few blocks from the Vienna State Opera, offers 220 seats in a modernized art nouveau format of bright colors, bentwood chairs, and an occasional statue of a merry-go-round horse. A sidewalk terrace extends the seating capacity of the restaurant. The menu features the usual café drinks, such as coffee, tea, wine, and beer, plus good Viennese cookery with a few international dishes thrown in for variety. Meals cost from 120 AS ($6.38).

Demmer's Teehaus, 5 Mölkerbastei (tel. 63-59-95), serves 30 different kinds of tea, plus dozens of pastries, cakes, toasts, and English sandwiches. This is under the same management as the excellent Buffet Trześniewski, previously recommended. However, the teahouse gives you a chance to sit down and enjoy your drink and snack. Teas begin at 30 AS ($1.60). The establishment is open Monday to Friday from 9 a.m. to 6 p.m., from 9:30 to 12:30 p.m. on Saturday.

Chapter IV

SIGHTS, SHOPS, NIGHTLIFE OF VIENNA

1. What to See
2. Where to Shop
3. Vienna After Dark

"ASIA BEGINS at the Landstrasse." Prince von Metternich, the Austrian statesman who arranged the marriage of Napoleon and Marie-Louise of Austria, made that now-famous remark to suggest the power and influence of the far-flung Austrian Empire whose destiny was linked with that of the Habsburgs from 1273 to 1918.

After deliverance from the dreaded plague and the equally dreaded Turks, Vienna entered into a great period of power and prosperity which reached the zenith of empire under the long reign of Maria Theresa from 1740 to 1780. Many of the sights I'll describe shortly are traced directly to that great empress of the Age of Enlightenment. She welcomed Mozart to her court at Schönbrunn when he was only six years old, a child prodigy indeed.

At the collapse of the Napoleonic Empire, Vienna took over Paris's long-held position as "the center of Europe." The crowned heads of Europe met for the now-legendary Congress of Vienna in 1814-1815. But so much time was devoted to galas that a remark made by Prince de Ligne became famous in its day: "The Congress doesn't make progress, it dances."

In this chapter we'll explore this legendary city of gemütlichkeit, beginning first with its many sightseeing attractions—most of which are a holdover from its days of empire—and going on to take in its many shopping possibilities as well as its exciting nightlife and cafés, plus practical facts which will help you enjoy your Vienna visit.

1. What to See

Vienna stands today, as it always has, as a crossroads between West and East (it's only 44 miles from the Iron Curtain). After New York and Geneva, it's the third city of the United Nations. It's also the home of many international organizations.

You can spend a week here and you'll have just touched the attractions of this multifaceted international city. I'll skim only the highlights, and even seeing what's listed below will take more than a week of some fast-paced walking.

Many readers will not have the time to spend seeing Vienna as it deserves to be seen. Some visitors will have only a day or two, and with those people in mind, I've compiled a list of the major attractions which no traveler should miss, however brief the stay in Vienna. If this guidebook awarded stars, I'd rate the following sights three stars each: the Inner City, Ringstrasse, Schönbrunn Palace, Hofburg Palace, Belvedere Palace, Kunsthistorisches Museum, and St. Stephen's Cathedral.

These top-rated sights are each previewed below, together with others I consider the two- or one-star attractions of Vienna. But before we visit them in detail, let's skim the highlights of Vienna's sights on a walking tour.

A WALKING TOUR OF IMPERIAL VIENNA: There are hundreds of potential itineraries through the architectural wonders of Vienna. However, this two- to three-hour walking tour will give you at least an exterior view of many of them. Place names in boldface are explained in detail in other sections of this guide. This tour is mainly designed to reveal lesser known sights which are best seen from the outside, on foot. Later, you can pick and choose the attractions you most want to revisit.

Our tour begins at the southernmost loop of the beltway, the **Ringstrasse,** which encircles most of the historic core of the city. From a stance in front of the most obvious symbol of Viennese culture, the **Staatsoper** (State Opera House), proceed one block northward on the most famous pedestrian street of Austria, the Kärntnerstrasse. This tour will eventually take you past this street's rows of glamorous shops and famous houses, but, for the moment, turn left behind the arcaded bulk of the Opera House onto the Philharmonikerstrasse. On the right-hand side, you'll see the lushly carved caryatids and globe lights of Vienna's best-known hotel, the **Sacher.** If you're interested, a confectionary store with a separate streetside entrance sells portions of the hotel's namesake, the Sachertorte, which can be shipped anywhere in the world.

A few steps later you'll find yourself amid the irregular angles of the Albertinaplatz where you can enjoy a "mélange" of coffee with a cap of whipped cream at the **Café Mozart,** lying just a few storefronts off to the right. Immediately opposite the café, behind an undistinguished facade, is one of Vienna's best known buildings, the headquarters of the **Albertina Collection.** A monumental staircase built into its side supports an equestrian statue which dominates the square. Its inspiration was Field Marshal Archduke Albrecht in honor of a battle he won in 1866. One of the many baroque jewels of Vienna, the Lobkowitz Palace lies adjacent to the Albertinaplatz at 2 Lobkowitzplatz. (Its position is confusing because of the rows of buildings partially concealing it. To get there, walk about 50 paces to the right of the Albertina Collection.)

At the far end of the Lobkowitzplatz, take the Gluckgasse past a series of antique shops filled with art deco jewelry and silverware. At the end of the block, at the Tegetthoffstrasse, go left. About 40 paces later, you'll be in front of the deceptively simple facade of the Church of the Capuchin Friars (see **Tombs of the Habsburgs**). Originally constructed in the 1620s, its facade was rebuilt in a severely simple design following old illustrations in 1935. Despite its humble appearance, the church contains the burial vaults of every Habsburg ruler since 1633. The heavily sculpted double casket of Maria Theresa and her husband, Francis I, are flanked with weeping nymphs and skulls, but capped with a triumphant cherub uniting the couple once again in love.

The portal of this church marks the beginning of the Neuer Markt whose perimeter is lined with rows of elegant baroque houses. The square's centerpiece is the partially dressed river goddess of the Donner fountain. Holding a snake, she is attended by four laughing cherubs struggling with fish. The waters flowing into the basin of the fountain are provided by four allegorical figures representing nearby tributaries of the Danube. The fountain is a copy of the original which was moved to Belvedere Palace. It was commissioned by the City Council in 1737, executed by Georg Raphael Donner, but judged obscene and immoral when viewed for the first time by Maria Theresa. Today, it is considered one of Austria's masterpieces of baroque sculpture.

Now, take the street stretching west from the side of the fountain, the Plankengasse, where a yellow baroque church fills the space at the end of the street. As you approach it, you'll pass arrays of shops filled with alluringly old-fashioned merchandise. Even the pharmacy at the corner of the Spiegelgasse has a vaulted ceiling and rows of antique bottles. The store at no. 6 Plankengasse, as well as its next-door neighbor at the corner of Dorotheergasse, are well stocked with museum-quality antique clocks, many of which ticked their way through the dying days of the early 19th century. Turn left when you reach the Dorotheergasse, past the turn-of-the-century Italianate bulk of no. 17. Therein lies one of the most historic auction houses of Europe, the **Dorotheum,** established in 1707.

About a half block later, turn right into the Augustinerstrasse, whose edge borders a labyrinth of palaces, museums, and public buildings known as the **Hofburg.** The grime-encrusted grandeur of this narrow street is usually diminished by the traffic roaring past its darkened stone walls. Despite that modern intrusion, this group of buildings is the single most impressive symbol of the former majesty of the Viennese Habsburgs. In about half a block, you'll arrive at the Josefsplatz, where a huge equestrian statue of Joseph II seems to be storming the gate of the Palffy Palace (no. 5). Its entrance is guarded by two pairs of relaxed caryatids who seem to be discussing the horseman's approach. Next door, at no. 6, is another once-glittering private residence, the Palavicini Palace. A few steps later, a pedestrian tunnel leads past the **Spanish Riding School.** The district becomes increasingly imperial, filled with slightly decayed vestiges of a long-ago empire whose baroque monuments are flanked with outmoded streets and thundering traffic.

The Michaelerplatz now opens to your view. Opposite the six groups of combative statues struggling with their own particular adversaries is a streamlined building with rows of unadorned windows. Known as the Loos House (no. 3 Michaelerplatz), it was designed in 1910 and immediately became the most violently condemned building in town. That almost certainly stemmed from the unashamed contrast between the lavishly ornamented facade of the Michaelerplatz entrance to the Hofburg and what contemporary critics compared to "the gridwork of a sewer." Franz Joseph himself hated the building so much that he used the Michaelerplatz exit as infrequently as possible so that he wouldn't have to look at the building, which faced it.

A covered tunnel which empties into the center of the square takes you beneath the Hofburg complex. Notice the passageway's elaborate ceiling where spears, capes, and shields crown the supports of the elaborate dome. Cars seem to race beside you, making this one of the most heavily embellished traffic tunnels in the world. An awesomely proportioned series of courtyards reveal the Imperial Age's addiction for conspicuous grandeur. Continuing straight through the passageway, you'll eventually emerge beneath the magnificent curves of the Haldenplatz. Its carefully constructed symmetry seems to dictate that each of the magnificent buildings which border it, as well as each of its equestrian statues and ornate lampposts, seems to have a well-balanced mate. Gardens stretch out, flowering in summer, in well-maintained splendor.

Enjoy the gardens if you want, but to continue the tour put the rhythmically spaced columns of the Hofburg's curved facade behind you and walk cater-corner to the far end of the palace's right-hand wing. At the Ballhausplatz notice the Chancellery at no. 2. It's a very elegant building, yet its facade is modest in comparison with the lush ornamentation of its royal neighbor. The events that transpired within this building influenced the course of European history hundreds of times since it was erected in 1720. Here, Count Kaunitz plotted with Maria Theresa again and again to expand the influence of her monarchy. Prince Metternich used these rooms as his headquarters during the Congress of Vienna in 1814 and 1815. Many of the decisions made here were responsible for the chain of events leading to World War I. In 1934, Dollfuss was murdered here. Four years later, Hermann Göring forced the ouster of the Austrian cabinet with telephoned threats of a military attack with calls made to an office in this building. Rebuilt after the bombings of World War II, this battle-scarred building has housed Austria's Foreign Ministry and its Federal Chancellor's office since 1945.

Walk along the side of the Chancellery's adjacent gardens, along the Lowelstrasse, until you reach the **Burgtheater** or national theater of Austria. Notice the window trim of some of the buildings along the way, each of which seems to have its own ox, satyr, cherub, or Neptune carved above it. At the Burgtheater, make a sharp right-hand turn onto the Bankgasse. The ornate beauty of the Palais Liechtenstein, completed in 1706, is on your right, at no. 9. A few buildings farther on, stone garlands and glimpses of crystal chandeliers are visible at the Hungarian Embassy, at no. 4-6 on the same street.

Now retrace your steps for about a half block until you reach the Abraham a Sancta Clara Gasse. At its end, you'll see the severe Gothic facade of the **Church of the Minorities** in the Minoritenplatz. Its 14th-century severity contrasts sharply with the group of stone warriors struggling to support the gilt-edged portico of the baroque palace facing it.

Walk behind the blackened hulk of the church to the curve of the building's rear. At this point, some maps of Vienna might lead you astray. Regardless of the markings on your particular map, look for the Leopold-Figl-Gasse and walk down it. You'll pass between two sprawling buildings, each of which belongs to one or another of the Austrian bureaucracies, which are linked with an above-ground bridge. A block later, turn right onto Herrengasse. Within a few minutes, you'll be on the by-now-familiar Michaelerplatz. This time you'll have a better view of **St. Michael's Church,** where winged angels carved by Lorenzo Mattielli in 1792 fly above the entranceway and a single pointed tower rises. Turn left (north) along the Kohlmarkt, noticing the elegant houses along the way: no. 14 houses **Demel's,** the most famous coffeehouse of Vienna; no. 9 and no. 11 bear plaques for Chopin and Haydn, respectively. At the Graben, turn right. The plague column you see in the center has chiselled representations of clouds piled high like whipped cream, dotted profusely with statues of ecstatic saints fervently thanking God for relief from the plague.

A few feet before the plague column, turn left onto the Jungferngasse and enter what is probably my favorite church in Vienna, **St. Peter's** or Peterskirche.

Return to the Graben, passing the papal tiaras at the base of the plague column. A few steps later, pass the bronze statue of a beneficent saint leading a small child in the right direction. You might, at this point, want a sandwich at the famous **Buffet Trześniewski,** 1 Dorotheergasse, off to the right. Continue your way down the Graben to Stock-im-Eisen. Here two pedestrian thoroughfares, the Graben and the Kärntnerstrasse, meet, both under the spire of **St. Stephen's Cathedral.** To your right, notice the sheet of curved Plexiglass bolted to the corner of an unobtrusive building at the periphery of the square. Behind it are the preserved remains of a tree which used to grow nearby. In it, 16th-century blacksmiths drove a nail for luck each time they left Vienna for other parts of Austria. Today the gnarled and dusty log is still covered with an almost uninterrupted carapace of angular nails.

Now, first encircle and then enter the soaring Gothic majesty of St. Stephen's Cathedral. When you exit, turn left after passing through the main portal, passing once again the nail-studded stump in Stock-im-Eisen, and promenade down the pedestrian thoroughfare of the Kärntnerstrasse. Notice especially the exhibition of art objects on the second floor of the world famous glassmaker, **Lobmyer,** at no. 26.

If you still have the energy, make a two- or three-block detour off the Kärntnerstrasse, turning left on the Johannesgasse. The severe facade of no. 8 contains an exhibition of religious folk art. A few steps farther, baroque carvings which include stone lions guard the 17th-century portals of the Savoy Foundation for Noble Ladies (no. 15) where well-born damsels sometimes struggled to learn "the gentle arts of womanhood."

As you retrace your steps back to the shops of the Kärntnerstrasse, you might hear the strains of music cascading into the street from the Vienna Conservatory of Music, which also lies within the Johannesgasse. Turn left as you reenter the Kärntnerstrasse, enjoying the views until you eventually return to the point of origin, the State Opera House.

THE INNER CITY: *Inner Stadt,* the inner city, is the tangle of streets of the old town from which Vienna grew in the Middle Ages. Much of your exploration will be confined to this area. It is encircled by the boulevards of "The Ring" and the Danube Canal. The main street of the inner city is the Kärntnerstrasse, most of which is a pedestrian mall. The heart of Vienna is the Stephansplatz, the square on which St. Stephen's Cathedral sits.

RINGSTRASSE: In 1857, seeing no further need for the old walls which had girdled old-town Vienna for several centuries, Emperor Franz Joseph ordered them torn down and replaced by a series of grand buildings and a wide promenade. Ringstrasse, or Ring Boulevard, was laid out between 1858 and 1865, an elegant horseshoe curve 2½ miles long, one of the grand boulevards of Europe, overhung with leafy trees. The emperor got his wish—a boulevard worthy of an empire that controlled some 50 million people.

A cross-section of architectural styles was used in constructing the buildings on the Ringstrasse, ranging from Greek to Gothic. The street name changes eight times around the boulevard, and along it you'll pass the Stadtpark, the State Opera House, the Burggarten, the Hofburg Palace, the Volksgarten, the Parliament, the Rathaus, the Burgtheater, the University of Vienna, and the Museum of Fine Arts. The Viennese call this pastiche of architecture *Ringstrassenstil.* They refer to the Ringstrasse simply as "The Ring."

You can circle the boulevard in one of the Viennese red trolleycars, but some people walk from one end to the other. If you wish to do that, the starting point is Aspernplatz by the Danube Canal. Along the way—for a rest—you can stroll into one of the parks (perhaps the Stadtpark), where you might hear Viennese music in summer as you relax at an outdoor café.

THE PALACES OF VIENNA: On your sightseeing tour of Vienna, I suggest that you start with the once-royal palaces, perhaps first—

Schönbrunn Palace

A Habsburg palace of 1441 rooms, Schönbrunn (tel. 83-36-46) was designed by those masters of the baroque, the von Erlachs. It was built between 1695 and 1700, ordered by Emperor Leopold I for his son, Joseph I, with Leopold directing the architects to design a palace whose grandeur would surpass that of Versailles. However, Austria's treasury, drained by the cost of wars, would not support the ambitious undertaking, and the original plans were never carried out.

When Maria Theresa became empress, she had the original plans changed greatly, and Schönbrunn looks today much as she conceived it, with delicate, feminine rococo touches designed for her by Austrian Nikolaus Pacassi. It was the imperial summer palace during Maria Theresa's 40-year reign, from 1740 to 1780, being considered by the empress as a fit place for her 16 children, six of whom did not live to grow up. Schönbrunn was the scene of great ceremonial balls and lavish banquets. During the 1814-1815 Congress of Vienna, fabulous receptions were held here. At the age of six, Mozart performed in the Hall of Mirrors before Maria Theresa and her court, and the empress held secret meetings with her chancellor, Prince Kaunitz, in the Chinese Room.

Franz Joseph was born at Schönbrunn, and the palace was the setting for much of the lavish court life carried on when he was emperor. He spent the last years of his life at Schönbrunn. The last of the rulers of the House of Habsburg, Karl I, signed his abdication document here on Nov. 11, 1918.

Napoleon, when Emperor of France, stayed here in 1805 and 1809. A melancholy footnote to the connection between the arrogant Bonapartes and the House of Habsburg is revealed in the brief life history of the son of the Emperor Napoleon and his second wife, Marie-Louise, daughter of Franz I of Austria. The boy, hailed by his father as "King of Rome" but officially known as the Duke of Reichstadt, lived at Schönbrunn—but not entirely from choice. The Austrian minister of foreign affairs, Metternich, who had for his own Machiavellian reasons arranged the marriage of Napoleon and Marie-Louise, ordered what was tantamount to imprisonment for the young duke—house arrest at Schönbrunn. The palace was no doubt the best of all possible worlds in which to be incarcerated, but the "King of Rome" was still in custody there upon his death in one of the splendid guest rooms at the age of 21.

Schönbrunn Palace was damaged in World War II by Allied bombs and by occupation troops, but restoration has obliterated the scars.

In complete contrast to the grim, forbidding-looking Hofburg, Schönbrunn Palace, done in "Maria Theresa ochre," has **formal gardens,** laid out in 1705, embellished by the Gloriette, a marble summerhouse topped by a stone canopy on which the imperial eagle is mounted. The so-called Roman Ruins consist of a collection of marble statues and fountains, dating from the late 18th century when it was fashionable to simulate the ravaged grandeur of Rome. The park, which can be visited until sunset daily, was laid out by Ferdinand of Hohenburg and contains many lovely fountains and heroic statues, often depicting Greek mythological characters.

The **State Apartments** are the most stunning display within Schönbrunn Palace. Much of the interior ornamentation is in 23½-karat gold, and many porcelain tile stoves are in evidence. Of the 40 rooms which you can visit, particularly fascinating is "The Room of Millions," decorated with Indian and Persian miniatures and considered to be the grandest rococo salon in the world. Much of the palace is in the rococo style, done in reds, white, and gold. You get to see the apartments once lived in by Franz Joseph and his ill-fated empress, Elizabeth, and the lavish rooms in which guests of the royal family were housed. Three of the rooms in Franz Joseph's quarters were decorated by the painter Joseph Rosa. You'll be shown the bleak chamber and the spartan iron bedstead in which the aged Franz Joseph died in 1916.

From the statistics you'll be told as you tour the palace, you learn that there are scores of kitchens but only two bathrooms dating to the beginning of the century. Before that, even before the time of Franz Joseph, rooms of the palace were used for this purpose, but there was no plumbing. However, these rooms are not on the tour.

Guided tours lasting 45 minutes are narrated in English but only at the indicated times given on the timetable. The imperial apartments are open from 9 a.m. to noon and from 1 to 5 p.m. in summer, to 4 p.m. in winter. Admission is 50 AS ($2.66) for adults, 10 AS (53¢) for children.

Evening tours combined with a concert are given at special rates in July and August, beginning at 7:15 p.m. For detailed information about the concerts, such as programs, times, and sale of tickets, get in touch with Kulturamt der Stadt Wien, 5 Friedrich Schmidt Platz (tel. 42800, ext. 2713).

On the ground floor of the east wing of the main building are the **Bergl Rooms** and the **Crown Prince Rooms.** These consist of four rooms with wall and ceiling murals by Johann Bergl, a painter in the second half of the 18th century, and three rooms in which an exhibit traces the history of Schönbrunn Palace. The rooms are open from 9 a.m. to noon and 1 to 5 p.m. May 1 to September 30. Admission is 15 AS (80¢) for adults and 5 AS (26¢) for children.

The palace is closed January 1, November 1, and December 24.

Well worth seeing is the **Schlosstheater,** or Palace Theater, which is still the setting for performances in summer. Marie Antoinette appeared on its stage in pastorals during her happy youth, and Max Reinhardt, the celebrated theatrical impresario, launched an acting school here.

Adjacent to the palace is the **Wagenburg,** or coach house (tel. 82-32-44), with a fine display of imperial coaches from the 17th, 18th, and 19th centuries. The coronation coach of Karl VI, which was pulled by eight white stallions, is here. It was used for a total of seven Habsburg coronations. Also to be seen are coaches ridden in by Franz Joseph and his wife Elizabeth, and by Napoleon and his wife Marie-Louise. The grim funeral coach of Franz Joseph is also on display. The children's phaeton you will see was built for Napoleon's son. The Wagenburg is open from 10 a.m. to 5 p.m. (until 4 p.m. in winter), costing 10 AS (53¢) for admission. It's closed Monday.

The oldest zoo in Europe, **Tiergarten Schönbrunn** (tel. 82-12-36), dating from 1752, is in the grounds of Schönbrunn Palace, open daily from 9 a.m. to 6 p.m. at the latest, changing with the seasons. Maria Theresa liked to take breakfast here. The zoo has new modern enclosures.

The Schönbrunn **botanical gardens** are also open to visitors.

To reach the palace, take the underground U-4 green line to the Schönbrunn stop. For the zoo, get out at the Heitzing stop.

Hofburg Palace

The winter palace of the Habsburgs, known for its vast, impressive courtyards, the Hofburg (tel. 57-55-54) sits in the heart of Vienna. To reach it (you can hardly miss it), head up the Kohlmarkt into Michaelerplatz, which is decorated with two enormous fountains embellished with statuary. This complex of imperial edifices, the first of which was constructed in 1279, grew and grew as the empire did, so that today the Hofburg Palace is virtually a city within a city. The earliest parts were built around a courtyard, the **Swiss Court,** named for the Swiss mercenaries who used to perform guard duty here. This most ancient part of the palace is at least 700 years old.

Hofburg's complexity of styles, not always harmonious, is the result of each emperor's having added to it according to his own tastes and taking away some of the work of his predecessors. So grand were the architect's plans for the 20th-century changes that the empire had ended before they could be carried out. The palace, which has withstood three major sieges and a great fire, is called simply *"die Burg,"* or "the palace," by Viennese. Of its more than 2,600 rooms, fewer than two dozen are open to the public.

The Imperial Treasury, the **Schatzkammer** (tel. 52-63-99), reached by a staircase from the Swiss Court, is considered the greatest treasury in the world. It is divided into two sections: the Imperial Profane and the Sacerdotal Treasuries. One part displays the crown jewels and other imperial riches, and the other, of course, contains ecclesiastical treasures.

The most outstanding exhibit in the Schatzkammer is the imperial crown, which dates from 962. It is so big that even though padded, it was likely to slip down over the ears of a Habsburg at a coronation. Studded with emeralds, sapphires, diamonds, and rubies, this 1,000-year-old symbol of sovereignty is a priceless treasure, a fact recognized by Adolph Hitler, who had it taken to Nürnberg in 1938 (the American army returned it to Vienna after World War II ended). Also on display is the imperial crown which was worn by the Habsburg rulers from 1804 to the end of the empire. You will see the saber of Charlemagne and the holy lance from the ninth century, a sacred emblem of imperial authority which in medieval times was thought to be the weapon that pierced the side of Christ on the cross. The Agate Bowl was once believed to be the Holy Grail.

Among great Schatzkammer prizes is the Burgundian Treasure seized in the 15th century, rich in vestments, oil paintings, gems, and robes. This loot is highlighted by artifacts connected with the Order of the Golden Fleece, that romantic medieval order of chivalry. You will also see the coronation robes of the imperial family, some of which date from the 12th century. The cradle of the "King of Rome," son of Napoleon and his Austrian second wife Marie-Louise, is in the Empire style in silver, pearl, and gilt.

The Schatzkammer is usually open Monday, Wednesday, and Friday from 10 a.m. to 3 p.m., on Tuesday and Thursday from 1 to 5 p.m., and on Sunday from 9 a.m. to 1 p.m. It's closed on Saturday. Admission is 25 AS ($1.33). The treasury may not actually be open at the time of your visit, as it is being massively restored. However, while it is closed, some of its exhibits may be seen in the Museum of Fine Arts.

The Hofburg complex also includes the **Reichskanzleitrakt,** or Imperial Chancellery, where the emperors and their wives and children lived on the first floor. To reach the **Kaiserappartements** (Imperial Apartments), you enter via the rotunda of the Michaelerplatz. The apartments are richly decorated with tapestries, many from Aubusson. The court tableware and silver are magnificent, revealing the pomp and splendor of a bygone era. Leopoldinischer Trakt, or Leopold's apartments, date from the 17th century. You can't visit the quarters once occupied by Maria Theresa as they are now used by the president of Austria.

These Imperial Apartments seem to be more closely associated with Franz Joseph than with any other emperor, probably because of his long reign. His wife, Elizabeth of Bavaria, lived here too when she wasn't traveling, which actually was most of the time until her fatal stabbing by an assassin in Switzerland. Elizabeth believed in keeping fit and had a room where she worked out. She was a vain empress, refusing to sit for portraits after she turned 30. You'll see the "iron bed" of Franz Joseph, who claimed he slept like his own soldiers. Maybe that explains why his wife spent so much time elsewhere!

Guided tours of the Kaiserappartements, lasting half an hour, are conducted in English in summer from 8:30 a.m. to 4:30 p.m., to 1 p.m. on Sunday and holidays. Admission is 25 AS ($1.33) for adults, 10 AS (53¢) for children.

Construction of **Die Burgkapelle** (Palace Chapel) in the Gothic style started in 1447 during the reign of Emperor Frederick III, but it was subsequently massively renovated in a rich baroque style. From 1449 it was the private chapel of the royal family. Today the Burgkapelle is the scene of the Hofmusikkapelle, an ensemble consisting of the Vienna Boys' Choir and members of the Vienna State Opera male chorus and orchestra, performing works by classical and modern composers. Masses (performances) are held every Sunday and on religious holidays at 9:15 a.m. from January 1 to May 25, June 1 to June 29, September 21 to December 25, and December 28. Written applications for reserved seats should be sent at least eight weeks in advance of the time you wish to attend, but send no checks or money. The cost per seat ranges from 50 AS ($2.66) to 120 AS ($6.38). For reservations, write to **Verwaltung der Hofmusikkapelle**, A-1010 Vienna, Hofburg. If you failed to reserve in advance, you may be lucky enough to secure tickets from a block sold at the Burgkapelle box office every Friday from 5 p.m. on, but the queue starts lining up at least a half hour before that. Or you might settle for standing room (it's free).

The Vienna Boys' Choir boarding school is at Palais Augarten, 1 Obere Augartenstrasse.

Neue Burg, called the New Château, was the most recent addition to the Hofburg complex. Construction was started in 1881 and continued until work was halted in 1913. The palace was the residence of Archduke Franz Ferdinand, the nephew and heir apparent of Franz Joseph, whose assassination at Sarajevo set off the chain of events that led to World War I.

Neue Burg now houses four museums. One collection devoted to arms and armor is considered second only to that of the Metropolitan Museum in New York. It is in the **Waffensammlung** on the second floor of the New Château. You'll see crossbows, swords, helmets, and pistols, plus armor, mostly the property of the emperors and princes of the House of Habsburg. Some of the exhibits, such as scimitars, were captured from the Turks as they fled the scene of their losing sieges of Vienna. Of bizarre interest is the armor worn by the little Habsburg princes, who had to learn the martial arts at a very early age.

The Waffensammlung is open weekdays except Tuesday from 10 a.m. to 4 p.m. and on Saturday and Sunday from 9 a.m. to 1 p.m. Admission is 20 AS ($1.06).

Another section, called **Musikinstrumentensammlung,** is devoted to old musical instruments, mainly from the 17th and 18th centuries, but with some from the 16th. Some of the instruments, especially pianos and harpsichords, were played by Brahms, Liszt, Mahler, and Beethoven. The hours and admission charge are the same as for the Collection of Arms and Armor.

The **Ephesos-Museum,** or Museum of Ephesian Sculpture (tel. 93-45-41), is also in Neue Burg. Here the prize exhibit is the 11 marble reliefs of Ephesus (now part of Turkey) once owned by the co-regent with the Emperor Marcus around A.D. 161. The remains of a good-size marble frieze from the monument to Lucius Verus depict battle scenes from the Roman wars. The museum is open from 10 a.m. to 4 p.m. Monday through Friday, except Tuesday when it is closed. Sunday hours are from 9 a.m. to 4 p.m. Admission is 20 AS ($1.06).

Visit the **Museum für Völkerkunde** (Ethnographical Museum) (tel. 93-45-41) if for no other reason than to see "Montezuma's treasure," three flamboyant feather robes which the mighty Aztec emperor is supposed to have given Cortés when the Spanish conquistador went to Mexico. The museum is open from 10 a.m. to 1 p.m. on Monday, Thursday, and Friday, to 5 p.m. on Wednesday, and from 9 a.m. to 1 p.m. on Sunday, Saturday 10 a.m. to 1 p.m. Closed Tuesday. Admission is 15 AS (80¢).

Also in the Hofburg complex is the **Österreichische Nationalbibliothek,** or Austrian National Library (tel. 52-52-55), entrance on Josefplatz where you'll see an equestrian statue of Joseph II. The royal library of the Habsburgs was established in the 14th century, but the present building was constructed between 1722 and 1726. It was ordered by Karl VI and designed by those masters of the baroque, the von Erlachs. The Great Hall is a thing of ornate splendor, with frescoes by Daniel Gran. Part of the collection here belonged to Prince Eugene of Savoy during his lifetime. Many of the texts in the library date from the Middle Ages and even the Dark Ages. There's also a collection of thousands of rare autographs of both the famous and the forgotten.

The library may be visited daily, except Sunday and holidays, May to September from 10 a.m. to 4 p.m. (off-season from 11 a.m. to noon). Admission is 20 AS ($1.06).

The **Albertina** (tel. 52-42-32), entrance at 1 Augustinerstrasse, is another Hofburg museum, this one showing the development of graphic arts since the 14th century. Housing one of the world's greatest graphic collections, the museum was named for a son-in-law of Maria Theresa. The most outstanding exhibit in the Albertina is the Dürer collection, although what you will see are copies, the originals being shown only on special occasions. See, in particular, Dürer's *Praying Hands,* which has been reproduced throughout the world. The some 20,000 drawings and more than 250,000 original etchings and prints include work by such artists as Poussin, Fragonard, Rubens, Rembrandt, Michelangelo, and Leonardo da Vinci. Prince Eugene of Savoy collected many of the graphics displayed here.

The Albertina is open Monday, Tuesday, and Thursday from 10 a.m. to 4 p.m., until 6 p.m. on Wednesday, and until 2 p.m. on Friday. On weekends it's open from 10 a.m. to 1 p.m. (except closed on Sunday in July and August). Admission is 15 AS (80¢).

Augustinerkirche (Church of the Augustians), 3 Augustinerstrasse (tel. 52-33-38), was constructed in the 14th century as part of the Hofburg complex to serve as the parish church of the imperial court. In the latter part of the 18th century it was stripped of its baroque embellishments and returned to the original Gothic features. The Chapel of St. George, dating from 1337, which you enter from the right aisle, is a mausoleum in which are 54 urns containing the hearts of Habsburgs. The chapel is open from Easter till the end of September from 2 to 2:30 p.m. on Monday and from 10 a.m. to 12:30 p.m. Tuesday through Friday. It's closed weekends and holidays. The tomb of the favorite daughter of Maria Theresa, Maria Christina, is also here, but there's no body in it. The princess is actually buried in the Capuchin Crypt, which I will describe later in this section under "Tombs of the Habsburgs." The richly ornamented empty tomb here was designed by Canova and is considered one of his masterpieces.

This church is a place of death but also of life. Maria Theresa married François of Lorraine here in 1736, and the Augustinerkirche was the site of other royal weddings: Marie Antoinette to Louis XVI of France in 1770, Marie-Louise of Austria to Napoleon in 1810 (by proxy—he didn't show up), and Franz Joseph to Elizabeth of Bavaria in 1854. Some of the great church music of Vienna is performed at this church on Sunday morning.

A bittersweet nostalgia seems to permeate the **Spanische Hofreitschule** (Spanish Riding School), a reminder of the fact that horses were an important part of both imperial and everyday life for many centuries, with their care and training a matter of pride and honor. The school is in the white, crystal-chandeliered ballroom in an 18th-century building of the Hofburg complex, designed by J. E. Fischer von Erlach. There I always marvel at the skill and beauty of the sleek Lippizaner stallions as their adept trainers put them through their paces in a show which is the same now as it was four centuries ago. These are the world's most famous and most classically styled equine performers. Many North Americans have seen them in the States, but to watch the Lippizaners move to the music of Johann Strauss or a Chopin polonaise in their "airs above the ground" dressage in this, their home setting in Vienna, is a pleasure you should not miss.

Performances usually take place on Sunday at 10:45 a.m. and on Wednesday at 7 p.m., except in January, February, July, August, and December. Between mid-April and June and in September and October, short performances are held at 9 a.m. on Saturday. Reservations must be made in advance, as early as possible. Order your tickets for the Sunday show from the Spanish Riding School, 1 Michaelerplatz (tel. 52-18-36), or through your travel agency. Tickets for Wednesday and Saturday shows can be ordered only through a booking or travel agency. Prices for seats are 120 AS ($6.38) to 350 AS ($18.62); for standing room, 90 AS ($4.79). Children under 3 are not admitted, but those from 3 to 6 can attend free with adults.

Training sessions may be visited daily except Sunday in February, except Sunday and Monday from March till June and September till November. Tickets with no advance reservations for the training sessions can be purchased at door 3, Josefplatz, costing 45 AS ($2.39) for adults, 15 AS (80¢) for children.

Stallburg, which you enter at 2 Reitschulgasse, is a combination art gallery and stables for the Spanish Riding School, a somewhat unusual association. The structure in the Hofburg complex was begun in 1558 and was once the home of Emperor Maximilian. It consists of three floors of galleries opening onto a Renaissance-style courtyard. Maximilian II transformed the ground floor into stables for his horses, and despite heavy damage from Allied bombs in 1945, restoration has since allowed the stabling here of the Spanish Riding School's Lippizaners. You may visit the stables Wednesday and Saturday from 2 to 4 p.m., on the Sunday and holidays with performances from 12:15 to 12:45 p.m. (on those days with no performances from 10 a.m. to noon). Cost of the visit is 10 AS (53¢).

Tombs of the Habsburgs

Kaisergruft (Capuchin Crypt), Neuer Markt (tel. 52-68-53), was the burial place of the imperial family of Habsburgs for some three centuries. The vault is below the Kapuziner Church which was built between 1622 and 1632. Capuchin friars guard the final resting place of the Habsburgs, where 12 emperors, 16 empresses, and dozens of archdukes are entombed. But only their bodies are here. Their hearts are in urns in the St. George Chapel of the Augustinerkirche in the Hofburg complex, and their entrails are similarly enshrined in a crypt below St. Stephen's Cathedral.

Most outstanding of the imperial tombs is the double sarcophagus of Maria Theresa and her consort, the Emperor Francis I (François of Lorraine). Before she joined him on a permanent basis, the empress used to descend into the tomb by elevator to visit the gravesite of her beloved Francis. The "King of Rome," the ill-fated son of Napoleon and Marie-Louise of Austria, was buried here in a bronze coffin after his death at the age of 21. (Hitler managed to anger both the Austrians and the French by having the remains of Napoleon's son transferred to Paris in 1940.)

Emperor Franz Joseph was interred here in 1916, a frail old man who outlived his time and died just before the final collapse of his empire. His wife, Empress Elizabeth, was buried in the crypt following her assassination in Geneva in 1898, as was their son, Archduke Rudolf, who committed suicide at Mayerling. Archduke Franz Ferdinand, heir apparent to Franz Joseph at the time of his assassination at Sarajevo, and Karl I, the last of the Habsburg rulers, were not entombed in the Kaisergruft. Karl I was buried in Madeira where he lived in exile after the fall of the Habsburgs. Countess Fuchs, the governess who practically reared Maria Theresa, lies in the crypt although she was not a Habsburg. (The empress bestowed this burial honor on the countess.)

The crypt may be visited daily from 10 a.m. to 3 p.m. for 20 AS ($1.06) admission. To find the Kaisergruft, head for Neuer Markt. The entrance is to the left of Kapuziner Church.

Belvedere Palace

Lying to the southeast of Schwarzenberg Palace on a slope above Vienna, approached through a long garden with a huge circular pond, Belvedere Palace (tel. 78-41-58) was designed by Johann Lukas von Hildebrandt, who is considered the last major Austrian baroque artist. Built as a summer home for Prince Eugene of Savoy, Belvedere consists of two palatial buildings the design of which foretokens the rococo. The pond reflects the sky and the palace buildings, which are made up of a series of interlocking cubes. The interior is dominated by two great, flowing staircases.

Unteres Belvedere (Lower Belvedere), entrance at 6 Rennweg, was the only part lived in by Prince Eugene, known for his brilliant military strategy and a professor to Frederick the Great. The prince resided here from the time of its construction, complete with Orangery, which took from 1714 to 1716. He never lived in **Oberes Belvedere** (Upper Belvedere), which was started in 1721 and completed in 1723. It is entered at 27 Prinz-Eugen-Strasse.

The Gold Salon in Lower Belvedere, one of the most beautiful rooms in the palace, was selected by Prince Eugene as the site of his death. The legendary conqueror of the Turks breathed his last in 1736 in the salon in an elaborate baroque bed. Following his death, the Habsburgs took over the palace. Anton Bruckner, the composer, lived in Upper Belvedere until his death in 1896, and the palace was once the residence of Archduke Franz Ferdinand who was slain in 1914. In May 1955 the peace treaty recognizing Austria as a sovereign state was signed in Upper Belvedere by foreign ministers of the four powers which occupied this country at the close of World War II—France, Great Britain, the United States, and the Soviet Union.

Today visitors can come to the splendid baroque palace, enjoying the superb view of the Wienerwald (Vienna Woods) from the terrace and passing the regal formal French-style garden to go between Unteres and Oberes Belvedere to see the art collections now open to the public in both.

Lower (Unteres) Belvedere has a wealth of sculptural decorations and houses the **Österreichisches Barokmuseum** (Museum of Baroque Art). Here are displayed the original sculptures from the Neuer Markt fountain, the work of Georg Raphael Donner who died in 1741. During his life, Donner dominated the development of Austrian sculpture of the 18th century, well founded in Italian art. On the fountain, four figures represent the four major tributaries of the Danube. Works by Franz Anton Maulbertsch, an 18th-century painter, are also exhibited. Maulbertsch, strongly influenced by Tiepolo, was considered the most original and the greatest Austrian painter who lived in his century. He was best known for his iridescent colors and flowing brushwork.

Another section is the **Museum mittelalterlicher Österreichischer Kunst** (Museum of Medieval Austrian Art) in the Orangery. Here you'll see works from the Gothic period. One Tyrolean Romanesque crucifix dates from the

12th century. Outstanding works include seven panels by Rueland Frueauf, scenes from the life of the Madonna.

Upper (Oberes) Belvedere was turned into **Österreichische Galerie des 19, and 20. Jahrhunderts** (the Austrian Gallery of 19th- and 20th-Century Art) (tel. 78-41-58-0) in 1954. In a large salon decorated in red marble you can see the 1955 peace treaty, mentioned above. Many paintings of the Biedermeier period in Austria are in this gallery. The west wing is devoted to art turned out during the long reign of Franz Joseph. Among outstanding works is *The Entrance of Charles V into Antwerp*, painted by Hans Makart. Also on display are many pictures by Gustav Klimt, who died at the end of World War I at the very collapse of the Austro-Hungarian Empire. Klimt was a founder of the Secession movement in art. See *Adam and Eve*, one of his most celebrated works. Klimt's student, Egon Schiele, who also died in 1918, is represented. *Death and the Girl* is one of his better known paintings.

The work of one of Austria's most noted artists, Oscar Kokoschka, can be seen here. Although most of the painter's life was spent in Britain to which he fled when the Nazis entered Vienna in 1938, becoming a naturalized citizen of the United Kingdom, Kokoschka is viewed as the greatest contemporary Austrian artist. He attempted to express psychological confusion and the solitude of women and men. The artist died in 1980.

Belvedere Palace is open daily from 10 a.m. to 4 p.m., until 1 p.m. on Friday. On Sunday and holidays, hours are from 9 a.m. to noon. It's closed Monday. Admission is 15 AS (80¢). One-hour guided tours in English are conducted in summer.

THE MUSEUMS OF VIENNA: There are those who say that all of the inner city of Vienna is virtually a museum. That's true. Much of the city is to be enjoyed by strolling through its streets enjoying the monuments and squares, but in some cases you'll want to find out what's behind those grandiose facades, what hidden treasures they protect. The many buildings actually operating as museums will let you do just that.

Admission to all municipal museums is free throughout the year. Children up to the age of 14 are admitted free to most national museums. From September 1 to April 30, admission is free on Saturday, Sunday, and public holidays; from October 1 to March 31 at the Museum of Fine Arts (Kunsthistorisches Museum) and the Museum of Military History (Heeresgeschichtliches Museum).

If your schedule allows for a visit to only one, make it the—

Kunsthistorisches Museum

The Museum of Fine Arts, the Kunsthistorisches, 1 Maria-Theresien-Platz, across from the Hofburg Palace (tel. 93-45-410), is housed in a huge building which contains many of the fabulous art collections gathered up by the Habsburgs when they added new territories to their empire. Acquisitions range from the art of ancient Egypt and Greece up to the 20th century. The museum is rich in works of Dutch, German, Flemish, French, and Italian painters, with representation of many of the greatest European masters, such as Velásquez and Titian.

Among notable works from the German, Dutch, and Flemish schools are Roger van der Weyden's crucifixion triptych, a Memling altarpiece, and Jan van Eyck's portrait of Cardinal Albergati. But it is the works of Pieter Brueghel the Elder for which the museum is renowned. This 16th-century Flemish master is known for his sensitive yet vigorous landscapes. He did many lively studies of the life of the peasants, and his pictures today are almost a storybook of life in his time. See especially his *Children's Games* and *Hunters in the Snow*, one of his most celebrated works. Don't confuse this artist with his son, Pieter Brueghel the Younger, also an artist.

Many visitors go to the gallery which displays the work of Van Dyck especially to see his *Venus in the Forge of Vulcan*. Rubens, naturally, comes in for a big, lavish display. You'll see his *Self-Portrait* and *Woman with a Cape*, for which he is said to have used the face of his second wife, Helen Fourment. Rubens brings a robust Flemish enthusiasm to the museum's galleries in both religious and allegorical works. Great pride is, of course, taken in the Rembrandt collection, which includes two remarkable self-portraits as well as a moving portrait of his mother and one of his son Titus. Holbein the Younger, who lived in England, painted *Jane Seymour*, third wife of Henry VIII.

For me, other than revisiting the works of Brueghel, the thrill of any trip to Vienna is seeing the Kunsthistorisches Museum's aggregation of the works of Albrecht Dürer, the German painter and engraver (1471–1528), known for his imaginative art and his painstakingly detailed workmanship. Here you will see his noted *Blue Madonna*. He was also known for his realistic landscapes as best seen in *Martyrdom of 10,000 Christians*. Dürer was a true Renaissance man.

The glory of the French, Spanish, and Italian schools is also to be seen in this Vienna museum, having often come into Habsburg hands as "gifts." Represented are Titian by his *A Girl with a Cloak*, Veronese by the *Adoration of the Magi*, Caravaggio by his *Virgin of the Rosary*, Raphael by *The Madonna in the Meadow*, and Tintoretto by his painting of Susanna caught off guard in her bath when the Peeping Tom elders came along. One of my all-time favorite painters is Il Giorgione, and here I can gaze long at his *Trio of Philosophers*. If you have only a short time to spend in this museum, I suggest that you skip many galleries if necessary just to see the work of Velásquez, the 17th-century Spanish artist often referred to as a "painter's painter." Some of his pictures of the court of Philip IV of Spain are exhibited.

One whole section of galleries is devoted to the works of ancient Egypt, Greece, and Rome. Don't miss seeing the tiny Egyptian hippopotamus. There is a noteworthy assemblage of cameos in onyx, some of which belonged to Emperor Augustus. There are also Etruscan antiquities on display.

In a sculpture and applied arts section, you can drool over the celebrated gold salt celler by Benvenuto Cellini, which was made for Francis I and is a Renaissance goldwork masterpiece. Here you'll also see a large collection of tapestries, some going back to early medieval times, and ivory horns from the ninth century. Perhaps you'll fancy a rococo breakfast service which was used by Maria Theresa and her big brood of young Habsburgs. Finally, there's a numismatic exhibit, with many medals left over from the Austro-Hungarian Empire.

The museum is open from 10 a.m. to 6 p.m. Tuesday to Friday, from 9 a.m. to 6 p.m. on Saturday, Sunday, and holidays. The galleries are also open from 7 to 9 p.m. on Tuesday and Friday. All are closed Monday. Admission is 20 AS ($1.06).

On Maria-Theresien-Platz where the Kunsthistorisches Museum is situated stands a glorious concoction, a memorial constructed in 1888 to honor the long reign of Maria Theresa, with important statesmen clustered at the feet of the empress.

Uhrenmuseum der Stadt Wien

The Municipal Clock Museum, 2 Schulhof (tel. 63-22-65), has a wide-ranging assemblage of timepieces, some ancient, some modern, some in between. Housed in what was once the Obizzi town house, the museum dates from 1690 and displays clocks of all shapes and sizes. Clock collectors from all over Europe and America come to gaze and perhaps to covet. See Rutschmann's astronomical clock made in the 18th century. There are many cuckoo clocks and a gigantic timepiece which was once mounted in the tower of St. Stephen's.

The museum is open Tuesday to Sunday from 9 a.m. to 12:15 p.m. and from 1 to 4:30 p.m. Admission is free.

Historisches Museum der Stadt Wien

The Historical Museum of Vienna, on the Karlsplatz (tel. 42-804), is a fascinating but apparently little-visited collection. History buffs seek it out, however, finding here the full panorama of the history of the old city unfolded, beginning with the settlement of prehistoric tribes in the Danube basin. Roman relics, artifacts from the reign of the dukes of Babenberg, and a wealth of leftovers from the Habsburg sovereignty are here, as well as arms and armor from various eras. A scale model shows Vienna as it looked in the Habsburg heyday. You'll see pottery and ceramics from the Roman era forward, 16th-century stained-glass windows, mementos of the Turkish sieges of the city in 1529 and 1683, and even Biedermeier furniture. There's also a section on Vienna "between the wars."

The museum is open daily except Monday from 9 a.m. to 4:30 p.m. (The second floor is closed from noon to 1:15 p.m.)

Akademie der bildenden Künste

When I'm in Vienna, I always make at least one visit to this academy of fine arts, 3 Schillerplatz (tel. 57-95-16), to see the *Last Judgment* triptych by the incomparable Hieronymous Bosch. In this work, the artist conjured up all the demons of the nether regions for a terrifying view of the suffering and sins that mankind must go through. There's more here than that, however, and you'll have the opportunity to see many Dutch and Flemish paintings, some from as far back as the 15th century, although the academy is noted for its 17th-century art. The gallery boasts works by Van Dyck, Rembrandt, Botticelli, and a host of other artists. There are several works by Lucas Cranach the Elder, outstanding being his *Lucretia,* completed in 1532, which some say is as enigmatic as *Mona Lisa.* Rubens is represented here by more than a dozen oil sketches. You can see Rembrandt's *Portrait of a Woman* and scrutinize Guardi scenes from 18th-century Venice.

Hours are from 10 a.m. to 2 p.m. on weekdays (except Wednesday, when the gallery is open from 10 a.m. to 1 p.m. and from 3 to 6 p.m.). On weekends it's open from 9 a.m. to 1 p.m. It's closed Monday. Admission is 10 AS (53¢).

Niederösterreichisches Landesmuseum

That polysyllabic name simply identifies the Museum of Lower Austria, 9 Herrengasse (tel. 63-57-11), housed in a 17th-century palace. Exhibits trace the story of life in Vienna from prehistoric times. Roman objets d'art, folkloric artifacts, Viennese antiques, regional costumes, and ecclesiastical works of art, including an altarpiece from Roggencorf, vie for attention here.

The museum is open Tuesday to Friday from 9 a.m. to 5 p.m.; Saturday from 9 a.m. to 2 p.m.; Sunday from 9 a.m. to noon; closed on Monday and from mid-July to September. Admission is 15 AS (80¢).

Österreichisches Museum für Volkskunde

The Austrian Museum of Folklore, 15-19 Laudongasse (tel. 43-89-05), dating from the late 19th century, brings vividly to life the domestic affairs of the

Austrian people of earlier times. You'll see how people lived in the remote east Tyrol and all the way to Lake Constance through some completely furnished farmhouse rooms, much baroque and religious art, and regional dress, among the exhibits. Artifacts depict a way of life—much of it already gone—made meaningful through well-arranged displays. Many painted chests, porcelain stoves, old toys, and puppets reveal how people lived. The biggest and most impressive crib collection in the country is here, as well as a fascinating toboggan display.

Open from 9 a.m. to 3 p.m. daily, to noon on Saturday, and to 1 p.m. on Sunday, the museum is closed on Monday. Admission charge is 15 AS (80¢).

Österreichisches Museum für angewandte Kunst

The Museum of Applied Art, 5 Stubenring (tel. 72-56-96), has a rich collection of tapestries, some from the 16th century. Of special interest is a Persian carpet depicting *The Hunt.* The most outstanding assemblage of Viennese porcelain in the world is here, as are some 13th-century Limoges enamels. Exhibits include much Biedermeier furniture and other antiques, glassware and crystal, an Oriental display, outstanding objects of "Wiener Werkstätte," and large collections of lace and textiles. One hall is devoted to art nouveau.

You can see these displays of applied art from 10 a.m. to 4 p.m. daily, until 6 p.m. on Thursday, and until 1 p.m. on Sunday. The museum is closed on Monday and Saturday. Entrance costs 10 AS (53¢).

Museum Moderner Kunst

The Museum of Modern Art, 1 Fürstengasse (tel. 34-12-59), was opened in 1979. Built between 1698 and 1711, the edifice, one of the most splendid in Vienna, was the home of the Prince of Liechtenstein. It is lavish with baroque adornment on the first floor. The permanent collection shows works of international modern art from 1900 on to the present and is especially rich in surrealism, object art, photo-realism, and abstract art.

Hours are daily from 10 a.m. to 6 p.m. (except Tuesday when it's closed). Admission is 15 AS (80¢).

Museum des 20 Jahrhunderts

This modern museum lying in the Schweizergarten (tel. 78-25-50) was opened in 1962 in the pavilion built for the 1958 World's Fair in Brussels by Karl Schwanzer. Now it is used for ever-changing exhibits of international modern art, and there is an important sculpture garden outside the museum. Hours are daily from 10 a.m. to 6 p.m. except Wednesday when it is closed. Admission varies according to the exhibit being shown, ranging from 10 AS (53¢) to 30 AS ($1.60).

Heeresgeschichtliches Museum

Vienna's Museum of Military History in the Arsenal (tel. 78-23-03), is the oldest state museum building in Vienna, constructed from 1849 to 1856. Mostly, of course, the military history of the Habsburgs—their glittering triumphs and their defeats—is delineated. A glass case in the center of the Hall of Glory (Ruhmeshalle) contains the six orders of the House of Habsburg which Franz Joseph wore on all public occasions. The colors are faded and the pins and other fasteners almost worn away from use. I find fascinating the Sarajevo room, with mementos of the assassination of Archduke Franz Ferdinand and his wife on June 28, 1914, the event which ignited the smoldering kindling and set off the deadly bonfire of World War I. The archduke's bloodstained uniform is displayed, along with the bullet-scarred car in which the royal couple rode on that fateful day. Many exhibits relating to the navy of the Austro-Hungarian Empire may be seen. You'll also view frescoes depicting important battles, including those fought with the Turks in and around Vienna.

The museum is open daily from 10 a.m. to 4 p.m. (except Friday when it's closed). A 10 AS (53¢) admission fee is charged.

The Horological Museum

Vienna's clock museum, 2 Schulhof (tel. 63-22-65), founded in 1917, is based mainly on clocks from the collections of Maria Ebner-Eschenbach and Rudolf Kaften. Of the 3,000 unusual timepieces which the museum owns, fewer than 1,000 are placed on display at one time, so you may want to make repeat visits. In an elegant baroque town house, the collections, arranged in rooms on three floors of the building, range from musical and "picture" clocks to cuckoo clocks, rococo long-case clocks, and a pocket-watch exhibit in which beautiful and delicate 18th- and 19th-century workmanship can be seen. The history of clock-making is graphically displayed, with timepieces arranged on the various levels of the house in chronological order. The museum is open Tuesday through Sunday from 9 a.m. to 12:15 p.m. and 1 to 4:30 p.m. Admission is free, and guided tours are offered.

THE CHURCHES OF VIENNA: The houses of worship are so inviting that even nonbelievers may want to attend on their Vienna visit, if not for the rich baroque decoration of crystal chandeliers and trompe l'oeil ceilings, then for the magnificent music of Mozart, Bach, Haydn, perhaps Bruckner. Many former Gothic churches have a massive baroque overlay, although some have been relieved of this decoration and put back to their original simpler style. If you spent a week visiting the churches of Vienna you still wouldn't have seen them all. If your stay here is relatively brief, I suggest you look at the first two recommended below, and then see others if you have more time. I'll begin with the king of them all—

St. Stephen's Cathedral

Lying in the very heart of the city on Stephansplatz, a bustling intersection where legend has it that if you wait long enough you'll see anybody you're looking for in the city, St. Stephen's Cathedral (tel. 53-25-61-563) was founded in the 12th century in what even in the Middle Ages was the town's center. The church was the result of a new basilica being built on the site of a Romanesque sanctuary.

Stephansdom, the German name for this church, was virtually destroyed in a 1258 fire which swept Vienna, and toward the dawn of the 14th century the Romanesque basilica gave way to a Gothic building. The cathedral suffered terribly in the Turkish siege of 1683 but then was allowed to rest until the Russian bombardments of 1945, with the Germans bringing more destruction when they continued to fire on Vienna from the outskirts as they fled the city. During these most recent depredations the wooden roof of St. Stephen's was heavily bombed, but it has been replaced with a steel structure. The steeple, rising to some 450 feet, has come to symbolize the very spirit of Vienna. Reopened in 1948 after restoration from war damage, today the cathedral is considered one of the greatest Gothic structures in Europe, rich in woodcarvings, altars, sculptures, and paintings.

The west door, in the Romanesque style, called Giants' Doorway *(Riesentor)*, is one of the oldest parts of the main building, having been spared from the 1258 fire. It is richly embellished with statuary. The mammoth bell of St. Stephen's, Pummerin or Boomer Bell, largest in the country, was originally cast from cannons left behind by the fleeing Turks after their failed siege of 1683. I'm sure the bell was sufficiently blessed to remove any heretical taint from the metal. Or perhaps some tinge remained, to be released in the fire of 1945, for the bell fell and shattered then, since replaced by a bell donated by Upper Austria.

The 352-foot-long cathedral is inextricably linked with Viennese and Austrian history. It was here that Mozart was buried in 1791 in a "pauper's funeral," and it was on the cathedral door that Napoleon posted his farewell edict in 1805.

The pulpit of St. Stephen's was carved from stone by Anton Pilgrim, his enduring masterpiece. But the chief treasure of the cathedral is the carved wooden Wiener Neustadt altarpiece dating from 1447, richly painted and gilded, found in the Virgin's Choir. See also the curious tomb of Emperor Frederick III in the Apostles' Choir. Made of a pinkish Salzburg marble in the 17th century, the tomb is carved with hideous little hobgoblins trying to enter and wake the emperor from his eternal sleep. The entrance to the catacombs or crypt is on the north side next to the Capistran pulpit. You can visit it from 10 a.m. to 4:30 p.m. for 20 AS ($1.06). In the crypt you'll see the funeral urns which contain the entrails of 56 members of the Habsburg family. (As I said earlier, the hearts are inurned in the St. George Chapel of the Augustinerkirche and the bodies entombed in the Capuchin Crypt of the Kapuziner Church.)

You can climb the south tower of St. Stephen's, 344 steps, which dominates the Viennese skyline and from which you have a view of the Vienna Woods. Called Alter Steffl (Old Steve), the tower with its needle-like spire was built between 1350 and 1433. From it, watchkeepers of earlier days kept vigil over the city. So well known is Old Steve that the Viennese refer to the entire cathedral as Alter Steffl. If you're game to climb the tower, you can do so from March to the end of September from 9 a.m. to 5:30 p.m. and from October to mid-November until 3:30 p.m.

The north tower (Nordturm) was never finished to match the south one, but was crowned with a Renaissance tower in 1579. You can reach it by elevator April to the end of September from 9 a.m. to 6 p.m. and October to the end of March from 8 a.m. to 5 p.m. at a charge of 30 AS ($1.60). You view a panoramic sweep of the city and the Danube.

St. Maria am Gestade

This church at Passauer Platz, the Church of Our Lady of the Riverbank, was once just that, with an arm of the Danube flowing by it, making it a favorite place of worship for fishermen. But the river was redirected, and now the church draws people by its beauty. A Romanesque church on this site was rebuilt in Gothic style between 1394 and 1427. The western facade is in the flamboyant Gothic style, with a seven-sided Gothic tower surmounted by a dome which culminates in a lacelike crown. This tower has long been an Old Town landmark.

The church's most remarkable treasure is in the Chapel of St. Clement, an altarpiece made in 1460. See the panels depicting the Coronation of the Virgin and the Annunciation. In the interior are many pieces of Gothic statuary and superb woodcarving.

St. Maria am Gestade was much damaged during Turkish sieges, both in 1529 and 1683.

Church of the Teutonic Order

Die Deutschordenkirche and its treasury, Schatzkammer des Deutschen Ordens, both at 7 Singerstrasse (tel. 52-11-656), will stir thoughts of the Crusades in the minds of history buffs, but the relics of vanished glory may make some visitors wish they had been among the nobility of the Middle Ages.

The Order of the Teutonic Knights was a German society founded in 1190 in the Holy Land, and this is the church they built in Vienna in 1395. The building did not share in the baroque madness that swept the city following the Counter-Reformation, so you see it pretty much as it was originally, a Gothic church dedicated to St. Elizabeth. A choice feature is the 16th-century Flemish altarpiece standing at the main altar which is richly decorated with woodcarving, much gilt, and painted panel inserts. Many knights of the Teutonic Order are buried here, their heraldic shields still mounted on some of the upper walls.

In the treasury of the knights on the second floor of the church, you'll see mementos such as seals and coins illustrating the history of the order, as well as a collection of arms, vases, gold, crystal, and precious stones. These were very wealthy knights. Also on display are the charter given to the Teutonic Order by Henry IV of England and medieval paintings. A curious exhibit is a Viper Tongue Credenza, said to have the power to detect poison in food and render it harmless.

The treasury can be visited from 10 a.m. to noon and from 3 to 5 p.m. except on Monday. Admission is 15 AS (80¢).

St. Peter's Church

Called Peterskirche, this church dominates Peterplatz. It's the second-oldest church in Vienna, but the spot on which it stands may well be the *oldest* Christian church site. Many places of worship have stood here, the first believed to date from the second half of the fourth century. Charlemagne is credited with having founded a church on the site (late eighth or early ninth century).

The present St. Peter's, the most lavishly decorated baroque church in Vienna, was designed in 1702 by Gabriel Montani. Von Hildebrandt, the noted architect who designed the Belvedere Palace, is believed to have finished the building in 1732. The fresco in the dome is a masterpiece by J. M. Rottmayr, depicting the Coronation of the Virgin. The church contains many frescoes and much gilded carved wood, plus altarpieces which are the work of many well-known artists of the time.

St. Rupert's Church

The oldest church in Vienna, Ruprechtskirche, stands at Ruprechtsplatz where it has been since 740, although much that you see now, such as the aisle, is newer—from the 11th century. It's believed that much of the masonry from a Roman shrine on this spot was used in the present church. The tower and nave are Romanesque, the rest Gothic. St. Rupert is the patron saint of salt merchants of the Danube.

The church is not always open to the public, so if you really want to see it, I suggest you attend service on Sunday.

Church of St. Charles

Construction on Karlskirche, opening onto Karlsplatz, dedicated to St. Charles Borromeo, was begun in 1716 by order of Emperor Charles VI. Black plague swept Vienna in 1713, and the emperor made a vow to build the church if the disease would abate. Work on the structure was begun by that master of the baroque, Johann Bernard Fischer von Erlach, who labored from 1716 to 1722. His son Joseph Emanuel completed it between 1723 and 1739. The lavishly decorated interior was given to the people by the father and son leaders in the baroque field.

The well-known ecclesiastical artist, J. M. Rottmayr, painted many of the frescoes inside the church from 1725 to 1730. The green copper dome of Karlskirche is a lofty 236 feet high, a dramatic landmark on the Viennese skyline. Two columns, spin-offs from Trajan's Column in Rome, flank the front of the church, and there is also a statue by Henry Moore.

The Church of the Jesuits

Built at the time of the Counter-Reformation, the Jesuitenkirche at Dr. Ignaz-Seipel-Platz is rich in baroque embellishments, which is no surprise as it was constructed between 1627 and 1631 when the baroque craze in churches was sweeping the city. This was the university church, dedicated to the Jesuit saints, Ignatius of Loyola and Franciscus Xaverius. It was built at the order of the emperor, Ferdinand II. The rich high-baroque decorations (galleries, columns, and the trompe l'oeil painting on the ceiling which gives the illusion of a dome) were added from 1703–1705, after the Thirty Years War and the Turkish siege of Vienna had ended. The embellishments were the work of Jesuit laybrother, the Roman Andrea Pozzo, at the orders of Emperor Leopold I. The redecorated church was dedicated to the Assumption of the Virgin. See Pozzo's painting of Mary, behind the main altar.

In July the church is a central point of the **Spectaculum,** a summer festival held by the Society for Music Theatre in the Old University District. Baroque operas are performed in the church, with other segments of the Spectaculum performed elsewhere. Information about this event is available from the **Society for Music Theatre,** 19 Türkenstrasse (tel. 34-01-99).

Church of St. Michael

Michaelerkirche on Michaelerplatz can date some of its Romanesque portions to the early 1200s. The exact date of the chancel is not known, but it is probably from the mid-14th century. Over its long history this church has felt the hand of many architects and designers, resulting in a medley of styles, not all harmonious. Perhaps only the catacombs would be recognized by droppers-in from the Middle Ages.

Most of the present look of St. Michael's dates from 1792, when the facade was done in the neoclassical style typical of the time. The spire, however, is from the 16th century. The main altar is richly decorated in baroque style, and the altarpiece, entitled *The Collapse of the Angels,* is the last major baroque work done in Vienna. The year was 1781.

Church of the Minorites

If you're tired of baroque ornamentation, visit Minoritenkirche on Minoritenplatz, a church of the Friar Minor Capuchins, a Franciscan order also called the Minorite friars (inferior brothers, so called to emphasize their humility). This church, begun in 1250 but not completed until early in the 14th century, had its tower damaged by the Turks in their two sieges of Vienna, and then it fell prey to baroque architects and designers in the 18th century. But in 1784 Ferdinand von Hohenberg ordered that the baroque be removed and the simple lines of the original Gothic church returned, complete with Gothic cloisters. Inside you'll see a mosaic copy of da Vinci's *The Last Supper.*

Church of the Piarist Order

Work on Piaristenkirche, on Jodok-Fink-Platz, which is more popularly known as Piaristenplatz, was launched in 1716 by the Roman Catholic teaching congregation known as Piarists (fathers of religious schools), but the church was not consecreated until 1771. Some of the designs submitted during that long period are believed to have been drawn by von Hildebrandt, the noted architect who designed the Belvedere Palace, but many builders had a hand in things during the decades between construction start and consecration.

Despite the time lag and the many alterations during construction, this church is noteworthy for its fine, classic facade. Frescoes by F. A. Maulbertsch, done in 1752, adorn the inside of the circular cupolas.

Church and Court of the Scots

Heinrich, a Babenberg ruler who died in 1177, during his reign founded a "monastery of the Scots," Schottenhof in Freyung, in 1155. The monks were in fact Irish, but who was inclined to point out an error to a medieval monarch? So Schottenhof was and still is the "Courtyard of the Scots" and Schottenkirche the "Church of the Scots." Although it suffered much damage in the late Middle Ages, the church always bounced back and has survived massive alterations done in the 17th century, plus a major facelift which gave it its present appearance in 1880, the heyday of the empire. In the art gallery in the abbey, you'll see paintings showing Vienna in the Middle Ages.

Kirche am Hof

This most exuberantly baroque of all Vienna's churches is called "The Church of the Nine Choirs of Angels." With the Germanic penchant for expressing a name by stringing all the words together, I'm glad they simply call this church by its am Hof location rather than using a literal translation.

The church was constructed between 1386 and 1403 by Carmelite monks in the Gothic style. However, when the Jesuits took it over early in the time of the Counter-Reformation, they made many architectural changes, so that today it bears a simple baroque facade which was completed in 1692. In a chapel inside the church you can see a fresco by Franz Anton Maulbertsch, perhaps the greatest and most original of the 18th-century Austrian painters.

Kirche am Hof has a place in history. It was here that Franz II, seeing the end of the Holy Roman Empire approaching, proclaimed the Austrian Empire in 1804. It was well that he did. Just two years later the Holy Roman Empire, brought forth with great fanfare in 962, ceased to exist.

VIENNA WOODS: Yes, dear reader, there really are Vienna Woods. They weren't simply dreamed up by Johann Strauss as the subject of musical tales in waltz time. The Wienerwald is a land of gentle paths and trees several thousand acres in size in a delightful hilly landscape. If you stroll through this pleasant area, a weekend playground for the Viennese, you'll be following in the footsteps of Strauss and Schubert. Beethoven, when his hearing was failing, claimed that the chirping birds, trees, and leafy vineyards of the Wienerwald made it easier for him to compose.

A round trip through the woods, which lie to the south and west of Vienna, takes about 3½ hours by car, a distance of some 50 miles. You leave the city on the Eichenstrasse. Even if you don't have a car, the woods can be visited relatively easily on your own. Board trolleycar no. 1 near the State Opera House, going to Schottenring. There you must switch to tram no. 38 (the same ticket is valid) going out to Grinzing, the village that is the site of the famous heurigen, or wine taverns. At Grinzing you can board a bus that goes through the Wienerwald to Kahlenberg (see below). The whole trip costs about 45 AS ($2.39) and takes about 1½ hours each way. You might rent a bicycle nearby to make your own exploration of the woods.

Many of the attractions of the Wienerwald will be described in Chapter V, "Lower Austria."

When you go to the Vienna Woods by public transportation, after you reach Grinzing (if you can resist the heurigen), you board bus no. 38A up the hill to **Kahlenberg** on the northeasternmost spur of the Alps (1,585 feet). If the weather is fair and clear, you can see all the way to Hungary and Czechoslovakia from here. At the top of the hill is the small Church of St. Joseph where King John Sobieski of Poland stopped to pray before leading his troops to the defense of Vienna against the Turks. For one of the best of all views overlooking Vienna, go to the right of the Kahlenberg restaurant. From the terrace there, you'll have a panoramic sweep, including the spires of St. Stephen's.

Many Austrian visitors from the country, a hardy lot, walk along a footpath to the suburb of Nussdorf and Heiligenstadt, perhaps along the very path Beethoven trod when he lived there. At Nussdorf, it's possible to take a trolleycar, designated D, which will return you to the heart of Vienna.

THE PARKS OF VIENNA: When the weather is fine, the typical Viennese shuns city parks in favor of the Wienerwald, brought to the notice of the world by Johann Strauss in his celebrated work, "Tales from the Vienna Woods." But if you're an aficionado of parks, you'll find some magnificent ones in Vienna, where there are more than 4,000 acres of garden and parks within the city limits and no fewer than 770 sports fields and playgrounds. You can, of course, visit Schönbrunn Park and Belvedere Park when you tour those once-royal palaces.

Of the parks of Vienna, tastefully laid out by municipal authorities, I will highlight only the most popular, beginning with—

Stadtpark: This lovely garden is on the site of the slope where the Danube used to overflow into the inner city, before the canal was constructed. It can be reached from the Ring or from Lothringer-Strasse. Many memorial statues stand in the park, perhaps the best known being the one to Johann Strauss, Jr., composer of operettas and waltzes, including "The Blue Danube Waltz." (His father was also a noted musician.) Here too are monuments to Franz Schubert and to Hans Makart, a well-known artist whose work you'll see in churches and museums.

The Kursalon, an elegant café-restaurant, sits at the south end of the Stadtpark. Here you can sit at a garden table and often enjoy a concert of Viennese music as you sip the local wine.

Volksgarten: Next to the Burgtheater, visited elsewhere in this book, the people's park was laid out on the site of the old city wall fortifications and can be entered from Dr.-Karl-Lueger-Ring. It's the oldest public garden in Vienna, dating from 1820. Here too there are many monuments. One to Franz Grillparzer, the poet, was sculptured in 1889. A memorial to the assassinated Empress Elizabeth dates from 1907. Construction of the so-called Temple of Theseus, a copy of the Theseion in Athens, was begun in 1820.

Burggarten: From the Burgring, you can enter this former garden of the Habsburg emperors, built soon after the Volksgarten was completed. There is a monument to Mozart in this park as well as an equestrian statue of Franz I, beloved husband of Maria Theresa. The only open-air statue of Franz Joseph in all Vienna is here. The Burggarten lies next to the Neue Hofburg. There's a statue of Goethe at the park entrance.

Botanischer Garten: Exotic plants from all over the world, many extremely rare, are found in the Botanical Garden of the University of Vienna at 14 Rennweg (78-71-01), next to Belvedere Park, from which it can also be entered. The botanical garden grew out of a place where medicinal herbs were planted on orders from Maria Theresa. The garden may be visited from mid-April until the first of October from 9 a.m. to dusk, but always call before going if the weather is inclement as the garden may be closed. No admission is charged.

Donaupark: The entrance to this, the Danube Park laid out in 1964 between the Danube and the Old Danube which was diverted from its original course, is on Wagramer Strasse. The 247-acre park was converted from a garbage dump by municipal authorities. It's visited mainly by those who wish to go up to the 828-foot tower where there is a rotating café-restaurant, offering superb vistas of the city. There's an observation platform at 560 feet. Two express elevators take people to the top of the tower for 33 AS ($1.76) per person. The café revolves quickly, the restaurant taking more time. The tower is open from 9 a.m. till midnight (from 10 a.m. till 11 p.m. in winter). For information, phone 23-53-68.

The Prater

Since 1766, when Emperor Joseph II opened the Prater to the public, this extensive tract of woods and meadowland lying between the Danube River and the Danube Canal has been Vienna's favorite recreation area. Joseph, son and co-ruler of Maria Theresa, a liberal reformer and humanist, didn't always come up with changes everybody liked, but when he declared that "everybody shall be allowed to walk, ride, and drive in the Prater at their pleasure," he came up with a winner. Before that the area had been used mostly as a hunting preserve and riding ground for the aristocracy. People still hunted in the wooded section until the reign of Franz Joseph.

Perhaps the coming of too many people drove all the game away, because from the time it was opened to the public, a collection of booths, amusements, and restaurants sprang up in the Prater and drew many visitors. In its early years it was a gathering place for the carriage trade too. Even the emperor and empress came here—when they could get in!

The Prater is considered the birthplace of the waltz. It was first heard here in 1820, introduced by Johann Strauss (the elder) and Josef Lanner. However, it was under Johann Strauss the Son, who became known as "the king of the waltz," that this music form reached its greatest popularity.

The best known part of the huge park is at the end nearest the entrance from the Ring. Here you'll find the **Riesenrad,** the giant ferris wheel, one of the landmarks of Vienna, constructed in 1897, 220 feet at its highest point. If you saw the film *The Third Man,* you may recall this ferris wheel in the scene where it appeared that Orson Welles was going to murder Joseph Cotten.

Just beside the Riesenrad is the terminus of the Lilliputian railroad, the 2.6-mile narrow-gauge line which operates in summer using vintage steam locomotives. The amusement park, right behind the ferris wheel, has all the typical entertainment facilities—roller coasters, merry-go-rounds, tunnels of love, games arcades, whatever.

The Prater is not a fenced-in park, but not all amusements are open all year. The season lasts from March or April until October, but the Riesenrad operates from the beginning of March until November 1. A ride on it costs 35 AS ($1.86) for adults, 20 AS ($1.06) for children. Some of the more than 150 booths and restaurants stay open in winter, including the pony merry-go-round and the gambling places.

The **Prater Museum** (tel. 24-94-32) has historical exhibits, including carousel figures and posters, illustrating the 200-year history of the park. Located in the Planetarium building near the ferris wheel, the museum is open on Saturday, Sunday, and public holidays from 2 till 6:30 p.m.

The Prater is also a sports center with swimming pools, riding schools, and race courses here and there between woodland and meadows. International soccer matches are held in the Prater stadium.

To reach the Prater, take either streetcar no. 1 from the Ring or the U1 subway to Pratersten. If you drive here, don't forget to observe the "No Entry" and "No Parking" signs which apply from 3 p.m. on daily. The place is usually jammed on Sunday afternoon in summer. I suggest you schedule your visit at some other time.

HOMES OF FAMOUS MEN: Many of the residences once occupied by celebrated personages in Vienna, most often composers, have been made into museums and opened to the public. It's a privilege for the music lover to see the rooms once lived and worked in by his or her particular favorites. But dwelling places of noted persons outside the music world are also preserved. For instance, you may visit the apartment where the originator of psychoanalysis wrote of his revolutionary studies.

If you're a Beethoven fancier and want to see where this genius lived, you'll have to do a bit of footwork, as he seems never to have stayed long in one place. He was evicted from several of his dwellings because of a habit he had of composing at 3 o'clock in the morning. His music may have been heavenly, but it probably came off as pretty hellish to neighbors who preferred to spend the night hours sleeping.

You can visit one of his residences where the landlord was tolerant (or the neighbors hard of hearing!), the **Pasqualati House,** 8 Mölker Bastei (tel. 63-70-665). The building dates from the 1790s, and Beethoven lived there—on and off—from 1804 to 1814. He is known to have composed his Fourth, Fifth, and Seventh Symphonies here, as well as *Fidelio* and other works.

There isn't much to see except some family portraits and the composer's scores, but you may feel it's worth the climb to the fourth floor (there's no elevator). You may visit the apartment daily except Monday from 10 a.m. to 12:15 p.m. and 1 to 4:30 p.m.

Haydns Wohnhaus (Haydn's House), 19 Haydngasse (tel. 56-13-07), is where Franz Josef Haydn conceived and wrote his magnificent later oratorios *The Seasons* and *The Creation*. He lived here from 1797 until his death in 1809. Haydn gave lessons to Beethoven here. There's also a room in this house, which is a branch of the History Museum of Vienna, honoring Johannes Brahms. Hours are from 10 a.m. to 12:15 p.m. and 1 to 4:30 p.m. Tuesday through Sunday. There's no admission charge.

The **Mozart-Wohnung** (Figarohaus), or Mozart Memorial, is at 5 Domgasse (tel. 52-40-722), in a 17th-century house, called the House of Figaro because Mozart composed his opera *The Marriage of Figaro* here. The composer's life in this house from 1784 to 1787 was a relatively happy period in what was otherwise a rather tragic life. It was here that he often played chamber music concerts with Haydn, whose home we have just visited. Later, Mozart was not to have such a fancy address as this one on Domgasse. Over the years he lived in a dozen houses in all, which became more squalid as he aged. He died in poverty and was given a blessing at St. Stephen's Cathedral in 1791, then buried in St. Marx Cemetery.

The Domgasse apartment has been turned into a museum. Hours are from 10 a.m. to 12:15 p.m. and 1 to 4:30 p.m. daily except Monday.

The **Schubert Museum** (Schubert's birthplace) is at 54 Nussdorferstrasse (tel. 34-59-924). The composer, son of a poor schoolmaster, was born in 1797 in a house built earlier in that century. Many Schubert mementos are on view. The house is open from 10 a.m. to 12:15 p.m. and 1 to 4:30 p.m. daily except Monday. Schubert's last residence was in his brother's house, 6 Kettenbruckengasse (tel. 57-39-072), and the room in which he died at the early age of 31 has been made into a memorial.

"The king of the waltz," Johann Strauss, Jr., lived at the **Johann-Strauss-Wohnung**, 54 Praterstrasse (tel. 24-01-21), for a number of years, composing "The Blue Danube Waltz" here in 1867. Now part of the History Museum of Vienna, the house is open from 10 a.m. to 12:15 p.m. and 1 to 4:30 p.m. daily except Monday.

The **Sigmund Freud apartment**, 19 Berggasse (tel. 31-15-96), with its dark furniture (only part of it original), lace curtains, and collection of antiquities, gives you the feeling that the doctor might walk in at any moment and tell you to make yourself comfortable on the couch. His velour hat, dark walking stick with ivory handle, and other mementos are to be seen in the study and waiting room he used during his life here from 1891 to 1938. When Hitler staged his takeover of Austria, the so-called Anschluss, Freud fled these quarters to seek safety in London.

You may visit the apartment from 9 a.m. to 1 p.m. Monday to Friday, from 9 a.m. to 3 p.m. on weekends. Admission costs 20 AS ($1.06) for adults, 10 AS (53¢) for children above the age of ten. The museum also has a bookshop where souvenirs are available, including a variety of postcards of the apartment, books by Freud, posters, prints, and pens.

TOURS: The two Vienna sightseeing companies, **Cityrama Sightseeing Tours** and **Vienna Sightseeing Tours**, offer a wide range of trips for visitors. If sufficient notice is given, you can be picked up at your hotel for all but the mini-tours.

Cityrama conducts nonstop tours lasting about 1½ hours each at 9:45 a.m. and 2:45 p.m. daily from Stephansplatz and at 10 a.m. and 3 p.m. daily from Johannesgasse.

Vienna Sightseeing Tours (Wiener Rundfahrten), 4/11 Stelzhamergasse (tel. 72-43-83), offers many tours, ranging from a 1½-hour **Vienna—Getting Acquainted** trip to a two-day luxury excursion to Budapest and a flight across the Alps to Innsbruck. The getting-acquainted tour, costing 150 AS ($7.98) for adults, 50 AS ($2.66) for children, is a favorite with visitors who are pressed for time and yet want to see the most important sights of the city. It takes you past the historic buildings of the Ringstrasse—the Opera House, Hofburg, museums, the House of Parliament, City Hall, Burgtheater, the university, and the Votive Church—and into the heart of Vienna to St. Stephen's Cathedral, as well as Belvedere Palace, St. Charles Church, and the Musikverein (Vienna Philharmonic Orchestra building). Tours leave the Opera House daily at 10:30 and 11:45 a.m. and at 3 and 4:30 p.m.

Another popular excursion, lasting about 3½ hours, **Vienna Woods Impressions,** leaves from the Opera House and takes you to the towns of Perchtoldsdorf and Mödiing, passing by the Höldrichsmühle, where Franz Schubert composed many of his beloved *Lieder,* going to the Abbey of Heiligenkreuz, a center of Christian culture since medieval times. The commemorative chapel in the village of Mayerling reminds visitors of the tragic suicide of Crown Prince Rudolph, only son of Emperor Franz Joseph, and his mistress. The tour also takes you for a short walk through Baden, the spa once a favorite summer resort of the aristocracy. Tours start and end at the Opera House, leaving at 1 p.m. daily and costing 230 AS ($12.24) for adults, 50 AS ($2.66) for children.

A **Grand City Tour,** which includes a visit to Schönbrunn and Belvedere

Palaces, leaves the Opera House daily at 9:30 and 10:30 a.m. and at 2:30 p.m., lasting approximately three hours and costing adults 290 AS ($15.34); children, 100 AS ($5.32).

A visit to the **Spanish Riding School,** where the world-renowned Lippizaner horses are trained, is offered daily Tuesday through Saturday, leaving the Opera House at 9:30 a.m., except in July and August. The charge is 350 AS ($18.62) for adults, 100 AS ($5.32) for children. On some Saturdays there's a special short performance by the Lippizaners, for which a 50 AS ($2.66) supplement is charged. Also on this tour, you will take a short stroll through the old city and visit the Museum of Fine Arts.

Perhaps you'll have time to make an eight-hour trip along the Danube, going to Wachau by bus and boat and tasting the wines produced in this area since Roman times. From the end of March until October 31 this tour leaves daily at 9:30 a.m., cutting the schedule to every Thursday and Sunday from November 1 to March 31. The price is 800 AS ($42.56) for adults, 400 AS ($21.28) for children.

2. Where to Shop

Visitors find much of interest to buy or just to look at in Vienna's shops, where you'll see handicrafts produced in a long-established tradition of skilled workmanship. Popular for their beauty, quality, and reasonable prices are petit-point items, hand-painted Wiener Augarten porcelain, work of gold- and silver-smiths, handmade dolls, ceramics, enamel jewelry, wrought-iron articles, leathergoods, and many other items of value and interest.

The main shopping streets are in the city center (first district). Here you'll find **Kärntnerstrasse,** between the Opera House and Stock-im-Eisen-Platz; the **Graben,** between Stock-im-Eisen-Platz and Kohlmarkt; **Kohlmarkt,** between the Graben and Michaelplatz; and **Rotensturmstrasse,** between Stephansplatz and Kai. There are also **Mariahilferstrasse,** between Babenbergerstrasse and Schönbrunn, one of the longest streets in Vienna; **Favoritenstrasse,** between Südtiroler Platz and Reumannplatz; and **Landstrasser Hauptstrasse.**

Shops are normally open Monday through Friday from 9 a.m. to 6 p.m. and on Saturday from 9 a.m. to noon. Small shops close at noon for lunch. Railroad station shops in the Westbahnhof and the Südbahnhof are open from 7 a.m. to 11 p.m., offering groceries, smoker's supplies, stationery, books, and flowers. These two stations also have hairdressers, public baths, and photo booths.

Vienna's antique shops hold what seems to be a limitless treasure trove, and you can find valuable old books, engravings, etchings, and paintings in secondhand shops, bookshops, and picture galleries.

The state-owned **Dorotheum,** 19 Dorotheergasse (tel. 52-31-29), is the oldest auction house in Europe, dating from 1707 when it was founded by the emperor, Joseph I, as an auction house where impoverished aristocrats could fairly (and anonymously) get good value for their heirlooms. If you're interested in what is being auctioned off, you give a small fee to a *Sensal,* one of the licensed bidders, and he or she will bid in your name. The Dorotheum is also the scene of many art auctions, and there are 16 subsidiaries in other districts, plus large private galleries and antique dealers.

You may find a little of everything at the **Flohmarkt** or flea market, in the vicinity of the Naschmarkt, near the Kettenbrückengasse underground station. It is held every Saturday from 8 a.m. to 6 p.m. except on public holidays. Naturally it's customary to haggle over the price, and the Viennese have perfected that skill.

The **Naschmarkt** itself is a vegetable and fruit market, the "Covent Garden of Vienna," which has a lively scene every day. To visit it, head south of the Opera district. It's at Linke and Rechte Wienzeile.

Ö. W. (Österreichische Werkstatten), 6 Kärntnerstrasse (tel. 52-24-18), is a big, well-run store that sells hundreds of handmade art objects from Austria. You'll find an especially good selection of pewter, along with enameled jewelry, glassware, brass, baskets, ceramics, and serving spoons fashioned from deer horn and bone. Be sure to keep wandering through this place, as there are three floors and a friendly staff. Even if you skip the other stores of Vienna, check this one out.

Trachten Schlössl, 2 Kohlmarkt (tel. 63-92-34), is one of Vienna's most fabulous women's clothing stores, where the decor is as elegant as the garments. The dozen or so saleswomen are charming and very helpful. It opened as recently as 1982 in a three-story town house where the in-house fitters (all three of them) work in rooms opening off the wrought-iron stairwell connecting the three floors. You'll see the most exotic Biedermeier sofas and chairs in Vienna against a background of marble floors, wood paneling, and pink- and cream-colored walls. Many of the clothes are custom-made, and include suits in Austrian suede or English tweed. Austrian and English winter coats are sold, along with lots of accessories, including scarves and umbrellas. The clothes are not as expensive as you might think.

Popp & Kretschmer, 51 Kärntnerstrasse (tel. 52-78-01). The staff here is usually as well dressed and elegant as their clientele, and will, if you appear to be a bona fide customer, offer coffee, tea, or champagne as you scrutinize the carefully selected merchandise. The store contains three carpeted levels of dresses for women, along with shoes, handbags, and a small selection of men's belts, briefcases, and travel bags. The establishment is opposite the Opera, near many of the grand old hotels of Vienna.

Lanz, 10 Kärntnerstrasse (tel. 52-24-56), is a well-known Austrian store which specializes in haute couture in Austrian folkloric clothing. It has a rustically elegant format of wood paneling and brass chandeliers. Most of their stock is for women, although they do offer a limited selection of men's jackets. Clothes for toddlers begin at sizes appropriate for a six-month-old child, while women's apparel begins at size 36 (American size 7).

Gerold and Co., 31 Graben (tel. 52-22-35), is the best bookstore in Vienna for English-language publications. The sales personnel are very helpful, and you can often pick up many titles not readily available elsewhere.

J. & L. Lobmeyr, 26 Kärntnerstrasse (tel. 52-21-89). If during your exploration of Vienna you should happen to admire a crystal chandelier, there's a good chance that it was made by this company. It was designated in the early 19th century as a purveyor to the Imperial Court of Austria, and it has maintained an elevated position ever since. The company is credited with designing and creating the first electric chandelier in 1883. It has also designed chandeliers for the Vienna Opera, the Metropolitan Opera in New York, even the Assembly Hall in the Kremlin.

Behind its art nouveau facade on the main shopping street of town, you'll see at least 50 chandeliers of all shapes and sizes. The store also sells hand-painted Hungarian porcelain, along with complete breakfast and dinner services. They'll also engrave your family crest on a wine glass if you want it, or sell you one of the uniquely modern pieces of sculptured glass from the third-floor showroom. The second floor is a museum of some of the outstanding pieces the company has made since it was established in 1823.

Mary Kindermoden, 14 Graben (tel. 52-79-03), is—at last!—an inexpensive store specializing only in children's clothing with a regional twist. If you've thought about buying your nephew a pair of lederhosen or a dirndl for your niece, this is the place to go. In the heart of the old city, near St. Stephen's Cathedral, the establishment has two floors of well-made garments which even include lace swaddling clothes for a christening. Most garments are for children aged 10 months to 14 years, although lederhosen (which are adorable if you can get junior to wear them) are available for children 10 months to 8 years. The staff speaks English and seems to know how to deal with children.

Albin Denk, 13 Graben (tel. 52-44-39), is the oldest remaining porcelain store doing continuous business since its establishment in 1702. Its clients have included the Empress Elizabeth, who saw the shop in almost the same format you'll see it in today. The decor of the three low-ceilinged rooms is beautiful, as are the thousands of objects from Meissen, Dresden, and other regions. With such a wealth of riches it's hard to make a selection, but the staff will help you.

The jewelry store, **A. E. Köchert**, 15 Neuer Markt (tel. 52-92-91), is where the fifth generation of the family which served as court jewelers until the end of the House of Habsburg maintains the same fine workmanship of their ancestors. The store, founded in 1814, is in a 16th-century building which is protected as a monument. The firm has designed many of the crown jewels of Europe, but the staff still gives attention to customers looking only for such minor purchases as charms for a bracelet. Köchert also has a store at 1 Goldschmied (tel. 52-58-28).

3. Vienna After Dark

Come to the cabaret . . . or the heurigen or the disco or the casino—whatever turns you on in the nightlife scene. Vienna has a little bit of everything and a lot of some late-evening entertainment activities to pursue after you've been to the theater or opera and perhaps topped it off with a fine dinner. Now you're ready to play. You can dance, go to shows, gamble, listen to music, and smile a lot in gemütlich nighttime Wien.

Liquor costs pretty much the same in all the clubs. Sometimes a cover charge is imposed, especially when live entertainment is offered. Often it's only 125 AS ($6.65), but it may be higher if you go for erotic specialties. Financially, it's better to drink beer in nightspots than hard liquor as the latter is expensive—from 85 AS ($4.52) for scotch.

FASHIONABLE BARS: The **Eden Bar**, 2 Liliengasse (tel. 52-74-50), is perhaps the top chic rendezvous spot in Vienna, often drawing local society figures as customers. It's open from 10 p.m. to 4 a.m., but if you show up much before midnight you may have the place to yourself. The Eden is a popular après-théâtre stop, and if there's a foreign celebrity in Vienna, he or she is likely to visit here. A live band plays for dancing.

New Splendid Bar, 3 Jasomigrottstrasse (tel. 63-15-15), rivals the Eden as a fashionable watering spot and keeps the same hours—10 p.m. to 4 a.m.—making it a good place to drop in for a nightcap. A live band, usually from Milan or some other place "south of the border," plays for dancing in this three-tiered room. The New Splendid also attracts celebrities.

DISCO: **Queen Anne**, 12 Johannesgasse (tel. 52-02-03). Lots of colorful people have dropped into the Queen Anne nightclub and disco (the leading one in town), including Joan Fontaine, German playboy Gunther Sachs, the Princess of Auersperg, and Jimmy Page of Led Zeppelin. It is considered one of Vienna's foremost "hot spots." The club has a big collection of the latest Stateside and Italian records, as well as occasional musical acts performed by singers ranging from Mick Jagger lookalikes to jungle imitations of Watusi dancers. The brown doors with brass trim are open from 9 p.m. to 4 a.m. Sunday through

Thursday and from 8 p.m. to 5 a.m. Saturday and Sunday. Drinks cost from 85 AS ($4.52). There is no cover charge.

Take Five, 3 Annagasse (tel. 52-32-76), is one of the city's leading discos, with an international clientele. Mostly recorded music is played at this nightspot just off the Kärntnerstrasse. The disco is open from 10 p.m. to 4 a.m. every day except Sunday and Monday. There's no cover charge. Beer costs 75 AS ($3.99); scotch and soda, 95 AS ($5.05).

Atrium, 10 Schwarzenbergplatz (tel. 65-35-94), was Vienna's first disco. For a long time it was the "in" place for university students, but a more diversified crowd is now found at this disco-cum-wine tavern, although many students still come here. Customers can savor the smoke-gets-in-your-eyes atmosphere from 10 p.m. to 3 a.m. on Monday; from 8 p.m. to 3 a.m. on Thursday and Friday; from 8 p.m. to 4 a.m. on Saturday; and from 8 p.m. to 2 a.m. on Sunday. It's closed Tuesday and Wednesday. Admission is 50 AS ($2.66), and beer costs from 40 AS ($2.13).

It's called **New Scotch,** but except perhaps for the whisky you might drink, there's not much Scottish ambience at this disco and coffeehouse at 10 Parkring (tel. 52-94-17), in Vienna's most fashionable area, next to the Hilton, Intercontinental, and SAS Palace hotels and quite near the exclusive and famous shopping street, the Kärntnerstrasse. The establishment, open from 11 a.m. to 6 a.m., is a popular place for society figures and intellectuals to meet. Furnished luxuriously, it has the most sophisticated technical equipment, such as a hydraulic stage and fancy neon lights. Near one of the three bars downstairs, a monumental waterfall creates an adventurous, romantic atmosphere. Upstairs, the coffeehouse is a cozy, relaxing place.

For a change, drop in at the **Triangel,** 8 Wiesingerstrasse (tel. 53-32-71), which has similar high standards and is under the same management as the New Scotch. In addition, it offers Italian specialties. It's open daily from 11:30 a.m. to 2:30 p.m. and 5:30 p.m. to 4 a.m.

Capt'n Cook, 23 Franz-Josefs-Kai (tel. 63-13-81), is one of the top discos in Vienna, with one of the city's best DJs. It's a large, comfortable place where you can sit at the bar if you prefer. The disco is open Monday through Thursday from 8 p.m. to 2 a.m. and Friday through Sunday from 8 p.m. to 4 a.m. A cover charge of 50 AS ($2.66) is levied at the door, but then the first drink costs only 10 AS (53¢), with subsequent libations costing 50 AS ($2.66).

Chattanooga, 29a Graben (tel. 52-41-86), offers one of the most popular sidewalk cafés along the Graben in summer. Inside, the decor of its restaurant is like that of a railroad car in the Gay '90s, with formally dressed waiters working feverishly behind glass counters. It has been under Max Funk's ownership for a quarter of a century. Aside from such drinks as beer at 22 AS ($1.17), they serve cheeseburgers and simple meals from 65 AS ($3.46) to 180 AS ($9.58). The real reason for coming here, however, is the disco downstairs. You'll get a modernized view of the generous proportions of old Vienna in the wide mirrored staircase leading to the half-rounded room with its maroon velvet niches. Stylized white tree trunks sprout from the floor to the sophisticated decor of the ceiling (displays are likely to change for certain musical acts). The entrance fee is usually 10 AS (53¢). Drinks start at 70 AS ($3.72) for a cola. This is the only dining establishment in the city that is open seven days a week from 8 a.m. to 2 a.m. (to 4 a.m. on Saturday), during which time all items on the menu are available. Its location on the Graben puts it in the very center of the city.

Sowieso, 1 Grashofgasse (tel. 52-12-36), contains two restaurants, a disco, and a backgammon club. Specialties in the restaurant include spare ribs, chili con carne, and an additional 15 dishes as part of the daily menu. The first restaurant is open from 5 p.m. to 2 a.m., while the disco and the second restaurant are open from 8 p.m. to 4 a.m. The gambling club opens at 5 p.m., closing at 4 a.m. Whisky in all sections begins at 80 AS ($4.26).

JAZZ: Right next door to Take Five, described above, is the **Tenne,** 3 Annagasse (tel. 52-57-08), where live groups play jazz music for listening or for dancing on a floor with a circle of boxes hovering above. Tenne has a log cabin ambience with lots of farm equipment, such as ox yokes, making up the decor. Waitresses wear tight-fitting dirndls. Admission is 16 AS (85¢), and beer goes for 60 AS ($3.19). The place is open daily except Monday at 8 p.m., closing at 3 a.m. weekdays, 2 a.m. Sunday.

EROTIC NIGHTCLUBS: **Casanova Revue Bar,** 6 Dorotheergasse (tel. 52-98-45), is considered *the* leading nightclub of Vienna. The top bands of Europe perform here. There are two shows nightly in the erotic revue theater, starting at 9:30 p.m. and at midnight. Between times, you're entertained by acrobats, magic acts, and naked women swinging through simulated spiderwebs. For the revue theater, entrance for standing room is 200 AS ($10.64) and a table costs 240 AS ($12.77) per person. A separate nightclub with "pretty ladies" accepts guests from 8 p.m. to 6 a.m.

    Moulin Rouge, 11 Walfischgasse (tel. 52-21-30), was for years the leading nightclub of Vienna, but there's serious competition for that slot today. If you're window-shopping, you can see pictures of the "artists" who will later disrobe for you during a show in this "red mill" modeled after the original Moulin Rouge in Paris, with curved walls, clapboard siding, and windmill. In the pictures you view from the sidewalk the girls are stark naked, so there's no surprise awaiting you if you decide to go into the club's lavishly decorated room which has two tiers of seating. The show is presented from 11 p.m. to 2:30 a.m., with the bar being open from 10 p.m. to 6 a.m. The entrance fee of 75 AS ($3.99) is only the beginning of the charges here. Beer costs 200 AS ($10.64), scotch and soda going for around 250 AS ($13.30). Girls come in all shades here. If you're a halfway presentable single male and willing to pay the price, you won't have to wait long for companionship.

    Another leading nightclub, **Renz,** 50 Zirkusgasse (tel. 24-31-35), is a bit out of the way, being near the Prater. The art of disrobing is practiced to perfection here, with ecdysiastic artistes from all over the world and in all skin hues likely to be featured. Sometimes, even, a renowned headliner (with clothes on) will appear on stage. The club is open seven nights a week, with live music beginning at 10 (the bar opens at 9:30 p.m.). The first show starts at 11 p.m., the main one at midnight. The action continues until 5 a.m. There's no entrance fee, but drinks cost 200 AS ($10.64).

YOUNG AND PUNK: **Peter's "B,"** 12 Rauhensteingasse (tel. 53-39-40), is a place where Boy George would probably feel just as much at home as do any of the motorcycle buffs who parade, helmets in hand, through the quadruplicate rooms which comprise this mid-city neobohemian haven. Some guests never advance beyond the ground-floor bar area, where Victorian accessories, including an old-fashioned gramophone, contribute to the visual distractions. Upstairs, mostly by candlelight, you can admire an iconoclastic collection of colored illustrations scattered among the pair of bars, the comfortable sofas, the café tables and chairs, and the burgeoning plants. Fixed-price meals begin at around 70 AS ($3.72). Of course, you won't be out of place if you decide just to drink, a beer costing from 30 AS ($1.60). The establishment is open weekdays beginning at 10:30 a.m. and on Saturday and Sunday from 5 p.m. Closing varies, depending on the evening, from 2 to 4 a.m. On rare occasions, there's live entertainment.

A LANDMARK BEERHALL: The **Esterházykeller,** 1 Haarhof (tel. 63-34-82), is a famous beerhall where the ancient bricks and scarred wooden tables are permeated with the aroma of endless pints of spilled beer. An outing here isn't recommended for everyone, although to its credit no one ever feels sloppily dressed at the Esterházykeller. If you decide to chance it, choose the left-hand entrance (while facing it from the street), grip the railing firmly, and begin your descent. A promenade through this establishment's endless recesses and labyrinthine passages could provide views of the faces you may have thought only appeared in movies. Wine, a specialty, costs from 14 AS (75¢) a glass. Order a bottle if you plan to stay a while. The place is open Monday through Friday from 11:30 a.m. to 10 p.m. On weekends, hours are from 3:30 to 9 p.m.

SONG AND DANCE: **Fledermaus,** 2 Spiegelgasse (tel. 52-84-38), has an all-German cabaret supplementing a live band and disco. The cabaret begins at 8 p.m., ending at 10 p.m. Between that hour and 4 a.m., the band alternates with disco music. A cover charge of 150 AS ($7.98) is levied at the door, and each drink costs 120 AS ($6.38). At the end of the evening, a 15 AS (80¢) "music charge" is added to all drink bills. The place is open nightly except Sunday.

GAMBLING: **Spiel-Casino Wien,** Estherhazy Palace, 41 Kärntnerstrasse (tel. 52-48-36), which opened in 1968, is the most expensive casino in Austria. Its admission is 150 AS ($7.98), but that entry fee provides you with that amount in gambling chips. You'll need to show your passport to get in (and they're strict about that!). The casino itself is one flight above street level. The minimum stake at any game is 50 AS ($2.66). You can charge up to $600 worth of chips to a Diner's Club credit card, providing you do so over a three-day period. You'll see gaming tables for French and American roulette, blackjack, and chemin de fer. The club opens at 4 p.m.

THE HEURIGEN: These wine taverns on the outskirts of Vienna were introduced in Chapter II, under "Food and Drink." These gardens of vintners lie principally in Grinzing (the most popular district) or in Sievering, Neustift, Nussdorf, or Heiligenstadt. They have been celebrated in operettas, films, and song.

In some of the more basic taverns the schilling-wise Viennese bring their own *heurigenpackerl,* a picnic composed mainly of cold cuts, cheese, some chicken, always a sausage, and hard-boiled eggs. But many of these so-called heurigen have grown into elaborate restaurants.

If you don't want to pack your own lunch or dinner but wish to economize, you can bring along inexpensively priced picnic packages sold at many a deli in Vienna. However, you can bring your own lunch into only the simpler worker's type of wine cellars, where the proprietor is content just to sell wine. Often his wife and family prepare food which they'd like to sell, however.

The most-visited section, **Grinzing,** lies at the edge of the Vienna Woods. Once it was a separate village until it was overtaken by the ever-increasing city boundaries of Vienna. Much of Grinzing remains unchanged, as it looked in the days when Beethoven lived nearby and composed music. It's a district of crooked old streets and houses with thick walls which are built around inner courtyards that are often grape arbors sheltering gemütlich Viennese wine-drinkers on a summer night. The playing of zithers and accordions lasts long into the night.

Which brings up another point. If you're a motorist, don't drive out to the heurigen. Police patrols are very strict, and you're not to be driving with more than 0.8% alcohol in your bloodstream. It's much better to take public transportation. For example, to go to Grinzing from the heart of Vienna takes only about half an hour.

Take trolley line no. 38 to Grinzing; no. 41 to Neustift am Wald, or trolley car no. 38, the same as for Grinzing, to Sievering, which is also reached by bus 39. Heiligenstadt is reached by underground line U-4.

At a typical heurige you can spend an evening, ordering a liter of wine and snacks, for about 250 AS ($13.30).

I'll lead off with some of my favorites, although you may find dozens more on your own.

Passauerhof, 9 Cobenzlgasse (tel. 32-63-45). One of Vienna's well-known wine taverns maintains an old-fashioned ambience little changed since the turn of the century. Some of its foundations date from the 12th century. Menu specialties include such familiar fare as tafelspitz, an array of roasts, and plenty of strudel. You can order a glass or bottle of wine, perhaps a meal costing from 95 AS ($5.05).

Grinzinger Hauermandl, 20 Cobenzlgasse (tel. 32-20-444), in Grinzing, is a rustic inn where many of the guests are lively Viennese escaping their city for an evening in the suburbs. You'll enter through a garden where you'll notice a gypsy wagon perched on the roof. The farm-style cookery includes noodle soup with liver dumplings, as well as a selection of dishes so hearty they could fortify you for a day's work in the vineyards. A quarter liter of wine (about two glasses) costs around 25 AS ($1.33), while à la carte meals range from 130 AS ($6.92) to 240 AS ($12.77).

Altes Presshaus, 15 Cobenzlgasse (tel. 32-23-93), in Grinzing, is the oldest heurige in Grinzing, with an authentic cellar which you should ask to see. The interior is filled with wood paneling and antique furniture, giving the place lots of character. It's closed Sunday, from November through February, and every Thursday until 5 p.m. The garden terrace blooms throughout most of the summer. Meals cost from 130 AS ($6.92) to 280 AS ($14.90); wine from 25 AS ($1.33).

Mayer, 2 am Pfarrplatz (tel. 37-12-87), in Heiligenstadt, is a historic house, some 130 years old when Beethoven composed sections of his Ninth Symphony while living here in 1817. Today Viennese music replaces the melodies that may have filled the house during Ludwig's era. However, the same kind of fruity dry wine is still sold to guests in the shady courtyard of the well-kept rose garden. Menu items, aside from the new wine, include grilled chicken, savory pork, and a lavish buffet of well-prepared country-style food. Reservations are suggested. It's open daily from 4 p.m. to midnight. The owner, Franz Mayer, spends part of his time working with the Austrian Ministry of Agriculture. Meals cost from 175 AS ($9.31).

Alt Sievering, 63 Sieveringer Strasse (tel. 32-58-88), is one of several attractive heurigen in this pleasant suburb of Vienna. The owner, Walter Slupetzky, serves not only excellent new wine, but prepares such specialties as game, lamb, fish, soufflés, dessert pancakes, strudels, and cakes. A fixed-price meal, which you can eat in summer under the trees, costs around 75 AS ($3.99), while à la carte meals range from 175 AS ($9.31). The restaurant is open from 9 a.m. to 11 p.m. except Tuesday and Wednesday. If you prefer beer, the house keeps three different types on tap.

Killermann, 22 Sonnbergstrasse (tel. 86-81-81), in Perchtoldsdorf, wasn't a heurige until Luki and Marina Killermann transformed a century-old building into the attractive establishment you see today. The tasteful interior is painted in clear colors, the service is friendly and efficient, and the food is a savory blend of gratinées with broccoli, ham, and cheese sauce or potatoes, meat, and vegetables, scampi in butter and garlic, a favorite veal dish, all kinds of country meats, sauerkraut, fresh salads, and noodles, much of it embellished with heaps of butter and sour cream. For dessert, try the Salzburger nockerl. Reservations are suggested. It's closed Sunday and Monday and from the day before Christmas until the end of the first week of January, as well as during most of July and August. The cost of a meal is from 175 AS ($9.31).

CULTURAL VIENNA: The cultural life of Vienna is set to music. This has been true for a couple of centuries or so, with the city being a lure to composers and librettists, musicians and music lovers even up to today. There's plenty of room for music in Vienna, and you can find places to enjoy everything from chamber music to pop, from waltzes to jazz. You'll find small discos and large concert halls, as well as musical theaters. And if you should (how could you?) tire of tuneful, atonal, or whatever musical sounds, then there's drama from classical to modern to avant garde, among other attractions. Below I'll describe just a few of the better known spots for cultural recreation. There are many others for you to find on your own if you're in Vienna long enough.

The four state theaters—Staatsoper (State Opera House), Volksoper, Burgtheater (National Theater), and the Akademietheater—are all reached by the same phone number, 53-24-0. The season is generally from September until June. Tickets for all state theater performances, including the opera, are available by writing to the **Österreichischer Bundestheaterverband,** 1 Goethegasse, A-1010 Vienna, from points outside Vienna. Orders must be received at least 12 days in advance of the performance to be booked. Advance orders from Vienna are not accepted. Otherwise you can purchase your ticket at the box office, the **Bundestheaterkasse,** 3 Hanuschgasse, which is open from 9 a.m. to 5 p.m. on weekdays and from 9 a.m. to noon on Sunday.

A highlight of the cultural season is the **Vienna Festival,** usually from May 20 to June 20. During this important European event, Vienna is likely to stage at least 1,000 performances. This is not just a music festival—theater and other activities are offered too. For instance, Clown Town at the Prater draws entertainers from all over the continent. The State Opera is the centerpiece of the festival. The Theater an der Wien is the official festival house, and there's a good chance you'll get to see Beethoven's *Fidelio* here.

The Major Halls

If your German is halfway passable, try to see a play by Arthur Schnitzler if one is being staged during your visit. This mild man, who died in 1931, was the most characteristically Viennese of the Austrian writers. Through his works he gave the Imperial City the charm and style more often associated with Paris. Whenever possible I attend a revival of one of his plays, such as *Einsame Weg* (The Solitary Path) or *Professor Bernhardi*. My favorite is *Reigen*, on which the film *La Ronde* was based. Schnitzler's plays are often performed at the Theater in der Josefstadt (see below).

The **Staatsoper,** or State Opera House, is considered one of the three most important in the world, and the upkeep is apparently a necessity to the Austrians, as its operation is estimated at a cost to the taxpayers of some million schillings a day! When the opera house, at 2 Opernring, was originally built in the 1860s, criticism of the structure so upset one of the architects, Eduard van der Nüll, that he killed himself. At the end of World War II, despite other pressing needs such as for public housing, Vienna started restoration work on the opera house in 1945, finishing it in time to celebrate the country's independence from occupation forces in 1955.

With the Vienna Philharmonic Orchestra in the pit, some of the leading opera stars of the world perform here. In their day, Richard Strauss and Gustav Mahler worked as directors. Daily performances are given from the first of September until the end of June. Standard prices are from 400 AS ($21.80) to 1,800 AS ($95.76), but these may vary for special events. Tickets can be purchased up to seven days before each performance from 9 a.m. to 5 p.m. Monday through Saturday and 9 a.m. to noon on Sunday, at 3 Hanuschgasse near the opera house (tel. 5324-2655). Guided tours of the Staatsoper are conducted at 9, 10, and 11 a.m. and at 1, 2, and 3 p.m. in summer, usually at 3 p.m. in winter.

Volksoper, 78 Währingerstrasse (tel. 53-240), the folk opera house, presents lavish productions of Viennese operettas and other musicals from the first of September until the end of June on a daily schedule. Tickets are generally from 100 AS ($5.32) to 500 AS ($26.60). During July and August, performances of opera and operetta are given three times a week at prices ranging from 100 AS ($5.32) to 800 AS ($42.56).

Burgtheater, the National Theater, 2 Dr.-Karl-Lueger-Ring, produces classical plays in German. Work started on the original structure in 1874, but the theater was destroyed during World War II and has since been rebuilt. It is the dream of every German-speaking actor to appear here.

Akademietheater, 3 Lisztstrasse, the largest theatrical concern in Europe, specializes in contemporary works. The Burgtheater company often performs here.

Theater an der Wien, 6 Linke Wienzeile (tel. 57-96-32), opened on the night of June 13, 1801, and ever since that time fans have been able to enjoy both opera and operetta presentations here. This was the site of the première of Beethoven's *Fidelio* in 1805; in fact the composer once lived in this building. The world première of *Die Fledermaus* was also given here. Invariably, every year an article appears in some newspaper proclaiming that Theater an der Wien was the site of the première of Mozart's *The Magic Flute*. However, considering that the first performance of that great work by Mozart was in 1791 while this theater did not exist until 1801, that première would have been a neat trick. During the years of occupation after World War II, when the Staatsoper was being restored after heavy damages, the Vienna State Opera made Theater an der Wien its home. Tickets for performances cost from 90 AS ($4.79) to 500 AS ($26.60).

Schlosstheater at Schönbrunn Palace, mentioned earlier, is a gem of a theater in a regal setting, which opened in 1749 for the entertainment of the court of Maria Theresa. The architecture is a medley of baroque and rococo, and there's a large, plush box where the imperial family sat to enjoy the shows. Today anyone who has the price of a ticket—generally from 120 AS ($6.38) to 320 AS ($17.02)—can see a show if he or she is in Vienna in the summer. Opéra comique is often presented.

Other Theaters

The **Volkstheater,** 1 Neustiftgasse (tel. 93-35-01), opened in 1889 and has a long tradition of a classical repertoire, from Ibsen to Strindberg, Nestroy, and Raimund. Modern plays and comedies are also presented. The season is from September to the end of June. Tickets cost from 40 AS ($2.13) to 340 AS ($18.09).

The **Vienna English Theatre,** 12 Josefsgasse (tel. 42-12-60), is the only English-speaking theater on the continent. It was established in 1963 and proved so popular that it's been around ever since. Many international celebrities have appeared on the stage of this neobaroque theater building, and many

British actors perform here. Princess Grace of Monaco played here, before her tragic death, in a performance to raise money for charity. Occasionally works of American playwrights are presented.

Theater in der Josefstadt, 26 Josefstädter Strasse (tel. 42-51-27), is a typically Viennese theater, which presents, among other works, contemporary social comedies and classical plays. Under the aegis of Max Reinhardt, who took it over in 1924, this became one of the most outstanding theaters in the German-speaking world.

Count yourself fortunate if you get to hear a concert by the Wiener Philharmoniker at the **Musikverein,** 3 Dumbastrasse (tel. 65-81-90). The box office is at 6 Karlsplatz.

Konzerthaus, 20 Lothringerstrasse (tel. 72-12-11), is another major concert hall, this one with a trio of auditoriums. The "Concert House" was built just before the outbreak of World War I.

Chapter V

LOWER AUSTRIA

"THE CRADLE of Austria's history," Lower Austria, or Niederösterreich, is the biggest of the nine federal states which make up the country today. This province, crisscrossed by the Danube, is in fact named *Lower* Austria because the great river flows east into it. It may seem to you more like *Upper* Austria because of its geographic location, much of it being north of the rest of the country. The 7,402 square miles of the state are bordered on the north and east by Czechoslovakia, on the south by the province of Styria, and on the west by Upper Austria. It lies virtually on the doorstep of Vienna, the state capital of this province of 1½ million living souls as well as the nation's capital.

This historic nucleus of the Austria of today was once a heavily fortified land, as some 550 fortresses and castles—many still standing but often in ruins—testify. The medieval dynasties of the Kuenringers and the Babenbergers had their hereditary estates here, and it was through Lower Austria that the legendary Nibelungen passed. Many monasteries and churches, ranging from the Romanesque and Gothic eras up to the much later baroque abbeys, are found here.

The province is filled with vineyards, and in summer it's rich in festivals, not only of music and operetta but also of classical and contemporary theater.

It's relatively inexpensive to travel in Lower Austria, with a drop of at least 30% below the prices you encounter in Vienna, just visited, or in such places as Salzburg and Innsbruck which will be explored further on in this book. This price differential explains why many people, especially those from other Austrian provinces, visit in Vienna but stay at one of the neighboring towns in Lower Austria. Parking is also accessible in the outlying towns. However, you mustn't expect always to have a private bath if you want to check into an old inn.

Lower Austria is divided into five distinct districts, the best known being the **Wienerwald** (Vienna Woods) completely surrounding Vienna.

Another district, **Alpine Lower Austria**, lies about an hour's drive south of Vienna. With mountains up to 7,000 feet high, this area has been greatly developed in the past few years and has a system of mountain railways, chair lifts, and cable cars, as well as hundreds of miles of hiking paths.

The **foothills of the Alps**, beginning about 30 miles west of Vienna, comprise a district extending to the borders of Styria and Upper Austria. This area has some 50 open-air swimming pools that are busy in summer and nine chair lifts which go up to the higher peaks, such as Ötscher and Hochkar, each around 6,000 feet.

A celebrated section is the **Waldviertel-Weinviertel,** a viertel being a traditional division of Lower Austria. The viertels in this case are the woods *(wald)* and wine *(wein)* areas. They contain thousands of miles of marked hiking paths and, of course, many mellow old wine cellars.

Another district, **Wachau-Nibelungengau,** is of historical and cultural significance. In fact it's considered one of the most historic valleys in Central Europe. It is a land of castles and palaces, of abbeys and monasteries. For centuries it has also been known for its wine making. Lying on both banks of the Danube, this area begins about 40 miles west of Vienna.

Some 60% of the grape harvest of Austria is produced in Lower Austria, stretching from the rolling hillsides of the Wienerwald to the terraces of the Wachau. Many visitors to the country like to take a "wine route" through the province, stopping off at cozy taverns to sample the vintages from Krems, Klosterneuburg, Dürnstein, Langenlois, Retz, Gumpoldskirchen, Poysdorf, and other spots.

Lower Austria has 12 spa resorts, of which Baden is the most celebrated. Innkeepers make families with children especially welcome at these resorts. Most hotels accommodate children up to 6 years old free. Between ages 7 and 12, they are given 50% reductions on the listed prices for adults. Many towns and villages have facilities designed especially for the amusement of children.

In short, Lower Austria is a good place to go for a family holiday.

1. The Wienerwald

The Vienna Woods—romanticized in operetta, literature, and the Strauss waltz—have already been introduced in the sightseeing section of Vienna. The woods stretch all the way from Vienna's city limits to the foothills of the Alps to the south.

You can hike through the woods along marked paths or else drive through at a leisurely pace, stopping off at country towns to sample the wine and the local cuisine, usually hearty, filling, and reasonable in price. The woods are filled with wine taverns and cellars, and on weekends with Viennese and a horde of foreign tourists, principally German. I advise you to make any summer visit on a weekday. Perhaps the best time of year to go is September and October, the months when the grapes are harvested from the terraced hills.

If you don't want to go on your own, a popular tour out of Vienna will take you to the Wienerwald and Mayerling. It goes through the Vienna Woods to the Castle of Liechtenstein and the old Roman city of Baden, with an excursion to Mayerling where Crown Prince Rudolf and his mistress died violent deaths. You'll also go to the Cistercian Abbey of Heiligen-Höldrichsmühle-Seegrotte. A boat ride on Seegrotte, the largest subterranean lake in Europe, is included.

This tour is operated by **Vienna Sightseeing Tours**, 4 Stelzamergasse (tel. 72-46-83). It runs from April 1 to October 30 at 9:30 a.m. and 2:30 p.m., taking about four hours. The cost is 350 AS ($18.62) for adults, 100 AS ($5.32) for children. The price includes admission fees and a guide.

KLOSTERNEUBURG: Lying on the northwestern outskirts of Vienna within easy reach of the capital, Klosterneuburg is an old market town in the major wine-producing center of Austria. The Babenbergs founded the town practically at the gates of Vienna in the eastern foothills of the Vienna Woods, making it an ideal spot to enjoy the countryside and also to participate in the cultural and entertainment activities of Vienna, seven miles southeast.

A Roman stronghold occupied the site of the town in the first century A.D.
Klosterneuberg Abbey (Stift Klosterneuberg) which lies to the east of the Upper Town is considered the most significant abbey in the country and is the major sightseeing attraction of the town. The abbey church dates from 1114, but the first of the Gothic west towers was not constructed until the end of the 14th century. The abbey has magnificent stained-glass windows, also dating from that century. The altar of the church is from 1181 and contains more than 50 biblical scenes in enamel. The most outstanding exhibit in Stift Klosterneuburg is the altarpiece by Nicolas of Verdun in the Chapel of St. Leopold. The abbey apartments are richly furnished with many empire antiques.

The abbey may be visited daily from 9:30 to 11 a.m. and from 1:30 to 4 p.m. On Sunday it's open only in the afternoon. Admission is 30 AS ($1.60).

The abbey came into its glory when the ruling family of Austria, the Babenbergs, moved here from Melk and built a grand residence, remnants of which are preserved in the Albrechtsberger abbey. After the royal residences were moved to Vienna the abbey declined in power and prestige, but it was revived in the 18th century by Emperor Charles VI, who came up with an ambitious architectural scheme—to build a pompous residence and monastic edifice which would rival El Escorial, the celebrated palace built by Philip II of Spain on the outskirts of Madrid. This grandiose building scheme was never completed, but the monastery was finally finished in the 19th century, looking as you will see it today.

The abbey has an old restaurant, Stiftskeller, where you can dine well at moderate prices. The restaurant has a historic wine cellar. If you don't choose to eat here, you can patronize one of several heurigen in the district, enjoying good wine and simple country food.

Austrians and tourists gather in Klosterneuberg annually to celebrate St. Leopold's Day on November 15.

The area code for Klosterneuburg is 02243.

Food and Lodging

Schlosshotel Martinschloss, 34-36 Martinstrasse (tel. 7426), is the historic baroque castle on the banks of the Danube that was owned by the Trapp family (did you see *The Sound of Music?*) between 1924 and 1938. Before that the 1766 castle was held by a British naval officer, Sir John Whitehead, who developed the world's first submarine torpedo from experiments he performed in the castle's swimming pool. The castle was renovated after the Second World War, as the Russians had virtually ruined it during their occupation. Today it's a comfortable and glamorous hotel, and most of its well-furnished bedrooms contain private baths. Singles range from 850 AS ($45.22) to 1,500 AS ($79.80), while doubles cost from 550 AS ($29.26) to 1,000 AS ($53.20) per person, with a buffet breakfast included.

Hotel/Restaurant Josef Buschenreiter, 188 Wiener Strasse (tel. 2385), is a modern white-walled hotel with metal window frames and a mansard roof above the balcony on the fourth floor. A terrace on the roof and an indoor swimming pool provide diversion for the hotel guests, who will also find a contemporary bar area in contrasting earth-colored patterns. Singles range from 480 AS ($25.54) to 650 AS ($34.58), while doubles cost 320 AS ($17.02) to 420 AS ($22.34) per person, depending on the plumbing. Breakfast is included, and half board can be arranged for an additional 110 AS ($5.85) per person daily.

Pension Alte Mühle, 36 Mühlengasse (tel. 7788), is housed in an uncomplicated two-story building with a red tile roof and a facade of yellow paint and iron balconies. The breakfast room is simple to the point of being spartan, although a comfortable restaurant-café in the same building has upholstered banquettes and a sunny modern decor of bright colors and conservative designs. The Veit family, the owners, charge between 310 AS ($16.49) and 430 AS ($22.88) in a single and between 240 AS ($12.77) and 380 AS ($20.22) per person in a double, with breakfast included.

PERCHTOLDSDORF: This old market town with colorful buildings, referred to locally as Petersdorf, is one of the most visited spots in Lower Austria when the Viennese make the wine tour. You'll find many heurigen, where you can sample local wines and enjoy good, hearty cuisine. Perchtoldsdorf is not as well known as Grinzing, which is actually within the city limits of Vienna, but many discriminating visitors find it less touristy. It has a Gothic church, and part of its defense tower is from the early 16th century. A vintners' festival is held annually in early November. Local growers make a "goat" from grapes for this festive occasion which attracts many Viennese.

The area code for Perchtoldsdorf is 0222.

Where to Dine

Restaurant La Tour, 17 Hochstrasse (tel. 86-47-63). Residents of the countryside often come here to celebrate special occasions, and many of the gastronomes of Vienna come here as if on a pilgrimage. Chef Karl Mühlberger concocts a deliciously fresh array of specialties, each dish prepared whenever possible from local ingredients. Your repast might include marinated crayfish with sweetbreads, a parfait of gooseliver with apples cooked in brioche, filet of turbot in a tarragon-flavored cream sauce, followed by a dessert mousse of sweet and bitter chocolate. À la carte dinners range between 170 AS ($9.04) and 680 AS ($36.18), while fixed-price menus range from 300 AS ($15.96) to an expensive extravaganza costing around 900 AS ($47.88). The restaurant is closed for lunch on Monday and Saturday and also shuts down every Sunday evening at dinnertime. Otherwise, it is open for lunch and dinner every day of the week.

Killerman, 22 Sonnbergstrasse (tel. 86-81-81). Austrian charm at its best is part of the rewards of a meal in this comfortable restaurant directed by members of the Killerman family. There has been a wine restaurant on this spot since 1880. Today, much of the antique aura remains. However, food items have been updated to include such dishes as green noodles with veal and garlic-flavored scampi; nevertheless, many traditional dishes are also offered. Tempting caloric desserts follow, and a glass or bottle of Austrian wine might accompany your meal. À la carte dinners cost between 120 AS ($6.38) and 480 AS ($25.54). Meals are served daily except Sunday, Monday, and during the month of August.

MÖDLING: The Viennese use this place as a resort. Quite old, it lies at the beginning of the Brühl Valley and still has a medieval core, the Hauptplatz. The Rathaus (town hall) dates from 1548. Beethoven wrote his *Missa Solemnis* here in 1818.

About a 15- to 18-minute drive from Mödling is **Schloss Liechtenstein.** The castle was built originally in the 12th century, but that one was largely demolished in one of the Turkish sieges. Construction on the present schloss began in 1820. You can visit a relic of the old castle, however, a Romanesque chapel dating from 1165.

Another popular excursion from Mödling is to **Schloss Laxenburg,** a short drive to the east. In the complex, surrounded by a baroque park, are an old castle from the 14th century and a new one. The Neues Schloss, once used by the Habsburgs as a summer residence, has been turned over to an institute. Yet another mock Gothic castle from the 19th century has been converted into a restaurant. Mainly, however, the place is visited for its park, once the hunting ground of the dukes of Austria but now the home of protected wild game. True to the baroque ideal, the park is studded with statuary and "temples."

The area code for Mödling is 02236.

Food and Lodging

Hotel/Restaurant Babenbergerhof, 6 Babenbergergasse (tel. 22246), is a three-story rectangular building painted a deep Maria Theresa ochre with a garden restaurant extending out behind it. On a summer night the owner, Karl Breyer, stretches lights below the large trees in the garden, while in winter the indoor ambience is one of well-maintained modernity. Rooms are comfortably furnished and well maintained. Singles range from 210 AS ($11.17) to 520 AS ($27.66), while doubles go from 400 AS ($21.28) to 820 AS ($43.62). Prices include breakfast.

HINTERBRÜHL: Instead of staying in Mödling, you might prefer to drive to the neighboring hamlet of Hinterbrühl, where you'll find a good hotel and food. The village is only a 20-minute drive from Vienna. This is no more than a cluster of bucolic homes, much favored by the Viennese who want to escape the city for a long weekend. Hinterbrühl holds memories of Schubert, who wrote *Am Brunnen vor dem Tore* here.

The area code for Hinterbrühl is 02236.

Food and Lodging

Hotel/Restaurant Höldrichsmühle, 34 Gaadner Strasse (tel. 26274), has been painted a pastel pink since the era when Schubert stayed here, and it still has much of its old allure. Singles, all comfortably furnished, range from 500 AS ($26.60) to 680 AS ($36.18), while doubles cost 800 AS ($42.56) to 950 AS ($50.54), with breakfast included. Prices depend on the plumbing and the size of the accommodation. The restaurant connected to the hotel is one of the best in the village. Viennese often make the 20-minute ride from the heart of the city to eat under the linden trees of the restaurant's terrace. In winter they find the Biedermeier-filled interior cozy and inviting. Specialties of the chef include fresh trout, roast veal with corn salad, an array of venison dishes in season, and many varieties of fish, including eel. Reservations are suggested, and à la carte meals range from 150 AS ($7.98) to 320 AS ($17.02).

GUMPOLDSKIRCHEN: From Mödling, you can take the wine road, or *weinstrasse,* to Gumpoldskirchen, a town celebrated for its Gumpoldskirchner wine, a Viennese favorite. Along the main street are heurigen. Like Perchtoldsdorf, this village is preferred by many Viennese to Grinzing. Go to any of the wine taverns whose doors are open, and chances are you'll be served not only delectable white wine of the town but food as well, all at reasonable prices.

The area code for Gumpoldskirchen is 02252.

Where to Dine

Weinstadl, 42 Jubiläumsstrasse (tel. 62218), is a rustically cozy establishment with wood tables, big flasks of local wine, and a friendly reception given by the unpretentious staff. The room here is vast, usually with live music, in a building that in olden days was used to store the abundant harvests that came from this region. You can sit in an upper level if it's open on the night you happen to visit, which might be a good idea since the music near the bandstand can be rather loud. The chef is known for his grills, turning out an especially good tournedos. The produce is fresh, and the food is well presented. The restaurant is closed from January 10 to February 10 and on Sunday. It's open only in the evening, and reservations are suggested. À la carte meals range from 150 AS ($7.98) to 350 AS ($18.62).

Weinbergschenke, Pfaffstätten (tel. 88540). The ambience here is low key, informal, and gutbürgerlich, with copious amounts of the local wine consumed by the hearty clientele. Whether you appreciate the noise level will depend a great deal on your degree of joviality. The food is well prepared, wholesome, and filling, the fare consisting of country specialties made with pork, ham, beef, and veal. À la carte meals range from 100 AS ($5.32) to 250 AS ($13.30). The restaurant is closed on Monday. They also rent out seven double rooms at a cost of 550 AS ($29.26).

GUNTRAMSDORF: In your search for a charming place to stay in the Wienerwald, with the atmosphere typical of the area, the following recommendation near Gumpoldskirchen might be considered. The hamlet lies at the very doorstep of the Wienerwald.

The area code for Guntramsdorf is 02236.

Food and Lodging

Jagdhof, 41 Hauptstrasse (tel. 52-2-25). The limited number of rooms here are tastefully decorated and comfortable. The hotel is identified by a wrought-iron bracket hanging over the front door with a medieval-style sign announcing the locale. Singles go for 380 AS ($20.22) and up, while doubles, depending on the size, cost from 560 AS ($29.79) to 620 AS ($32.98), with breakfast included. All units have private bath.

Much of the reputation of the establishment, however, revolves around its well-known restaurant. Under the vaults of an old farmhouse, it abounds in rustic atmosphere, and has a cuisine which is so well prepared that many of the clients return again and again. Menu items include Canadian salmon with dill sauce, rack of lamb with beans and cabbage, and a tender array of veal dishes. Dessert might be an unusual ice cream flavored with kiwi, lemon, and vodka. The restaurant is closed Monday and occasionally on Sunday, depending on the season. À la carte meals range from 140 AS ($7.45) to 370 AS ($19.68).

TULBINGER-KOGEL: This is a small hamlet a short drive from Vienna whose main virtue seems to be its wooded rolling hills and the autumn foliage, which can be spectacular. Dozens of Viennese make the drive here to escape the congestion of their capital.

The area code for Tulbinger-Kogel is 02272.

Where to Stay

Berghotel Tulbinger-Kogel (tel. 7391) sprawls like an 18th-century château across a wide vista of forested land. Its walls are white, and the symmetrically sloping roofline comprises a single row of prominent gables. An outbuilding with surrounding balconies provides modern accommodations as well as a calm and beautiful view of the nearby region. Prices per person, based on double occupancy, range from 200 AS ($10.64) to 480 AS ($25.54), with a single supplement of 160 AS ($8.51) per person daily. The hotel has the finest restaurant in the area and the most copious wine list in the country.

HEILIGENSTADT: Once a fairly remote and isolated wine-growing village, Heiligenstadt is really a suburb of Vienna today. It is visited chiefly for its connection with Beethoven, who came here hoping that a sulfur spring to which miraculous powers were attributed could help him recover his hearing. In 1802, the composer wrote a letter, the "Testament of Heiligenstadt," in the house at 6 Probusgasse, which painfully documents his hopelessness about his rapidly approaching deafness. This house is open from 10 a.m. to 4 p.m. on weekdays, from 2 to 6 p.m. on Saturday, and from 9 a.m. to 1 p.m. on Sunday. Closed Monday.

For a few months in 1817, Beethoven lived at 2 Pfarrplatz in a 17th-century house which has been turned into a heurige.

HEILIGENKREUZ: This most ancient Cistercian abbey in Austria, dating from 1135, lies in the village of the Sattelbach about ten miles to the west of the spa in Baden. Called the Abbey of the Holy Cross, the church, founded by Leopold III, was built in the 12th century, but there has been an overlay of Gothic and baroque in subsequent centuries, with some stained glass from the 14th century still in place. The abbey was once ravished by the Turks, but much of the complex was reconstructed in the 17th and 18th centuries. However, the Romanesque and Gothic cloisters date from 1220, with some 300 pillars of red marble, a striking display. There's also a gallery of Teutonic baroque paintings and a library.

Some of the dukes of Babenberg were buried in the 1240 chapter house, including Duke Friedrich II, the last of his line, who died in 1246.

Tours are offered from 9 to 11:30 a.m. and from 1:30 to 6:30 p.m. (until 4:30 p.m. in winter), except on Sunday and public holidays when hours are from 11 to 11:30 a.m. and from 1:30 to 5:30 p.m. Admission is 30 AS ($1.60).

MAYERLING: This beautiful spot in the heart of the Wienerwald, to the west of Baden and 2½ miles from Heiligenkreuz, was the setting in 1889 for a grim tragedy which altered the line of succession of the Austro-Hungarian Empire and shocked the world. On a snowy night, Archduke Rudolf, only son of Emperor Franz Joseph and Empress Elizabeth, and his mistress, Maria Vetsera, were found dead in the hunting lodge at Mayerling and called suicide victims.

Rudolf was locked into an unhappy marriage, and neither his father nor Pope Leo XIII would allow, through annulment, breaking the matrimonial bonds. At the time of his death Rudolf was 30 years old. He had met Maria at a German embassy ball when she was only 17. Because of the young archduke's liberal leanings and sympathy for certain Hungarian partisans, he was not popular with his country's aristocracy, which of course gave rise to lurid speculation about the deaths, not only in the press but also in books and in films, as to whether the couple actually killed themselves or were the victims of cleverly designed assassination.

Franz Joseph, grief-stricken at the loss of his only son, ordered the hunting lodge torn down and had the Carmelite nunnery built which still occupies the lodge site.

As it turned out, if Rudolf had lived he would have succeeded to the already-tottering Habsburg throne in 1916 in the middle of World War I, shortly before the collapse of the empire.

The area code for Mayerling is 02258.

Food and Lodging

Hotel-Restaurant Marienhof (tel. 379) is a Belle Époque–style establishment in the midst of the hunting territory most preferred by Crown Prince Rudolf. The original part is a three-story structure with white stucco walls and a brown tile roof with matching shutters, somewhat removed from the other buildings of the village. The owners, Johann and Cäcilia Hanner, have enlarged their place by adding a new building, bringing the room total to 72, with 33 units in the new structure. In the new part, all rooms are equipped with complete bath, radio, TV, phone, mini-bar, and balcony. Singles rent for 450 AS ($23.94) to 580 AS ($30.87), while the rate for a double room ranges from 320 AS ($17.02) to 480 AS ($25.54) per person. Half-board costs an additional 160 AS ($8.51) per person per day. The hotel has such amenities as a sauna, a solarium, a tennis court, and table-tennis facilities. Guests can enjoy Austrian specialties such as homemade sweets and coffee on the sunny terrace. The hotel also has two restaurants and a bar where you can spend the evening in an agreeable and cozy atmosphere.

2. Baden bei Wien

Czar Peter the Great of Russia is credited with ushering in the golden age of Baden as a spa around the dawn of the 18th century. The Soviet army used the resort city as its headquarters from the end of World War II to the end of the Allied occupation of Austria in 1955. But there's not much Russian about Baden, the dowager empress of health spas in Europe.

The Romans, who didn't miss many of the natural attractions in sections of Europe into which they moved, began in A.D. 100 to visit and enjoy what they called Aquae, with its 15 thermal springs whose temperatures are up to 95° Fahrenheit. You can still see the Römerquelle (Roman spring) in the Kurpark which is the center of Baden today.

This lively casino town and spa in the eastern sector of the Vienna Woods was at its most fashionable in the early part of the 18th century, but its appeal for royalty, aristocracy, sycophants, musicians, and intellectuals continued for much of the 19th century. For years the resort was the summer residence of the Habsburg court. In 1803, when he was still Francis II of the Holy Roman Empire, the monarch (who became Francis I of Austria when the vast empire originated by Charlemagne ended in 1806) began annual summer moves to Baden, a practice which ended only at his death in 1835.

Where the court went, there went the most outstanding musicians and artists of the age. Even before the spa was "discovered" by Emperor Francis, however, Mozart spent time in Baden, and it is here that he is said to have composed his *Ave Verum*. Schubert is supposed to have done creative work at this spa, and Beethoven, who lived in Baden for three summers, worked on his Ninth Symphony in this peaceful town surrounded by forests and vineyards.

At **Beethoven's house,** 10 Rathausgasse (tel. 48419), a little museum has been set up, open from 9 to 11 a.m. and 3 to 5 p.m. daily, except Thursday, in summer. In winter it's open only on Tuesday, Thursday, and Saturday. Admission is 15 AS (80¢).

During the Biedermeier era (mid to late 19th century), Baden became known for its Schönbrunn yellow (Maria Theresa ochre) Beidermeier buildings which still contribute to the spa city's charm. The Kurpark, Baden's center, is handsomely laid out and beautifully maintained. Public concerts performed here keep alive the magical music of the great Austrian composers.

The bathing house complex was constructed over the location of more than a dozen sulfur springs. In the complex are some half dozen bath establishments, plus two outdoor thermal springs.

Emperor Karl made this town the Austrian army headquarters in World War I, but a certain lightness of heart persisted in the Austrians and in the life of Baden. It was the presence of the Russians during post-World War II years that brought about the lowest ebb in the resort's fortunes. The Soviets did little to encourage luxurious spa resort vacations and casino gambling.

Among sights in Baden there's a celebrated death mask collection at the **Städtisches Rolletmuseum,** 1 Weikersdorfer (tel. 48-2-55). The Trinity column at the Hauptplatz commemorates the lifting of the plague that swept over Vienna and the Wienerwald in the Middle Ages.

The resort (officially named Baden bei Wien to differentiate it from other Badens *not* near Vienna) is some 15 miles from the capital city. An old and rather flamboyant streetcar is the best—or at least, the most romantic—way to go. However, the resort is also connected to Vienna by rail and bus lines.

The area code for Baden bei Wien is 02252.

FOOD AND LODGING: The **Grand Hotel Sauerhof zu Rauhenstein,** 11-13 Weilburgstrasse (tel. 41251). Ludwig van Beethoven once took Karl Maria von Weber to lunch here "in happy and joyful spirits." Today it's considered a place where comfort and a sense of history go hand in hand. It was formerly a recreational center for Austria's imperial officers. The exterior has been restored to its former grandeur. It rambles across a wide expanse of lawn in a three-story neoclassical format with steeply sloping slate roofs. Few of the original furnishings remain, although the management has collected a handful of vintage Biedermeier sofas and chairs to fill the starkly elegant public rooms, where portraits of Franz Joseph in all stages of his life decorate the pure white walls. There's a collection of Russian icons in glass cases and a series of medieval halberds along the walls of the richly decorated, farmer's-style restaurant.

In the depths of this historic building is a windowless wine cellar, as well as a copy of a Roman covered courtyard whose vaulted ceiling is supported by eight chiseled columns. A plaque announces that Beethoven wrote his "Wellington Sieg" here and that the premises served as a sanitorium in World War I and as a Russian headquarters after World War II.

The 87 bedrooms all contain private baths and comfortable modern decor. Depending on the season and the accommodation, single rooms range from 1,100 AS ($58.52) to 1,300 AS ($69.16), while doubles cost from 1,500 AS ($79.80) to 1,800 AS ($95.76), with breakfast included. Half board costs an additional 190 AS ($10.11) per person. On the premises, you'll find two tennis courts and a jogging course. A golf course is nearby. Under the brick vaulting of one of the older sections, the management has installed a 40-foot swimming pool.

Clubhotel Baden (Schloss Weikersdorf), 9-11 Schlossgasse (tel. 48301), has all the massive beams you'd expect in such an old building, along with arched and vaulted ceilings which are sculpted into unusual sinuous patterns. The oldest part of the hotel has an Italianate loggia stretching toward the manicured gardens, and an inner courtyard with stone arcades and a flagstone pavement. Even the rooms in the newer section have repeated the older section's arches and high ceilings, with a constant reappearance of ornate chandeliers and antique (or reproduction) furniture. The nearby sports facility has an indoor swimming pool, tennis courts, a sauna, a whirlpool, and massage facilities. On the premises you'll find a charming baroque bar and two restaurants. Accommodations are handsomely furnished and most comfortable. Singles range from 750 AS ($39.90) to 950 AS ($50.54), while doubles cost from 620 AS ($32.98) to 820 AS ($43.62) per person daily. Breakfast is included in these rates, and all units contain private bath.

Hotel Gutenbrunn, 22 Pelzgasse (tel. 48171). If what you want is an elegant old-world hotel with lots of original architectural features, this might be the one for you. The pink-and-white facade has a hexagonal tower at one of its corners, and a slate roof capped with a baroque steeple. The interior has a skylit reception area with a double tier of neoclassical loggias, all of them focusing on the hanging chandelier in the center. Rooms are well furnished and maintained. Singles rent for 850 AS ($45.22), while doubles cost 1,350 AS ($71.82) to 2,200 AS ($117.04), with breakfast included. You'll find a sauna and a swimming pool on the premises, plus a restaurant which provides half board for an additional 180 AS ($9.58) per person daily. The hotel is connected to the city spa facilities by a passage.

Hotel Herzoghof, 5 Theresiengasse (tel. 48395), is an elegant cream-colored hotel across from the city park. The complicated detailing of its 19th-century facade hints at the old-fashioned decor inside, where Oriental rugs, stained glass, and high ceilings evoke another era. On the premises is a small outdoor swimming pool, a garden terrace, and a pink and white dining room capped with a skylight. The hotel also offers an array of hydrotherapy and spa facilities.

The conservatively comfortable bedrooms contain a scattering of reproductions of antiques, as well as private bath. Half board is obligatory even for overnighters at a cost of 185 AS ($9.84) per person in addition to the room rate. High season tariffs are 1,300 AS ($69.16) in a double and 1,000 AS ($53.20) in a single, with breakfast included. Off-season reductions are granted.

Parkhotel, 5 Kaiser-Franz-Ring (tel. 44-3-86), is an elegantly contemporary hotel in the middle of an inner-city park dotted with trees and formal statuary. The high-ceilinged lobby is dramatically contemporary, with a stone marble floor padded with thick Oriental carpets and ringed with richly grained paneling. Most of the sunny bedrooms have their own loggia overlooking scores of century-old trees. Each contains a private bath, radio, TV, and mini-bar. Depending on the season and the room assignment, singles cost between 810 AS ($43.09) and 1,000 AS ($53.20), while doubles are priced between 1,150 AS ($61.18) and 2,100 AS ($111.72), with breakfast included. Half board is another 200 AS ($10.64) per day. The hotel also contains a heated indoor swimming pool, two Finnish saunas, a restaurant, a coffeeshop, and a concrete terrace overlooking the park. Private parking is available. Anna-Maria Meizl, the attractive manager, is familiar with American guests because of the contingents of visitors from Los Angeles who come here every year.

Krainerhütte (tel. 44511) stands five miles west of Baden at Helenental, on its own tree-filled grounds. Run by J. Dietmann and his family, it's a large, A-frame chalet with rows of wooden balconies stretching across the front. The interior has well-worked wooden surfaces and more detailing than you might expect in such a modern hotel. There are separate children's rooms and play areas. Depending on the season, singles rent for 1,000 AS ($53.20) to 1,100 AS ($58.52). Doubles cost from 860 AS ($45.75) to 920 AS ($48.94) per person. All tariffs include breakfast. In the cozy restaurant or on its terrace, you can dine on international and Austrian cuisine, with fish and deer from the hotel grounds offered on the menu. On the premises, you'll find an indoor swimming pool, a tennis court, a sauna, and an exercise room. Hiking in the owner's forests, hunting, and fishing are possible. Bus service to Baden is available all day.

Badner Stüberl, 19 Gutenbrunnstrasse (tel. 41232), an old-fashioned coffeehouse in the center of the older section of Baden, is filled with black and red upholstery and unusually designed lighting fixtures. Specialties of the house include generous proportions of a Stroganoff dish which is searched out by visitors from Vienna, along with a green salad garnished with chicken, and pork and beef steaks grilled to savory tenderness. Frau Ackerl, the experienced chef, prepares many of the noodles and desserts herself. À la carte meals range from 105 AS ($5.59) to 160 AS ($8.51). The establishment is closed Tuesday.

NIGHTLIFE: The major attraction, of course, is the **Casino in Spa Park** (tel. 44496), which opens daily at 4 p.m. Here you can play roulette, blackjack, and baccarat. On Wednesday night, and also on Saturday and Sunday, many Viennese come down to Baden for a night of gambling, drinking, and eating. They are often most fashionably dressed.

3. Wiener Neustadt

When you head south from Vienna on the Südautobahn, Wiener Neustadt, a former imperial city, might be your first stopover. Called Allzeit Getreue because of its loyalty to the throne, this thriving business city between the foothills of the Alps and the edge of the Pannonian lowland has a strong historical background.

Unfortunately, Wiener Neustadt was a popular target for Allied bombs during World War II, because it lay at the point where the routes from Vienna diverge, one going to the Semmering pass and the other to Hungary via the Sopron gate. The presence here of a military academy which turned out officers for the Austrian army for some 200 years may have been an added attraction to bombers. German Gen. Erwin Rommel, "the desert fox," was the academy's first commandant during the Nazi era. At any rate, bomb the city the Allies did—more than any other town in the country. It's estimated that some 60% of its buildings were leveled.

The town was founded in 1192, when its castle was built by Duke Leopold V of the ruling house of Babenberg. He had it constructed as a citadel to ward off attacks of the Magyars from the east. From 1440 to 1493 Austrian emperors lived at this fortress in the southeast corner of what is now the old town. Maximilian I, called "the last of the knights," was born here in 1459 and lies buried in the Church of St. George in the castle. It was Maria Theresa who in 1752 ordered that the structures comprising the castle be turned into a military academy.

You can visit the **Church of St. George** (St. Georgskirche) daily from 8 a.m. to 4 p.m. The gable of the church is adorned with more than 100 heraldic shields of the Habsburgs. It's noted for its handsome interior, decorated in the late Gothic style.

Neukloster, a Cistercian abbey, was founded in 1250 and reconstructed in the 18th century. The New Abbey Church (Neuklosterkirche), on Ungargasse near the Hauptplatz, is Gothic with a beautiful choir. It contains the tomb of the Empress Eleanor of Portugal, wife of Friedrich III and mother of Maximilian I. Mozart's *Requiem* was first presented here in 1793.

Liebfrauenkirche, on the Domplatz, was once the headquarters of an episcopal see. It's graced by a 13th-century Romanesque nave, but the choir is Gothic. The west towers have been rebuilt.

In the town is a **Recturm,** a tower in the Gothic style said to have been built with the ransom money paid for Richard the Lionhearted.

The area code for Wiener Neustadt is 02622.

FOOD AND LODGING: Hotel Corvinus, Ferdinand Porsche Ring (tel. 4134), is a dramatically designed modern hotel with a color scheme of white and weathered bronze. It sits in a quiet neighborhood near the city park. Its 68 rooms have all of the modern comforts in a decor of patterned bedspreads and solid colors. Inside you'll find an ultramodern bar area, a parasol-covered sun terrace, and a lightheartedly elegant restaurant with big sunny windows. Singles cost 660 AS ($35.11), while doubles rent for 900 AS ($47.88), with breakfast included. Children under 12 stay in their parents' room for free.

Hotel/Restaurant Forum, 2 Heimkehrerstrasse (tel. 4918), is a comfortable 37-room hotel near the railway and bus stations. Bedrooms are cheerfully papered and usually high-ceilinged, while the outdoor terrace restaurant and the indoor bar area are attractive gathering spots. Doubles cost 650 AS ($34.58) per night, while singles go for 350 AS ($18.62).

Restaurant Porsche, 90 Neunkirchnerstrasse (tel. 35-91-44). Years ago a garage mechanic opened a small restaurant above his shop so that his clients would have a place to wait. Today the shop is the biggest Volkswagen-Porsche workshop in the city, and the restaurant has evolved into a high-quality and popular eatery filled with garage and race-car memorabilia (the silverware, for example, is engraved with the initials V.W.). The daily menus are solid, hearty, and what the Austrians call "honest." The savory and uncomplicated selections include veal steak Ticino style, a nourishing beef soup, and a wide range of generously served gutbürgerlich dishes. The restaurant doesn't "run" on Saturday. Fixed-price meals cost 80 AS ($4.26) to 260 AS ($13.83), while à la carte dinners range from 120 AS ($6.38) to 300 AS ($15.96).

Witetschka, 1 Allerheiligenplatz (tel. 3109). This small and tasteful café was long ago used by Austrian Protestants as a meeting place. Today it's a trendy hangout on one of the city's most beautiful squares. Much of the menu is devoted to café items, such as ice cream, elaborate pastries (try the crêpes Suchard), and coffee drinks. Coffee is priced from 18 AS (96¢) to 32 AS ($1.70), pastries from 22 AS ($1.17). It's closed Sunday.

4. Semmering

One of the best-known places for skiing in Austria, Semmering, at an elevation of 3,200 feet sheltered by forests of firs and mountain ranges, is just over an hour by car or train from Vienna. It's a romantic spot in summer and a choice location for winter sports when snow blankets the area. The resort, built on terraces, is perched around the Semmering pass which divides Lower Austria from Styria.

An international resort, called by the Austrians a *kurort,* a fresh-air spot rather than a mineral springs spa, Semmering is considered by doctors to be ideal for the health of patients, and there are many rest homes in the vicinity.

In winter guests can ski at the ski centers at Semmering-Hirschenkogel or Spital am Semmering. In this region, you find Raxalpe and Schneeberg, two of the highest mountains in Lower Austria. They are separated by the Höllental, or Valley of Hell. This misnamed valley is really a lovely, wild spot, lying to the northwest of Semmering. The Schwarza River creates the gap between the two mountains.

If you don't want to stay right in Semmering, you'll also find accommodations in **Puchberg,** and **Reichenau,** which is like a summer spa. It has a direct cable-car hookup which will take you up to the Rax.

Puchberg, at the foot of the Schneeberg, is a quiet, tranquil place which has a rack railway to take you right into the mountain range. It will take a full day for an excursion up to Schneeberg. The train from Puchberg climbs to the Hochschneeberg terminus in about an hour and 20 minutes. A hotel (see below) is perched on the mountainside. From the terminus, you can go by foot to the

Kaiserstein (6,760 feet), from which you're rewarded with a vista of the Alps and a panoramic sweep of the Raxalpe, a limestone massif which attracts many climbers. It is riddled with tunnels. From its upper belvedere you can see a sweep of the Semmering mountains to the south, the Kaiserstein to the north, and the Valley of Hell, also to the north.

Departures from Puchberg on the mountain railway in summer are at 7:40 and 11:40 a.m. and at 3:45 p.m. Return trips are at 1:35 and 4:15 p.m. The round-trip fare is 150 AS ($7.98).

The area code for Semmering is 02664; for Puchberg, 02636; and for Reichenau, 02666.

FOOD AND LODGING: The **Hotel Panhans**, 32 Hochstrasse (tel. 8181). The sprawling white facade of this hotel shelters both the most glamorous and the highest accommodation in town. Capped with a green roof, and filled with marble and an elaborate re-creation of art nouveau detailing, it contains 70 well-furnished bedrooms as well as dozens of privately owned apartments. The establishment was built in 1888, but almost completely reconstructed in 1982. Today, it often hosts conventions from throughout Austria.

On the premises are an indoor pool, exercise room, a restaurant, and a coffeehouse, along with a dramatic cocktail bar and disco outfitted with Oriental trappings and painted a shade of blue-gray. Depending on the season and the view, singles cost between 650 AS ($34.58) and 900 AS ($47.88), while doubles range between 500 AS ($26.60) and 760 AS ($40.43) per person, with breakfast included. Half board is another 145 AS ($7.71) per person daily.

Kurhaus Dr. Stühlinger (tel. 447) receives guests in a four-story building with large arched windows on the ground floor, horizontal rows of wooden balconies, an angular modern extension sided with glass, and landscaping which makes it seem taller than it actually is. You'll enter through the grand loggia extending off the front of the building. The public rooms are streamlined, filled with curved lines and big windows. A basement swimming pool and a host of health facilities are available, sometimes for an extra charge, to guests. The rooms are clean and filled with 1950s-style wooden furniture and lots of natural light. Because of the health treatments which usually go with a room at this establishment, full board is encouraged. With all meals included, singles rent for 585 AS ($31.12) to 800 AS ($42.56), while doubles cost 680 AS ($36.18) per person daily.

Pension Daheim (tel. 382) is a gracefully embellished chalet with green shutters and a series of gables that look out over the valley below. The interior is filled with pleasant wooden furniture and warmly patterned fabrics. The establishment is directed by the Hahnl-Steeger family, who charge from 180 AS ($9.58) to 290 AS ($15.34) per person in either a single or double room. Prices depend on the plumbing and the view.

Hotel/Pension Belvedere, 60 Hochstrasse (tel. 270), is a four-story building with a gabled roofline and a series of arches repeating themselves in the ground-floor windows and in the second-floor loggias. A formal garden grows abundantly off to one side, while a café with parasols has been placed near the stone walls of the ground floor. On the premises you'll find a small swimming pool and sauna. Rooms with private bath range from 410 AS ($21.81) to 480 AS ($25.54) per person daily, while bathless units cost around 360 AS ($19.15) per person. The Englschall family are your congenial hosts.

Gartenhotel Alpenheim, 55 Villenstrasse (tel. 322), is a well-designed chalet with a modern annex extending toward the downhill side of a forested hill. You'll find an indoor swimming pool, as well as a comfortable bar area with upholstered chairs and rustic details. Singles range from 340 AS ($18.09) to 400

AS ($21.28), while doubles cost from 320 AS ($17.02) to 380 AS ($20.22) per person daily. All units have phone, radio, and a TV outlet. The Steiner family will give you a hearty welcome.

At Puchberg

Forellenhof Wanzenböck, 20 Losenheim (tel. 22-05-11). From the front, you'll see a curved series of windows capped with a sloped roof and an upper-level terrace. A more conventional modern wing stretches off to the side, accented with flagstone walls and blue-green fir trees. The interior has wrought-iron wall sconces, pine paneling with arched niches for religious art, and lots of hunting trophies. The earth-toned bedrooms are filled with comfortable contemporary furniture. An in-house swimming pool has imaginative metal cutouts of giant fish fastened to one of the brown tile walls. As the name of the hotel would imply, the Wanzenböck family are the owners. They charge 345 AS ($18.35) to 425 AS ($22.61) per person for a room and full board during the ski season, depending on the plumbing.

Hotel Puchbergerhof (tel. 2278) is a mellow old building with a stucco facade highlighted with golden illustrations, slate gables, and honey-colored wooden shutters. The backyard is filled with flowers and well-kept greenery, while the simple interior has wooden paneling which, on the wall areas, is sometimes stenciled with regional designs. The cozy bedrooms sometimes have wooden ceilings and an occasional carved headboard. The 40 rooms range from 260 AS ($13.83) to 300 AS ($15.96) in a single and 480 AS ($25.54) to 540 AS ($28.73) in a double, with breakfast included. Edith Resch-Stickler, the charming hostess, works hard to make her guests comfortable.

Berghaus Hochschneeberg (tel. 2257) is a solidly built masonry house which can be reached only by a cog railway on a path up through alpine meadows. The hotel is perched over a steep cliff, and might be an ideal place to get away from it all. There are only two trains a day from the terminal at Puchberg which go to a station (Hochschneeberg) five minutes away from the hotel. They leave at 9 a.m. and at noon. On Friday and Saturday there's a train at 3:45 p.m. as well. The ride to the hotel takes an hour and a half. Guests are received from April 1 to October 30. Josef Schanner charges from 250 AS ($13.30) per person for full board in this isolated spot.

At Reichenau

Alpenhotel Knappenhof (tel. 3633) is an alpine chalet covered with yellow stucco and wooden slats. Its shutters are forest green, and from the parasol-dotted sun terrace you'll have a view of the rock-covered mountains in the distance. Aside from the sauna and indoor swimming pool there's a choice of a wide range of health facilities, including underwater massage and diet therapy. The bedrooms are filled with simple blond furniture and cheerful warm colors. The charges are from 320 AS ($17.02) to 380 AS ($20.22) per person per day in either a double or a single room. Prices include a buffet breakfast. In winter, there's an additional charge of 35 AS ($1.86) daily for heat.

Gasthof Flackl (tel. 2291) is a country chalet hotel with balconies covered in summer with flowers. Inside you'll find a green ceramic oven, chalet chairs, wooden ceilings, and a terracotta floor. The Flackl family charges 200 AS ($10.64) to 310 AS ($16.49) in a single and 310 AS ($16.49) to 480 AS ($25.54) in a double, with breakfast included. Prices depend on the plumbing.

5. The Southeast Corner

You might want to consider anchoring in the very southeast corner of Lower Austria, at the doorway to Burgenland. There are several good spots to select from, all off the beaten track and all with good food and reasonable prices. Places I'll recommend are patronized by Austrians and are hardly known to foreigners. All of them are easily reached by driving south from Wiener Neustadt. They are to the east of Semmering.

First, I'll take you to—

BAD SCHÖNAU: This small spa has baths said to be helpful to persons with circulatory troubles. Outside the town is Krumbach Castle (2,000 feet), a medieval fortress which saw action in the Turkish siege of Austria in 1683.

The area code for Bad Schönau is 02646.

Food and Lodging

Kurhotel Bad Schönau, 1 Am Kurpark (tel. 25850). One of its facades is designed like a futuristic opera house, with sleek horizontal lines of arched windows looking out over a sun terrace and jets of water. It stretches over a wide expanse of green lawns and has evenly spaced balconies leading into comfortable bedrooms with lots of light. An indoor swimming pool is covered with a slanted roof and has a full wall of big windows. On the premises you'll find a wide range of massage and health facilities, as well as dining and drinking areas that are inviting and appealing. Prices range from 510 AS ($27.13) to 565 AS ($30.06) per person in a single or double, with breakfast included. All accommodations contain private baths.

MÖNICHKIRCHEN: On the road from Vienna to Graz where good accommodations are not as plentiful as one might wish, the following recommendation— roughly at the halfway point in your trip—might be handy either for food or lodging or both.

The area code for Mönichkirchen is 02649.

Food and Lodging

Hotel Pension Robert Reidinger (tel. 242) is a boxy cement building with flower-covered rows of balconies separated from one another with masonry dividers. Inside you'll find comfortable rooms, a sauna, an elevator, and a quiet location guaranteed to afford you a pleasant night's rest. Singles range from 230 AS ($12.24) to 290 AS ($15.34), while doubles cost 215 AS ($11.44) to 290 AS ($15.34) per person, with breakfast included. The hotel is closed from November until just before Christmas.

6. The Marchfeld

When you travel through Lower Austria in the autumn, you see signs at little inns advertising wild game on the menu, with such graphics as a defenseless stag depicted cornered by hunting dogs. Or you might see pheasant and quail strung up for proper aging. A lot of this game comes from the Marchfeld, a rich agricultural plain lying to the east of Vienna in the direction of the Iron Curtain. The Marchfeld, called "the fertile granary of Austria," was under Soviet domination during the occupation years.

The "fertile granary" lies roughly between the River March and the Danube, which, with all due respect to Strauss, is a muddy brown rather than a beautiful blue. The plain lies on the border between Lower Austria and the Slovakia section of Communist Czechoslovakia. The Marchfeld is not one of the scenic sections of Austria, but it is historically significant, having been a battleground on many occasions. Here the Austrians fought the Magyars (Hungarians), the Turks, and even the forces of Napoleon.

While you're still based in Vienna, you can explore much of this area on a long morning's drive, leaving the city on the right bank of the Danube via Route 9 and heading toward Bratislava in Czechoslovakia. You'll have to have a visa as well as your passport if you cross the border.

On your drive, a good stopover might be—

FISCHAMEND: I suggest you explore in the morning and return to this town for lunch, as it's the site of the oldest fish restaurant in Austria. Many Viennese make culinary pilgrimages here to partake of its cuisine (see below). A market town with an early 16th-century tower, Fischamend lies on the Fischa River.

The area code for Fischamend is 02232.

Where to Dine

Fischrestaurant Merzendorfer (tel. 314) is supposed to be the oldest restaurant in Austria specializing in fish, all of which are deliciously and conscientiously prepared. If you've wanted to try eel (with fennel or dill sauce, for example) or fish from the Danube, as well as carp, Serbian-style fogasch, trout, sheat-fish, or pike-perch with anchovy butter, this is the place to come. You might begin your meal with an Austrian roe soup. The restaurant is small, pleasant, cozy, with an outdoor terrace filled with plants in summer. Lunch is served from 11 a.m. to 2 p.m. while dinner is offered from 5:30 to 10 p.m. The restaurant is closed Sunday evening, all day Monday, and from the day before Christmas until January 6. It's also closed during all of August. À la carte meals begin at 225 AS ($11.97).

For your next sightseeing stop, you might take a look at some Roman ruins by driving to—

PETRONELL: In an open-air museum (not very spruced up) you can see the remains of several houses built in Roman times, along with some interesting mosaics.

Nearby are the partially excavated ruins of **Carnuntum,** a Roman city of some 45,000 inhabitants, maybe more, which thrived between the second and the fourth centuries A.D. Signs direct you to the ruins of two amphitheaters, where plays are presented in summer. The smaller and older of the two was surpassed by the one built in the second century which held an estimated 10,000 spectators. Near it are the ruins of a triumphal arch, also built in the second century.

BAD DEUTSCH–ALTENBURG: The **Museum Carnuntinum** stands in this spa town, a neighbor of Petronell. Near the spa complex, the museum contains the most interesting of the Roman artifacts excavated at Carnuntum. Museum hours are 9 a.m. to 5 p.m. Admission is 25 AS ($1.33).

ROHRAU: Four miles on from Petronell is Rohrau, where a 16th-century castle houses one of the most important private art collections in Austria. Called the **Harrach Gallery,** it has an impressive aggregation of art and is particularly rich in paintings from the Spanish and Neapolitan baroque period. The gallery is open to the public April through November daily except Monday from 10 a.m. to 5 p.m. Admission is 40 AS ($2.13).

Music lovers come to Rohrau because it was where Joseph Haydn, son of a wheelwright, was born in 1732. Haydn wrote some 104 symphonies, perfecting the classical sonata form. The **Haydn House,** a modest thatched cottage, contains mementos, including original scores. It's open daily except Monday from 10 a.m. to 5 p.m., charging an admission of 15 AS (80¢).

Even if you're not going on to Czechoslovakia, you might want to continue toward the border to the old town of—

HAINBURG: As nations developed and boundaries between countries were fixed, border towns naturally became defensive citadels. Hainburg was no exception. Its great moment in history was long ago, during the Middle Ages, but it still has a ruined castle and some fortified gateways, and part of the 13th-century wall that circled the town still stands. The Wiener Tor gateway is also from the 13th century. There are many vintage houses, in Gothic, Renaissance, and the ubiquitous baroque style.

Haydn attended school in this town, which lies between two cone-shaped hills overlooking the Danube. A fountain is dedicated to the composer.

GROSSENZERSDORF: If you don't want to drive back to Vienna for the night, you can stay in this hamlet north of the Danube, in an area immediately east of the capital city. The village is partially enclosed by its former fortified wall, and nearby battlefields haunt the communal memory—at Aspern in 1809 Napoleon suffered his first defeat in the field, and through this sector the Red army and the retreating Nazis fought in the closing weeks of World War II in Europe.

The area code for Grossenzerdorf is 02249.

Food and Lodging

Hotel am Sachsengang (tel. 29010) is a rambling, recently constructed building with a gently sloping roof and an elegantly crafted wood-trimmed interior. The indoor swimming pool is sunny and spacious, with scattered café tables to permit you to take coffee beside the water. An outdoor terrace faces a tree-lined canal. The hotel has a sauna, an indoor swimming pool, a whirlpool, a massage, and a tennis club. There are 54 comfortable bedrooms, all with private bath or shower, direct-dial phone, and mini-bar. Singles rent for 620 AS ($32.98) to 750 AS ($39.90), depending on the season, while doubles, on the same basis, range from 950 AS ($50.54) to 1,200 AS ($63.84). The rates include a buffet breakfast, service, and taxes. Guests can enjoy the Hotelgalerie, upstairs from the lobby, an elegant and exclusive lounge where a selection of Viennese coffees is served.

Taverne, Hotel am Sachsengang (tel. 29010), is an elegant restaurant dotted with wood detailing and handsomely rustic touches, and is a part of the above-named hotel. Many of the featured dishes come in puff pastry, including Hungarian fogosch and rack of lamb. Other specialties include veal parma, wild venison, and a wide range of desserts, all of them served on blue-and-white porcelain. Fixed-price meals range from 190 AS ($10.11) to 460 AS ($24.47), while à la carte meals cost anywhere from 195 AS ($10.37) to 360 AS ($19.15). From May to October, live gypsy music is played in the restaurant.

Farther along, still on the north bank of the Danube, you can visit—

ECKARTSAU: This tiny hamlet has had its moment in history. It was to an imperial hunting lodge here that Emperor Karl I and the royal family fled in the last days of the empire, when the Habsburg sovereignty collapsed in 1918. The baroque lodge was built in 1722. You are allowed to stroll through the gardens and some display rooms, run by the Federal Forestry Administration and open daily except Monday from 9 a.m. to 5 p.m. Admission is 25 AS ($1.33).

DEUTSCH-WAGRAM: Should you become fascinated by the Marchfeld, you can drive along a more northerly route from Vienna, reaching the village of Deutsch-Wagram in about 20 minutes. Many memories of Napoleon are here, especially at the hotel recommended below.

The area code for Deutsch-Wagram is 02247.

Food and Lodging

Hotel Marchfelderhof (tel. 2243) is a beautiful hotel with lots of atmosphere, replete as it is with historic artifacts, valuable paintings, and carefully worked rustic detailing. It was established in 1912, and is today directed by the Bocek family, who charge 230 AS ($12.24) to 330 AS ($17.56) for a single and 430 AS ($22.88) to 480 AS ($25.54) in a double, depending on the plumbing. Only a few of the units have private baths. You'll find a disco, a souvenir shop, a restaurant (see below), and an art nouveau café on the premises.

Restaurant Marchfelderhof (tel. 2243) is one of the best restaurants in the region. It has a gemütlich and cozy decor of polished wood, hunting artifacts, warmly tinted textiles, and oil paintings which add an elegant and rustically appropriate note. Some of the accessories, such as a mandolin and a coal miner's lamp hanging from the ceiling, add a lighthearted touch. A garden terrace with a cherub-capped fountain is pleasant on a summer afternoon, while the musical entertainment of the evening sometimes includes a harpist. Specialties on any given night might be avocado sections with oysters in a spicy sauce, filet of wild venison, all the meat dishes you can think of, and a satisfying array of desserts. Portions are more than generous. The restaurant is closed Monday, and reservations are suggested. Fixed-price meals range from 145 AS ($7.71) to 460 AS ($24.47), while à la carte dinners cost from 150 AS ($7.98) to 520 AS ($27.66).

7. The Weinviertel

The Weinviertel, or wine district, referred to in my introduction, lies to the north of Vienna, a rich wine-growing territory between the Danube and the closely guarded Austria-Czechoslovakia border. On one of the most pleasant drives to be made in the environs of Vienna, you not only go through the vineyard district but you also pass many castles, often in ruins, which evoke the tumultuous Middle Ages.

You can stop in somnolent old market towns that seem light years removed from bustling Vienna. Many of the little towns have beautiful churches, and scenic views abound. The people who inhabit the district appear to lead relaxed and peaceful lives.

Your tour might take you to—

KORNEUBURG: This town, like Vienna, has a landmark column commemorating deliverance from the plague. It also has the Augustinerkirche, a rococo church built in 1773. A tower from the 15th century crowns the Rathaus (town hall).

A short distance from the town center is a castle fortress, **Burg Kreuzenstein,** rebuilt after being virtually demolished by the Swedes in 1645. Reconstruction was launched in 1874 and carried on into the 20th century. Some objets d'art are on exhibit. The castle is open daily except Monday from 9 a.m. to 5 p.m. for a 25-AS ($1.33) admission charge. You can enjoy the café and restaurant on the premises from which a fine vista unfolds.

From Korneuburg, I suggest that you continue on to the little town of—

EGGENBURG: One of the most beautiful little towns in the Weinviertel, Eggenburg, lying on the Schmida, was encircled by fortified walls in the 15th century. You can still see the defense towers and gates. Its castle, now in ruins, evokes thoughts of past grandeur. The parish church, dedicated to St. Stephen, has two Romanesque towers. On the main square, the Hauptplatz, stands a pillory dating from the 16th century. It's only there to look at today. Look for the **Gemaltes Haus** (painted house). The Krahuletz Museum, which has some prehistoric relics, is only of minor interest.

Towns near the border might intrigue you. One is—

RETZ: This well-known wine village lies near the Thaya Valley, almost in the Bohemian hills of Czechoslovakia. Retz is distinguished by fortified towers and ramparts, two gate towers dating from the 13th century. The center of this wine district town is the main square, or Hauptplatz, where a stately column dedicated to the Holy Trinity stands. The houses on the square are much photographed. The Rathaus (town hall) was reconstructed in the 16th century. The church, a Gothic Dominican structure, is noteworthy. The town also has an 18th-century windmill.

Many Viennese drive to Retz, mostly on Sunday, to take tours of the **wine cellars** of the town. Tours are conducted at 1:30 p.m. on weekdays and at 10 and 11 a.m. and 2 and 3 p.m. on Sunday. Each takes about an hour and costs 30 AS ($1.60). For advance information on these tours, telephone 23-79.

If you head east along the Thaya River, you come to—

LAA: This 13th-century town, very near the Czechoslovakia border, was once heavily fortified. Some of its walls still stand, and there's an ancient fortress. Also, there is an early Gothic parish church and a castle where you can see an armor collection from the 15th century.

Close by are some wine-growing towns, including **Poysdorf,** which is quite near the heavily fortified border.

On your way back to Vienna from Laa, you might enjoy a stopover at—

MISTELBACH: This charming old town, not far from Czechoslovakia, is in the northeast corner of Austria. Its Gothic-style parish church is from the 15th century. The *karner* (charnel house or bone house) is even older, from the 12th century. Mistelbach also has a baroque castle, built in 1725.

Mistelbach's area code is 02572.

Food and Lodging

Zur Goldenen Krone, 15 Oberhofer Strasse (tel. 27-295). Walter Heindl is the engaging owner of this wine tavern and hotel. The outside has a faded ochre facade and tall, old-fashioned windows which let in lots of light. Singles range from 250 AS ($13.30), while doubles cost 200 AS ($10.64) to 240 AS ($12.77) per person daily. The wood-paneled restaurant has a wall-size illustration of one of Austria's royal families, and lots of comfortably intimate nooks and crannies. Specialties include game and veal dishes, all of them cooked in a regional style. À la carte meals range from 95 AS ($5.05) to 225 AS ($11.97).

8. The Wachau-Danube Valley

If you plan to journey along the Danube, I recommend taking a paddleboat steamer in summer. You can travel by armchair, lounging on the deck along this longest river in Central Europe. (The Volga holds "longest river" title for the continent.)

If you're really "doing the Danube," as some travelers do, you can begin your trip at Passau, West Germany, and go all the way to the Black Sea and across to the Crimean Peninsula, stopping over at Yalta, scene of the famous, now controversial, meeting of Roosevelt, Churchill, and Stalin. However, the Vienna to Yalta portion of the trip alone takes nearly a week and few travelers have that kind of time to devote to it.

Therefore most visitors limit themselves to a more restricted look at the Danube, taking one of the many popular trips offered in Vienna. If you go westward on the river, your first stop might well be at **Klosterneuburg,** which was previewed as an excursion in the environs of Vienna (see Chapter V under sight-seeing attractions).

Cityrama Sightseeing, 1 Börsegasse (tel. 63-66-19) in Vienna, offers Wachau-Danube Valley tours from May 1 to October 31 on Monday, Wednesday, Friday, and Sunday.

Verkehrsbüro, Austrian Travel Agency Inc., 5 Opernring (tel. 56-00-0) in Vienna, offers Wachau-Danube Valley tours daily from early April to October 27 starting at 9:30 a.m. and on Thursday and Sunday from November 1 to April 3, also departing at 9:30 a.m., lasting about eight hours and costing 800 AS ($42.56) per person. The tour takes you from Vienna to Krems, with the boat trip on the river lasting about two hours. You have lunch on board, arriving soon after at Melk Abbey. From there, a bus takes you to Dürnstein before your return to Vienna.

Of course, you can do a Wachau-Danube Valley land tour in your own car. Some of the sights lie a few miles from the river, so if you're a serious sightseer an automobile will give you far more freedom to explore on your own.

Actually, the Wachau is that part of the Danube Valley lying between Krems and Melk, about 50 miles to the west of Vienna. It's possible to reach this far-western tip of the Wachau, where many visitors come to see Melk Abbey, taking a train from Vienna to Melk and then a river trip between Melk and Krems.

Scenic experts consider the Wachau one of the most beautiful parts of Austria, where competition for top rating is keen. Throughout this part of the Danube Valley you'll pass ruins of castles reminiscent of the Rhine Valley.

Stopovers along your route by car could include some of the following places, beginning with—

TULLN: This is one of the most ancient towns in Austria, originally being the naval base, Comagena. Later a center for the Babenbergs, who ruled Austria before the Habsburgs, Tulln, on the right bank of the Danube, is called "the flower town" because of the masses of blossoms you'll see in spring and summer. It is the place, according to the saga of the Nibelungen, where Kriemhild, the Burgundian princess of Worms, met Etzel, king of the Huns.

The twin-towered parish church (*pfarrkirche*) grew out of a 12th-century Romanesque basilica dedicated to St. Stephen, as was the cathedral in Vienna. Its west portal is from the 13th century. A Gothic overlay added in its early centuries gave way in the 18th century to the baroque craze that swept the country. A 1786 altarpiece commemorates the martyrdom of St. Stephen. Ogival vaulting was used in the chancel and the nave. Adjoining the church is the **karner** (charnel house or bone house). This funereal chapel is actually the major sight of Tulln, considered the finest of its kind in the entire country. Built in the mid-13th century in the shape of a polygon, it is richly decorated, with capitals and arches. The Romanesque dome is adorned with frescoes.

The Tulln area code is 02272.

Food and Lodging

Hotel/Restaurant Römerhof Stoiber, 66 Langenlebarnerstrasse (tel. 2954), was built in 1973. It has a simple modern facade of white walls and unadorned windows, with a prominent sign announcing its name. The interior is warmly outfitted with earth colors, a macramé wall hanging, and hanging lighting fixtures. A wood-ceilinged restaurant serves well-prepared meals in an attractively rustic setting. The comfortable bedrooms rent for 320 AS ($17.02) in a single and 500 AS ($26.60) in a double, with breakfast included. All units have private baths. Specialties of the hotel's restaurant include Wiener schnitzel, veal cutlets in a barbecue sauce, and roast or grilled pork dishes. Complete meals average around 180 AS ($9.58).

Zur Rossmühle, 12-13 Hauptplatz (tel. 2411). Occupants of the elegant dining room of this baroque hotel might have made the trek from Vienna for one of the chef's well-prepared meals. Dinner tends to be the social focal point of the weekend here. Specialties include breast of chicken in a raspberry vinegar sauce, salmon or gooseliver in puff pastry, tempting veal and fish dishes, along with high quality wines. À la carte meals cost between 170 AS ($9.04) and 480 AS ($25.54), with set dinners ranging between 420 AS ($22.34) and 700 AS ($37.24). Many choose to spend the night in one of the establishment's well-furnished bedrooms, where rates range between 480 AS ($25.54) and 600 AS ($31.92) per person. The place is closed in January.

Farther along you come to—

TRAISMAUER: This old market town hardly merits a stopover, but it does have a ring of town walls, partially preserved, and a Renaissance castle that was once the property of the archbishops of Salzburg. Its Wiener Tor dates from the 16th century.

A drive of about seven miles will take you to a more interesting spot, the—

HERZOGENBURG MONASTERY: Founded in the early 12th century by a German bishop from Passau, this Augustinian monastery has a long history with some illustrious highlights. The present complex of buildings comprising the church and the abbey was reconstructed in the baroque style. That master of baroque, Fischer von Erlach, designed some of the complex. The art painted in the high altar of the church is by Daniel Gran, and the most outstanding art owned by the abbey is a series of 16th-century paintings on wood, displayed in a room devoted to Gothic art. The monastery is known for its library containing more than 80,000 works.

Guided tours lasting an hour take visitors through the monastery from the first of April until the end of October from 9 a.m. to noon and from 1 to 5 p.m. for an admission of 25 AS ($1.33). There's a wine tavern in the complex where you can drink the product of local grapes.

ST. PÖLTEN: Most guidebooks omit St. Pölten, which is today mainly an industrial town and rail link on the line from Linz to Vienna. But this is not only an important rail junction, it's also a city of culture and tradition, its origins going back to the time it was a Roman village known as Aelio Cetio. It lies on the left bank of the River Traisen which connects to the Danube 12½ miles to the north, passing along Traismauer, visited above.

The cultural heyday of St. Pölten, an episcopal see in the province which lies in the foothills of the Alps, was the 18th century, but many devotees today appreciate its special treasures. Daniel Gran, the painter, and Jakob Prandtauer, the architect, lived here and some of their works remain. These two loom large in the art and architectural annals of Austria.

For your tour of the old town, head for the Domplatz, which, as its name indicates, is dominated by a **cathedral** of early Gothic style. The present structure supplanted a Romanesque church built on the site in the mid-12th century. However, some of the original edifice remains. One of the cathedral's towers is crowned by a baroque onion-shape dome. Prandtauer worked on designs for the interior, and there are ceiling paintings by Gran.

The second most important square in the old town is the Rathausplatz where you will of course find the Rathaus (town hall), dating from the 16th century, and also a colony of baroque houses. To the north of the square is a Franciscan church known for outstanding altarpieces by Kremser Schmidt, the noted baroque artist from Krems (see below).

Another interesting sight is the **Institute of the English Maidens** (Institut der Englischen Fraulein) on the Linzerstrasse. The charming baroque building dates from 1715. A portrait of the Virgin by Lucas Cranach the Elder is exhibited in one of the altars.

The area code for St. Pölten is 02742.

Where to Dine

Maria Kern, 41 Harlanderstrasse (tel. 81-1-17). Establishments like this hold few illusions about innovating their menu with fancy new recipes or adding trendy new decorations. This place remains much as it was years ago, with a conservatively flavorful menu, including such dishes as huntsman's soup, an array of roasts, and stuffed roll of pork, along with traditional Austrian desserts. À la carte meals cost from between 105 AS ($5.59) and 280 AS ($14.90), while fixed-price menus start at a most reasonable 80 AS ($4.26). The establishment is open for lunch, and dinner daily except Wednesday.

Back along the Danube, continue on to one of the major sightseeing targets of the Wachau-Danube Valley—

KREMS: In the eastern part of the Wachau on the left bank of the Danube lies Krems, a city some 1,000 years old. The city today encompasses Stein and Mautern, once separate towns (see my recommendation of a restaurant in Mautern).

Krems is a mellow town of courtyards, old churches, and ancient houses in the heart of the vineyard country, with some partially preserved town walls. Just as the Viennese flock to Grinzing and other suburbs to sample new wine in heurigen, so do the people of the Wachau come here to taste the vintners' products which are new in Krems earlier in the year than in the Vienna area.

The most interesting part of Krems today is what was once the little village of **Stein.** Narrow streets are terraced above the river, and the single main street, Steinlanderstrasse, is flanked with houses, many from the 16th century. The Grosser Passauerhof, 76 Steinlanderstrasse, is a Gothic structure decorated with an oriel. Another house, at 84 Steinlanderstrasse, which combines Byzantine and Venetian elements among other architectural influences, was once the imperial toll house. In a troubled era, the aristocrats of Krems barricaded the Danube and extracted heavy fines from the river traffic. Sometimes the fines were more than the hapless victims could pay, so the townspeople just confiscated the cargo.

The parish church (*pfarrkirche*) of Krems is somewhat overadorned, rich with gilt and statuary. Construction on this, one of the oldest baroque churches in the province, began in 1616. In the 18th century Martin Johann Schmidt painted many of the frescoes you'll see inside the church. In the Altstadt, or old town, the **Steiner Tor,** a 1480 gate, is a landmark. The town's Rathaus (town hall), from 1549, has an oriel.

The **Historisches Museum der Stadt Krems** (Historical Museum of Krems; tel. 25-11, ext. 339) is in a restored Dominican monastery. The abbey is in the Gothic style from the 13th and 14th centuries. It has a painting gallery displaying the works of Martin Johann Schmidt, a well-known 18th-century artist better known as Kremser Schmidt (mentioned earlier).

The complex also has an interesting **Weinbaumuseum** (wine museum) where artifacts, many quite old, gathered from the vineyards along the Danube are exhibited.

The historical museum is open from around Easter until the middle of November. Hours are 9 a.m. to noon and 2 to 5 p.m. (9 a.m. to noon on Sunday). It's closed on Monday. Admission is 25 AS ($1.33).

The area code for Krems is 02732.

Food and Lodging

Parkhotel Krems, 19 Edmund-Hofbauer-Strasse (tel. 32-66), is a large, glass-walled hotel with a wooden canopy stretching out over the front entrance. After registering in a simply paneled modern reception area, you'll be able to choose between a meal in the airy café or on its terrace, the restaurant, or in what is my personal favorite, the Wachauer-Keller. This room caters as much to the local population as to the hotel guests, and has a rustically timbered decor of chalet chairs, red-checked curtains, and red tablecloths. The waitresses, all of whom wear regional garb, will bring you local and Austrian specialties which include fish from the Danube and wine from the Wachau district. Single rooms here cost 475 AS ($25.27) while doubles rent for 385 AS ($20.48) per person, with breakfast included. All units contain private bath.

Hotel/Restaurant Am Förthof, 8 Donaulände (tel. 33-45), in the Stein sector of the city, is a big-windowed building with white stucco walls between each of its flower-covered wooden balconies. A rose garden surrounds the base of an al fresco café, while the inside is decorated with Oriental rugs and a scattering of antiques amid the newer furniture. On the grounds is an outdoor swimming pool bordered in stone. The high-ceilinged bedrooms, with complete bath or shower, foyer, phone, and shared balcony, rent for 450 AS ($23.94) per person, with a single room supplement of 200 AS ($10.64). Half board is offered for 600 AS ($31.92) per person. At dinner, hotel guests have a choice of main dishes, including contemporary cuisine or traditional Austrian cooking.

Restaurant Bacher (tel. 29-37), at Mautern, 2½ miles away from Krems, is a friendly restaurant with an elegant dining room and a well-kept garden. Liesl Wagner, the engaging owner, cooks à la Paul Bocuse, serving an imaginative array of the freshest possible ingredients. Specialties include crabmeat salad with nut oil, zucchini stuffed with fish, and two kinds of sauces, plus a changing collection of creatively prepared foods. Dessert might be beignets with apricot sauce and vanilla ice cream. She has won awards for her cuisine, as her enthusiastic clientele will tell you. À la carte meals range from 200 AS ($10.64) to 500 AS ($26.60). Reservations are strongly advised, and the restaurant is closed Monday and Tuesday from November to April. A limited number of bedrooms, each attractively furnished, are offered for 330 AS ($17.56) in a single and for 260 AS ($13.83) to 290 AS ($15.34) per person in a double.

DÜRNSTEIN: Less than five miles from Krems is the loveliest town along the Danube, Dürnstein, which draws throngs of tour groups in summer. Terraced vineyards mark this as another Danube wine town. Once fortified, its walls are partially preserved.

The ruins of a castle fortress, 520 feet above the town, are a link with the crusades. It was here that Leopold V, the Babenberg duke ruling the country at that time, held Richard the Lionhearted of England prisoner in 1193. It seems that Richard had insulted the powerful Austrian duke in Palestine during one of the frequent religious forays of the Middle Ages to get the Holy Sepulcher and its appurtenances into Christian custody. The story goes that when Richard was trying to get back home, his boat went on the rocks in the Adriatic and he tried to sneak through Austria disguised as a peasant. Somebody probably turned stool pigeon, but at any rate, the English monarch was arrested and imprisoned by Leopold.

For quite some time nobody knew exactly where Richard was incarcerated in Austria, but his loyal minstrel companion, Blondel, had a clever idea. He went from castle to castle, playing on his lute and singing Richard's favorite songs, particularly where it seemed as though somebody important might be held prisoner. The tactic paid off, the legend says, and at Dürnstein Richard heard the voice of the minstrel singing and took up the lyrics in reply. This discovery forced Leopold to transfer the English king to another castle, this one in the Rhineland Palatinate, but by then everybody knew where he was, so Leopold set a high ransom on the Plantagenet head which was eventually met, and Richard was set free.

The castle was virtually demolished by the Swedes in 1645, but you can visit the ruins if you don't mind a vigorous climb (allow an hour). The castle isn't so much, but the view of Dürnstein and the Wachau is more than worth the effort.

Back in the town, take in the principal artery, Hauptstrasse, which is flanked by richly embellished old residences. Many of these date from the 1500s and have been well maintained through the centuries. In summer the balconies are filled with flowers.

The 15th-century *pfarrkirche* (parish church) also merits a visit. The building was originally an Augustinian monastery and was reconstructed in baroque when this style swept Austria. The church tower is considered the finest one in baroque in the whole country. There is also a splendid church portal. Kremser Schmidt, the noted baroque painter mentioned earlier, did some of the altar paintings.

Dürnstein's area code is 02711.

Food and Lodging

Richard Löwenherz (tel. 222) is built into what was once an abbey. Classified today as one of Austria's "Romantik" hotels, it's filled with antiques, Renaissance sculpture, and elegant chandeliers. The vaulting of some of the ceilings rests on exposed stone columns, while the paneling in other rooms is well polished and mellow. An arbor-covered sun terrace with restaurant tables extends toward the Danube, and will give you a chance to see the other residents of the hotel enjoying the view. Best of all, the hotel offers a swimming pool where you'll be able to see the reflection of the apse of a medieval church in its waters. The spacious bedrooms, especially those in the balconied modern section, are tastefully filled with lighthearted furniture and cheerful, unobtrusive colors. Singles range from 580 AS ($30.87) to 950 AS ($50.54), while doubles cost from 900 AS ($47.88) to 1,300 AS ($69.16), with breakfast included. The restaurant offers excellent local wines as well as fish from the Danube among its many regional specialties.

Hotel Schloss Dürnstein (tel. 212). The baroque tower of this Renaissance castle rises above one of the most colorful parts of the Danube. It used to be owned by the princes of Starhemberg, but today it's one of the best furnished hotels in Austria, with a series of intricate architectural details. Inside you'll see white ceramic stoves, immaculately maintained vaulted ceilings, parquet floors, Oriental rugs, gilt mirrors, and oil portraits of elaborately dressed courtiers. Below the ochre facade of one of the wings, an ivy-covered wall borders the water of a swimming pool. The real beauty of the grounds, however, is found on the shady terrace a stone's throw from the river whose traffic stimulated the construction of this building more than 350 years ago.

The restaurant is outfitted with velvet armchairs with cabriole legs. Here you'll be served well-prepared dishes from the kitchen of an experienced chef. With half board included, regular singles cost from 1,020 AS ($54.26) to 1,300 AS ($69.16), while doubles range from 800 AS ($42.56) to 1,060 AS ($56.39) per person. One of the hotel's most elegant rooms, with rare antiques, beautiful upholstery, and beds worthy of Napoleon, goes for 1,400 AS ($74.48) per person nightly. The hotel is open only from March 22 until November 10.

Gartenhotel Pfeffel (tel. 206) is a black-roofed, white-walled hotel whose angularity is partially concealed by the well-placed shrubbery growing around it. Most of the pleasant rooms have private balconies. The public rooms are invitingly furnished with contemporary pieces, usually clustered around a wintertime fireplace. Leopold Pfeffel, the congenial owner, charges from 380 AS ($20.22) to 600 AS ($31.92) in a single and from 300 AS ($15.96) to 400 AS ($21.80) per person in a double, with breakfast included. Half board is included for an additional 125 AS ($6.65) per person.

Gasthof-Pension Sänger Blondel (tel. 253) is a lemon-colored, charmingly old-fashioned hotel with green shutters and clusters of flowers gathered at the windows. Its name is derived from the faithful minstrel who searched the countryside until he found Richard the Lionhearted imprisoned at Dürnstein. Aside from the good and reasonably priced restaurant, Sänger Blondel offers 18 rooms to travelers, costing 550 AS ($29.26) in a single and 410 AS ($21.28) per person in a double, with breakfast included. All rooms have shower or bath and toilet. If you dine in the restaurant on Tuesday, you can enjoy zither music.

After exploring Dürnstein most visitors rush on to Melk, but if you have more time to spend in this beautiful area there are other sights in the immediate vicinity. These include—

WEISSENKIRCHEN: This is a celebrated wine town in the heart of the vineyards of Wachau which lie along the Danube. You'll see many old houses, but Weissenkirchen's main attraction is its fortified Gothic **pfarrkirche,** or parish church, from the 15th century. The builders had the church fortified in 1531, fearing that the Turks would take Vienna and pose a threat to areas to the west of the capital. From one of the belvederes here you have an excellent view of the Danube Valley. A car-ferry crosses the river here.

The **Wachaumuseum** (Wachau Museum; tel. 2268) also merits a visit. The Teisenhofer-Hof, once a patrician house, was also fortified in the 16th century. It has a charming courtyard and arcades extending out to support a canopied gallery. The museum is devoted to the history of the region. It's open from the first of April to the end of October from 10 a.m. to 5 p.m., except Monday. Admission is 20 AS ($1.06).

Weissenkirchen has some of the finest food in the Wachau (see below), so you may want to schedule a luncheon stop here.

The area code for Weissenkirchen is 02715.

Food and Lodging
Raffelsbergerhof (tel. 2201), at Weissenkirchen, is the former headquarters of one of the river's traffic controllers. It's been renovated to its Renaissance integrity, and converted into a tastefully decorated hotel, with a pretty garden and contemporary touches in the comfortable bedrooms. The Anton family, your hosts, charge from 360 AS ($18.62) to 420 AS ($22.34) per person in a single or double. The place is closed from November until April.

Florianihof (tel. 2212), at Wösendorf, is a beautifully old-fashioned house decorated with taste and rustic furniture. Specialties of the house include such gutbürgerlich dishes as blutwurst and sauerkraut, zucchini and chicken cream soup, and cabbage noodles with ham. Reservations are suggested, and the establishment is closed all day Thursday and on Friday until 6 p.m. À la carte meals range from 130 AS ($6.92) to 275 AS ($14.63).

JOCHING: As an alternative to Weissenkirchen, you can turn off the main Wachau route deep into vineyard country to the little hamlet of Joching, area code also 02715, where you'll find the following establishment.

Where to Dine

Jamek (tel. 2235) is named after its owner, Josef, who, in addition to fermenting excellent wine, is also a masterful chef. The restaurant is in an old house covered with flowers. Someone will bring you a different glass for each of the wines you order to match an excellent cuisine which includes what is reputed to be the best blutwurst in the region, as well as sauerkraut, goose, duck, venison, pork dishes, black bread, veal schnitzel, filet of lamb with basil, and zucchini in a cream sauce flavored with dill. You might prefer on a warm day to eat in the flowering garden, although the inside is also cozy. À la carte meals range from 250 AS ($13.30) to 300 AS ($15.96), and reservations are suggested. Jamek is closed from mid-December to mid-February and for the first week of July. Otherwise, it's open Tuesday to Saturday from 11 a.m. to 11 p.m.

Back along the wine route, you might consider a stopover in—

SPITZ: Southward along the Danube in the direction of Melk is Spitz, a sleepy little market town celebrated for its grapes and characterized by its terraced vineyards. It is at its most beautiful in spring when hundreds of fruit trees are in bloom.

Spitz has the ubiquitous ruined castle and is noted for its ancient houses, many owned by vintners. Balconies of the houses are filled with masses of geraniums in spring and summer. A walk along the Schlossgasse will permit you to see some of the town's finest buildings. The Gothic *pfarrkirche* (parish church) is from the 15th century. The well-known baroque painter, Kremser Schmidt, worked on the altar.

The Spitz area code is 02713.

Food and Lodging

Hotel Wachauer Hof (tel. 303) is a large gabled building with white walls and a pleasant situation near vineyards and other buildings. Attractively furnished singles rent for 240 AS ($12.77), while doubles go for 350 AS ($18.62) to 510 AS ($27.13), with breakfast included. The staff is friendly and helpful. The hotel is open from April to October.

Mühlenkeller, 1 Auf der Wehr (tel. 352). Some of the foundations of this wine restaurant date from the 11th century. From the thickness of some of the walls, you can imagine that much of the rest of the building is almost as old. Menu items include a conservative but flavorful medley of Teutonic specialties, including a roast of pork with noodles and cabbage, along with grilled blood sausage and a fattening array of strudels. À la carte menus range between 60 AS ($3.19) and 200 AS ($10.64), with fixed-priced dinners costing from 90 AS ($4.79) and 170 AS ($9.04). The restaurant is open for lunch and dinner daily except Wednesday and for dinner only on Thursday. It also takes a long Christmas break.

From here, a car ferry will take you and your vehicle over to the Danube's right bank.

SCHÖNBÜHEL: On the right bank of the Danube in one of the most idyllic settings of the Wachau, some three miles before you reach Melk, stands the castle of Schönbühel, built in the early 1800s. It was erected on a rocky ledge commanding a view of the valley and of Melk. An architect was allowed to create a fantasy of onion-shaped domes and "pepperpot" towers on the castle.

Finally, you arrive at one of the chief sightseeing goals of every pilgrim to Austria—

MELK: Some 55 miles from Vienna on the right bank of the Danube, Melk marks the west terminus of the Wachau. **Melk Abbey,** one of the finest baroque buildings in the world, and the **Stiftskirche,** or abbey church, are the major attractions today. However, Melk has been an important place in the Danube Basin since establishment of a Roman fortress on a promontory looking out onto a tiny "arm" of the Danube. Melk also figures in the *Nibelungenlied,* in which it is called Medelike.

The rock-strewn bluff where the abbey now stands overlooking the river was the seat of the Babenbergs who ruled Austria from 976 until the Habsburgs took over. In the 11th century Leopold II of the House of Babenberg presented Melk to the Benedictine monks, who turned it into a fortified abbey. It became known as a center of learning and culture, and its influence spread all over Austria, a fact that is familiar to readers of the bestseller, *The Name of the Rose,* by Umberto Eco. However, it did not fare well during the Reformation, and it felt the fallout from the 1683 Turkish invasion, although it was spared from direct attack when the armies of the Ottoman Empire were repelled at the outskirts of Vienna. The construction of the new building began in 1702, just in time to be given the full baroque treatment.

Most of the design of the present abbey was by the baroque architect Jakob Prandtauer. Its marble hall, called the Marmorsaal, contains pilasters coated in red marble. A richly painted allegorical picture on the ceiling is the work of Paul Troger, whose work is distinguished by his blue coloring. The library, rising two floors, again with a Troger ceiling, contains some 80,000 volumes. The Kaisergang, or emperors' gallery, 650 feet long, is decorated with paintings of the rulers of Austria, the most notable of which is the prominently displayed likeness of Maria Theresa.

Despite all this adornment in the abbey, it still takes second place in lavish glory to the Stiftskirche, the golden abbey church, damaged by fire in 1974 but now almost completely restored, even to the regilding with gold bullion of statues and altars. Richly embellished with marble and frescoes, the church has an astonishing number of windows. Many of the paintings are by Johann Michael Rottmayr, but Troger also had a hand in decorating the church. The Marble Hall banquet room next to the church was also damaged by the fire but has been restored to its former ornate elegance.

Visitors can make arrangements to tour the monastery on their own by phoning 2312, ext. 232, but the best opportunity to see it is to take a tour with an English-speaking guide. Melk is still a working abbey, and you may see blackrobed Benedictine monks going about their business or schoolboys rushing out the gates.

Guided tours of the abbey complex are from 9 a.m. to noon and from 1 to 4 p.m. in April, May, and October, till 5 p.m. in summer. Otherwise, the tours are at 11 a.m. and 2 p.m. Admission is 30 AS ($1.60).

Everybody heads for the terrace for the view of the river. Napoleon probably used it for a lookout when he made Melk his headquarters during his campaign against Austria.

Food and Lodging

Hotel Stadt Melk, 1 Hauptplatz (tel. 2475), is a four-story beflowered hotel with a gabled roof, white stucco walls, and a position just below the yellow baroque walls of the town's palace. The pleasant restaurant has leaded-glass windows in round bull's-eye patterns of greenish glass, while the simply furnished bedrooms are clean and comfortable. There's a sauna on the premises. Singles rent for 450 AS ($23.94) per person, while doubles go for 280 AS ($14.90) to 380 AS ($20.22) per person daily, with breakfast included. Half board is another 140 AS ($7.45) per person daily.

9. The Nibelungengau

Austrians call one section of the Danube Valley the Nibelungengau, a name which brings a nostalgic "Once upon a time . . . " feeling even to those only vaguely familiar with the legend of Siegfried and his struggle to steal the treasure of the Nibelungen, a tribe of dwarfs, and awaken the enchanted princess, Brunhild. The *Nibelungenlied* is that German epic poem, probably written about A.D. 1200, which set down household legends that had been centuries in the making. After the gold hoard was taken from the dwarfs, the name Nibelungen was given to the followers of Siegfried, the Burgundian kings who acquired the treasure after Siegfried's death.

In Teutonic tradition, the epic of the Nibelungen enjoys a renown equaled only by that of King Arthur in England.

The Nibelungengau is that part of the Danube Valley lying beyond the Wachau to the west. Here you'll find—

PÖCHLARN: This river town, which still has remnants of its medieval walls, is today a focal point of tourist attention in June. Visitors from all over Europe and America come to attend a festive pageant, complete with bonfires, which briefly turns back the clock to the Middle Ages. In the *Nibelungenlied,* Pöchlarn was Bechelaren, where the margrave, Rüdiger, entertained the Burgundian kings who were going east to face the king of the Huns (really Attila). The Erlauf River flows into the Danube at Pöchlarn.

Two miles north of the town stands **Hohenstein Castle** at Arstetten. The baroque chapel here, a parish church since the 17th century, contains the tombs of two people who figured prominently and tragically in the history of the 20th century—Archduke Franz Ferdinand, heir to the throne of Austria, and his wife. Their assassinations at Sarajevo (now a Yugoslavian city) on June 28, 1914, touched off events that led to World War I.

MARBACH: A ferry connects this little village with the right bank of the Danube. Summer tourists visit it, but otherwise it's a fairly sleepy little market town.

However, from here you can take a steep, 2¼-mile drive up to—

MARIA TAFERL: At this little summer resort, a fantastic view of the Nibelungengau unfolds. The hamlet is known for its pilgrimage church, designed by Jakob Prandtauer, the architect of Melk Abbey. A Celtic sacrificial stone can be seen outside.

Maria Taferl's area code is 07413.

If you'd like to anchor in this bucolic little spot, I have the following recommendations:

Food and Lodging

Hotel Krone (tel. 6355) has an elegantly detailed pseudo-baroque facade stretching out in two separate wings, each of them with a modernized mansard roof. The interior has a paneled bar area where you might decide to have a predinner drink below the light from the brass chandeliers, plus an opulent dining room with a splendid view of the Danube. Bedrooms are rustic and comfortable, costing from 290 AS ($15.34) to 440 AS ($23.41) per person, based on double occupancy. Occupants of singles pay 70 AS ($3.72) supplement. An indoor swimming pool, a rooftop sun terrace, and a whirlpool and sauna are part of the facilities.

Hotel Kaiserhof (tel. 6355), under the same management as its sister hotel, the Krone, has a large outdoor swimming pool within sight of the twin baroque towers of a nearby church. The facade is pleasantly simple, with attractive shrubbery and colorful flowerboxes, an imposing entrance area, and a summertime cold buffet which is sometimes served on the spacious lawns outside. An outdoor terrace offers panoramic views of the Danube. Prices are the same as for the Hotel Krone.

PERSENBEUG: Near the end of the Nibelungengau is Persenbeug, a market town across the river from Ybbs with a bridge connecting the towns. Persenbeug was built in 1617 at a loop at the Danube on a rocky ledge overlooking the river. Persenbeug Castle, a Habsburg imperial residence, was the birthplace of "the last of the Habsburgs," Karl I, who died in exile in Madeira in 1922. The river you can see from here has been dammed by a power station.

If you take the bridge across the dam, you'll arrive at—

YBBS: On the right bank of the Danube, this old town lies near the mouth of the Ybbs River. You can still see the remains of its medieval walls. The town, which may or may not have grown up on the site of a Roman fort, has a Gothic church.

The area code for Ybbs is 07412.

Gourmet Dining

Villa Nowotni, 3 Trewaldstrasse (tel. 2620). The imaginative chef of this well-known restaurant works hard to combine the tenets of nouvelle French cuisine with traditional Austrian ingredients. The result is a gastronomic citadel which attracts diners from all over Europe and America. In a decor filled with art nouveau accessories and immaculate napery, a team of well-trained waiters serves such specialties as trout Stroganoff with fresh asparagus, variations on quail, and deliciously prepared dishes from the mainstream of Austrian cuisine.

The offerings change frequently, but the menu degustation gives appreciative diners small portions of an almost unending variety of imaginative courses which change seasonally, based upon the availability of ingredients. Reservations are most important, and the restaurant is open every day of the week except Monday. Full à la carte repasts range from 200 AS ($10.64) to 385 AS ($20.48), while fixed-price meals go between 300 AS ($15.96) and 600 AS ($31.92).

10. The Ybbs and Erlauf Valleys

In the far-western section of Lower Austria are two little-known—at least to North Americans—valleys containing a number of charming old towns and villages as well as beautiful scenery. To explore the Erlauf Valley, called "one of the few backwaters left in Europe," you can head south from Ybbs, going toward the celebrated Styrian resort of Mariazell.

Your first stop along this route might be at the brewery town of **Wieselburg,** which has an old church and castle.

If you continue along the same route, soon you'll reach **Pürgstall,** which also has an old church and castle.

In a short time you'll reach **Scheibbs,** which is bigger than Wieselburg or Pürgstall. Remnants of the town walls have survived ever since the Middle

Ages, and a tower gate and some houses date from the Renaissance. The parish church is in the Gothic style, and—you guessed it—there's a castle, this one from the 16th century.

From Scheibbs, you can drive to **Gaming,** a little summer resort noted for its former Carthusian monastery, Marienthorn, built in 1330 and dissolved by order of Emperor Joseph II in 1782. The church, from 1332, is in the "high Gothic" style.

At Erlauf Lake you can take a road which connects with the upper part of the Ybbs Valley. I recommend heading for **Lunz am See,** a market town and small summer resort on Lunzer lake. It has a celebrated Gothic parish church from the early years of the 16th century.

Along the Ybbs River, about 6½ miles from Lunz, lies **Göstling,** a very tiny summer resort. Many travelers pass through, going another 5¼ miles to Lassing where they connect with the **Hochkar Alpine Road.** This is less than 6 miles long and reaches a height of 4,720 feet. At the end of the road you can go the rest of the way by chair lift almost to the summit of Hochkar at 5,931 feet. From this vantage point you'll have a panoramic view of the countryside.

Your chief target in the Ybbs Valley should be—

MAIDHOFEN AN DER YBBS: This mellow old place in the lower part of the valley got its city charter in 1288. The early economy of the town was based on work in the forges with iron mined in the Erzberg. Many houses here are from the 1400s and 1500s. Gables and oriels were common in early house construction, as were arcaded courtyards.

The Rathaus, or town hall, has such an arcaded court. The parish church, built in 1510, is in late Gothic style. The **stadtturm** (tower) was erected in 1542 to commemorate the town's victory over the Turks. The exact moment of the Turkish defeat, shortly before noon, was "frozen for eternity" in the tower's clock dial. A nearby castle was the summer home of the Baron de Rothschild for some years of the 19th century.

The pilgrimage church of **Sonntagberg,** rising five miles north of the town, is the most distinguishing landmark to be seen in the Ybbs Valley. The church was built in 1706 by Jakob Prandtauer, the noted baroque architect.

STEINAKIRCHEN AM FORST: For one of the most spectacular accommodations not just in the valley but in all of Austria, consider the following 12th-century castle, which lies in a forest setting in the foothills of the Alps with a superb view of the Danube Valley.

Ernegg, the site of the castle, is a satellite of Steinakirchen, lying about ten miles south of the Vienna/Salzburg motorway (take the Ybbs exit). It's about a 90-minute drive from Vienna. By railroad, take the train to Amstetten.

The area code for Steinakirchen am Forst is 07488.

Food and Lodging

Schloss Ernegg (tel. 214) is on the outskirts of Steinakirchen am Forst. It's hard to imagine a more idyllic hotel: it's isolated from the nearest village, which is one mile away. From the outside it looks like a cross between a medieval fortress and a baroque pleasure palace, and once you're inside you'll realize that it's actually a bit of both. Constructed originally in the 12th century, it has an inner courtyard whose three floors of arcades rest on chiseled granite columns, elaborate public rooms whose salmon-colored walls reflect off the white tile ceramic stoves, and an impressive collection of rugs, antiques, and oil paintings. The dining room has a high ceiling, pink napery, well-prepared food, and a collection of hunting trophies.

There are only 20 bedrooms in the castle open to the public. The hotel maintains a private stable, whose horses are available for the use of guests. You'll also find tennis courts and a heated swimming pool in the nearby village. A nine-hole golf course is on the grounds. Clay pigeon shooting and trout fishing can be arranged nearby. The daughter of the last Count of Auersperg is today in charge of the hotel, charging from 440 AS ($23.41) to 580 AS ($30.87) per person daily, based on double occupancy with half board included. Occupants of singles pay a supplement of 120 AS ($6.38) daily. The castle is open from the first of May until October. In July and August there's an additional supplement of 120 AS ($6.38) per person daily.

AMSTETTEN: This is a busy commercial town of light industry on the Ybbs River, but it makes a convenient stopover in this part of the province, as it has some fine accommodations and good food. Its parish church is from the 14th century.

Amstetten's area code is 07472.

Food and Lodging

Hotel Hoffman, 2-4 Bahnhofstrasse (tel. 2516), is an imposing 19th-century hotel, constructed with a combination of Victorian and baroque elements which render it grandly imperial in a faded sort of way. It has a square cupola above a complicated roofline, plus well-embellished laurel wreaths crowning the top of the single third-floor lunette window. Some of the inside rooms still have rustic timbers and old-fashioned decor, although the bedrooms have been modernized into a slickly contemporary format. Near the train station, the hotel has a country-style dance bar which is popular with local residents on weekends. Singles range from 260 AS ($13.83) to 340 AS ($18.09), while doubles go from 450 AS ($23.94) to 850 AS ($45.22), with breakfast included. There's a parking garage on the premises.

Hotel/Restaurant Gürtler, 13 Rathausstrasse (tel. 2765), is an inner-city hotel with boldly outlined windows and a stucco facade. The interior has paneling, wrought-iron detailing, and strong colors which look pleasingly accommodating to the drinkers and diners who congregate in the restaurant. The contemporary bedrooms have patterned wallpaper and comfortable beds. The friendly atmosphere is what makes this place successful. Singles rent for 200 AS ($10.64) to 290 AS ($15.34), while doubles cost 370 AS ($19.68) to 520 AS ($27.66), with breakfast included. Streetside rooms tend to be noisy, so get a unit facing the courtyard if available. The restaurant serves well-prepared specialties which include, for example, grilled and pan-fried seafish, plus a daily menu that often has nouvelle cuisine touches. Try the pork cutlet with a spicy orange and apricot sauce, a variety of velvety-smooth cream soups, and a tempting list of pastries. À la carte meals range from 110 AS ($5.85) to 220 AS ($11.70), while fixed-price meals go from 70 AS ($3.72) to 190 AS ($10.11). The restaurant is closed on Monday.

Paradiesgartl, 104 Haabergerstrasse (tel. 2694) has green shrubs surrounding it and a Mediterranean ambience of relaxed conviviality. The food is well prepared and attractively served. Desserts are made fresh daily (the strudel is divine). Main courses are likely to include roast ham, veal, fish, and pork dishes. À la carte meals range from 75 AS ($3.99) to 150 AS ($7.98). The owner, Heribert Schlemmer, also offers ten comfortable bedrooms, all with shower or bath. The price per night, including an Austrian breakfast, ranges from 280 AS ($14.90) to 320 AS ($17.02) per person.

St. George's Stub'n (tel. 332), in St. Georgen (Ybbsfelde), is a country-style rendezvous point for local gourmets. The menu is unusual, emphasizing light recipes that have been strongly influenced by nouvelle cuisine. The menu changes almost daily, although staples of the establishment include the chef's gourmet salad, polenta noodles, rack of lamb local style, and a host of other specialties, culminating with a piece of apple strudel. Fixed-price meals range from 145 AS ($7.71) to 420 AS ($22.34), while à la carte meals range between 125 AS ($6.65) to 250 AS ($13.30). The place is closed on Thursday.

HAAG: Sometimes called Stadt Haag, this is my most remote recommendation in the province. It lies in the far-western reaches of Lower Austria. Actually, it's not inconvenient, being just off the autobahn to Linz. You might prefer to stop here instead of going on into busy Linz. Haag is only a short drive from Amstetten (visited above), and it may well suit your taste if you're looking for an overnight stay in an "undiscovered" Austrian village.

The Haag area code is 07434.

Food and Lodging

Gasthof Schafelner, 11 Hauptplatz (tel. 2411), is a lime-green baroque building, with white trim and steeply sloping tile roof. The interior has elegantly upholstered straight-back chairs clustered beneath the vaulted arches of the dining room, and a less formal weinstube paneled in wood with chairs that might be called "country Biedermeier." Restaurant specialties include mousse of smoked trout, lamb sausages on lentils, homemade herb noodles with fresh mushrooms, saddle of venison with bread dumplings and cranberries, filet of veal with morels and roast potatoes, roast duck with red cabbage and potato dumplings, and sweetbreads in Austrian white wine sauce. Desserts might include soufflé of cottage cheese in orange sauce and coffee mousse with rum sauce. An average meal will cost 325 AS ($17.29). The restaurant serves Tuesday till Sunday from 11 a.m. to 3 p.m. and from 6 p.m. to midnight. It's closed for part of January.

A limited number of rooms are available, costing from 175 AS ($9.31) to 225 AS ($11.97) per person in singles or doubles, with breakfast included. Only four of the accommodations have private showers.

11. The Ötscher Mountains

To the south of St. Pölten, lying between the Eisenerz Alps and the Vienna Woods, are alpine foothills known as the Ötscher mountains or massif. The Austrians jealously guard for themselves this popular area, which is unspoiled and certainly not yet overbuilt or filled with tourist lures. If you appreciate beautiful scenery and a tranquil way of life, you'll enjoy this area.

After leaving St. Pölten, the first stop will be—

LILIENFELD: This was once a huge Cistercian abbey in the Traisen Valley, founded by one of the Babenberg dukes named Leopold in 1202 when Romanesque was in flower, but many baroque architects worked on it through the years. The tomb of that Leopold is here. Lilienfeld has one of the most celebrated libraries in Lower Austria, dating from 1704. Inside the abbey is an art gallery, and the cloisters have 13th-century pillars of red marble. Some of the stained glass is from the 14th century. The abbey church is Gothic. A park surrounds the complex.

Tours are conducted from 8 to 11 a.m. and from 2 to 5 p.m. for a fee of 25 AS ($1.33).

At **Freiland,** an industrial town at the confluence of the Turnitz and the Traisen, you can take one of the area's most scenic drives.

ANNA BERG: This small hamlet lies at the top of a pass. It is known for its church of pilgrimage dating from the 14th century. The church later received, as did practically every other building in Austria, a baroque overlay.

12. The Waldviertel

To the north of the Wachau and the "land of the Nibelungen" lies the Waldviertel, not to be confused with the already-visited Weinviertel. That was a trip to the land of the grapes. In the Waldviertel you'll meet forests. From Krems, in the Danube Valley, you can begin your exploration of this history-rich region, much of which can be visited in a day's sightseeing trip, and return to Krems or nearby Dürnstein for the superior food and lodging as night falls.

The area abounds with castles, many in ruins. Two rivers, the Thaya and the Kamp, cross it. Waldviertel means forest sector, and the region lives up to its name, with many wooded uplands as well as river valleys.

Your first stop might be at—

LANGENLOIS: Standing at the top of the Valley of Kamp, Langenlois, six miles from Krems, is known for vineyards from which a good, dry white wine called Schluck is made. In this old market town, complete with Gothic church, you should visit the old buildings of the Altstadt (old town), taking in, among other attractions, a column built in the 13th century to commemorate deliverance from the plague. Many houses dating from the 16th century have arcaded courtyards. Others are from the 17th and 18th centuries, and you'll note differences in building styles. Often the houses are richly painted in pastels, including Maria Theresa ochre.

The area code for Langenlois is 02734.

Where to Eat

Weinschlössl, 1 Dimmelgraben (tel. 3154). Much of the wine served here is produced in the establishment's own wine presses, which lie just a short distance from the dining room. This is very much a family-run enterprise, where no one will mind if your chief ambition is just to savor a glass or a bottle of the most recent vintage.

If dining is your intention, however, you will find a menu filled with tempting items. These include varieties of ham flavored with sherry or madeira, broccoli in a pungent wine sauce, cucumber soup, cabbage strudel with garlic cream sauce, and several veal dishes. For dessert, you might prefer a portion of the local cheese or else one of the homemade pastries. A la carte repasts are priced from 85 AS ($4.52) to 245 AS ($13.03).

The restaurant closes its doors between late January and mid-March and between mid-November and the end of December. The rest of the year, it closes Monday through Wednesday.

From Langenlois, the road heads north through the Kamp Valley to—

GARS AM KAMP: This market town, perched on the east bank of the river, enjoys a modest summer visitor traffic. The Rathaus (town hall) is from the late 16th century.

A much more appealing destination is the romantic town of—

HORN: The major business hub of the eastern Waldviertel, Horn has many buildings of historic interest, including a castle built in the Middle Ages which was given a much later architectural overlay. Armed with a good map, you can set out on many excursions from Horn, especially if you're interested in castles.

Rosenburg Castle, built in the 12th century, has a large courtyard where tournaments were held when knighthood was in flower. Apartments of the edifice, which stands on a rocky slope, contain antiques and much weaponry. Visitors are allowed through only on conducted tours, from 9 a.m. to noon and from 1 to 5 p.m. Admission is 35 AS ($1.86).

Even more important is the nearby **Abbey of Altenburg,** founded in 1144. Reconstruction on this Benedictine religious house began in 1650 and lasted for almost a century. The design of the abbey was the masterpiece of Joseph Mungenast. As the taste for baroque swept the land during that time, the abbey was of course not spared, with the result that some parts of the facade, with onion-shaped domes, appear Byzantine. The lowest point in the abbey's history was when it was used as a barracks for Soviet soldiers during 1945 and 1946.

The abbey cupola was frescoed by the noted baroque painter Paul Troger, whose work I have already mentioned in this chapter. In the crypt are macabre paintings illustrating *The Dance of Death*. The abbey church and its buildings are open April through October from 9 a.m. to noon and from 1 to 5 p.m. for an admission of 30 AS ($1.60). You pay another 20 AS ($1.06) to see the treasury of the abbey, with antiques, objects in gold and silver, and statuary.

From Fuglau, a road leads to **Greillenstein Castle,** which dates from the 14th century although the present structure is more 16th century. Contained within is a Criminal Law Museum, with exhibits of instruments of torture. The property has been the traditional seat of the counts of Kuefstein. You can visit the castle April through October from 9 a.m. to noon and from 1 to 5 p.m. Admission is 30 AS ($1.60).

For your final visit in the Waldviertel, I suggest—

ZWETTL: Many remains of the old city walls, studded with towers and gates, can still be seen in this major hub of traffic and business lying at a loop of the Kamp River near the Ottenstein Dam in the northern sector of the Waldviertel. Two miles northeast of the town lies **Zwettl Abbey** (tel. 2391), a Cistercian religious house founded in 1138, now an architectural mélange of Romanesque, Gothic, and baroque. Its choir, in the late Gothic style, is one of its chief treasures. The cloister is intriguing, with both Romanesque and Gothic touches. The church, whose baroque tower pierces the sky, was built in the 14th century but now has 18th-century overlays. Paul Troger, the noted painter, did pictures on the altarpieces.

The abbey complex is open from the first of May until mid-September from 10 a.m. to noon and from 2 to 5 p.m. The rest of the year the hours are the same except that closing is at 4 p.m. On Sunday it opens at 11 a.m. Admission is 25 AS ($1.33).

BURGENLAND

THE EASTERNMOST and the newest province of Austria, Burgenland is a little border region between East and West which came into being in 1921, formed of German-speaking border areas of what had been Hungary in the Austro-Hungarian Empire and for centuries before that. It's the start of a large, flat steppe (*puszta*) that reaches almost to Budapest, but it also lies practically on the doorstep of Vienna. The province shares a western border with Styria and Lower Austria, and its long eastern boundary separates it from its former fatherland, Hungary.

This area has suffered greatly from wars over the centuries—from tribal ages through long years when it was a part of the Roman Central European country Pannonia, to efforts to add it to the Ottoman Empire, and up to the war-torn times in this century. Burgenland joined Austria after a vote of its citizens in the aftermath of World War I, although when the vote was taken in 1919, its capital, Ödenburg, now called Sopron, chose to remain with Hungary. This accounts for the narrow corridor between the northern and southern parts of the province. The Hungarian city of Sopron actually lies to the west of Lake Neusiedl (Neusiedler See, in German), an important part of Burgenland. Sopron represents a far penetration of what used to be called the Iron Curtain into Austria. The Russians occupied Burgenland from 1945 to 1955, and few of its citizens seemed sorry to see them depart.

Called "the vegetable garden of Vienna," Burgenland is mostly an agricultural province, also growing such products as wheat and fruit. It is noted for its wines, producing more than one-third of all the wine made in Austria. The province is a point where the vast Hungarian plain gradually modulates into the foothills of the eastern Alps, 29% of its area being covered by forest and 7% of its agricultural lands composed of vineyards. Its Pannonian climate means hot summers with little rainfall, but the winters are moderate. For the most part you can enjoy sunny days from early spring until late autumn.

Besides the 2% of the Burgenland population that is Hungarian, many other citizens of the province are not typically Austrian. Some 10% belong to the Croat ethnic group which settled here in the 16th century after fleeing their southern Slav homes before the advance of Turkish armies which brought fear and pillage through the countryside in their path. For hundreds of years the Croats, Hungarians, and German-speaking people have lived together in this area, but the ethnic and religious variety is still reflected in customs, language, dress, legends, folk songs, and folklore. Many Burgenlanders interested in maintaining their traditions wear the traditional garb of their ancestors on Sunday.

This mixture of ethnic stock has resulted in a regional cookery that is among the best in Europe. It has of course been heavily influenced by its eastern neighbors, especially Hungary, as you'll appreciate when you savor gulasches and strudels, as well as goose dishes. Much wild game lives in the wooded areas of Burgenland and is often featured on menus.

The capital of Burgenland, **Eisenstadt,** is a small provincial city which was for many years the home of Joseph Haydn, and the composer is buried here. Each summer there's a festival at **Mörbisch,** using **Lake Neusiedl** (Neusiedler See) as a theatrical backdrop. Neusiedl is the only steppe lake in Central Europe. If you're here in summer, you'll most certainly want to explore it by motorboat. Lots of Viennese are attracted to Burgenland on weekends for sailing and/or birdwatching.

Accommodations in this province are extremely limited, but they're among the least expensive in the country. It's relatively unknown to North Americans, which I consider a pity and recommend that you add it to your itinerary. Like Lower Austria, Burgenland contains many fortresses and castles, often in ruins, but you'll find a few castle hotels in the romantic style, as well as some rather high-class spa establishments with all the modern amenities. **Bad Tatzmannsdorf** is the most important spa in the province, with the best facilities. Or perhaps you'll prefer to settle into a *gasthof*-type place. The spa season in Burgenland lasts from April to October.

This small province is connected to Vienna by both train and bus services. It's estimated that you can drive through it in about 2½ hours. You can also travel between Eisenstadt, capital of the province, and Lake Neusiedl by bus.

1. Eisenstadt

In the early 1920s when Burgenland joined Austria it was a province without a capital, its former seat of government, Ödenburg (now the far-western Hungarian city of Sopron), having voted to remain a part of Hungary. In 1924, realizing that they needed a provincial capital, Burgenlanders agreed on Eisenstadt for the honor. This small town at the foot of the Leitha mountains is only 31 miles southeast of Vienna, at the beginning of the great Hungarian plain. The town is surrounded by vineyards and forests and has lots of fruit trees. It's a convenient stopover for exploring Lake Neusiedl, six miles to the east.

Even before assuming its new role, however, Eisenstadt was not unknown. Mainly it was renowned as the place where the great composer Joseph Haydn lived and worked while under the patronage of the Esterhazys, a powerful family who ruled Eisenstadt and its surrounding area. For a good part of his life (1732–1809) Haydn divided his time between Eisenstadt and the Esterhazy Castle in Hungary. Prince Esterhazy eventually gave the composer his own orchestra and a concert hall in which to perform.

Schloss Esterhazy, the Eisenstadt château of the Esterhazy princes in which Haydn worked, was built on the site of a medieval castle. The Esterhazy clan was a great Hungarian family with vast estates. They claimed descent from Attila the Hun. The Esterhazys helped the Habsburgs gain control in Hungary. So great was their loyalty to Austria that when Napoleon offered the crown of Hungary to Nic Esterhazy in 1809, he refused it.

The schloss, built around an inner courtyard, was designed by the Italian architect Carlone, and fortified because of its strategic position. Carlone started work on the castle in 1663, but subsequently it was remodeled by many other architects, resulting in sweeping alterations to its appearance. In the late 18th and early 19th centuries it was given a baroque pastel facade. On the first floor, the great baronial hall was made into the Haydnsaal, where the composer conducted the orchestra Prince Esterhazy had provided for him and often performed his own works before the Esterhazy court. The walls and ceilings of this concert hall are elaborately decorated, but the floor is of bare wood, which, it is claimed, is the cause of the room's acoustical perfection.

Today, much of the castle is used by officials in administering the affairs of Burgenland, but the Haydnsaal is open to the public. Guided tours, lasting 25 minutes, are conducted, for a minimum of ten persons. Tours leave hourly from 9 a.m. to 5 p.m. (from 10 a.m. to 4 p.m. in winter). Admission is 10 AS (53¢) for adults, 5 AS (27¢) for children.

Haydn House, 21 Haydn-Gasse, the little Eisenstadt home of the composer from 1766 to 1778, has been made into a museum honoring its former tenant. It is open May to October from 9 a.m. to noon and 1 to 5 p.m. Admission is 15 AS (80¢). Although he appeared in court nearly every night, Haydn actually lived very moderately when he was at home. However, the home wasn't exactly bleak, as he had a little flower-filled courtyard. The museum has collected mementos of Haydn's works and life.

If you want to pay your final respects to the memory of Haydn, follow Hauptstrasse, which will connect you to Esterhazystrasse leading to the **Bergkirche** (Church of the Calvary), containing Haydn's tomb, built of white marble.

Until 1954 only the composer's headless body was here. His skull was in the Music Museum in Vienna, where curious spectators were actually allowed to feel it. Haydn's head was stolen a few days after his death and did not get back together with his body for a total of 145 years! The story of how the head traveled from one owner to another—eventually even being sold—before finally, I hope, coming to rest with the other part of Haydn's remains at Eisenstadt is a long and complicated one.

To honor another composer, Franz Liszt, you can leave Eisenstadt going south on the road to the small village of **Raiding.** There the **Liszt Geburthaus,** or Franz Liszt birthplace, is now a museum containing many mementos of the composer's life, including an old church organ he used to play. Liszt's father worked as a bailiff for the princes of Esterhazy, and this was his home when little Franz was born in 1811. The museum is open from Easter until the end of October from 9 a.m. to noon and from 1 to 5 p.m., charging an admission of 15 AS (80¢).

Near Eisenstadt at **St. Margarethen** is an outdoor sculpture gallery with monumental stone art at a quarry. Sculptors have done carvings on the site instead of taking the material for their artwork back to their studios.

Eisenstadt's area code is 02682.

FOOD AND LODGING: **Rosenberger Hotel Burgenland,** Schubertplatz (tel. 5521), is a dramatically designed contemporary hotel with a modified mansard roof, white stucco walls, and big windows. The comfortable bedrooms have lots of light, wood-grained headboards, and simple furniture. A swimming pool, a sauna, two restaurants, and a café are on the premises. With breakfast included, singles rent for 620 AS ($32.98) to 720 AS ($38.30), while doubles range from 860 AS ($45.75) to 1,020 AS ($54.26), depending on the season. All accommodations have private bath, TV, radio, and mini-bar. Half board is another 150 AS ($7.98).

One of the best restaurants in Burgenland is the in-house **G'wū-stöckl,** open daily from noon to 2:30 p.m. and from 6 to 11 p.m. Of bright, airy, modern design, it specializes in such dishes as cabbage soup, veal steak with fresh vegetables, and a host of other platters sometimes influenced strongly by the kitchens of Hungary. Fixed-price meals range from 190 AS ($10.11) to 550 AS ($29.26), while à la carte meals go from 160 AS ($8.51) to 300 AS ($15.96). Reservations are suggested.

Parkhotel Mikschi, 38 Haydngasse (tel. 4361), is a modern hotel in the center of town. Its prominent balconies shelter big windows and look out over a sunny garden. Inside, the contemporary public rooms have a wintertime fireplace encased in modern brick with a copper hearth. Singles rent for 590 AS ($31.39), while doubles go for 790 AS ($42.03), with a buffet breakfast included. All rooms have bath, refrigerator, phone, and wall-to-wall carpeting.

Hotel Eder Zum Goldenen Adler, 25 Hauptstrasse (tel. 2645), is a cozily decorated family-style guest house filled with wooden furniture, deer antlers, and iron chandeliers. A garden terrace is surrounded with a thick wall of greenery, while the simple bedrooms are clean and comfortable. Singles rent for 240 AS ($12.77) to 290 AS ($15.34), while doubles range from 195 AS ($10.37) to 290 AS ($15.34) per person. The hotel's restaurant serves hot and cold Austrian and Hungarian specialties at reasonable prices.

2. Lake Neusiedl

This lake, called Neusiedler See in German, is a true steppe lake lying in the northern part of Burgenland. It has been described as strange and mysterious, and is certainly like no lake familiar to North Americans. It was part of a body of water that once blanketed all of the Pannonian Plain. Today it's only about six feet deep at its lowest point, and the wind can shift the water dramatically, causing parts of the lake to become dry at times. A broad belt of reeds encircles the huge expanse of lake, about 115 square miles. It's roughly between 4¼ and 9¼ miles wide, and about 22 miles long. If you're tall enough you could walk across it, but I'm not recommending that!

Because of the curvature of the earth, the middle of the lake is about 80 feet higher than the longitudinal axis. The Neusiedler See possesses no natural outlets. Its water is slightly salty, and the plants and animal life here are unique in Europe. This is the meeting place of alpine, Baltic, and Pannonian flora and fauna. Some 200 different species of birds inhabit the lake area, resting on its reeds, including the Rust stork.

Destinations along the lake include:

ILLMITZ: This old *puszta* (steppe) village lying on the east side of the lake has grown into a town which does a slight tourist business in summer. This is steppe country, and a tourist brochure issued by the town pictures the most characteristic part of the landscape, a traditional rural Hungarian-type well with long wooden poles which are used to draw up water.

Leaving Illmitz and heading toward the border, you come to the village of **St. Andrä bei Frauenkirchen,** where you'll see thatch houses. The little town is known for its basket-weaving, so you might want to drive here for a shopping expedition.

A short drive farther will take you to **Andau,** which became the focus of world attention in 1956 during the Hungarian uprising. It was through this point, almost on the border, that hundreds of Hungarians dashed to freedom in the West, fleeing the grim massacres of Budapest.

From the town you can see the closely guarded border, with its forbidding barbed-wire fences and watchtowers on the Communist side, where guards are prepared to shoot Hungarians who might attempt to escape. This is not a particularly happy place for a vacation, but it's a fascinating piece of geography between the East and the West.

What makes the place intriguing, however, is that the surrounding marshy area of this remote sector of Austria, called **Seewinkel,** is a haven for birds and contains many rare flora, plus many small *puszta* animals. This is a large natural wildlife sanctuary. You'll see a few windmills and expanses of reeds which are used to make roofs and shelters.

This area, very different from the celebrated Austria of alpine and Wienerwald lore, is little known to North Americans, and therefore a visit here can qualify as an offbeat adventure. For devotees of geography, it's a fine part of Central Europe for exploration, with sights you won't see elsewhere.

The area code for Illmitz is 02175.

Food and Lodging

Heurigenrestaurant/Pension Rosenhof, 1 Floriangasse (tel. 2232), is a charming baroque building in an agricultural area a block from the main highway running through the center of town. Its gold and white facade includes an arched gateway, which takes visitors into a rose-laden courtyard filled with arbors. A tile-covered sister building, capped with platforms for storks' nests, contains the cozy bedrooms. Doubles cost from 450 AS ($23.94) with breakfast included.

In an older section is the pleasant wine restaurant where the star attraction is the recent vintage produced by the Haider family's wine presses. Many of your fellow diners live in the neighborhood, and they enjoy the Hungarian and Burgenlander specialties as much as you do. In the evening, musicians fill the air with gypsy music.

Gasthof Zentral, Obere Hauptstrasse (tel. 2312), in spite of its name, does not contain overnight accommodations. However, its pleasant restaurant is well worth the stopover. On sunny summer days, a member of the Kroiss family will offer a table on the shaded garden terrace, unless you prefer a place in the impeccably clean wood-trimmed dining room. Both fish specialties and Hungarian dishes, along with traditional Austrian food, are offered. Full meals cost from 180 AS ($9.58).

HALBTURN: North of St. Andrä, if you go through Frauenkirchen you reach the hamlet of Halbturn, which lies within a stone's throw of the Austria-Hungary border. Here you'll find a lovely baroque concoction designed by the architect Lukas von Hildebrandt, which was used as a summer palace by Empress Maria Theresa and her large brood. It's surrounded by well-laid-out park grounds forming a handsome setting for this landmark of luxurious imperial living, standing in curious contrast to the sparsely settled, bleak villages in the far-western extremities of Hungary.

This was originally a hunting lodge which was destroyed by the Turks during the siege of 1683 and rebuilt by Hildebrandt in the 18th century. It was again partially burned in 1949 in the postwar era when it was part of the Soviet-occupied zone. In the central hall is a ceiling painted by F. A. Maulbertsch, done in 1765 and considered his masterpiece.

Visits are possible in summer from 9 a.m. to noon and from 1 to 5 p.m. for an admission of 25 AS ($1.33).

PODERSDORF: If you head west from Frauenkirchen, you reach Podersdorf am See, one of the finest places for swimming on the mysterious lake, as its shoreline is relatively free of reeds. This attracts visitors, and the little town has become a modest summer resort. The parish church in the village is from the late 18th century. You'll see many storks nesting atop chimneys, and some of the cottages have thatch roofs. The Viennese like to drive out here on a summer Sunday to go for a swim and also to purchase wine from the local vintners.

Podersdorf's area code is 02177.

Food and Lodging

Haus Attila, 1 Strandplatz (tel. 415), sits directly on the water. Its light-grained balconies are concealed with a brake of trees. The bedrooms are comfortable, clean, and filled with livable furniture. In the basement you'll find a well-stocked wine cellar where a member of the Karner family might take you for a visit. Apartments rent for 320 AS ($17.02) to 420 AS ($22.34) per person daily, with breakfast included.

Gasthof Seewirt, 1 Strandplatz (tel. 415), stands close to the Haus Attila. This pleasant hotel sits at the edge of the lake, with a wide expanse of deserted marshland close by. The bedrooms are comfortable and the public rooms include a rustically modern restaurant, a café terrace, and an indoor sauna. Doubles cost from 270 AS ($14.36) to 360 AS ($19.15) per person daily.

Gasthaus Karner, 14 Neusiedlerstrasse (tel. 256). There are more modern hotels closer to the lake, but few of those offer the old-fashioned charm of this one. It sits on a centrally located street a few blocks from the lake. Its windows are ringed with country baroque trim which attractively offsets the dark green facade and white trim. A restaurant inside offers wholesome Teutonic food and old-fashioned recipes. Per person rates in a comfortably furnished single or double range from 180 AS ($9.58) to 220 AS ($11.70), with breakfast included.

KITTSEE: On to the north in the direction of Bratislava, Czechoslovakia, is the Austrian border town of Kittsee, where a Count Esterhazy (of the same family that ruled in Eisenstadt and sponsored the composer Haydn there) had a baroque castle erected, beginning in 1730. Toward the southeast sector of the village is the Czechoslovakian frontier.

En route to Bratislava is a colony of residential houses with a startling name for this area—**Chicago.** It was named by an emigré who likened the pace of construction to what he'd known as a laborer in Chicago, Illinois.

NEUSIEDL AM SEE: At the top of Lake Neusiedl on the north bank lies this popular stopover, which is likely to be crowded on summer weekends. Water sports prevail here, and sailboats can be rented. The parish church, in the Gothic style, is noted for its "ship pulpit." A watchtower from the Middle Ages still stands guard over the town, although it's no longer manned. Many vineyards cover the nearby acreage. If you plan to be here on a weekend in summer, I advise you to make a reservation ahead.

The area code for Neusiedl am See is 02167.

Food and Lodging

Hotel Wende, 40 Seestrasse (tel. 8111). Its walls are dotted with maps of Burgenland, and many menu items in its dining room are recipes from the region. The place is actually a complex of three sprawling buildings, each interconnected with rambling corridors dotted with conference rooms and contemporary accessories. Set at the edge of town, on the road leading to the water, the hotel is almost a village unto itself.

The aura is one of clean but slightly sterile propriety, although the indoor pool and sauna, along with the glass-enclosed clubhouse, add notes of diversion. The in-house restaurant is well known, offering such dishes as wild game in season, rumpsteak Hotel Wende, several pork specialties, veal piccata, and roast beef Esterhazy style. Full meals cost from 380 AS ($20.22).

Depending on the room assignment and the season, comfortably furnished bedrooms cost from 340 AS ($18.09) to 600 AS ($31.92) in a single and from 450 AS ($23.94) to 510 AS ($27.13) in a double. Both the hotel and restaurant are closed for the last week in January and the first week in February.

Gasthof zur Traube, 9 Hauptplatz (tel. 423), stands on the bustling main street of town. The pleasant restaurant on the ground floor is illuminated with leaded-glass windows and filled with country-style trim and wrought-iron table dividers. You can stop in for a meal or else book one of the cozy upstairs bedrooms for an overnight stay (you have to register at the bar in back of the restaurant). Franz Rittsteuer and his family are the owners. With breakfast included, they charge 240 AS ($12.77) in a single and 480 AS ($25.54) in a double. Unlike many guesthouses in Burgenland, this one remains open all year.

PURBACH AM SEE: If you take the road south from the area around the northern tip of Lake Neusiedl, your first stopover might be in this little resort village which has some decent accommodations. Purbach is also a market town, and you can buy Burgenland wine in the shops. Some of the town walls, built against invading Turks, still stand.

The area code for Purbach am See is 02683.

Food and Lodging

Am Spitz (tel. 5519). The main building of this hotel has unusual baroque embellishments rounding out the angular sections of the frontal gable. When you enter you'll see unusual stucco detailing in the rounded columns of the restaurant and bar area, lots of weathered timbers and ceiling beams, and a scattering of antiques. The Hölzl-Schwarz family are your efficient hosts here, charging from 300 AS ($15.96) in a double. Many of the accommodations have panoramic views of the lake. The adjoining restaurant, rustically decorated, is one of the best places in the region for Burgenland cookery. Specialties include chicken soup, bacon salad, lamb cutlets with potatoes and spinach, and an array of local wines. À la carte meals cost from 300 AS ($15.96). Reservations are suggested, and the gasthof is closed from mid-December through February.

Nikolauszeche (tel. 5514). In a niche high above the rest of the baroque decor, someone has placed a statue that looks more like the Madonna than the namesake of this establishment, Saint Nicholas. The food, however, is authentically regional, attracting a wide cross section of Austrians, many of whom travel from Vienna. Once here, they can order the rich bouillon or cabbage soup, the Hungarian fogosch, and the chef's special ham crêpes, plus selecting from a well-chosen wine list. The gypsy music can sometimes be overwhelming. If you seek privacy and quiet, you can gravitate to an interior courtyard, finding a quiet corner for an intimate conversation. The restaurant is closed Wednesday, and à la carte meals cost from 400 AS ($21.28). Reservations are suggested.

Leaving Purbach and taking the road south toward Eisenstadt, you can veer off on a secondary road southeast along the lakeshore to our final destinations, which are also provided with limited accommodations. The first stopover is at—

RUST: This colorfully named summer resort—famous for its stork nests built on chimneys throughout the town—stands right on the lakeshore. The heart of Rust is an old town section that is well preserved and immaculately ready for your inspection. Its walls were built in 1614 as protection against the Turks.

The little resort has a gemütlich atmosphere, especially on weekends. Summers tend to be hot, and the water of the lake is warm. Sailboats and windsurfers are rented for touring the Neusiedler See, where the shallowness of the waters relieves you of much fear of drowning, except for small children.

Rust might be called the capital of the Burgenland lake district. The town lies in a rich setting of vineyards which produce the celebrated Burgenlander grape. If it's available, you should try the Blaufränkisch, a red wine which seems to be consumed entirely either locally or by the Viennese, who flock to the area and often return home with bottles of the wine of the region. Sometimes you can go right up to the door of a vintner's farmhouse, especially if a green bough is displayed, and sample wine and buy it on the spot, as at a heurige.

On my last visit during August, the taverns in the town had lively gypsy music. Some local residents, when the wine is in their blood, like to dance in regional costume wearing high boots. You're left with the distinct impression that you're in Hungary.

The Rust area code is 02685.

Food and Lodging

Seehotel Rust (tel. 381), one of the most attractive hotels in the lake district, is well designed and modern, set on a grassy lawn at the edge of the lake. It has an appealing series of connected balconies, rounded towers that look vaguely medieval, and a series of recessed loggias set into the slope of the roofline. The ceiling beams of the big-windowed restaurant sweep dramatically up toward the central lighting fixture, while a series of floor-mounted lamps curve over many of the immaculate tablecloths like spokes of an umbrella. Food items include tafelspitz with chive sauce, calf brains with a honey vinegar, watercress soup, and sole meunière.

On the premises of the hotel are an indoor swimming pool, a sauna, two tennis courts, and a bar area. The pleasant bedrooms are decorated with a combination of white plaster and blond wood. A gypsy band sometimes provides the evening's entertainment. À la carte meals in the restaurant range from 300 AS ($15.96). Bedrooms cost from 790 AS ($42.03) to 950 AS ($50.54) in a single and 585 AS ($31.12) to 720 AS ($38.30) per person in a double, with half board included.

Hotel Sifkovits, 8 Am Seekanal (tel. 276), offers a concrete and stucco facade fashioned into sloping rows of well-planted balconies. An older wing has a format of red tile roofs and big windows which sometimes cover entire walls. The bedrooms get a lot of sun and are comfortably streamlined. Other facilities include a sauna, an exercise room, a café, a sun terrace, and outdoor tennis courts. Singles range from 215 AS ($11.44) to 510 AS ($27.13), while doubles cost from 215 AS ($11.44) to 460 AS ($24.47) per person. Prices, of course, depend on the season and the accommodation.

Eselmühle (tel. 2223) at St. Margarethen is an interesting and summer fun establishment built around a defunct water wheel. It's about two miles from the center of Rust, and you'll probably find that the food is worth traveling the distance. You'll be greeted with the strains of live Hungarian music, which will certainly whet your appetite for the country-style hors d'oeuvres. These might include paprika-flavored pork, thinly sliced ham, and smoked eel. Soups include classic Burgenland varieties, often heavily spiced, and a delectable Hungarian fish soup called halaszle. Marinated meat dishes include sauerbraten with homemade noodles and sauerkraut. Many of the clients are local residents, who pay about 360 AS ($19.15) for dinner. Reservations are suggested, and the restaurant is open until midnight.

MÖRBISCH: Our final stopover along the lake, near the Hungarian border, is this charming little, typical Burgenlander lakeside hamlet. There's a small bathing beach and mineral springs, the water of which is bottled for sale. The town fills up in August when the lakeside outdoor theater presents operettas such as *The Merry Widow*. Wine-tasting festivals are also a Mörbisch feature, especially on Sunday when the Viennese flock here.

With such excitement and festivity, it's hard to accept that the grim, closely guarded Hungarian border is so near by.

The area code for Mörbisch is 02685.

Food and Lodging

Hotel Steiner (tel. 8218) has an attractively simple cream-colored facade with one recessed balcony covered with flowers. With 110 beds, it's big enough usually to have an empty room, but quiet enough to afford relaxing comfort. The Steiner family, your hosts, rent rustically modern bedrooms, where singles range from 400 AS ($21.28) to 440 AS ($23.41) and doubles from 330 AS ($17.56) to 440 AS ($23.41) per person, depending on the plumbing and the season. On the premises are a sauna, a heated swimming pool, and an appealing restaurant.

South of Eisenstadt lies one of the most romantic and charming accommodations in all of Burgenland. It's at—

3. Drassburg

Hotel Schloss Drassburg (tel. 02686/2220). Parts of this castle date from the 14th century, although what you'll see today is an 18th-century facade of ochre paint and white trim. It's owned by the Baroness Maria von Patzenhofer, who rents about 30 of the bedrooms to paying guests. The vaulted interior is lavishly equipped, usually in an antique style with a heavy emphasis on the baroque. Near the Hungarian border and some ten miles south of Eisenstadt, the estate includes about two dozen acres of parkland designed by Le Nôtre, the landscape architect of Versailles.

The water of the indoor swimming pool surrounds a few of the masonry columns that support the overhead vaulting. There's also an outdoor pool, plus tennis courts. Persons interested in horseback riding often book in here for long weekends, although even overnight guests can rent a horse from a nearby stable. Singles range from 440 AS ($23.41) to 680 AS ($36.18), while doubles cost from 400 AS ($21.80) to 600 AS ($31.92) per person. All units contain private baths. An excellent breakfast costs an additional 100 AS ($5.32) per person.

4. Forchtenstein

After leaving the lake district, you can head south from Eisenstadt toward the narrow "waistline" of the province, a small corridor between north and south Burgenland created when Ödenburg, then the capital (now the Hungarian far-western frontier city of Sopron), voted to remain with the fatherland and be ruled by Budapest. Many of the people of Forchtenstein grow fruit.

Visitors come here chiefly to get a look at **Forchtenstein Castle**, lying in Burgenland, nine miles southeast of Wiener Neustadt in Lower Austria. From a belvedere here you can see as far as the great plain of Hungary. The castle was constructed on a rock on orders of the counts of Mattersdorf in the 13th century. The Esterhazy family had it greatly expanded around 1636.

The castle saw action in the Turkish sieges of Austria, both in 1529 and in 1683. You can see a handsome collection of armory here, some captured from the fleeing Turks. But they didn't all get away. Turkish prisoners carved out of the rock the castle cistern, more than 450 feet deep. There's also a display of "memorabilia of the hunt," as it is described here.

The castle may be visited from 10 a.m. to 5 p.m. (to 4 p.m. in winter). Admission is 29 AS ($1.53).

Forchtenstein's area code is 02626.

FOOD AND LODGING: Gasthof Sauerzapf, 9 Rosalienstrasse (tel. 8217), is a long grange-like building with two stories of weathered stucco, renovated windows, and a roofline that's red on one side and black on another. The updated interior is cozy and appealing, albeit simple, and is kept immaculately. Franz Sauerzapf and his family charge 160 AS ($8.51) in a single and from 160 AS ($8.51) to 180 AS ($9.58) per person in a double, with breakfast included. Prices depend on the plumbing and the season. The gasthof is closed in October. The in-house restaurant serves good food and a full array of local wines.

Gasthof Wutzlhofer, 12 Rosalia (tel. 32-45-11). The view from the rooms of this family-run stucco guest house encompasses all of the valley and many square miles of forested hills. Inside you'll find a late 1950s–style decor. In keeping with that spirit, you'll even find a jukebox in the striped and wood-paneled bar area. Herbert Wutzlhofer, the owner, charges from 140 AS ($7.45) to 160 AS ($8.51) per person, in either a single or a double, with breakfast included. Prices depend on the plumbing and the accommodation.

Reisner (tel. 3139) serves garden-fresh vegetables in a rustic setting, with especially good steaks. The main dining room is perfectly acceptable, but my favorite is the cozily rustic stüberl, which seems to be preferred by the locals as well. You might enjoy trout filet served with a savory ragoût of tomatoes, zucchini, potatoes, and basil, or the sautéed sweetbreads with beans and a yogurt-vinaigrette dressing over cabbage. À la carte meals range from 120 AS ($6.38) to 320 AS ($17.02). The restaurant is closed on Wednesday, and reservations are suggested otherwise.

5. Bernstein

This little market village lying in the Valley of the Tauchen is known for its castle, which ranks along with the just-visited Drassburg Castle for providing the most dramatic accommodations in Burgenland (see below).

Bernstein is also known for its serpentine stone, a jet-green stone sometimes called Bernstein jade. Workers polish the stone here, and it can be purchased in the shops, although much of it is shipped around the world. It's shaped into ornaments of many different types.

The area code for Bernstein is 03354.

WHERE TO STAY: Hotel Burg Bernstein (tel. 220). Initially constructed during the era of Charlemagne (around A.D. 800), most of the castle you will see today was built in the 13th century, with thick stone walls and towers, plus small windows along the outer walls. The owners were so preoccupied with defending themselves from invaders that they even surrounded the 120-meter-deep well with a defensive stone tower.

In 1953 this rich piece of history was converted into a hotel and furnished with antiques appropriate to its status as a historic monument. Its dining room has a stone floor and an ornate baroque ceiling. Most of the bedrooms are baronial and are filled with beautiful pieces of craftsmanship.

The castle is said to have a resident ghost. Its long-ago former owner, a medieval lord, Graf Uilaky, reportedly returned home from a siege somewhere in Hungary only to discover his wife in bed with one of the male servants. He slashed out the heart of the hapless servant, but for his adulterous wife he showed he was no women's liberation advocate. He sealed her up in her bedroom and left her there to die of thirst and starvation. Her "ghost" is still reported to roam the place on dark nights.

Singles cost 450 AS ($23.94) while doubles go for 900 AS ($47.88), with breakfast included. The hotel is open from April through September.

6. Bad Tatzmannsdorf

The best known spa of the province, nine miles south of Bernstein, lies in a heavily forested valley. Its springs and baths, said to be beneficial to certain cardiac patients and for female ailments, have been used for centuries. Many Hungarians from Budapest spent part of their summers here in earlier, freer times.

Naturally, the resort has a Kurpark, where on a summer evening entertainment is likely to be presented. There's also an open-air museum where many ancient structures moved from the surrounding valley have been placed on exhibit.

The area code for Bad Tatzmannsdorf is 03353.

FOOD AND LODGING: Parkhotel (tel. 287) is constructed in a modern format of several different beige and white sections connected together in a flowering garden. Many of the rooms have private balconies, which open into the comfortable and pleasing sleeping areas with lots of paneling and tasteful furniture. The public rooms are padded and upholstered with built-in banquettes in buff-colored velvet near big windows, while an outdoor café affords a relaxing getaway on a warm day. The Anderle family are the distinguished owners of this hotel, charging 480 AS ($25.54) in a single and 820 AS ($43.62) to 950 AS ($50.54) for a double, with breakfast, taxes, and service included. Half and full board are offered only for stays of seven days or more.

Hotel Zum Kastell, 6 Joseph Haydnplatz (tel. 428). On a summer day, guests of this attractive, modern hotel gather on the sun terrace or on one of the private balconies attached to their bedrooms. Many of the private accommodations are decorated in firecracker colors such as hot orange, along with autumn browns. Seats in the dignified restaurant are usually fashioned in a banquette format around circular tables, with cluster chandeliers hanging near the arched windows. A less formal restaurant is cozily outfitted with terracotta tiles and upholstered wooden chairs. Many of the summertime guests have moved in for a week or more as part of their annual vacations, but if you want to stay for just a night, singles rent for 315 AS ($16.75) to 380 AS ($20.22), while doubles range from 315 As ($16.75) to 345 AS ($18.35) per person, with breakfast included.

Hotel/Pension Sonnenhof, 33 Parkstrasse (tel. 417), is a big-windowed, balconied hotel set on a hillside with a view of a collection of old farmhouses in the distance. Maria Janisch is the kindly owner of this simple but well-maintained establishment, charging from 225 AS ($11.97) to 275 AS ($14.63) per person in a double, with a continental breakfast included. Half board is offered for another 85 AS ($4.52) per person daily.

7. Heiligenkreuz

If you're looking for a tranquil hideaway, this is it! No one will ever find you in this, one of the most remote places recommended in this guide (not to be confused with Heiligenkreuz, the Cistercian Abbey west of Baden). This little town lies in the far-southern tip of Burgenland, right next to the Hungarian frontier, near the confluence of the Raab and the Lafnitz. There are many thatch houses in the area, which is known and treasured by the Austrians. If a North American turns up here, it's considered a rarity.

Heiligenkreuz is near a battle site where General Montecuccoli defeated the Turks in 1664, a fact honored by Rainer Maria Rilke, the noted German epic poet, in *The Cornets.*

From this peaceful town, you can head for nearby Hungary or Yugoslavia, although a visa is required to enter either country.

The Heiligenkreuz area code is 03325.

FOOD AND LODGING: **Gasthof Edith Gibiser** (tel. 216) is one of my favorite hotels in the region. Thanks partly to the concerned service given by the namesake of the hotel, it's a pleasant and well-maintained place to stay during your tour of Burgenland. The exterior is a symmetrical white country-style villa with comfortable horizontal lines and pink and white detailing around each of the rectangular windows. The interior is tastefully paneled in a format of modern rusticity. Rooms are comfortably and attractively furnished, with singles ranging from 175 AS ($9.31) to 260 AS ($13.83), while doubles cost from 220 AS ($11.70) to 320 AS ($17.02) per person, with breakfast included. For half board, she charges 380 AS ($20.22) to 420 AS ($22.34) per person. Four private cottages are available in the garden.

The adjoining restaurant serves well-prepared meals on beautiful china, and is usually filled with flowers. Specialties of the house include cabbage soup, fried pike-perch, and steak Cordon Rouge (stuffed with goose liver and served with fresh mushrooms). Meals cost between 75 AS ($3.99) and 340 AS ($18.09). The restaurant is open all day long every day of the week (except Monday during the period from November until May).

SALZBURG

A BAROQUE CITY on the banks of the Salzach River, Salzburg, set against a mountain backdrop, is the beautiful capital of the Austrian province of Land Salzburg. The city and the river were so named because many of the early residents earned their living in the salt mines in the region. The site of Salzburg was once the Roman town of Juvavum.

This "heart of the heart of Europe" is the city of Mozart, who was born here in 1756. The composer's association with the city beefs up tourism even today, providing major revenue to the area.

This fact carries a certain irony, because Mozart wasn't all that appreciated in Salzburg in his lifetime. But since his death almost 200 years ago, his image seems to be everywhere. A square bears his name. A statue in its center honors him. A music academy is named for him. And of course his music dominates the Salzburg Festival. Too bad he couldn't have been more honored when he was still around to enjoy it. He died in Vienna on December 5, 1791, and the sad truth is that the body of the 35-year-old musical genius was carried in a pauper's hearse to a common grave in the cemetery of St. Marx in the Austrian capital.

The old town of Salzburg lies on the left bank of the river where a monastery and bishopric were founded in 700. From that start, Salzburg grew in power and prestige, becoming an archbishopric in 798. In the heyday of the prince-archbishops, the city became known as the "German Rome." The little province known as **Land Salzburg**, of which Salzburg is the capital, still occupies much the same space in the mountains of west-central Austria as shown on maps of the Middle Ages designated as "church lands." It was in the Holy Roman Empire, a part of Germany until it was joined to Austria in 1816 after the Congress of Vienna.

Salzburg is a city of 17th- and 18th-century houses and for the most part, has a worldwide reputation for the grandeur of its architecture. Much of that work was done by those masters of the baroque, Fischer von Erlach and Lukas von Hildebrandt.

As well as being the scene of the celebrated Salzburg Festival, this is where

Max Reinhardt staged Hugo von Hoffmannsthal's miracle play *Everyman* (*Jedermann*, in German) in 1920, an event which has become a tradition.

Salzburg lies a short distance from the Austria-West Germany frontier, so it's convenient for exploring many of the nearby sightseeing attractions of Bavaria. On the northern slopes of the Alps, the city is at the intersection of traditional European trade routes and is well served today by air, autobahn, and railroad.

The area code for Salzburg and its suburb of Aigen is 0662. For Anif, it is 06246, and for Bergheim 06222.

AN ORIENTATION: Most visitors head for the **old town,** which lies on the left bank of the Salzach, that part stretching from the river to the Mönchsberg. This is a section of narrow streets (many from the Middle Ages) and slender houses. This part of Salzburg is in complete contrast with the town constructed by the Prince Bishops, which lies between the Neutor and the Neugebäude. The bishops created a town of magnificent buildings and large, airy squares.

The heart of the old section, on the left bank of the Salzach, is the **Residenzplatz,** with its splendid Unterberg marble baroque fountain.

The newer part of town is on the right bank of the Salzach, below the **Kapuzinerberg,** which is the right bank counterpart of the Mönchsberg. This peak rises 2,090 feet, and is a lovely woodland.

Mönchsberg itself, to the west of Hohensalzburg, is a mountain ridge slightly less than two miles long. It rises over the old town.

1. Practical Facts

TRANSPORTATION: City buses: A quick, comfortable service is provided through the center of the city from the Nonntal car park to Sigmundsplatz, the city center car park. Service is Monday to Friday from 9 a.m. to 6 p.m., Saturday from 9 a.m. to noon. Fares are 10 AS (53¢) for one ride for an adult, 5 AS (26¢) for a child.

Reduced-fare tickets may be purchased at the local railway station (opposite the main railway station), at the ticket counter of the cable train up to Hohensalzburg Fortress, from conductors of the lift to Mönchsberg, and in 91 tobacco shops in the city which are specially marked. These tickets are sold in blocks of five and ten at a reduction of 20% off the regular fare.

For **information** on all bus transportation, telephone 71-2-10. *Be warned:* Buses stop running at 11 p.m.

Taxis: You'll find taxi ranks scattered at key points all over the city center and in the suburbs. Salzburg Funktaxi-Vereinigung (radio taxis) office is at 27 Rainerstrasse (tel. 76-1-11). To order a taxi in advance, telephone 74-4-00.

Horse-drawn cabs (fiacres): At Residenzplatz. Four persons pay 280 AS ($14.90) for a half-hour ride, 550 AS ($29.26) for an hour's jaunt.

USEFUL INFORMATION: The **City Tourist Office** is at 7 Auerspergstrasse (tel. 74-6-20 or 71-5-11). The **Land Tourist Office,** where you can get information on the Land Salzburg province, is at 1 Mozartplatz, opposite the Mozart monument (tel. 41-5-61).

You'll find the main **railway station** at 17 Südtiroler Platz (tel. 70-5-51). **Flughafen Salzburg,** the airport, is at 95 Innsbrucken Bundestrasse (tel. 45-3-23).

Information on various problems or answers to **emergency** needs are available by telephone as follows: police—133; fire—122; ambulance—144. The

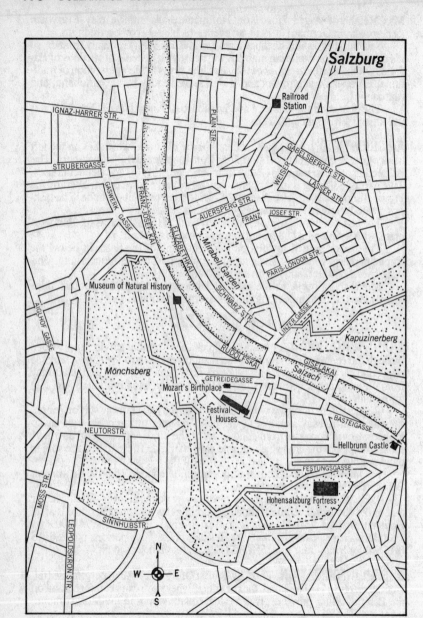

Salzburg

Medical Emergency Center, at 8a Paris-Lodron-Strasse (tel. 75-3-50), is open from 7 a.m. Saturday to 7 a.m. Monday and on public holidays.

For information on medical **doctors, specialists, and dentists,** call Ärzte-kammer für Salzburg, 2 Schrannengasse (tel. 71-3-72 or 71-3-28); Österr. Dentistenkammer, 22 Bergstrasse (tel. 73-9-06).

Drugstores are open Monday to Friday from 8 a.m. to 12:30 p.m. and from 2:30 to 6 p.m., on Saturday from 8 a.m. to noon. For night or Sunday service, shops display a sign giving the address of the nearest pharmacy open.

Banks are open Monday to Friday from 8 a.m. to noon and from 2 to 4:30 p.m. Money can be changed at the main railway station daily from 7 a.m. to 10 p.m. and at the airport from 9 a.m. to 4 p.m.

The **American Express** office, 5 Mozartplatz (tel. 42-5-01), is open Monday to Friday from 9 a.m. to 5:30 p.m., on Saturday from 9 a.m. to noon.

The main **post office** is at 9 Residenzplatz (tel. 44-1-21). The post office at the main railway station is open all year 24 hours a day.

If you need help from the **U.S. Consul General,** you'll find the Consulate General of the United States of America at 51 Giselakai (tel. 28-6-01), open Monday to Friday from 9 to 11 a.m. and 2 to 4 p.m.

Lost something? Try the Police Headquarters and **Lost Property Office,** 1 Churfürststrasse (tel. 44-5-57).

Parking: To park downtown, try the City Center parking facility in Mönchsberg, open day and night. On the right bank there's the Mirabell car park on Mirabellplatz, open from 7 a.m. to midnight. The Raiffersen facility, 13-15 Schwarzstrasse, keeps the same hours as Mirabell. There are attended car-parking facilities at Hellbrunn, Franz-Josef-Kai, Glockingasse, and the airport.

Car breakdown service needed? Try SAMTC (Salzburg Automobile Service), 102 Alpenstrasse (tel. 20-5-01/24); or ARBÖ (Motorists Association), 9 Münchner Bundesstrasse (tel. 0662/33-6-01), 7 a.m. to 7 p.m. daily. The emergency number is 1-2-3.

If you need to wash clothes, you'll find **"laundrettes"** available: Constructa, 10 Kaiserschutzenstrasse, opposite the main railway station (tel. 76-2-53); and Norge, 16 Paris-Lodron-Strasse (tel. 76-3-81).

2. Where to Stay

Some of the finest accommodations, particularly the schloss hotels or even converted farmhouse pensions, lie on the outskirts of Salzburg, within an easy drive of the city. However, for the most part they're suitable only for motorists. If you don't have a car, then you may want to consider one of the hostelries right in the city—within walking distance of all the major sightseeing attractions. If you're driving, you may want to read Chapter VIII before selecting a hotel. Since the hotels of Salzburg are often very crowded in the summer (and are impossibly booked during the Salzburg Festival in August), many travel-wise Europeans reserve one of the less expensive accommodations in "Land Salzburg," from which they then drive into Salzburg.

THE DELUXE CHOICES: The **Goldener Hirsch,** 37 Getreidegasse (tel. 84-85-11), wins the award as the finest hotel in Salzburg. It's so steeped in legend and history that the mention of its name in Austria evokes instant recognition. It sits in an enviable position in the old city, a few buildings from Mozart's birthplace. The hotel is composed of three medieval townhouses joined together in an intimate labyrinth of rustically elegant hallways and staircases. Sections of the thick walls date from 1407 and required extensive renovations after Count Emmanuel and Countess Harriet von Walderdorff took over the buildings after World War II.

Today their son Johannes is the alert general manager whose clientele is considerably more sophisticated than it was when the place was set up as an inn in 1564. The hotel is built on a small scale, yet it absolutely reeks of patrician elegance which is enhanced by the superb service of the staff, many of whom are dressed in gray and forest-green Styrian suits. The decor throughout the hotel, from its huntsman-style bar to its impeccably elegant restaurant (see my dining recommendation) includes alpine antiques, stag horns, and well-crafted wood and stone detailing.

This is the kind of hotel where you can dial a staff member for virtually anything from flowers to theater tickets. If you arrive by car, you can double park in front of the Getreidegasse entrance or at the Sigmundsplatz entrance, and a staff member will take your vehicle to the hotel's garage.

Rooms are beautifully furnished and maintained, renting for 1,600 AS ($85.12) to 2,200 AS ($117.04) in a single and 2,100 AS ($111.72) to 4,000 AS ($212.80) in a double. All prices are slightly higher at the time of the Salzburg Festival.

The **Salzburg Sheraton Hotel,** 4 Auerspergstrasse (tel. 79-32-10), one of the crown jewels in the Sheraton chain, opened in 1984 in a desirable location about 10 pedestrian minutes from the Mozartplatz. An older hotel was demolished to make room for the dignified new structure, half of whose 165 bedrooms look out over the formal Mirabell Park. The Austrian architect who designed this place took pains to incorporate it into its 19th-century neighborhood, specifying that the exterior be capped with a mansard roof and that the casement windows be ringed with elaborate trim. As you enter, the lobby opens to reveal a plushly intimate piano bar outfitted in alluring designs of burnished brass, richly grained wood, art nouveau trappings, and sun-flooded views of the garden. What might be the best-valued luncheon buffet in town is served in the cream-and-crystal Mirabell Room, which is rapidly earning its place among the best restaurants of Salzburg. A less formal bistro offers daily specials, wine, and beer in wood-lined cubbyholes illuminated with iron street lamps.

Each bedroom contains its own private bath, with floor-to-ceiling tiles designed by Valentino, built-in headboards, concealed mini-bar, thick wall-to-wall carpeting, color TV, radio, phone, and an array of in-house movies. The more expensive accommodations have silky wallpaper and are filled with elegant copies of Biedermeier furniture.

The hotel is the largest in Salzburg, but because of its personalized service it seems much smaller. It's connected with a corridor to the city swimming pool with its sauna and adjacent conference center. Joggers or strollers can unwind in the nearby park, while motorists will appreciate the hotel's underground garage.

None of this luxury comes cheaply. Low-season rates range from 1,200 AS ($63.84) to 1,900 AS ($101.08) in a single and between 1,850 AS ($98.42) to 2,500 AS ($133) in a double. High-season rates range from between 1,900 AS ($101.08) and 2,800 AS ($148.96) in a single and between 2,500 AS ($133) and 3,600 AS ($191.52) in a double. An extra bed can be set up in any room for 600 AS ($31.92). These tariffs include a generous buffet breakfast.

Hotel Bristol, 4 Markartplatz (tel. 73-5-57). The bar of this 19th-century hotel has terrazzo floors and Oriental rugs in an ambience of concealed lighting, light-grained paneling, and discreet piano music. The bedrooms range from upper-class functional to opulently baroque, with embellished ceilings and crystal chandeliers. The armchairs in the public rooms are comfortably upholstered in brown leather, and afford a vantage point for viewing the enormous paintings, some of which should probably be in a museum.

The cream-colored baroque facade of the hotel encompasses a view of the Hohensalzburg Fortress and the Mirabell Gardens. As you'd expect from such an elegant hotel, each of the rooms has its own bath. Singles cost from 1,700 AS ($90.44) to 2,000 AS ($106.40), while doubles range from 2,500 AS ($133) to 3,600 AS ($191.52), with breakfast included.

During high season, which is at Easter, for a few days in mid-June, and from late July till early September, the hotel requests that guests take half board.

Hotel Schloss Mönchstein, 26 Am Mönchsberg (tel. 841-36-30), is a Teutonic-style manor house on top of a rocky outcropping above the center of Salzburg. Because of its height it affords panoramic views of the city, which you might enjoy from one of the well-appointed salons after a day of sightseeing. The ochre exterior is a pastiche of watchtowers, step gables, and big windows, some of which curve in the direction of the elaborate gardens.

Also on the premises you'll find an elegant restaurant and bar, Paris Lodron, with discreetly patterned red-and-white wallpaper and leaded-glass windows, a tennis court, a wedding chapel, and a garden terrace overlooking a magnificent statue of Apollo in the private park.

Each of the bedrooms has a private bath, direct-dial phone, color TV, radio, mini-bar, and hairdryer, and in the suites an electronic safe. Singles range from 1,400 AS ($74.48) to 2,200 AS ($117.04), while doubles cost from 2,500 AS ($122) to 5,500 AS ($292.60), with breakfast included. Half board is offered for 500 AS ($26.60) per person extra, depending on your menu choice.

If you're driving, take Müllner Hauptstrasse north along the quays, turning left as soon as you pass a church (this will be Müllner Church on Augustinergasse). Follow the direction you're being funneled into, and take the next left-hand turn up a winding road (you'll see signs leading you to the hotel). An easier way, if you're on foot, is to take the Mönchsberg-lift. This is a grimly decorated elevator traveling the vertical distance from the Anton Neumayr Platz (center of the old town) up to the top of the Mönchsberg, five minutes' walking distance from the hotel.

Hotel Kobenzl, Salzburg-Gaisberg (tel. 20-2-75), is a country-style inn on Gaisberg mountain, about seven miles from the heart of Salzburg. If your intention is to stay outside of the crowded city, this might be a good choice. Its exterior has half-timbered detailing, fieldstone masonry, big windows with a panoramic view over Salzburg, and weathered wooden balconies. The air here is mountain pure, the amenities are top-notch, and the decor is tasteful and attractive.

The Herzog family prepares a savory cuisine, which has appealed to everybody from Werner von Braun to Austrian President Kreisky. A swimming pool is on the premises, and a public bus runs to and from the city. The hotel has an indoor pool and a sauna. Bedrooms contain complete baths, TV, safes, phones, radio-clocks, and hairdryers. Charges, which include a buffet breakfast, are 1,400 AS ($74.48) to 2,200 AS ($117.04) in a single, from 2,400 AS ($127.68) to 3,600 AS ($191.52) in a double, and from 3,400 AS ($180.88) to 4,400 AS ($234.08) in an apartment, taxes and service included. Half board can be arranged for 300 AS ($15.96) per person extra. An à la carte menu can be enjoyed in the dining room or on the terrace. The hotel is open from March to the end of October.

Hotel Osterreichischer Hof, 5-7 Schwarzstrasse (tel. 7-25-41), is a palatial white hotel on the right bank of the Salzach. It has a magnificent view across the water to the old town, plus an interior decor of wrought iron, grand staircases, potted palms, Biedermeier and Victorian antiques, big windows, and Oriental rugs. Built about a century ago, it has attracted a clientele that has numbered some of the most powerful figures in Europe.

Among the restaurants inside, my favorite is the wood-paneled Zirbelzimmer, whose craftsmanship is admirable. Other facilities include a piano bar and a garden terrace. The 130 well-furnished rooms range from 900 AS ($47.88) to 1,550 AS ($82.46) in a single and from 1,300 AS ($69.16) to 4,300 AS ($228.76) in a double, with breakfast included. Prices depend on the season and the room assignment, the most expensive double price being for a suite.

Schloss-Hotel Klessheim, Siezenheim (tel. 850-8770), is a neoclassical villa which was built originally for the brother of Franz Joseph in 1882. After Hitler took over Austria, he ordered that the palace be fixed up for him to have as a private retreat, perhaps intending to journey over from Berchtesgaden, but these plans never worked out. It was later used as a vacation home for top-ranking military brass during the American occupation of Austria. Since 1957, it has been a beautiful castle hotel, and, among others, it has received former presidents Richard Nixon and Gerald Ford.

Open only in summer, it contains more than two dozen rooms, about 16 of which have private bath. It has a nine-hole golf course, a swimming pool, a tennis court, and a large surrounding park. On the outskirts of Salzburg, it lies less than four miles from the center. Bed and breakfast costs from 750 AS ($39.90) to 1,200 AS ($63.84) in a single and from 1,000 AS ($63.20) to 2,200 AS ($117.04) for a double. Half board is offered for an additional 220 AS ($11.70) per person daily.

FIRST-CLASS HOTELS: Hotel Fondachhof, 46 Gaisbergstrasse, Salzburg-Parsch (tel. 20-9-06), is one of the most pleasing hotels at the foot of Gaisberg. It was built as a manor house 200 years ago in a baroque format of mustard-yellow walls, white trim, and a steep red-tile roof. It was made into a hotel in 1950, and today affords quiet and secluded lodgings to guests in spring and summer only (from March to October). Many of the bedrooms look down on a gazebo set close to the flowered sun terrace. On the grounds you'll find sculpted fountains, a heated swimming pool, and a sauna. Many of the accommodations are furnished with antiques, while the architectural detailing inside includes stone columns and decorative ceramic stoves. Singles range from 700 AS ($37.24) to 1,300 AS ($69.16), while doubles cost from 1,600 AS ($85.12) to 2,800 AS ($148.96), with breakfast included. Prices depend on the season.

Maria Theresien Schlössl, 87 Morzgerstrasse, Salzburg-Hellbrunn (tel. 84-12-44). An archbishop ordered this castle built in the early part of the 17th century, and there's still a vague feeling of the ecclesiastical in the proportions of the lemon-colored baroque facade with curved gables. It became a hotel about three years before Hitler annexed Austria. Lying on the southern outskirts of the city, it's more a manorial home than an actual castle. In fact it was once an outbuilding of the neighboring Hellbrunn Palace. It's set in spacious park-like grounds, through which guests wander freely, inspecting the well-manicured gardens. There are 15 bedrooms, some dozen of which have private bath. The friendly and helpful staff serves good food, which includes both German and French specialties. Well-furnished singles range from 550 AS ($29.26) without bath to 800 AS ($42.56) to 1,100 AS ($58.52) with bath. Doubles with bath rent for 1,500 AS ($79.80) to 2,100 AS ($111.72). Apartments for two persons cost 2,300 AS ($122.36) to 2,700 AS ($143.64), those accommodating four persons going for 2,700 AS ($143.64) to 2,900 AS ($154.28). Prices include breakfast.

Hotel Kasererhof, 6 Alpenstrasse (tel. 21-2-65), is composed of two mustard-colored baroque buildings connected with a low passageway. The main building was built in 1642 on land that had previously belonged to an archbishop. A nearby chapel, which is part of the hotel, was constructed 35 years later, and is still filled with museum-caliber pieces from the 18th century. The public rooms are outfitted with cozily contrasting patterns of flowered upholstery over Oriental rugs. The Günther family do everything they can to make a visitor's stay pleasant. They charge 910 AS ($48.41) to 1,360 AS ($72.35) in a single and 1,800 AS ($95.76) to 2,600 AS ($138.32) in a double.

Hotel Winkler, 7 Franz-Josef-Strasse (tel. 7-35-13), can be recognized by the huge sign stretching above the honeycomb concrete of its rectangular facade. The contemporary bedrooms are outfitted with discreet colors, big windows, and romantic touches which sometimes include gilded headboards in baroque patterns. Singles range from 850 AS ($45.22) to 1,050 AS ($55.86), while doubles cost from 1,500 AS ($79.80) to 2,500 AS ($133), with breakfast included. The hotel is outside the old town, near many 19th-century buildings, in a commercial section. It accepts tour groups, who have their own dining room.

Bayerischer Hof, 1 Kaiserschützenstrasse (tel. 54-1-70). Set within a two-block walk of the railway station, this streamlined hotel often hosts groups visiting from other parts of the Teutonic world. The attractively modern lobby is paneled with light-grained oak and carpeted in a pleasing shade of blue-gray. The 60 bedrooms are well-insulated refuges from the surrounding commercial neighborhood. The establishment opened in 1985, and since then has done a thriving business in each of the three in-house dining rooms. With breakfast included, singles range from 830 AS ($44.17) to 1,000 AS ($53.20), while doubles cost between 1,200 AS ($63.84) and 1,650 AS ($87.78), depending on the season. Fixed-price meals are offered from 200 AS ($10.64).

THE MIDDLE RANGE: **Hotel Stieglbräu,** 14 Rainerstrasse (tel. 77-6-92), is a comfortable, contemporary hotel within a five-minute walk of the main train station, in the Mirabell section of Salzburg. Facilities include two pleasant restaurants and a salad bar for light snacks. The 50 bedrooms are simply furnished, with big windows, clean sheets, snug beds, and private baths. The hotel has its own parking lot, which will solve at least one of your problems in traffic-congested Salzburg. Singles range from 650 AS ($34.58) to 840 AS ($45.22), while doubles go from 1,050 AS ($55.86) to 1,500 AS ($79.80), with breakfast included.

Hotel Mozart, 27 Franz-Josef-Strasse (tel. 72-2-74), angles itself around a street corner a few blocks south of the train station. Its facade of beige stucco contains modern weatherproof windows which let in plenty of light to fill the simply furnished bedrooms, each of which has its own private bath and phone. Singles cost 980 AS ($52.14), while doubles go for 1,380 AS ($73.42), with breakfast included. The hotel is owned and operated by the Ast family.

Hotel Pitter, 6-8 Rainerstrasse (tel. 78-5-71), has an impressive gray stucco facade which angles around a curve in its street. The lower floors have restrained neoclassical detailing around their windows. The huge lobby area has beautifully polished square columns of red porphyry and a marble floor. One of the three inviting restaurants contains a wood-paneled bar, while a daytime café provides a place to read the local newspapers. The Fellner family with their two sons are the owners of this hotel, where attractively furnished singles or doubles rent for 600 AS ($31.92) to 900 AS ($47.88) per person, depending on the season.

Hotel Restaurant Gablerbräu, 8 Linzer Gasse (tel. 73-4-41), is an inviting hotel built in three six-story sections. The end sections are rust-colored with white trim, while the center part has been painted a beige pink, with arched windows on the ground floor and wrought-iron detailing on its imposing facade. Inside you'll find three pleasant restaurants: one with vaulted ceilings and green and yellow murals, another covered with wrought-iron detailing, and a third—the least formal of all—which is a beer hall. Not far from the right bank's Markartplatz, the hotel offers well-appointed rooms for 600 AS ($31.92) to 750 AS ($39.90) in a single and 1,050 AS ($55.86) to 1,300 AS ($69.16) per person in a double, with breakfast included. All prices depend on the season and the plumbing.

Flughafen Hotel, 105 Innsbrucker Bundesstrasse (tel. 87-1-23), might be the ideal choice if you're arriving on a late flight into Salzburg. Close to the airport, it has comfortable and modern bedrooms, many with views of the city. The public rooms are tastefully appointed in leather, wood, and chrome, with colorful carpeting, while the good restaurant serves well-prepared food in a verdant setting. Singles cost from 450 AS ($23.94) to 600 AS ($31.92), while doubles range from 700 AS ($37.24) to 1,100 AS ($58.52), with breakfast included. Half board is offered for another 200 AS ($10.64) per person daily.

Hotel Kasererbräu, 33 Kaigasse (tel. 42-4-45), has a distressed stucco facade and baroque ornamentation around each of its windows. It's in one of the old town's most colorful neighborhoods, a few blocks from the cathedral. The building has sections dating from the 13th century, plus a collection of baroque and Biedermeier furniture that goes well with the Oriental rugs and embellished plaster ceilings. The dining room is rustically alpine, while some of the bedrooms have painted regional furniture covered with provincial floral motifs. Singles range from 500 AS ($26.60) to 850 AS ($45.22), with doubles costing from 900 AS ($47.88) to 1,650 AS ($87.78), breakfast included. Prices depend on the plumbing and the season, and half board is offered for another 150 AS ($7.98) per person daily.

Hotel Johann Strauss, 37 Makartkai (tel. 34-6-19), is an ochre-colored hotel on a pedestrians-only square near the river. You might want to rest after a day of sightseeing on its flower-covered terrace which offers a view of the old town. The simple contemporary bedrooms have patterned carpeting in autumnal colors and private baths. The dining room is pleasant and not overly decorated, serving well-prepared food. Depending on the plumbing and the season, singles range from 450 AS ($23.94) to 850 AS ($45.22), while doubles go from 850 AS ($45.22) to 1,500 AS ($79.80), breakfast included.

Hotel Wolf-Dietrich, 7 Wolf-Dietrich-Strasse (tel. 71-2-75), is composed of two neoclassical town houses joined together with an updated ground-floor facade. The lobby area is covered in Oriental rugs, with unbroken modern paneling accented with brass detailing. The smallish bedrooms are appealing and cozy, while parts of one of the two restaurants are outfitted in alpine carving and graceful pine detailing. An indoor swimming pool is covered with mirrors and unusual murals of Neptune chasing a sea nymph. Comfortably furnished doubles cost 1,050 AS ($55.86) to 1,500 AS ($79.80), while singles range from 650 AS ($34.58) to 850 AS ($45.22), with breakfast included.

Hotel Auersperg, 61 Auerspergstrasse (tel. 71-7-57), is a rectangular building with a gently sloping roof and a prominent curved wall of big windows, behind which is a restaurant. The establishment lies between the rail station and the Kapuzinerberg, within a three-minute walk of the center of town. Pleasantly equipped singles range from 470 AS ($25) to 840 AS ($44.69), while doubles go from 355 AS ($18.87) to 680 AS ($36.18) per person, with a buffet breakfast, service, and taxes included, the prices depending on the season and the plumbing.

Hotel Stein, at Staatsbrücke (tel. 74-3-46). You'd never know it by looking at its renovated stucco and stone exterior, but there has been an inn on this site since 1399. The interior is the kind of spacious and airy place where you'll feel at ease. The big-windowed bedrooms are conservatively furnished in comfortable chairs and sofas. One of my favorite spots here is the rooftop terrace, where you can sip coffee or wine while listening to the splashing of a fountain as you take in the baroque buildings of old town. With breakfast included, singles range from 460 AS ($24.47) to 700 AS ($37.24), while doubles go from 750 AS ($39.90) to 1,200 AS ($63.84).

Hotel Europa, 31 Rainerstrasse (tel. 73-2-93), is an angular, skyscraping concrete building rising from a tree-dotted area a short walk from the main station. On the 14th floor you'll find a panoramic restaurant serving an international cuisine, while a less expensive snackbar on the ground floor might be a good stopover for lunch. The contemporary bedrooms are tastefully decorated, with vivid color schemes whose tones are sometimes repeated on the ceilings. Each of the 104 rooms has its own private bath, as well as radio and mini-bar. A TV is available on request. Singles range from 860 AS ($45.75) to 1,050 AS ($55.86), while doubles cost from 1,200 AS ($63.84) to 1,700 AS ($90.44), with breakfast included. Half board is offered for an additional 200 AS ($10.64) per person daily.

Hotel Drei Kreuz, 9 Vogelweiderstrasse (tel. 72-7-90), has a ground-floor series of aluminum-framed windows set into the kind of porous rock that Salzburg is built of. The upper floors are a two-toned combination of yellow stucco and terracotta colored panels. At the reception area you'll be greeted with a friendly smile and a wall-size illustration of a view of medieval Salzburg. The restaurant has some of the most massive beams I've seen in this part of Austria, along with a cozy bar and a gemütlich decor of rustic tables and chairs. The bedrooms are tasteful and well furnished. The name of the hotel derives from the three crosses of the Kapuzinerberg nearby, which was the site for public executions centuries ago. Well-furnished singles range from 850 AS ($45.22), and doubles cost 1,200 AS ($63.84), breakfast included.

BUDGET HOTELS: **Hotel Elefant,** 4 Sigmund-Haffner-Gasse (tel. 43-3-97), is a well-established family-run hotel near the Rathaus in the old city. It is in one of the most ancient buildings of Salzburg, a house more than 700 years old, in a quiet alley off the Getreidegasse. In the lobby, you'll see a pink-and-white marble checkerboard floor as well as a 400-year-old marquetry cabinet. One of my favorite rooms is the vaulted Bürgerstüberl, where high wooden banquettes separate the tables and where the chairs are comfortably curved. You might like to dine in the historic Ratsherrnkeller, a room which in the 17th century was called the wine cellar of Salzburg. The well-furnished and high-ceilinged bedrooms rent for 390 AS ($20.75) to 520 AS ($27.66) in a single and 650 AS ($34.58) to 1,200 AS ($63.84) in a double, depending on the plumbing and the season. Breakfast is included in the prices.

Hotel Fuggerhof, 9 Eberhard-Fugger-Strasse (tel. 20-4-79), is a family-run boarding house on the south slope of the Kapuzinerberg. From the outside it looks like the secluded mountain home of a wealthy industrialist, with three stories of curved walls, stone detailing, and cone-shaped roofs. A kidney-shaped swimming pool is set among pine trees near the hotel's entrance. The furnishings are comfortably rustic, often painted in regional designs or richly grained with baroque carvings. Each of the bedrooms has a private bath, refrigerator, phone, and radio. Herta Kammerhofer, your congenial hostess, charges from 650 AS ($34.58) to 850 AS ($45.22) in a single and from 900 AS ($47.88) to 1,800 AS ($95.76) in a double, the higher price being for a suite. Breakfast is included in all the tariffs. The hotel has an elevator, a laundromat, and a sauna.

Hotel Weisse Taube, 9 Kaigasse (tel. 41-7-83). The reception area lies behind a stone-trimmed wrought-iron and glass door a few steps from the Mozart-platz. It's ideally located for sightseeing but not for private car parking. Constructed in 1365, it's been owned by the Haubner family since 1904. Some of the public rooms maintain the massive ceiling beams of their original construction, but the 30 bedrooms, all with bath or shower, are for the most part renovated and comfortably streamlined. Singles range from 650 AS ($34.58) to 750 AS ($39.90), while doubles go from 1,000 AS ($53.20) to 1,350 AS ($71.82), with breakfast included. On the premises you'll find an elevator, a television room, and a bar.

Hotel Garni Reiter, 8 Mirabellplatz (tel. 77-6-17), is a solidly constructed hotel whose interior is filled with wood paneling. You'd think the building was older than it is, except for the construction dates carved into some of the ceiling beams (1974 and 1977). The hotel is well situated on the Mirabellplatz, about five pedestrian minutes from the old city. The bedrooms are unpretentious and outfitted in autumnal colors of beiges, yellows, and browns. Singles rent for 650 AS ($34.58) while doubles cost 1,000 AS ($53.20), with breakfast and free parking included.

Hotel Blaue Gans, 43 Getreidegasse (tel. 841-3-17), has an ash-colored facade and a convenient location in the old city near the underground garages of the Mönchsberg. On the ground floor you'll find an informal beer hall. The narrow sidewalk outside is barely wide enough to walk three abreast. The bedrooms are cozy and comfortable, mostly with bathroom or shower and toilet. Each one has a direct-dial phone, and there is a TV lounge for residents. Singles rent for 350 AS ($18.62) to 550 AS ($29.26), with doubles costing from 350 AS ($18.62) to 950 AS ($50.54). Breakfast and taxes are included in the rates, which depend on the plumbing and the season.

Hotel Neutor, 8 Neutorstrasse (tel. 44-1-54), presents a gray and white elliptical facade, lots of windows, and a faded modern format. Views from the contemporary bedrooms (where you'll usually find a padded quilt covering the comfortable bed) include the Mönchsberg and the Untersberg. Rates range from 390 AS ($20.75) to 550 AS ($29.26) per person. All units contain private bath.

THE BEST OF THE GUESTHOUSES: A pension or guesthouse in Salzburg does not necessarily indicate economy. They can be luxurious, rated five stars, or of a more modest class, comparable to (but often better than) a third-class hotel. I'll lead off with the most expensive. If you're on a strict budget, read from the bottom of the list.

Dr. Wührer's Haus Gastein, 25 Ignaz-Rieder-Kai (tel. 22-5-65). From many of the windows of this prosperous-looking Teutonic villa, lying in a verdant area east of the city's center, you can spot colonies of ducks paddling behind a screen of riverside saplings. The establishment is officially classified as a hotel; however, a stopover in one of its ample bedrooms is similar to a stay in an upperclass private home. During the annual music festival, the place is likely to be filled with musicians, some of them famous, who appreciate the spacious flowering garden, a stage setting for breakfast or afternoon tea.

The interior is sparsely but pleasantly filled with conservative furniture and plush Oriental carpets. The three-story building was originally constructed as a private residence in 1953, then later converted by a local dentist into a 12-room guesthouse. His wife, who returned to the university in her mid-50s to obtain a doctorate of philosophy, is nominally in charge of the establishment. But the person a guest is likely to encounter at check-in is the Wührer's beautiful daughter, Colette.

Many of the bedrooms contain private balconies, and each is equipped with a renovated private bath. With breakfast included, summer prices range from 1,000 AS ($53.20) to 1,600 AS ($85.12) per person. In winter tariffs are reduced to between 650 AS ($34.58) and 900 AS ($47.88) per person.

Haus Ingeborg, 9 Sonnleitenweg (tel. 21-7-49), is a small and luxurious alpine chalet in a secluded area northeast of the old town. It has a slope-roofed facade of reddish-colored wood and white stucco. The interior is outfitted with well-crafted details such as exposed ceiling beams, a riserless staircase of glowing hardwood, and a geometrically paneled ceiling. Some of the bedrooms are furnished with special accessories such as baronial beds. On the premises you'll find an outdoor swimming pool and a sauna. All the handsomely equipped bedrooms contain private baths as well. Singles rent for 1,400 AS ($74.48) to 1,600 AS ($85.12), while standard doubles cost 1,680 AS ($89.38) to 2,080 AS ($110.66), with breakfast included. More expensive suites are also rented. Fritz and Inge Oberrauch are your hosts, and they keep their place open from the first of March until the end of October.

Haus Arenberg, 8 Blumensteinstrasse (tel. 77-1-74). Staying in a place like this gives you the chance to enjoy the best of the Austrian countryside while being a short car ride from the old city. On a fieldstone foundation, the two balconied stories have a format of white stucco and wood detailing. Parts of the interior are completely covered in blond paneling, while the panoramic breakfast room is accented with hunting trophies and Oriental rugs. The view from the comfortable bedrooms usually encompasses the nearby city. All units have private baths. Singles cost from 600 AS ($31.92) to 720 AS ($38.30), while doubles range from 950 AS ($50.54) to 1,200 AS ($63.84), depending on the season. Breakfast is included in the rates.

Hotel Pension am Dom, 17 Goldgasse (tel. 42-7-65), is a rustically decorated family-run guest house a few steps from the Residenzplatz. The Bachleitner family, your hosts, charge from 920 AS ($48.94) to 1,020 AS ($54.26) with private bath. Breakfast is included in the tariffs.

Pension Wolf, 7 Kaigasse (tel. 843-4530), near the Mozartplatz, dates from 1429. It's built of stucco with big shutters, and in a location that couldn't possibly be more ideal. Red polished stone steps lead to the wood-ceilinged first-floor reception area. This hotel is usually full, even in off-season, so make reservations way in advance. The interior is rustically cozy, with a few baroque touches, such as an embellished ceiling, which make it inviting and appealing. The sunny bedrooms rent for 750 AS ($39.90) in a single and for 650 AS ($34.58) per person in a double, breakfast included.

Pension Am Eschenbach, 21 Hellbrunner Strasse (tel. 20-3-47). One of the best parts about this country-style guest house is the welcome provided by the kindly owner, Elisabeth Elwischger. The public rooms are filled with an eclectic mixture of 19th-century paintings, formal sculpture, and cozy contemporary furniture. The high-ceilinged bedrooms have painted designs on the furniture and are outfitted in cheerful colors. Singles cost around 420 AS ($22.34) to 500 AS ($26.60), while doubles range from 630 AS ($33.52) to 1,080 AS ($57.46). There are some apartments and a bungalow available for up to five persons as well. Breakfast is included in the price.

Pension Helmhof, Lieferinger Hauptstrasse (tel. 33-0-79), is an appealingly rustic stucco chalet with flowered balconies and a stone-trimmed sun terrace. Rooms are comfortably furnished and well kept, and the staff is hospitable. Singles cost from 350 AS ($18.62) to 400 AS ($21.80), while doubles range from 460 AS ($24.47) to 600 AS ($31.92), with breakfast included. Prices depend on the plumbing.

Pension Adlerhof, 25 Elisabethstrasse (tel. 75-2-36). Only the second and third floors of this guest house near the train station retain their original baroque embellishments. The windows of the first and fourth floors have been stripped and re-covered with polished marble and gray stucco. The result is a pastiche of styles which eventually reveals a cozy interior with high ceilings. It's filled with wooden furniture with occasional painted designs, plus lots of folkloric touches which include an occasional hunting trophy. The Pregartbauer family charges from 230 AS ($12.24) to 310 AS ($16.49) in a single and from 380 AS ($20.22) to 550 AS ($29.26) in a double, breakfast included. Prices depend on the season and the plumbing, and half of the units have a private shower.

Hotel/Pension Goldene Krone, 48 Linzer Gasse (tel. 72-3-00). My favorite part of this family-run guest house is the ivy-covered walls of its big sun terrace, where a member of the Egger family will serve you coffee after a tiring day in the city. Only a few minutes from the Staatsbrücke, the hotel offers comfortably outfitted bedrooms with patterned carpeting and wooden furniture. Singles rent for 310 AS ($16.49) to 450 AS ($23.94), while doubles cost 480 AS ($25.54) to 700 AS ($37.24). Breakfast is included in these rates. Prices depend on the plumbing and the season.

Food and Lodging at Anif

Romantik Hotel Schlosswirt (tel. 21-75) is a country inn on the outskirts of Anif, four miles from the center of Salzburg and a half mile from the autobahn's exit at Salzburg-Süd. It was founded in 1607, and with its flagstone floors, thick walls, and a pleasing collection of local artifacts and hunting trophies, has done a thriving business ever since. It's so well known that Austrians sometimes drive all the way from Innsbruck to dine here.

The bedrooms, whether in the main building or in the L-shaped annex, are furnished mainly with Biedermeier furniture, with patterned wallpaper and flowerboxes at the windows. If you're a late riser, be warned that traffic beginning at 7 a.m. might disturb you if you're housed in the annex, which is right on the highway.

All rooms have private bath and are well equipped. Singles range from 560 AS ($29.79) to 700 AS ($37.24), while doubles go from 900 AS ($47.88) to 1,300 AS ($69.16), depending on the season. Rooms come with a generous breakfast buffet with wurst, cheese, and coddled eggs.

Dinner is an elegant experience. Menu items include matjes herring with dill, an array of wild game in season, duckling in orange sauce, and many traditional fish dishes. A kindly English-speaking hostess in regional dress will help you with translations. Fixed-price meals begin at 220 AS ($11.70), with à la carte dinners costing from 250 AS ($13.30) to 400 AS ($21.28).

Hotel Friesacher (tel. 20-75) is an elegant, elongated chalet with a hipped roof, a long expanse of gables, and natural-grained wooden balconies covered with flowers. It has an older building a few steps away, which serves as a well-furnished annex to the main hotel, with flowering lawns scattered in between. The entrance hall to the main building has an intriguing variety of blue-gray and rust-colored marble covering the floor, and a wooden ceiling muting the light from the big windows. Throughout the hotel you'll find unusual artifacts, intimate corners, and friendly service provided by the Friesacher family. Each of the spacious bedrooms has its own bath, renting for 480 AS ($25.54) to 520 AS ($27.66) in a single and for 750 AS ($39.90) to 850 AS ($45.22) in a double. Apartments are offered for around 1,050 AS ($55.86).

Food and Lodging at Aigen

Gasthof/Pension Doktorwirt, 9 Glaserstrasse (tel. 22-9-73), a chalet with prominent gables, a red tile roof, and white stucco walls, lies on the southern edge of Salzburg, within ten minutes by car from the old city. The adjoining restaurant produces many of the sausages it serves, as well as a collection of tempting pastries. The decor is rustic, sunny, and pleasant, with lots of wood detailing. On the premises is an outdoor swimming pool with a view of the mountains. The cozy bedrooms rent for 420 AS ($22.34) to 520 AS ($27.66) in a single and for 660 AS ($35.11) to 850 AS ($45.22) in a double, breakfast included. By car, exit from the autobahn at Salzburg-Süd, or if you don't have a car you can reach the place from the center of Salzburg by taking city bus line 7, which has buses running every ten minutes.

Food and Lodging at Bergheim

Hotel Gasthof Gmachl (tel. 52-1-24) lies four miles from the center of Salzburg. It looks like a private chalet home of a prosperous business person, with an interior embellished with carved stone and octagonal ceiling panels. In one of the public rooms, a massive hearth burns under a stone and stucco overhang. The 60 beds are contained in interesting and cozy rooms, some of them with sloping paneled ceilings and lots of homey individualized touches. On the premises you'll find three sand tennis courts, an indoor heated swimming pool, a sauna, and 2½ miles away, a riding stable (for which you will have to pay extra, of course). Singles rent for 700 AS ($37.24) to 795 AS ($42.29), while doubles cost 950 AS ($47.88) to 1,500 AS ($79.80), with breakfast included.

3. Where to Dine

Salzburg has a wide range of restaurants in all price ranges. But two special desserts you'll have to sample while there include the famous Salzburger nockerln, a light mixture of stiff egg whites, as well as the elaborate confection known as the Mozart-Kugeln, with bittersweet chocolate, hazelnut nougat, and marzipan. You'll also want to taste the beer in any one of the numerous Salzburg breweries.

THE UPPER BRACKET: **Goldener Hirsch**, 37 Getreidegasse (tel. 84-85-11). Even if this restaurant only served the clients of its adjoining hotel (see my hotel recommendation) it would still attract the brightest luminaries of the international music and business community. The fact is, however, that dozens of the fans of this place travel a long distance to eat in the authentically renovated ambience of an inn established in 1407. It's staffed with a superb team of chefs and waiters in an atmosphere of elegantly restrained simplicity. Specialties include parfait of smoked trout in a mustard dill sauce, grilled hare, veal in saffron sauce, and many more dishes, all beautifully served and impeccably prepared. À la carte meals range from 250 AS ($13.30) to 550 AS ($29.26). The restaurant is open every day, and reservations are suggested.

Restaurant Alt-Salzburg, 2 Bürgerspitalgasse (tel. 841-4-76), is one of the bastions of intensely formal Austrian service. The predominant colors are red and white, in a wood-ceilinged room crafted to reveal part of the chiseled rock of Mönchsberg. The crystal here shines, the waiters are formally dressed (often better than the clients), and the food choices include tomato mousse with shrimp, parfait of calves' liver, quenelles of veal kidneys Calvados in a chervil sauce, and saddle of hare with mushrooms. The restaurant is open from 11:30 a.m. until 2 p.m. and 6:30 to 11 p.m. (till midnight during August). It's closed in February. Meals generally cost from 400 AS ($21.80). The restaurant is closed on Sunday, and reservations are suggested on the other nights of the week.

Zum Eulenspiegel, 2 Hagenauerplatz (tel. 84-31-80), is housed in a white-and peach-colored building at one end of a quiet cobblestone square in the old city. Inside you'll find five rooms on three different levels, all of them rustically but elegantly decorated. Management seems to have no problem with allowing clients to pick their favorite rooms, so feel free to look around. A bar area on the ground floor might be a pleasant place for an apéritif.

After that, you'll climb a stone staircase whose stucco walls are loaded with unusual art objects. The menu features a table d'hôte priced at 400 AS ($21.80) and 450 AS ($23.94). It might include cream of zucchini soup, along with many classic dishes such as tafelspitz, Salzburger nockerln, and perch filet. À la carte meals cost approximately the same as the set dinners. The restaurant is open from 11:30 a.m. to 2 p.m. and 6 to 11 p.m.; however, the bar is open from 10 a.m. to midnight daily. Renate and Helmuth Wienerroither, who go on vacation in November, are the polite and friendly owners of the place.

THE MIDDLE RANGE: G'würzmühl, 9 Rainbergstrasse (tel. 46-3-56). Sixty years ago this cozy restaurant was used as a spice mill (that's what its name means in German). Now it offers an array of specialties such as a concoction of lobster and crabmeat in a dill cream sauce with buttered rice, along with trout dumplings, mock turtle soup, two kinds of schnitzel, peppersteak Madagascar, and veal chop Du Barry. The kitchen will also serve a children's menu as well. The restaurant, charging from 300 AS ($15.96) and up for a meal, is open every day except Tuesday from 11:30 a.m. to 3 p.m. and 6 p.m. to midnight. In August it remains open every day. The location is about five minutes from the center of town.

Hagenauerstuben (Stranz & Scio), 14 Universitätsplatz (tel. 42-6-55). Melodies composed by this building's most famous occupant might accompany your before-dinner drink in this pleasant restaurant. It's accessible from the rear entrance of the building where Mozart was born. Many visitors never get beyond the street-level bar, where snacks and drinks are served in a 14th-century room with stone floors and a vaulted ceiling, plus a changing exhibition of modern lithographs and watercolors. At the top of a narrow flight of stone steps, you'll discover an austere trio of thick-walled rooms decorated with a ceramic stove and wooden armoires. A central serving table holds an array of salads and hors d'oeuvres, which are served by a brigade of handsome waiters in candy-striped shirts.

If you can find a free table, you can dine informally in the downstairs bar. The upstairs rooms are so popular that reservations are essential. The limited menu includes such items as a salad of salmon roe with cucumber, fresh asparagus vinaigrette, chicken liver mousse with fennel and citrus, mushroom strudel, several kinds of roasts, schnitzels, and stuffed pork cutlets. Wines are available by the glass, carafe, or bottle. Full meals range from between 300 AS ($15.96) and 500 AS ($26.60) per person, and are served between 10 a.m. and 11 p.m. on weekdays (on Saturday from 9 a.m. to 2 p.m.); closed Sunday.

Stiftskeller St. Peter (Peterskeller), 1-4 St. Peter-Bezirk (tel. 84-12-68). There's a legend that says that Mephistopheles met with Faust in this tavern, which isn't that far-fetched considering that it was established by Benedictine monks in A.D. 803. In fact it's the oldest restaurant in Austria, and is housed in the abbey of the church which supposedly brought Christianity to Austria. Aside from a collection of baroque banqueting rooms, open only for special occasions, the establishment contains an inner courtyard with vaults cut from the living rock, a handful of dignified wood-paneled rooms, and a brick-vaulted cellar with a tile floor and rustic chandeliers.

In addition to the wine fermented from the abbey's vineyards, the tavern serves such menu items as cheese soup with white wine and ham, filet of pork in a roquefort cream sauce with rice, roast duckling, and a combination plate of sausages, pork chops, semolina dumplings, potatoes, and sauerkraut. An unusual dessert might be curd dumplings with plum jam. Meals cost from 175 AS ($9.31) to 300 AS ($15.96), and the restaurant is open every day of the week all day until 1 a.m., and hot food is served until midnight. It's closed on Monday from the first of November until just before Easter.

Restaurant Hohensalzburg, in the Hohensalzburg Schloss (tel. 41-7-80), offers a chance to dine at the former stronghold of the prince-archbishops of Salzburg (see the sightseeing attractions). The restaurant is in the castle, which is perched on a block of Dolomite rock. You are 400 feet above the Salzach, and naturally you'll have a panoramic view.

Three times a week this gutbürgerlich restaurant is host to a folkloric music group which performs every Tuesday, Thursday, and Friday from 8:30 to 10:30 p.m. Also, during the summer, evening concerts of Mozart's music are presented daily. All week long, clients enjoy such specialties as grilled pork, grilled steak with pearl onions and pepperoni, veal dishes, schnitzels, fish, and fowl. The restaurant, charging from 200 AS ($10.64) to 350 AS ($18.62) for a typical meal, is open from March until the end of October from 10 a.m. to 8 p.m. (until 11 p.m. at the time of the festival in July and August).

Daimler's Beisl, 17 Giselakai (tel. 74-3-12). My favorite seats in this interesting restaurant are those in the window niches, where you'll have a view over most of Salzburg. The place has a kind of low-key elegance that's relaxed and informal, and especially appealing when accompanied by the specialties of the house, which include trout soup with salmon dumplings, lamb and game dishes, pork filet with mint-flavored butter, and a small but select range of stylishly presented other courses. You help yourself to the cheese and salad buffet, after selecting a wine from an extensive list. Desserts are appropriately caloric. The friendly and attractive personnel will serve you à la carte meals, ranging from 130 AS ($6.92) to 300 AS ($15.96) for a typical repast. Reservations are suggested, and the restaurant is closed on Sunday.

Purzelbaum, 7 Zugallistrasse (tel. 27-8-43). During the Salzburg Festival, you're likely to see some of the most dedicated music lovers in Europe congregating around the small square tables of this sophisticated bistro. It's near a duck pond in a residential neighborhood not frequently visited by tourists at the bottom of a steep incline leading up to Salzburg Castle. There's a cramped corner of the bar reserved for visitors who only want to drop in for a drink. Most guests, however, reserve a table in one of the trio of rooms filled with marble buffets from a French buttery, an art nouveau ceiling from a now-defunct café in Paris, and panels painted a heavenly shade of blue-green.

Habitués begin their meal with one of the daily champagne-based cocktails, then order a glass or a bottle of vintage wine which the owners import from five different countries. A set menu costs 370 AS ($19.68), with à la carte meals costing from 500 AS ($26.60). Menu specialties include three kinds of filet with homemade noodles, chateaubriand with a tarragon sauce, cream of smoked trout soup, tournedos Henri IV, and a rack of lamb in a cabbage sauce. If you order coffee, it will emerge steaming hot from a chrome espresso machine made in 1943 in Italy.

The restaurant is open every day except Sunday from noon to 2 p.m. and from 6:30 to 11 p.m. During the Salzburg Festival, it remains open seven days a week.

Restaurant K & K (Stiegl-Bräu-Keller), 2 Waagplatz (tel. 41-1-56), is on a giant square in the old city, with three different sections, each with a separate ambience. From the street you'll see an elaborate wrought-iron and gilt bracket holding a sign. You'll go down a massive stone staircase to reach the cellar bierkeller, which is a marvel of another time's masonry (it was built 900 years ago). The stube on the ground floor is candlelit, with a wood-paneled ambience.

Upstairs is the restaurant, which is divided by a flagstone-covered hallway into three separate eating areas, with dozens of stone accents crafted from both the porous rocks of Salzburg and beautiful slabs of salmon-colored marble. The diners here tend to be better dressed, and the atmosphere is slightly more formal. The three restaurants serve warm food from 11 a.m. to 2 p.m. and 6 to 10 p.m. They're also open for drinks and snacks from 9 a.m. till midnight in summer and from 10 a.m. to midnight in winter. Fixed-price meals cost 150 AS ($7.98) and 280 AS ($14.90). Menu items in the three restaurants include such specialties as perch, trout, roast filet of beef in a cognac cream sauce with fresh mushrooms and green peppercorns, tafelspitz, and breast of chicken in a curry cream sauce, along with grilled lamb and an array of seafood.

THE BUDGET RANGE: Weinhaus Moser, 3 Wiener Philharmoniker Gasse (tel. 841-136), is a smoke-stained winehouse with vaulted ceilings, paneling that looks polished from the backs of generations of drinkers, and the most unusual collection of overhead chandeliers in Salzburg. You'll also see a green ceramic oven, friendly uniformed waiters, and if you stop in before noon, groups of senior citizens sitting around gossiping as they drink coffee.

Menu items include typical Austrian dishes such as zander (pike-perch), tafelspitz, veal filet with späzle, seasonal wild game, schnitzels, peppersteak with zucchini, and Salzburger nockerl. Set meals begin at 90 AS ($4.79), while à la carte dinners range from 120 AS ($6.38) to 150 AS ($7.98). Warm food is served from 11 a.m. to 2:30 p.m. and 5:30 p.m. until midnight (on Saturday, from 10 a.m. to 2:30 p.m.). In August the wine house is open all day from 11 a.m. to midnight.

Krimpelstätter, 31 Müllner Hauptstrasse (tel. 32-2-74). The grimy neighborhood around this 500-year-old restaurant bustles with traffic, but inside a visitor can enjoy a decor virtually untouched by the modern world. Unlike other establishments which were originally built as private houses, this one was designed and constructed as an inn, with chiselled stone columns to support the vaulted ceilings and heavy timbers grown dark with smoke. In summer the roses and trellises of the establishment's beer garden attract up to 300 visitors at a time.

If you want a snack, a beer, or a glass of wine, head for the paneled door marked "Gastezimmer" in the entry corridor. If you're looking for a more formal, less visited area, a trio of cozy antique dining rooms sit at the top of a flight of narrow stone steps. The menu offers the same dishes in each of the different areas. Specialties include venison parfait with broccoli and a dill-flavored cream sauce, a Christmastime version of roast goose, venison gulasch with polenta, a schnitzel of wild hare and spinach dumplings. Full meals begin at 150 AS ($7.98). Service is every day except Monday, and drinks and snacks are available during all open hours. Full meals, however, are served only between 11:30 a.m. and 2 p.m. and between 6 and 10:30 p.m. when it would be wise to make a reservation.

Hotel Stadtkrug, 20 Linzer Gasse (tel. 73-5-45), is a rustic and attractive restaurant which is part of a hotel on a narrow street in the old city. The layout is unusual, with a kitchen opening off the hotel's reception area and with a dining room that contains a stone staircase leading from the back to the large arched window in front. Wooden tables are set on two tiers, illuminated by gilded wooden chandeliers with pink shades. The fixed-price meals are a good bargain at 90 AS ($4.79) and 125 AS ($6.65), with a long list of à la carte specialties, usually priced from 195 AS ($10.37) up. These include mixed grills, gulasch, peppersteak, and Salzburger nockerl. One of the featured specialties is trout meunière, the ingredients of which come from the exposed trout tank that bubbles in the entrance vestibule. There are also daily blackboard specials. The restaurant is open from 11 a.m. to 11 p.m. seven days a week.

Restaurant Zum Mohren, 9 Judengasse (tel. 842-387). A statue of an exotic-looking Moor sits atop the wrought-iron sign announcing the entrance to this restaurant. The house that contains it was built in 1423, with much of the original masonry still showing. You'll have to descend a flight of gray stone steps to reach the three distinctly different eating areas, the best of which is on the right as you enter. The ceilings are made either of vaulted stucco or of well-crafted paneling. You'll see many replicas of Moors, with or without a gold earring, either in bas-relief or in full-rounded sculpture. A third area, on the left as you enter, is more cave-like, with an orange ceramic stove and a low ceiling.

The staff is friendly yet attractively formal. Meals range from 150 AS ($7.98) and up, and might include entrecôte Parisian style, filet mignon with broccoli and béarnaise sauce, grilled lamb chops, a good selection of cheese, and lots of rich desserts. The restaurant is open every day but Sunday from 11 a.m. to midnight, and the chef stops serving hot food after 11 p.m. It is closed in November.

Sternbräu, 23 Griesgasse (tel. 42-1-40). You'll enter this establishment through a cobblestone arched passageway leading off a street in the old city. The place seems big enough to have fed half of the old Austro-Hungarian army, in a series of rooms that lead one after another in varying degrees of formality. The Hofbräustübl is a rustic fantasy of square masonry columns with a massive format of hand-hewn beams and wood paneling. The other rooms have such accessories as sea-green tile stoves, marble columns, and oil paintings.

In addition to the different rooms, you'll also be able to eat in the chestnut-shaded beer garden, which is usually packed on a summer's night, or else under the weathered arcades of an inner courtyard. Daily specials, which are served by a battalion of aproned waiters, include typically Austrian dishes such as Wiener schnitzel, some trout recipes, cold marinated herring, Hungarian gulasch, hearty peasant soups, and lots of other gutbürgerlich selections. À la carte meals begin at 150 AS ($7.98), and the restaurant is open from 8 a.m. to midnight every day.

Mundenhamer Bräu, 2 Rainerstrasse (tel. 75-6-93). As you enter this warm-hued paneled restaurant, you'll pass by an elongated stainless-steel counter which almost looks like something from a delicatessen. There are several different seating areas, of which my favorite is the big-windowed section with a view of a city park. Meals cost 160 AS ($8.51), with à la carte dinners for around 200 AS ($10.64). Menu items include Salzburger cream schnitzel, paprika cutlets, mushroom ragoût, and a specialty of the house called Mundenhamer potpourri, a mixed grill for two persons. The menu is in English, and the portions are large. The restaurant lies near the main train station.

Bratwurstherzl, 7 Sigmundsplatz (tel. 84-15-17). Partly because of its glamorous association to the Goldener Hirsch Hotel, of which it is a part, and partly because it offers such good value, this place is usually jammed with kibitzing local residents. You'll descend a few steps from the sidewalk into a pair of cozily proportioned rooms, one of which is paneled and timbered. Both are filled with publicity photographs of musicians who have come here to dine. In addition to the beer and wine served in liberal quantities, the establishment offers a 150 AS ($7.98) fixed-price meal whose components change daily. À la carte meals, ranging from between 120 AS ($6.38) and 350 AS ($18.62), might include such dishes as a ragoût of venison, an array of sausages, a mousse of smoked trout in cabbage sauce, and roast hare. The place is open every day, and gets especially crowded on weekends.

Bastey-Brasserie & Crêperie, 7 Kaigasse (tel. 41-1-80). Its location on the ground floor of the Pension Wolff, a short walk from the Mozartplatz, is ideal. Its leaded windows look out just above the level of the sidewalk, illuminating an àlpine decor of exposed wood and scarlet napery. In many ways, the place is perfect for seekers of a light meal unencumbered with heavy sauces and starches. It prepares 13 different kinds of crêpes, ranging from zucchini with tomato to chili with cheese. The kitchen also prepares special salads, everything from Caesar to niçoise. You can also order such items as a steak sandwich, or a half dozen snails, each accompanied by a glass of wine or beer. Full meals cost from 220 AS ($11.70), with snacks and salads going for less. The establishment is open from noon to 2:30 p.m. and from 6 p.m. to midnight daily except Sunday.

Jugoslawisches Restaurant, at Hotel Weisses Kreuz, 6 Bierjodlgasse (tel. 45-6-41), has a facade of stone blocks that are almost hidden on a very small, village-style street just south of the cathedral. A grape arbor shelters the front terrace, where summertime tables have been set out for relaxed guests. The cuisine is both Viennese and Balkan, and includes Serbian bean soup, boiled beef, Wiener schnitzel, mutton chops, roast beef in a cream and onion sauce, and peppersteak. More exotic specialties include Serbian gulasch soup, moussaka, fried mincemeat loaf Serbian style with pickled peppers, and Dalmatian steak with Serbian rice and stuffed cabbage, along with a Serbian-style risotto. An average meal costs from 180 AS ($9.58), and the restaurant is open from 11 a.m. to midnight.

In the hotel, all the bedrooms have complete baths. Singles rent for 580 AS ($30.87) and doubles for 840 AS ($44.69). All tariffs include breakfast, tax, and use of the garage.

Schloss Stube Mirabell, 4 Mirabellplatz (tel. 73-7-73). In a distant wing of the magnificent pink and white baroque palace giving this restaurant its name, you'll find a small and intimate square dining room with a high vaulted ceiling and a pictorial mural of a medieval city. A tiny beer garden is set on the cobblestones in front, separated from the sidewalk by an attractive row of potted ivy and evergreen trees. The clientele tends to be a silent crowd of older local residents at certain times of the day. The price is right: from 125 AS ($6.65) for a traditional meal. It serves from 10 a.m. to 7 p.m. Monday to Saturday.

4. The Cafés of Salzburg

Cynics in the festival city sometimes complain that there isn't a lot to do in Salzburg except drink endless cups of thickened coffee while waiting for someone at the next table to be brilliant about art or music.

But that isn't the perception of everyone. A hometown friend of mine told me that the peak emotional experience of her trip to Europe happened while seated at a café table in the Mozartplatz. The combination of the baroque setting, the strains of a string orchestra, the Austrian pastry half eaten on her plate, and the companionship of a close friend made her realize that she was suddenly living her fantasy of what culture, art, and beauty are all about.

Don't leave Salzburg without some significant time in one of the world-famous cafés of the inner city. Descriptions of some of my favorites immediately follow.

Café Tomaselli, 9 Alter Markt (tel. 44-4-88), was established in 1703. It opens onto the cobblestone pavement of one of the most charming squares of Salzburg. Aside from the summertime chairs placed outdoors, you'll find a high-ceilinged square room with many tables, small crystal lighting fixtures, and lots of what look like elegant conversations. Another more formal room to the right of the entrance has oil portraits of well-known 19th-century Salzburgers in oval frames hung one above another. The crowd is chic. A waiter will probably show you a pastry tray filled with 40 different kinds of cakes, which you are free to order or not as you see fit. Other menu items include omelets, wursts, ice cream, and a wide range of drinks. Pastries cost from 20 AS ($1.06) to 30 AS ($1.60) and coffee from 21 AS ($1.18) to 30 AS ($1.60). The café is open from 7 a.m. to 9 p.m., from 8 a.m. to 9 p.m. on Sundays and holidays.

Restaurant Café Winkler, 32 am Mönschberg (tel. 84-12-15) reached by the elevator *(aufzug)*, offers a magic view of the old city, excellent traditional cuisine and cellar, and friendly service. Lunch, coffee and cake, afternoon tea, and dinner are offered, with dance music during the summer, in the contemporary surroundings of this typical continental first-class restaurant. Lunch costs from 200 AS ($10.64), an a la carte dinner from 350 AS ($18.62), and coffee and cake from 65 AS ($3.46). The establishment is open Tuesday through Sunday from 11 a.m. to midnight.

Kaffeehäferl, 6 Universitätsplatz (tel. 84-32-49), is constructed in an arcaded gray and white format of stucco walls set onto columns made of the porous rock that supports many of the buildings of Salzburg. This establishment attracts members of both the business and art communities of the city. The interior is simpler and more modern than you'd expect. Masses of ceramic pots are displayed in cases on one of the far walls. A specialty of the house is fleckerl with ham, which is served in addition to the wide selection of coffee, wine, and pastries. Coffee costs from 17 AS (90¢), with the price the same for the average pastry. The café is open Monday to Friday from 9 a.m. to 7 p.m., on Saturday to 6 p.m., and on Sunday in summertime from noon to 6 p.m. (in winter, Sunday hours are from 2 to 6 p.m.).

Schatz-Konditorei, 3 Getreidegasse (tel. 42-7-92), is an oldtime Austrian confectioner. The cobblestones in front of its 19th-century wood-and-glass facade are from the 14th century. Almost everything is made from traditional recipes, my favorite of which is the well-known Mozart-Kugeln, a combination of pistachio, marzipan, and hazelnut nougat, all of it dipped in chocolate. Clients are free to try any of the pastries with coffee at an indoor café table or to purchase them for consumption elsewhere. A pastry costs 12 AS (64¢) to 30 AS ($1.60) and coffee from 14 AS (75¢) to 25 AS ($1.33). Some varieties of pastry, including the Mozart-Kugeln, are mailed around the world. They're open from 8:30 a.m. to 6:30 p.m. weekdays, from 8 a.m. to 1:30 p.m. on Saturday. During festival performances in summer they're open full time on Saturday.

Konditorei Ratzka, 45 Imbergstrasse (tel. 70-9-19), is a small shop ten minutes from the center of town. Herwig Ratzka is the owner and pastry chef, and by all accounts he's a master at his craft. He uses the freshest ingredients to produce about 30 different pastries every day. Since the cakes are made fresh every day, much of the selection is gone by late afternoon. So for an insight into what's for sale, go early in the day. Prices begin at 30 AS ($1.60). Mr. Ratzka requests that clients not smoke in the shop, which is open Wednesday to Friday from 8 a.m. to 12:30 p.m. and from 1:30 to 5 p.m. (on Sunday, from 9 a.m. to 5 p.m.). It's closed on Monday and Tuesday and for two weeks in January, two weeks in June, and two weeks in September.

Café Glockenspiel, Mozartplatz (tel. 41-4-03). Its location on one of the most colorful squares of Salzburg has made this café the most popular and the most frequented in the city. Management keeps about 100 tables with well-maintained white armchairs in front of the café. If the day is warm enough, you might want to spend an afternoon in one of the chairs, particularly on the days when there is live chamber music. Immediately after entering you'll find yourself face to face with a glass case filled with every high-calorie delight west of Vienna.

The rooms opening on either side are upholstered in gray and pink, with big arched windows overlooking the statue in the square. A restaurant upstairs, with an even bigger pastry case than the one downstairs, is tastefully decorated in browns and beiges, with a big balcony. The restaurant offers such specials for lunch as gulasch of veal with dumplings, boiled rump of beef with roast potatoes and a chive sauce, and roast sausages with sauerkraut. Midday meals cost from 150 AS ($7.98). For dinner, you can sit on the balcony and look out over Salzburg's famous buildings while you enjoy Austrian and international specialties. Prices are from 250 AS ($13.30). Many people come here just for the drinks and pastries. Coffee costs 30 AS ($1.60); tea, 22 AS ($1.17); and beer, 30 AS ($1.60). There are many varieties of coffee, including Maria Theresa, which has orange liqueur in it.

Café Bazar, 3 Schwartzstrasse (tel. 74-2-78), is as deeply entrenched into Salzburg's social life as practically anything else in town. It has a regular clientele which includes persons from all walks of Austrian life, many of whom usually sit in the same section of the café and order practically the same item every time they visit.

It's housed in a pink stucco, palace-like building with many baroque features across the river from the main section of the old town. The inside is high ceilinged and vaguely art deco, with light-grained wooden walls covered with marquetry designs.

You'll occasionally see someone with a Franz-Joseph mustache wearing a gray flannel Styrian suit with loden trim, but a growing number of the clients are young, trendy, and fashionable, and would probably be much at home at a café in London or Paris.

Menu items include an array of salads, sandwiches, and omelets. Coffee prices range from 20 AS ($1.06), while pastries go from 18 AS (96¢) to 30 AS ($1.60). It's closed on Sunday.

Café Papageno, 14 Pfeifergasse (tel. 41-1-06), is a gemütlich hangout for an under-26 crowd. It's named after the comic character from Mozart's *Magic Flute,* whose statue stands in the nearby Papageno-Platz. The inside has wooden ceilings, comfortable banquettes, and a crowd of young people in couples or groups. The ambience is welcoming, and the food items include snacks such as hamburgers and salads. Beer costs from 25 AS ($1.33).

5. What to See

The old town lies between the left bank of the Salzach River and the ridge known as Mönchsberg, which rises to a height of 1,650 feet and is the site of Salzburg's gambling casino. The main street of the old town is **Getreidegasse,** a narrow little thoroughfare lined with five- and six-story burghers' buildings. Most of the houses along the street are from the 17th and 18th centuries. Mozart was born at no. 9 (see below). Many lacy-looking wrought-iron signs are displayed, and a lot of the houses have carved windows.

You might begin your tour at the **Mozartplatz,** with its outdoor cafés. From here you can walk to the even more spacious **Residenzplatz,** where torchlight dancing is staged every year, along with outdoor performances.

The **Residenz** (former archepiscopal residence) (tel. 41-5-61), on the west side of the Residenzplatz, just north of the Domplatz, was the seat of the Salzburg prince-archbishops after they no longer felt the need of the protection afforded in the gloomy Hohensalzburg Fortress on Mönchsberg (see below). The

Residenz dates from 1120, but work on the series of palaces in its present form, which comprised the ecclesiastical complex of the ruling church princes, began in the late 1500s and continued until about 1782. The lavish rebuilding was originally ordered by Archbishop Wolfgang (usually called "Wolf") Dietrich. The Residenz fountain, from the 17th century, is one of the largest and most impressive baroque fountains to be found north of the Alps.

The child prodigy, Mozart, often played in the Conference Room for guests. In 1867 Emperor Franz Joseph received Napoleon III here, and in 1871 Kaiser Wilhelm I was also a state guest at the Residenz. More than a dozen state rooms, each richly decorated, are open to the public. Conducted tours are given through these rooms daily from July to September at 10, 10:30, 11, and 11:30 a.m. and 1, 1:30, 2, 2:30, 3, 3:30, 4, and 4:30 p.m. October to June, hours are 10 and 11 a.m. and 2 and 3 p.m. Admission is 15 AS (80¢) for adults, free for children.

On the second floor you can visit the **Residenzgalerie** (tel. 8042, ext. 2770), an art gallery founded in 1789, now containing works mainly from the 16th to the 19th centuries displayed in 15 historical rooms. The some 200 paintings on exhibit include the art of Rembrandt, Rubens, Brueghel, Titian, Waldmüller, Maulbertsch, Poussin, Bordone, Troger, Vernet, Makart, Rottmayr, and Barbieri, among others. Gallery hours are 10 a.m. to 5 p.m. daily. Admission is 20 AS ($1.06) for adults, 10 AS (53¢) for persons from 15 to 18 years old, and free for children.

Concerts are often presented in the Residenz ballroom, and official receptions are held here. Special art exhibitions are frequently arranged in the sumptuous salons.

Across from the Residenz stands the celebrated **Glockenspiel,** with its 35 bells. You can hear this 18th-century carillon at 7 a.m., 11 a.m., and 6 p.m. Conducted tours are offered weekdays at 10:45 a.m. and at 5:45 p.m. from November 1 to March 15 for 10 AS (53¢) for adults, 5 AS (26¢) for children under 14.

At the south side of the Residenzplatz, where it flows into the **Domplatz** centered by a 1771 statue of the Virgin, stands the Dom, the **Salzburg cathedral,** world-renowned for its 10,000-pipe organ. The original building from 774 was superseded by a late-Romanesque structure erected from 1181 to 1200. When this edifice was destroyed by fire in 1598, Prince-Archbishop Wolf Dietrich followed up the start of work on the Residenz by commissioning construction of a new cathedral. His overthrow prevented the finishing of the project. His successor, Archbishop Markus Sittikus Count Hohenems, commissioned the Italian architect, Santino Solari, with the building of the present cathedral, which was consecrated in 1628 by Archbishop Paris Count Lodron.

Considered by some people the "most perfect" Renaissance building in the Germanic countries, the cathedral has a marble facade and twin symmetrical towers. The mighty bronze doors were created in 1959. The themes are Faith, Hope, and Love. The interior is in rich baroque with elaborate frescoes, the most important of which, along with the altarpieces, were designed by A. Mascagni of Florence. In the cathedral you can see the Romanesque font at which Mozart was baptized. The dome was damaged during World War II and restored by 1959. In the crypt, traces of the old Romanesque cathedral which once stood on this spot have been unearthed. These excavations can be viewed by the public Easter to October daily from 9 a.m. to 5 p.m. Admission is 10 AS (53¢) for adults, 7 AS (37¢) for children.

The treasure of the cathedral and a parade of the "arts and wonders" of the archbishops collected in the 17th century are displayed in the **Dom Museum,** open from mid-May to mid-October weekdays from 10 a.m. to 5 p.m., on Sunday and holidays from noon to 5 p.m. Admission is 20 AS ($1.06) for adults, 5 AS (26¢) for children 6 to 15.

The allegorical play *Everyman*, by Hoffmannsthal, is performed in the Domplatz at the Salzburg Festival. Based on my experience, if you attend a performance of this miracle play, bring your raincoat.

Stiftskirche St. Peter is the church of St. Peter's Abbey and Benedictine Monastery, founded by St. Rupert in 696. The church, once a Romanesque basilica with three aisles, was completely overhauled in the 17th and 18th centuries in an elegant baroque style. The west door dates from 1240. The tomb of St. Rupert is here. The church is richly adorned with art treasures, some altar paintings being by Kremser Schmidt. The Salzburg Madonna in the left chancel is from the early 15th century.

St. Peter's Cemetery (Petersfriedhof, in German; tel. 84-45-78) lies at the stone wall that merges into the rock called Mönchsberg. Many of the aristocratic families lie buried here as well as many other noted persons, including Nannerl Mozart, sister of Wolfgang Amadeus. Four years older than her better known brother, Nannerl was also an exceptionally gifted musician. You can see the Romanesque Chapel of the Holy Cross and St. Margaret's Chapel, dating from the 15th century. The cemetery and its chapels are rich in nostalgia, monuments to a way of life long vanished.

Conducted tours are given through the early Christian catacombs in the rock above the cemetery every 30 minutes May to September from 10 a.m. to noon and 1 to 5 p.m., and every hour October to April from 11 a.m. to noon and 1:30 to 3:30 p.m. The tour costs 10 AS (53¢) for adults, 8 AS (43¢) for children.

The Kollegienkirche, or Collegiate Church, opening onto Universitätsplatz, an open-air marketplace, was built between 1694 and 1707 for the local (Benedictine) university founded in 1622, designed by the great baroque architect, Fischer von Erlach. The university, disbanded in 1810, was refounded as the modern University of Salzburg in 1962. The main university is in the suburb of Nonntal. There are a few university buildings in the area of the church, and part of the former seat of learning is a fine library and reading room. This is von Erlach's finest and largest Salzburg church and one of the most celebrated baroque churches in Austria (and that's saying a lot). Altar paintings are by Rottmayr.

The **Hohensalzburg Fortress** (tel. 41-5-61), stronghold of the ruling prince-archbishops before they moved "downtown" to the Residenz to live, towers 400 feet above the Salzach River on a rocky Dolomite ledge. The massive fortress crowns the Mönchsberg and literally dominates Salzburg. Work on Hohensalzburg began in 1077 and was not finished until 1681, during which time many builders of widely different tastes and purposes had a hand in the construction. This largest completely preserved castle left in Central Europe has bastions for the cannons needed in the strife-torn Middle Ages when the odor of sanctity was often mixed with the odor of gunpowder. Functions of defense and state were combined in this fortress for six centuries.

The elegant state apartments once lived in by the prince-archbishops and their courts are on display. Coffered ceilings and much intricately constructed ironwork are of interest. See, in particular, an early 16th-century porcelain stove in the Golden Room.

A **Burgmuseum** which has been installed is distinguished mainly by its collection of medieval art. Plans and prints tracing the growth of Salzburg are on exhibit, as well as instruments of torture and many Gothic artifacts. The Salzburger Stier, or Salzburg bull, is an open-air barrel organ built in 1502 which plays melodies by Mozart and his friend Haydn for daily concerts following the Glockenspiel chimes. The **Rainermuseum** has displays of arms and armor. The late Gothic, beautiful St. George's Chapel, dating from 1501, has marble reliefs of the apostles.

Conducted tours of the Hohensalzburg Fortress and museums are given every 15 minutes May to September from 9 a.m. to 5:30 p.m., and every 30 minutes October to April from 9:30 a.m. to 3:30 p.m. Admission is 25 AS ($1.33) for adults, 7 AS (37¢) for children 6 to 15.

You should visit Hohensalzburg even if you're not interested in the fortress, just for the experience of the view from the terrace. From the Reck watchtower you get a panoramic sweep of the Alps. Also, the Kuenberg bastion has a fine view of the domes and towers of Salzburg, looking from here like a riot of baroque architecture.

There are several ways to reach the fortress. If you're athletic you can follow one of the paths or lanes leading to it, or you can come on foot from Kapitelplatz by way of Festungsgasse or else from Mönchsberg via the Schartentor. I like to take the funicular from Festungsgasse at the station in back of the cathedral. The round trip costs 21 AS ($1.18) for adults, 10.50 AS (59¢) for children, and it runs every ten minutes during daylight hours (the trip takes six minutes). You can't go to the fortress by car.

West of Hohensalzburg Fortress is **Mönchsberg.** This heavily forested ridge extending for some 1½ miles rising above the old town has fortifications dating from the 15th century. Several panoramic vistas can be seen from it, and a lovely view of Salzburg is possible from Mönchsberg Terrace just in front of the Grand Café Winkler where the casino is located. Three express elevators from along Gstättengasse take you to the terrace daily May 1 to September from 7 a.m. till 3 a.m., October 1 to April 30 from 7 a.m. till 2:30 a.m. For adults the fare is 15 AS (80¢) for a round trip. Children's fare is 7.50 AS (40¢) round trip.

The **Mozart Museum,** Mozart's Geburtshaus (Mozart's birthplace), 9 Getreidegasse, is a typical old burgher's house. Leopold Mozart lived on the third floor of this structure from 1747 to 1773, and it was here that Wolfgang Amadeus was born on Jan. 27, 1756, a date all Salzburgers know.

The apartment contains a number of mementos. The child prodigy Mozart, who began composing at the age of four, wrote his early works here. You can see the small violin on which he played and his childhood spinet.

You can visit this birthplace of Salzburg's most renowned citizen May 1 to October 1 from 9 a.m. to 7 p.m. and January to May 1 and October 1 to December from 9 a.m. to 6 p.m. Admission is 30 AS ($1.60) for adults, 15 AS (80¢) for children.

It's also possible to visit **Mozart's Wohnhaus,** his residence, at 8 Makartplatz, the Mozart family home from 1773 to 1787. The house was rebuilt after World War II damage. All that remains of the original are the entrance and the Tanzmeistersaal (dance master's hall). The house is open to visitors June 1 to September 30, Monday to Saturday from 10 a.m. to 4 p.m. Admission is 20 AS ($1.06) for adults, 10 AS (53¢) for children.

Mirabell Gardens, on the right bank of the river, laid out by Fischer von Erlach and now a public park, are the finest baroque gardens in Salzburg. They are studded with statuary and reflecting pools. Some of the marble balustrades and urns were also designed by von Erlach. There's also a natural theater. As you wander in the gardens at your leisure, be sure to visit the bastion with fantastic marble baroque dwarfs and other figures, by the Pegasus Fountain in the lavish garden west of Schloss Mirabell (coming up). From the gardens is an excellent view of Hohensalzburg Fortress. The marble statues make Mirabell Gardens virtually an open-air museum.

Mirabell Palace (Schloss Mirabell) was built originally as a luxurious private residence called Altenau. Prince-Archbishop Wolfgang Dietrich had it constructed in 1606 for his mistress and mother of his children, Salome Alt. Not much remains of the original grand structure. Lukas von Hildebrandt rebuilt the schloss in the first quarter of the 18th century, and it was modified after a great fire in 1818. The official residence of the mayor of Salzburg is now in the palace, which is like a smaller edition of the Tuileries in Paris. The ceremonial marble "angel staircase" with sculptured cherubs, carved by Raphael Donner in 1726, leads to the Marmorsaal, a marble and gold hall now used for concerts and weddings. Candlelit chamber music concerts are staged here.

Admission is free to both the gardens and the palace, which lie just off the Makartplatz.

You can also visit **Salzburger Barockmuseum** (tel. 77-4-32) in the orangery in the Mirabell Gardens. Here European art of the 17th and 18th centuries is displayed, with works by Giordano, Rottmayr, Bernini, and Straub, among other artists in the Rossacher collection. Hours all year are 9 a.m. to noon and 2 to 5 p.m. Tuesday to Saturday, 9 a.m. to noon on Sunday and holidays. Admission is 20 AS ($1.06) for adults, 10 AS (53¢) for children.

The **Friedhof St. Sebastian** (St. Sebastian Cemetery) in Linzergasse was commissioned by Prince-Archbishop Wolf Dietrich in 1595, to be laid out like an Italian *campo santo*. Tombs of Mozart's wife, who endured many hardships, and of his father, Leopold, are here. In the middle of the cemetery is St. Gabriel's Chapel, wherein lies the mausoleum of the now-notorious Dietrich. The interior of his sarcophagus is lined with multicolored porcelain.

To reach the cemetery, you take steps modeled after those in the Italian style up from **St. Sebastian's Church.** The original late Gothic edifice dated from the early 16th century. It was rebuilt and enlarged in 1749, decorated in the rococo style. Destroyed by fire in 1818, it was later reconstructed. The 1752 rococo doorway remains from the old church building. Paracelsus, the Renaissance doctor and philosopher who died in 1541, is entombed here.

Nonnberg Convent, reached by a flight of steps at the end of the Kaigasse, founded about 700 as a Benedictine nunnery by St. Rupert, is the oldest existing convent on earth. St. Rupert's niece, St. Erentrudis (or Ehrentrude), was the first abbess. The convent is a storehouse of treasures, with elaborate woodcarvings. There's also a museum of sacred relics. In the abbey church, in late Gothic style, is the tomb of St. Erentrudis. The St. John Chapel over the gateway displays a Gothic altarpiece from the late 15th century. An underground passage leads from the convent to Hohensalzburg Fortress.

The **Franciscan Church** (Franziskanerkirche), near the Domplatz, was built to replace St. Mary's parish church which was destroyed by fire in 1167. The present edifice was consecrated in 1223, the Romanesque nave dating from that year. In the 17th century the house of worship was rebuilt, and now is one of the most interesting churches of Salzburg stylistically, having Romanesque and Gothic styles as well as rococo and baroque elements in its architecture and decoration.

The **Festspielhaus,** or Festival Hall, 1 Hofstallgasse (tel. 42-5-41), was once the stables for the court, designed by Wolf Dietrich and built in 1607. Today it's the center for the major musical events of Salzburg, cultural activity reaching its peak at the August festival. Standing at the rear of Kollegienkirche which is on Universitätsplatz, the small old hall has superb ceiling paintings by Rottmayr. The modern hall seats 2,300 spectators. The major concerts and big operas are performed here during the festival. Many outstanding Austrian artists contributed works to decorate the modern Festival Hall.

Guided tours are given Monday to Friday at 11 a.m. and 3 p.m. and on Saturday at 11 a.m. in May and June; Monday to Friday at 11 a.m. and 3 p.m. in

September; Monday to Friday at 3 p.m. and on Saturday at 11 a.m. from October to April; and Monday to Saturday at 2 p.m. during the Easter Festival. There are no guided tours in July and August. Admission is 25 AS ($1.33) for adults, 10 AS (53¢) for children.

On the right bank of the Salzach at 26 Schwarzstrasse is the **Mozarteum** (tel. 73-1-54), founded almost a century after the composer's birth. In this building (constructed just before World War I) the first Mozart festival took place in 1922. There are two concert halls and a vast library of works about and by the composer. In the garden is the **Magic Flute House,** a little wooden structure in which Mozart composed *The Magic Flute* in 1791. It was shipped here from the Nachtmarkt in Vienna. In 1970 the Mozarteum was designated as the College of Music and the Performing Arts.

The Magic Flute House may be visited Monday to Friday July 1 to August 31 from 11 a.m. to noon for 30 AS ($1.60) per person.

Also on the right bank is the "other hill" of Salzburg, the **Kapuzinerberg,** a forested area rising more than 2,000 feet. Today this area is a lovely park. A Capuchin friary was built here in the closing year of the 16th century, constructed inside an old fortification from the Middle Ages. On the south side of the hill is a handsome street, Steingasse, from medieval times, and the Steintor, which was once a gate in the walls of Salzburg. The author of "Silent Night," Joseph Mohr, was born here in 1792.

From vantage points on the Kapuzinerberg you can see into Bavaria.

IN THE ENVIRONS: The environs of Salzburg are outstanding, and to explore them fully you'll need to refer to the information contained in Chapter VIII of this book, "Land Salzburg." The area is a setting of beautiful old romantic castles, charming villages, glacial lakes, salt mines, ice caves, and some of the most spectacular alpine scenery in Europe. But before going on to Land Salzburg, I'll describe a few attractions to be found right on the doorstep of the city.

Schloss Hellbrunn (Hellbrunn Palace), about three miles south of the city, is a popular spot for outings from Salzburg. It's at the end of Hellbrunnerstrasse off Alpenstrasse. Also to be seen here is the Hellbrunn Zoo. The palace dates from the early 17th century, built as a hunting lodge and summer residence for Prince-Archbishop Marcus Sitticus. The zoo was formerly the palace deer park.

The palace **gardens,** the oldest baroque formal gardens in all Europe, are known for their trick fountains. As you walk through, take care. You may be showered when and from a source you least suspect. In some of the contrived fountain play, spurts of water shoot out from unlikely spots, such as from antlers. More than 100 figures in a mechanical theater are set in motion by a clockwork movement to the music of an organ, powered by water.

The rooms of the schloss are furnished and decorated in 18th-century style. See, in particular, the banqueting hall with its *trompe l'oeil* ceiling. There's also a domed octagonal room that was used as a music room and reception hall.

The **Salzburg Folklore Museum** is housed in the Monatsschlösschen, the original hunting lodge of Schloss Hellbrunn. Mementos of life in Land Salzburg are on display.

Conducted tours of the castle, trick fountains, and folklore museum are given from 9 a.m. to 4 p.m. April 1 to April 15; to 5 p.m. April 16 to April 30 and September 1 to September 15; to 5:30 p.m. May to August. From September 16 to September 30, hours are 9 a.m. to noon and 1 to 4:30 p.m., to 4 p.m. in October. Admission is 35 AS ($1.86) for adults, 17 AS (90¢) for children. The gardens, orangery, and pheasantry may be visited free.

Castle concerts, together with a visit to the trick fountains and the historic wine cellar, are given on Wednesday and Saturday (occasionally on Monday) in July and August, beginning at 7:30 p.m. Adults pay 180 AS ($9.58) and children 100 AS ($5.32).

In the same setting, a natural gorge forms the **Stone Theater** where the first opera performed in the German-speaking world was presented in 1617. A Hellbrunn Festival is held in the gardens, palace, and theater in August.

In 1961 the Hellbrunn Zoo (tel. 41-1-69) was opened, stretching around the western slope of the hill, with low fences allowing the public close views of the zoo's mainly alpine animal denizens. As this was the deer park for the prince-archbishops, there are still large herds of stags and their families grazing on their ancestral acres. The zoo is open all year. Visiting hours are 9 a.m. to 4 p.m. October to March, to 6:30 p.m. April to September. Admission costs 30 AS ($1.60) for adults, 7 AS (37¢) for children.

It's only about a 20-minute drive from the heart of Salzburg to Hellbrunn Palace, and if the weather is good, many visitors prefer to walk the three miles. If you drive, turn off Alpenstrasse at the Mobil gas station. Or you can take an "H" bus, which makes the run in about 18 minutes.

About ten miles east from the center of Salzburg is **Gaisberg**, which at 4,250 feet is one of the best places for views of the Salzburg Alps. Much of the road leading here is hewn out of rock. You can take a bus to the Gaisbergspitz or summit from which you see almost a full panorama. On a clear day you can see into Chiemsee in West Germany and to the Dachstein massif. In summer the bus leaves Mirabellplatz by St. Andrew's Church at 9 a.m. or at 11 a.m. The trip takes about an hour.

To reach **Untersberg**, about 7½ miles from Salzburg, you head south out of the city toward Berchtesgaden in West Germany, the retreat of Hitler during his days of power. At the St. Leonhard junction, turn right and drive to the platform of a cable-car station. The funicular goes to the Untersberg summit (6,020 feet), from which you have a panoramic view of the Salzburg Alps. A marked path leads to the Salzburger Hochtron (6,100 feet), highest Austrian peak in the Untersberg massif.

Funicular service March 1 to June 30 and September 16 to October 31 is from 9:15 a.m. to 4:45 p.m., July 1 to mid-September from 8:30 a.m. to 5:30 p.m., and December 25 to February 28 from 10 a.m. to 4 p.m. The fare is 125 AS ($6.65) for a round-trip ticket, 70 AS ($3.72) for children.

The **Church of Maria Plain**, about 2½ miles north of Salzburg, is the most important pilgrimage church in the vicinity of the city. Construction on the twin-towered baroque church started in 1671, and it's lavishly embellished. To reach Maria Plain you head out Plainstrasse, eventually turning right onto Plainbergweg. If you take the tram it's about 45 minutes further on foot. Many people prefer the view from here at night.

From Maria Plain you can continue on about nine miles northwest to another pilgrimage church at **Oberndorf**. This village lying on the Salzach River is where Joseph Mohr wrote the carol "Silent Night" on Christmas Eve in 1818. A memorial chapel was built here in 1937.

Mattsee, 14 miles from Salzburg, is a small resort for city residents, on the shores of Niedertrumer See, Obertrumer See, and Grabensee. Many tombstones from the 14th century have been found in the cloister of a 13th-century collegiate church here. To get to Mattsee, head out on Plainstrasse and the Itzlinger Hauptstrasse. You'll go through the hamlets of Bergheim, Lengfelden, and Elixhausen to reach it.

In the Tennengau, a division of the Salzach Valley south of Salzburg, a major attraction is—

Hallein

The second-largest town in Land Salzburg, (visited in detail in the upcoming chapter), Hallein, once a center for processing the salt from the mines of Dürrnberg, was a prize possession of the prince-archbishops of Salzburg. Today it's an industrial town on the Salzach River, and tourists pass through it on the way to the Dürrnberg mines.

On the north side of the Hallein parish church are the former home and tomb of the man who composed the music for Father Joseph Mohr's Christmas carol "Silent Night," Franz-Xaver Gruber, a schoolteacher, who died in 1863.

The **Dürrnberg Salt Mines** are the big lure, forming one of the most popular attractions in Land Salzburg, usually visited on day-trips from Salzburg. On guided tours, visitors walk downhill from the ticket office to the mine entrance, then board an electric mine train which takes you deep into the caverns. From there, you go on foot through deep galleries, changing levels by sliding down polished wooden slides. You exit the mine on the train that brought you in. An underground museum traces the history of salt mining back into remote time.

Tours are conducted daily May to October from 8 a.m. to 5 p.m., lasting about 1½ hours. Admission is 85 AS ($4.52) for adults, 45 AS ($2.39) for children.

Hallein is connected to Salzburg, ten miles away, by both train and bus service. From here there's a cable railway to Dürrnberg, although many Germans and Austrians prefer to walk to the mines, the trip taking about an hour. Cable railway fare for a round trip is 56 AS ($2.98) per person.

Phone 06245/3511 for more information. There is a new road from Hallein directly to a large parking lot near the ticket office.

Also in the Salzburg environs is the Pongau basin, described in the Land Salzburg chapter coming up, a division of the Salzach Valley. An outstanding attraction, most often visited on day trips from the city, is the—

Eisriesenwelt

Some 30 miles south of Salzburg by train is the "World of the Ice Giants," the largest known ice caves in Europe. The caves, opening at some 5,500 feet up, stretch for about 26 miles, although only a portion of that length is open to the public. You'll see fantastic ice formations at the entrance, extending for half a mile.

To reach the Eisriesenwelt, head for Werfen, a village that is the center for exploring the ice caves. It also contains **Castle Hohenwerfen** which was founded in the 11th century and frequently reconstructed. It is one of the most important castles in Land Salzburg and is visible for miles around. It's open in summer to visitors.

If you come by train from Salzburg, you can take a taxibus from Werfen's Hauptplatz (main square), going 3½ miles by mountain road to the same point you'll reach if you're traveling in your own car, rising from 1,600 feet to 3,000 feet. You have to take a cable car to the entrance of the caves, which involves a 15-minute walk along a shady path with stunning views to the lower station. The round-trip cable-car ride costs 70 AS ($3.72) for adults, 35 AS ($1.86) for children to this point.

Tours begin at the Dr.-Friedrich-Oedl-Haus at 5,141 feet, from which you walk to the actual entrance. Tours take about two hours and cost 55 AS ($2.93) for adults per person, 30 AS ($1.60) per child. Conducted tours are given every hour from May to October from 9:30 a.m. to 3:30 p.m. In July and August, the schedule is accelerated if demand justifies it. For information, phone 06468/248.

Eisriesenwelt is on the western cliffs of the Hochkogel, towering over the Salzach Valley. You can imagine you're in the kingdom of the Ice Queen as you pass through this underground ice wonderland, which looks as if fairies had decorated their frozen precincts, adorning them with icy figures that look almost man-made and with frozen waterfalls. The climax of this chill underworld tour is the spectacular Ice Palace. It's too bad visitors can't explore the entire 26-mile length of the cave, but such a venture is extremely dangerous and cannot be permitted.

Allow about 5½ hours for the entire trip from Werfen and back. Dress warmly, and wear shoes appropriate for hiking.

Even if you don't want to go underground, I recommend making the drive as far up toward the caves as you can go, as the scenery along the way is truly splendid.

TOURS: A **City Sightseeing Tour** is offered daily at 9:30 a.m., 11 a.m., noon, and 3 p.m. from Mirabellplatz, taking about two hours and costing 180 AS ($9.58). This tour highlights both the old and modern parts of the city, beginning with Mirabell Palace, passing the Congress Hall, Mozarteum, and Landestheater. You cross the main bridge to the left bank of the Salzach River and go past the oldest bakery, the Horse Pond, the Festival Hall, St. Peter's Church, the Salzburg Cathedral, and the Residenz.

You must take your passport along for the afternoon **excursion to Berchtesgaden and Königsee.** The trip, beginning daily at 2 p.m. and returning about 6 p.m. from April 1 to October 31, costs 220 AS ($11.70). You leave from Mirabellplatz and tour neighboring Bavaria, going past Hellbrunn and Anif Palaces en route to Hintereck (3,000 feet), from which you have a good view of Hitler's "Eagle's Nest." The guide explains matters of interest about der Führer's aerie. The tour takes you down to Königsee where you can make a brief cruise on the lake if you wish. Next you go to Berchtesgaden, formerly a salt-mining town and now a popular summer resort, before returning to Salzburg.

Another interesting half-day trip is an afternoon **excursion to the lake district, Salzkammergut,** which leaves Mirabellplatz daily at 2 p.m. from April 1 to October 31, returning around 6 p.m. The cost is 200 AS ($10.64). You're driven through the outskirts of Salzburg, passing the pilgrimage church of Maria Plain and going to Mondsee, warmest of the lakes in the Salzkammergut area, and into Upper Austria. You stop for tea at the celebrated White Horse Inn in the market town of St. Wolfgang, also visiting the 15th-century church there. This scenic tour brings you back to Salzburg via the summer resort of Fuschl.

A **Sound of Music Tour** leaves from the American Express office, 5 Mozartplatz (tel. 42-5-01), daily except Sunday all year, at 9:30 a.m. and 2 p.m., costing 240 AS ($12.77) and lasting three hours. The tour revitalizes the celebrated movie *The Sound of Music,* which shows how the Trapp family escaped from Austria when the Nazis took over, making their way to the United States. On this tour you're shown palaces, squares, and other settings that were used in the film.

Another, slightly longer **Mountain Picnic Tour,** arranged by Bob's Special Tours, Münchnerhof, 3 Dreifaltigkeitsgasse (tel. 72-4-84), provides a lot for your money. For just 240 AS ($12.77), plus your lunch cost (see below), you can be picked up at your hotel or pension free, in time to leave Salzburg on the tour at 9 a.m. or 2 p.m. You'll be returned after about four hours either to the old town (Neutor) or the main railway station. The trip takes you past the major *Sound of Music* sites, including Schloss Leopoldskron, through the Bavarian Alps for a one-hour stop at Berchtesgaden, where you will get to enjoy an indoor or outdoor concert (depending on the weather). You'll go to remote, peaceful Untersberg Nature Park.

Participation in the picnic is optional, but for only 50 AS ($2.66) you get a variety of cheese and cold cuts, fresh vegetables and fruit, and dark farmer's bread, with lemon tea. Picnic time is at noon for the morning tour, at 5 p.m. for the afternoon trek. If the weather is inclement, you have lunch for 50 AS ($2.66) at a cozy mountain inn.

On the tour route are Anif, the West German border, Marktschellenberg, Berchtesgaden, Bischofswiesen, Bayerisch Gmain, and Grossgmain. You must take your passport on this tour.

You can make reservations for the Mountain Picnic Tour at the reception desk of your hotel or pension or at ticket office Polzer, 4 Residenzplatz; Salzburger Landesreisebüro, 13 Schwarzstrasse; or Neubaur travel and ticket office, 14 Getreidegasse in the arcade.

There are numerous other tour possibilities, including full-day excursions to Grossglockner Glacier and other points of interest.

6. Where to Shop

Salzburg, being a much smaller city, obviously doesn't have the wide range of merchandise that Vienna does. However, if you're not going on to the Austrian capital, you may want to patronize some of the establishments recommended below, most of them opening at 9 a.m. and staying open until 6 p.m. Note that a number of them, especially the smaller places, take a one- or two-hour break for lunch. The stores also close down on Saturday afternoon and all day on Sunday.

Good buys in Salzburg include souvenirs of Land Salzburg, dirndls, lederhosen, petit-point, and all types of sports gear. Getreidegasse is a main shopping thoroughfare, but you'll also find some intriguing little shops on the Residenzplatz.

Original Trachten Wenger, 2 Munzgasse (tel. 41-3-59), is one of the best shops in Salzburg for elegantly traditional clothing. The gracious and sophisticated owner, Edith Hagn, will direct her in-house fitter to alter any garment within two hours, so you can buy it in the morning and wear it that evening at dinner. Dozens of well-made dirndls, skirts, and women's coats hang from racks in this well-furnished store. Couturier made-to-order garments can be created from patterns and individualized fabrics. The English-speaking staff do everything they can to be of assistance. Accessories include umbrellas, belts, scarves, and gloves. The store is near the river in the old town.

Jahn-Markl, 3 Residenzplatz (tel. 84-26-10), is a small and elegant store with a forest-green facade trimmed with brass and wrought-iron detailing. In the center of the old town, it carries lederhosen for both men and women, leather skirts, and a full line of traditional Austrian coats and blazers. The less expensive items are usually sold off the racks that stretch high above the clients' heads. More expensive items are usually made to order in four weeks and can be mailed anywhere in the world for an additional charge. Some children's clothing is available as well, along with hats, belts, and gloves.

Salzburger Heimatwerk, Am Residenzplatz (tel. 84-41-19), is one of the best places in town to buy native Austrian handicrafts. It's a dignified stone building in the least crowded section of the Residenzplatz, with a discreet (and hard to see) sign announcing its location. Items for sale include Austrian and silver garnet jewelry, painted boxes, candles, woodcarvings, copper and brass ceramics, tablecloths, and patterns for cross-stitched samplers in alpine designs. A special section sells dressmaking materials such as cotton, silk, and wool fabrics in Tyrolean designs, with dressmaker patterns that can be adapted for the eventual size of the garment. Wherever you go in this interesting store, be sure to keep exploring until you've seen every room.

Sporting Goods Dschulnigg, 8 Griesgasse (tel. 42-3-76), is an uppercrust emporium for clothes, guns, fishing equipment, overcoats for both men and women, intricately patterned sweaters in alpine colors, a collection of fur-lined hats, and many kinds of sporting goods. Queen Elizabeth II and Prince Phillip have been photographed on a shopping expedition here. You can get hunting rifles in Austria without a license (but not pistols or revolvers), although the Customs officers back home might present a problem. Be sure to climb to the second floor if you're interested.

Slezak, 8 Makartplatz (tel. 73-5-68), near Mozart's house, sells gloves, skirts, leather goods, umbrellas, suitcases, sweaters, belts, and leather and suede jackets for men, and has a good selection of all these items.

Schatz-Konditorei, 3 Getreidegasse (tel. 42-7-92). Already covered in the café section of this chapter, this establishment is an excellent pastry shop and one of the few in Salzburg that will mail cakes to foreign clients. The specialty of the store is the highly acclaimed Mozart-Kugeln, a concoction of pistachio, marzipan, and hazelnut nougat, dipped in chocolate. It might make a nice present for the friends or relatives you left behind. Packages of this gourmet delight can be air-mailed to North America.

Gollhofer Herrenmode, 10 Getreidegasse (tel. 42-1-75), is a large store selling quality clothing for men and women. It has a high-ceilinged spacious format with lots of modern paneling and a collection of merchandise that includes sports jackets, leather garments, and women's shoes. This is more of a large downtown store than an intimate boutique.

Brüder Fritsch, 42 Getreidegasse (tel. 47-5-51), sells leather goods to an up-market clientele. The contents of the store are expensive, filling two floors. Both Celine and Gucci are represented here.

Musikhaus Pühringer, 13 Getreidegasse (tel. 43-2-67), sells recorders, classical records, and tapes, plus Mozart recordings by many different artists from many different countries. The store is appropriately located a few buildings away from Mozart's birthplace. It also sells guitars made in Germany, Italy, and Japan.

Lobmeyr, 20 Schwartzstrasse (tel. 73-1-81), is the Salzburg branch of the famous store in Vienna. Among a wide range of crystal goblets and elegant china, it includes some of the prettiest breakfast services I've seen, many of them made in Hungary.

Lanz, 4 Schwartzstrasse (tel. 74-2-72), is a well-stocked store across the river from the old town. The format is rustically modern, with one of the widest collections of long-skirted dirndls in town, in dozens of different fabrics and colors. Men's clothing includes loden-colored overcoats. The store also sells dirndls for little girls, women's shoes, and hand-knitted sweaters.

J. B. Neumüller, 3 Rathausplatz (tel. 41-4-29). In wintertime this store sells children's toys. In summer the stock changes, the shelves filling up with handcrafted souvenirs such as mugs, cowbells, and rustic art objects.

7. Salzburg After Dark

FESTIVAL: In 1986 the **Salzburg Festival**—one of the premier music attractions of Europe—celebrated its 66th season. The composer Richard Strauss founded the festival, aided by the director Max Reinhardt and the writer Hugo van Hofmannsthal. Details on this festival are available by writing the Austrian National Music Festivals, Suite 207, 545 Fifth Ave., New York, NY 10017 (tel. 212/697-0656), before the middle of May. After that, make direct inquiries to the box office of the Salzburg Festival, Festspielhaus, A 5010 Salzburg, Austria (or telephone 84-24-51 for information).

Festival tickets are in great demand, and there never are enough of them. Don't arrive expecting to get into any of the major events unless you've already purchased tickets. Travel agents can often get tickets for you, and you can also go to branches of the Austrian Tourist Office at home or abroad. Hotel concierges, particularly at the deluxe and first-class hotels of Salzburg, always have some tickets on hand, but they most often ask outrageous prices for them, depending on the particular performance you wish to attend. At first-night performances of the major productions, remember that evening dress is *de rigueur*.

An annual event is Hofmannsthal's morality play *Everyman*, which is staged outside the cathedral in the Domplatz. Concerts are likely to be conducted in the Rittersaal of the Residenz Palace (Mozart also conducted here) and in the marble salon of Mirabell Palace (Mozart's father, Leopold, conducted here). The Salzburg Marionette Theater (see below) also presents performances. Ballet is likely to be performed by the Vienna State Opera Ballet with the Vienna Opera Chorus and the Vienna Philharmonic. Operas (certainly Mozart, and most likely Richard Strauss and Beethoven) are also accompanied by the Vienna Philharmonic. International soloists—such big names as Luciano Pavarotti—are invited annually, and the London Symphony or the Berlin Philharmonic are also likely to be invited.

Tickets begin at 65 AS ($3.46) for standing room at one of the serenade concerts, going up to 3,000 AS ($160) for the choice opera seats.

Most performances begin fairly early in the evening, and sometimes there are morning and afternoon performances. These annual events overshadow any nightlife you might find in Salzburg, where clubs rise and fall fairly rapidly.

OTHER CONCERTS: As mentioned, the **Salzburger Marionetten Theater,** 24 Schwarzstrasse (tel. 7-24-06), presents shows of operas and operettas, running from Easter through September (there are also special shows at Christmas). These puppets perform both opera and ballet and are a delight to both adults and children. Usually they present Mozart operas. Seats are likely to range from 230 AS ($12.24) to 300 AS ($15.96). The theater was founded in 1913, and since that time has been one of the most unusual—and enjoyable—theatrical entertainments in Salzburg. You may forget that marionettes are on stage, it's that realistic.

The **Salzburger Landestheater,** 22 Schwarzstrasse (tel. 7-40-86), doesn't always play for summer visitors, but if you're in Salzburg from September until some time in June, you can see its regular repertoire of operas (not just Mozart) and operettas. On my last visit, for example, I saw a thrilling performance of Giuseppe Verdi's *La Traviata*. In August, performances are given for the Festspiel.

All year round you can go to the tourist office in Salzburg and pick up a list of musical events that are being presented when you're there, even if you should arrive in January. In fact the annual **Mozart Week** is in January. Summer chamber music concerts are most often offered at the Residenz and Mirabell Palace.

Music, especially organ concerts, is also presented at the **Mozarteum,** 26 Schwarzstrasse (tel. 7-31-54).

If you're not a music lover, you may prefer some casino action instead.

DISCOS: Discos are still alive, but not doing that well in Salzburg. Sometimes admission fees of about 30 AS ($1.60) are charged, and drinks usually go from 60 AS ($3.19) to 80 AS ($4.26).

One of the leading discos is in the suburb of Anif, just outside the city limits. It's the **Friesacher Stadl,** 57 Anif (tel. 24-11), a substantial-looking country house set about 100 yards away from a busy highway in Anif. You'll enter a dimly lit room loaded with paneling, wooden tables, and rustic artifacts. The bar area, which is usually a good place to meet people, stretches toward the small dance floor, where many of the couples dance in each other's arms, even to the disco/folkloric music. This is a popular rendezvous point for Salzburg and all its suburbs, and there's rarely a cover charge.

Other leading discos include **Disco Seven,** 7 Gstättengasse (tel. 84-41-81), and **Pavillon,** 72 Morzget Strasse (tel. 84-13-21). There's more disco dancing at the **Old Grenadier,** 2 Ursulinenplatz (tel. 84-37-18), which is usually open daily except Sunday from 9:30 p.m. to 4 a.m. You might also try the gyrations at **Disco-Tyrol,** 4 Wolf-Dietrich-Strasse (tel. 7-62-79), which is open from 9 p.m. to 3 a.m. It can squeeze in as many as 250, most often a very international crowd.

LATIN AMERICAN MUSIC AND DINING: Mexicano Keller (Hotel Blaue Gans), 43 Getreidegasse (tel. 84-24-91), is a popular evening spot in Salzburg, offering Latin American music and Mexican food. The cuisine includes both enchiladas and chili con carne, along with five different steak dishes, such as carne asada Acapulco. Fondue Mexicano is another specialty, served for two persons. Sangría is available as well, and meals cost from 250 AS ($13.30). The decor looks like a combination of an Austrian wine cellar and a ranch south of the (American) border, with a vaulted stone ceiling and rustic ranchero-style banquettes. The cellar is closed on Tuesday and Wednesday.

GAMBLING: If you're interested in either losing or winning a fortune, you can head for the **Spiel-Casino** which sits along with the Café Winkler on Mönchsberg (tel. 45-6-56). You can reach it by an elevator at the bottom of the hill. As you enter you'll find gaming tables where you can play roulette, baccarat, and blackjack, as well as the inevitable slot machines. The casino might be a way to pass a few evening hours in Salzburg, if only for the sake of the view from the top.

You must take your passport because they're very strict about this—no exceptions are allowed. All employees speak English. The casino is open from 7 p.m. to 2 a.m. weekdays, with late closings of 4 a.m. on Saturday and Sunday. In exchange for an entrance fee of 130 AS ($6.92), the management will give you gaming tokens worth 150 AS ($7.98). If you come in your own car, there is free parking for 12 hours for casino guests in the Mountain Garage North.

Casino Fallenegger, 14 Bayerhamerstrasse (tel. 71-1-69), a five-minute ride from Old Town, is a wide-ranging entertainment complex about half a mile east of the Salzach River. Its facilities include a summertime athletic complex, four outdoor tennis courts, and an inviting collection of sun terraces with waiter service. Also on the premises are two restaurants, a disco, two indoor tennis courts, a sauna, and several bars. You'll enter the site through a central courtyard, which is closed on one side by shrubbery and a rustic post-and-lintel construction capped with a sign that looks like something from the American Southwest.

One of the bars has a forest-green decor, Oriental rugs, and a pleasantly masculine well-appointed ambience of green leather and polished wood. Other places to have a drink overlook the indoor tennis courts. Drinks are also served in a pine-walled billiard room. The Zirbenstube serves gutbürgerlich food in a rustic, pleasantly woodsy atmosphere, while another restaurant has a high wood-covered ceiling, Oriental rugs, and an inviting bar area. Drinks throughout the complex range from 50 AS ($2.66), while meals in the restaurant go from 250 AS ($13.30) to 500 AS ($26.60).

A rustic disco (the **Casino-Alm**) is one of the oldest surviving ones in Salzburg, founded in 1955. Its cozily rustic format of sloped ceilings and open fireplaces sometimes gets crowded in the evening, and it's open every day except Sunday from 9 p.m. to 3 a.m. You'll find adjoining rooms and offshoot areas attached to many of the places described.

BEER GARDENS: Casinos not for you? My recommendation for one of the most enjoyable and authentic evenings in Salzburg is to pay a gemütlich visit to the **Augustiner Bräustübl,** 4-6 Augustinergasse (tel. 3-12-46), the most famous beer gardens in Salzburg. In winter guests retreat inside to one of several large beer halls, but in fair weather the beer-drinking fraternity spills out into the leafy chestnut garden to "taste the brew." The brew, incidentally, is excellent, and it's served daily from 3 to 11 p.m. The activity gets loud and raucous, especially when the young men from Munich invade on their summer tours south from neighboring Bavaria. To get there, you climb a steep, narrow cobblestone street and go through an austere stone entranceway, passing statues of ecstatic saints and happy cherubs.

After descending a baroque staircase whose ceiling frescoes evoke images of a Habsburg palace, you'll come face to face with about a dozen kiosks, where you can buy carry-away portions of salads, wursts, sandwiches, and pretzels. Farther on, you choose one of the thick stoneware mugs from the drying racks and carry it to the beer tap, paying the cashier as you go. A full liter costs from 30 AS ($1.60) to 36 AS ($1.92), depending on the type of brew you select. Smaller mugs are available if you just want to sip and watch the crowd. You take your own mug to one of the trio of cavernous rooms *(saals)* nearby. This place has been known to squeeze in some 2,200 beer-drinkers (the busiest night on record). Toward the end of the evening, take care not to slip on the suds which spill onto the tile floor near the taps.

The place got its name from the old Augustinian monastery which was taken over in 1835 by the Benedictines whose monastery is at Michaelbeuern. They are only responsible today for the parish church in Mülln, across the street from the Bräustübl, in which they have a small financial interest.

Stiegelbrau Keller, 8-10 Festungsgasse (tel. 84-26-81). To reach this place, you'll have to negotiate a steep cobblestone street which drops off on one side to reveal a breathtaking view of Salzburg. Part of the establishment is carved into the rocks of Mönchsberg mountain, so all that is visible from the outside is a gilded iron gate and a short stairway of porous stone. The cavernous interior is open only in summer when, along with hundreds of others, you can drink beer and eat traditional bierkeller food such as sausages and schnitzels. But, mainly, you can attend performances of the Alpinia Folkloric Club. Its members offer a "Salzburger Abend" every Wednesday and Saturday night at 8:15, which includes 2½ hours of yodeling and Schuhplattln dancing, all of which is accompanied with music from brass bands and zithers. Seats cost around 125 AS ($6.65) and should be booked in advance.

LAND SALZBURG

THE GEOGRAPHIC BORDERS of Land Salzburg may appear to be a fantasy—the work of a mapmaker gone haywire—but actually the boundaries of this lofty province in the high Alps follow the dictates of Mother Nature. Craggy mountains, deep valleys, winding rivers, lakes, and rolling foothills, plus a little political expediency, all had their effect on the cartographers' pens. This Bundesland (state, or province) of Austria takes in some 2,762 square miles. It's known for its beautiful waterfalls, including the Krimml Falls, the most important cataract in the eastern Alps.

This is a land of both summer and winter sports, with such celebrated spas as Badgastein and such renowned ski resorts as Zell am See, Kaprun, and Saalbach. You can select resorts right on the lakeside or else mountain hotels at celestial levels. You'll be better suited to the activities of this province if you're athletic.

Instead of staying in Salzburg, especially during the crowded, hotel-scarce months of festival time, you might prefer to anchor into one of the resorts described below and commute to the province's capital city. You'll find the prices far cheaper and the living much easier if you don't mind the drive. (You won't necessarily have to go into the city *every* day.)

Accommodations are wide ranging. If you want deluxe, you'll find it. If you want a mountain hut or just a *zimmer* (room) in one of the local houses—usually perched in some idyllic spot—these are available too. A few castle hotels, some of the finest accommodations in Austria, are found in Land Salzburg, to suit those who have traditional and romantic tastes and don't always demand the latest in plumbing fixtures.

The terrain directly around Salzburg is flat, but most of Land Salzburg is mountainous. Always inquire about local weather conditions before embarking for a day's sightseeing, particularly if you're going to be traversing one of those lofty alpine highways. The highest mountain range in Austria, the Hohe Tauern, lies on the southern fringe of Land Salzburg. A national park, the Hohe Tauern encompasses one of the most beautiful areas of the eastern Alps, still mainly undeveloped. The core of the park is formed of mighty mountains, steep rock faces, glaciers, and glacier streams, one of which contains the Krimml Falls mentioned above. The park's periphery comprises mountain meadows, alpine pastures, and protective woods. Visitors to the park are required to treat the plants and animals with respect.

The Tauern Highway is one of the most important roads going from north to south over the Alps. Vehicles pass through two tunnels while traversing the highway. The Tauerntunnel is 4 miles long and the Katschbergtunnel 3¼ miles.

Because many of the alpine highways are feats of engineering, requiring enormous investment of capital and paralyzingly expensive upkeep, tolls are charged. They're not excessive, but are vital to keeping some scenic splendors open to the public.

Of course, Land Salzburg is a skier's paradise. The season begins about ten days before Christmas and usually lasts until Easter or beyond, depending on snow conditions. Skiing on some of the lofty plateaus is possible all year long.

Kaprun, Saalbach, and Zell am See are celebrated resorts, long established *and* expensive. However, in the true spirit of the *Dollarwise* guides, I've sought out less familiar and even undiscovered places—many known only to the Austrians and an occasional German tourist—for this book. Many establishments we'll visit, particularly the smaller, off-the-beaten-track resorts, are making their debut in a guide (in any language).

Long cut off from the rest of the world but now accessible because of modern engineering achievements, some of the sections of Land Salzburg still cling tenaciously to their traditions. Old costumes and folklore still flourish in the province, although who can say whether the present generation—heavily influenced by U.S. styles, music, or whatever—will want to keep the traditional ways alive into the next century?

The quickest way to reach the province of Land Salzburg is to fly into Salzburg, then go by train, bus, or private car to one of the resorts. If you're really in a hurry, you can take an air taxi from the capital to either Zell am See or Badgastein.

Many excursions leave from Salzburg and go into Land Salzburg, but frankly I think it's much more fun if you do it on your own. Most of the people involved in tourist services speak English, and you can travel in relative security and comfort, perhaps making discoveries of your own. You might even prefer to take a Postal Bus which goes to *all* regions, even if you have a private car.

Of course, during your tour of Land Salzburg, you can easily stray toward the West German frontier. In many places you'll be very near the border, and in fact in your exploration you might have to cross that border once or twice. That should pose no problem. Often, if you don't look suspicious, the border guards will wave you across without even looking at your passport.

One of the most interesting sections to explore in west-central Austria is the Salzkammergut lake country. This is a narrow-waisted corridor in Land Salzburg between Bavaria and Upper Austria. Parts of it will be explored in other sections of this guide. Essentially, it's a land for those who like clear alpine air and blue mountain lakes, the country of *The Sound of Music*.

Salzkammergut, incidentally, means "domain of the salt office." Many parts of the area grew rich from mining salt—and also gold.

1. Badgastein

The premier spa of Austria and one of the great spa towns of Europe—that's Badgastein. The local tourist industry is said to have been founded by

Frederick, Duke of Styria, who came here in the 15th century for treatment of a gangrenous wound. The duke was healed, and the word spread. Badgastein had made its way onto the medieval tourist map.

In more modern times, royalty and aristocrats put it back on the spa map when they flocked here around the turn of the century to "take the waters." And good waters they are—radioactive springs with healing properties. The curative effect of Badgastein's springs is not only due to their natural heat from deep under the earth but also to the radium emanation called radon.

Badgastein lies on the north slope of the Tauern massif in one of the most dramatically beautiful spots in all of Austria. The spa town climbs steep hillsides split by the foaming waters of the tumbling Gasteiner Ache. Hotels, many with water piped in directly from the Ache, adorn the steep slopes formed by the cascading waterfall. The spa's indoor swimming pool is carved into a rock filled with the radon waters.

With its pristine alpine air, skiing equaling that of St. Moritz in Switzerland, 18 hot springs for thermal hydrotherapy, and a mountain tunnel which has been called "the world's only natural giant sauna," Badgastein is considered by many people to be the pinnacle of mountain spa resorts.

Those who want to "take the cure" in the natural sauna go to **Böckstein,** two miles to the south, where the thermal galleries (underground passageways) are in an abandoned goldmine. A small train takes those seeking treatment to the various chambers.

Badgastein began its resort existence as a summer retreat, but is now also a center for winter sports. It contains the finest hotels in Land Salzburg province, and a big convention center attracts large crowds from many places.

Besides the delightful natural scenery of the town and its environs, you can see the **Nikolauskirche,** a 15th-century church with well-preserved Gothic frescoes, a late Gothic stone pulpit, and baroque altars and tombs. In the **Haus Austria,** you can view a mineral collection and see slides and photographs along with artifacts in mining and hunting exhibitions. Hours are from 10:30 a.m. to noon and 3:30 to 6 p.m. daily. Admission is 15 AS (80¢) for adults. Children up to 10 years are admitted free.

In summer there are things to do other than swimming in thermal baths or taking advantage of concomitant activities. There are saunas, massages, gymnastics, and sunning in the solarium. You can go golfing (on a nine-hole course), play tennis, ride horseback, go on mountain outings, or make excursions, perhaps in a fiacre (horse-drawn trap). Cableways and chair lifts (see below) are not only for winter sports crowds. In summer they'll take you to places from which you can view the magnificent world of the Hohe Tauern.

There's quite a lot of evening entertainment in Badgastein, both in summer and in winter, with cabaret, theater, folkloric events, and other activities.

In winter, however, most visitors are drawn here for the fine skiing possibilities, with three principal areas for skiers, where world championships and world-cup races are held. In 1958 Graukogel, one of the main areas, was the site of the world championships for skiers.

Graukogel (8,224 feet), to the east of the valley, is reached by bus from Badgastein. A chair lift takes skiers to the halfway station, from which they go the rest of the way by drag lift. Expert European skiers prefer these slopes in the afternoon. A round-trip ticket for the lift costs 150 AS ($7.98). There is a mountain restaurant at the halfway station. This is a favorite starting point for alpine walking tours.

On the west side of the valley rises **Stubnerkogel** (7,310 feet), reached by a four-seat gondola. However, it takes a chair lift and a couple of drag lifts to reach the top station. The round trip costs 150 AS ($7.98). There is a mountain

restaurant with a marvelous view. Easy mountain walks are possible here.
Kreuzkogel (8,800 feet) is at **Sportgastein,** which lies five miles up the valley to
the south of the village of Böckstein, site of the tunnel sauna mentioned above.
It's about a 20-minute bus ride from the heart of Badgastein. A chair lift will
take you to the halfway station, with a drag lift taking you on up to Kreuzkogel's
top station. Sportgastein offers high-altitude bowl skiing. Besides the well-
equipped skiing facilities here, including cross-country runs, you can also enjoy
indoor horseback riding or trekking, indoor tennis on sandy courts, alpine curling, ice skating, and walks on beautiful winter paths away from traffic.

You can drive from Badgastein to Sportgastein along the Gasteiner Alpine
Road at elevations ranging from 3,000 to 4,766 feet. The toll charge is 30 AS
($1.60) per person; children under 15, free. In winter, the ski season ticket in-
cludes the road toll.

The area code for Badgastein is 06434.

UPPER BRACKET HOTELS: **Grand Hotel de l'Europe** (tel. 37010). Even
though it was opened in 1906, it wasn't completed until three years later, which
was probably the time it took to finish the marble columns and majestic symmetrical facade. Emperor Franz Joseph and Wilhelm II came here often, making it
one of the leading hotels of Badgastein until its decline during the Russian occupation and the years that followed.

It was eventually closed in 1969, but on New Year's Eve of 1982, Liza Min-
nelli celebrated the reopening of the glamorously renovated hotel with a gala act
that's still talked about in the region. Today the hotel is outfitted with elegant
velvet walls, masses of crystal chandeliers, and dozens of original paintings by
Austrian artists. The Wiener Saal is filled with art nouveau murals and well-
prepared cuisine.

A more rustic restaurant, the Ritterstüberl, has stained-glass windows and
good food. A Biedermeier building nearby offers guest apartments and another
restaurant, the Vinothek, in the 16th-century cellars below ground level. Singles range from 1,300 AS ($69.16) to 1,900 AS ($101.08), while doubles go from
1,300 AS ($69.16) to 3,000 AS ($159.60), with breakfast included. Rates depend on the season. Children under 12 stay free in their parents' room.

Hotel Elisabethpark (tel. 2551). The ceilings of this hotel are as varied and
unusual as anything else you are likely to find in Austria. They include sections
covered with heavily textured knotty pine as well as rooms crowned with Moorish patterns of geometric greens and reds. One of the sitting rooms has a white
ceiling with iridescent gray-blue wallpaper and elegant marble detailing around
the windows. The public rooms stretch on and on, which is not surprising since
this hotel is a vast, sprawling collection of buildings, with a white exterior, lots of
balconies, and a series of hallways that are often decorated with unusual paintings, hunting trophies, and regional antiques. A thermally heated swimming
pool on the premises, a sauna, and a host of massage therapies are part of the
health facilities here. In well-furnished rooms, tariffs range from 1,150 AS
($61.18) to 1,250 AS ($66.50) in a single and from 1,900 AS ($101.08) to 2,100
AS ($111.72) in a double, breakfast included.

Der Kaiserhof (tel. 2544). You'll discover the yellow facade of this opulent
hotel in a woodland setting, a short stroll away from the heart of the spa. This is
a sister to the Grand Hotel. Der Kaiserhof dates from 1909, with all the exterior
and interior detailing you'd expect from a fin-de-siècle palace. It lies along the
tree-shaded Kaiser Wilhelm II Promenade, named after the German emperor
who loved to stroll along here with his entourage.

The 76 rooms are individually decorated with period furniture and their
own private baths. Some of them also contain private balconies, and even the

ones that don't have windows big enough to take in a panoramic sweep of the Gasteiner Valley and the mountains beyond.

In addition to the grand salons, the hotel has a cluster of tiny sitting rooms, each with a distinctive character, usually with overstuffed chairs, select antiques (some of them with imperial associations), and high ceilings. The excellent food served in the deluxe dining room includes both Viennese cookery and international specialties. Singles range from 1,350 AS ($71.82) to 1,525 AS ($81.13), while doubles go from 1,225 AS ($65.17) to 1,400 AS ($74.48) per person, with full board included. Prices depend on the season, of course.

Parkhotel Bellevue (tel. 25710) offers a vast expanse of covered balconies turned toward the most scenic part of the nearby mountains. Viewed from the downhill side, it looks like a glittering collection of windows and extensions, with a generous covering of ivy over the foundations of many of them. The hotel includes a 400-year-old alpine hut near the ski slopes, with a rustic bar area and a smoke bonnet supported by carved wooden posts. In the main building an elegant series of public rooms is colorfully and tastefully filled with Oriental rugs, painted ceilings, and comfortable niches.

The bedrooms are spacious, well furnished, and sunny, usually with big balconies and beautiful lighting fixtures. An American-style bar offers live music, while an indoor thermal swimming pool is graced with copies of ancient Roman sculptures. A full range of massage therapies are available for an additional fee. Rates, based on double occupancy, range from 950 AS ($50.54) to 1,300 AS ($69.16) per person, with full board included, the tariffs depending on the season and the plumbing. Residents of single rooms pay an additional supplement of 150 AS ($7.98) per day. Prices are slightly higher between December 20 and January 6.

Hotel Weismayr (tel. 25940) sits prominently in the center of town, rising grandly in a series of milk-white stories, each embellished with neoclassical ornamentation. The roof is fashioned of green copper, while the street level has been modernized to include cafés and kiosks. The main sitting room is a blend of browns and reds, with Oriental rugs, comfortable settees, wing chairs, and high ceilings. The elegant high-ceilinged dining room is decorated in shades of blue and white. A terrace café is dotted with parasols and plants, with a sunny exposure that is ideal for a midday coffee. Well-furnished singles range from 900 AS ($47.88) to 1,000 AS ($53.20), while doubles cost 800 AS ($42.56) to 900 AS ($47.88) per person daily. The hotel is sometimes closed during part of April and May and for all of November.

Hotel Wildbad (tel. 2443) stands out from the collection of buildings around it because of its dark-yellow facade and its flat-roofed construction of big windows and prominent balconies. Views from the wood-detailed bedrooms usually offer splendid vistas of the valley. The public rooms are pleasant and up to date. On the premises you'll find a sauna and a range of physical therapy services, as well as a terrace sundeck with chaise longues and café tables. Located in the center of the village, close to the indoor thermal pools and the ski lifts, the hotel charges from 650 AS ($34.58) to 850 AS ($45.22) in a single and from 590 AS ($31.39) to 760 AS ($40.43) per person in a double, with half board included. G. Hoertnagl, owner and manager, sees to it that excellent food is provided, with a superb salad buffet and a buffet breakfast.

Hotel Habsburgerhof, Kaiser-Wilhelm-Promenade (tel. 2561) is a comfortable hotel built in 1964 on a sunny hillside somewhat removed from the center of town. Each of the contemporary bedrooms faces southwest, and each one has a wood-covered private balcony with a view of the valley and the resort. Inside you'll find a heated swimming pool, a sauna, a flowered café terrace, and a modern panoramic dining room. The immaculately clean bedrooms rent for 855 AS

($45.49) to 1,010 AS ($53.73) in a single and for 2,150 AS ($114.38) to 2,260 ($120.23) in a double. The hotel is open from December to March and June to September.

MIDDLE-BRACKET HOTELS: Hotel Salzburgerhof (tel. 2037) sits amid towering pine trees on a rise above the rest of the spa town. It looks like a 19th-century balconied building with a later series of stories added on top, one of which holds an indoor swimming pool. Much of the interior, including the reception area and bar, is covered with paneling and small accents of vivid color. Anny and Helmut Lercher, the owners, charge from 700 AS ($37.24) to 950 AS ($50.54) per person, with half board included, depending on the season. The hotel is closed between October 1 and December 17.

Hotel Straubinger (tel. 20120) is a 365-year-old traditional hotel in the center of town, where Franz Joseph, the emperor, used to stay. Inside you'll find an American bar, two dining rooms, a sun terrace, a reading room with a small library, and a massage service. The food is well prepared, and the service, directed by Karl-Michael Rödhamer, is friendly and professional. In well-furnished rooms, singles range from 600 AS ($31.92) to 850 AS ($45.22), while doubles cost from 1,050 AS ($55.86) to 1,600 AS ($85.12), with full board included.

Kurhotel Miramonte (tel. 2377) sits on the landscaped side of an alpine hill, with a panoramic view of the valley from the hotel's downhill side. It's surrounded with wooden balconies in their full natural grain, which contrasts prettily with the white walls of the superstructure. A big terrace has sun umbrellas jutting up from the extended roof of the second floor. Inside, the public rooms are elegantly simple, with Oriental rugs that cover even the tile floors of the rustic bar and weinstube area. Sauna, massage services, and hydrotherapy services are available for an additional fee. Singles range from 720 AS ($38.30) to 890 AS ($47.35), depending on the plumbing and the season, while doubles (all of which contain private bath) cost from 820 AS ($43.62) to 890 AS ($47.35) per person daily, including full board.

Hotel Grüner Baum (tel. 25160) is a complex of five chalet-style buildings surrounding a grassy area in the Kötschach Valley on the outskirts of Badgastein. The oldest building has, during its long history, offered hospitality to Kaiser Wilhelm and to the Empress Elisabeth, the former Shah of Iran, and Arturo Toscanini, Arthur Schopenhauer, Charles Laughton, and King Ibn Saud. The oldest parts of the building are exquisitely crafted of local woods, sometimes with charmingly elaborate regional carving, with hunting trophies beneath the beamed ceilings.

The hotel sits at the starting point for four kilometers of cross-country ski trails, and will rent equipment to guests. It has a beginner's slope nearby, with a T-bar lift, as well as facilities for bowling, curling, shooting, and boccie, plus both indoor and outdoor heated swimming pools. There's a dancing bar as well as organized weekly activities.

The bedrooms are cozily rustic, with wood paneling and sometimes a recessed sleeping alcove in some of the singles. With full board included, per-person prices, based on double occupancy, range from 650 AS ($34.58) to 1,500 AS ($79.80), depending on the season and the plumbing. The supplement for occupants of a single is 75 AS ($3.99).

Hotel Germania (tel. 2247) is a six-story, high-ceilinged hotel set onto a hillside with a view of the valley. Its cream-colored salons are filled with cozy easy chairs and Oriental rugs, while its bar and dining area are outfitted in an inviting series of low-slung chairs and hanging contemporary lamps. A more formal dining room has about the biggest arched windows in Badgastein, gilt and crystal chandeliers, and clean white napery. An indoor swimming pool is on the premises. Singles range from 445 AS ($23.67) to 1,055 AS ($56.13), while doubles cost from 635 AS ($33.78) to 985 AS ($52.40) per person, with full board included. The hotel is open from December to March and May to September.

Hotel Savoy (tel. 2588) is a roadside hotel with dramatic terraces and big expanses of glass covering some of the windows. Inside is a covered swimming pool, a sauna, and a graceful series of public rooms with high ceilings, crystal chandeliers, and attractive antiques. Some of the floors have marble coverings, others contain Oriental rugs, and most of the rooms are tastefully filled with pleasing fabrics and colors. Tennis courts are nearby. With full board included, singles range from 750 AS ($39.90) to 850 AS ($45.22), while doubles go from 610 AS ($32.45) to 820 AS ($43.62) per person, depending on the season.

Hotel Krone (tel. 2330) is designed like an Italian villa, with arched windows on the ground floor and French windows opening onto iron balconies on the front, sides, and back. The high-ceilinged interior alternates light-grained paneling with white plaster walls, and a refreshing series of colors are used in the pink- and green-accented dining room. Pleasantly furnished singles range from 400 AS ($21.28) to 480 AS ($25.54), from 390 AS ($20.75) to 440 AS ($23.41) per person in a double.

Schillerhof (tel. 2581) sits in a clearing on the side of a forested hill above Badgastein. Its symmetrical construction encompasses wings on either side of the main section, which is covered with horizontal rows of wooden balconies. The interior has big windows, warmly tinted public rooms, and a panoramic restaurant. An outdoor swimming pool is flanked with chiseled stone walls, while the bedroom walls are sometimes covered with light-grained planking. With half board included, rates in a double range upward from 680 AS ($36.18) per person in a room with bath or shower. An additional supplement of 150 AS ($7.98) per day is charged for single occupancy.

Meranhaus (tel. 2328). An engraving in the Biedermeier-furnished lobby shows a view of the hotel shortly after it was built as a summer retreat in 1828 for Archduke Johann. Today the hotel, owned by Count A. v. Meran, has been expanded, elongated, and enlarged, yet much of the original charm remains. My favorite room is the pine-covered sitting salon, with a green ceramic stove, a vivid Oriental rug, and round-framed portraits. Several of the bedrooms are filled with delicate Victorian-era chairs and good settees and dressers, some of which, if they could talk, would remember the visit of Empress Elisabeth during the summer of 1886. The hotel is closed from early October till just before Christmas and during most of April. Rooms with private bath rent for 700 AS ($37.24) to 800 AS ($42.56) per person, depending on the season, although accommodations without bath are cheaper.

BUDGET HOTELS: Hotel Mozart (tel. 2686) is an unusual hotel designed in the 19th century with half-rounded stone projections extending toward the front, a long veranda on the ground floor, and a gabled mansard roof on top of which an additional story was later added. The inside has beautifully patterned Oriental rugs in muted colors covering the floor of the wood-paneled lobby area, as well as crystal chandeliers hanging from the detailed plaster ceiling. Some of the 70 comfortably furnished rooms have private bath, although there are thermally heated baths on each floor, costing 90 AS ($4.79). Bed and breakfast ranges from 185 AS ($9.84) to 225 AS ($11.97) in a single and from 320 AS ($17.02) to 350 AS ($18.62) in a double, depending on the plumbing and season.

Kurhaus Alpenblick (tel. 2087) is a chalet with a wing stretching off to one side containing a comfortable collection of balconied bedrooms. These are decorated with an eclectic collection of furniture, which includes Oriental rugs, heavy simple wooden headboards, richly upholstered chairs, and big windows with views of the mountains. In the timbered and beamed dining room, well-prepared meals are served by a friendly staff. A swimming pool is outside on the grounds near a small mountain stream. The 38 rooms rent for 350 AS ($18.62) to 625 AS ($33.25) in a single and for 350 AS ($18.62) to 550 AS ($29.26) per person in a double, with breakfast included, tariffs depending on the season and plumbing.

Haus Gerke (tel. 2378) is a graceful old chalet-style hotel, with a hip-roofed upper section covered with green and white shutters and weathered planking, plus a lower section embellished with yellow stucco and gray masonry. The inside is filled with Oriental rugs, high ceilings with hanging painted chandeliers, marble fireplaces, and oil paintings. The bedrooms have 1950s-style wood-grained furniture and comfortable beds, some of which are recessed into curtained sleeping compartments. Singles range from 280 AS ($14.90) to 350 AS ($18.62), while doubles rent for 480 AS ($25.54) to 650 AS ($34.58), depending on the plumbing and the season. Breakfast is included in the price.

BEST FOR DINING: **Jörg Wörter's Vinothek** (tel. 37016). To reach this place, you'll have to negotiate first a hilly road leading into town and then a steeply inclined driveway heading toward the parking lot of this pleasantly proportioned baroque house. Its yellow and white walls match those of the Hotel Europa next door.

The country rustic interior sits on a 17th-century foundation, with lots of handcrafted accents ringing the pleasant room. Herr Wörter concocts the best specialties at the resort, each made from patrician ingredients designed to tempt both the eye and palate. After a champagne cocktail, you can opt for rack of lamb with cabbage, gooseliver terrine in brioche, crab strudel, wild trout with mushrooms, tafelspitz, calves' brains, and roast venison with a kohlrabi and salmon garnish. Dessert might be a papaya slice with a ragoût of cherries.

A la carte meals average 720 AS ($38.30), with a fixed-price menu featured at 560 AS ($29.79). Reservations are necessary, and the restaurant is closed every Sunday and from the end of April till mid-May and from mid-October till about a week before Christmas.

THE LEADING CAFÉ: **Restaurant Gastein,** in the Kongresshaus (tel. 2982), is a popular café designed in an international decor. Except for the language of the menu, you'll find it easy to forget where you are, since a place this modern could as easily be an upper-class establishment in Sydney, New York, or Johannesburg. Still, it's a relaxing place for a midafternoon cup of coffee and perhaps a pastry or ice cream. Coffee costs from 20 AS ($1.06) to 32 AS ($1.70), with pastries beginning at 20 AS ($1.06) going up to 25 AS ($1.33). It's open all day every day of the week.

AFTER DARK: The center of nightlife—and the chicest spot to be seen at the spa and winter sports center—is the **Spiel-Casino Badgastein** (tel. 2121). Here you can play roulette, baccarat, and blackjack, but you'll need a passport to get in. The summer season lasts from June 1 until mid-September, and the winter season is from Christmas until the end of January. The casino opens daily at 5 p.m.

At the height of the season, most of the clubs charge from 85 AS ($4.52) for a hard-liquor drink, from 50 AS ($2.66) for beer.

One of the most popular discos in town is at the already-recommended **Hotel Weissmayr.** This place attracts a generally young and affluent crowd.

Another popular disco, **Mahlhäusl,** is beneath the Hotel Söntgen (tel. 2235), a three-minute walk from the Cure and Congress Centre. This is an intimate rendezvous point, attracting a young crowd.

If you want more conventional dancing, head for the **Hotel Elisabethpark,** already recommended. This is an elegant nightlife retreat, and most of its patrons are well dressed.

Another elegant choice on the après-ski circuit is the also recommended **Parkhotel Bellevue,** where guests often linger in its alpine tavern, enjoying drinks, candlelight, and an open fire. Its American bar has live music in season, a band playing for dancing couples.

2. Bad Hofgastein

Lying five miles from Badgastein, halfway to Dorfgastein (coming up), is another resort, Bad Hofgastein (2,850 feet), an old established spa and long a rival of Badgastein for the tourist schilling.

Bad Hofgastein is tinier than Badgastein, but it's almost as charming, and in general its hotels are less expensive. The little resort is actually almost a satellite of the larger spa, as the radioactive waters of Badgastein are pumped to its neighbor. Some hardy visitors like to follow a marked footpath between the two towns, the trip taking about 2½ hours. As a resort unit, Badgastein and Bad Hofgastein welcome at least as many visitors as does Salzburg—maybe more.

The **pfarrkirche** (parish church) of this tiny village is late Gothic, dating from the end of the 15th century, although it has a baroque altar. Some sights, such as old houses with turrets, evoke thoughts of the gold-mining days in the Gastein Valley. In the 16th century the nearby goldmines made Bad Hofgastein the rival of Salzburg in wealth. A rich mining family lived at the 15th-century **Weitmoserschlössl,** which has now been converted into a restaurant.

The most popular ski area hereabouts is the **Schlossalm,** which can be reached by mountain railway (board a train in the parking section). Skiers or just plain sightseers are transported to Kitzstein, where a chair lift takes over. Expect long lines of prospective passengers in the height of the season. The Schlossalm area has two chair lifts and eight drag lifts. The mountain station Kleine Scharte is at 6,120 feet, and there is a mountain restaurant with a panoramic view. Round-trip fare for the station is 150 AS ($7.98).

Bad Hofgastein, about 55 miles south of Salzburg, is on the town railway and federal road 167 and is served by Postal Buses.

The area code for Bad Hofgastein is 06432.

UPPER BRACKET HOTELS: Kur- und Sporthotel Moser (tel. 6209), on the main square of town, has sections dating back to the 12th century. You'd never know it from a quick glance at the facade, which is pleasantly balconied with yellow accents above the red street-level awnings. The interior, however, is vaulted and cozy, with lots of old exposed wood, heavy beams, Oriental rugs, and a tapestry. The furnishings are rustic and regional, with lots of homey touches such as racks of pewter above the banquettes of the dining room. The sunny bedrooms, all with private bath, rent for 650 AS ($34.58) to 750 AS ($39.90) per person, with full board included. Prices depend on the season. The hotel has private parking, and guests have the use of a roof garden for sunning. For evening relaxation, you can choose an intimate lounge and terrace dining, or you may prefer the cozy cellar facilities for dining and dancing.

Grand Park Hotel (tel. 6356) rises majestically in a contemporary adaptation of a chalet. It's in its own birch-filled park, with a swimming pool and lawn chairs on the grassy lawns around it. The interior is filled with stone and polished-wood accents, plush carpets, and modern touches of bright colors and polished brass, all of which combine for a pleasant feeling of well-being. An indoor pool under a soaring timbered roof is only one of the many sports and health-oriented facilities. Handsomely furnished singles range from 550 AS ($29.26) to 1,300 AS ($69.16), while doubles cost 600 AS ($31.92) to 1,350 AS ($71.82) per person with full board included. The hotel is open all year.

Hotel Carinthia (tel. 8374) is a large solid-looking chalet, with flowered balconies on all sides and regional-style painted detailing on the corner mullions and around some of the windows. The interior has elegant and unusual touches, such as brass sheathing above the stone curves of the fireplace, the tucked-away corner bar, and the luminous modern chandeliers in the high-ceilinged dining room. The colors of the spacious bedrooms are coordinated in pleasing combinations such as reddish violet with beiges and browns in a contemporary decor of style and comfort. In addition to the indoor swimming pool the hotel has a wide range of massage and hydrotherapy regimes. Singles range from 750 AS ($39.90) to 830 AS ($44.17), while doubles cost from 690 AS ($36.71) to 790 AS ($42.03) per person, with full board included.

Hotel Palace Gastein (tel. 67150) is a 200-room luxury hotel with an elevator, situated in a quiet, sunny spot a few minutes' walk from the resort center. Guest rooms all have shower or bath and toilet, radio, telephone, and balcony. The tastefully furnished units cost from 650 AS ($34.58) to 1,300 AS ($69.16) in a single, from 590 AS ($31.39) to 1,200 AS ($63.84) per person in a double, all tariffs including full board. Facilities guests may use include the thermal indoor pool, sauna, solarium, hotel ski-bus to the Schlossalm funicular railway, hairdresser, cosmetic salon, bars, a chimney bar, a Vienna coffeehouse, a supervised kindergarten, and a lively nightclub. There is a daily program of entertainment and activities.

Hotel Norica, Bachbauergasse (tel. 8391), in the pedestrian zone, is dramatically designed in such a way that the flowered balconies angle themselves directly toward the sun. A spacious sun terrace is covered with potted shrubs. A rounded hearth inside illuminates the art objects and striped banquettes of one of the public rooms, while the dining room is spacious, with friendly service.

An in-house disco, a curved bar, tennis, and an indoor thermal swimming pool, plus a wide range of other sports, offer plenty of distractions. The light-toned, good-size bedrooms have wood accents and modern bath. Full board is recommended here, as the food is of a good standard and served in large portions. Full-board rates go from 1,090 AS ($57.99) to 1,455 AS ($77.41) in singles and from 780 AS ($41.50) to 1,275 AS ($67.83) per person in doubles.

MODERATE AND BUDGET HOTELS: **Hotel Sendlhof** (tel. 3510) is a family-run hotel with six big-windowed floors, each surrounded with balconies and potted flowers. An outdoor heated swimming pool lies across the lawn. The interior has heavily recessed rectangular designs in the ceiling's paneling, large windows with attractive curtains, cozy fireplaces with masonry detailing, and lots of extra touches such as ceramic stoves and painted detailing below some of the massive arches. Management sometimes provides live zither music in the evening.

The bedrooms are elegant and cozy, each of them with lots of exposed wood and a private bath. Singles range from 680 AS ($36.18) to 780 AS ($41.50), while doubles cost from 620 AS ($32.98) to 720 AS ($38.30) per person, with full board included. Most of the units have private balconies. The hotel is open from December to March and May to October.

Hotel Astoria (tel. 6277) is a generously proportioned five-story building with a simple white and wood-balconied facade and an interior that has been renovated into a contemporary format of streamlined furniture and warmly inviting colors. An indoor swimming pool is encircled with molded furniture. Rates range from 500 AS ($39.90) to 800 AS ($42.56) per person, depending on the season and the plumbing. Prices include full board. The Astoria is open from December to October.

Hotel St. Georg (tel. 6100) has an elegant country-house atmosphere, with attractive en suite bedrooms and family apartments, designed for the discerning guest. Bedrooms have complete bath, phone, and TV connection, and rent for 580 AS ($30.87) to 820 AS ($43.62) per person. The surcharge for single occupancy is 125 AS ($6.65). Tariffs include a buffet breakfast, a four-course dinner, service, heating, and taxes. Tempting Austrian cuisine is served in the Salzburg country-style restaurant, with special diets being catered for. Guests have the use of an indoor swimming pool, sauna, solarium, steam bath, and massage and cosmetic treatments. Secure parking is available in the hotel garage.

Kurhotel Osterreichischer Hof (tel. 62160). One of the many charming aspects about this family-run hotel is the regionally styled portal, which is surrounded with yellow and gold painted detailing, a theme repeated around many of the chalet's windows. A balconied extension with the same detailing stretches out behind. Both sections have the added benefit of angled stone buttresses reaching as high as the second-floor windows. The interior contains a heated pool, a range of massage therapy rooms, warmly tinted public rooms, and simple and attractive bedrooms, many of them with wood paneling. Sometimes they're surprisingly spacious, and often have good views over the valley. Singles range from 550 AS ($29.26) to 700 AS ($37.24), while doubles go from 500 AS ($26.60) to 650 AS ($34.58) per person, depending on the plumbing and season. Half board is included.

Kurhotel Germania, 14 Kurpromenade (tel. 232). Although this is a modern hotel, it has some beautifully maintained Victorian antiques (including an exquisite collection of armchairs) filling some of the big-windowed public rooms. If your unit has a balcony—and many of the pleasant and sunny bedrooms here do—you'll have a view of the houses and barns of the valley below. The facade of the hotel rises in a symmetrical series of white walls and wooden balconies, with summertime parasols adding accents of color to the white walls. A full range of massage and hydrotherapy services are available inside. With full board included, singles range from 690 AS ($36.71) to 730 AS ($38.84) while prices in a double are from 640 AS ($34.05) to 690 AS ($36.71) per person. Tariffs depend on the plumbing. The hotel is open from December to October.

Kur- and Sporthotel Alpina, 11-17 Parkstrasse (tel. 84750), looks like a double chalet, with symmetrical rooflines that peak above rows of wooden balconies. The interior is as tasteful and warm as anything you'll find in town, with attractive color schemes. A heavily beamed ceiling covers the illuminated waters of the heated indoor swimming pool, while the lobby area is lit with pin spotlights shining from the overhead beams. The sunny bedrooms rent for 750 AS ($39.90) to 950 AS ($50.54) in a single and 766 AS ($40.75) to 950 AS ($50.54) per person in a double, full board included. The hotel is closed between the end of October and the middle of December.

Kurhotel Völserhof, Kurpromenade (tel. 8288), rises five balconied stories above a flowering garden near the edge of town. In summertime the areas above the windows of the second-floor restaurant are covered with masses of red flowers, while the arched windows on the ground floor are surrounded with meticulously painted regional designs. Much of the interior alternates areas of white with full-grained areas of wood. The city's recreation center is a five-minute walk from the hotel, and the terminus of the funicular is ten minutes away. The Lang family, your hosts, close the hotel from mid-October to mid-December.

Doubles rent for around 500 AS ($26.60) to 650 AS ($34.58) per person daily, with breakfast included.

Kurpark Hotel, 17-21 Kurgartenstrasse (tel. 8436), is a wood and stucco alpine-style house discreetly concealed behind the trees that grow close around it. The garden terrace is one of the establishment's main social centers on a sunny day. Inside, the public rooms are filled with angular furniture and neutral colors, while the bedrooms tend to be covered with flowered wallpaper and furnished with modern pieces. An annex nearby offers bathless rooms at lower rates. Bathless doubles rent for 285 AS ($15.16) to 495 AS ($26.33) per person, doubles with bath costing from 425 AS ($22.61) to 630 AS ($33.52). Half board is included in the prices. A resident of a single room is charged a supplement of 80 AS ($4.26).

WHERE TO DINE: The **Café-Restaurant Weitmoser-Schlössl** (tel. 6601) is near the departure point of the Schlossalmbahn, and because of its position on a steep hillside, affords a good view of the valley below. Parts of it date from the 14th century, although today you'll just be grateful for the warmth of the place in winter and for the shaded terrace surrounded by mountain ash trees in summer. You can lunch or dine on mainly Austrian specialties. Meals cost from 175 AS ($9.31). If you only want coffee, tea, snacks, or afternoon schnapps, you'll find a full array of these items, as well as a lot of other clients who seem to sample a bit of everything. Coffee costs 20 AS ($1.06) to 33 AS ($1.76), while pastries range from 32 AS ($1.70) to 45 AS ($2.39). It's closed on Monday.

AFTER DARK: For your big night on the town, you can take a free taxi from Bad Hofgastein to Badgastein to gamble at the **casino,** already recommended.

Otherwise, you can stay right in Bad Hofgastein, dancing at its discos, enjoying open fires in its taverns, or else dancing more formally at the hotels that import live bands in season. The tourist office will tell you the latest information about which hotels or clubs are likely to have nightlife at any given time, as schedules and programs fluctuate.

Most hard drinks cost from 80 AS ($4.26), and no one forces more on you than you want.

Among the hotels, one of the best centers for après-ski life is the **Hotel Norica** (see above). You can just drop in for a drink at its bar, or else patronize one of its restaurants, including the Schneckenthurm-Häusl, the Egghaus-Stübl, or the Kitscher Grill. The young at heart will go below to the Vision, a disco. There's also nightly dancing to a band at the **Palace Gastein** (see above).

For your afternoon après-ski drink, visit the **Café Weitmoserschlössl,** which is installed in the 15th-century castle (already mentioned) that was once the home of a gold-mining family.

READER'S NIGHTLIFE SUGGESTIONS: "I particularly enjoyed going to the **Tenne Club** near the heart of Bad Hofgastein, where you can sit on the balcony overlooking the dance floor. They have live bands in season. I also found the **Tennistreff** great fun, with its tennis and squash courts, but especially for the folk singing and the jazz which is presented some nights. The alpine version of pizza is tasty here. Another spot for dancing is the **Glücknerkeller,** and if you're in the mood to disco, I recommend **Manfred's,** with its tiny dance floor and intimate bar. It's near the river. Some of these spots may be closed between seasons, but you can usually find some of them open both summer and winter" (Alan Deer, Erie, Pa.).

3. The Pongau

Badgastein and Bad Hofgastein, already explored, are part of a section of Land Salzburg known as the Pongau. It's one of several parts of an alpine valley called Salzach. The Pongau basin, heart of the Salzach Valley, lies between Werfen and Golling downstream and between Taxenbach and Lend upstream. The Pinzgau section (coming up) of the Salzach Valley is in the southwest.

The Pongau's most frequented tourist route is through the **Gastein Valley,** of which Badgastein and Bad Hofgastein are a part. For many centuries the Gastein Valley has been celebrated for its hot springs, and in more recent times it has also become known as a winter sports center, this phase of activity developing mainly after World War II. As a consequence, many old spas such as Badgastein suddenly find themselves overrun with skiers in winter.

The **Radstädter Tauern** region is the second most popular section of the Pongau. It sprawls across five mountains and four valleys, with a mammoth expanse of skiable terrain from St. Johann to Obertauern. In between, you'll find that Wagrain, Flachau, Altenmarkt, and Radstadt are all well provided with hotels. You might find a car convenient in the Radstädter Tauern. However, most of it can be reached by lifts and runs.

DORFGASTEIN: This pleasant alpine village (2,750 feet) in the Gastein Valley is both a winter and a summer resort, its tranquil ambience attracting many who shun the more commercial atmosphere of Badgastein and Bad Hofgastein. You'll find an assortment of hotels and gasthof-type places here, as well as an open-air swimming pool heated by solar energy.

Dorfgastein is popular with Austrian families who, in winter, can park the small fry all day at a ski kindergarten while the grownups enjoy the ski runs and slopes. In fact the resort has many faithful habitués who resent its increasing popularity. The ski circus comprising Dorfgastein and Grossarl offers four chair lifts and 15 T-bar lifts to slopes of varying challenges, and there is also a natural toboggan run and a curling rink. A Gastein ski pass is valid for all cable cars and lifts in the Gastein valley, and the ski bus is free of charge.

The village has a **parish church** (*pfarrkirche*) "updated" in the baroque style but originally built in the 14th century.

You can take a bus from the heart of the village to the lower station of the chair lift, the trip taking less than an hour. The lift takes you to Wengeralm, and from there you can go by another lift to Kreuzkogel (6,690 feet).

Another popular attraction is the stalactite cavern, **Entrische Kirche,** 48 miles from Salzburg. Ascent from Klamstein takes more than half an hour to reach these partly water-bearing, stalactite, and dry caves. Total length is two miles on three levels. The caves are open daily except Monday from March 20 to October 20 from 10 a.m. to 6 p.m. Conducted tours last an hour. Admission is 42 AS ($2.23) for adults, 28 AS ($1.49) for children.

The area code for Dorfgastein is 06433.

Food and Lodging

Hotel/Restaurant Römerhof (tel. 209) has four floors of well-built wood and stucco, designed like an expanded version of a chalet. Constructed in 1966, it sits near the site of a 12th-century tower which served after 1421 as a shelter for men and horses. The Hasenauer family maintains accommodations considerably more comfortable than those written about in the medieval annals.

The interior is decorated with wood beams, wrought-iron embellishments, and rustic furniture. The exterior walls of the pleasant, wood-paneled, restaurant are covered with painted floral designs. A public swimming pool and the departure point for the cable cars are each a five-minute walk from the hotel. Per-person rates, with breakfast included, range from 325 AS ($17.29) to 500

AS ($26.60) in a single and from 300 AS ($15.96) to 420 AS ($22.34) in a double. Prices depend on the season and the plumbing.

Hotel Kirchenwirt (tel. 251) is a large, cozy, and tastefully decorated chalet hotel a few steps from the village church. Its wood-paneled restaurant can be viewed through the arched stucco windows of the ground floor, while the public rooms are filled with Oriental rugs, comfortable chairs, and a dramatically coffered ceiling.

The bedrooms are spacious and comfortable, often with unusual shapes and many wood accents. The bar area is den-like and intimately rustic, with provincial artifacts hanging from the walls. The building has its own elevator and is maintained by the Köstinger family. Rates range from 550 AS ($29.26) to 590 AS ($31.39) per person, with half board included. Prices depend on the season and the plumbing.

Après-Ski

When darkness falls on the slopes, the after-dark circuit starts buzzing. Nightlife (and there is some) is fairly restrained, taking place for the most part in the lounges and bars of the hotels, many of which have open blazing fires.

The most popular place seems to be the **Hotel Kirchenwirt,** already recommended. Its nighttime diversion is the K-Keller, which has an open burning fireplace and dancing to disco music. In season the place becomes very gemütlich.

Also popular is the **Hotel Römerhof,** recommended above. It not only has two lounge bars, but two stüberls as well. The Hasenauer family maintains a lively, friendly atmosphere.

The cost of an evening out in Dorfgastein is usually much cheaper than in Badgastein and Bad Hofgastein, with most drinks costing from 65 AS ($3.46).

GOLDEGG:
Lying on a small lake dominated by a castle from the 14th century, Goldegg, reached by going through Schwarzach, is about an 18-minute bus ride from St. Veit im Pongau. Schwarzach is at the western end of the Pongau. Goldegg, both a winter and a summer sports resort, is known also for its peat baths.

The castle, once owned by the counts of Galen, now shelters the **Pongau Folk Museum,** where you can see displays of old rural utensils and a collection of tools used in early-day occupations. Guided tours are conducted May 1 until the end of September every Thursday at 3, 4, and 5 p.m. and October 1 to April 30, only one tour a week is conducted, every Thursday at 2 p.m. Adults are charged 15 AS (80¢); children, 8 AS (43¢). For information, phone 81-1-70.

Goldegg's area code is 06415.

Food and Lodging

Hotel Gesinger Zur Post (tel. 81-0-30) consists of two country-style buildings, both with flowered balconies and window boxes, plus a pleasant lakeside location with a view of the mountains. The interior is outfitted with painted regional furniture, polished pine paneling, homey detailing, and lots of comfort. Under the rafters of what was probably a barn the hotel has installed a dancing nightclub, complete with hanging lanterns and lots of intimate corners. Congenial hosts Raimund and Hertha Gesinger do everything they can to make guests comfortable. The cozy bedrooms are equipped with spacious private bath, and usually have enclosed sleeping compartments behind full-length curtains. Rates range from 475 AS ($25.27) to 775 AS ($41.23) per person, based on double occupancy, depending on the season. In a single, a supplement of 50 AS ($2.66) daily is charged.

Hotel/Pension Neuwirt (tel. 8114) sits on the side of a hill in the center of the village. The approach road to the hotel will take you around the back side of a miniature religious shrine. The big ground-floor windows let lots of light flood into the public rooms. Many guests enjoy a sun terrace built into stone columns above the downhill side of the building. The interior has lots of country-style charm, heavy ceiling beams, and hand-painted murals set into wooden frames. The Mayr family, your hosts, charge from 450 AS ($23.94) to 550 AS ($29.26) per person in a double, depending on the plumbing and the season. These prices include full board. Singles pay a surcharge of 50 AS ($2.66) per day.

Hotel Lärchenhof, 24 Weng (tel. 8169), is pleasantly surrounded with weathered balconies and green lawns. The ground-floor restaurant has lots of exposed light-grained wood and big windows, while elsewhere on the premises is a dancing bar along with a rustic drinking area adorned with cut saplings stripped of their bark and nailed into rustic table dividers. The cozy bedrooms rent for 400 AS ($21.28) to 450 AS ($23.94) per person, depending on the season, with full board included. The hotel is open from December to October.

Hotel Seehof (tel. 8137) is filled with the kind of rustic artifacts and local painted furniture that many of us could spend weeks looking for in antique shops. It sits on the lake, which reflects the chalet's forest-green shutters and the many flowerpots on the hotel's balconies. The bedrooms are contemporary and warm, often with private balconies and sloping paneled ceilings. The modern baths are tiled in autumnal colors, with wood detailing and big mirrors. An outdoor sun terrace sports red-and-white checked tablecloths and sun parasols. In summer many guests enjoy the private lakeside beach, while in winter the hotel rents ski equipment for the nearby slopes. A sauna is on the premises. Each of the accommodations has its own private bath, and rents for 500 AS ($26.60) to 720 AS ($38.30) per person, depending on the season, with half board included. An in-season disco, filled with a decor of rustic beams and farmer's implements, affords a pleasant place for a drink.

The owner, Mr. Schellhorn, is leader of the ski-tracking school of Goldegg. Here you can find 36 miles of some of the best ski tracks of the Salzburg country.

WAGRAIN: At 2,750 feet, Wagrain, in the vicinity of Salzburg, lies in a sunny valley amid lush green meadows and forests in summer and fine ski runs in winter. It's the hometown of the poet Karl-Heinrich Waggerl, whose memory is honored with a folklore museum, open June to September on Monday from 3 to 6 p.m., on Saturday from 4 to 6 p.m., and on Sunday from 10 a.m. to noon. Admission is free. This tiny resort is in the three-valley ski round point of Flachau-Wagrain-St. Johann, with open skiing ground protected against avalanches.

From mid-December to mid-April some 60 miles of mechanically prepared downhill runs are open, suitable for everybody from beginners to intermediates, and there's a ski school in the area. Three chair lifts and 11 drag lifts are available. The top station that can be reached is at 6,600 feet. You can go to Flachau, the neighboring resort, by chair lift.

For nonskiers Wagrain offers rambling trails, tobogganing, folkloric evenings, Austrian curling, and horse-drawn sleigh rides in winter. Summer visitors can use the chair lifts for sightseeing, and they can swim in a heated outdoor pool or take advantage of one of the four tennis courts.

The area code for Wagrain is 06413.

Food and Lodging

Hotel Alpina, 108 Kirchboden (tel. 8337), is a white stucco chalet with balconies and a low-lying extension that stretches off down the hillside. One of the public rooms contains a white brick fireplace with a large metallic hood—a pleasant place for a drink if a fire is burning. On the premises is a rustic bar, as well as a sauna and an indoor pool with big glass windows looking out onto the snow-covered hillside. Your hosts, the Wiesbacher family, rent their sunny bedrooms from 625 AS ($33.25) to 900 AS ($47.88) for a single and from 400 AS ($21.28) to 850 AS ($45.22) per person in a double, with half board included. The hotel is closed from early October until the beginning of December, with special discounts available between early December and Christmas.

Hotel Wagrainerhof (tel. 8204). Local residents say that you can tell what time it is by the direction of the shadows that fall from the ornate eaves of this enlarged chalet. You'll enter through a pointed arch into which some craftsman has skillfully inserted a door of patterned brass. Inside you'll find a high-quality series of cozy rooms with thick carpeting, burnished paneling, and art objects. A rustic bar often has live music, while the gemütlich restaurant is filled with homey touches. The in-house café has standing brass lamps and a cross-beam ceiling. Located in the center of the village, the hotel is owned by the Rötzer family, who charge from 580 AS ($30.87) to 635 AS ($33.78) per person, with full board included. The hotel is open from December to October.

Alpengasthof Kirchboden (tel. 8202) is a solidly constructed chalet with cutout patterns on its three tiers of balconies, arched windows on its ground floor, and a flowered sun terrace with red and yellow parasols. The interior is covered in many areas with natural-grained wood, while some of the thick beams are reinforced with wrought-iron straps. A fieldstone fireplace is capped with a timbered mantelpiece. The view encompasses most of the village of Wagrain. With half board included, per-person rates range from 400 AS ($21.80) to 620 AS ($32.98), depending on the season and the exposure. All rooms have private bath.

The adjoining restaurant is excellent. The well-prepared specialties tend to be regional (palatschinken, Pariser schnitzel), along with good appetizers and a fine selection of cheese). Fixed-price meals cost from 125 AS ($6.65) to 150 AS ($7.98), while à la carte ranges from 135 AS ($7.18) to 300 AS ($15.96).

Gasthof Grafenwirt (tel. 8230) is a pleasant three-story villa with white walls and lots of ivy growing up the side. A walled garden is a pleasant place for a summertime drink. The inside is accented with lots of recently applied paneling, rustic artifacts, and brightly contrasting patterns. The smallish bedrooms have painted furniture and a minimum of other decoration, but are comfortable nevertheless. Singles range from 380 AS ($20.22) to 450 AS ($23.94), while doubles go from 330 AS ($17.56) to 400 AS ($21.28) per person, breakfast included. The gasthof is open from December to March and from June to September.

The in-house restaurant is one of the better ones in the region. Colorfully decorated with pretty chandeliers and wrought-iron accents, it serves standard Austrian specialties such as liver noodle soup, beef goulash, and Tyrolean-style liver. Fixed-price meals range from 85 AS ($4.52) to 120 AS ($6.38), while à la carte meals cost 85 AS ($4.52) to 300 AS ($15.96) Half or full board can be arranged for residents of the hotel.

Gasthof Enzian (tel. 8502), built in 1974-1975, is a chalet hotel with big balconies, lots of wood trim, and panoramic windows looking out over the surrounding green area. The bedrooms usually have white walls, autumnal colors, and patterned curtains. A few steps away, two smaller buildings constructed in the same style hold more accommodations. The 32 bedrooms rent for 420 AS ($22.34) to 520 AS ($27.66) in a single and 375 AS ($19.95) to 475 AS ($25.27) per person in a double, with breakfast included. The place is open from December to October.

FLACHAU: This member of the trio of resorts which includes Wagrain and St. Johann im Pongau is just five miles southwest of Altenmarkt, in a lovely position in the Enns Valley, on the motorway. From the village, you can go by chair lift to Griesskareck at 6,530 feet.

Flachau, known heretofore mainly to Europeans, is just beginning to attract more international skiers. Hence the prices are fairly reasonable.

The area code for Flachau is 06457.

Food and Lodging

Hotel Pongauerhof (tel. 242). The balconies of this stucco-and-wood chalet only extend part of the way across the facade, interrupted as they are with an extension stretching toward the front. This allows the cheerful bedrooms inside to be more spacious than those in the other hotels in the region. The public rooms are busily filled with contrasting patterns and designs, with lots of paneling and hanging light fixtures. Rates range from 550 AS ($29.26) to 620 AS ($32.98) per person, with half board included. The hotel has a sauna, a solarium, and a recreation room.

The in-house restaurant is often sought out by the local residents. Snails are a specialty of the chef, who also prepares a full line of snacks, including pizzas and various salads (often without lettuce) at the daily salad bar. Full meals are also available, and main courses are likely to include pork Wiener schnitzel and marinated roast pork (sometimes garnished with a cabbage salad). A wide variety of Austrian beer is on tap as well. Fixed-price meals range from 135 AS ($7.18) to 175 AS ($9.31), while à la carte dinners go from 150 AS ($7.98) to 300 AS ($15.96).

Hotel Alpenhof (tel. 205) has a pleasing exterior design, where the balconies have thick timbers running vertically up the front of the solidly constructed chalet. In summertime the café terrace offers a resting point in the shadows of the flowers on these balconies. In winter guests prefer to bathe in the sunny indoor pool or enjoy the rustic wood-covered interior. The contemporary bedrooms are simple and sunny, renting for 390 AS ($20.75) to 730 AS ($38.84), with half board included. Prices depend on the plumbing, the exposure, the season, and whether or not the unit has a balcony. The restaurant is especially worth the visit. Specialties of the house include grilled filet of pork in a cream sauce, as well as roast marinated pork and an array of veal dishes. The hotel is closed from mid-April to mid-May and from October 20 to December 5.

Hotel Tauernhof (tel. 3110) has two almost identical chalet-like sections connected by a glassed-in series of public rooms. The proportions are generous and comfortable, with a rustic decor of heavy timbers, hanging lamps, warm colors, and indoor fireplaces. On the premises you'll find a bowling alley, an indoor pool, a dancing bar, a sauna, outdoor tennis courts, and an inviting restaurant. Rates in a double range from 680 AS ($36.18) to 900 AS ($47.88) per person, with full board included. The hotel is owned by Willi Schorn.

Forellenhof (tel. 273) is a wood-and-stucco chalet with a gently sloping roof and a pleasing facade of recessed balconies and symmetrical detailing. From the café sun terrace, clients can look at the pink and white walls of the onion-domed church next door. The interior is attractive and cozy, with lots of handcrafted paneling and dozens of extra touches, such as stained-glass inserts, hanging ornate lamps, and an occasional niche containing a statue. Under the heavy overhead beams of the ceiling you can enjoy well-prepared regional cuisine. An octagonal indoor swimming pool is sheltered below a wooden ceiling that is supported by an unusual series of curved laminated beams. A sauna and a whirlpool are also on the premises. The sunny bedrooms rent for 420 AS ($22.34) to

775 AS ($41.23) per person based on double occupancy, with half board included. Prices depend on the season and the exposure, and all units contain private bath. Residents of singles pay a surcharge of 75 AS ($3.99). The Krauthauf family are your conscientious hosts.

ST. JOHANN IM PONGAU: The third of the three-valley trio of summer and winter resorts, including Wagrain and Flachau, St. Johann im Pongau (there's a larger St. Johann in Tyrol) lies 38 miles from Salzburg on the sun-drenched terrace on the right bank of the river. The town's twin-towered **parish church** (*pfarrkirche*) was built in 1855, but use of the site for a house of worship dates from the year 924.

The winter sports season here lasts from December to April. There are some 52 lifts and cable cars in the tri-resort area, plus some 60 miles of prepared runs. This best known ski lift network in the Salzburg mountains is called Drei-Täler-Skischaukel, or three-valley ski swing.

If you're a nature lover, St. Johann is a good base for many excursions, such as to the **Grossarlbach Valley** to the south of the town and to the mouth of **Wagrainer Tal** to the north.

Just three miles south of St. Johann im Pongau is the most important gorge of the eastern Alps, the spectacular **Liechtensteinklamm,** which attracts more visitors to its three-quarter-mile length than any other such site. A path has been blasted through the gorge, and during about a 45-minute trek you can climb up a mammoth cauldron with rock walls some 1,000 feet high. At its tiny waist the gorge is only 12½ feet wide. A tunnel leads to the waterfall with a drop of about 200 feet at the gorge's end.

To reach the Liechtensteinklamm, go three miles by road to Grossarl. The road to the gorge is marked. From there, count on about an hour by foot. The gorge may be visited from May 10 to the first Sunday in October from 8 a.m. to 5 p.m. Admission is 20 AS ($1.06).

The area code for St. Johann im Pongau is 06412.

Food and Lodging

Hotel Prem, 1 Premweg (tel. 6320), is a comfortably proportioned yellow stucco house styled like the home of a wealthy farmer. It sits in the middle of town, near all the sports facilities, with a nearby annex that holds the overflow from the main hotel. You'll recognize this place by the red and white horizontally striped shutters, which look almost like racing stripes, especially to the skiers who stay here in winter. The hotel is about three buildings away from the Haumbaumlifte chair lift. Inside, the public rooms are cozy, with a regional decor that includes a ceramic stove and well-oiled paneling. The hotel is frequently booked throughout the winter. Year-round prices range from 450 AS ($23.94) to 550 AS ($29.26) per person, breakfast included. For full board, add an extra 125 AS ($6.65) per person.

Pension Monika, 2 Liechtensteinkammstrasse (tel. 411), a ten-minute walk from the train station at the southern edge of St. Johann, has weathered pine siding and a double row of balconies festooned with flowers. The sunny interior has lots of wood trim and comfortable furniture. The cuisine is prepared by the owners themselves, the Rudolf Wedl family, who charge from 320 AS ($17.02) to 350 AS ($18.62) per person for bed and half board, based on double occupancy. Singles pay a 35 AS ($1.86) supplement per day.

Alpenland (tel. 70-2-10). As its name implies, this wood-lined establishment offers the closest thing to a total alpine fantasy in town. Against a background of burnished pine, a corps of pretty waitresses in dirndls serve a wide selection of Austrian wines, beer from the tap, and well-prepared mountain dishes. Try, for example, a tangy peppersteak, veal Cordon Bleu with parsley potatoes, liver dumpling soup, and the homemade bread. Fixed-priced menus go for 155 AS ($8.25), and à la carte meals start at about the same price.

RADSTADT: Between the Dachstein massif in the north and Radstädter Tauern to the south lies Radstadt, at the beginning of the 13½-mile Radstädter Tauern Road to the pass, which has been used since Roman days as a way north through the mountains.

The town, built by a prince-archbishop of Salzburg, has many handsome patrician houses. Some other features of its past, including town walls, have been preserved. The skyline is distinguished by a trio of large towers built in the 16th century. Its **pfarrkirche** (parish church) is from the 14th and 15th centuries. In the churchyard stands a late Gothic **Schustersäule** (cobbler's column) from 1513.

Radstadt, for a long time a summer resort, now has been developed as a winter sports attraction. Many excursions from here are possible to the satellite resorts of Altenmarkt, Filzmoos, and Obertauern (coming up).

Radstadt's area code is 06452.

Food and Lodging

Sporthotel Weissenbacher (tel. 590) is skillfully landscaped into the side of an alpine meadow. A flight of stone-trimmed stairs will lead you first to the raised sun terrace, with its views of the many flowers surrounding the balconies, and then into the well-decorated public rooms. These are awash with comfortable niches, mellow paneling, and rustic conviviality. A full range of sporting pastimes lies within a short distance of the hotel. One of the foremost attractions is a network of some 15 kilometers of freshwater streams in the region, which are said to be filled with an angler's dream of eel, trout, and carp. Per-person rates, with full board included, range from 580 AS ($30.87) to 660 AS ($35.11), depending on the season. All the accommodations contain private baths. The in-house restaurant is one of the best in the village. Filled with hunting trophies and covered with old paneling, it serves specialties that are both regional and Italian. Reservations are suggested. The hotel is open from December to October.

Gasthof Pertill, 4 Schwemmberg (tel. 471), is a small, family-run inn set on the side of a mountain 300 yards above Radstadt. The view from the sun terrace encompasses the village and the valley. The inside is as rustic and cozy as you'd expect. The Kocher family charges 220 AS ($11.70) per person for bed and breakfast, and 340 AS ($18.09) per person with half board included, in units with private bath.

Alpengasthof Seitenalm (tel. 490) is a well-designed complex of chalets two miles (via good roads) from the center of Radstadt. The main building has a dining room whose high ceiling is supported by massive vertical timbers. For skiers who want to be close to the slopes, or for mountain climbers in summer, the hotel rents rooms in its rustic Kurzenhof, which is about a mile and a half away near the hotel's T-bar lift. An outdoor swimming pool and nearby horseback riding provide distraction, along with fishing, hiking, shooting, and table tennis. You'll also find a sauna on the premises.

The bedrooms are individually decorated with good taste and lots of homemade touches. Sometimes in summer you might want to eat in the country-style Grill Hut, assembled from logs notched together, while zither music accompanies your meal. The Arnold family have been the owners for three generations.

Rooms cost 235 AS ($12.50) to 260 AS ($13.83) per person, breakfast included. The Seitenalm is open from January to April and June to October.

ALTENMARKT: Some two miles west of Radstadt lies this sleepy provincial hamlet, sometimes called Altenmarkt in Pongau (2,790 feet). It's popular with Austrian families who come here to take advantage of the good accommodations available at reasonable prices and to enjoy swimming, skiing, and other sports typical of the region.

Of interest is the **parish church** *(pfarrkirche)* with an 18th-century statue of the Virgin.

The area code for Altenmarkt is 06452.

Food and Lodging

Hotel Urbisgut (tel. 7227) is a symmetrical double chalet connected with a balconied center section. The exterior walls have been decorated in some areas with regional painted designs. The cozy interior has painted furniture in some of the bedrooms and a bar area that sometimes is one of the most active and convivial places in nighttime Altenmarkt. Emma and Bartl Bittersam, the convivial owners of this place, charge from 350 AS ($18.62) to 420 AS ($22.34) per person, with half board included. The hotel is open from December to October.

Gasthof Markterwirt (tel. 420) is one of my favorite places in town, located in a three-story chalet with weathered facing and white shutters. It's next door to the village's baroque church. Aside from having cozy and comfortable rooms, the gasthof serves as one of the village's social centers. The café has big windows and a woodsy modern decor, where you might want to stop for coffee even if you're just driving through town. The Kellerstüberl has a vaulted ceiling, cozy ambience, and painted designs on the white plaster. In addition, the Alte Küche, the main dining room, and the Gaststube, as well as the outdoor sun terrace, are inviting places to stop for a drink or a meal. The Schneider family, your hosts, charge 280 AS ($14.90) to 300 AS ($15.96) per person in a single or double with breakfast included. Open December to October.

Lebzelter Stub'n (tel. 503) is an accommodating restaurant whose prices are low enough for a large family and whose specialties are so varied that guests can enjoy a different dish every day of the week. Wednesday, for example, is fondue day. Tuesday is strudel day. In addition to that, the restaurant serves thick and savory steaks, tafelspitz, tiroler Gröst'l (sautéed potatoes, onions, boiled meat, and bacon), blutwurst, lamb, fish, and venison dishes. A member of the Kohlmayr family is always on the premises, serving, in addition to everything else, pizzas. À la carte meals range from 95 AS ($5.05) to 350 AS ($18.62). The restaurant is open every day of the week from 11 a.m. to 11 p.m., but closes in May and again in October.

FILZMOOS: A still-unspoiled resort 50 miles south from Salzburg, Filzmoos (3,465 feet) lies at the foot of the 8,000-foot Bischofmütze, a section of the Dachstein massif.

Filzmoos is a good starting point for many excursions, as well as for walking tours. In winter you can ride in horse-drawn sleighs (ask at your hotel), practice curling and ice skating, and go skiing. The resort has a good ski school, along with 16 ski lifts and many fine slopes, some of which are suitable for beginners, others for the most experienced of skiers. From here you can try the Dachstein Glacier runs about 7½ miles away, via the scenic Höhenstrasse.

Ski areas include Rossbrand (5,250 feet), which lies to the south of Filzmoos. This section is serviced by a drag lift. Rettenstein (5,380 feet), to the north of the resort, is the second most popular area. Its drag lift is in two stages.

The third ski section is Grossberg (4,590 feet), also to the north of Filzmoos, served by a chair lift. It has runs for all grades of skiers.

You'll find the innkeepers here, for the most part, friendly and hospitable. The area code for Filzmoos is 06453.

Food and Lodging

Sporthotel Filzmooserhof (tel. 232) is the balconied chalet between the village church and the public swimming pool. Sports enthusiasts will find lots to do, since the public facilities for golf, mini-golf, and tennis are close at hand, as well as access to the ski slopes. One of the hotel's exterior walls has a hand-painted illustration of a man carrying a child across a stream, which guests can study while sipping coffee on the sun terrace. The interior is cozy, rustic, and filled with sunny colors. In winter the Webinger family charges from 420 AS ($22.34) to 570 AS ($30.32) per person, with full board included.

The adjoining restaurant is one of the better establishments in the village, serving international dishes such as scampi, steak, and schnitzel, and a collection of regional dishes which, even if you speak German, you'll have difficulty translating. The staff will help you, especially with the names of some of the Bosnian dishes, which include a well-prepared sour cream soup with potatoes. Both the restaurant and the hotel are closed from Easter till mid-May and from mid-October until mid-December.

Hotel Alpenkrone (tel. 280). One of the best times to view this hotel is in summer, when masses of alpine flowers cluster in the meadow nearby. Constructed in two parts, the chalet hotel has balconies facing the jagged mountains and an interior decoration which makes ample use of light-grained wood paneling. The doors to the bar area are wrought of straps and plates of solid iron, strong enough to keep anyone in (or out) for a long time. The dancing bar is a popular local hangout. The charge per person for full board ranges from 350 AS ($18.62) to 600 AS ($31.92) daily.

Hotel Hanneshof (tel. 275). The bedrooms in this comfortable chalet hotel have windows as big as those in any hotel in town, as well as spacious balconies, lots of paneling, and a series of colorful public rooms designed around open hearths and ornate wrought-iron chandeliers. The hotel was constructed in 1974, with careful attention to all the modern amenities, including a big indoor pool and a sauna. Well-furnished rooms range in price from 300 AS ($15.96) to 400 AS ($21.28) per person, breakfast included. The Hanneshof is open from December to April.

Alpenhotel Wurzer (tel. 220). The Wurzer family are your hosts in this family-run hotel near the village church. From the front the hotel looks like an old-fashioned slope-roofed chalet, with one end of the facade devoted to a country baroque painted design of what might be called the tree of life. The more contemporary backside looks out over a rolling grassy lawn. Constructed in 1959, the hotel is full of beautifully crafted paneling and cozy public rooms. Per-person rates with half board included range from 325 AS ($17.29) to 380 AS ($20.22), depending on the season. Accommodations with private balcony go for a supplement of 20 AS ($1.06) per person. Tariffs, otherwise, depend on the season and plumbing.

Après-Ski

In season live bands are brought in, and there is the inevitable collection of discos. The **Hotel Alpenkrone**, already recommended, is one of the most popular stops on the after-dark circuit. Young skiers especially are drawn to its

Königskeller disco, where all drinks cost about 65 AS ($3.46). Also you might ask about the next "fondue evening."

The also-recommended (see above) **Sporthotel Filzmooserhof** may attract you if you like your music live. A band plays for dancing until 3 a.m.

Another one of the hotels just recommended, the **Hanneshof,** has the Kaminstube, which also offers disco dancing.

OBERTAUERN: This winter and summer resort at 5,930 feet lies at the top of an old Roman road which divides Land Salzburg from Carinthia (see Chapter XII). The unspoiled resort is about 60 miles from Salzburg. It can be reached by train from Radstadt or else by Postal Bus. A car isn't really necessary here, as you can easily get around on skis in winter and on foot in summer. The people of Obertauern are friendly, and the tourist office is helpful.

In the vicinity is the **graveyard of the nameless ones,** the burial place of bodies recovered from the mountain area over the centuries, most of them victims of avalanches. The cemetery is near the Tauern Pass and dates from the 16th century.

One of the newest ski resorts in Land Salzburg, Obertauern has become an international sports center, with both ski and chair lifts, plus a cable car. A ski school is in business, with state-qualified instructors, and there are children's ski courses, plus a ski kindergarten.

The elevation at the top of the pass ensures that the snow is good and the season extra long. You can ski from November until the end of May at this "snow-proof" resort, with its ski circus. It's easier on one side, steep on the other, letting you ski all around the village.

Obertauern's area code is 06456.

Food and Lodging

Alpenhotel Perner (tel. 236). There's so much variety to the many sections of this mountainside hotel that it almost gives the impression of a long series of balconied railroad cars strung together. The interior is appealingly outfitted with hewn beams and timbers, often with carved detailing, as well as accents such as stained-glass insets and both stone and wrought-iron embellishments.

The public swimming pool is connected to the hotel via an underground passage, and covered tennis courts are close nearby. The friendly and engaging owners of this place are Erich and Maria Perner. High-season rates, with full board included, range from 840 AS ($44.69) to 950 AS ($50.54) for singles and from 750 AS ($39.90) to 990 AS ($52.67) per person for doubles. The dancing bar sees a lot of wintertime action, often with live music. The Perner is open from December to April and July to September.

Hotel Kristall (tel. 323) has a chalet facade and a two-story balconied extension angling attractively off to one side. The contemporary interior has lots of rustic touches, including a fireplace whose hood is fashioned from curved and textured stucco. The bedrooms usually have good views of the mountains, pleasing wooden furniture, and springtime colors in the curtains, bedspreads, and wall-to-wall carpeting. Guests enjoy well-prepared meals under the coffered ceiling of a panoramic dining room. With breakfast included, rates range from 370 AS ($19.68) to 400 AS ($21.28) per person for double occupancy. All units have private baths. Occupants of a single pay a surcharge of 50 AS ($2.66) daily. Open December to April and July and August.

Clubhotel Kärntnerland (tel. 271) is a cream-colored balconied building with painted embellishments in regional patterns covering its stucco walls. It sees itself as more of a private club than a resort hotel, with attentive service provided by the Günter Kanduth family. Inside you'll find a library, an open hearth, and two restaurants, one of them a rustic keller and the other a high-ceilinged paneled room with comfortable upholstered armchairs and colorful napery. The bedrooms are warmly intimate, often with contrasting patterns and cozy colors. Winter rates, with half board included, range from 450 AS ($23.94) to 540 AS ($28.73) in singles and from 440 AS ($23.41) to 540 AS ($28.73) per person in a double, depending on the plumbing. In summer, the bed-and-breakfast rate is from 200 AS ($10.64) to 250 AS ($13.30) per person.

Berghotel Pohl (tel. 397) is a white-walled chalet with wooden balconies in front of two of its four stories. An extension on the ground floor has oversize glass windows, behind which is the small but elegant restaurant. A rustically modern bar area has red accents and lots of wood, while the smallish bedrooms have simple and comfortable furniture. The hotel is in the heart of the ski-lift station, a short distance from the center of the village. High-season rates range from 610 AS ($32.45) to 680 AS ($36.18) per person for full board. Open from December to April.

Hotel Kohlmayr (tel. 282). As you approach this well-run hotel it looks like a pleasantly situated chalet, with stucco walls and several rows of wooden balconies with matching shutters. You'll soon realize, however, that the entire construction rests on top of a glass-walled foundation that contains the heated swimming pool with its view of the mountains. The rest of the hotel is tastefully and rustically filled with paneling, cozy bric-a-brac, and pleasing colors. Also on the premises are a sauna and a fitness room. The spacious sunny bedrooms look out over an alpine vista, and are sometimes divided into two sections with a full-length curtain which you can close if you plan to sleep late. With breakfast included, doubles rent for 540 AS ($28.73) to 650 AS ($34.58) per person, while singles range from 540 AS ($28.73) to 725 AS ($38.57), depending on the season.

Hotel Edelweiss (tel. 245). Once you sit down at the bar in this imaginatively decorated hotel you're likely never to leave. That's because the bar stools hang from a ceiling beam like children's swings and, in addition, mold themselves to the contours of your back. Other niches within the hotel's public rooms include Hitchcock-style rocking chairs placed beside the rustic fireplace, whose semicircular metallic bonnet exposes the flames to three sides of the room. A heated swimming pool and sauna are pleasant places to relax in before dinner in the restaurant or the brasserie, which might be followed by nighttime dancing. The contemporary bedrooms are sunny and filled with autumnal colors. They rent for 600 AS ($31.92) to 1,100 AS ($58.52) in a single and for 585 AS ($31.12) to 1,000 AS ($53.20) per person in a double. These prices include half board. The hotel is open only in winter.

Après-Ski

Nightlife is very limited, but there is some. Many skiers, mostly European, go to bed by ten so they'll have an early chance on the slopes. Prices of most drinks average around 65 AS ($3.46).

One of the best places for after-dark diversions is the **Alpenhotel Perner,** already recommended. In their "Stage Coach," a dance band keeps the joint jumping.

The **Hotel Edelweiss,** again recommended previously, also occasionally has dancing to live music.

But the most fun is likely to be found at the **Gasthof Taverne,** where a ski expert, Mr. Oberhumer, and his sons welcome you in a real gemütlich atmosphere. They feature Tyrolean music and dancing. The place has plenty of atmosphere (it was actually converted from a stable).

4. The Tennengau

The Tennengau, named for the Tennen massif, is one of the divisions of the Salzach Valley to the south of Salzburg. It's characterized by rolling hills and many woodlands. Often you'll see waterfalls, of which those outside the town of Golling are the most visited.

As you leave Salzburg going south on the left bank of the Salzach River you'll pass through Anif, a section already previewed in the environs of Salzburg (Chapter VII). You'll find some excellent, old romantic accommodations in Anif, if you'd like to live on the immediate outskirts of the provincial capital.

If you don't want to stay in the Tennengau region, you might consider it as a day's exploration from Salzburg, its chief sight being the Dürrnberg Salt Mines outside Hallein. See the previous chapter. However, if you'd like to anchor in the district—in either summer or winter—the town that is most blessed with accommodations in a wide range of prices is Abtenau (sometimes called Bad Abtenau), which for decades has been known mainly as a winter ski business.

Much of the Tennengau area, especially the houses with their gables and window boxes of geraniums, will remind you of Bavaria.

GOLLING: The major attraction drawing visitors to Golling, 7½ miles south of Hallein, is the **Gollinger Wasserfall** (Golling waterfall), 1½ miles outside the little resort, plus about a ten-minute walk in addition. The waterfall is between Golling and Kuchl, 17 miles from Salzburg. Visits to the wasserfall, which tumbles down more than 500 feet over a rock wall, are from May to October daily, a tour taking about an hour. Admission is free.

You can also visit the **Salzach Gorge** near Golling. It's an hour's walk from Golling up to Pass Lueg. You can visit the gorge from May to October daily. Allow about an hour. Adults are charged 15 AS (80¢); children, 10 AS (53¢).

In Golling you can visit the castle with its chapel and folklore collection. You'll see remains of cave bears, fossils, and copies of rock drawings, plus views of the village in old pictures. Visiting hours are June to September on Wednesday, Saturday, and Sunday from 9 a.m. to noon. Admission is 15 AS (80¢) for adults, 5 AS (27¢) for children.

Many visitors use Golling as a base for enjoying the varied sports facilities in the nearby mountains.

For Golling, the area code is 06244.

Food and Lodging

Hotel Stern (tel. 220) sits in a row of picture-book houses in the center of the village. It has arched windows on the ground floor, three floors of embellished windows above that, and a wrought-iron bracket holding a sign out over the street. The interior is filled with rustically modern furniture, while the bedrooms are cozy and comfortable. Singles range from 350 AS ($18.62) to 425 AS ($22.61), while doubles go from 300 AS ($15.96) to 400 AS ($21.28) per person, with half board included.

Many of the region's gourmets know about the in-house restaurant. Its specialties include dried alpine beef, sliced wafer-thin and served with pearl onions and pickles, filet steak, filet Stroganoff, and an Austrian version of the Italian saltimbocca (veal schnitzel stuffed with ham and served with a savory sauce). There's also an array of seafood which includes mussels prepared in several different ways. Fixed-price meals cost 100 AS ($5.32) and 135 AS ($7.18), while à la carte dinners cost from 125 AS ($6.65) to 375 AS ($19.95). The restaurant is closed every Monday between October and April, and reservations are suggested otherwise.

OBERALM: The main reason for visiting this little hamlet, which lies near Hallein and Salzburg, is to stay at the castle hotel recommended below.

However, if you're sightseeing in the area you might want to stop to see the **parish church** *(pfarrkirche)*, which is Romanesque with Gothic extensions. It has a magnificent high altar from 1707 by J. G. Mohr. The church is embellished with baroque furnishings and has heraldic tombstones. See the funereal shield from 1671.

Oberalm's area code is 06245.

Food and Lodging

Schloss Haunsperg (tel. 2662) is an early 14th-century castle, decorated with towers and interior ornamentation. The outside is restrained, with a grayish-pink covering of stippled stucco with white trim. A small but ornate baroque chapel adjoining the hotel has a wrought-iron gate separating the vestibule from the inner sanctuary, along with plenty of gilt embellishments. The public rooms include a series of vaulted corridors, each furnished with antiques and rustic chandeliers, several salons with parquet or flagstone floors, and a collection of antiques. My favorite is the second-floor music salon. Many of the accommodations are divided into suites of two or three rooms plus private bath, along with some doubles with bath also. The owners, the von Gernerth-Mautner Markhof family, charge from 625 AS ($33.25) to 860 AS ($45.75) per person, breakfast included. A tennis court is on the premises.

ABTENAU: A small town nestling at the foot of the Kogel, Abtenau is known for its Gothic church. The little town, 30 miles from Salzburg, can be reached by bus from Golling in the Salzach Valley. It does mostly a summer business, but some winter trade has been developing. The minor spa is closed in winter.

Summer holiday visitors enjoy the mountain landscape through which to tour, strolling on forest paths, canoeing, playing tennis, horseback riding, swimming, and watching cheerful folkloric entertainment. You can hire guides for climbs in the Tennengebirge, but allow a whole day for this activity. A chair lift goes from Abtenau to the Karkogel at 3,950 feet.

During the winter months guests often assist in feeding the deer. Abtenau offers skiing, tobogganing, horse-sledge rides, ice skating, and swimming in a covered pool.

There are some 60 miles of quiet hiking trails and fitness runs.

The area code for Abtenau is 06243.

Food and Lodging

Windhofer's Hotel/Restaurant Post (tel. 209) has lots of rustic artifacts scattered throughout its country-style interior, including an ox yoke positioned below a hay-filled manger hanging from the ceiling of the intimate bar area. The Windhofer family has positioned an old iron-and-wood postal cart in the lobby, which is today filled with flowers. Summer guests might enjoy the terrace below the balconies of the pleasant chalet, whose smallish bedrooms are comfortable and clean. A covered swimming pool is nearby. A member of the family will sometimes organize bus excursions to sights in the area.

With half board included, rates range from 430 AS ($22.88) to 480 AS ($25.54) per person per day based on double occupancy, with singles paying a supplement of 65 AS ($3.46).

Breakfasts are buffet style and generous, but the evening meals are particularly inviting and well prepared, served in a gemütlich room with a big ceramic stove and lots of niches. Specialties include rumpsteak Tyrol, Indian-style veal, onion-flavored roast of beef, and fresh salads. À la carte meals range from 100 AS ($5.32) to 275 AS ($14.63).

Hotel Roter Ochs (tel. 2259) sits on the village's central square, across from the church. The sides of the building are covered with red, gold, and gray geometric illustrations, while the front has paintings of village characters who appear to be dancing and leaping over the sides of the wooden balconies. The public rooms are modern and simple, and some of the comfortable bedrooms have carved headboards and rustic furniture. Live folkloric music and dancing are part of the entertainment provided in the beer and wine room, Zum Stacherl. You'll find a wide variety of accommodations, ranging from bathless singles to more elaborate units with private bath, phone, radio, mini-bar, and balcony. The price per person ranges from 380 AS ($20.22) to 480 AS ($25.54) for half board, based on double occupancy. Tariffs depend on the accommodation and the season. Singles pay a supplement of 90 AS ($4.79) per day.

Sporthotel Gasthof Moisl (tel. 2232) is a prosperous-looking building in the middle of the town, with a backside dotted with short masonry columns and carriage lamps and a front side covered with regional paintings, wooden balconies, and heavily overhanging eaves. The interior is filled with heavy coffered ceilings, curved half timbering, rounded stucco columns, and an unusually shaped central fireplace in the baroque style. A scattering of carved regional antiques adds to the appeal of the hotel, along with an inviting collection of bar and restaurant areas. On the premises is an indoor shooting range, plus an indoor swimming pool with a big-windowed view of the rest of the village, along with a bowling alley and fitness room. Singles range from 650 AS ($34.58) to 900 AS ($47.88), while doubles cost from 600 AS ($31.92) to 950 AS ($50.54) per person, with full board included. The hotel is open from December to October.

Gasthof Weisses Rössl (tel. 2302) has glass and wrought-iron doors guarding the entrance, adding an appeal to the skillfully lit beamed ceiling of the entrance hall of this chalet hotel. The bedrooms are filled with alpine furniture, most of it painted in forest green and blue-gray, with doorways decorated to match. The Eder family are your hosts in this pleasant hotel, where each of the accommodations has a private bath, renting for 400 AS ($21.28) per person, based on double occupancy, with half board included. Single occupancy carries a 50 AS ($2.66) surcharge. The hotel also rents apartments by the week in a building down the street.

Gasthof/Pension Ledererwirt (tel. 2269) was originally a village house with a flagstone roof, pink walls, lime-green shutters, and masses of flowers. Years ago someone added a modern extension which today dominates the smaller building, but also provides additional accommodations. The comfortable bedrooms rent for 275 AS ($14.63) to 360 AS ($19.15) per person, based on double occupancy, with a buffet breakfast included. Half board is another 100 AS ($5.32) per person daily.

PUCH-THURNBERG: This small spa catering mainly to Europeans lies at an altitude of 2,600 feet, 7½ miles south of Salzburg. Here you can breathe in mountain air full of ozone and clear the city pollution from your lungs. Puch-Thurnberg is known for its ultramodern curative and rehabilitation therapies.

The area code for Puch-Thurnberg is 06245.

Food and Lodging

Kurhotel Vollererhof (tel. 3232) sits imposingly on a hillside with its balconies turned toward one of the most panoramic views in the region. A parasol-dotted sun terrace is surrounded by fir trees. The indoor swimming pool is angled toward the view, which swimmers can see through large windows. The public rooms are elegant and tasteful, with a kind of restrained dignity to many of the high ceilings and cozy niches.

The bedrooms have chaise longues near the wooden railings of their balconies. A toboggan run and a small ski lift are on the hotel's grounds. Another building, the Landhaus, charges slightly lower rates for its rooms. For accommodations in their two buildings the Eberlein family charge 750 AS ($39.90) to 915 AS ($48.69) per person, with full board included. Prices depend on the season and the accommodation.

5. The Pinzgau

The Pinzgau section of Land Salzburg stretches east from the Gerlos Pass to the Gastein Valley, with the Salzach River flowing through. To the south lies Hohe Tauern and to the north the Kitzbühel alpine region.

This is a very special area for skiing, especially the twin villages of **Saalbach** and **Hinterglemm,** which lie at the end of a valley ringed by a horseshoe of mountains laced with more than 40 ski lifts. The chief resort of the Pinzgau, **Zell am See,** is treated separately (see below). Another outstanding ski resort in the Upper Pinzgau region is **Kaprun.** The **Grossglockner Road** begins in Pinzgau (see below).

The Austrians call the Upper Pinzgau Valley the Oberpinzgau. This was one of the most isolated regions of the country until massive hydroelectric works opened it to the world. But the Upper Pinzgau areas, from a touristic point of view, isn't as lively as the resorts, such as Saalfelden, of the Mittelpinzgau, or Middle Pinzgau. This area runs along the **Steinernes Meer,** or "sea of stone," marking the frontier of Bavaria, part of West Germany.

LOFER: Ideally situated in a setting of forests, valleys, and mountain rivers, Lofer is an old market town, with a **Bauerntheater** (peasant theater) and a Gothic-style **pfarrkirche** (parish church). The church tower dominates the town with its two onion-shape domes. Many of the houses are decorated with oriels, as much of the architecture was inspired by nearby Bavaria.

Lofer is both a health resort and a ski center, offering friendly hospitality as well as native tradition and rural charm. It's known for its peat-water and mud baths and its Kneipp cures. The fog-free area around Lofer is suitable for walking in both summer and winter. There are a tennis court, skating rink, miniature golf course, and enclosed swimming pool.

A ski school is operated here, and there are nine T-bar lifts. A chair lift will deliver you to the Sonnegg-Loderbühel at 3,290 feet and the upper station of the Loferer Alm, 4,600 feet. Rising in the background of the town are the Loferer Steinberge and the Reiter Steinberge.

A popular excursion is to the pilgrimage church, **Maria Kirchenthal** (see St. Martin, below). You can also visit the **Lamprechtsofen Cavern,** Austria's deepest water-bearing cave, on the road from Lofer to Weissbach, about 37 miles from Salzburg by bus. A guided tour takes about 40 minutes. Admission is 25 AS ($1.33) for adults, 12 AS (64¢) for children

The area code for Lofer is 06588.

Food and Lodging

Hotel Bräu (tel. 2070) has a lemon-colored facade, white neoclassical ornamentation around each of the windows, and voluptuously curved wrought-iron balconies on the second floor. It's in the center of the village. If you don't see it as you approach it on the narrow flagstone-covered sidewalk, you'll recognize it by the ornate curved bracket (it's shaped like the garlanded head of a mythical bird) extending out over the pavement. Parts of the hotel were constructed in

1639, and from a view of the antiques inside it's easy to get a sense of the era of its construction.

The modern parts of the hotel have made every effort to offset the antique appearance of the older sections. A persimmon- and lime-colored bar area is an unusual study in modern design, while the entrance hall is covered with marble floors and discreet geometric designs. The bedrooms are usually filled with painted alpine furniture and a romantic selection of colors. Prices for a single are 900 AS ($47.88) to 1,020 AS ($54.26), while doubles are charged 800 AS ($42.56) to 920 AS ($48.94) per person, all prices including full board. Rates quoted depend on the season.

The garden restaurant is one of the most charming places in town for a meal, and you can easily move into the rustic dining room when it turns cold. Specialties include a delectable soup of smoked trout, roast pork in a gorgonzola cream sauce served with green spätzle, and tafelspitz, while desserts might feature a variety of fresh strudels. A la carte meals range from 160 AS ($8.51) to 350 AS ($18.62). Fixed-price dinners cost from 120 AS ($6.38).

Haus Gertraud in der Sonne (tel. 203) is a wood-covered chalet with red and white shutters. It's set high on a mountainside, in a solitary position among fir trees which gets a lot of sunshine. Access to the hotel can be made via a winding alpine road, where Haus Gertraud is the last stop. The Blüml family maintains a private rope tow up a beginner's ski slope, or advanced skiers can reach more challenging slopes from the nearby ski lift.

In winter or summer a terrace provides a wooden deck where guests can usually get a suntan. The colorful and cozy interior has a rustic bar area with rows of exposed shingles serving as a roof and evenly spaced rows of honey-colored planks covering the walls of many of the bedrooms. Singles range from 475 AS ($25.27) to 700 AS ($37.24), while doubles cost 460 AS ($24.47) to 610 AS ($32.45) per person, with full board included. Open from December to April and June to September.

Hotel Gasthof Post (tel. 3030) is a gracefully painted chalet with two-dimensional colored embellishments surrounding each of the facade's windows. It also has carved wooden balustrades serving as the balcony railings and lots of flowers. Guests rarely check out of this place without having coffee on the street-level sun terrace, where a view of the village street life is presented just beyond the summer bed of yellow marigolds. The decor inside contains lots of aged wood and a few well-placed ceramic stoves.

The comfortable bedrooms rent for 550 AS ($29.26) to 710 AS ($27.77) per person, based on double occupancy, and 620 AS ($32.98) to 800 AS ($42.56) for a single. Prices, which include full board, depend on the plumbing and the season.

The adjoining restaurant is charmingly filled with all the rustic detailing you'd expect in such an old house, coupled with a gemütlich feeling. Specialties of the house include a ragoût of fresh venison, trout, pork cutlets, and a tempting array of fish and meat dishes.

Hotel St. Hubertus (tel. 266). You'd never guess that this beautifully painted chalet is as big as it is, but actually it stretches for dozens of yards behind the regional designs and balconies of its facade. The spotlessly clean interior has ceilings almost universally made of wood—at least in the public rooms—and a simple attractive decor of wooden chairs with upholstery in autumnal colors. Each of the comfortable bedrooms has its own private bath, and many of them contain balconies. With full board included, doubles rent for 460 AS ($24.47) to 510 AS ($27.13) per person, while singles cost from 500 AS ($26.60) to 540 AS ($28.73), depending on the season. The Grissesman family will give you a fine welcome from December to October.

ST. MARTIN BEI LOFER: This tiny hamlet is visited for its pilgrimage church, a large baroque edifice in a romantic setting called **Maria Kirchenthal**. The building was designed by the renowned master of the baroque J. B. Fischer von Erlach. The church has a museum displaying votive pictures from the 17th to the 19th centuries.

The church, one mile west of the village, is reached by a toll road open only in summer, a passenger car costing 35 AS ($1.86) both ways, or you can make an hour's walk from Lofer (see above).

The **Vorderkaser Gorge** can be visited from St. Martin. A 1½-mile road connects the gorge with the Mittelpinzgau Road near the Vorderkaser bus stop. The gorge may be seen daily from the first of May until the end of October. A visit costs adults 20 AS ($1.06); children, 10 AS (53¢).

SAALBACH AND HINTERGLEMM: This internationally celebrated tourist resort, at an elevation of 3,290 feet, places emphasis on relaxation, recreation, and sports—both summer and winter.

From spring until late in the autumn many quiet walks or more extended hikes are possible, as well as mountaineering, riding, bowling, mini-golf, and tennis. You can swim in a nearby lake, where surfing and sailing are also possible. There are some 160 miles of well-laid-out footpaths. A kindergarten caters exclusively to children of people on holidays.

Saalbach has seen rapid growth as a winter sports resort in recent years, with numerous lifts in close proximity to the center of town. There's one cable car big enough to carry 100 passengers, along with 40 tow and chair lifts. Tobogganing is popular too, as are ski-bobbing, sleigh rides, and curling in the clear, alpine winter. Many cross-country ski tracks emanate from here.

Saalbach is a twin resort to **Hinterglemm,** which lies about an eight-minute car ride to the west, at the head of the valley. Often the region is spoken of as a unit—the Saalbach-Hinterglemm ski area. The resorts are linked by a lift system and a ski bus. The area has a surprising variety of well-groomed slopes and deep-snow runs. The major lift, the Schattberg cableway, leaves from the heart of Saalbach, taking skiers to the top station (6,560 feet) where there's an excellent restaurant with a suntrap terrace and a panoramic vista. Of course summer visitors can also take the cableway to enjoy the scenery.

The Saalbach-Hinterglemm visitors' racing course is available to enthusiasts from Tuesday to Sunday between 10 a.m. and noon and 2 and 4 p.m., with slaloms, giant slaloms, and parallel slaloms being held. Both resorts have ski schools and provide ski circus runs.

Saalbach has fine shops where you can find traditional Austrian clothing as well as chic apparel for dress or sports. Local arts and crafts shops are also of interest to visitors.

Saalbach can be a good center for exploring the neighboring resorts of Kaprun and Zell am See.

The area code for Saalbach and Hinterglemm is 06541.

The Resort Hotels

Hotel Sonnleiten (tel. 402) is a multi-sectioned balconied hotel with a series of gently sloping rooflines and a format that looks like a greatly expanded chalet. It's on the ski slopes a short distance above the village, and parts of the hotel are attractively angled to create a varied facade of many different planes. Some sections of the interior have high modern ceilings supported by massive sloping beams. Management often has a fire going, even in summertime, near the curved bar.

The dining room is large, with a paneled ceiling and wooden chairs. On the premises you'll find tennis courts and an outdoor swimming pool which is heated in winter. (Many guests take a warm dip and then roll around in the snow!) With full board included, singles range from 890 AS ($47.35) to 1,120 AS ($59.58), while doubles cost from 790 AS ($42.03) to 1,070 AS ($56.92) per person, depending on the season and the exposure of the room. All of the accommodations contain private bath. The hotel is open from December to March and May to September.

Ingonda (tel. 262). Built as late as 1980, this hotel and restaurant exudes an aura of well-established, even antique, prosperity. It was named after the attractive brunette wife of the owner, Dietmar Scheyerer, who works hard to make the establishment one of the most comfortable at the resort. Aside from its five-star restaurant, the social center is a rambling pine-covered bar occupying an extended corner of the elegantly rustic lobby. There, an intricately crafted softwood ceiling casts a mellow glow over the leather chairs and Oriental carpets.

The hotel contains 47 well-furnished bedrooms, each with its own bath, TV, radio, phone, and balcony. Most residents at this year-round hotel opt for half-board plans: between 650 AS ($34.58) to 1,225 AS ($65.16) per person in a double in low and shoulder season, rising to 1,400 AS ($74.48) to 1,500 AS ($79.80) per person in high or winter season. Singles pay a supplement of 350 AS ($18.62) on the same plan.

Skiers appreciate the proximity of the hotel to any of the village's trio of ski lifts, a one-minute skiborne trek from the entrance. The hotel has its own Jacuzzi, sauna, solarium, and massage facilities, plus a well-recommended restaurant. There in a setting of chalet chairs and burnished paneling guests enjoy such specialties as scampi flambéed in gin, filet of beef jambalaya, tender cuts of well-seasoned beef, and homemade strudels. Meals cost from 200 AS ($10.64) to 600 AS ($31.92) if you're dropping in to dine (reserve in season for a table, of course).

Hinterhag (tel. 291) is an unusual and appealing hotel set on the side of an alpine hill a short distance from the center of town. It's composed of at least five different sections, all of them balconied and built in a chalet style, connected into an architectural unit that might be your headquarters during your stay in Saalbach. In addition to a large collection of paneled and timbered public rooms, the hotel maintains a combination art nouveau café and art gallery. When I was last there the paintings were a dreamy collection of pastel-tinted water colors, but the collection changes frequently.

The story of the construction of this oft-expanded hotel is documented in photographs on one of the walls of the public rooms. The cuisine is the finest at the resort (see the dining recommendations coming up). The varieties of light-hearted activities for wintertime guests bring repeat business. The bedrooms have lots of exposed wood and an occasional wry touch, such as a nun's head extending over a bed's headboard, seemingly looking down at whatever might be happening. Sepp and Evi Fersterer, both avid skiers, are your hosts. They charge from 650 AS ($34.58) per person in either summer or winter, including a buffet breakfast. The hotel is closed between April 1 and July 1 and from September 30 until mid-December.

Hotel Glemmtalerhof at Hinterglemm (tel. 7135) rises six stories, all of them in a chalet style, above the central street of the village. The street level of the hotel contains a few small shops as well as the front entrance. Inside you'll find gemütlich and cozy public rooms, sometimes accented with fireplaces and lots of exposed wood. A covered swimming pool has big windows and sun chairs, while the public tennis courts are a few buildings away. The decorator here used a combination of knotty-pine paneling and conservatively modern accessories for an attractive and appealingly rustic format. The bedrooms are the kind of place where you'll be tempted to linger. They're covered with mellow pine and invitingly lit. A coffeeshop, two bars, a nightclub, and a choice of restaurants are part of the facilities. Depending on the season, singles range from 930 AS ($49.48) to 1,080 AS ($57.46), with doubles costing from 890 AS ($47.35) to 1,040 AS ($55.33) per person, with full board included. The hotel has a dozen family apartments. Open December to October.

Hotel Bauer (tel. 2130) presents lots of visual distraction. You'll see a mixture of colors and patterns, all of them invitingly cozy. In summer many guests sit on the flowered terrace in front, while in winter they move into the happily cluttered public rooms, which are large, containing lots of niches for secluding oneself with a book or a friend. In the center of town, the hotel maintains a chalet annex a few minutes away, closer to the ski slopes. The annex contains rooms similar to the ones in the main buildings, as well as a snackbar which skiers find convenient. Singles range from 900 AS ($47.88) to 960 AS ($51.07), while doubles cost from 840 AS ($44.69) to 920 AS ($48.94) per person, with full board included. The hotel is open from December to October.

Hotel Saalbacher Hof (tel. 7111) has one of the prettiest chalet facades in town. It's embellished with heraldic paintings, masses of summertime flowers, and on top of the lower of the two sloping rooflines, an open-sided stork's tower supported by a single stout post. The interior is dignified, restrained, and baronial, with a big stone fireplace in the attractively formal main salon, acres of chestnut-colored paneling, and pleasingly bold Oriental rugs. A wide grassy lawn with a view of the onion dome of the village church leads down to the outdoor heated swimming pool.

The Dschulnigg family provides live music for dancing at five-o'clock tea and in the evening. You'll find three different restaurant and bar areas, my favorite of which has masonry walls and hanging lamps shaped like enormous pewter double-handled tankards. The accommodations in a nearby annex are similar to the ones in the main house. Rates range from 520 AS ($27.66) to 620 AS ($32.98) per person, based on double occupancy, and singles go from 580 AS ($30.87) to 720 AS ($38.30). Heating, service, and taxes are included in the prices.

Berger's Sporthotel (tel. 577). If you arrive in midwinter, the ambience is almost like that of a giant house party which almost never ends, the guests of which tend to be refugee urbanites celebrating their once-a-year vacation. On the premises are a boutique and dress shop, a small heated indoor swimming pool, a two-tiered restaurant and disco with a central marble-covered dance floor, a stüberl, and a cellar bar with live music and intimate lighting. In the center of Saalbach, the hotel can be recognized by its wooden balconies and its big yellow sign. Rates range from 1,220 AS ($64.90) to 1,320 AS ($70.22) in a single, from 1,020 AS ($54.26) to 1,120 AS ($59.58) per person in a double, with full board included in all the tariffs. Prices depend on the season, and each of the comfortable and brightly colored bedrooms has its own bath. Open only from January to April.

Hotel Kristiana (tel. 253) is one of my favorite hotels in Saalbach. It has a facade that bristles with jutting balconies, the horizontal supports of which have been intricately cut into pleasing patterns. On one corner, just above the sun terrace, an artist has executed a series of etched panels designating what might be the different seasons in Saalbach.

The interior is a rustic fantasy of carved beams and well-polished paneling, several open fireplaces, and comfortable, well-planned rooms, each with its own private bath. A sauna is on the premises, while tennis courts and an indoor swimming pool are just around the corner. Johann Breitfuss and his family are your accommodating hosts at this pleasant hotel. Depending on the season, prices are from 610 AS ($32.45) to 940 AS ($50.01) per person for half board, based on double occupancy. Singles pay a surcharge of 150 AS ($7.98) per day.

Alpenhotel Saalbach (tel. 666) is a big modern hotel with a design reminiscent of a chalet. It has painted detailing around some of the windows on the lower floors, lots of wooden balconies, and a facade divided into several different sections. A disco in the basement is one of the attractions, as well as a cozy, well-furnished interior. This includes a collection of country artifacts, several fireplaces (one of which juts pleasantly into the room and is capped with a conical stucco chimney), a popular bar with enough unusual details and enough people to make you want to linger, and a cellar with regional folk music.

A long narrow indoor pool capped with what looks like hand-hewn ceiling beams is part of the sports facilities, along with a sauna, exercise room, a whirlpool, and a solarium. Apartments are available for extended stays, sleeping between two and six guests. For shorter stays, singles range from 520 AS ($27.66) to 1,300 AS ($69.16) daily, while doubles go from 475 AS ($25.27) to 1,250 AS ($66.50) per person. Prices depend on the season. The Thomas family are your hosts.

Hotel Panther (tel. 227). When the flowers are out in full force the balconies of this hotel are stunning. Even when they're not, the exterior is invitingly rustic, with solidly constructed wooden balconies, heavy overhanging eaves, and an open-sided tower, ideal for a stork's nest, crowning the roof. One of the village's popular discos is reached by a separate entrance clearly marked on the outside of the building.

The interior is generously covered with well-crafted paneling, tile floors, and Oriental rugs. One of the salons has white walls, a massive beamed ceiling, and an unusual painted sculpture of a warrior with a shield. The hotel is only a few steps from the cable car and within skiing distance from the bottom of the slopes. The Gasteiger family are your hosts, charging from 450 AS ($23.94) to 550 AS ($29.26) per person, based on double occupancy, with full board included. Prices depend on the plumbing and the season. The hotel is open from December to September.

Hotel Kristall (tel. 376) is a pleasant family-style chalet in the center of Saalbach. Its five stories contain well-furnished bedrooms, many of them wallpapered in light patterns of gray and white, with furniture that sometimes looks as if it came from a private home. The public rooms are either rustic and heavily timbered or filled with modern and flamboyant colors and big windows. One area looks like a Victorian pub complete with globe lights. On the premises you'll find an indoor pool, a sauna, a fitness room, and frequent live entertainment. The owners charge 790 AS ($42.03) to 990 AS ($52.67) per person daily based on double occupancy, with full board included. Singles, also with full board, cost from 850 AS ($45.22) to 1,030 AS ($54.80). Open from December to March and May to September.

Gasthof Unterwirt (tel. 274) has a modern balconied addition set at right angles to the main house. The overall effect is pleasant and relaxed, a feeling helped by the rustic decor of the ceiling beams, ceramic tile stoves, and full-grained paneling. Paul Kröll and his family are the accommodating owners, charging 640 AS ($34.05) to 900 AS ($47.88) in a single and 620 AS ($32.98) to 830 AS ($44.17) per person in a double, with full board included. Prices depend on the season, the plumbing, and the exposure. Open from November to September.

Hotel "Haus Wolf" at Hinterglemm (tel. 346). If you're interested in ski lessons, this might be an ideal hotel since the local ski school makes its headquarters here. The hotel is right beside the Reiterkogel cable car in a pleasant chalet with wooden balconies and a first-floor sun terrace. The interior is covered with wood paneling, some of it crafted into curved and geometric designs. The vertical columns supporting the ceilings are made either of wood or stone, while many of the homey touches include shelves with hand-painted plates just below ceiling level.

In winter fires burn beneath copper-sheathed chimneys, and guests often congregate in one of the several bars and restaurants. A smaller annex provides comfortable accommodations, often filled with painted furniture, a short distance away. Prices range from 550 AS ($29.26) to 760 AS ($40.43) per person, depending on the plumbing and the season. Full board is included in the rates. The hotel is open from December to March and May to September.

Where to Dine

Hinterhag-Alm, at the Hotel Hinterhag (tel. 291), is considered by some gourmets to be among the best restaurants in Austria. The award-winning chef, Peter Huber, uses ingredients from the mountains that wouldn't ordinarily be used anywhere else. One example is a local variety of stinging nettles which, when properly prepared, make a delicious flavoring for dumplings, salads, and soups. Some of his recipes are updated versions of very old local dishes. He uses large quantities of cabbage, reaching perfection in the cabbage soup. Dandelion greens, which are used in salads, as you'd expect, also might turn up in a honeyed dessert parfait. Specialties also include whortleberry omelets, sometimes suggested as an appetizer, as well as mountain-style roast mutton flavored with thyme. The restaurant is closed from April 1 till June 15 and for all of October and November. À la carte meals range from 175 AS ($9.31) to 425 AS ($22.61). Reservations are suggested.

Zur Dorfschmiede, at Hinterglemm (tel. 7408), appears nondescript, scattered over several floors, but inside you'll find a Teutonic retreat of glowing pine, wrought iron, and gemütlich warmth. Portions are copious, flavorful, and worth the trip even if you're staying in Saalbach. You won't find anything very exotic, but the traditional dishes are satisfying. The peppersteak comes steaming and rich and might be followed by a richly caloric chocolate-flavored palatschinken. À la carte meals cost from 100 AS ($5.32) to 325 AS ($17.29).

Après-Ski

Saalbach is one of the liveliest centers in Land Salzburg for après-ski and nightlife.

First, for coffee, tea, or pastries, you might drop in at one of the many cafés in town. In Saalbach, the **Galerie Café** (tel. 242) is housed in a modernized chalet faced with white stucco on a sloping street in the center of the resort across from the Hotel Ingonda. Inside, bentwood chairs, expositions of art, and tempting pastries lure visitors. The artwork changes frequently, but you'll find that the caloric sweets, concocted by Evi-Fersterer, are inevitably there, luring some of the trendiest of skiers. Coffee costs from 24 AS ($1.27), with pastries ranging from 24 AS ($1.27) to 30 AS ($1.60).

In Hinterglemm, try the **Café Glemmtalerhof** (tel. 7135).

The **Saalbacher Fassl** (tel. 7309) is another café-restaurant, and it has dance music and is open every day from 10 a.m. to 10 p.m. It's beyond the Hochalm lift at Hinterglemm.

The **Kristall Keller,** to the right of the entrance to the already-recommended Hotel Kristall, draws an attractive young crowd to its lively bar where in high season a live band plays for dancing. In addition its Bacchus Weinstube is considered "the meeting point in Saalbach."

The **Hotel Panther,** also recommended previously, shelters one of the most popular discos in the village. It's the Zum Herrn Karl, an American-style music bar which shows video films daily.

If you want more local entertainment, consider the Kuhstall Bar at the also recommended **Alpenhotel**. It only has a two-man Tyrolean band, but they manage to sound like a dozen musicians and they keep the place lively. The setting is rustic with beamed ceilings.

One of my favorite spots is the **Hotel-Gasthof Neuhaus,** where a two-man Zigeuner band entertains the skiers after a hard day on the slopes. This is one of the friendliest places on the nighttime circuit of Saalbach.

Among the major hotels, the Sportkeller Night Club Disco at the recommended **Sporthotel** is very festive for those who like their après-ski with a good band and a good drink (maybe more than one). Sportsmen are very fond of the place.

The après-ski crowd shuttles back and forth between Saalbach and Hinterglemm, and after a few drinks the resorts merge into one.

In Hinterglemm, a good spot is the Knappenhof Knappenkeller of the **Knappenhof Tirolerhof** (tel. 529). Grilled food is served until 3 a.m., and most often there is live music for your dancing and entertainment pleasure. Sometimes Tyrolean music is interspersed between the more modern sounds.

Also at Hinterglemm, the **Hotel Glemmtalerhof,** also recommended, has perhaps the most gemütlich atmosphere of any place in the village. The Almbar, a small, intimate disco, stays open very late, and the Glemmerkeller Apéritif Bar is just the place to order a fondue any time before midnight. The show room, however, is Harlekin Dancing, where well-known international bands often appear in season.

If you're seeking a rustic, charming setting, try the previously recommended **Landhaus Wolf** at Hinterglemm. Some of the most attractive and fun-loving people in the area gather here around the fire. The decor might be called "Come to the Stable."

In recent years the nightlife prices of Saalbach and Hinterglemm have almost caught up with the high tariffs of Zell am See, and you're likely to spend from 80 AS ($4.26) for a drink in most of the taverns and clubs recommended above. There is rarely a cover charge, unless a name band happens to appear.

SAALFELDEN: An old market town in the Middle Pinzgau, Saalfelden is set against a background of towering mountains. Lying in a broad valley formed by the Saalbach River, this is a good center for touring the **Steinernes Meer,** or "sea of stone," a karstic limestone plateau which the Austrian government has turned into a nature reserve.

Although Saalfelden is primarily a summer resort, winter sports areas in the mountains are within easy reach.

The town has a **pfarrkirche** (parish church) with a Gothic crypt beneath the choir and a late Gothic triptych in the presbytery.

At **Ritzen Castle,** which dates from 1563, a local museum (Heimatmuseum) is devoted to life in the Pinzgau region. Here you'll see a rich collection of Christmas cribs by the artist Xandl Schläffer, exhibited in four rooms. Another hall displays a collection of pictures and ecclesiastical art. The museum is open Wednesday, Saturday, and Sunday from 2 to 4 p.m. (daily in high season). Admission is 20 AS ($1.06) for adults and 10 AS (53¢) for children.

Saalfelden's area code is 06582.

Food and Lodging

Hotel Dick (tel. 2215) is a long four-story building with unusual geometric designs around the windows and heraldic paintings on the white front section.

The reception hall has Louis XIII-style chairs and dark paneling, while the rest of the interior has high coffered ceilings and bright colors. In the back yard a heated swimming pool is the gathering place in summer. The featured bedroom has 18th-century furniture and a painted ceiling, but the other units contain pleasant furniture quite a bit newer.

Doubles rent for 450 AS ($23.94) to 520 AS ($27.66) per person, with half board included. Singles go for an additional 75 AS ($3.99) surcharge per night. Prices depend on the season, and all the accommodations are equipped with private bath. The adjoining restaurant serves unusual specialties, such as Japanese gulasch, plus a wide variety of fresh fish. Someone told me that the chef goes out to catch them himself in his free time.

Restaurant Schatzbichl, 82 Ramseiden (tel. 3281), is an alpine country house known for its cuisine. The recipes are usually derived from formulas used for generations by the area's grandmothers, and are served by local waitresses dressed in colorful regional garb. Specialties are often placed in a copper pan directly onto your table, while members of your party dig in with forks and serving spoons.

You might enjoy Kasfarfeln (thick consommé with cheese, onions, chives, and dumplings) or Schottnocken (served in a big pot with spätzle, smoked cheese, chives, and onions), or finally my favorite, Erdäpfelgröstl (a big pot with potatoes, broth, sausages, onions, and chives).

You can get here by car, because the restaurant lies off a road dug into the valley of Maria Alm. But if you're adventurous, you can walk here in an hour and a half from Maria Alm, which might make a pleasant midday excursion. Be sure to call ahead for a reservation. À la carte meals range from 115 AS ($6.12) to 320 AS ($17.02). The restaurant is closed November 3, December 5, and in April.

LEOGANG: This is really an off-the-beaten-track little hamlet known principally to the Austrians and Bavarians. In the general vicinity of Saalfelden, it's so undiscovered that you can enjoy quietness and tranquility here. Leogang is both a summer and a winter resort, lying at an elevation of 2,750 feet, in the Middle Pinzgau. Many day excursions are possible from here, including one to the "sea of stone" mentioned above.

The Leogang area code is 06583.

Food and Lodging

Hotel Krallerhof (tel. 246) is designed in a combination of antique rural styles (which include painted baroque detailing around some of the windows) and late 20th-century adaptations such as an A-frame roof over part of the front section. The result is a pleasing combination of old and new, with an interesting sprinkling of contemporary sculpture thrown in. Because of its isolation from other buildings in the village, you'll be able to imagine that the sun terrace stands at the edge of a virtual wilderness, which goes as far as the dramatic peaks of the nearby Leoganger Steinberge.

The popular double-tiered nightclub inside is appealingly decorated with lofty ceilings, gently sloping exposed stairways, and hand-carved paneling. Regional live music can often be heard. The bedrooms usually have checked curtains and wood ceilings. They rent for 665 AS ($35.38) to 785 AS ($41.76) per person, based on double occupancy, with full board included. Prices depend on the plumbing, the room assignment, and the season. Singles pay from 715 AS ($38.04) to 845 AS ($44.95) for full board. On the premises is an indoor and outdoor swimming pool, plus a ski school and a small ski lift for beginners. Open from December to October.

KAPRUN: Both a summer resort and a winter ski center as are most towns in the area, Kaprun is known for its high glacier skiing. The town is hardly the most attractive or the most atmospheric in Land Salzburg, but serious skiers don't seem to mind that. It's about a 12-minute run from Zell am See, which is easily reached by bus.

The surrounding area takes in the Valley of Kaprun and its magnificent dams. It includes an ascent to the Kitzsteinhorn (9,612 feet), which can be quite complicated, involving Postal Buses, funiculars, and cableways. Always have your routes outlined at the tourist office with a detailed area map before you set forth. An English-speaking staff member there will supply the best possible routing and provide you with the most up-to-date hours, costs, and types of services likely to be available at the time of your visit. Also, you can learn about weather conditions from that source. For example, after mid-October, tours to the valley of the dams may not be possible. However, a visit to Kitzsteinhorn is an attraction in both summer and winter.

The **Kitzsteinhorn** will probably be first on your list of things to see. To reach the summit, you can go by cable car, transferring to the Salzburger Hütte at the Restaurant Alpincenter, where you can enjoy lunch with a view. The Alpincenter (8,020 feet), incidentally, is the largest ski area in Austria. You can also reach the mountain by taking the underground funicular and changing at the Alpincenter. Don't forget that traffic gets very heavy here in winter.

The bottom station of this glacier railway is at an elevation of 2,784 feet and the top one is at 9,087 feet. Not only can you ski from the Alpincenter, but you can also take glacier and mountain tours.

It's best to purchase a day ticket—round trip, naturally—for both the cable railway and the glacier lift, costing 280 AS ($14.90), as the railway goes only to the second platform of the cableway. You get off the train at that station and board a cableway which will swing west, coming to a stop near the summit of Kitzsteinhorn. This station is called the Gletscherbahn.

You'll find the Panoramatunnel cut through the mountains, as well as the Aussichtsrestaurant (talk about dining with a view!). You'll also be able to see Grossglockner, the neighboring mountain and the highest in Austria at 12,340 feet. The tunnel measures some 1,000 feet on the south side of the mountain, opening onto a panoramic gallery from which the view of Grossglockner is possible.

The **Kapruner Tal,** or Valley of Kaprun, is visited in summer to see its dams, which form a dramatic mountain sight. These dams, constructed in tiers, were originally built as part of the World War II recovery act, the U.S.–financed Marshall Plan. Experts from all over the world come here to study these hydroelectric constructions, considered brilliant feats of engineering genius. Trips are possible from the middle of May until around the middle of October, depending on weather conditions.

From Kaprun you can take a road to see the mammoth wall of the Limbergsperre (Limberg Dam). At the Gletscherbahn cable-car station, you can go all the way to the Kitzsteinhorn, already described. From the Limbergstollen car park, you can take a shuttle bus to the lower station of the Lärchwand funicular. At the upper platform you'll have a magnificent view of the Limberg Dam rising nearly 400 feet. The dam holds back water to form the Upper Mooserboden reservoir.

You can go along the valley by Postal Bus, passing through some 1½ miles of tunnels, to the Mooser Dam. A view of the Wasserfallboden lake reservoir (5,480 feet) is possible from here. The reservoir holds more than 18,500 million gallons of water.

You can see the two dams, the Moosersperre and the Drossensperre, which combine to form the Mooserboden reservoir, capable of holding nearly 19 million gallons of water. These hydroelectric plants have reservoirs surrounded by glaciers of the Glockner range.

An inclusive ticket to visit the plants costs 140 AS ($7.45) in high season, 130 AS ($6.92) in off-season. This covers the cost of transport from the Limbergstollen or Kesselfall car parks as far as Mooserboden and back. The ice-covered peaks of the High Tauern can be seen from the dams.

The area code for Kaprun is 06547.

Food and Lodging

Sporthotel Kaprun (tel. 8625) is a large chalet with a gently sloping roof and flowered balconies. It's near the cableway stations at the southern exit of Kaprun. Built in 1977, it has an attractive format of paneled ceilings, big windows, and spacious public rooms. These include a sauna, a children's playroom, and a game room. You'll also find exercise machines and table tennis tables nearby, plus at least one bar area.

The bedrooms are modern, and some areas are covered with paneling. With full board included, rates range from 640 AS ($34.05) to 700 AS ($37.24) per person.

Menu items in the adjoining restaurant read like a "Who's Who" of international geography. They include recipes from the Pacific (veal steak Hawaii), the Far East (Chinese fondue), and India (a range of curry dishes). If you like steak tartare, it's succulent here. Steaks are also elegantly presented at your table in a copper pan.

Hotel zur Burgruine (tel. 8306) is a rambling, three-story building set on a hillside, with a design somewhat like that of a chalet. Its public rooms have high ceilings with huge timbers crisscrossing them, beautifully notched and skillfully joined together. On the premises is an indoor pool with a rustic ceiling, plus a sauna, an exercise room, and a large restaurant whose specialties are well-flavored grilled meats. A member of the Heinze family will be glad to tell you about excursions in the region. Rooms range in price from 650 AS ($34.58) to 750 AS ($39.90) in a single and 550 AS ($29.26) to 620 AS ($32.98) per person in a double, according to the season and plumbing, with full board included.

Hotel Orgler (tel. 8205) is a cream-colored house with flowered balconies in the middle of the village. Slightly isolated from its neighbors, it offers peace, quiet, and a pleasantly rustic interior of high ceilings, heavy beams, and chalet furniture. A sauna, a solarium, and a day café are all on the premises, as well as a sunny dining room. Each of the bedrooms has its own bath, and many of them contain their own balconies as well. Half-board rates in a double range from 500 AS ($26.60) to 580 AS ($30.87) per person, depending on the season. Singles pay a 45 AS ($2.39) surcharge. The hotel has a tennis center with indoor and outdoor courts and a squash court, an 18-hole golf course, and a sauna.

Gasthof zur Mühle (tel. 8254) is a white-walled chalet with wooden balconies and five floors of cozy rooms. On a quiet road in an isolated part of the village, it contains a sauna, table tennis facilities, and a comfortable TV room. It's owned and operated by the Nindl family, who charge from 465 AS ($24.74) to 530 AS ($28.20) per person in a double, with full board included. The full-board single cost is 505 AS ($26.87) to 570 AS ($30.32) daily. A covered swimming pool in a nearby hotel is available to guests at zur Mühle.

Gasthof Hotel Tauernhof (tel. 8235). Elise Mayerhofer and her family run this L-shaped chalet with the painted illustrations and the prominent balconies. Constructed in the recent past, the establishment contains comfortable bedrooms, a restaurant, and a wine cellar. With full board included, doubles cost from 380 AS ($20.22) to 440 AS ($23.41) per person. Singles pay a daily surcharge of 30 AS ($1.60).

Barbarahof (tel. 7248) is adjacent to its sister hotel, the Tauernhof. The windows of its front bedrooms are gently angled to allow more of the sunlight to penetrate behind the flowered balconies. Inside you'll find a covered swimming pool, a sauna, a separate breakfast room, a fitness room, and an elevator. Each of the accommodations has a private bath, phone, TV, and radio. Rates in a double range from 360 AS ($19.15) to 400 AS ($21.28) per person, depending on the season, with breakfast included. Singles carry a daily surcharge of 60 AS ($3.19).

Grabner's Gasthof Gletscherblick (tel. 8293) is a small, family-run guest house with flowered balconies and a sunny terrace. A bus stops in front of the house to transport guests to the village. Inside the gasthof you'll find gutbürgerlich cookery, a kellerbar, and a café. The comfortable bedrooms are clean, with lots of exposed wood. Rooms rent for 400 AS ($21.28) per person either single or double, with full board included.

Krefelderhütte (tel. 621-361) is a mountain lodge in lonely isolation above the village at 7,545 feet. It's an elongated three-story house with wood siding. It sits next to a rocky outcropping near the ski slopes, with an amiable direction provided by the Rattensberger family. Simply furnished doubles rent for 360 AS ($19.15) per person. Half board costs an additional 75 AS ($3.99) per person, a super-bargain. The hotel is closed in June and October, and almost constantly booked during Easter, Christmas, and New Year's.

Alpincenter (tel. 8300) is a sturdily built wood-and-concrete hotel near the terminus of the ski lift at the middle station of the Kitzsteinhorn railway, some 8,000 feet up the mountain. The interior is modern and rustic, with lots of heavy exposed beams, a central fireplace with curved stools pulled up in a circle around it, and a series of clean and attractive public rooms, usually filled with sports enthusiasts. This hotel makes week-long offers that include a six- or seven-day ski pass, but for the daily rate, half board ranges from 395 AS ($21.01) to 445 AS ($23.67) per person, with single occupants paying a daily surcharge of 75 AS ($3.99).

Zirbenstüberl (Hubertus) (tel. 8504). Many visitors consider the pine-paneled walls of this place a tempting refuge from the weather and the hordes of visitors who descend upon Kaprun. Hans Brudermann is the guiding light, producing a nouvelle cuisine of impeccably fresh ingredients. Specialties include crayfish with watercress, sweetbreads with basil-flavored noodles, venison with a dressing of wild mushrooms, and a house version of chicken breast with cabbage, followed by an assortment of desserts made fresh daily. Fixed-priced menus range from 300 AS ($15.96) to 500 AS ($26.60), with à la carte meals in the 200-AS ($10.64) to 400-AS ($21.28) range. In winter reservations are necessary, and the stube is open every day except Monday (also closed for two weeks in September and again in October).

Après-Ski

Kaprun has its own relatively modest nightlife, but should you ever get bored you can always take the shuttle bus over to Zell am See for much more excitement. Nightlife reaches its peak in Kaprun on Friday and Saturday nights, and on other nights you might like to turn in with a good book . . . or whatever.

The **Sporthotel Kaprun,** already recommended, is the scene of the most action, offering dancing to either disco records (the latest hits from the U.S.) or else live bands, often imported from Italy. You might begin your evening with a Chinese fondue dinner or an Indonesian-style rijsttafel, that ceremonial feast of the Dutch colonists.

Your evening in Kaprun might begin relatively modestly—and early—by dropping into **Morokutti** (if you can find a seat) for one of those mouthwatering Austrian pastries. Sometimes the **Nindl Café** has folkloric evenings and dancing, which you'll definitely want to see and participate in.

You can also attend tea dances in the late afternoon at the **Baum tavern,** later enjoying disco action at the **Salzburger Keller.**

Many skiers like to spend their evening sitting and drinking around an open fire. Nearly all hotels and pensions welcome outside guests.

Drink prices are about the same in all these establishments, beginning at 75 AS ($3.99).

MARIA ALM: The village of Maria Alm, three miles east of Saalfelden at an elevation of 2,600 feet, is both a summer and a winter resort. Lying at the foot of the Steineres Meer, the karstic limestone plateau called the "sea of stone," now a nature reserve, Maria Alm holds many attractions for warm weather visitors, including chair-lift rides to heights presenting glorious alpine vistas, a 35-mile network of marked pathways for walks in shady woods and across wide romantic grassways, tennis, and mini-golf.

The surrounding mountains attract skiers in winter. Together with Hintermoos and Hinterthal, Maria Alm forms a large avalanche-free winter sports area, with continuous snow cover from the beginning of December to the end of April.

The church spire in Maria Alm rises to 276 feet.

Maria Alm's area code is 06584.

Food and Lodging

Hotel Norica (tel. 491) is a four-story roadside chalet, with all the balconies and rustic detailing you'd expect. The cozy interior is comfortable, filled with alpine timbers (some of them decorative), knotty paneling, and conference facilities. A heated indoor swimming pool and a sauna, along with a wind-sheltered sun terrace, are part of the facilities. The location of this hotel, near the ski lifts, makes it ideal for skiers. Each of the rooms has a large bath. Singles range from 910 AS ($48.41), while doubles cost from 810 AS ($43.09) per person, with full board included.

The adjoining restaurant is definitely an above-average place at which to eat. Menu items include scampi Café de Paris, peppersteak Madagascar, filet Stroganoff, and roast pork Singapore style. The restaurant is open seven days a week, and reservations are a good idea.

Restaurant Arcade, 9 Hinterthal (tel. 828-235), is a small and intimate restaurant loaded with personalized touches. The decor, both inside and out, is one of regionally inspired handiwork. The clientele is local and loyal, although the establishment draws a large number of vacationers as well. Menu items include delicately flavored specialties such as watercress soup, filet of beef in a paprika-rosemary sauce, trout in a Riesling sauce, and turbot with a chive sabayon. Dessert items are too lengthy to list, but one of the most popular is a walnut parfait. À la carte meals range from 190 AS ($10.11) to 400 AS ($21.28), while fixed-price dinners cost 300 AS ($15.96) to 600 AS ($31.92). Reservations are important. The restaurant is closed during all of May and from early October until just before Christmas.

Almer Heurigen Keller (tel. 615). Easy to find in the basement of a building right in the center, this country-style wine cellar has hosted many personalities whose names are known throughout the Teutonic world. You'll find a good selection of wine and a solidly appealing cuisine prepared by Mr. and Mrs. Hans Haller. To accompany your bottle of wine, you might enjoy one of the house schnitzels, sausages with cabbage, or an array of snacks and salads from the buffet. The cellar is open every day except Tuesday. It's closed from mid-April till the end of May and from the end of October to mid-December. À la carte meals cost 80 AS ($4.26) to 300 AS ($15.96), depending on your appetite and tastes.

MAISHOFEN: This is actually a little satellite outpost of Zell am See where you might choose to anchor if you want to stay in the area, yet escape the frenetic pace that overtakes the larger resort in the height of both the winter and the summer seasons. Maishofen has convenience and tranquility, with all the sights and attractions of Zell am See at its doorstep.

The Maishofen area code is 06542.

Food and Lodging

Gasthaus Schloss Kammer (tel. 8202). From the outside this place looks more like a prosperous bourgeois house than a castle. But for romantics, a small room in the main building might be a perfect hideaway. Most of them get lots of sun and are furnished with antiques or reasonably good copies, along with some baroque fireplaces or ceramic stoves. You can stay here for 400 AS ($21.28) per person for complete board. Or, especially if you're a family, the Neumayer family will rent you an apartment in a neighboring annex, suitable for two to six persons.

In the main hotel the public rooms have old photographs and lots of carved statues. The dining room is one of the most sought after in the region. Most of its plaster ceiling is supported by massive stone columns and old vaulting. A green ceramic stove provides heat to offset the winter winds blowing against the small-paned windows. The noodles are homemade, accompanying such main dishes as roast pork, roast venison, gulasches, and a variety of tempting stews. À la carte meals range from 85 AS ($4.52) to 185 AS ($9.84). The restaurant is closed on Tuesday.

BRUCK AN DER GROSSGLOCKNERSTRASSE:
The starting point for Grossglockner Road (coming up) is at this little mountain resort, which becomes a lure to skiers when the snow falls. In summer the Grossglocknerstrasse brings lots of vehicular traffic through the village, standing at an elevation of 2,485 feet. Bruck's **parish church** *(pfarrkirche)* is from the 19th century.

From here visitors go up to **Schloss Fischhorn** for one of the most celebrated views in the area. Another excursion is to **Taxenbach,** 7½ miles away. Some 15 minutes from that point, you reach **Kitzloch Gorge,** where you can take a 45-minute tour from May 1 until the end of October, costing adults 20 AS ($1.06); children, 5 AS (27¢).

The area code for Bruck an der Grossglocknerstrasse is 06545.

Food and Lodging

Hotel Lukashansl (tel. 458) has an unusual facade of white stucco with beige detailing and avocado-colored shutters. The windows are small and are surrounded with detailing in country baroque. A member of the Peter Mayr family has cultivated a grape arbor near the café terrace, which is separated from the road by a row of potted shrubs. An annex with flowered balconies juts off to one side of the main building with parking space beside it. Half-board rates range from 400 AS ($21.28) to 425 AS ($22.61) per person, based on double occupancy, while singles cost 500 AS ($26.60). The hotel is especially popular in winter.

RAURIS: Motorists entering the Rauris Valley from Taxenbach come upon Rauris, which was a goldmining town in the Middle Ages. Many of the elegant old houses in the town are from that era.

The **Rauriser Talmuseum**, in the Nationalparkgemeinde Rauris, exhibits popular art and artifacts left over from the goldmining heyday of the town. The collection is in honor of Ignaz Rojacher, founder of the Sonnblick Observatory. The museum is open all year, with guided tours daily at 10 a.m. and 4 p.m. Admission is 20 AS ($1.06) for adults and 10 AS (53¢) for children.

Rauris (2,600 feet) is a summer excursion and a winter ski resort. You can take chair lifts to the Kreuzboden at 4,280 feet and the Jack-Hochalm at 4,820 feet.

For Rauris, the area code is 06544.

Food and Lodging

Sporthotel Rauriserhof (tel. 213) is a large, modern hotel which, if you could see it from the air, looks like two huge chalets connected by a central corridor and a series of low-lying sports facilities. The outdoor tennis courts are a few steps away, and immediately next to them are two indoor tennis courts. Other facilities include a sauna, a swimming pool, a bowling alley, and at the end of a tiring day of sports and play, a collection of cozily paneled bars, backgammon rooms, crackling fireplaces, and intimate corners. The place is fun, interesting, and could be a central point for a prolonged stay exploring the region's footpaths.

Well-furnished singles cost 770 AS ($40.96), while doubles go for 730 AS ($38.84) per person, with full board included. The in-house restaurant is worth a special trip. Aside from its Austrian specialties, international fare includes snails, crabmeat soup, and entrecôte Café de Paris. Gutbürgerlich selections feature well-prepared game, schnitzels, roasts, and pork cutlets in vodka sauce. Fixed-price meals range from 85 AS ($4.52) to 135 AS ($7.18), while à la carte dinners cost 95 AS ($5.05) to 325 AS ($17.29). It's open every day.

Restaurant Schüttgut, Wörth (tel. 403), is authentic enough to make you feel like one of the prosperous local farmers. The restaurant used to be a rough-timbered farm building, constructed in the 16th century, until it was transformed into this charming establishment run by Mr. and Mrs. Anton Hubers. The service is personalized, and you are likely to feel a gemütlich warmth before the end of your meal. Specialties are wholesome, filling, and regional. À la carte meals range from 75 AS ($3.99) to 170 AS ($9.04). It's open every day.

MITTERSILL: The major town of the Upper Pinzgau region (Oberpinzgau), Mittersill, at an elevation of 2,590 feet, is at the intersection of ancient trade routes, with buildings rich in tradition. Surrounded by three lakes and 30 miles of alpine brooks, with many beautiful paths for summer walking and hiking, the town is also a popular winter sports center.

Skiers can go to the main skiing area of Pass Thurn-Kitzbühel, where one ski pass allows use of any of the 56 ski lifts and a ski bus.

The glaciers of Hohe Tauern south of the village are part of the national park system, which you can visit.

Mittersill has two churches built in the baroque style in the mid-18th century. Schloss Mittersill, from the 16th century, is privately owned and cannot be visited.

There's a local **museum** in the Felber Tower (tel. 4441), where a varied collection of Pinzgau peasant furnishings is exhibited, as well as many minerals, tools, and other artifacts. It also shows ecclesiastical art. The museum is open from June 1 until the end of September Monday to Friday from 9 a.m. to 5 p.m., on Saturday and Sunday from 1 to 5 p.m. Admission is 20 AS ($1.06) for adults, 5 AS (27¢) for children.

Mittersill's area code is 06562.

Food and Lodging

Hotel Schloss Mittersill (tel. 4523). The Gothic chapel attached to this prosperous-looking house is frequently used for marriage ceremonies, which eventually spill over into the main hotel. The hotel is about a 20-minute walk from the center of the village and is easily accessible by car. You'll recognize it by its patterned red and white shutters and its roofline with three tiers of small-windowed gables. The public rooms are stately, with vaulted ceilings and thick walls pierced with triple sets of arched Gothic windows. A library/sitting room has stone detailing and paneling darkened long ago by frequent polishing. My favorite room has a massively timbered ceiling, pure-white walls, a stone fireplace, and lots of hunting trophies.

Each of the bedrooms is individually furnished, sometimes with built-in closets of knotty pine. Singles range from 350 AS ($18.62) to 800 AS ($42.56), while doubles cost from 500 AS ($26.60) to 1,300 AS ($69.16), with breakfast included. Half board goes for additional 160 AS ($8.51) per person daily.

Gasthof Bräurup (tel. 216) is a historical white-walled house with four floors of wood-grained shutters and a surrounding grassy lawn. The interior has rustic touches which include lots of burnished paneling, ceramic stoves with unusual hand-painted illustrations, shelves of antique pewter, and a scattering of large regional antiques. The bedrooms are usually large and furnished with large windows and more furniture than you'd expect. The elevator is big enough to accommodate wheelchairs. The rates per person in double rooms range from 325 AS ($17.29) to 500 AS ($26.60), which includes half board. Singles pay a daily surcharge of 65 AS ($3.46).

My favorite room is the richly paneled rectangular restaurant with the hand-carved baroque finials at the corner of the walls and ceiling. In the center is a round panel bristling with sheaves of grain carved into the glowing hardwoods. The inn is in the center of the village.

Hotel/Restaurant Pass Thurn (tel. 34611), built in an area convenient to skiers, is large, balconied, imposing, and covered on the outside with wood detailing. The rustically elegant interior has a collection of painted armoires and chests in the public rooms that deserve a second look, a heavily beamed two-story bar and restaurant in a separate building, and cozy eating and drinking areas where you'll run into sports enthusiasts. Depending on the season, the rate per person in a double ranges from 400 AS ($21.28) to 420 AS ($22.34), with full board included. Residents of singles pay a daily surcharge of 40 AS ($2.13). All units contain private bath. Open December to October.

NEUKIRCHEN AM GROSSVENEDIGER: Lying near Wald in Pinzgau at an

elevation of 2,800 feet, in a setting of alpine woods and meadows, fields and forest paths, Neukirchen's sunny terraces afford a view of 15 mountain peaks, including the Grossvenediger, the Kleinvenediger, and the Geiger. Many alpine hikes can be arranged by the Oberpinzgau school of mountaineering.

The village has a late Gothic church with a 14th-century fresco. You can also see the **Castle Hochneukirchen** here, dating from the 16th century. The present schloss was built on the site of a much older structure that was destroyed.

Like nearly all resorts in Land Salzburg, Neukirchen is a ski center in winter and a holiday resort in summer.

The area code for Neukirchen am Grossvenediger is 06565.

Food and Lodging

Hotel Gassner (tel. 6232) is a large hotel built chalet style in two sections joined together by a series of balconied rooms. A sun terrace rests on massive stone columns above a parking lot, and the hotel is slightly outside the central part of the village. The interior is contemporary and rustic, with lots of comfortable banquettes and full-grained polished planking decorating the ceilings and walls. The indoor pool is big enough to swim laps in, while the spacious bedrooms are simple, cozy, and comfortable. Also on the premises is a sauna, and the hotel has easy access to the nearby ski slopes. Usually a crackling fire will be waiting for you after your return from a winter's day outdoors. Charges per person in doubles range from 400 AS ($21.28) to 440 AS ($23.41), with full board included. Prices vary according to the plumbing and the season. Occupants of singles pay a supplement of 35 AS ($1.86) daily. The hotel is open from December to October.

Gasthof/Pension Kammerlander (tel. 231) is a large, four-story hotel with a concrete exterior, painted white, wraparound balconies, and heavy overhanging eaves. Not far from the village church, the gasthof is owned by the Kammerlander family, who do everything they can to welcome guests to their comfortable hotel. The interior includes masonry detailing, lots of wood, art objects, and a comfortably inviting restaurant and bar area with red tablecloths, hanging lamps, and well-prepared Austrian-style food. Tariffs per person for double occupancy are 460 AS ($24.47) to 530 AS ($28.20), with full board included. For a single, a supplement is charged, ranging from 40 AS ($2.13) and 60 AS ($3.19) daily. Prices depend on the plumbing, the season, and the room assignment.

Alpengasthof Rechtegg (tel. 6329). The Kröll family are your friendly hosts at this hillside chalet, where the views from the windows are spectacular. The panoramic restaurant on the downhill side has a well-planted sun terrace on top, and someone has accommodatingly built a rooftop covered platform for any happenstance stork who feels like living there. The public rooms are cozy and sunny, while the bedrooms look like something from a private home, with combinations of knotty pine and textured white walls that are pleasing. With half board included, rooms with private bath rent for 325 AS ($17.29) to 400 AS ($21.80) per person, while bathless units go for 225 AS ($11.97) to 300 AS ($15.96) per person, depending on the season.

WALD IM OBERPINZGAU: Wald, a summer and winter resort at a 2,900-foot

elevation, occupies one of the most beautiful sites in the Upper Pinzgau. The village lies at the junction of the old road from the Gerlos Pass, and from it you can see the glacial peaks of the Grossvenediger massif. In its churchyard you'll find gravestones carved out of rare minerals.

In summer, Wald is a good center for easy footpaths and climbs in the national park. From here, you can enjoy alpine hunting and trout fishing. Also, a hang-gliding school may attract you.

Skiing and other sports lure winter visitors. A ski school prepares you to try the 25 miles of slopes. About 18 major lifts reach three skiing areas where snow is virtually guaranteed well past Easter. Skiing is possible at elevations ranging from 4,800 feet to 6,500 feet. There are also any number of easy footpaths. Hotels here can organize toboggan runs, riding, horse-sleigh rides, and curling.

The Wald im Oberpinzgau area code is 06565.

Food and Lodging

Jagdschloss Graf Recke (tel. 6417). This elegant red-roofed mansion was built in 1926 as the personal hunting lodge of the Silesian family of the Count von der Recke. At the time they owned the hunting rights in what is today the nearby Austrian National Park of Hohe Tauern. The best time to see this place might be in summer, when a thick layer of wildflowers covers the grounds around it. A curved swimming pool lies just beyond the stone foundation. The famous guests who stayed here in the 1920s and 1930s would make a long (and perhaps notorious) list, although today the hunting trophies that fill the interior are the only reminder of their presence. Tennis, horseback riding, alpine hunting, and trout fishing, plus proximity to the miles of footpaths in the region, along with the dozens of ski lifts all around, are part of the benefits of this well-run hotel.

With half board included, singles rent for 650 AS ($34.58) to 800 AS ($42.56), while doubles cost 550 AS ($29.26) to 700 AS ($37.24) per person, depending on the plumbing and the season. Some of the suites and apartments are more expensive. An extra bed can be set up in any room for an additional fee which almost matches the per-person rate for the room itself.

The handsome restaurant is worth a detour, especially if you're fond of game or freshly caught fish. Many of the fish are caught in the nearby wilderness. Fixed-price meals range from 160 AS ($8.51) to 375 AS ($19.95), while à la carte dinners cost from 150 AS ($7.98) to 350 AS ($18.62).

Walderwirt and Märzenhof (tel. 8216). Everyone has a choice in life, and in this case you'll be able to choose between two different buildings on either side of the street. The older of the two was built in 1770, and still maintains the vaulted ceilings, heavy timbers, and some of the painted antiques of the year of its construction. The modern section has streamlined wooden balconies, an indoor pool, tennis courts, lots of paneling, and an open fireplace whose massive hanging chimney is made of small plates of iron riveted together.

Bedrooms cost approximately the same in the two buildings, and they're connected by an underground passage in case you can't decide which you like better. Prices per person, based on double occupancy, range from 550 AS ($29.26) to 650 AS ($34.58) with full board included, depending on the season and the plumbing.

The restaurant is contained in the older section. It has old paneling, smallish windows, and a ceramic stove. The food comes in copious quantities, and is the kind of gutbürgerlich fare best enjoyed with a few beers. Many of the cheese selections come from the region. À la carte dinners range from 85 AS ($4.52) to 250 AS ($13.30).

KRIMML: This village in the far-western extremity of Land Salzburg is visited mainly by those wishing to explore **Krimml Falls.** The German name for this scene of iridescent splendor is Krimmler Wasserfälle. These falls, the highest in Europe, are spectacular, dropping 1,250 feet in three stages. They lie to the south of the Gerlos Pass, which connects the Salzach Valley in Land Salzburg with the Siller Valley in the Tyrolean country. Krimml, mainly a summer resort, is the best base for exploring the falls. The village is in a heavily forested valley called Krimmler Ache, between the Kitzbühel Alps and the Hohe Tauern.

If you're coming from Salzburg, figure on some 95 miles by train. There's also bus service from Zell am See. If you're traveling by car you have a choice of leaving your vehicle at the car park at the south of the village and making a 30-minute walk to the lower falls, or taking the Gerlos Pass toll road, open from June 1 to September 30. The toll is 8 AS (43¢) for adults and 4 AS (21¢) for children. Visits to the falls are possible from May until October.

Most visitors allow about 3½ hours to explore the entire falls area. On a sunny day, try to visit the Wasserfälle around noon when they are at their most spectacular. On summer nights the waterfalls are likely to be floodlit on Wednesday, depending on weather conditions.

Wear good, sturdy shoes, and since viewing points are always shrouded in spray, a raincoat will come in handy.

After you've seen the lower falls, if you want to see the second stage, count on another 12-minute walk. From there it's only a five-minute jaunt to the third and final stage for viewing the cataracts. There are also paths leading to the fourth and fifth viewing points. The middle part of the falls can be seen at the sixth and seventh lookouts. At the Bergerblick, you'll have your greatest view of the waterfalls, reached by continuing another 20 minutes from the seventh viewing point. If you wish, you can go on to the Schettbrücke (4,800 feet) for a look at the upper cascades.

Krimml is also visited in winter, because good skiing is offered at Gerlosplatte (5,600 feet), seven miles away. The waterfalls lie under a deep ice layer during the winter. If you like to drive along high alpine roads, you can take the Gerlos Road leading from the Krimml Waterfalls to the Gerlos Pass where it joins the road to Zell an Ziller in Tyrol. A single trip costs passenger cars a toll of 80 AS ($4.26).

Krimml's area code is 06564.

Food and Lodging

Gastehaus Hanke (tel. 279) is a contemporary, solidly built two-story chalet. It has white walls, wood balconies, and heavy overhanging eaves. The tasteful interior has much wood paneling and lots of cozy touches. The bedrooms are warmly modern and rustic. An indoor heated swimming pool is on the premises. A café and restaurant with painted detailing around the windows and a busy sun terrace are in a separate building. Comfortably furnished singles cost 290 AS ($15.34); doubles, 265 AS ($14.10) per person. Some three-person apartments are available as well. Breakfast is included in these prices, and each unit contains a private bath.

Alpengasthof Krimmler Tauernhaus (tel. 8327). This wood-sided hotel is built on the grassy flatlands of a high alpine valley. Two streams rush by at a safe distance on either side of the green shuttered building, whose only neighbors are a few barns and storage sheds. The interior is charming, with a timbered restaurant decorated with red-and-white checked curtains, musical instruments, and an antique polychrome crucifix hanging from the old paneling on the walls. You'll be tempted to spend your days outdoors, and there are plenty of nearby footpaths to accommodate you. Half board costs 385 AS ($20.48) per person. Few of the rooms have private bath. Adolf and Franziska Geisler are your hosts.

Hotel Klockerhaus (tel. 208) is a peaceful double chalet with wooden balconies, gently sloping rooflines, and a central section two stories high. The restaurants inside are timbered, covered with natural-grained pine, and filled with chalet-style chairs and tables. The spacious bedrooms are outfitted with regionally painted furniture with flowered panels set into natural pine frames. Rates in a double range from 300 AS ($15.96) to 380 AS ($20.22) per person, with half board included. Singles pay a daily supplement of 50 AS ($2.66). Prices depend on the plumbing and the season.

Gasthof Schönmoosalm (tel. 272) is a roadside hotel consisting of two chalets joined together in the middle like Siamese twins. The airy dining room has a coffered ceiling, tile floor, and pink napery. The hotel is small, containing only 22 beds, but the location is quiet and sunny, and the accommodations have a view of the mountains. The Eder family, your hosts, charge 300 AS ($15.96) per person in winter and 260 AS ($13.83) per person in summer, with breakfast included.

Gasthof Krimmlerfälle (tel. 203) is a pretty four-story house with sea-green shutters and wood siding covering the third and fourth floors. In summertime the balconies are covered with pink and red flowers. The dining room is laid out below a wooden ceiling whose planks are arranged in a circular pattern above the modern upholstered chairs. The simple rooms are tasteful and comfortable. They range in price from 345 AS ($18.35) in a single and from 300 AS ($15.96) per person in a double, with breakfast included. Your congenial hosts are the Schöppl family.

6. The Grossglockner Road

Grossglocknerstrasse, the longest and most splendid alpine highway in Europe, and one of the outstanding tourist attractions on the continent, will afford you one of the greatest drives of your life.

The hairpin turns and bends of the Grossglockner Road have been called "the stuff Grand Prix is made of." It's believed that this was the same route through the Alps used by the Romans, although this was forgotten until 1930 when engineers building the highway discovered remains of the work of their road-building predecessors done some 19 centuries earlier. The highway, representing engineering genius, was finished in 1935. It was the one that such countries as Switzerland and France copied years later when they built their own alpine highways.

It runs for nearly 30 miles, beginning at Bruck an der Grossglocknerstrasse (see above) at 2,483 feet, via Fusch/Grossglocknerstrasse, and heading toward Ferleiten, Hochmais, and Fuschtörl through Hochtortunnel, where the highest point is 8,220 feet, to Guttal and Heiligenblut (4,267 feet) in Carinthia.

The actual mountain part of the road stretches for some 13½ miles, usually at about 6,500 feet. It has a maximum gradient of 12%.

Many visitors prefer to take the bus over this spectacular stretch, but if you feel that your driving is good enough, you can do it by private car. Because of the high altitudes, the road is only passable from mid-May to mid-November. Always check with some authority about the road conditions before considering such a drive, especially in spring and autumn. A single trip in a passenger car costs a toll of 250 AS ($13.30). The toll is collected either at Ferleiten or at Heiligenblut. In summer there is regular Postal Bus service running from such places as Zell am See and Salzburg.

After leaving Bruck, you enter the Fuscher Valley going south, and along the way you'll be rewarded with breathtaking alpine scenery. Four miles from the Hochtortunnel on the north side, you can branch off onto the Edelweiss-Strasse, going along for about 1½ miles to the car park at the **Edelweiss-Spitze** (8,433 feet). Here you'll see a panorama of 37 10,000-foot peaks. At Edelweiss-Spitze is an observation tower, going up to more than 8,450 feet.

One of the interesting detours along the road is to the stone terrace of the **Franz-Josefs-Höhe.** It's named for the emperor who once had a mansion constructed here in the foothills of the Pasterze Glacier. The stretch from Gletscherstrasse to Franz-Josefs-Höhe (7,770 feet) is some five miles long, branching off near Guttal. This road lies above the Pasterze Glacier, opposite the Grossglockner (12,430 feet). The Pasterze, incidentally, is the largest glacier in the eastern Alps, 5½ miles long.

If you're traveling in spring and autumn, it might not be possible to take detours to the Edelweiss-Spitze or the Franz-Josefs-Höhe if heavy snow falls. If you do take the side trip to the latter site, avoid arriving there around midday.

On a bright sunny day in summer the place is literally mobbed. It has an outstanding view of the majestic Grossglockner.

It's possible to descend from Freiwandeck to Pasterze Glacier by taking a funicular from May until the end of September. Service is every hour from 8 a.m. to 4 p.m.

7. Zell am See

Founded by monks around the middle of the eighth century, the old part of Zell am See lies on the shore of the Zeller See (Lake Zell), with a backdrop of mountains. Zeller See is a deep glacial lake filled with clear blue alpine water. The town today is the most important resort in the Middle Pinzgau, a district that has already been previewed. Zell is popular and fashionable in both summer and winter. It's also a center for those who'd like to get an early start and travel the Grossglockner alpine highway, described above.

Unlike most resorts in Land Salzburg, Zell am See has some old buildings worth exploring. These include **Kastnerturm,** or the constable's tower, the oldest building in town, dating from the 12th century. It was once used as a grain silo.

The town's **parish church** (*pfarrkirche*) is an 11th-century Romanesque-style structure. It has, however, a late Gothic choir from the 16th century.

Castle Rosenberg is also from the 16th century. It was once an elegant residence of South Bavaria. Today it houses the Rathaus (town hall), with a gallery. There's a tower at each of the four corners, and a round tower.

The **folklore museum** is in the old tower, the Vogtturm, near the town square. Old costumes are displayed in the museum, and many artifacts on exhibit show the traditional way of life in earlier Land Salzburg. The museum is open Monday, Wednesday, and Saturday from 4 to 6 p.m., charging no admission.

Zell is as well equipped for summer and for winter sports as are the competitive resorts of Kaprun and Saalbach.

For winter visitors, snow conditions in the Zell area are usually ideal from December all the way to the end of April. Zell am See attracts beginner and intermediate skiers but, surprisingly, more nonskiers it seems—people who like the attractions of the resort in winter and the bustling life even if they never take to the slopes. They do take the chair lift (sans skis) for the magnificent alpine scenery. Skiing is possible at elevations ranging from 3,000 feet to 9,000 feet.

Sports fans gravitate to the Kur- und-Sportzentrum, an arena northwest of the resort housing a mammoth indoor swimming pool as well as a sauna and an ice rink. Sometimes in cold weather, the lake is frozen over. Aircraft, presumably lightweight ones, have been known to land on the Zeller am See in the dead of winter.

Although known as a winter sports center, Zell am See seems to attract even more visitors in the peak summer months. **Lake Zell,** which has been called "the cleanest" lake in Europe, is warm, maintaining an average temperature of some 70° Fahrenheit in summer. The lake is 2½ miles long and 1 mile wide. Motorboats can be rented for tours. You can go along a footpath from the town to the bathing station at Seespitz, the walk taking about half an hour.

Schmittenhöhe, at 6,450 feet, towers to the west of Zell am See. You can go up the mountain in four different ways, with even more choices for ways to descend. In summer the hardy and hearty have been known to climb it in four hours. I suggest, however, that you take the cableway. The view from here is one of the finest in the Kitzbühel Alps, the majestic glacial peaks of the Grossglockner range being only part of the celestial heights you'll see on your excursion. You can have lunch at the Burghotel at the upper station.

From the west side of Zell am See you can take a four-seater cableway to the middle station. From here you can connect with several lifts that will take you to the upper platform. A sun terrace at the upper station is popular in both summer and winter. (Don't be surprised to see bare breasts even in February.)

It's about one mile up Schmittenhöhe. Figure on about 1¾ hours for your round trip, plus another 18 minutes by cable car. In summer service is every half hour. A round trip costs 150 AS ($7.98) per adult.

You can also take the Sonnalm cableway (entrance near the Schmittenhöhe terminus) to Sonnalm at 4,540 feet. You'll find another restaurant here. From Sonnalm, it's possible to go by chair lift to Sonnkogel (6,020 feet) and by drag lift to Hochmais (5,665 feet). From the eastern part of Lake Zell you can take the chair lift up to Ronachkopf (4,875 feet).

From Zell am See you can also take a funicular to Kaprun (see above), at the foot of the Kitzsteinhorn, for glacier and year-round skiing. In fact some of the most spectacular excursions possible from Kaprun can be made easily on tours from Zell am See (refer to the Kaprun description for more details).

The area code for Zell am See is 06542.

FOOD AND LODGING: The **Grand Hotel Zell am See,** 4 Esplanade (tel. 2388). From the time the first visitors began coming to Zell am See, there has been a "grand hotel" on this desirable lakefront site. Today's hotel is the newest (and third) manifestation of that time-honored tradition. An older hotel was demolished in 1984 to make room for this brainchild of a group of Swedish financiers. Basing their new design on late Victorian models, they built a wedding cake extravaganza of mansard roofs and cream-colored stonework whose elaborate cornices and moldings are reflected in the cold waters of the lake.

A blazing fire and a receptionist dressed in regional costume greet winter visitors in the marble-trimmed lobby. Most of the accommodations are private apartments, whose prices vary according to the size and accessories. Each contains a small but efficient kitchen, a wood-burning fireplace, a closet-size clothes dryer in which to hang wet ski clothes, red marble floors, Chinese carpets, and a duplex format of twin floors connected with a winding staircase. Some of the more expensive suites also have private saunas and whirlpools.

Accommodations are priced according to their exposure, their square footage, and their extras. With breakfast included, the least imposing twin rents for 600 AS ($31.92) per person in low season, rising to 1,150 AS ($61.18) in high (winter) season. Singles in low season begin at 700 AS ($37.24), going up to 1,300 AS ($69.16) in high. Half and full board are available for another 335 AS ($17.82) to 480 AS ($25.54) per person daily, respectively.

The two in-house restaurants merit a special visit, even if you're a nonresident. The less formal dining room offers panoramic seating in an elegant crescent-shaped room overlooking the lake. Menu specialties include terrine of veal with a celery salad, poached sweetbreads in a champagne sauce, duck breast salad with lentil sprouts, and filet of trout with horseradish. Set meals are attractively priced at 180 AS ($9.58) and 210 AS ($11.17). The more formal restaurant, Hintertasche, offers intensely cultivated meals whose menu changes daily. Norbert Payr, the head chef, concocts set dinners for between 380 AS ($20.22) and 600 AS ($31.92), with à la carte repasts beginning at 700 AS ($37.24). Specialties include chicken breast in a fennel-flavored ragoût, polenta and salmon soup, and veal filet with a shellfish risotto. The rooftop bar (Wünderbar) is reviewed separately under après-ski.

Diversionary activities change with the seasons. They include squash courts, massage facilities, an indoor pool with an adjacent sauna and whirlpool, a high-ceilinged disco called "the Grand Slam," and a private grass-covered beach with its own sun terrace for summer tea parties. There's also tennis, along with golf, mountainside ski lifts, horseback riding, waterskiing, and a separate ski school annexed to the hotel.

Hotel Salzburger Hof, 11 Auerspergstrasse (tel. 2828). You'll get a glimpse of the handcrafted interior of this hotel through the glass doors leading inside. A polychrome wood statue of what might be an archbishop is fastened to a background of carved pine in the lobby. The most elegant piece of wrought iron in town serves as the entrance to the dining room.

In the salon a blazing fire is housed in an unusual brick-lined stucco fireplace, which guests enjoy under heavily timbered ceilings. The Holleis family maintains the pleasant outdoor garden with its sun terrace. You'll recognize the hotel by its chalet design and its location near the lake. A sauna, a Jacuzzi, and a heated indoor swimming pool are on the premises.

With half board included, rates per person in a double range from 600 AS ($31.92) to 1,150 AS ($61.18), depending on the season. Singles cost an additional 110 AS ($5.85) per day. All units contain a private bath.

Hotel Zum Hirschen (tel. 2447). The Pacalt family are the congenial and hard-working owners of this balconied hotel with its white walls, wood trim, and central location. You'll enter from the street through a double doorway angled into a corner of the building, whose renovated interior has lots of wood accents, a central heating stove in white stucco and dark-green tiles, along with a combination of modern furniture that blends well with the painted armoire in the main salon. A covered heated swimming pool has an unusual border of smooth river rocks, with a sauna and steambath close at hand. The hotel charges 750 AS ($39.90) to 1,050 AS ($55.86) per person in a double, with full board included. Singles pay a surcharge of 50 AS ($2.66) daily.

Restaurant Zum Hirschen is connected to the hotel. The setting is one of light-grained paneling, immaculate napery, and wholesome rusticity. Specialties include fresh lavarits from the nearby lake, mountain game, and homemade pâté. If that doesn't appeal to you, you might try creamed chipped veal with the Swiss-style rösti, a range of schnitzels and pork dishes, as well as roast veal in a burgundy sauce or perhaps entrecôte Café de Paris. The chef also prepares that traditional Franz Joseph favorite, tafelspitz. The service is friendly and efficient. À la carte meals range from 180 AS ($9.58) to 500 AS ($26.60).

Hotel Porschehof (tel. 7248) is a charming chalet in a woodsy area a few minutes' drive from the center of town. The main salon inside has a gently vaulted ceiling, painted chests, and wrought-iron lighting fixtures. You'll find several attractive fireplaces, my favorite of which has a pleasingly scaled fieldstone construction with an arch for the fire itself and a tapering pyramid for the chimney. The rest of the building's detailing includes ceramic ovens, beamed ceilings, rustically alpine dining room chairs, and the kind of inviting bar area where you can enjoy a drink before dinner. On the premises are a solar-heated indoor pool, a sauna, a fitness room, and massage facilities. Rates range from 500 AS ($26.60) to 750 AS ($39.90) per person, based on double occupancy, and half board pension costs another 125 AS ($6.65) per person daily. Singles pay a supplement of 50 AS ($2.66) per day. Each of the units has a private bath, and almost all of the accommodations contain private balconies.

Clima Seehotel, 1 Esplanade (tel. 2504), is an imposing building with a crescent-shaped terrace above the curved windows of the panoramic first floor. The hotel sits directly on the water, with several floors of white walls, yellow window trim, and at least one well-placed skylight. The bedrooms behind the mansard-style gables on the top floor have an especially good view, and all units have private bath/shower and toilet, radio, phone, and TV connection. The charge ranges from 650 AS ($34.58) to 900 AS ($47.88) per person based on double occupancy, with a supplement of 150 AS ($7.98) daily charged for one person. Half board costs another 75 AS ($3.99) per person daily.

Schmittenhöhe (tel. 2489). The ski lifts leading to the top of this mountain will deposit you a few steps from the door of this cozy hotel. The only buildings nearby are the isolated village church and those connected with the ski lifts, so much of your nighttime activity will be centered within the hotel. The format is pleasant, well furnished, warm, and intimate, with blazing fireplaces, lots of paneling, good food, and superb views from the bedrooms. An "Ice Bar" and a buffet attract lots of daytime visitors as well. Singles range from 580 AS ($30.87) to 640 AS ($34.05), while doubles cost 520 AS ($27.66) to 580 AS ($30.87) per person, with full board included. Prices depend on the plumbing and the season. The hotel is open from December to October.

Hotel St. Hubertushof, Thumersbach (tel. 31160), is a large sprawling hotel that's designed like a collection of balconied chalets clustered in a single unit. The sober, elegant decor attracts many repeat visitors, and the staff is efficient and friendly. The flat-roofed dance bar which juts forward into the parking lot is one of the area's popular nightspots. The hotel is in one of the sunniest spots of the resort. Its bedrooms are large, comfortable, and rustic. Erna Hollaus, the host, charges from 460 AS ($24.47) to 620 AS ($32.98) in a single and from 450 AS ($23.94) to 620 AS ($32.98) per person in a double, all tariffs including full board. The hotel is closed between November 1 and mid-December.

The menu in the adjoining restaurant includes specialties from around the world, as well as a few regional grandmother-style recipes. Meals are well prepared and beautifully served, and might be followed by one of the chef's flaming desserts. Fixed-price meals range from 110 AS ($5.85) to 180 AS ($9.58), while à la carte dinners cost from 115 AS ($6.12) to 325 AS ($17.29).

Hotel St. Georg, 10 Schillerstrasse (tel. 3533), will greet you with one of the prettiest facades in town. Roughly half of the front is devoted to finely drawn country baroque designs around the windows. The other half of the exterior has flowered balconies, curved awnings, and a parapet covered with thick cedar shingles. The rustically romantic interior is filled with beamed ceilings, antique wrought iron, and old painted chests. On the premises are an indoor swimming pool, a sauna, and several cozy bars.

The restaurant has vaulted plaster ceilings, hunting trophies, wrought-iron wall sconces, and a circular open fireplace which acts as a focal point for the entire room. For visitors not on the board plan, à la carte meals range from 125 AS ($6.65) to 400 AS ($21.28) and might include oxtail soup, a ragoût of fresh mussels, fresh fish from the Zellersee, and medallions of fresh crayfish. With full board, singles range from 820 AS ($43.62) to 1,120 AS ($59.58), while rates in a double go from 810 AS ($43.09) to 1,020 AS ($54.26) per person, also with full board. Prices depend on the season, and each unit has a private bath. Open December to April and June to October.

Sporthotel Alpin (tel. 3576) is a contemporary chalet whose balconies almost completely surround it. It was designed in such a way that cars can drive up to the front entrance on a concrete platform cantilevered above the hillside slope. The elegant and sporty interior has big sunny windows, a warmly tinted decorative scheme with wine-colored accents, and lots of beamed ceilings. On the premises are a large indoor pool, a sauna, and massage facilities.

Since the hotel lies slightly outside the village, it has both an excellent view of the lake and easy accessibility to the ski lifts. The well-proportioned doubles contain private bath, radio, phone, color TV, and mini-bar. With full board included, they rent for 950 AS ($50.54) to 1,330 AS ($70.46) per person, with occupants of singles paying from 1,070 AS ($56.92) to 1,430 AS ($76.08).

The handsome restaurant has immaculate napery, lots of plants, and big windows. Specialties include both Austrian and international foods which range from wild game to scampi to nouvelle cuisine dishes. If you happen to be around during one of the suckling pig banquets or one of the elaborate farmer's buffets, a uniformed chef will stand behind the heavily laden table to assist you.

Hotel Waldhof (tel. 2853) is a country-style hotel with lots of weathered planking and balconies. Just outside the sun terrace you'll find an outdoor pool. A warmly decorated cellar bar, filled with alpine timbers and colored lights, often has dancing with live music both at 5 p.m. and later in the evening. The other public rooms are tastefully filled with Oriental rugs, big windows, and wood accents. The hotel, run by Joseph Loferer and his family, is about five minutes from the center of town. It charges 780 AS ($41.50) to 850 AS ($45.22) per person in a double, including full board. Singles pay a daily surcharge of 80 AS ($4.26).

Hotel/Restaurant Neue Post (tel. 3773). One of the best parts of this hotel is the dozens of details carved into the wood of the heavy ceilings of both the public rooms and the bedrooms. The interior has cozy wintertime fireplaces and huge hanging chandeliers fashioned of wrought iron and gilt. The outside of the building has lots of balconies, an enlarged central gable, and a painted design under the side of the roof peak. The spacious bedrooms rent for 650 AS ($34.58) to 930 AS ($49.48) per person, with full board included. All units have private bath. Prices depend on the season, the size, and the exposure. The supplement for single occupancy is 80 AS ($4.26) a day.

Sporthotel Lebzelter (tel. 2411) is a pretty balconied hotel with subdued ornamentation around its windows and shutters, and under the overhang of the eaves. Sections of the hotel are 500 years old, and the best view of the oldest parts is in the vaulted stone cellar, which the Schandlbauer family has converted into a bar. Details inside include an old-fashioned stove made of a combination of plaster and green ceramic tiles, chalet-style chairs, lots of paneling, and rustic artifacts. My favorite room is the Sport-Stüberl, whose attractive clientele somehow looks even better in the reflected glow from the polished wood paneling. Prices, based on double occupancy with half board included, range from 575 AS ($30.59) to 645 AS ($34.31) per person, depending on the season and the plumbing. Singles pay a surcharge of 40 AS ($2.13) per day. Open December to March and June to September.

APRÈS-SKI: Zell am See has one of the liveliest après-ski scenes in Land Salzburg. No one puts on airs here, and the clubs and taverns are very informal and getmütlich, with most hard drinks costing from 85 AS ($4.52) up.

Perhaps the friendliest place after the sun sets is the already-recommended **Sporthotel Lebzelter.** Many times the word "keller" or "cellar" is used in Austria to evoke the atmosphere of a real cellar when it's merely the mock. But at the Lebzelter the cellar is genuine, with a vaulted stone ceiling. Attractive young skiers, mainly European, gravitate here at night, enjoying the booze.

Wünderbar, Grand Hotel (tel. 2388). The canopy of glass which shelters this glamorous bar from the snow and rain is set at the pinnacle of the Grand Hotel's mansard roof. A less imaginative architect might have considered this eyrie to be little more than wasted space, but in this case it welcomes some of the most fashionable après-skiers in town. Sixty persons can sit comfortably here, enjoying the live piano music and watching the light change upon the rock face of the nearby mountains.

Hotel Waldhof, also recommended, has a typical tavern with regional artifacts. Often a local musician—attired in lederhosen and red stockings—will play for skiers (the women invariably wear pants) who like to dance on the small floor.

A typical Austrian stüberl is found at the **Gasthof Alpenblick,** lying in the satellite hamlet of Schüttdorf on the road to Kaprun. Zither music is usually played for your enjoyment here every evening in season.

The major disco action is usually at the **Pinzgauer Diele,** where you can dance until the wee hours. You might also try **Wurzelkeller.**

In addition to the above-mentioned establishments, there are countless taverns willing to welcome you around their open fire and give you a mug of chilled beer or something more potent.

8. The Flachgau

One of the chief attractions of the Flachgau district is **Wolfgangsee** (Lake Wolfgang) which lies mainly in Land Salzburg, although its major center, St. Wolfgang, is in Upper Austria. The chief Land Salzburg resort on the lake is St. Gilgen. Many people visit Lake Wolfgang on day trips from Salzburg, as it lies within easy commuting distance.

The most celebrated lake in the Salzkammergut, Wolfgangsee is 6 miles long and 1¼ miles wide. The northwest shores are fairly inaccessible.

The Flachgau is a relatively flat area in the environs of Salzburg, dividing Styria, another Austrian province, from Bavaria in West Germany. This section, unlike many of the districts of Land Salzburg to which I've previously introduced you, is strictly a summer resort area for those who enjoy lakeside holidays.

FUSCHL AM SEE: Fuschlsee, of all the lakes in Land Salzburg, is closest to the festival city. It lies to the east of the provincial capital. Salzburgers frequent it heavily, particularly on summer weekends. You may choose to stay in Fuschl am See as an alternative to Salzburg at any time of the year but especially during the festival season. From here you can explore Wolfgangsee.

Lake Fuschl is ringed by woodland. In fact sections bordering the lake comprise a nature reserve. The lake is only 2½ miles long and less than a mile wide. It lies to the northwest of Lake Wolfgang. Fuschl, strictly a summer resort, lies on the eastern strip of the lake.

The area code for Fuschl am See is 06226.

Food and Lodging

Parkhotel Waldhof (tel. 342) is a first-class chalet hotel with a sprawling facade of flower-bedecked balconies as well as a curved series of bay windows. The interior has wood detailing, stone columns, knotty-pine paneling, leaded windows set in diamond-shaped panes, and crackling open fireplaces. On the premises and grounds are a shooting gallery with rifles set on stationary tripods, a high-ceilinged swimming pool, a sauna, a grassy lawn with frontage on the lake, massage facilities, and table tennis. Guests go on guided nature walks which often end up with the guide leading his charges to his local tavern.

Each of the individually furnished bedrooms has its own bath, as well as a collection of elegantly comfortable furniture. With full board included, the charge for rooms ranges from 560 AS ($29.79) to 700 AS ($37.24) in a single and from 560 AS ($29.79) to 950 ($50.54) per person in a double. There are two comfortable guest houses nearby. With breakfast included, singles at these facilities cost from 275 AS ($14.63) to 375 AS ($19.95), while doubles range from 200 AS ($10.64) to 375 AS ($19.95) per person. Breakfast is served in the guest houses while half board—arranged for an additional 175 AS ($9.31) per person —can be enjoyed in the hotel's main dining room. All three establishments are directed by members of the Ebner family.

Sporthotel Leitner (tel. 565) and **Stefanihof** (tel. 371) are two hotels both owned by the Leitner family. The older of the two is a hip-roofed, green-shuttered building with a prominent dining room jutting out toward the lake. The more modern of the two has a streamlined format of modern windows and a few wood-trimmed balconies. Singles range from 530 AS ($28.20) to 570 AS ($30.32), while doubles cost 510 AS ($27.13) to 530 AS ($28.20) per person, with full board included. Prices depend on the plumbing and the season.

Brunnwirt (tel. 236) is one of the region's leading restaurants, serving light and well-prepared meals to vacationing gourmets from as far away as Vienna. Housed in a 15th-century building loaded with atmosphere, it receives a healthy business from urbanites who motor here on the autobahn. The cuisine is light textured and inspired by Austrian regional recipes. The kitchen staff is directed by Frau Brandstätter, who insists on strictly fresh ingredients.

Specialties include game dishes, veal, lamb, and a range of other foodstuffs which appear on the frequently changing daily menu. Portions are generous. Herr Brandstätter will probably help you select a wine, and the clientele seems to have a good time. Fixed-price meals cost from 300 AS ($15.96) to 550 AS ($29.26), while à la carte dinners range from 135 AS ($7.18) to 400 AS ($21.28). The restaurant is closed all day Tuesday and on Wednesday until 6 p.m. It has an annual closing during the first two weeks of February and for the first two weeks of October.

HOF BEI SALZBURG: About 15 minutes from Salzburg on Lake Fuschl is this resort which has long drawn the aristocrats of Salzburg because of its private hunting and fishing preserves. There's a nine-hole golf course. You can fish for trout or rent boats for a tour of the lake. The setting is one of mountains, woods, and alpine lake water. From here it's easy to explore not only Fuschlsee but also Wolfgangsee and Mondsee.

Like the suburb of Anif (see Chapter VII), Hof bei Salzburg might be considered for its traditional and romantic accommodations, especially at festival time in August when hotel rooms are virtually impossible to obtain in Salzburg.

Hof bei Salzburg's area code is 06229.

Food and Lodging

Hotel Schloss Fuschl (tel. 253). The main section of this castle built in 1450 has the proportions of a city building, with a simple facade of unadorned windows and a height that's greater than its width or depth. It was the former hunting lodge of the prince-archbishops of Salzburg, who cultivated the gardens on the peninsula jutting into Lake Fuschl and who, over the course of time, gradually transformed it from a semi-fortress into a pleasure palace.

Among its former guests were Nehru, Eleanor Roosevelt, and Khrushchev. In World War II, von Ribbentrop selected the schloss as his headquarters. Later, Mussolini came here to meet with Nazi leaders.

The interior is dotted with elegant, sometimes baronial fireplaces, along with timbered ceilings, stone columns, and handcrafted stonework. The swimming pool, dedicated to the mythical figure of Diana, is found under the plastered vaulting of the ground floor.

According to the price you want to pay, you can rent either a modern room inside the hotel, part of a cozy bungalow on the surrounding grounds, or a luxurious suite fit for a prince and studded with valuable antiques. Singles range from 1,400 AS ($74.48) to 1,500 AS ($79.80), while doubles go from 2,000 AS ($106.40) to 2,450 AS ($130.34). An apartment or a two-person bungalow costs from 3,800 AS ($202.16) to 4,100 AS ($218.12). All accommodations contain private baths, and prices include a buffet breakfast. Half and full board are available for an additional 400 AS ($21.80) and 850 AS ($45.22), respectively.

The restaurant is one of the most frequented and highly praised in Austria, with a clientele that includes many of the country's leading politicians and industrialists. Designated long ago as a Relais de Campagne, it has several elegant rooms from which to choose, all decorated in excellent taste with dozens of antiques and paintings. One of the rooms is outfitted in pale blue and pink, not unlike a Viennese pastry. The view encompasses much of the lake and sometimes a vista of Salzburg.

Menu items from the handwritten carte include lobster terrine with caviar, homemade noodles with goose-liver pâté, and summer truffles, plus a host of seasonally adjusted specialties. Klaus Fleischhacker is the chef, Martin Adlgasser is the wine steward, and their combined efforts produce meals which are known throughout the region. Reservations are almost essential. À la carte meals range from 250 AS ($13.30) to 650 AS ($34.58), while fixed-price dinners go for 375 AS ($19.95) to 850 AS ($45.22).

Jagdhof am Fuschlsee (tel. 372) was an outbuilding of a nearby feudal castle. Originally a 16th-century farmhouse, it's in the authentic style that many 20th-century Austrian buildings are modeled after. The public rooms have evenly spaced timbers supporting the massive ceiling beams, with many contemporary and practical updates such as comfortable chairs, hanging lights, tile floors, and glass display cases. Part of the decoration consists of masses of hunting trophies and some 1,000 pipes. Management has also added two bowling alleys.

Rates range from 550 AS ($29.26) to 620 AS ($32.98) in a single and from 820 AS ($43.62) to 1,000 AS ($53.20) in a double. All the comfortably furnished bedrooms have a private bath, so prices depend on the season. Half board is available for another 175 AS ($9.31) per person. The dining room is filled with rustic artifacts, heavy beams, and a loyal and conservative clientele. A specialty of the chef is pike terrine with green sauce, which could be followed by a wide variety of fish and game dishes. Fixed-price meals cost 150 AS ($7.98) and 225 AS ($11.97), while à la carte dinners go for 150 AS ($7.98) to 400 AS ($21.80). Reservations are suggested.

Gasthof/Pension Nussbaumer (tel. 275) is a recently constructed country hotel, set against an alpine meadow, with a big asphalt parking lot on two sides. On the premises are an indoor heated pool, a sauna, and comfortable public rooms with honey-colored ceiling paneling, inviting banquettes, and lots of sunny windows. An elevator is part of the conveniences, as well as outdoor tennis courts, and a grassy children's playground. The hotel sits just beside a wintertime ski lift. The charge is from 440 AS ($23.41) per person, based on double occupancy, with full board. The supplement in a single is 60 AS ($3.19) daily. Open December to October.

OBERTRUM: Lying on the northern part of Lake Obertrum, about ten miles to the north of Salzburg, Obertrum is a popular holiday resort, offering bathing in the lake, water sports, sailing, fishing, tennis, horseback riding, and in winter, ice sports. It's also a good center for many hikes and excursions in a beautiful district.

Incidentally, the lake virtually joins Mattsee and Grabensee, separated only by narrow tongues of land.

The Obertrum area code is 06219.

Food and Lodging

Braugasthof Sigl (tel. 212). This hotel, along with the nearby brewery, has been owned by the same family since 1775. In the center of the village, it's housed in a distinguished-looking hip-roofed building with lots of chimneys, a row of gables, and a distinctive yellow-and-white facade. In summer, flowers bloom in the boxes near the rounded tower at one of the corners and also in the arched windows on the ground floor.

The interior has a very old carved clothing chest, along with a sprinkling of other antiques. The comfortable bedrooms usually have conservative furnishings and a scattering of homey touches. The hotel is open only from May to September, charging from 250 AS ($13.30) to 280 AS ($14.90) for a single and from 235 AS ($12.50) to 265 AS ($14.10) per person for a double, breakfast included.

If you're a beer lover, you'll gravitate to the earthy, unpretentious restaurant adjoining this hotel. You'll have a chance to sample each of the beers brewed in the region, as well as a solid country cooking that goes with the brew. Management features week-long specials of, for example, wild game, depending on the season and the availability of ingredients. Desserts are satisfyingly rich, often containing their share of schnapps. À la carte dinners go from 75 AS ($3.99) to 230 AS ($12.24).

Gasthof Neumayr, 8 Dorfplatz (tel. 302), is a centrally located, hip-roofed guest house with a facade of yellow stucco, forest-green shutters, and an arched entryway leading into a rustically old-fashioned interior. The hotel has 30 rooms, mainly with private shower. The rate is 350 AS ($18.62) in a single and from 320 AS ($17.02) per person in a double.

The food served in the rustic stube is good enough to attract diners from Salzburg. Specialties of the establishment include fish, especially trout. For an appetizer, you may prefer the matjes herring or liver noodle soup. Other main dishes include an onion-flavored roast beef. À la carte meals range from 90 AS ($4.79) to 250 AS ($13.30), while fixed-price dinners go from 100 AS ($5.32) to 155 AS ($8.25). The restaurant is closed every Tuesday from November to March.

ST. GILGEN: This leading lakeside resort of Land Salzburg lies at the western edge of Wolfgangsee. In the summer it's filled mainly with Austrians and Germans enjoying the indoor swimming pool and bathing beach.

Once St. Gilgen was one of the strongholds of the prince-archbishops of Salzburg, and in a sense the aristocratic tradition continues even today, as many of the fashionable and wealthy from Salzburg maintain mountain villas here. Parties at festival time tend to be lavish. You're lucky if you get an invitation.

The town has many Mozart connections. In the vicinity of the Rathaus (town hall) is the house in which Anna Maria Pertl was born in 1720. She was to become Mozart's mother. After the composer's sister, Nannerl, married Baron Berchtold zu Sonnenberg, she also settled in St. Gilgen. The **Mozart Fountain,** built in 1927, stands on the main square in front of the town hall.

The area code for St. Gilgen is 06227.

Food and Lodging

Parkhotel Billroth (tel. 217), a mile from town, sits imposingly on its own spacious grounds. One wing was designed in a white-walled villa style, with the main section looking more like an overblown chalet. The view from the bedrooms and from the parasol-dotted sun terrace takes in the lake and the mountains beyond. The hotel has its own lakeside beach, with a floating sun raft ideal for bathing (especially since it's connected to the shoreline). It has its own outdoor tennis courts and easy access to the ski lifts. Some of the public rooms are baronial, with dark paneling, Oriental rugs, and wide, gently sloping staircases. Bathless rooms rent for 450 AS ($23.94) to 650 AS ($34.58) per person, while units with private bath cost 440 AS ($23.41) to 750 AS ($39.90) per person. Prices depend on the accommodation and the season. Breakfast is included.

Hotel Zur Post, 8 Mozartplatz (tel. 239), is the comfortably proportioned hotel on the main square of town. It was established in 1415, and aside from the charm of the thick walls and heavy timbers, it has a high level of comfort and efficient and friendly service directed by the Hinterberger family. The interior has been updated so frequently it's difficult in some places to see the original building. Everything is nonetheless comfortable, clean, and pleasant. Someone has painted murals of village life under some of the ceiling's vaults, while parts of some of the wood ceilings are ornately decorated with paint and inlays. A swimming pool with a lake scene on the far wall is part of the lure.

The well-furnished bedrooms rent for 230 AS ($12.24) to 450 AS ($23.94) per person, with breakfast included. Prices depend on the plumbing and the season. The hotel is closed from early November till December 10.

The in-house restaurant is worth a stopover. Aside from its view over the center of the resort, it has a romantic ambience with a ceramic tile oven along with good food such as farmer's gulasch, pork cutlets, and an exotic rumpsteak served with mandarin orange slices and kiwi à la nouvelle cuisine.

Hotel Radetzky-Hof (tel. 232) is a centrally located house that's easy to recognize thanks to its orange shutters and its lighthearted designs painted onto a gray-and-white facade. The interior is simple and elegant, in good taste, and filled with comfortable, pleasing chairs and colors. Some of the ceilings are timbered, others are vaulted, but there's usually lots of exposed wood and a cozy feeling of well-being. With full board, singles go for 470 AS ($25) to 570 AS ($30.32) and doubles for 460 AS ($24.47) to 570 AS ($30.32) per person. The hotel is open in December and January and from May to September.

Grossgasthof/Hotel Kendler (tel. 223) is a contemporary chalet set onto a well-maintained lawn. Many of the pleasant bedrooms have their own balconies, and most of them contain a private bath. The main salon has a high beamed ceiling, a massive ornate chandelier, and cozy easy chairs scattered over a collection of intricately patterned Oriental rugs. Singles with bath range from 400 AS ($21.28) to 420 AS ($22.34), while doubles with bath rent for 390 AS ($20.75) to 410 AS ($21.81) per person, with full board included. Open December to October.

Café/Pension Nannerl (tel. 368). An 18th-century name deserves an 18th-century ambience, and that's exactly what you'll see in this charming old-style coffeehouse which happens to be named after Mozart's sister. The furnishings are something you might have found in a wealthy farmer's house around 1801, and the food served includes the most delicious (and most caloric) in the repertoire of Austrian pastries, including Sacher torte, poppy tart, and Malakoff tart, each mouthwatering, each baked fresh every day and served in generous slices. Pastries range from 20 AS ($1.06) to 30 AS ($1.60), while coffee costs 15 AS (80¢) to 25 AS ($1.33).

STROBL: The flower gardens along the shore of Lake Wolfgang make this small resort a potent lure in summer. Strobl lies on the southeast side of the lake, almost opposite St. Gilgen at the western end. For a relatively undiscovered little lakeside village it has much appeal, mainly because of its romantic setting. The road to St. Wolfgang in Upper Austria branches off here.

The area code for Strobl is 06137.

Food and Lodging

Hotel Stadt Wein (tel. 381) is a modern hotel with floor-depth windows and stone detailing. The interior is attractively outfitted in tasteful colors (the bar is painted forest green) and occasional rustic details such as a ceramic stove in the dining room. The sunny and airy rooms rent for 510 AS ($27.13) to 570 AS ($30.32) per person, single or double, with full board. Prices depend on the season, and all the units contain private baths.

Parkhotel Seethurn (tel. 202). One side of this big balconied hotel faces the edge of the village, where residents can admire the elaborate regional designs painted on part of the facade. The other end looks out over a well-maintained lawn area. The roof of the swimming pool is supported with massive laminated timbers, while the rest of the public rooms are elegantly and rustically laid out with wood furniture, big fireplaces, and coffered ceilings. Full-board prices range from 810 AS ($43.09) to 1,000 AS ($53.20) per person, depending on the season and the view. All accommodations contain private baths.

EUGENDORF: If you're touring in the Flachgau, you'll find good food at the following recommendation.

Landgasthof Holznerwirt (tel. 8205). Johann and Eveline Bimminger are the genteel owners of this hip-roofed chalet near the onion dome of the village church. They pride themselves on serving a traditional menu of such specialties as three kinds of roast, tafelspitz, and veal dishes. A buffet at 250 AS ($13.30) per person includes stews, warm cabbage salads, an array of meats, and assorted breads. Full meals cost around 175 AS ($9.31). If you're touring in the area, it makes a fine dining choice.

9. The Lungau

A heavily forested district in the southeastern part of Land Salzburg, Lungau can be visited easily on a day trip. The section is beginning to develop as a winter sports center now that the Tauern highway has opened up the valley. However, in spite of its at times sun-drenched slopes, the Lungau is one of the chilliest parts of Austria in winter.

TAMSWEG: The principal town of the Lungau, whose people show a healthy respect for tradition, is Tamsweg, with a 1570 Rathaus (town hall) and a baroque pfarrkirche (parish church). This was once a Roman town, and some ruins remain. The pilgrimage **Church of St. Leonard,** enclosed by defensive walls, is a Gothic edifice known for its stained glass, including a unique "golden window."

You can visit the **Lungauer Folklore Museum,** which has fine pieces of provincial furniture and collections of paintings and weapons. The museum is open May to October daily except Monday from 10 a.m. to noon and from 2 to 5 p.m. Guided tours are given every hour. Admission is 20 AS ($1.06) for adults, 10 AS (53¢) for children.

From Tamsweg, you might want to visit **Moosham Castle** at Unternberg, first mentioned in documents in 1256. This was formerly a fortress of the prince-archbishops of Salzburg. Its most outstanding feature is the lower courtyard. Its schloss chapel has a late Gothic triptych. A folkloric museum in the castle is open January 1 until mid-June and from mid-September until the end of October daily except Monday from 10 a.m. to 3 p.m. In summer it's open from 10 a.m. to 4 p.m. Admission is 30 AS ($1.60) for adults, 25 AS ($1.33) for children.

MAUTERNDORF: This is an old market town going back 1,000 years, and today it's both a summer resort center and a mecca for skiers in winter. It lies on a highway to the northwest of the Tauern Pass. From here you can take a cableway to Speiereckhütte (6,805 feet).

Mauterndorf Castle, erected on the ruins of a fort which stood here in

Roman times, dates from 1253. Parts of it were extended in the 14th and 15th centuries. It contains a chapel with frescoes from the 14th century and a winged altarpiece, circa 1450. You can visit the keep and a local museum. They're open in May, June, and September from 3 to 5 p.m. and in July and August from 10 a.m. to noon and 2 to 5 p.m.; closed Tuesday. Admission is 25 AS ($1.33).

Mauterndorf's **pfarrkirche** (parish church) has a sumptuous baroque altar from 1702.

Mauterndorf's area code is 06472.

Food and Lodging

Hotel Elisabeth (tel. 7365). The position of this hotel at the edge of the village marks the beginning of acres of farmland, most of which you can see from the windows of your well-furnished bedrooms. The hotel is one of the most elegant in town, outfitted like a private home with lots of balconies, a pleasing hip-roof design, and alpine furniture. The hospitable hosts, members of the Spreitzer family, charge from 690 AS ($36.71) to 970 AS ($51.60) for a single and 670 AS ($35.64) to 880 AS ($46.82) per person for a double, with half board included. All accommodations contain a private bath.

On the premises you'll find a sauna, an indoor pool, a dancing bar, and a hairdresser. The in-house restaurant offers a wide range of flambés and fondues, as well as Austrian and international specialties.

Hotel Post (tel. 7316), the most atmospheric choice in town, is a four-story white building with a dignified façade and solid proportions. It is situated in a beautiful square close to the 12th-century castle and provides an excellent center for walking and motoring in the Lungau valleys and mountains. The hotel's interior has lots of 16th-century touches. The dining room, which serves international cuisine and local specialties, is elegant, with immaculate napery and leather-upholstered chairs. In summer, guests retreat to a courtyard garden. Depending on the plumbing and the season, singles range from 400 AS ($21.80) to 500 AS ($26.60) and doubles from 350 AS ($18.62) to 550 AS ($29.26) per person, these tariffs including full board.

Gasthof Steffner-Wallner (tel. 7214) is a cozy hostelry owned by the Steffner-Wallner family. The interior is pleasantly outfitted with painted furniture and lots of plants. The charges for full board, based on double occupancy, range from 320 AS ($17.02) to 390 AS ($20.75) per person. Singles pay a daily surcharge of 40 AS ($2.13). All units contain private baths. The gasthof is open from December to April and June to October.

Gasthof/Pension Neuwirt (tel. 7268) is announced by its wrought-iron bracket extending over the pavement in front of the mustard-colored facade. The bedrooms inside are cozy, colorful, and warm. Rates in doubles range from 300 AS ($15.96) to 390 AS ($20.75) per person, depending on the season, the plumbing, and the room assignment. Full board is included in the above prices. On the premises are a swimming pool and table-tennis facilities.

MARIAPFARR: This little town, at an elevation of 3,675 feet, becomes lively in winter when it fills up with skiers. Mariapfarr lies in an area of Austria renowned for its variety of runs and for attracting cross-country skiers. There are some 80 miles of beautifully placed tracks. It's possible to rent heavy skis and boots on the spot in the town's shops.

Mariapfarr has long been known for its pilgrimage church, dating from the 13th and 14th centuries. This Gothic **pfarrkirche** (parish church) is decorated with wall paintings and has an exceptional winged altar in the late Gothic style. Its 14th-century frescoes include Saint Mary, Protectress with Man of Sorrows, the only known representation of its kind.

The area code for Mariapfarr is 06473.

Food and Lodging

Hotel Haus Carinth (tel. 235). Karl-Peter Dindl is the accommodating owner of this pleasantly isolated double chalet. Both wings of the hotel have hip roofs, balconies, and impressive views. The interior has all the rustic comfort you'd expect, as well as an invitingly dark decor of masonry, wood wall coverings, and comfortable furniture. On the premises are a tennis court, heated outdoor pool, and a sauna. Rates, based on double occupancy, range from 400 AS ($21.80) to 600 AS ($31.92) per person, with half board included. Single rooms cost about 30% more than the rate per person in a double.

Chapter IX

UPPER AUSTRIA

1. Linz
2. The Mühlviertel
3. Attersee and Mondsee
4. St. Wolfgang and Bad Ischl
5. Hallstatt
6. The Traunsee
7. Wels
8. The Southeast Corner
9. Steyr and Enns
10. Stops Along the Danube
11. Schärding and Braunau

TOO OFTEN NEGLECTED by North Americans who may be unaware of its charms, Upper Austria contains some of the country's most beautiful scenery. It is a land of mountains, scenic valleys, and lakes, with Styria and Land Salzburg to its south and Bavaria on the west. Its northern parts border the Bohemian forest in Czechoslovakia. Its eastern neighbor is Lower Austria, traditionally called its twin. The Austrian name of this province is Bundesland–Ober Österreiche, since it lies nearer to the source of the Danube, which cuts across both provinces, than does Lower Austria.

Upper Austria has three different types of landscape. In the north are the granite and gneiss hills which are separated in the center of the province by the Valley of the Danube. There are also the limestone Alps and the Salzkammergut lake district, about a 30-minute drive from Linz, which crosses into Upper Austria. Here you'll find the most breathtaking scenery in the entire area. You can center at the Attersee, the Mondsee, the Traunsee, and the Wolfgangsee, part of the latter being in Land Salzburg.

Boating is fine on these lakes *(sees),* but if you like to swim, know that the *see* water here is not as warm as you'll find in Carinthia (Chapter XII). There are farms and fruit trees in the lake district. The cider of the region is excellent and competes with wine for popularity among the local inhabitants.

Except for Linz, the provincial capital, Upper Austria is a choice location for nature-lovers. Most of its towns are small, and although there's much industry, it doesn't blight the province with grime. Industrial installations are often discreetly hidden away as is usually the case in Switzerland.

Bad Ischl, once a retreat of the Austrian imperial court, is perhaps the most fashionable spa attraction. Most of the hotels are in the Salzkammergut region, but in all towns and villages you can find one or two moderately priced to inexpensive inns. There are few deluxe accommodations, although several old castles have been turned into "romantik" lodging places. Most of the hotels around the lakes are open only in summer months, and May is an ideal time to visit. These areas tend to be overrun with visitors, especially Germans, in the peak months of July and August.

The ski areas of Upper Austria are not much known to the North Americans visiting this country, as they lie for the most part in the southeast corner. The Dachstein is another major ski area. If you like to ski and don't demand massive facilities and a lot of après-ski festivity, you'll find the emerging ski resorts of this province far less expensive than the more celebrated resorts in the Tyrol and Zell am See in Land Salzburg.

If you're coming into the region, you can fly to the Linz international airport served by planes from main points in Europe or to Salzburg, from which train service is good into Upper Austria. To remote places where trains don't go, an excellent local Postal Bus service takes over. If you're driving, you can reach the province easily by the autobahn from Vienna.

It's also possible to take steamer service on the Danube between Passau in West Germany and Linz, but these boats operate only in summer. By steamer, you can continue on from Linz along the Danube into Lower Austria, to Vienna, and on to Budapest or even the Black Sea, as mentioned earlier. At certain times of the year you can make an excursion on the Danube leaving from the Linz marina.

1. Linz

This provincial capital of Upper Austria, about 116 miles northwest of Vienna, is the third-largest city in the country after Vienna and Graz. It is the biggest port on the Danube, which widens out considerably here to become a majestic thoroughfare. Three bridges connect Linz with the suburb of **Urfahr,** on the left bank of the river. If you enter the country from Passau, West Germany, Linz might be your gateway to Austria.

Linz was the site of a Roman castle and settlement, Lentia, in the first century A.D., and by the Middle Ages it had become a thriving center of trade through its position on the river. Emperor Friedrich III lived here from 1489 to 1493. The city now lies also on a direct rail route between the Adriatic and Baltic Seas. It was here that Austria's first railroad terminated. Because of these factors, Linz became an industrial and manufacturing center, with blast furnaces and steel factories. These were built up rapidly after Hitler seized Austria in 1938, and the Nazis also established chemical plants here. This industrial upsurge led to massive destruction by Allied bombs, with reconstruction being started after 1945.

Like Frankfurt in West Germany, Linz became known in the days of the empire for its trade fairs. It has been the seat of a bishop since 1785. Its heyday, at least with the aristocracy, came in the 18th century, after which it experienced a cultural decline.

Linz today, however, is one of the leading cultural centers of Austria, although nowhere near the level of Vienna and Salzburg. The city's name appears in numerous Germanic songs, and many notable figures have come from or been connected with Linz, including native son Anton Bruckner, the composer. Mozart composed and dedicated a symphony to the city, and Beethoven wrote his Eighth Symphony here. Franz Schubert described with pleasure his holidays in Linz. Goethe, who had a romance with a Linz fräulein, dedicated one of his most lyrical works "to the beautiful girls of Linz."

Napoleon lived here three times—in 1800, 1805, and 1809. The first steel airplane was constructed at Linz by the Schiessl brothers.

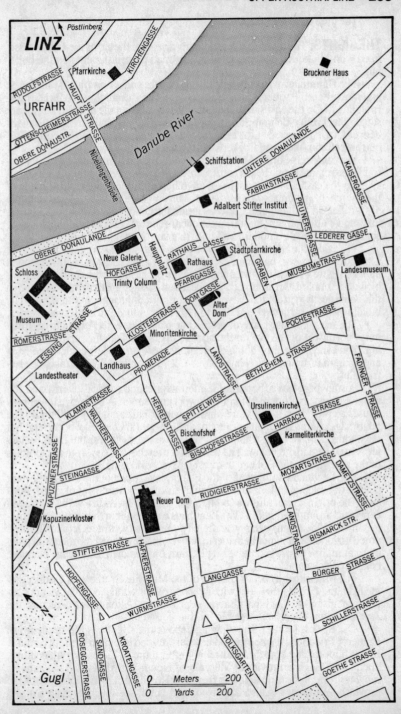

The area code for Linz is 0732.

THE SIGHTS: The most popular shopping district in the city is the **Landstrasse,** filled with boutiques, sometimes with Victorian embellishments on the buildings.

The **Hauptplatz** was the original marketplace and is now one of the biggest and most beautiful squares in all Europe, with baroque and rococo facades surrounding it. On the east side is the rathaus (city hall). In the heart of the square stands the **Trinity Column,** like the column in Vienna, built in 1723 to mark deliverance in the case of Linz from plague, fire, and invasion by the Turks. This marble column, the Dreifaltigkeitssaule, rises 85 feet.

Martinskirche, or St. Martin's Church, is the most ancient church in Austria in its original form. It was constructed by Charlemagne in the eighth century, near the castle on the remains of a Roman wall. Mention was first made of the church in written records in 788. St. Martin's is considered a good example of Carolingian architecture. Frescoes inside the church date from the 15th century, and it also contains masterpieces of baroque art. This edifice is in dramatic contrast with the ultramodern buildings that surround it.

The concert hall, called **Bruckner Haus** in honor of Anton Bruckner, the Linz-born composer, has an elliptical facade of glass and steel with a wooden interior where a raised dais accommodates an orchestra whose conductors have included Leonard Bernstein and Herbert von Karajan. Concerts presented in this acoustically perfect hall have been transmitted throughout the world. The building was constructed from 1969 to 1973 as a cultural and conference center.

The most popular place of pilgrimage from Linz is to **Pöstlingberg,** three miles northwest of the city on the north bank of the Danube, up a very steep hill. You can get there by going out Rudolfstrasse on the left bank of the river and taking a turn right onto Hagenstrasse. If you don't have a car, take the electric railway.

Pöstlingberg has a botanical garden with exotic tropical plants, and the summit terrace is a riot of blooming flowers in summer. A defensive tower now houses a grotto with a miniature railway, which makes a hit with children. The pilgrimage church is visited because of an 18th-century carved wood Pietà, but most tourists make the ascent mainly to take in the view over the Danube Valley. Linz is spread out below. The panorama stretches all the way to the foothills of the Alps and to the Bohemian forest in Czechoslovakia.

The **Landhaus,** southwest of the Hauptplatz, is one of the most important landmark buildings of Linz and headquarters of the government of Upper Austria. The original structure was built in the latter 16th century with an arcaded courtyard around a fountain. The Landhaus was rebuilt in the early 19th century. In the 17th century this was the city's university, where Johann Kepler, noted astronomer and mathematician, taught and developed the theory of planetary motion. The present university of Linz, on the north bank of the Danube, bears Kepler's name.

The **Minoritenkirche,** or Church of the Minorite Brothers, is Gothic, dating from the 13th century, but with a rococo overlay done in 1758. An art masterpiece inside is the high altar by Bartolomeo Altomonte, depicting the Annunciation. There are three red marble side altars.

The **Schloss** (castle), standing high above the river, was the residence of Emperor Friedrich III when he and his court resided in Linz in the 15th century. It was built for the emperor and rebuilt after a fire in the early 19th century. Today it houses the Provincial Museum of Upper Austria, which has exhibits ranging from prehistoric artifacts from the Roman era to the local art of the province. Weaponry is also displayed, and you'll see much popular art and folkloric exhibitions showing how the people of Upper Austria used to live. There's a gallery of paintings, none outstanding, from the 19th century. Many Gothic and Renaissance interiors have been reproduced. A railway museum is also to be seen at the castle.

You can visit the parts of the castle open to the public Wednesday through Saturday from 10 a.m. to 1 p.m. and from 2 to 6 p.m., from 9 a.m. to 1 p.m. on Sunday. It's closed Monday and Tuesday.

Alter Dom on Domgasse, the biggest baroque church in the city and formerly the cathedral of Linz, was constructed by the Jesuits around the latter part of the 17th century. You mustn't judge this church by its relatively simple exterior. The inside warms up considerably with pink marble columns, an intricately carved pulpit, and much statuary. The high altar is a concoction bedecked with marble images. Bruckner was the organist of this church for 12 years, and the annual Bruckner festival is centered here. Two other composers who worked in Linz are honored at the same time—Mozart, who composed his Linz symphony (No. 36 in C, K.425) here, and Beethoven, who wrote his Eighth in Linz.

The **Neue Galerie der Stadt Linz** (new gallery), 15 Blütenstrasse, is in the industrial suburb on the left bank, Urfahr, already referred to. Paintings shown are mostly by Austrian and German artists of the 19th and 20th centuries. You can visit daily from 10 a.m. to 6 p.m., to 1 p.m. on Sunday, and to 10 p.m. on Thursday. Admission is 20 AS ($1.06).

Priesterseminarkirche, or seminary church, is a small place of worship dedicated to the Holy Cross. Dating from the early part of the 18th century, the building plans were the work of Johann Lukas von Hildebrandt, the celebrated architect. The church is worth a visit just to see its richly decorated interior.

EXCURSIONS: Of possible short trips out of Linz, the most popular is to the **Abbey of St. Florian,** about a 12-mile trek. The abbey, largest in Upper Austria, is one of the major attractions of the province, an outstanding example of baroque architecture.

Augustinians have occupied a building of some sort on this site since the 11th century, although the structures you see today are baroque, having been under construction from 1686 to 1751. St. Florian was a Christian martyr, killed by being drowned in the Enns River around 304. As a saint he is often called upon by the faithful to protect their homes against flood and fire. The abbey was constructed over his grave.

The greatest composer of church music in 19th-century Austria, Anton Bruckner, a native of Linz born near the present abbey site in 1824, became the organist at St. Florian as a young man and composed many of his world-renowned masterpieces here. Although he went on to greater fame in Vienna, he was granted his wish to be buried at the abbey church underneath the organ he loved so well at St. Florian. You can visit the crypt, as well as the room where the composer lived for about a decade.

Carlo Carlone was originally in charge of rebuilding the abbey in the baroque style, the job being started in 1686, and the progress was continued by others.

The western exterior of the abbey is crowned with a trio of towers. The doorway is especially striking. As you enter the inner court, you'll see the **Fountain of the Eagle.** In the library, said to contain some 140,000 books and manuscripts, are allegorical ceiling frescoes by Bartolomeo Altomonte. The marble salon honors Prince Eugene of Savoy for his heroic defense of Vienna against a major siege by the Turks. The ceiling paintings here depict the Austrian victory over the "infidels."

The **Altdorfer Gallery** is the most outstanding feature of the abbey, surpassing even the imperial apartments. Well-known works of Albrecht Altdorfer, born in 1480, a master of the Danube school of painting, are displayed. Altdorfer was a warm, romantic contemporary of Dürer, to whom he is often compared. He did more than a dozen paintings for the abbey's Gothic church, his panels depicting, among other scenes, the martyrdom of St. Sebastian.

The **imperial apartments**, called the Kaiserzimmer, are reached by climbing a splendid staircase. Once Pope Pius VI stayed here. A whole host of royalty has occupied these richly decorated quarters, and you're allowed to visit the royal bedrooms of the emperor and empress.

The **abbey church**, designed by Carlone, has twin towers rising to 260 feet. The decoration is rich—maybe too rich. It's distinguished by columns of pink marble, quarried near Salzburg. Lavish stucco decoration was used in the interior, and the pulpit is in black marble. The choir stalls are heavily gilded and rich with ornamentation and carving. You should allow about an hour for a tour.

You must go with a guide to visit the abbey. Tours are conducted April to October at 10 and 11 a.m. and 1:30, 3, and 4 p.m. Otherwise, you must write to the abbey for permission to visit. Admission is 30 AS ($1.60).

One of the most macabre outings from Linz is to **Mauthausen**, 16 miles down the Danube from the provincial capital, the village of the quarries that once supplied the granite for paving stones in Vienna. The Nazis used the quarries, about two miles northwest of the village, as a concentration camp in World War II. It was also an extermination center, where Austria's Jewish population was dramatically and horrifyingly reduced in number in the darkest days of the war. Not only were Austrian Jews exterminated at this camp but thousands of other so-called undesirables were also annihilated—homosexuals, gypsies, whatever.

The government of Austria does not hide the scene and its reminders of these atrocities. The camp's site was declared a national monument in 1949, and often schoolchildren are brought here and given descriptions of what went on in this notorious camp. Various countries who lost citizens have erected memorials outside the camp to honor the dead. It's believed that the Nazis killed some 200,000 victims here, although exact figures are not available. It may have been even more.

You can visit the huts where the condemned, most of whom almost surely knew their ultimate fate, were kept. You are also led down the infamous "Stairway of Death" which the prisoners took on their last walk. To visit the ghastly site is a shattering experience, but still people come here to be painfully reminded of a cruel and savage era.

It takes about 1½ hours to take a tour of the camp, which is open February 1 to mid-December from 8 a.m. to 4 p.m. (to 3 p.m. off-season). Admission is 20 AS ($1.06).

Besides traveling to Mauthausen from Linz, you can visit the site via commuter train from Vienna, the ride taking about 45 minutes.

WHERE TO STAY: **Hotel Schillerpark**, 2-4 Rainerstrasse (tel. 554050), is the most prestigious modern hotel in town. It's in a futuristic mirrored building at the entrance to the downtown's pedestrian zone, about ten minutes on foot from the rail station. Inside you'll find a gambling casino (the center of nightlife in Linz), two bars, an elegant restaurant, a sauna, and a solarium. The lobby area is covered with slabs of polished marble, while the bedrooms are airy, sunny, and tastefully filled with streamlined furniture. Singles cost 1,200 AS ($63.84), while doubles rent from 1,500 AS ($79.80), with breakfast included. Each of the units has a private bath.

Tourotel, 9 Untere Donaulande (tel. 275075), is one of Linz's most prominent "skyscrapers," rising many stories above the ground in the center of the city. On the premises you'll find all the facilities of a large urban hotel, including a range of bars and restaurants, an indoor pool, and bedrooms with all the modern comforts. International bands often play at the hotel's nightclub. Singles cost 950 AS ($50.54); doubles, 1,200 AS ($63.84). Weekend rates are about 40% less.

Dom-Hotel, 17 Baumbachstrasse (tel. 278441), is ideally located in a quiet area in the center of town, only a few minutes' walk from the pedestrian precinct and the main station. The owners do all they can to maintain the hotel as a cozy stopping place, with lots of atmosphere. All of the bedrooms have bath, dial phone, radio, and color TV. Singles rent for 820 AS ($43.62) and doubles for 1,050 AS ($55.86). Tariffs include a buffet breakfast, service, and taxes. There is an apéritif bar on the ground floor, and international specialties are served in the restaurant. Free car parking is available.

Hotel/Restaurant Zur Lokomotive, 40 Weingartshofstrasse (tel. 54554), has a severe facade with practical, unadorned windows. Its interior is clean but stark, and it's very much of a no-frills kind of hostelry which provides shelter. Singles range from 350 AS ($18.62) to 490 AS ($26.07), while doubles go from 550 AS ($29.26) to 700 AS ($37.24), with breakfast included.

Hotel Ebelsbergerhof, 485 Wiener Strasse (tel. 42125), stands in the suburb of Ebelsberg, and is easy to locate because of its vivid pink facade. The interior is woodsy and elegant, with thick curtains, lots of handcrafted paneling, thick beams, and an upper-class ambience of well-being and fine cuisine. The bedrooms are papered in romantically flowered patterns, and each of them has its own bath. The 40 rooms rent for 750 AS ($39.90) in a single and for 1,200 AS ($63.84) in a double, breakfast included. A station wagon will pick you up at the airport if you arrange it in advance.

Hotel Prielmayrhof, 33 Weissenwolffstrasse (tel. 274131), is housed in a five-story distinguished-looking building slightly outside the center of town. It can be reached from the main train station by public bus. Its exterior is painted a vivid terracotta with white trim, while its streamlined and comfortable interior has been renovated into a tasteful modern format of white walls and exposed wood. Singles rent for 625 AS ($33.25), while doubles cost 780 AS ($41.50), breakfast included.

Hotel Wolfinger, 19 Hauptplatz (tel. 273291), is housed in a historic building on what is said to be the largest and best preserved baroque square in Europe. Its entrance is through an arcade a short distance from the Danube. If you take one of the front rooms, you'll see old-fashioned trams running through the center of the square. The reception desk is one flight above ground level. The management is casual, and the decor includes lots of homey touches which help to make the place a friendly oasis.

Parking is a problem, but management told me that police allow cars headed toward the hotel to traverse the pedestrian-only square to park in the inner courtyard. Doubles rent for 600 AS ($31.92) to 850 AS ($45.22), while singles cost 360 AS ($19.15) to 575 AS ($30.59), with breakfast included. Prices depend on the plumbing. The adjoining restaurant is one of my favorites in Linz (see my restaurant recommendations).

Hotel Mercure, 39 Wankmüllerhofstrasse (tel. 42361), lies about a mile and a half from the center, close to the Linz exit from the autobahn. Built in an attractively up-to-date format of big windows and sand-colored walls, the hotel offers modern comfort in warmly tinted rooms with all the conveniences. The public rooms are filled with padded and upholstered banquettes and include an elegant futuristic bar area. Singles cost 950 AS ($50.54), while doubles rent for 1,100 AS ($58.52). An extra bed can be set up in any room for an additional 350 AS ($18.62). All these prices include breakfast.

Hotel Mühlviertlerhof, 24-26 Graben (tel. 272268), has 28 comfortable rooms, all with a certain elegant rusticity and coziness, as well as private baths, phones, radios, and color TV. The Zangerle family members maintain their centrally located hotel (only 50 steps to the Hauptplatz) with charm and efficiency. The bedrooms are immaculately kept and quiet, providing views of the garden. Rates range from 400 AS ($21.28) to 700 AS ($37.24) in a single, with doubles going for 500 AS ($26.60) to 560 AS ($29.79) per person.

WHERE TO DINE: **Allegro,** 68 Schillerstrasse (tel. 669800), is an elegant restaurant near the vegetable markets at the train station. In addition to the live music that the management sometimes provides, the menu is set up like the movements of a concerto, labeled "overture," "intermezzo," "theme and variations," along with "finale." A first course might be the house specialty of jamosala, mint sauce, and tonic (they call it "Allegretto"). Other introductory items include smoked salmon, pampas-style peppered ham, several kinds of salad, and snails. Main courses might be a steak potpourri or one of several fresh fish dishes. One of the best desserts is the homemade strudel. Fixed-price meals range from 375 AS ($19.95) to 520 AS ($27.66), while à la carte goes from 200 AS ($10.64) to 350 AS ($18.62). The restaurant is closed on Sunday and from August 10 to August 31.

Schloss Puchenau, Puchenau (tel. 221515). There's a local legend that mentions a castle ghost, yet he (or she) certainly doesn't seem averse to the idea of a tastefully decorated restaurant in its former abode. From certain parts you'll be able to see the Danube, while the head chef prepares a collection of tempting specialties. You'd better phone ahead for reservations, since it's located in a nearby satellite village of Linz. A fixed-price menu is priced from 520 AS ($27.66), while à la carte dinners cost from 150 AS ($7.98) to 350 AS ($18.62). The restaurant is closed on Sunday and sometimes on Thursday.

Restaurant Primo Piano, Hotel Wolfinger, 19 Hauptplatz (tel. 273291). The menu is handwritten on a large sheet of handmade paper. The restaurant is one floor above ground level in this historic hotel building on the baroque main square of Linz, with a view over the spires of the two churches and the fountain in the center. The napery is dark pink, the carpeting is black, and an upright piano sits against one wall with a bowler hat and a piece of ragtime sheet music on top.

The rest of the room might be art nouveau or art deco, depending on where you look. However, if you gaze at the center of the plaster ceiling, the triple-cherub motif is pure baroque. Menu items include three kinds of spaghetti, onion soup, trout meunière, peppersteak, veal piccata, saltimbocca, and excellent desserts. Meals range upward from 220 AS ($11.70). The restaurant is open every day of the week for lunch and dinner, but on Sunday only coffee and drinks are served.

Kremsmünsterer Stuben, 10 Altstadt (tel. 282111). Many guests come here as much for the view of the very old building in which it is located as for the cuisine itself. The food, however, has quickly made it one of the culinary rendezvous points of Linz. Chef Günther Preisberger trained in some of the most prestigious restaurants of Vienna, and today brings a flavorful mix of his own creation to the locale. The menu changes daily, but your meal might include delicately textured nouvelle cuisine dishes concocted with seafood, light meats, and superfresh vegetables. Set menus range in price from 175 AS ($9.31) to 525 AS ($27.93), with à la carte repasts costing from 125 AS ($6.65) to 350 AS

($18.62), depending on what you order. The establishment requires reservations, and is open daily except Sunday.

Restaurant Niccolai, 7 Klammstrasse (tel. 279028). For years Linzers joked that this was the only pizzeria in town directed by a real Italian. This cozy restaurant, however, offers much more than pizza, even though there are a dozen kinds of this pie, ranging from fish to meat to cheese to just about everything good in the Mediterranean repertoire. You might want to try the Italian pastas (the tortellini à la casa is good), saltimbocca, a range of fish dishes, and a variety of tempting cheeses and dessert. À la carte meals range from 110 AS ($5.85) to 320 AS ($17.02). The restaurant shuts down on Sunday.

Wachauer Weinhaus, 29 Pfarrgasse (tel. 74618). A baroque bas-relief of an ecstatic saint adorns the corner of this building near the old cathedral. The sign announcing this historic place is part of a wrought-iron bracket hanging over the cobblestone sidewalk. The smallest portion of any wine sold here is a quarter liter, which experience has taught me is about two full wine stems' worth. The wines from the Wachau region are featured, including five different kinds of white, four kinds of red, and one rosé, each priced from 25 AS ($1.33) per quarter liter. The establishment serves food from a limited menu priced from 150 AS ($7.98). Food items might include bean or gulasch soup, bratwursts, half a grilled hen, or free access to a self-service buffet. It's open daily except Sunday from 10 a.m. to closing.

Restaurant Stieglbräu zum Klosterhof, 30 Landstrasse (tel. 273373). If you're not sure where you want to sit inside this large homey restaurant, you'll see photographs of the various eating areas posted in the vestibule. In some of the rooms formally dressed waiters serve food under high ceilings, while in other rooms blue-jeaned youths in leather jackets, along with a scattering of older people, fill the air with smoke and loud talk. An aquarium in the pink and white stone vestibule swarms with live trout. The place was once the library of Kremsmünster Abbey. Meals cost around 175 AS ($9.31) and could include several kinds of schnitzels, half a hen cooked Viennese style, daily specials, Serbian bean soup, peppersteak, and for dessert, a Salzburger nockerl.

Hotel/Restaurant Mühlviertlerhof, 24-26 Graben (tel. 272269). In the heart of the old town you'll find a pleasant restaurant on the ground floor of this already-recommended hotel. There's more than one dining area, the biggest of which has wrought-iron hanging lamps and table dividers, vivid colors that could almost be Spanish, and heavy half-timbering between the renovated stucco walls. Fresh flowers are usually on the tables. Set meals range from 100 AS ($5.32) to 125 AS ($6.65), which usually include gutbürgerlich, seasonally adjusted menus as well as tafelspitz, several veal dishes, fish specialties, wild game, a knödelplatte, farmer's gulasch, with a dessert specialty known as topfenstrudel, as well as Salzburger nockerl and Linzer-cake. All the food, including the noodles, dumplings, and sausages, are handmade by the kitchen staff. À la carte meals range upward from 150 AS ($7.98).

Wienerwald, 22 Promenade (tel. 271419), is a branch of the famous chain restaurant that does more than any other to offer gemütlich ambience and rustic settings on a mass scale. This particular branch has a dark, woodsy interior with big arched windows overlooking a summertime beer garden. Menu items include a quarter or half a fried chicken, plus a variety of schnitzels, gulasches, steaks, and braised beef with potato noodles. The staff also offers a children's menu, as well as beer and wine. Full meals average around 175 AS ($9.31), but it's easily possible to dine for less.

THE CAFÉS OF LINZ: Café Traxlmayr, 16 Promenade (tel. 73353), is an old coffeehouse of the variety you imagined died at the end of World War I. It's next to a baroque palace on a wide ornamental boulevard, in a beige-and-brown building. Its outdoor sun terrace is protected by thick privets and geraniums in classical-style pots. It even has a fountain, designed to resemble a little boy playing with two gurgling fish, set into a wall out in front. The first thing you'll notice inside are the formally dressed staff (black and white tie are *de rigueur*), scurrying around with trays of coffee and cakes. The decor includes 1890s-style round marble tables, big mirrors, and crystal and gilt chandeliers. A rack of Austrian and foreign-language newspapers gives this place all the trappings of a Viennese coffeehouse, with elaborate pastries priced from 22 AS ($1.17) to 30 AS ($1.60) and coffee from 21 AS ($1.11) to 30 AS ($1.60). During cold weather, management serves some hot dishes such as gulasch soup.

Café-Konditorei Fritz Wagner, 15 Landstrasse (tel. 271765). The orange-and-brown facade of this small shop might not be too impressive, but the Linzer torte and the other pastries sold inside are heavenly. Owned by the same family for more than 80 years, the coffeeshop maintains a limited number of outdoor café tables during the summer, with more than 40 more seats available indoors. It's open Monday to Friday from 8 a.m. to 7 p.m. and on Saturday from 8 a.m. to 1 p.m. (closed Sunday). Linzer torte can be mailed to any country in the world.

Café-Konditorei Tautermann, 14 Klammstrasse (tel. 79680). The pastries from this small shop have won gold medals from contests held in places as far away as Brussels. You'll be able to buy fabulous-looking and tasting pastries, some of them with kiwi or regional fruits, from the ground-floor display cases. If you climb a simple flight of stairs you can order coffee in a sunny upstairs room with a view of the cathedral's spire. The café is open from 9 a.m. to 8 p.m. every day of the week but Tuesday. Aside from pastries, the upstairs also serves the Linzer torte along with ice cream and small cold dishes. Coffee costs from 21 AS ($1.19), pastries from 22 AS ($1.17).

Philipp Wrann, 6 Hofgasse (tel. 273288), is a well-known chain of pastry shops that specialize in the Linzer torte, that heavenly concoction of butter, nuts, chocolate, and in this case, gooseberry jam instead of raspberry jam, along with honey pies, candies, cakes, and chocolates. The company, which began in 1646, maintains five shops in Linz. Coffee is from 21 AS ($1.11); pastries, from 20 AS ($1.06) to 30 AS ($1.60).

Café am Park, Hotel Schillerpark, 2-4 Rainerstrasse (tel. 55405), seems to be the hottest place to go on a Sunday afternoon in Linz. If there's an equivalent of a sit-down singles bar, where everyone, and grandmother too, goes to watch, this is it. It's a big L-shaped room filled with belle-époque globe lights, mille-fleur carpeting in autumnal colors, upholstered bentwood chairs, and curtained glass windows overlooking the busy pedestrian traffic outside. You can get all the beverages you'd expect, as well as light snacks and wholesome meals, priced at around 160 AS ($8.51).

WHERE TO SHOP: O. Ö. Heimatwerk, 31 Landstrasse (tel. 73377), is an airy, sunny store with a stone floor, lots of handcrafted pine shelving, and a vaulted stucco ceiling dotted with pin spotlights. The entrance is under an arcade, although the shop windows face the busy pedestrian walkway of Linz's main shopping districts. Items for sale include local handicrafts such as pewter, intricately patterned silver, rustic ceramic pots, slippers, dresses, and a collection of dress-making fabrics in regional patterns, many of them in polka-dot.

Trachten Feichtinger, 9 Herrengasse (tel. 272824), has a decor of tasteful stucco curves and shiny wood floors. Its inventory includes a good selection of their own production of dirndls, suede skirts and jackets, and a full range of regional clothing, including sizes for men and women, girls and boys. This shop is open from 8:30 a.m. to noon and from 2 to 6 p.m. weekdays, and on Saturday from 8:30 a.m. to noon.

2. The Mühlviertel

This is a district of the Mühl River with pleasant hills for exploring. The Mühl is a small river that flows into the Danube at a point above Linz. The district, or viertel, lies between the Upper Austrian capital and the heavily guarded border of Czechoslovakia. To visit the district, leave Linz on the road to Bad Leonfelden (coming up). The road you'll take is lofty at certain points, reaching an elevation of 2,800 feet, and you'll see places where the hills have been quarried for granite. The tourist office in Linz will outline a route for you through these hills, the entire round trip lasting some 4½ hours—longer if you want to take your time.

If you're touring and would like to stop over, the chief town of the Mühlviertel is—

FREISTADT: Once a thriving little town on the route followed by salt traders from the alpine districts to reach Bohemia, Freistadt lies in the northeastern section of the Mühlviertel. Remnants of the town's watchtowers, gates, and fortified walls can still be seen. On the large, rectangular main square, the **Hauptplatz,** you'll find the church of St. Catherine, dating from the 14th century. A baroque overlay was added in the 17th century, but the church was rebuilt in the Gothic style. An onion-shape dome crowns the parish church.

Schloss Freistadt, with a 175-foot high keep, shelters the **Mühlviertler Heimathaus,** a provincial museum known for its collection of decorated glass engraved with gold.

The area code for Freistadt is 07942.

Food and Lodging

Gasthof Deim (Zum Goldenen Hirschen), 8 Böhmergasse (tel. 2258). The outside of this hotel has a series of neoclassical pilasters, corner mullions, and triangular window pediments, all clustered close together and accented with contrasting colors of reddish-brown and white. The interior ceilings are usually vaulted, with stone ribs supported by massive masonry columns. Furnishings are simple, and collections of hunting trophies and wrought-iron implements hang from the plaster walls. The cozy bedrooms have the kind of color schemes you can live with (mustards and russets) and lots of exposed wood. A garden sun terrace offers summertime drinks. With full board included, singles rent for 320 AS ($17.02) to 400 AS ($21.28), while doubles cost from 315 AS ($16.75) to 385 AS ($20.48) per person, depending on the plumbing.

KEPERMARKT: On the left bank of the Feldaist, north of the Danube, is the old town of Kepermarkt, about six miles south of Freistadt. A visit to the two towns can be ideally combined in a half-day excursion from Linz. Kepermarkt lies between the Mühlviertel and the Waldviertel, which was explored in the chapter on Lower Austria.

Kepermarkt is visited chiefly for its **Church of St. Wolfgang,** a Gothic edifice known for its altarpiece in the chancel, back of the main altar. You may be staggered at the size of it, as it appears to be about 42 feet high, with life-size figures. The carved part is of natural limewood. It's not only big, it's also beautiful to look at. Regrettably, the sculptor of this handsome work, dating from the latter part of the 15th century, is unknown. Otherwise he would have earned a place for himself in books devoted to ecclesiastical art. It is believed that the altarpiece was originally painted, but that is not the case today.

BAD LEONFELDEN: A small spa 13 miles to the west of Freistadt, Bad Leonfelden is known for its mud baths and the Kneipp treatment. It's mostly familiar only to Europeans, but you might want to make it a center for exploring Upper Austria if you book at one of the accommodations listed below. The spa has a pilgrimage church dating from the latter part of the 18th century.

A chair lift will take you to **Sternberg**, at 3,590 feet the loftiest point in the Mühlviertel. Once there you'll find a lookout tower and a panoramic sweep of the area. The spa has been customarily visited by summer travelers, but lately some winter skiers have been seeking it out.

You'll find prices reasonable here.

Bad Leonfelden's area code is 07213.

Food and Lodging

Gasthof Böhmertor (tel. 231) was designed in a modern format using lots of glass and steel, with a balconied section containing comfortable bedrooms. The large indoor pool and the sauna are bigger than you'd ordinarily expect. A range of massage facilities are also offered. The restaurants and bars inside are wood paneled and cozy, with hanging lamps and lots of color. Singles range from 240 AS ($12.77) to 360 AS ($19.15), while doubles cost from 410 AS ($21.81) to 575 AS ($30.59), with breakfast included.

Pension Angel, 132 Kurhausstrasse (tel. 429), offers clean, simple rooms and a friendly oldtime management which does everything it can to make your stay comfortable. There's a swimming pool on the premises, as well as an elevator, plus 54 beds in comfortable bedrooms, mainly with private bath. Singles without bath cost from 320 AS ($17.02), while doubles range from 290 AS ($15.34) to 340 AS ($18.09) per person, with breakfast included. The more expensive doubles have a private bath.

NEUFELDEN: Lying in the Grosse Mühl Valley, Neufelden has been a market town since the 13th century. Today it's known by the Austrians primarily as a little holiday resort in the Mühlviertel. The town has some lovely baroque buildings as well as a parish church from the 15th century. A wildlife park containing many different birds of prey is to the west of the town.

The Neufelden area code is 07282.

Food and Lodging

Mühltalhof (tel. 258). Many of the balconies of this charming hotel look out over an artificial lake that comes close to the hotel's flowered sun terrace. A private beach extends right to the stone wall at the water's edge. On the premises are tennis courts, a children's playground, and a sauna. The inside is decorated with tasteful furniture, coffered ceilings, and lots of extra touches. This hotel is a good choice for families traveling with children, especially since the relaxed management does what it can to make your holidays pleasant. Each of the comfortable rooms has its own bath. Singles cost from 500 AS ($26.60), while doubles range from 450 AS ($23.94) to 470 AS ($25) per person, with full board included. Prices depend on the season and the accommodation.

AIGEN IM MÜHLKRIES: A little market town enjoying a modest claim as a summer resort, Aigen lies in a forested area in the northwestern corridor of the Mühlviertel. From the resort, you can visit **Schlagl** (1,845 feet), an abbey built in 1218 and reconstructed centuries later. Its formerly Gothic church now flowers in the baroque style.

Aigen is surrounded by some of the most beautiful scenery in Upper Austria. From many of the panoramic belvederes you can look into Czechoslovakia. The area code for Aigen im Mühlkries is 07281.

Food and Lodging

Sporthotel Almesberger (tel. 213). The Gruber family will be your hosts in this modern hotel complex which wraps itself around two sides of a grassy area with a fountain in the middle. The interior is cozily outfitted with wooden beams and timbers, tasteful upholstery, and rustic furniture. The spacious bedrooms often have wood-covered ceilings and attractively contrasting patterns. Charges for a bed and half board range from 400 AS ($21.28) to 520 AS ($27.66) per person, based on double occupancy. Single occupants pay a daily surcharge of 50 AS ($2.66). Terms include service and taxes.

3. Attersee and Mondsee

The noted Salzkammergut, to the northeast of Salzburg, is the most explored part of Upper Austria, although portions of it spill into other provinces. In fact the parts we are about to consider are more often visited from Salzburg than from Linz.

Our first stopovers will be at a warm lake and a cold one. First, the cold one—

ATTERSEE: The largest lake in the Austrian Alps, Attersee comes alive in summer with the sporting crowd, when visitors flock to the resort town that bears the lake's name. Frankly, in my opinion the lake is too cold almost all the time for swimming (although polar bear club members may disagree), but it's a great draw to boaters in summer. An Austrian sailing club has its headquarters here.

Those interested in fishing will be attracted to the lake's clear alpine waters, as it holds trout, char, and in little tributaries, brook trout. At many guest houses along the shore you can have for dinner the fish you caught.

The blue-green *see* is 12½ miles long and about 1½ miles wide, with many orchards growing on its uplands. The government has built a road around the entire body of water. From the southern part of the lake, to the west of Burgau, you can take a 12-minute walk to a beautiful gorge, the **Burggrabenklamm,** with a waterfall, one of the most scenic sights along the Attersee.

Attersee's area code is 07666.

Food and Lodging

Hotel Oberndorfer (tel. 364) is a long, multi-sectioned hotel with a one-story extension stretching all the way to the edge of the lake. From the far edge of the sun terrace you can see the village church on the other side of the hotel. The bedrooms are sunny, carpeted, and comfortable, while the public rooms have more than their share of wood paneling and wrought iron. Singles rent for 320 AS ($17.02) to 490 AS ($26.07), while doubles go for 800 AS ($42.56) to 1,350 AS ($71.82), with breakfast included. Rates depend on the season and the room assignment. The much more expensive doubles have far better views and more elaborate plumbing. Open March to October.

NUSSDORF AM ATTERSEE: This is a little lakeside village next to the better known holiday resort, Attersee, just recommended. Nussdorf, in a central position on the lake, is a small holiday place enjoying mainly a summer trade. There are tennis courts, a sailing school, boats for rent, fishing, and folkloric concerts. The area code for Nussdorf am Attersee is 07666.

Food and Lodging

Bräugasthof Aichinger (tel. 8007) is a pleasant four-story rectangular building with a long garden stretching through flowering trees to a sunny lawn. A wellhouse with constantly flowing water is the first thing you'll see from the quiet street on the hotel's downhill side. Inside, the builders added stone accents, such as a rounded column to support the vaults of the breakfast room, as well as a dome-capped green tile oven studded with ceramic rosettes. The comfortable and practical bedrooms are outfitted with every comfort. Singles rent for 320 AS ($17.02) to 420 AS ($22.34), while doubles cost from 280 AS ($14.90) to 400 AS ($21.28) per person, with breakfast included. Prices depend on the season and the plumbing.

WEISSENBACH AM ATTERSEE: You'll find this tiny lakeside hamlet and mini-holiday resort on the southeastern corner of the lake. From here you can take a heavily forested, scenic road to a pass at **Weissenbach Sattel,** which has a chapel. Along this road you'll have a view of the Weissenbachklamm Gorge.

The Weissenbach am Attersee area code is 07663.

Food and Lodging

Hotel Post (tel. 240) is a balconied, white-walled hotel set at the edge of the lake. It's surrounded by trees, with a sun terrace stretching up to the edge of the water. Long rows of green-shuttered windows look out over iron railings onto the lake. In one of the public rooms stands a big ceramic stove with painted tiles. Modern furniture fills the tastefully appointed bedrooms, some of which have Oriental rugs as floor coverings. All units contain private baths. Depending on the season, patrons are charged 450 AS ($23.94) or 550 AS ($29.26) per person for bed and breakfast. Larger units, accommodating three to five persons, are available, costing from 400 AS ($21.28) to 550 AS ($29.26) per person. Half board goes for an extra 125 AS ($6.65) each. On the premises are tennis courts, two bowling alleys, a sauna, and sailing facilities. You can rent equipment for waterskiing and other water sports.

UNTERACH AM ATTERSEE: This lakeside hamlet is so small it doesn't appear on most maps, but it occupies one of the loveliest positions on the lake. It's on the right bank, across from Weissenbach, and it can be a base for exploring either Attersee or Mondsee.

The area code for Unterach am Attersee is 07665.

Food and Lodging

Hotel Georgshof (tel. 501) is a wood-and-stucco chalet set on a hillside. If you walk out onto the backyard's sun terrace, you'll realize that the hotel is actually bigger than it appears from the road. The exteriors of many of the windows are embellished with regional designs in yellow and brown. Inside you'll find a timbered and stuccoed bar area with chalet chairs and an angled serving area with alpine barstools. An indoor pool has a high ceiling and tile walls and floors. The bedrooms are spacious and comfortable. The Hollerwöger family, your hosts, charge from 380 AS ($20.22) for a single and from 680 AS ($36.18) in a double, including breakfast.

SEEWALCHEN AM ATTERSEE: At the northern extremity of Lake Atter (Attersee) is this small hamlet and holiday resort. It offers sailing and other water sports, but the main reason I'm recommending it is because of the following accommodation, one of the most pleasant stopovers in the Salzkammergut.

Seewalchen am Attersee's area code is 07662.

Food and Lodging

Gasthof Häupl (tel. 2249) is one of the most elegant hotels in the region, and it remains open all year. From the street side it has a pleasingly simple facade of white walls and a steeply sloped series of rooflines with long rows of interconnected gables. From the lake side the design literally blossoms into masses of flowers, set into boxes which hang from the handcrafted wooden balconies. The interior looks like a tastefully opulent private house. The paneling that covers many of the rooms glows softly in the reflected light from the wall sconces. In the light-grained bar the ceiling is crafted around baroque patterns and curves.

Well-furnished singles range from 650 AS ($34.58) to 1,200 AS ($63.84), while doubles cost from 1,000 AS ($53.20) to 1,500 AS ($79.80). These prices include breakfast and use of the sauna.

The rustic dining room is said to be one of the best in the region. It's accented with graceful curves of wrought iron, and the chef prepares such delicacies as roast goose with baby vegetables in a savory sauce. This could be followed by a dessert parfait of fresh prunes in a caramel sauce. Frau Häupl, whose family has run this place for the past seven generations, does most of the cooking, assisted by an able group of chefs. Fixed-price meals range from 180 AS ($9.58) to 660 AS ($35.11), while à la carte dinners cost from 150 AS ($7.98) to 450 AS ($23.94). The restaurant is closed Monday and in the period between October and April.

MONDSEE: "Moon Lake," or Mondsee, is considered one of the warmest lakes in the Salzkammergut. It's a crescent-shaped body of water which was named for the moon as long ago as Roman times. The Salzburg-Vienna autobahn runs along the south shores of this, the third-largest lake in the Salzkammergut district. In the background you can see the **Drachenwand** mountain and also the **Schafberg.**

The lake is sparsely settled, and if you want to find accommodations, you should head for the village which bears the lake's name, **Mondsee,** lying in the northwest corner. The village is popular in summer as a resort, with sailing schools and bathing beaches operating on the *see.*

A Benedictine abbey once was situated in Mondsee, dating from 748. However, Emperor Joseph II ordered the abbey dissolved in 1791, so the abbey church became the **parish church** *(pfarrkirche),* still a point of interest in the village. It's a 15th-century structure with an added baroque exterior, but its crypt is from the 11th century. The church was richly decorated by Meinrad Guggenbichler, a sculptor born in 1649. He designed seven of the more than dozen altars.

Part of the abbey is now the **Schloss Mondsee** (see below). The castle is adjacent to the church. The wedding scene in *The Sound of Music* was filmed here.

The town also has a small local museum, the **Heimatmuseum,** open from the first of May until the end of October from 9 a.m. to 5 p.m. daily, charging 20 AS ($1.06) for adults, 10 AS (53¢) for children. Local artifacts of life in the province in other days are displayed in what used to be chapels of the abbey. The history of the abbey is traced, and other works by Guggenbichler are displayed.

Of particular interest is the **Pfahlbaumuseum,** in the former cloisters of the abbey. Dedicated to prehistoric archeology, the museum traces the habitation by mankind from the time of neolithic man's construction of houses on pilings in the lake. Discoveries from as far back as 3000 B.C. up to the disappearance of prehistoric man in 1800 B.C. include pottery and stone carvings. The museum is open May 1 to the end of October from 9 a.m. to 5 p.m. daily. Admission is 20 AS ($1.06) for adults, 10 AS (53¢) for children.

You may also visit the **Mondseer Rauchhaus,** or smokehouse, a rustic wood chalet flanked by outbuildings. Farmers from the district came here to dry their crops. There is no chimney above the vaulted hearth. The smokehouse is open April until the end of October from 8 a.m. to 6 p.m. Admission is 18 AS (96¢) for adults, 10 AS (53¢) for children.

The area code for Mondsee is 06232.

Food and Lodging

Hotel/Restaurant Plomberg (tel. 3572) might remind you of a wealthy private home. It's dotted in dozens of places—even the bedrooms—with Oriental rugs, thick curtains, and lots of tasteful accessories which range from wrought-iron detailing to unusual art objects. The hotel sits above a stone wall that edges onto the lake. It's surrounded by deciduous trees and prosperous-looking villas. Bed and breakfast ranges from 500 AS ($26.60) to 750 AS ($39.90) per person daily.

The hotel doesn't offer full- or half-board plans, because most of the guests make their own plans during the day. The in-house restaurant serves outstanding food and is often considered among the best in Upper Austria. Karl and Monika Eschlböck have divided their restaurant into several cozy dining rooms, decorated with Oriental rugs and accented with heavy timbers and an occasional antique.

Mr. Eschlböck was an apprentice at Troisgros in France and carries much of that establishment's expertise into his own restaurant. The menu is long and includes unusual adaptations of Austrian recipes as well as such items as veal liver with tomatoes, a salad of mache and duck breasts, lotte with a mousseline sauce, an array of veal dishes, roebuck Corsican style, crab soup, and carp with a finely chopped mixture of gruyère, carrots, fennel, and potatoes. À la carte meals range from 150 AS ($7.98) to 650 AS ($34.58), while fixed-price dinners go from 475 AS ($25.27) to 900 AS ($47.88). Reservations are important.

Hotel/Restaurant Weisses Kreuz (tel. 2254). The only spots of color a visitor will see against the bare white walls of this elegant place are the bouquets of flowers arranged by the employees of owner Gustav Lugerbauer. Of course, there's a view from the dining room out over a pleasant garden, but the main focus of this place is on the food. Your meal might include veal cutlets with "baby" vegetables and a potato strudel, a salad of marinated fish, or baby lamb cooked with rosemary. The cabbage and the richly flavored mushrooms used in the preparation of some of the recipes are likely to have been picked that very day in the restaurant's garden. Dessert might be crêpes stuffed with grapes and nuts or else a cream-flavored soufflé with strawberry sauce.

Meals begin at around 160 AS ($8.51), but could easily go as high as 550 AS ($29.26), depending on your order. Reservations are necessary, and meals are served daily except Wednesday between mid-November and mid-December. A small number of conservatively furnished, thick-walled rooms are available for overnight guests, costing from 420 AS ($22.34) to 650 AS ($34.58) per person.

Seehotel Lackner, 33 Gaisberg (tel. 2359), is a rambling white hotel with balconies facing the lake and flowerboxes blossoming toward the street. The sun terrace has a covering of gray flagstones, while the interior is a rustic ensemble of modern furniture and wood accents. Comfortably furnished singles range from 550 AS ($29.26) to 580 AS ($30.87), while doubles cost 520 AS ($27.66) to 540 AS ($28.73) per person, with full board included. Prices depend on the season and the plumbing.

Grossgasthof Leitnerbräu (tel. 2219) has been owned by many generations of the Marschallinger family. You'll recognize it by its natural stucco facade with the white and pink geometric detailing around the windows. A wrought-iron bracket extends out over the candy-striped awning, holding a depiction of two lions drinking happily from a barrel. The interior is cheerfully rustic, with a green ceramic stove in the restaurant and a scattering of painted antique furniture. Prices are from 480 AS ($25.54) to 500 AS ($26.60) per person, with full board included. All accommodations contain private bath and are usually spacious and sunny. The hotel is open from December to October.

La Farandol, 150 Tiefgraben (tel. 3475). Much of the allure of this restaurant derives from the years its owners spent learning their craft in the French section of Switzerland. You'll probably be greeted at the door by Madame Buchschartner, whose talented husband modestly remains behind the scenes in the kitchen. From your eyrie above the lake, you can enjoy an array of specialties which change with the seasons. Your meal might include a terrine of chicken livers with coarsely textured homemade bread, fresh asparagus with sweetbreads in puff pastry, marinated filet of salmon with leaves of lettuce, and filet steak with a pepper-flavored sabayon. Most of the vintages on the sophisticated wine list come from France and Austria. Fixed-price and à la carte dinners range from between 180 AS ($9.58) and 420 AS ($22.34). Reservations are suggested. The restaurant is closed all day Monday and for lunch on Tuesday (also from the first week in January until the second week in February).

Café Frauenschuh (tel. 2312) is an establishment so famous that it's known by sweet tooths throughout the region for its delectable pastries and chocolates. In the middle of the village, it offers racks of fruited and chocolate-covered confections which you can eat on the spot or buy by the dozen to (supposedly) distribute among your friends back at the hotel. Coffee costs from 15 AS (80¢) to 26 AS ($1.38), while pastries run the range from 18 AS (96¢) to 30 AS ($1.60). The café is open every day of the week except Wednesday between October and April.

4. St. Wolfgang and Bad Ischl

The next two resorts, quite different in character, lie a short distance apart in the Salzkammergut.

St. Wolfgang lies on the Wolfgangsee, already visited in Chapter VIII, Land Salzburg. St. Gilgen in that province is a rival for St. Wolfgang, lying on the same lake but in Upper Austria. The province boundary crosses the lake.

Bad Ischl, once the summer residence of Emperor Franz Joseph, is the most fashionable spa in the lake district.

ST. WOLFGANG: In the midst of mountains in the Salzkammergut, Wolfgangsee is considered one of the most romantic lakes in Austria. Mountains and *see* join harmoniously to provide the setting for St. Wolfgang, a little holiday resort on the northeastern side of the lake below the Schafberg. Here in summer you can enjoy private bathing and other water sports, as well as frequenting the beach cafés. Hiking is possible in many directions.

There's also winter skiing in the hills, with snow from December to mid-March. The ski slopes are free of avalanches. You'll find facilities here for skating, curling, and horse sleighrides. Folkloric dancing is often presented as well.

In summer the resort is overrun with tourists, but there are two car parks at the entrance to the town. At certain times of the year I find it better to go to St. Wolfgang by boat, leaving from the landing stage at **Gschwendt** on the southern rim of the lake. Departures from mid-May to mid-October are usually hourly.

St. Wolfgang is the site of the celebrated **White Horse Inn** (see below), and the landscape has been called operetta-like, which is natural as the inn was the setting for Ralph Benatzky's operetta *White Horse Inn*, which brought glory to the town.

Long before it was a holiday resort, St. Wolfgang was a renowned pilgrimage center, having been so since the 12th century. The **Church of St. Wolfgang** is said to stand on the spot where St. Wolfgang built a hermitage on a rocky spur of land. The church, from the latter 15th century, is highlighted by the Michael Pacher altarpiece, a magnificent work from 1481, pictured in many Gothic art books. Pacher's altarpiece is luxuriantly adorned with panel paintings and masterfully carved figures. The main panel depicts the Coronation of the Virgin. Thomas Schwanthaler designed the double altar of the patron saint, Wolfgang, and John the Baptist.

You can visit the church May to September from 9 a.m. to 5 p.m., until 6 p.m. on Sunday and public holidays. Otherwise, its hours are from 10 a.m. to 4 p.m., from 11 a.m. on Sunday. Admission is 10 AS (53¢).

The most popular excursion from St. Wolfgang is to **Schafberg,** the view from the top being one of the best known and most sought in Upper Austria. Legend has it that you can see 13 lakes of the Salzkammergut from here, but I have never been able to do so. However, you're almost sure to have a good view of Mondsee and Attersee (which I've just introduced you to), and of course the entire Wolfgangsee. On a clear day you can see as far as the Berchtesgaden Alps of Hitler fame. As a backdrop to the view, you can gaze at the peaks of the Hollengebirge and the Dachstein with its glacier caps.

The whole trip to Schafberg takes about 4½ hours, nearly half by rack rail which operates from May to October. Once there, allow for about 30 minutes' walking. Departures are hourly mid-May to mid-June from 8:30 a.m. to 4:30 p.m., mid-June to mid-September from 7 a.m. to 6:25 p.m., and mid-September to mid-October from 8:30 a.m. to 6:20 p.m. A round trip costs from 175 AS ($9.31).

There's a hotel on the summit of the mountain, which rises to 5,850 feet.

The area code for St. Wolfgang is 06138.

Food and Lodging

Weissen Rössl (the White Horse Inn) (tel. 2306) was the setting used for a popular play *(Im Weissen Rössl am Wolfgangsee)* written in 1896 and adapted for the Berlin stage by a group of actors and directors who returned here to rewrite it in 1930. Actually, there has been an inn on this site since 1474, with continuous ownership by the Peter family since 1712.

This scene of the famous operetta absolutely reeks of romance and atmosphere. Its stippled yellow facade conceals a collection of carved antiques which are clustered into intimate conversational groupings. The public rooms are large and sunny, usually covered with wood and upholstered with pleasant and cheerful colors. The indoor pool has direct access to the wide lakeside sun terrace with its view of the village church.

On the premises are private tennis courts, a gymnasium, a sauna, sailing, waterskiing, and windsurfing facilities. In the evening the management usually provides live piano or zither music. A single room with bath or shower and toilet rents for 600 AS ($31.92) to 800 AS ($42.56), and doubles with complete baths go for 700 AS ($37.24) to 1,500 AS ($79.80). Junior suites are available for 1,500 AS ($79.80) to 1,800 AS ($95.76). A buffet breakfast, service, and taxes are included in the rates. The hotel is open from Christmas to the beginning of November.

Hotel Appesbach (tel. 2209). The entrance is through an arched portico covered with ivy, which brings you into a pleasant family-run hotel with plenty of character. About a mile from the center of town, the establishment is a collection of what looks like three separate yellow buildings with green shutters. They are joined together into a rambling complex set directly on the lake. The surrounding lawn area contains table-tennis equipment, outdoor chairs, and children's toys. The hotel has a tennis court, a small private beach, and facilities for sailboat rentals as well. It's closed in winter, reopening for business in April. Doubles with breakfast cost 750 AS ($39.90) to 1,100 AS ($58.52), while singles go for 500 AS ($26.60) to 575 AS ($30.59).

Sporthotel Wolfgangerhof (tel. 2237) is a modern balconied guest house with two elongated sections set at right angles to one another. A summertime café has been set up under a tree just outside the entrance. Inside you'll find a bar and several restaurants, as well as a swimming pool, sauna, and facilities for renting either bicycles or ski equipment. Per-person rates in doubles range from 350 AS ($18.62) to 450 AS ($23.94), half board included. The supplement in a single is 75 AS ($3.99) daily. Prices depend on the season and the plumbing.

Seehotel Cortisen (tel. 2376) is separated from the lake only by a solid stone wall which supports a sun terrace and a short expanse of well-maintained lawn. From the street side the first thing you'll see are the illustrations of regionally dressed couples that cover parts of the facade. Inside, the decor is rustically elegant, with well-crafted woodwork, richly patterned Oriental rugs, and lots of antique knickknacks.

The cozy bedrooms often have private balconies and are tastefully furnished with lots of well-detailed pieces. The Ballner family are your hosts at this pleasant oasis. They charge from 350 AS ($18.62) to 450 AS ($23.94) per person, based on double occupancy with breakfast included. Singles pay a daily surcharge of 75 AS ($3.99). Prices depend on the exposure of your room and the season. Half board costs another 150 AS ($7.98) per person daily. The hotel shuts down on Halloween for the winter months.

Hotel Tirol (tel. 3269) is a lakeside chalet that rises four flower-covered stories above a grassy area which serves as a combination beach, sun terrace, and café. The interior has lots of rustic ceiling beams and cozy alpine furniture, while many of the comfortable bedrooms have carved headboards, paneled closet doors, and lots of atmosphere. The bar area is especially inviting, with the bottles arranged in a wood, brick, and stucco combination that looks almost like a converted hearth. With half board included, per-person rates, based on double occupancy, range from 375 AS ($19.95) to 500 AS ($26.60) in accommodations without private bath. With bath, supplements range from 150 AS ($7.98) to 175 AS ($9.31) daily, and singles pay yet another daily surcharge of 150 AS ($7.98).

Hotel Belvedere (tel. 2302) is a cozy chalet hotel with a lakeside location and an interior filled with a scattering of Victorian antiques and ceramic stoves. One of the most pleasant places on the premises is the rustic covered café-terrace with a view of the lake. The hotel is open year round. Singles rent for 220 AS ($11.70) to 400 AS ($21.28), while doubles cost from 200 AS ($10.64) to 380 AS ($20.22) per person, with breakfast included. Prices depend on the plumbing and the season.

Hotel Eden, 40 Michael Pacher Strasse (tel. 2326), is a modern building with long rows of wooden balconies and a location on a hillside at the upper end of the village. The comfortable bedrooms are simply furnished, renting for 320 AS ($17.02) to 390 AS ($20.75) per person in a double and 380 AS ($20.22) to 400 AS ($21.28) in a single. The hotel is open in December and January and from April to October.

Gasthof/Pension Zimmerbräu (tel. 2204) has the kind of facade that will make you want to stop in for coffee. A big-windowed restaurant extends partly into the street, while someone has installed lots of gingerbread under the eaves.

You'll get the sense of a seaside town from the sun terrace of the two rustic beach huts whose foundations are built right into the lake. These also are accented with gingerbread and a wholesome sense of another era. The interior of the main hotel is simply and attractively furnished, with the kinds of floors that are easy to keep clean. The charges are 520 AS ($27.66) per person in a double, 540 AS ($28.73) in a single. Full board is included. The hotel is open in December and January and from March to October.

BAD ISCHL: The spa of Bad Ischl, one of the country's most fashionable watering places and the summer seat of Emperor Franz Joseph for more than 60 years, can be reached coming from Salzburg-Munich by leaving the motorway at Mondsee, heading along a well-constructed federal highway through the Salzkammergut, along Wolfgangsee and Mondsee. It's a 25-mile drive after you turn off the autobahn. Bad Ischl is easily accessible by daily bus and train service also. The spa establishments provide brine-sulfur mud baths for a variety of ailments.

The town, constructed on a peninsula between the Traun River and its tributary, the Ischl, still reflects a certain imperial conceit in its architecture, much of it left over from the heyday of the Austro-Hungarian Empire. The spa went into a decline after Franz Joseph stopped coming here in the first year of World War I, ending a practice he started in 1848 at the very beginning of his reign.

During imperial days the court was a magnet to musicians and artists, who depended on patronage from royalty and aristocracy for their bread and butter —and wine and caviar. Among those who made their way to Bad Ischl were Johann Strauss, Oscar Straus, Meyerbeer, Brahms, Bruckner, Lehar, Kálmán, Tauber, and Waldmüller.

Bad Ischl has surprisingly chic shopping even today, as you'll note if you go along the **Pfarrgasse.** This street comes to an end at the **Esplanade,** a shaded promenade where the most famous figures in Europe once strolled. The smart set of the 19th century shunned the sun. Wealthy salt merchants once lived along this promenade, and Maximilian, ill-fated Emperor of Mexico, was born in a royal dwelling here in 1832.

The former **Pump Room,** dating from 1831, is in the middle of town on the Ferdinand-Auböck-Platz. Many of the buildings seen on the platz are in the Biedermeier style. The 1753 parish church was rebuilt when Maria Theresa was empress.

Many riverside walks are possible at this spa, and you'll see lovely gardens and villas which attract viewers. **Lehar Villa** (tel. 2992) stands on the opposite bank of the Traun. Franz Lehar, the composer best known for his creation *The Merry Widow,* lived here from 1912 until his death in 1948. The villa is now a museum, open Easter and from mid-May to September 30 daily from 9 a.m. to noon and 2 to 5 p.m. Admission is 25 AS ($1.33).

The most important attraction of the town is the **Kaiservilla,** or imperial villa, in Kaiserpark (tel. 3241), close to the downtown area. Emperor Franz Joseph used this Biedermeier palace for 60 summers as a residence and center for recreation. Highlights in the villa are the Gray Saloon, where the Empress Elisabeth lived and which she left on July 16, 1898, to begin her trip to Switzerland where an assassin awaited her, and the emperor's study where he signed the *Manifest,* a declaration of war sparking off World War I. Tours are conducted May 1 through October 15 from 9:30 a.m. to noon and 1 to 4:30 p.m. Off-season, the villa is open Good Friday through Easter Monday and on weekends in April and October. Admission is 55 AS ($2.93).

The **Marmorschlössl** (tel. 4422), surrounded by the Kaiserpark, houses a photo-historic collection (Sammlung Frank). This tiny palace was used by Empress Elisabeth as a tea pavilion. It is open from 9:30 a.m. to 4:30 p.m. April 1 to October 31. Admission to the park is 20 AS ($1.06) and to the museum another 20 AS.

For a view of the overall area, you can take a cable car to Katrin Mountain (4,500 feet), a round trip costing 110 AS ($5.85). It's an easy walk from the mountain station to the summit, where there are restaurants. From the mountain, you have a view into the Salzkammergut, with dozens of lakes and mountain heights, even glaciers. The cable car does not operate from early April to early May and late October to early December.

Another tour is south of the spa to the **salt mine** (tel. 4231), which is open from mid-May to mid-September daily except Sunday from 9 a.m. to 5 p.m. Adults are charged 80 AS ($4.26) and children 40 AS ($2.13).

The tourist office at 6 Bahnhofstrasse (tel. 3520) will give you complete directions and information about all the sights in the immediate environs if you'd like to stay in the spa and make some day trips.

The area code for Bad Ischl is 06132.

Food and Lodging

Kurhotel Bad Ischl (tel. 4271), in the center of town, is a futuristic-looking hotel easy to recognize because of its multi-sectioned design of jutting angles and recessed balconies. Painted white, the hotel has a streamlined interior with neutral colors and lots of sunny, light-filled spaces. It was built between 1974 and 1976 with all the modern conveniences, including an underground garage, an indoor mineral water bath, a sauna, and a glistening collection of restaurants, plus massage and therapy facilities. A heated corridor leads directly to the famous spa. Singles rent for 850 AS ($45.22) to 920 AS ($48.94), while doubles cost 750 AS ($39.90) to 875 AS ($46.55) per person, with half board included. Each of the accommodations has a private bath, phone, radio, color TV, and private balcony.

Hotel Schenner, 9 Schulgasse (tel. 2327), is owned and managed by a family with the same name. Its interior is outfitted with stone detailing and plenty of exposed wood, as well as a conservatively rustic format that includes lots of wrought iron and a few hunting trophies. You'll recognize the building by its painted corner mullions and country baroque window detailing. There is a parasol-dotted sun terrace by the back lawn. The pleasant bedrooms are decorated in a comfortable selection of autumnal colors and usually have oversize tile bathrooms. Singles range from 600 AS ($31.92), while per-person rates in a double go from 525 AS ($27.93) to 595 AS ($31.65), with half board included.

Hotel Goldenen Schiff, 3 Stifterkai (tel. 4241), is a leisurely five-minute walk from the spa facilities. It sits directly on the river, housed in a simple white building taller than it is wide. The riverfront rooms usually contain balconies, while even those facing the street have an invitingly cozy decor of modern furniture and sunny colors accented with lots of exposed wood. The restaurants are outfitted with refreshing touches of green, blue, and red, and all have pleasant combinations of rough-sawed planking and smoothly polished wood. Christine Gruber is the congenial owner. She charges from 540 AS ($28.73) to 600 AS ($31.92) per person in a wide range of singles, doubles, and apartments, all with full board included.

Goldenes Hufeisen, 13 Pfarrgasse (tel. 3653). From the street side this family-run hotel has a restrained facade of pastel-colored stucco and white trim. From the garden side the building opens onto a green area with big sunny windows and parallel rows of wood-railed balconies. The beer garden adjoining the establishment is staffed with businesslike hausfraus and shaded with big trees.

The bedrooms are comfortable and clean. An annex holds the overflow from the main hotel and lies about three minutes away. Both buildings are in the center of the spa. The Abpurg family charge 425 AS ($22.61) to 525 AS ($27.93) per person, with full board included. Prices depend on the season and the plumbing.

Hotel Goldener Stern, 30 Kreuzplatz (tel. 3530), has one of the most memorable facades at the spa, covered with turquoise-colored stucco, white trim, and a white-walled rectangular tower jutting out from the corner. It's in the center of town, and while some of the public rooms have been renovated into a streamlined format of clean lines and modern paneling, the bedrooms retain much of their rustic allure. They're usually filled with painted furniture and wall-to-wall carpeting. Singles go from 640 AS ($34.05), while doubles cost from 560 AS ($29.79) per person, with full board.

Weinhaus Attwenger, 12 Leharkai (tel. 3327), is the rustically decorated wine tavern which, it's said, used to be a favorite of Bruckner and Lehar. It's very much an old-style decor that many more modern establishments try to duplicate. Even so, many summertime clients enjoy the riverside sun terrace where on a pleasant day the savory coffee and delectable pastries seem even more tempting. If you want a full meal, the menu includes a wide range of Austrian and international dishes. These feature medallions of veal chef's style, mussels in a savory sauce, and several kinds of fish. À la carte meals range from 135 AS ($7.18) to 375 AS ($19.95). Set menus cost from 140 AS ($7.45) to 260 AS ($13.83). Reservations are a good idea.

Konditorei-Café Zauner (tel. 3310) is the pastry shop and coffeehouse that anyone with a sense of history usually heads for after viewing the summer playgrounds of the former Habsburg monarchs. The only Austrian coffeehouse more famous than this is Demel in Vienna. The imperial court used to order their pastries here, and it used to be said that the easiest way to listen to the heartbeat of the empire during July and August was to eavesdrop on a nearby table at Zauner.

You can buy pastries from the gold and white rococo showroom (which has been renovated to handle the flood of summer tourists) or eat at the small round-topped tables in an elegant series of inner rooms. Menu items include sandwiches and salads as well as an extensive assortment of exquisitely prepared pastries. The café is open every day in summer between 8:30 a.m. and 6 p.m. From October to March it closes on Tuesday. Many of the items can be mailed as gifts. Coffee costs 20 AS ($1.06) to 28 AS ($1.49), while pastries range from 18 AS (96¢) to 30 AS ($1.60).

BAD GOISERN: This little spa town can be visited as an excursion from Bad Ischl, only six miles away, or else it can be used as a base for exploring this part of Upper Austria. Because it's much less well known than Bad Ischl, its prices are quite reasonable. Its little spa hotels offer good value for your schillings. The sulfurous spring waters of the spa contain iodine.

The resort attracts mainly Austrians and Germans who know of its quiet location in the Traun Valley. It's most popular in summer because of its good-size open-air swimming pool, but it does some winter business, being convenient to a toboggan run and ski lifts. Hikers like to base here, from where they can go up **Hochkalmberg** mountain (more than 6,000 feet high) in 4½ hours and **Predigstuhl** (4,190 feet) in 3 hours.

The area code for Bad Goisern is 06135.

Food and Lodging

Kurhotel Jodschwefelbad (tel. 8305) is a sprawling hotel and sanitorium with a modern format and a 100-year-old history in the treatment of rheumatic and skin disorders, especially psoriasis. Maintaining resident dermatologists on the premises, the hotel offers good accommodations to patients and tourists alike. A range of outdoor activities is in the region, and a thermally heated outdoor pool is on the premises. With full board included, singles rent for 680 AS ($36.18) to 780 AS ($41.50), while doubles go for 610 AS ($32.45) to 700 AS ($37.24) per person. Prices depend on the plumbing and the season.

Hotel Agatha-Wirt (tel. 8342), in the nearby hamlet of St. Agatha, is a romantic country hotel that was built in 1517. Today it has a humor-loving and friendly direction by the descendants of the family who bought it 200 years ago. It's designed with a steep hipped roof, lots of flowers, stone detailing around the entrance arch, and painted highlights around the corner mullions. The functional bedrooms inspire lingering and are suitable for other than just a good night's sleep. The headboards are often carved into regional patterns, and sometimes several kinds of wood are joined together for color contrast. If you're a light sleeper, avoid the units facing the street. Tennis, swimming, and ski facilities are all nearby. Rates for a room and half board range from 350 AS ($18.62) to 560 AS ($29.79), depending on the plumbing and the season. The hotel is usually closed for the first part of December.

Hotel/Café Goiserermühle (tel. 8206). The second floor of this square-based building is capped with a pyramid-shaped roof which comes to a point high above the immaculate lawns. The building is capped with a series of gables and a small tower surrounded by chimneys. The rooms have been renovated with all the modern comforts, costing 325 AS ($17.29) to 450 AS ($23.94) in a single and from 390 AS ($20.75) to 400 AS ($21.28) per person in a double, with full board included. The in-house restaurant serves well-seasoned steaks, schnitzels, and fish (especially trout) in a homey and rustic setting.

5. Hallstatt

Hallstatt, a small market town south of Bad Ischl, considered one of the most beautiful villages in Austria, is my favorite place in this province. It stands on the left bank of the dark, brooding Hallstättersee in the Salzkammergut, on the southernmost tip of the province, right at the border of Land Salzburg (see Chapter VIII) and Styria (see Chapter XIII). You may well drive through a part of Styria to reach the lake, going via Bad Aussee.

To reach Hallstatt you take a road through a tunnel in the mountain. Park your car in the car park and then go by foot past waterfalls to the traffic-free town. There are several large cascades in the area.

Hallstättersee is a narrow lake, about 5 miles long and 1½ miles wide at its broadest expanse, almost completely surrounded by mountains. Its waters are so dark they're often called black.

Now a modern town, Hallstatt is considered the oldest still-inhabited village in Europe, owing its importance and its longevity to the local deposits of salt. Its perch against a mountain on a rocky terrace overlooking Hallstättersee seems like a curious place to build a town, but this was the site of an early Iron Age culture dating from 800 to 400 B.C. Many Iron Age relics have been unearthed in the area. The mining of salt from the mountain behind Hallstatt was known among pre-Celtic tribes of 1000 B.C. It died out in medieval times but was revived by the Habsburgs and continues today.

Hallstatt's area code is 06124.

THE SIGHTS: The town of Hallstatt gave its name to one of the most important eras of prehistory. Some 1,000 tombs have been excavated in the area, which Austrians refer to as a "cradle of civilization." The 1,000 graves were of prehistoric people, who constructed huts on piles in the lake. Many of the artifacts excavated here—dating back to Neolithic times—are displayed in the **Museum of Prehistory,** 56 Seestrasse, open from the first of April until the end of October from 10 a.m. to 6 p.m. Admission is 25 AS ($1.33).

The center of this beautifully situated village, with views of the Dachstein mountain massif, is the Market Square, which contains 16th-century buildings. The lakeside terrace is from the 18th century. Hallstatt's streets are narrow and often steep.

You can visit the **pfarrkirche** (parish church), which is romantically situated, with the churchyard bordering the dark waters of the lake. The house of worship is a large structure from the latter part of the 15th century. It has a squat tower, but its unusually designed roof with overhanging eaves evokes thoughts of Oriental buildings. The church's most outstanding art treasure is a big altarpiece, the gift of a salt merchant (obviously a rich one). Ten years in the making, beginning in 1505, the altarpiece depicts the Virgin with Saint Catherine and Saint Barbara.

Visitors can also go to the **Chapel of St. Michael,** a Gothic church next to the parish church. The cemetery was so small that this *karner* (charnel house or bone house) had to be used, starting in the 17th century. Some 12 to 15 years after a body had been buried in the ground the bones were transferred to the charnel house. Some skulls bear markings of the date of their owners' deaths. Other signs reveal the age of the dead, and sometimes markings show the cause of death.

The **Heimatmuseum** (local museum) is open from 10 a.m. to 4 p.m. April 1 to April 30 and October 1 to October 31; from 10 a.m. to 6 p.m. May 1 to September 30, charging an admission of 25 AS ($1.33). The museum is in the oldest secular building in the village, the 14th-century **Hallstatt-Markt.** It contains exhibits of artifacts and details the history of the region.

Numerous cable cars and lifts are found in the town and surrounding area, as well as many walking paths or hiking trails. Mountain climbing is also possible, as Dachstein (9,820 feet) is in the vicinity, and the Dachstein Giant Ice Caves can be visited, although actually the mountain is more easily reached from nearby Obertraun (see below) than from Hallstatt. You can enjoy fishing on the Hallstättersee and in the Traun River, sailing, rowing, motorboating, swimming, and tennis. In winter Hallstatt is also a sports center, with snow from November to April. You can go skiing, sledding, curling, and ice skating, or hike along pleasant winter footpaths.

"Salt Mountain"

Lying above Hallstatt to the northwest is **Salzberg** (salt mountain), not to be confused with Salzburg, the city. The salt mines are still active and can be visited. Archeologists are constantly digging in this area and have unearthed many interesting finds.

To reach the mountain, you take the cableway from Lahn and make about a 20-minute walk after getting off. The funicular runs between 8 a.m. and 4 p.m., a round trip costing 55 AS ($2.93). Guided tours of the mines are conducted from the first of May to the end of September from 9 a.m. to 6 p.m., but you can't start the tour after 4:30 p.m. Admission is 75 AS ($3.99) for adults and 40 AS ($2.13) for children over 5 (children under 5 are not admitted). Dress warmly, and be sure to wear strong walking shoes for the 2¾-hour mine tour.

There's a restaurant and snackbar with a terrace and a belvedere letting you take in the view. Hikers go all the way from here to the **Iron Age cemetery,** a trip taking about 1½ hours. If you like to hike, the tourist office will outline a series of walks in the area. One goes along the Echerntal to **Waldbachstrub** at the top of the valley, with lovely waterfalls. You can also climb to the **Tiergar-**

tenhütte, which has a small inn, and on to the **Wiesberghaus,** 6,180 feet. After that, only the hardy continue to the **Simony-Hütte** at 7,230 feet, where there's another small inn lying at the foot of the Hallstatt Glacier. From Simony-Hütte, mountain climbers go up the **Hoher Dachstein,** the loftiest peak in the massif (9,820 feet), the climb taking 3½ hours.

The Dachstein Caves

These caves are among the most spectacular natural attractions of Upper Austria. To reach them, you can drive to Obertraun, where a sign in the vicinity will direct you to the lower station of the cableway that takes you to the caves. The cableway will deposit you at the intermediate platform (4,430 feet) on the Schönbergalm. From here it's about a 20-minute walk to the entrance to the caves.

Among the many attractions is the **Giant Ice Cave,** where even in summer the temperature is about 30° Fahrenheit. Be sure to dress for the cold. Among the ice cave's breathtaking features are the frozen waterfalls. You'll also see the so-called King Arthur's Cave and the Great Ice Chapel.

The ice cave is open from the first of May until mid-October from 8:30 a.m. to 4:30 p.m., a guided tour costing 45 AS ($2.39). If you also wish to visit the **Mammoth Cave,** a combined ticket costs 70 AS ($3.72). The Mammoth Cave has large galleries (subterranean passageways) cut through the rock by some ancient underground torrent. It takes about 1½ hours to go on a conducted tour of these caves. You're allowed to visit only a small part of the network of caves, which totals 23 miles in length, with a drop of 3,870 feet.

It's possible to go from the Schönbergalm station by cableway to the upper platform at a height of 6,920 feet. This is the **Hoher Krippenstein,** which offers an excellent panoramic view of the Dachstein massif. A chapel erected in the 1950s commemorates the accidental deaths here of 13 teachers and students. A round trip to Krippenstein costs 173 AS ($9.20). Service is about every hour from 9 a.m. to 4 p.m. You may have to queue up in summer when many visitors make the trip.

From Krippenstein you can take a cable car down to **Gzaidalm** (5,880 feet).

Another cave can be visited in the area of Hallstatt, the **Koppenbrüllerhöhle,** or Koppenbrüller Cave. A torrent crosses the cave, and its activity causes continual enlargement of the cavern. The Austrians have made galleries which you can traverse for a glimpse of these turbulent underground waters.

The Koppenbrüller Cave is reached from Gasthaus Koppenrast, two miles upstream from Obertraun. You have to go on foot for about an hour. Guided tours, lasting an hour, are conducted through the cave from the first of May until the end of September from 9 a.m. to 5 p.m. for a charge of 50 AS ($2.66).

The south wall of the Dachstein can also be explored. Take a cable car known as the Gletscherbahn (glacier road) up to **Hunerkogel.** To reach the cable car, leave from Schladming, going ten miles via Ramsau on a toll road. The 12-minute cable-car ride leaves from 8 a.m. to 5 p.m. At the upper belvedere (8,840 feet) a magnificent view spreads out before you. You'll be able to see the Grossglockner as well as the Salzkammergut Alps. At Hunerkogel it's possible to ski in summer on the Schladminger Gletscher (small glacier).

FOOD AND LODGING: Seehotel Grüner Baum (tel. 263) has a churchside location in a quiet spot between the lake and a baroque fountain in the center of town. It's capped with a hipped roof of hammered copper and has an ochre-colored facade with white, heavily bordered windows. Its simple and comfortable rooms are accented with wood trim and often get lots of sunshine. The hotel's sun terrace extends out over the water on a pier, where you can go swimming or simply lie on a chaise longue with a drink if you want to. Later in the day you can sample local lake fish in the restaurant or on the terrace. The hotel is closed between mid-October and May. The rest of the year it charges from 250 AS ($13.30) to 430 AS ($22.88) for a single and 480 AS ($25.54) to 865 AS ($46.02) for a double, with breakfast included. Prices depend on the plumbing and the accommodation.

Hotel Krippenstein (tel. 7129). Rarely have I seen such an inhospitable spot for a hotel—it stands on a rocky bluff which you can reach after taking three stages of cableways. It's billed as the tourist attraction with the highest elevation in all of Upper Austria. It looks like a concrete fortress as you approach it from the lichen-covered rocks below. In wintertime it's ideally suited for skiers, although the views of the glacier in summer are well worth the trip here. The 80 beds rent for 380 AS ($20.22) for a single, while rates in a double range from 380 AS ($20.22) to 420 AS ($22.34) per person, with half board included.

Under the same management is the **Schönnberghaus** (tel. 27323). This might be the ideal departure point for excursions to the ice caves of the Dachstein massif. Located at the end of the first stage of the Dachstein cableway, it's built entirely of wood, and offers a sunny terrace, a 100-seat restaurant, and 40 beds. Your neighbors in the next room might be one of the youth groups who sometimes rent out large blocks of beds for nature excursions. With half board included, the per-person rate is around 320 AS ($17.02) daily.

OBERTRAUN: This is a small village which because of its location is often overrun with visitors. It opens directly onto Hallstättersee at an elevation of about 1,960 feet. Obertraun is one of the most popular places to begin many sightseeing excursions in the district, especially to the Dachstein. For a rundown on tours, refer to the Hallstatt description (see above).

Skiers, including many from Great Britain, come here in winter to take advantage of several ski lifts in the area and to enjoy the slopes of the Krippenstein mountain mentioned above. Only the most dedicated skiers will wish to stay at Obertraun, as there is little après-ski activity here. Nonskiers will definitely want to seek out more exciting resorts in the winter. As a summer center, however, it's far livelier, being such a fine excursion base.

The area code for Obertraun is 06134.

Food and Lodging

Gasthof Zum Sarstein (tel. 331) is a pleasant roadside guest house with a pale-yellow facade in a verdant setting surrounded by trees. A café offers midday refreshment. The comfortable rooms rent for 200 AS ($10.64) for a single and 400 AS ($21.28) to 550 AS ($29.26) in a double, with breakfast included. Half board is also available. Open May to September.

GOSAU: This little village can be a happy alternative to staying at Hallstatt, as its prices are much more reasonable. Relatively little known, Gosau lies six miles west of Hallstättersee in the vicinity of the Gschütt Pass. Because it's in a ski region the village attracts winter business. Some of the Dachstein ski tours leave from here.

Gosau is also an ideal base for some summer touring. A road running south for about five miles leads to the Gosausee (Lake of Gosau), a mountain lake at 3,060 feet, encircled by steep rock walls. From here you can see the Gosau Glacier and the Dachstein (9,820 feet), surrounded by glaciers. The best view is from the lower lake.

It's popular to board a funicular going up to Gablonzer Hütte (5,200 feet), where you can enjoy snacks as you take in the view. The surrounding ski area is called the Swieselalm. A panoramic vista takes in the Hohe Tauern. Adventurers can climb to the top of Grosser Donnerkogel in about 2½ hours.

Gosau's area code is 06136.

Food and Lodging

Sommerhof (tel. 258) is separated from the road by a generous parking lot and a gracefully curved series of stone-flanked steps. From the sun terrace you can study the gold and white floral designs decorating the facade. You can also compare the artist's rendition to the masses of real flowers growing from the balconies. The interior has coffered wood ceilings painted in regional patterns, well-placed stone columns under beautifully illustrated arches, and cozy, well-furnished bedrooms, all of which contain private bath. Many of the local residents who come here to socialize in the evening still wear regional garb. With full board included, per-person rates range from 440 AS ($23.41) to 480 AS ($25.54), depending on the season and the plumbing.

Hotel-Pension Koller (tel. 207). The architecture of this Victorian-style building isn't the only unusual aspect about it. It sits on an expanse of lawn into which has been set a slate-ringed swimming pool. In the background rises a knife-edged series of jagged mountains. The hotel is built with arched loggias, recessed balconies, a series of hip and gabled roofs, and a feudal-style tower covered with cedar shingles. Forests come almost to the back door, but from the front the view is uninterrupted for several hundred feet. Inside you'll find winter fireplaces giving off a welcome warmth, plus a cozy weinstube and Sattelbar. The Koller family charges from 360 AS ($19.15) to 450 AS ($23.94) per person for half board, taxes included in the rates. Guests enjoy such special events as fondue evenings, candlelit dinners, and zither evenings.

6. The Traunsee

One of the biggest lakes in the Salzkammergut, the Traunsee is about 7½ miles long and some 2 miles wide at its broadest expanse, and lies to the east of the two major lakes already explored: the Attersee and the Mondsee. Three mountain peaks—Traunstein, Hochkogel, and Eriakogel—make a silhouette which Austrians call *Schlafende Griechin* (sleeping Greek girl). Some sections of the Salzkammergut road run along the western edge of the lake.

The most dramatic part of this road is from Ebensee, at the southwestern tip of the lake, to Trauenkirchen. This spectacular corniche had to be hewn out of rock. The Traunsee is ringed with a number of resorts, the chief town being Gmunden. There's lake steamer service in summer. To reach this lake from Bad Ischl (see above), you drive northeast along the Traun River.

Your first stopover along the Traunsee will be at—

EBENSEE: This resort town on the southern Traunsee lakeside draws visitors by its scenic splendors and its mild, constant climate. It's a good base for excursions into the mountains or along the lake.

For summer visitors there are natural bathing beaches, trips to the **Gassi Stalactite Cavern,** windsurfing, diving, fishing, and boating. In winter the alpine plateau in the nearby Hollengebirge massif offers 15½ square miles of ski area with practice slopes, descents into the valley, and ski hikes. This avalanche-free region has snow from December until April. There are eight ski lifts.

You can reach Ebensee by road from Bad Ischl (see above) or by train.

The Ebensee area code is 06133.

Food and Lodging

Hotel Post (tel. 208) is set far back from the street where it stands in the center of town near the Rathaus. Because it's designed like a chalet, many of the rooms have private balconies. The tasteful interior gives the impression of being older than it actually is. Parts of it have vaulted ceilings, lots of exposed wood, and unusual wall murals showing idyllic scenes of village life. The streamlined bedrooms have contemporary furniture and all the comforts you'd expect, including private bath. Singles range from 260 AS ($13.83) to 380 AS ($20.22), while doubles cost from 240 AS ($12.77) to 320 AS ($17.02) per person, with breakfast included. Prices depend on the season and the accommodation.

TRAUENKIRCHEN: Built on a peninsula out into the Traunsee on the western shore is this little summer resort village, once the support facility for a Benedictine abbey at the peninsula's tip. After the Benedictines, the Jesuits occupied the abbey until the 17th century.

If time permits, visit the baroque **pfarrkirche** (parish church). Its pulpit is shaped like a sailing vessel, sculptured figures depicting the catching of fish by Christ's disciples. Nearby is the 17th-century **Chapel of St. Michael.**

Trauenkirchen's area code is 07617.

Food and Lodging

Hotel Post (tel. 2307) is a friendly, balconied hotel with a ground-floor series of rounded arches which lead onto a popular daytime café terrace. Painted a pale yellow to set off the weathered balconies and the gray and white illustrations, the hotel sits on the main square of the village. Heinz and Renate Gröller are the attractive couple who run this spacious establishment. The public rooms are tastefully furnished, and the bedrooms have modern furniture, wall-to-wall carpets, and private baths. With half board included, rates in doubles range from 480 AS ($25.54) to 520 AS ($27.66) per person. Singles pay a daily surcharge of 75 AS ($3.99).

Hotel am Stein (tel. 203) is a rambling hotel which sits beside a lakeside road about a mile outside the village. It has its own private beach, as well as a terrace where guests can enjoy the sunshine with a cup of coffee or a drink. A Victorian-style pub in an English format of massive wood detailing and wrought-iron tables is also a disco, and there are two restaurants. Bedrooms, all with private bath, rent for 360 AS ($19.15) per person daily, with breakfast included. Half board is offered for another 110 AS ($5.85) per person per day. Ivelin H. Rabl is your congenial host. In July and August, the ferryboat stops at the hotel's landing stage.

GMUNDEN: This is one of the most popular summer resorts in the Salzkammergut, perched on the northern rim of the Traunsee with pine-green mountains as a backdrop.

Chestnut trees line the mile-long, traffic-free **Esplanade,** the town's chief attraction. You can walk from the **Rathausplatz** (town hall square) to the **Strandbad** (the lakeside beach), watching the many majestic swans glide serenely along the lake. In days of yore emperors and kings and members of the aristocracy strolled along the Esplanade and in the town's park, just as you can do today. The Welfen from Hannover, Württembergs, Bourbons, and diverse archdukes of Austria favored Gmunden as a pleasure ground, as did Franz Schubert, Friedrich Hebbel, and Johannes Brahms, among others.

The lake beaches are some of the best in the whole area, and in summer you can enjoy the varied lakeside activities, such as watching folkloric performances, dancing in discos, or relaxing in a cozy wine tavern or at an outdoor café. You can also bathe in the open-air swimming pool. Sailing, windsurfing, waterskiing, riding, and tennis are all available here. Perhaps you'd like to go mountaineering in the vicinity of this gemütlich town.

Gmunden, former center of the salt trade, has long produced Gmundner ceramics, and you'll see artistic work in faïence and green-flamed pottery.

A curiosity of the town is the **Orth Schloss,** or Palace of Orth, built on the Roman foundations of a small artificial island in the lake, connected to the town by a breakwater. Photographs of this palace are the most characteristic pictures taken of Gmunden, and one always graces the covers of tourist brochures luring visitors to the area. The gatehouse of the schloss, now the headquarters of an Austrian forestry school, is crowned by an onion-shape dome. To reach the schloss, you walk across a 140-yard-long wooden bridge. Once there, you go into an inner courtyard flanked by arcaded galleries.

The palace got its name from its occupant, Johann Orth, the assumed name of Archduke Salvator, nephew of Emperor Franz Joseph. Growing bored with the court life in Vienna, the archduke came here in 1878 to take up life as Johann Orth. Johann or Salvator, whichever, he died mysteriously off the coast of South America in 1891.

The **parish church** *(pfarrkirche)* of Gmunden was built in the 15th century and given the inevitable baroque overlay in the 18th century. Thomas Schwanthaler carved the main altar with scenes of the Three Kings of Orient (the Magi) in 1678.

From Gmunden you can go by cableway in 12 minutes to the top of the **Grünberg,** where you have a view down the Traunsee which has a fjord-like look at its southern end, with limestone rock faces rising almost vertically. The Dachstein completes the view. In winter, ski lifts, runs, and slopes on the Grünberg are easily reached. Also, curling, ice skating, and winter walks along the lake are available in Gmunden.

The Gmunden area code is 07612.

Food and Lodging

Parkhotel am See (tel. 4230) is a long, low-lying building capped with a red tile roof and an illuminated sign telling the name of the hotel. Between it and the lake someone has planted a rose garden and lots of begonias. The antiques inside include polychrome sculptures, painted double armoires, and gilt-covered 19th-century scroll-back chairs covered in pink satin.

One of my favorite rooms is the spacious lakeside restaurant, where you can sit either indoors or on the covered balcony where the first thing you'll see above your head is a verdant canopy of ivy. The Holzinger sisters maintain swimming facilities off a private pier. A Victorian-style bar is on the premises, where you might want to drink after returning from a five-minute walk to the center of town.

With full board included, singles rent for 620 AS ($34.58) to 880 AS ($46.82), while doubles cost from 545 AS ($28.99) to 800 AS ($42.56) per person, depending on the plumbing, the season, and the accommodation. The hotel is open from the end of May to the end of September.

Schlosshotel Freisitz (tel. 4905) sits on a hill overlooking the lake. Its design looks like a combination of a baroque private house and a Victorian-style hotel. Its dozens of architectural oddities include a crenellated tower with tall arched windows, wrought-iron window bars, and jutting parapets over many of the balconied windows, and a stone terrace built into the slope of the grass-covered hill.

The interior has been renovated and today incorporates lots of modern building materials with the older stone-accented design. However, many of the original vaulted ceilings remain. Singles rent for 650 AS ($34.58) to 790 AS ($42.03), while doubles go for 580 AS ($30.87) to 630 AS ($33.52) per person, with full board included. The hotel is open from April to October.

Seehotel Schwan (tel. 3391) is a beautifully detailed 19th-century hotel on the main square of town at the edge of the water. Its neoclassical design includes arched pediments above many of the windows, a gabled roof, and château-style corner towers. Painted white, like the bird it's named for, the hotel has a private mineral bath and a sauna on the premises. The well-furnished bedrooms are comfortable, and usually offer good views of both the town and the lake. Singles range from 360 AS ($19.15) to 750 AS ($39.90), while doubles cost from 600 AS ($31.92) to 1,250 AS ($66.50) per person, with breakfast included. Prices depend on the plumbing and the season.

Waldhotel Marienbrücke (tel. 4011) is a large, hip-roofed chalet with gables, balconies, and a pleasing facade of wood and stucco. Many of the clients are fishermen who spend part of their days angling for trout in the nearby river. Rates, with full board included, are around 475 AS ($25.27) per person.

Pension Haus Magerl, 18 Ackerweg (tel. 3675), has a long elegant facade with white full-length shutters which embellish a double row of balconied french windows. It sits in a grassy meadow with a view overlooking the lake. The clean and attractively simple public rooms have big, sunny windows and rustic wall coverings. On the premises are a sauna, an indoor pool, and a TV room. Prices range from 420 AS ($22.34) to 560 AS ($29.79) per person, with full board included.

Restaurant Wandl-Stuben (tel. 3884) lies in the center of town in a historic building with arcades. The inside is filled with dark paneling and lots of dimly lit niches, ideal for intimate conversations. By candlelight you read the menu, which offers one of the best assortments of food at the resort. Specialties include fresh lake fish, game, alpine lamb dishes, and a combination of old Austrian recipes and modern cuisine: oysters with mushrooms, butter, and onions, along with a host of regional specialties. Some of these feature savory and well-prepared meat dishes such as chateaubriand for two, medallions of pork in cream sauce, veal steak Luzern, and tournedos with a cognac cream sauce. Desserts include a range of warm sweets, such as banana flambé with chocolate sauce and walnut ice cream with plum-flavored whipped cream. Full meals cost from 225 AS ($11.97). The restaurant is open every day for lunch and dinner, except Monday between the months of October and May.

GRÜNAU IN ALMTAL:

It's not on the Traunsee, but Grünau in Almtal, lying to the east of that lake, with good accommodations and restaurants as well as a wildlife park, might be a good stopover for you. It's often less crowded in summer than resorts on the Traunsee, and it occupies a beautiful position in the Alm Valley.

The wide valley lies about 9½ miles east of our last stopover, Gmunden. To reach Grünau, you will pass through **Scharnstein,** which has a 17th-century castle housing the Austrian Museum of Criminal Law. About five miles southward, you come to this summer holiday resort. You'll find the celebrated **Kremsmünster Abbey** to the northeast, if you'd like to make a day's excursion.

Cumberland Wildlife Park (tel. 8205) lies four miles south of Grünau. Here you'll see otters, beavers, brown bears, and other animals. There's a restaurant at the park, plus a museum devoted to forestry.

If you continue on south along the Alm Valley, you'll reach Almsee, a lake at 2,810 feet.

The area code for Grünau in Almtal is 07616.

Food and Lodging

Romantik Hotel und Restaurant Almtalhof (tel. 8204) offers a fairytale setting which should appeal to nostalgics around the world. The four-story solidly built chalet has masses of live flowers covering the window boxes and decorative flowers painted onto the regional furniture scattered throughout the hotel. The decor is romantic, charming, and worthy of an extended stay. The intimate bedrooms offer coffered ceilings, elaborate wrought-iron chandeliers, and pink bedding that contrast with the light-grained pine of the wall paneling. The Leithner family charges from 500 AS ($26.60) to 550 AS ($29.26) for a single and from 450 AS ($23.94) to 550 AS ($29.26) for a double, with breakfast included.

The large and elegant dining room has well-polished slats of vertical paneling, stained-glass window medallions, and a collection of old pewter and hunting trophies. Menu items are traditional and Austrian. They include schnitzels, roast beef, roast pork, pork cutlets with apples, a selection of wild game, and an unusual salad with a dressing of yogurt and marinated cabbage. À la carte meals range from 150 AS ($7.98) to 350 AS ($18.62), while fixed-price dinners cost from 220 AS ($11.70) to 450 AS ($23.94). Both the hotel and restaurant are closed between early October and about a week before Christmas and from mid-January until the end of March.

Gasthof Deutsches Haus (tel. 802118) is a small, green-shuttered family-run hotel with two floors of cozy bedrooms. The ground-floor dining room has alpine furniture and a green tile oven under the beamed ceiling. The sun terrace looks out over a small lake, which is set in a quiet and restful location six miles from the nearest village. The restaurant serves home-style meals, with freshly caught lake trout prepared in several different ways. With half board included, per-person rates are around 280 AS ($14.90) per day. The hotel is open from the first of May until the end of September.

Pension Hochhaus (tel. 8241) offers 25 modern and comfortable bedrooms, all of which are maintained by members of the Schiefermayr family. Guests have free use of the large garden and its adjoining terrace. Charges range from 275 AS ($14.63) to 325 AS ($17.29) per person for half-board accommodations, depending on the season and the plumbing.

Restaurant Seehaus (tel. 802101) occupies an idyllic lakeside spot ten miles from the center of Grünau, which gives local residents the perfect excuse to make a midsummer excursion. The building is a long elegant construction that offers only one apartment to visitors, priced at 300 AS ($15.96) per person nightly, including breakfast. The rest of the time the Seehaus is mainly a restaurant, featuring gutbürgerlich regional fare served in generous portions, with meals costing from 250 AS ($13.30). The restaurant is open mid-April to mid-September from 9 a.m. to 6 p.m.

7. Wels

A flourishing town in Roman times, Wels lies on the left bank of the Traun River in the center of a large farm belt and is known today for its agricultural fairs. It can be reached by heading north from Gmunden after your visit there. It's also an easy drive southwest from Linz. Wels is most often used as a base for exploring the hinterlands, although it has some attractions of its own. In about 1½ hours you can walk through the town, seeing its chief sights.

The Wels area code is 07242.

THE SIGHTS: The **Stadtplatz** is considered one of the most architecturally harmonious town squares in Austria, with beautifully decorated facades of old houses and an intricately carved fountain. It is broad and cobbled. Most of the houses date from the 16th to the 18th centuries. The baroque-style **Rathaus** (town hall), built in 1748, is one of the most ornate buildings in the old town. The **Ledererturm,** dating from 1618, is the only tower remaining of those that once studded the town walls. Many homes or shops in the old town are held up by arches and passageways with vaulted ceilings.

Emperor Maximilian I died in Wels in 1519, stricken as he was traveling from the Tyrolean country to Wiener Neustadt. The house in which he died is called the **Kaiserliche Burg.** On Burggasse, it has been turned into a museum of minor importance. You can see the room in which the emperor breathed his last.

The **Stadtpfarrkirche** (town parish church) has a 14th-century Gothic chancel and three stained-glass windows from that same century. The entire church was once Gothic until baroque architects went to work on it. The Romanesque inner doorway is surmounted by a tower with a bulbous dome, dating from 1732.

Across from the church stands the **Salome Alt house.** She was the mistress and mother of the dozen children of Prince-Archbishop Wolf Dietrich who is encountered so frequently in Salzburg history. Following the disgrace and overthrow of this ecclesiastic, he retired to Wels.

On the Ringstrasse you can see what is left of **Schloss Pollheim,** where, the story goes, the shoemaker-poet Hans Sachs lived. Wagner is said to have based his character in *Die Meistersinger von Nürnberg* on Sachs.

Wels is a town which has moved into the future industrially, as witness its chemical plants, but it also clings to its imperial past.

FOOD AND LODGING: Hotel Greif, 50 Kaiser-Josef-Platz (tel. 5361), has a substantial-looking masonry facade in the center of town. The exterior hasn't been embellished in any way other than an occasional balcony, but the dining room inside has a renovated red and white Viennese-style decor of mirrors, crystal chandeliers, and high ceilings. Pleasantly furnished singles range from 350 AS ($18.62) to 700 AS ($37.24), while doubles cost 700 AS ($37.24) to 1,000 AS ($53.20) per room, with breakfast included.

Gasthof Bayrischer Hof, 23 Dr.-Schauer-Strasse (tel. 7214), is easy to recognize because of its elegant blue-and-white facade with neoclassical window treatments and a mansard tower extending upward from the building's exposed corner. The garden café is an inviting place to spend part of a warm midday. The simple bedrooms usually contain a wooden armoire and bedside tables, as well as an assortment of autumnal colors. The owner, Helmut Platzer, rents singles for 285 AS ($15.16) to 400 AS ($21.28) and doubles for 500 AS ($26.60) to 600 AS ($31.92).

Restaurant Wirt am Berg, 6 Berg (tel. 5059), was established in 1630 and has been in the same family since 1881. Prominent diners have included Field Marshal Göring, a host of Olympic champions, and the royal family of Monaco. Four kilometers outside Wels, the three-story restaurant is painted a deep yellow-orange and opens into a series of rustically decorated dining rooms with lots of hunting trophies.

On warm days you might prefer to eat under the chestnut trees on the brick-covered terrace. Wild game is the most popular item on the menu in hunting season, although at any time of year you can still enjoy an appetizer of terrine of wild deer with cumberland sauce, quail liver cocktail with vinaigrette sauce, or consommé of pheasant. This could be followed by venison ragoût, tafelspitz, veal or pork liver, or three kinds of schnitzels. Dessert might be a rum-flavored knockerl with nuts or a homemade flaky-crusted strudel. À la carte meals range from 150 AS ($7.98) to 430 AS ($22.88), depending on what you order. The restaurant also sells more than 100 kinds of wine. It's closed on Monday.

Café-Konditorei Urbann, 20 Schmidtgasse (tel. 6051), is the best-known café in town, offering a tree-shaded summer garden where you're likely to see all kinds of people, many of them local residents who show up every day for their usual cup of coffee and favorite pastry. Near the train station, the café prepares freshly made specialties such as handmade chocolate truffles, marzipan and nut kugeln, homemade gingerbread (wintertime only), and homemade jams and ice creams.

The place prefers not to be classified as a restaurant, but nonetheless serves sandwiches, toasts, and eggs. Coffee ranges from 18 AS (96¢) to 38 AS ($2.02), while pastries and ice creams average around 35 AS ($1.86) apiece. The Urban family has owned this place since 1853, and there was a candle and gingerbread shop on the premises from as early as 1630. It's open from 8 a.m. to 7 p.m. Monday to Saturday. The store is open on Sunday every season except summer from 9 a.m. to 7 p.m.

BAD SCHALLERBACH: This well-known Austrian spa lies nine miles northwest of Wels and can easily be visited on a half-day excursion, unless you want to anchor here and "take the cure." The spa is known for its hot sulfur springs. It has both indoor and outdoor swimming pools and is visited mainly in the summer months by an essentially European clientele.

Bad Schallerbach's area code is 07249.

Where to Dine

Grünes Turl, Gebersdorf (tel. 8163), was a farm complex first mentioned in a title deed in 1570. It was transformed by Herbert and Doris Ameshofer into a cozy restaurant which today combines well-prepared cuisine with an antique setting. It looks like an elongated white-walled building with two floors of flowered windows, a gently sloping roof, and a big sun terrace for afternoon meals. Food is usually served in the vaulted dining room whose ceiling is supported with short stone columns. Your dinner might include generous portions of pork medallions in an herb sauce, an array of fresh fish, a platter of seasonal venison, and most definitely, an old Austrian favorite, cabbage cream soup. Desserts are homemade and satisfyingly caloric. Full meals cost from 80 AS ($4.26) and 350 AS ($18.62), depending on your appetite and tastes.

TOURING THE ABBEYS: The two most popular excursions from Wels, to sites that are among the most outstanding sightseeing attractions of Upper Austria, will take you first to—

Lambach Abbey

In 1056 a Benedictine abbey was founded at Lambach, 10 miles southwest of Wels and about 15 miles north of the Traunsee. It stands at a point where the Traun River meets its tributary, the Ager. The once Romanesque monastery, which stands in the Marktplatz of the old market town, has changed its face since its early days, now showing a splendid baroque exterior. A towering marble gateway from 1693 leads into the first courtyard.

In the so-called ringing chamber, you can see one of the major attractions of the abbey, Romanesque frescoes from the 11th century. These works of art were once hidden but later discovered. They were restored in 1968 and put on public view, an event hailed by the Austrian press. The frescoes may be seen only on a guided tour May through mid-October from 9 to 11 a.m. and from 2 to 5 p.m. (opens an hour later on Sunday). Off-season hours are 10 a.m. to noon and 3 to 4 p.m. (again opens an hour later on Sunday). Admission is 15 AS (80¢).

The abbey's other attractions include a richly embellished library and a rather sumptuous refectory from the 18th century. There's also a painting gallery with, among other works, some notable pictures by Kremser Schmidt.

The abbey church was built in the 1650s, and its main altar is believed to have been designed by the celebrated baroque architect J. B. Fischer von Erlach. The only surviving monastic theater in Austria, built in 1746, is reached by a stairway.

Kremsmünster Abbey

Near Bad Hall, between the emerging hills of the Alps and the Danube River, overlooking the Valley of Krems, this Benedictine abbey was founded in 777. Two domed towers of the abbey church dominate the local skyline. This abbey, lying 22 miles southwest of Linz, was founded by order of Tassilo III, a Bavarian duke whose son Gunther was killed by a wild boar during a hunt. The abbey was erected to honor the memory of the duke's son. It was, of course, Romanesque, but in the 17th and 18th centuries the old abbey was given the baroque treatment.

The most outstanding feature of a tour through Kremsmünster is the **Fischbehalter,** or fish pond, built by the noted architect Carlo Antonio Carlone. It has five basins, each encircled by arcades, with statues that spout water. Figures depict everybody from Samson to Neptune.

In the cluster of abbey buildings the **Kaisersaal,** or hall of the emperors, has a collection of portraits of sovereigns of the Holy Roman Empire, painted by Altomonte at the end of the 17th century. One of the most outstanding works of art is a *Crucifixion* by Quentin Massys. The abbey still owns the chalice of Tassilo that was presented to the monks by the founding duke. It's the most ancient piece of goldsmith's work in either Austria or Bavaria, the duke's home. In the library is a celebrated manuscript, the *Codex Millenarius,* an 8th-century translation of the gospels.

An observatory tower rising nearly 200 feet has an exhibition of materials associated with astronomy and other sciences. This observatory has been called the first skyscraper in Europe.

Many noted men have been pupils at the abbey school, including the novelist Adalbert Stifter.

Tours are conducted through the abbey from Easter Sunday to the end of October at 9 and 10:30 a.m. and again at 2 and 3:30 p.m. Allow about three hours for a tour of "the whole works." Admission is 55 AS ($2.93).

BAD HALL: After leaving Kremsmünster Abbey, if you drive six miles southeast you'll find this well-known spa, whose iodine brine springs are among the most powerful in the heart of Europe. Its thermal park, covering nearly 90 acres, is beautifully landscaped.

You can visit the handsomely decorated **pfarrkirche** (parish church), from around the mid-18th century. Its vaulting is richly frescoed, and the baroque love of statues and cherubs is evidenced throughout.

On summer days, sacred-music concerts are presented here. You can learn the dates and hours of these recitals from the local tourist office.

The Bad Hall area code is 07258.

Food and Lodging

Schlosshotel Feyregg (tel. 2591) has been called one of the most beautiful castles in the pre-alpine regions of Austria. When it was built it served as the summer residence of the abbots from the monastery of Spital am Phyrn. The furnishings look like something from a museum and are usually accurate to the baroque origin of the castle itself. The bedrooms are large and also beautifully furnished. The entire hotel offers only about a dozen rooms, each of which has a private bath, renting for 550 AS ($29.26) per person, including breakfast.

Kurhotel (tel. 2611) is composed of four elegant villas a short distance away from one another in the middle of a 75-acre park just outside the center of town. This is the only hotel in Bad Hall with a complete inventory of cure facilities, administered by health care professionals. Each of the villas has a design which gives the impression that a grand duke will descend from a carriage in front of the portico at any moment. The interiors have been modernized but still evoke their former opulence, even though few of the original furnishings remain. The charges vary slightly for accommodations in the four buildings, but range from 600 AS ($31.92) to 970 AS ($51.60) for a single and from 600 AS ($31.92) to 1,030 AS ($54.80) per person in a double, with full board included.

Hotel Haller Hof, 27 Hauptplatz (tel. 2490), is a centrally located hotel designed around a concrete cube with a long, big-windowed extension stretching out back. The interior is filled with furniture which might have had its heyday in the late 1950s, although everything is clean and well-maintained by the capable owner, Ferdinand Lindinger. Singles range from 175 AS ($9.31) to 300 AS ($15.96), while doubles cost 400 AS ($21.28) to 525 AS ($27.93), depending on the accommodation, the plumbing, and the season. Breakfast is included in these tariffs. For clients staying less than three days the management adds another 20% to the above prices. The hotel is open only from the end of April until the end of October.

8. The Southeast Corner

After visiting the renowned Kremsmünster Abbey and Bad Hall, you can head south along the Steyr River into an area little known to North Americans —the southeast corner of Upper Austria, bordering Styria. This section where many discoveries await you is known as **Pyhrn-Eisenwurzen.**

If you're ready for lunch, you might want to stop at either Molln or Klaus, coming up.

MOLLN: After traveling along the Steyr River, you can veer southeast off Route 140 at Leonstein to the little hamlet of Molln (area code 07584) and this very fine restaurant.

Restaurant Martinsklause (tel. 2916). The specialties here are numerous, served in generous quantities and delicately flavored. They include pâté of trout with toast, homemade spiced ham with apple horseradish, veal medallions with fresh tarragon, salt pork "Upper Austria" with bread dumplings, apple dumpling with nuts in an apple wine sauce, and many different kinds of strudel. Average meals cost from 150 AS ($7.98) to 200 AS ($10.64). Warm food is served from 11 a.m. to 1:30 p.m. and from 6 to 8 p.m. However, the place is open from 8 a.m. to midnight for drinks and snacks.

KLAUS: In the heart of the Pyhrn-Eisenwurzen district, Klaus is a village set in the midst of some of the most splendid scenery in Upper Austria.

The hamlet, just north of the Klauser See, a beautiful lake, has developed into a popular resort since construction of the reservoir for the hydroelectric power station Klaus. Now a paradise for wild-water enthusiasts and also for canoeing more quietly along the river, Klaus has a special school for kayaking and paddling.

The area code at Klaus is 07585.

Food and Lodging

Hotel Schinagl (tel. 261). The painted illustration on the front of this partially balconied chalet is of a regionally dressed man and woman courting one another. The friendly ambience inside might encourage you to do exactly the same. On the premises is a rustically paneled stand-up bar, lots of big-windowed panoramas, and a series of comfortable chairs grouped into conversational units. Sporting facilities of the region will be described by Erich Mentil. Prices range from 525 AS ($27.93) to 590 AS ($31.39) per person, with full board included. Prices depend on the accommodation, the plumbing, and the season. An evening in the cellar bar is often devoted to live dance music.

VORDERSTODER: After passing by the Klauser See, you can make a detour into the high mountain valley known as **Stodertal**. It lies directly east of the Totes Gebirge mountain range. The upper part of the Steyr River flows through this scenic valley. You'll pass by the Stromboding Waterfall, which drops some 85 feet.

Along the way, you'll find a scenic stopover at the following recommendation:

Pension/Restaurant Stockerwirt (tel. 07564/8214) is beautifully situated on the slope of a hill with a view of the snow-covered mountains. The roof has a long expanse of interconnected gables, with a covering of red tile. The portico covering the entrance is fashioned of burnished sheet metal, hammered into graceful curves. The hotel on this site has been in the same family since 1664, although the format today has been significantly updated. You'll find a covered swimming pool on the premises, an immaculately clean kitchen serving well-prepared meals in a panoramic setting, and a vaulted entrance hall with lots of paneling. Charges, with full board included, range from 360 AS ($19.15) to 420 AS ($22.34) per person. Open December to October.

HINTERSTODER: The Steyr River wends its way through Hinterstoder, the valley's chief resort, which is so remote it has no through traffic. It's about four miles from the principal Linz/Graz artery. Lying directly under the Totes Gebirge massif, the town has combined with Windischgarsten (coming up) and Spital am Pyhrn to become an emerging ski resort area in Upper Austria. Hinterstoder has the widest range of accommodations, but if you're selecting a hotel, you might want to consider the possibilities of the other two villages, since the three resorts are within easy reach of one another.

Hinterstoder, which is both a summer and a winter holiday village, has a good ski school. A chair lift will transport you to Hutterer Böden (4,550 feet), the middle station on the ascent, where you'll find several ski lifts as well as a hotel. From here you can take a chair lift to Hutterer Höss (6,230) feet, where there's a mountain restaurant.

Another ski area, the Dietlgut-Bärenalm, lies about two miles from Hinterstoder at the far end of the valley. In winter a ski bus connects it to the center of the resort area. Once there you can take a double-chair lift to Bärenalm (3,950 feet), where you'll find another mountain restaurant.

The Hinterstoder area code is 07564.

Food and Lodging

Berghotel (tel. 54210) is shaped like a gently sloping pyramid, with flowered rows of parallel balconies in front of oversize bedroom windows. The hotel lies above Hinterstoder at the middle station of the chair lift, which shuts down every day at 5 p.m. You can get there by car, but in winter—their high season—you must use chairs. The hotel offers many sports and fitness facilities, including a gym, a sauna, and an indoor pool. Most of the private accommodations front a southern exposure and contain private baths, balconies, and a view of the well-maintained lawn that many of the guests use for midsummer sunbathing. The disco-keller, if it were located in your hometown, might become one of your preferred hangouts. The Jungreithmair family are the attractive and considerate owners of this hotel. They charge from 500 AS ($26.60) to 600 AS ($31.92) per person, with half board included. Prices depend on the season and the accommodation.

Sporthotel Stoderhof (tel. 5266) is the major hotel in the village, right in the center with a rambling modern format of white walls and a gently sloping gabled roof. A glass-walled greenhouse-type construction extends toward the sun terrace, behind which is an indoor swimming pool. Ilse and Erich Fruhmann might be the best loved innkeepers in Hinterstoder, and many guests believe that Ilse is certainly the most gracious hostess in the entire valley. At the same time her husband Erich is considered the best chef in the village. The hotel lies only a short distance from the chair lifts. The good-size rooms are comfortably furnished. With full board included, the cost per person in a double is 620 AS ($32.98). Occupants of a single pay another 50 AS ($2.66) per day.

Pension Dietlgut (tel. 5248) consists of one house with a series of adjacent outbuildings. The style is unabashedly romantic, with steep roofs, exposed cross-timbering, and an idyllic setting in a grassy area at the foot of a rocky cliff. It lies at the end of the valley. If you stay here it's best to have a car because of its distance from the village. The pension is known for its collection of hunting trophies which cover the walls of one of the antique-filled public rooms. In one of the sitting rooms the amber-colored paneling is arranged in an unusual and attractive pattern of random vertical and horizontal lines. The well-kept bedrooms rent for 440 AS ($23.41) to 570 AS ($30.32) in a single and 420 AS ($22.34) to 550 AS ($29.26) per person in a double. These prices include half board and depend on the plumbing and the season. The owners do much to make you comfortable.

WINDISCHGARSTEN: This resort lies in a sunny valley at an elevation of about 1,960 feet, about a half-hour drive from Hinterstoder, just visited. It's a typical Austrian village, with much old-fashioned charm and character, unspoiled so far by the inroads of modern tourism

Skiing is limited in winter, as this is only an emerging ski resort. A single chair lift goes to the highest station at 2,800 feet. The après-ski life here is unpretentious and not highly organized, but some does exist, especially in the cellars of the hotels. However, if you'd like a change of pace you can take a bus ride and be deposited at Spital am Pyhrn (coming up) in just 18 minutes.

With a lovely church spire piercing the winter sky and a blanket of snow covering the entire village for much of the winter, Windischgarsten is starkly picturesque, but I still prefer it in summer when the valley is green, the sun reflects off the russet-colored roofs, and the towering, snow-capped mountains form a dramatic background.

The area code for Windischgarsten is 07562.

Food and Lodging

Hotel Bischofsberg, 31 Edlbach (tel. 455), is a graceful collection of chalet-style buildings set on the side of a hill with a view over the mountains. On the downhill side of the hotel you'll find a rose garden flanking an outdoor pool. From the front you'll notice the summertime café terrace and the painted embellishments around each of the windows. The inside is decorated with enough rusticity to make anyone feel at home. In the center of one of the sitting rooms, a stucco and ceramic tile oven gives off wintertime heat below the heavy beams of the paneled ceiling.

The light from the big windows against one wall of the spacious restaurant not only illumines the pink and white napery on your table, but nourishes the potted trees growing in the center of the room. The Löger family (which has so many members that it's almost like a village in itself) are the owners and managers of this attractive hotel. With full board included, the charge is 485 AS ($25.80) to 630 AS ($33.52) per person. All rooms contain private bath, and there's also an indoor swimming pool.

Sporthotel Baumschlager (tel. 8282) is a pretty chalet directed by Hans and Gerda Baumschlager, who rank among the region's most experienced hoteliers. Part of the establishment's ground floor is accented with an arched arcade, the roof of which supports a popular café terrace. The third- and fourth-floor balconies are festooned with flowers that are reflected in the glass of the doors leading into the attractive bedrooms. On the premises is a swimming pool, plus an outdoor tennis court, a sauna, a solarium, a bar, and a restaurant, the latter specializing in venison, fish, and regional recipes. In season it serves such delights as fresh asparagus and strawberries. Rates average 500 AS ($26.60) per person daily, with half board included.

Hotel/Pension Schwarzes-Rössl (tel. 311) is a long-established hotel in the center of town. It's housed in an elegantly symmetrical gray building with a gabled roof, an arched entrance, and cleverly painted *trompe-l'oeil* embellishments around each of the rectangular windows. Inside, many of the ceilings are vaulted or timbered, with a scattering of painted antiques and a restaurant—one of the best in town—filled with alpine furniture.

The Baumschlager family are your gracious hosts. In addition to owning another well-recommended establishment nearby (the Sporthotel), Mr. Baumschlager was once a ski champion. With half board included, per-person rates average around 400 AS ($21.28) per day.

Food items in the restaurant are usually prepared in a temptingly old-fashioned style and served in big-portions. Specialties include schnitzels in cream sauce with noodles, marrow soup, and an array of grilled meats and fish. Fixed-price meals range from 100 AS ($5.32) to 185 AS ($9.84), while à la carte dinners cost from 110 AS ($5.85) to 250 AS ($13.30). The restaurant shuts down for most of November.

Hotel Blaue Sense (tel. 329) is a friendly, well-managed guest house in a modern format that was probably designed in the late 1950s. The interior has stone detailing, arched and vaulted ceilings, and lots of colorful contrasting patterns. The raised sun terrace is a popular place to eat. With full board included, the price is from 400 AS ($21.28) per person.

SPITAL AM PYHRN:
Spital was known as a stopover a long time ago on the ancient toll road that led over the nearby Pyhrn Pass on the road to Graz in Styria. The village, at 2,625 feet, lies close to Windischgarsten (see above).

In winter many skiers are attracted to Spital, where you can take a ski bus for about a mile to the foothills of the Pyhrn. There you board a mountain railway heading up Wurzeralm mountain and disembark at the Bergstation. The ride takes only eight minutes and the train can carry some 1,000 passengers per hour. The top station is at a lofty 4,700 feet. From Bergstation it's possible to go even higher, taking a double-chair lift to a height of 6,140 feet.

The **Alpenrose** is the center of most après-ski action. Otherwise attractions are limited, but you can always go over to Windischgarsten, just recommended. Chances are, however, that you'll visit Spital am Pyhrn in summer when it's at its most beautiful.

This village used to be the site of an abbey, and the **Stiftskirche** (abbey church) is well known. Work on it started in 1714 and continued for 16 years. Its baroque exterior is flanked by two towers. Kremser Schmidt did the paintings on the altarpieces of the side altars, and Altomonte painted some of the work on the colonnades in the then-fashionable *trompe-l'oeil* style.

Spital am Pyhrn's area code is 07563.

Food and Lodging

Hotel Alpenrose (tel. 225) is a well-established modern hotel with a two-story addition extending to the side of the main house. The public rooms are paneled and sunny, while the simple bedrooms are clean and filled with cheerful colors. An indoor swimming pool is five minutes away on foot. The Wesselitsch family are your hosts. Full-board rates (which in winter include free transportation from the hotel to the ski lifts) range from 350 AS ($18.62) to 370 AS ($19.68) per person, depending on the season, plumbing, and room assignment. The hotel is open from December to October.

Gasthof Vogel Händler (tel. 282) is a balconied chalet with painted illustrations on the facade as well as lots of flowers. It lies within a ten-minute walk of the train station. The unpretentious interior is paneled throughout many of the public rooms, while the bedrooms have big windows, and simple furniture. In summer a sun terrace offers a place to sit outside. A covered swimming pool and tennis courts are a few minutes away. Per-person rates, based on double occupancy, range from 300 AS ($15.96) to 350 AS ($18.62), with half board included. The supplement for a single is another 35 AS ($1.86) per day. Ingeborg Frech, the congenial owner, is happy to tell you about the sports facilities of the village.

9. Steyr and Enns

For another look at Upper Austria, we'll leave the southeast corner, heading north again via a route which, if followed on, would lead to Linz. Instead, however, we'll detour along the Enns River to visit two of the most ancient patrician cities of Austria.

These cities bear the names of the rivers that flow through the area, known as the Donau-Paum. The first such city to which I'll introduce you is Steyr and the second is Enns.

STEYR: The old town of Steyr was built on a tongue of land that juts out between the Enns and the Steyr Rivers. Three gates and a tower survive from the days when walls surrounded the town. The city's spread since its early days has taken it mainly along the Enns River. The boating crowd likes to visit here in summer, as this is the point of origin for many trips along both rivers.

Because of its name, visitors sometimes think that Steyr is in Styria, but even though that province also took its name from the Steyr River, the city is still very much in Upper Austria.

Steyr is the home of the well-known Steyr-Puch motorbike, and BMW trucks and bicycles are assembled here. But despite the factories, this is no grim industrial town. In its heyday it was considered a rival of Vienna, and the old town, particularly the major square which has many houses from the baroque era, makes it worth a stopover.

The Steyr area code is 07252.

The Sights

The **Stadtplatz** (town square) is one of the best preserved in Upper Austria and the city's most attractive feature. The street takes the shape of a plaza, and you'll see arcades as well as several balconied houses in both the Gothic and Renaissance styles. Most outstanding are the **Rathaus** (town hall) at no. 27 and the **Bummerlhaus** at no. 32. Construction on the rococo town hall, crowned by a slender tower, began in 1765. The Bummerlhaus was a private mansion built in the Gothic style. If possible, you should try to see inside some of the courts which were built as a part of these magnificent houses.

The **Dominikanerkirche,** or Dominican church, has a rich baroque interior, but it merits only a passing look. More intriguing is a street near the church, the colorful **Eisengasse,** which winds down to the Enns River.

The **Stadtpfarrkirche** (town parish church), on Pfarrgasse, dates from the middle of the 15th century, built in the Gothic style by the architect who designed St. Stephen's in Vienna to which it bears a resemblance. The church has some quite old stained glass. You'll see many ancient gravestones nearby in the **Pfarrhaus** (parish house), where Anton Bruckner composed his Sixth Symphony. A room in the house honors him.

You may also visit **Christkindl** (Christ Child), two miles west of Steyr, a well-known pilgrimage church in Austria. The baroque architects, Carlone and Prandtauer, designed Christkindl, which is painted a pinkish mauve. At Christmastime, children all over the world send letters to the *Wirtschaft,* a Christmas post office. If you send a self-addressed, stamped envelope, you'll receive a reply if your letter is addressed to Christkindl.

Food and Lodging

Hotel Minichmayr, 1-3 Haratzmüllerstrasse (tel. 23410). Views from the sun terrace of this old-world hotel encompass the confluence of two rivers and much of the old town. The hotel offers friendly service, excellent food, and comfortable bedrooms (the best of which have been renovated) in a sunny format of taste and style. With a buffet breakfast included, singles cost from 550 AS ($29.26) to 850 AS ($45.22), while doubles range from 420 AS ($22.34) to 550 AS ($29.26) per person. Guests have use of the sauna.

The Viertler family also directs the items served in the pleasant dining room. Specialties include fresh local river fish, a range of grilled and flambé-style meats, roasts, an excellent oxtail soup, and an array of solid, regionally inspired recipes. Fixed-price meals cost 160 AS ($8.51) and 220 AS ($11.70), while à la carte dinners cost from 100 AS ($5.32) to 250 AS ($13.30).

Linzerhaus (tel. 237) is a rustic hotel with a gently sloping roof and red and white striped shutters. You can reach it by cable car, which might be a good idea since it lies at an elevation of some 4,620 feet. The cozy interior offers the kind of rustic accommodations which you might appreciate after a strenuous day outdoors. Robert and Maria Danklmaier, your hosts, charge from 300 AS ($15.96) per person, with half board included.

Restaurant Ulrichsklause, at St. Ulrich (tel. 23459), would make a pleasant excursion from Steyr, particularly on a warm day when the view from its terrace encompasses the river and everything on the other side. In a satellite of Steyr, the restaurant serves specialties of venison, asparagus, mushrooms, and strawberries. You could begin your meal with puff pastry filled with ragoût, a portion of smoked ham, or a variety of fresh salads. Main courses include chipped veal in a wine and cream sauce with mushrooms and potatoes, filet of pike-perch, or charcoal-grilled steaks and cutlets. Dessert could be sweet cheese dumplings, rolled in buttered breadcrumbs, served with stewed prunes. Full meals range from 125 AS ($6.65) to 220 AS ($11.70), with hot dinners served from 11:30 a.m. to 2 p.m. and from 6 to 10 p.m. every day (except Sunday evening and all day Monday). The restaurant has a varied holiday schedule, so call before going there.

Café Rahofer, 9 Stadtplatz (tel. 24606), is an attractive modern café in the center of Steyr. Serving pastries, wine, coffee, and snacks, it's a popular hangout for shoppers, lovers, and just about everyone else in town. Coffee and pastries average around 18 AS (96¢) to 25 AS ($1.33) apiece. Closed Tuesday.

ENNS: The oldest town in Upper Austria, Enns stands on what was once the site of a Roman camp and later was the Roman city of Lauriacum, on the left bank of the Enns River, a short distance from where its water flows into the Danube. Enns was granted its charter in 1212. The **Rathaus** displays many artifacts from the Roman days of the town.

The **Stadtturm** (town tower), constructed in 1564 on orders of Emperor Maximilian II, still stands on the principal plaza, along with several old patrician houses in the baroque style. From the tower you have an excellent view over the old town and the river.

The **Pfarrkirche** (parish church) is Gothic with a double nave flanked with only one aisle. Pillars divide it into two sections, then into a trio of sections.

To the north of the town stands **Ennsegg Castle,** dating from the 16th century. Some five miles to the west of Enns lies the renowned Augustinian Abbey of St. Florian. (For information, refer to the sights in the environs of Linz.)

The area code for Enns is 07223.

Food and Lodging

Hotel Lauriacum, 5-7 Wiener Strasse (tel. 2315), presents a distinguished contemporary facade to a busy street in the center of Enns. The public rooms are filled with a combination of modern and rustic accessories, which include a ceramic tile oven, a coffered ceiling, and a collection of farm implements in one of the restaurants. Other rooms are invitingly contemporary, especially the plant-filled bar area where the stools look like oversize pin cushions set onto chrome columns. Management pays careful attention to its cuisine as well as to the well-being of its guests. The spacious and colorful bedrooms rent for 550 AS ($29.26) in a single and for 830 AS ($44.17) in a double, with breakfast included. Each of the accommodations has a private bath, and a sauna is on the premises.

10. Stops Along the Danube

Many of the major stopovers along the Danube, including Linz, have been explored in other parts of this guide. Other sections on the great river have been visited in Lower Austria (Chapter V) and in Vienna. However, the Danube offers several rewarding stopovers, besides Linz, in Upper Austria, including the following towns and villages.

Assuming you are picking up this trail at Passau, a border city of West Germany, and driving through the Danube Valley, I'd recommend a visit first to—

ASCHACH: This Danube town has associations with Dr. Faust. (See the description of Faust Schlössl below, where you can order a meal or spend the night —if you dare.) A bridge in the town spans the Danube, and you may be able to see from your bedroom window steamers plying the river. Aschach has many baroque houses from the 18th century.

Directly south of Aschach, you can visit the small town of **Eferding,** which was mentioned in the *Nibelungenlied.* Eferding has one of the finest restaurants in the area.

The Aschach area code is 07273.

Food and Lodging

Faust Schlössl (tel. 245). This medieval castle was used by tollkeepers of the powerful Schaumberg family, and later by a revolving series of noble families. The behavior of the residents so frightened the populace that it was soon rumored that the castle was not only haunted, but that it had been built by the devil for Dr. Faustus in a single night. In 1966 it was converted into a hotel with 50 rooms, each of which was designed with a private bath.

The arena of what had been a Roman theater was converted into the basin for an outdoor swimming pool. If you approach the castle from the river it will appear more massive and foreboding than it actually is, although the many wings, arcades, towers, and balconies certainly make an impressive combination of yellow stucco and red tiles.

The interior is surprisingly unpretentious, with few of the original furnishings remaining. The decor is simple, modern, and streamlined, except for an occasional rustic touch. Prices are from 250 AS ($13.30) to 280 AS ($14.90) per person, with breakfast included. Open March to December.

Restaurant Dannerbauer, Brandstatt (tel. 471), in the suburb of Eferding, is a popular restaurant which many locals drive long distances to reach. On weekends it gets so crowded you may have to wait for both a table and a waitress. The setting is gemütlich, and there's a view of the Danube.

If you like to drink, you might begin your meal with a taste of the local schnapps, which should certainly stimulate conversation at your table. Specialties include a Hungarian fish soup, perch filet in a Riesling sauce, a delicate filet of sole, and a range of well-prepared meat and game dishes. À la carte meals range from 180 AS ($9.58) to 420 AS ($22.34), while fixed-price dinners cost from 280 AS ($14.90) to a whopping 740 AS ($39.37). The restaurant is closed Monday and Tuesday and from mid-January until the end of the first week of February. Reservations are suggested.

Bypassing Linz and Enns, already visited, I recommend that you drive along the Danube to the far eastern border of Upper Austria. Here it's time for another stopover, this one in—

GREIN: Much of the economy of Grein, which lies on the left bank of the Danube, depends on shipping along the river. **Greinburg,** a schloss sheltering the Austrian Shipping Museum, stands to the west of the port. The castle, dating from the 15th century, has an inner court in the Renaissance style, with arcades.

In the **Stadtplatz,** a rococo theater from 1791, seating only about 150 spectators, has been preserved. This is the oldest known theater in Austria. Also on the Stadtplatz are several turreted houses. The **parish church** of Grein has an 18th-century altarpiece by Altomonte.

Grein's area code is 07268.

A Coffeehouse

Kaffeesiederei Blumenstraussl, 6 Stadtplatz (tel. 380), offers two separate dining rooms, both of them decorated in a glowing Biedermeier style. In summer the outdoor coffee garden is popular with almost everyone in town. The establishment lies close to the Rathaus, behind a well-preserved baroque facade. One of the rooms has a massive billiard table, a shiny ceramic stove, Empire-style hanging chandeliers, and country Biedermeier banquettes. You'll know when strawberries are in season by the wide range of pastries made with them as a primary ingredient. The Mozart torte is luscious, as well as the array of hot soups to warm up a cold day. Coffee costs 20 AS ($1.06) to 45 AS ($2.39), while pastries range from 15 AS (80¢) to 30 AS ($1.60) apiece. The café is closed all day Monday, until 2 p.m. on Tuesday, and during the month of October. The establishment also serves drinks, ice cream, and sandwiches.

ST. NIKOLA: On both banks of the Danube near the point where it enters Lower Austria is this 800-year-old town, about two hours by autobahn from Vienna. It's a good base for visiting Melk, the Wachau, and many castles, churches, and medieval towns in the general area, all about an hour's drive from St. Nikola.

The St. Nikola area code is 07268.

Food and Lodging

Hotel zur Post (tel. 8140) is composed of the union of a 17th-century central building with a small onion dome attached to the corner tower, plus a modern balconied extension. Practically none of the original furnishings or detailing remains, but the furnishings inside are tasteful, clean, and rustic, and set in a pleasing combination of white plaster walls and horizontal paneling. The Danzer family are your hosts, charging a peak 420 AS ($22.34) per person in a single or double, with full board included. All units contain private bath.

Donauhof (tel. 8107). The service and attitude of the Aigner family make this an especially attractive starting point for touring this part of Austria. Parts of the simple white hotel with the red tile roof and the modern extension are more than 400 years old. The public rooms are attractively furnished with painted armoires, chalet-style chairs, and rustic timbers. The bar area stocks practically everything from homemade wines to vintage cognacs. It has a comfortable 1950s-style decor, with round porthole-style windows cut into one of the walls.

The bedrooms are comfortable enough to spend time in, and sometimes they have provocatively dark walls to accent the imaginative color scheme. On the premises are a sauna, exercise room, and a garden terrace overlooking the Danube.

The in-house restaurant bakes many of its own pastries fresh every day, while the menu items include both Austrian and international specialties. Guests are welcome to fish in the hotel-owned waters or in the Danube, and if they catch anything, the hotel will prepare it for supper. The charge in a double is 260 AS ($13.83) per person, while singles cost 330 AS ($17.56), with breakfast included.

11. Schärding and Braunau

From the far-eastern border of Upper Austria, most visitors will go on into Lower Austria, following the Danube until it reaches Vienna. However, since that territory has been explored previously, we'll jump across the province to highlight some stopovers along its western border before going into the Tyrolean country.

Some towns and villages that merit exploration in this section include—

SCHÄRDING: Because of its beautiful old buildings—painted in pastels of gold, pink, yellow, and turquoise—Schärding is often called the romantic city of the baroque. It lies above the Inn River, about 11 miles south of the West

German city of Passau on the Danube, in a region of Upper Austria called the **Innviertel.** The Danube flows in the north, but in the west are the Inn and Salzach Rivers.

If much of the area in and around Schärding reminds you of Bavaria, it's no wonder. The Innviertel was part of Bavaria until it was ceded to Austria in 1779.

Schärding was once a fortified town, and remnants of the old walls stand today, along with some gates and towers. Its **parish church** *(pfarrkirche)*, like virtually every other old church in Austria, was once in the Gothic style but received a baroque overlay.

The area code for Schärding is 07712.

Food and Lodging

Forstinger's Wirthaus, 3 Unterer Stadtplatz (tel. 2302), has been a hotel since 1606 and has now attained four-star status. It is authentically rustic, with comfortable accommodations, completely renovated in 1985. All the bedrooms have bathroom, TV, safe, phone, and mini-bar. The charge is 400 AS ($21.28) in a single, from 400 AS ($21.28) to 700 AS ($37.24) in a double, all tariffs including breakfast. The inn's restaurant, known throughout the region for its gutbürgerlich fare, is furnished with beautiful rustic pieces, and the service is friendly.

Scheurecker (tel. 2651) is a charming old house with a view over the buildings of the central square of the village. It used to be called Zum Goldenen Löwen. The cozy bedrooms are attractively simple, renting for 310 AS ($16.49) to 340 AS ($18.09) in a single and 550 AS ($29.26) to 580 AS ($30.87) in a double. English is spoken.

BRAUNAU AM INN:

BRAUNAU AM INN: Lying on the right bank of the Inn River, Braunau, a very old town with several buildings from the Middle Ages still standing, has always been a frontier or border town. If you cross the bridge over the Inn you'll have to clear Customs, as you'll be in the small Bavarian village of Simbach.

The burghers' houses in Braunau date in part from the 16th and 17th centuries, but the most outstanding architectural treasure is **St. Stephen's Church,** with a large square tower rising 315 feet, the third-tallest tower in Austria. Inside you can visit the 15th-century Gothic chancel. In an adjacent chapel is the tombstone of a Passau bishop who died in 1485. See also its 16th-century baker's altar.

Braunau am Inn has the dubious distinction of being the birthplace of Adolf Hitler, although his name was Adolf Schicklgruber then. His father, Alois Schicklgruber, had been made a Customs inspector in Braunau in 1875. However, the town of Braunau was to be in the limelight much later in connection with its native son. When the Nazis were applying pressure on Austria before their complete takeover of the country, one of the most unlikely proposals made was that Braunau, because it was *Der Führer's Geburtsort* (native town), be ceded to Germany. Vague plans were in the air to turn it into a monument honoring the dictator's birth site.

After his takeover of Austria, Hitler made a "sentimental journey" to Braunau. He ordered his driver to take him to the Pommer Inn in which he had been born, but his caravan had a difficult time reaching the building because of cars full of onlookers which jammed the road. Historians recorded that when his car reached Braunau, "a jubilant crowd struggled to touch the vehicle as if it were some religious relic."

Today, neo-Nazis have made the little town and the house at 15 Salzburger Vorstadt, where Hitler was born in 1889, into a sort of pilgrimage goal for ultra-rightists of Austria, although this is frowned on by the Austrian government.

The former home of the Schicklgrubers is a brown-and-white building with a baroque facade.

The area code for Braunau am Inn is 07722.

Food and Lodging

Hotel Gann, 23 Stadtplatz (tel. 3206), is a distinctive-looking town house on the central square of the village. Its facade is painted a pearl gray-blue, while the heavy moldings around the neoclassical-style windows are pure white. The cellar bar is one of the most memorable places in town, partly because of the stone vaulting that soars over the gaily striped chairs and partly because of the patronage of many of the locals. The bedrooms have high ceilings and lots of cozily renovated comforts. Singles cost 280 AS ($14.90) to 340 AS ($18.09), while doubles rent for 700 AS ($37.24) to 900 AS ($47.88), with breakfast included.

Chapter X

INNSBRUCK AND TYROL

LAND OF ICE and mountains, of dark forests and alpine meadows where wildflowers bloom in the spring, of summer holidays and winter sports . . . that's Tyrol. Those intrepid tourists, the British, discovered its delights for holiday-makers and made it a fashionable destination for travelers in the last century. Now, however, the principal visitors are the Germans. Munich is only a few hours away, and even though Bavaria is itself one of the major tourist attractions of Europe, even the Bavarians head for Tyrol when they want a change of scenery.

Tyrol and its capital, Innsbruck, had an imperial heyday at the end of the Middle Ages, when the Habsburg, Maximilian I, often called "the last of the knights," was the Holy Roman Emperor. Castles dotted the countryside, many now only ruins.

With a population of about half a million Austrians occupying some 4,822 square miles, Tyrol was a much larger district at the turn of the century, until South Tyrol was lost to Italy in 1919. The lost portion was a large wine-growing area, considered the wealthiest part of Tyrol. This loss was a great blow for the

Tyrolean people who remained in Austria, as it separated many of them from relatives, friends, and sometimes livelihood.

By the same post-World War I treaty, East Tyrol, whose capital is Lienz, was separated from its sister, North Tyrol, of which Innsbruck is capital. The two are separated by a protuberance of the portion of Tyrol given to Italy which connects with a strip of Land Salzburg border. To the east of North Tyrol, the far larger portion of the split province, lies Land Salzburg. On its west is the Austrian province of Vorarlberg (to be visited in Chapter XI), to the north is Bavaria, West Germany, and to the south, Italy and a small part of Switzerland. East Tyrol is bordered by Carinthia on the east, Land Salzburg on the north, and Italy everywhere else.

Tyrol lies at the junction of several transcontinental links. The Valley of the Inn River, which I've divided into two sections, cuts across the northern part of the province. Many side valleys are offshoots of the major artery. The province is also known for its deep-blue alpine lakes, such as the Achensee and the Walchsee. The Drau River, rising in the Höhe Tauern Alps, runs through East Tyrol.

Tyrol is a province known for its folklore and colorful folk customs, including schuhplatter dancing, brass bands, and yodeling. It's also known for its Tyrol dress. Traditional garb topped off with tall hats (less common nowadays) used to be a special feature for both men and women, with the men being the more elaborately attired.

Today Tyrol is one of the most popular tourist regions of Europe, especially favored by Americans, who have to an extent supplanted the once firmly entrenched British holiday crowds. It didn't become a mecca for American tourists until shortly before World War I when rail magnate J. Pierpont Morgan spent time in Innsbruck and publicized the area when he returned home. Since World War II, the resorts of this province have made it a popular destination for American skiers.

Tyrol is the most frequented winter playground in all Austria. Many prefer its ski slopes to those of Switzerland. It has also produced great skiers, and names such as Toni Sailer have become household words. Skiers flock here for many months, but especially from mid-December until the end of March, reservations are at their tightest at the most fashionable resorts.

Glacier tours around May and June are a big attraction, with mountain climbers appearing in the summer months. Trout fishermen work the waters until the first sniff of autumnal air. July and August bring the most visitors to the province, many of them North Americans, so reservations are essential.

I recommend a private car for getting around, if you can afford it, but only for spring, summer, and fall. If you're not an experienced alpine driver, the other months of the year—especially at some of the remote places—can be hazardous. However, the province is well served by rail and bus connections.

1. Innsbruck

The Tyrol capital, Innsbruck (elevation 1,880 feet and population nearly 150,000), is considered one of the most beautiful cities of Europe. It has long been a center of commerce and traffic, as it lies at the junction of two important routes across the central Alps—a north-south and an east-west highway. It's easily reached by rail, air, or road.

The name Innsbruck means "bridge over the Inn," the Inn, of course, being the river that flows through the city, which lies at a meeting place of the Valley of the Inn and the Sill Gorge. As long ago as 1180 a little settlement on the river was moved from the northern bank to the site of the present old town

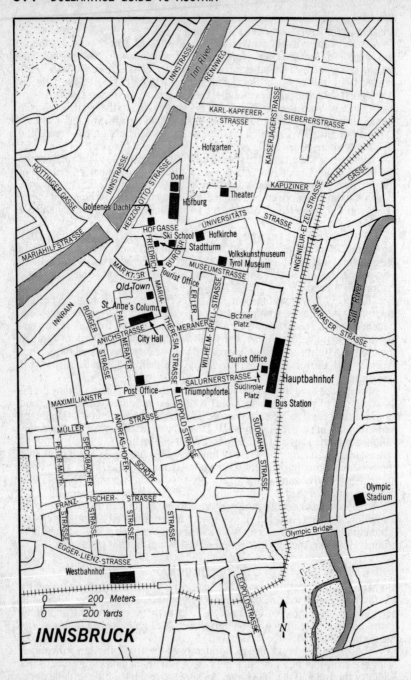

INNSTRASSE

Inn River

RENNWEG

KARL-KAPFERER-
STRASSE

Hofgarten

KAISERJÄGERSTRASSE

SIEBERERSTRASSE

KAPUZINER

GASSE

HÖTTINGER GASSE

INNSTRASSE

HERZOG-OTTO-STRASSE

Dom

Hofburg

Theater

STRASSE

Goldenes Dachl

MARIAHILFSTRASSE

HOFGASSE

Ski School

FRIEDRICH

BÜRGER

Hofkirche

Stadtturm

UNIVERSITÄTS

Volkskunstmuseum
Tyrol Museum

INGENIEUR-ETZEL-STRASSE

MARKT GR

MUSEUMSTRASSE

Tourist Office

Old Town

Sill River

AMRASER STRASSE

INNRAIN

BÜRGER

St. Anne's Column

MARIA-

ERLER

Bozner
Platz

FALL

THERESIA STRASSE

MERANER

WILHELM-GRELL-STRASSE

ANICHSTRASSE

MERAYER

City Hall

Tourist Office

Hauptbahnhof

STRASSE

SALURNERSTRASSE

Post Office

Triumphpforte

Südtiroler
Platz

Bus Station

MAXIMILIANSTR

LEOPOLD STRASSE

MÜLLER

ANDREAS-HOFER

STRASSE

SÜDBAHN

Olympic
Stadium

PETER-MAYR

SPECKBACHER

SCHÖPF

STRASSE

FRANZ-

FISCHER-

STRASSE

STRASSE

STRASSE

EGGER-LIENZ-STRASSE

Olympic Bridge

LEOPOLDSTRASSE

Westbahnhof

0   200 Meters

0   200 Yards

INNSBRUCK

N

(Altstadt). In 1239, as a part of Swabia Bavaria, it was granted its own "rights and privileges," and in 1420, Tyrol being by then part of Austria, Innsbruck became the capital of the province.

The city became celebrated throughout Europe during the sovereignty of the Holy Roman Emperor Maximilian I, the Habsburg mentioned above, called "the last knight." Under Maximilian, whose reign (1490–1519) signaled the end of the Middle Ages, Innsbruck reached the height of its cultural and political importance, and it's still the cultural center of the Tyrolean country. The city had its second imperial heyday some 300 years later, during the 40-year reign of Maria Theresa.

The beauty of Innsbruck has been protected by town planners who have seen to it that new structures in the inner city are in harmony with the Gothic, Renaissance, and baroque buildings already standing. Modern urban development spreads along the Inn River east and west, away from the historic areas.

The main street of the old town historic district is the **Herzog-Friedrich-Strasse,** which becomes the Maria-Theresien-Strasse, the main axis of the post-medieval new town. The old town becomes strictly pedestrian after 10:30 a.m., but that's all right, since the only way to see that part of Innsbruck is on foot.

In 1945, this city became the headquarters of the French zone of occupation.

Twice in a dozen years—in 1964 and 1976—the eyes of the world turned to Innsbruck when it hosted the Olympic Winter Games, leading to its becoming a winter sports center with the most modern facilities. Skiers who come to Innsbruck benefit twice: They stay in a cosmopolitan city called the jewel city of the Alps, and they ski on some of the choicest slopes of the world. Nonskiers and summer visitors can enjoy the sights of the medieval old town, the shops with Tyrolean specialties, and the many excursions into the environs.

The area code for Innsbruck and its nearby suburbs is 05222.

TRANSPORTATION: A network of three tram and 25 bus lines covers all of Innsbruck and its close environs. Tickets for single rides in the central area are 13 AS (69¢). A book of 5 tickets costs 46 AS ($2.48); and 10 tickets, 86 AS ($4.58).

Postal Buses leave from the Central Bus Station, next to the Central Railway Station, heading to all parts of Tyrol.

Taxi stands are in all parts of town, or you can call a radio cab (tel. 2-77-11 or 4-55-00).

You can take a ride in a **fiacre** (horse-drawn carriage) from in front of Tiroler Landestheater, Rennweg.

Parking: If you elect to use your own car for transportation in Innsbruck, you need to know something about parking. The fee for parking in the city center's short-term parking zones (marked by special signs) is 5 AS (27¢) for 30 minutes. The maximum length of time you can stay in one spot is 1½ hours. Parking vouchers can be bought in all post offices, at most tobacconists, and at the Tourist Office.

There are several multistory and underground car parks in Innsbruck.

PRACTICAL FACTS: The **Tourist Office** (Städtisches Verkehrsbüro), 3 Burggraben (tel. 25-7-15), will courteously supply you with a wealth of information to ensure that you will enjoy your Innsbruck and Tyrol visit. It's open Monday to Friday from 8 a.m. to noon and from 2 to 5:30 p.m., on Saturday from 9 a.m. to noon. If you have children with you, ask for the special guide book for the young.

Hotel information is available at the Central Railway Station (Hauptbahnhof) (tel. 23-7-66).

For **emergency** needs, you should know the following numbers: police, 133; fire, 122; ambulance, 144; mountain rescue service, 194.

For emergency medical service, call the **University Hospital,** 35 Anichstrasse (tel. 723-0).

The **Lost Property Office** is at the police station (Bundespolizeidirektion), 8 Kaiserjägerstrasse (tel. 26-7-21, ext. 341).

You can **exchange money** at banks in all parts of town Monday to Friday from 7:45 a.m. to 12:30 p.m. and from 2:30 to 4 p.m.; at the Tourist Office; and at the Central Railway Station (7:30 a.m. to 8:30 p.m. daily).

The **American Express** office, 3 Brixnerstrasse (tel. 22-4-91), is open Monday to Friday from 9 a.m. to 5:30 p.m. and on Saturday from 9 a.m. to noon.

The **Central Post Office** (Hauptpostamt), 2 Maximilianstrasse (tel. 26-7-61), is open 24 hours a day Monday to Saturday. The post office at the Central Railway Station, 1-3 Bruneckerstrasse, is open Monday to Saturday from 6:30 a.m. to 9 p.m.

SPORTS: Ski areas around Innsbruck are excellent for winter activity or for summer mountain walks and viewing. Five sunny snow-covered, avalanche-free areas around the capital of Tyrol are served by five cableways, 44 chair lifts, and ski hoists. More detailed information on skiing areas will appear later in this chapter.

In winter, the city is also known for bobsled and toboggan runs and ice-skating rinks.

In summer in Innsbruck you can enjoy tennis at a number of courts, golf on either an 18-hole or a nine-hole course, horseback riding, mountaineering, gliding, swimming, hiking, and shooting.

HOTELS: Always arrive with a reservation, as Innsbruck is said never to be out of season. Accommodations are scarce from June until the end of summer and from about mid-December to mid-April.

The Deluxe Category

Hotel Europa Tyrol, 2 Südtiroler Platz (tel. 35571). The facade of this elegant hotel was bombed in World War II and later rebuilt into the modern format you'll see today as you leave the train station. Now it's part of the Steigenberger chain and has been renovated into what is often considered the best hotel in Innsbruck.

The lobby is a high-ceilinged, formally paneled room with an English-style bar at one end and accents of green marble. The upholstery on many of the chairs is made of green leather, set off by the many valuable Oriental rugs. This is a very formal but friendly hotel, with a public image so important that Queen Elizabeth II used it during her stay in Innsbruck.

The uniformed staff is helpful in every way and will usually be willing to show you the heavily ornate yellow and white Barock Saal whose lunette paintings are worth a second look.

The 166 rooms rent for 1,050 AS ($55.86) to 1,500 AS ($79.80) in a single and 1,750 AS ($93.10) to 2,800 AS ($148.96) in a double.

Holiday Inn, 15 Salurner Strasse (tel. 36501), offers clean American-style accommodations in a typical Holiday Inn format. While this might not be the charming Tyrolean-style hostelry you'd fantasized about, it is nonetheless convenient, especially for motorists who find parking difficult in the inner city. The hotel has a garage and lies only two blocks from the central train station. Each accommodation is equipped with two double beds, a private bath, radio, phone, TV, and air conditioning. An indoor pool and sauna are on the premises, as well as several theme restaurants. The rates for single occupancy of a room are from 1,250 AS ($66.50) to 1,770 AS ($94.16), while tariffs for two persons range from 2,050 AS ($109.06) to 2,730 AS ($145.24), with a buffet breakfast included in all prices.

Hotel Innsbruck, 3 Innrain (tel. 34511), is a deluxe hotel in the center of the city near the Congress Center. Its facade is painted a vivid tangerine in a contemporary format of windows and op-art trim accenting the vertical rows of bay windows. The lobby has a marble floor and modern-style paneling and cluster chandeliers. On the premises are a big swimming pool, a bar, and a good restaurant. Rates in the handsomely furnished bedrooms range from 650 AS ($34.58) to 1,050 AS ($55.86) per person, with breakfast included.

First-Class Choices

Hotel Goldener Adler, 6 Herzog-Friedrich-Strasse (tel. 26334). Even the phone booth near the reception desk of this 600-year-old hotel is outfitted in an antique style, concealed behind an old panel. This hotel contains 31 rooms in a family-run format of leaded windows with stained-glass inserts, travertine floors, ornately carved Tyrolean furniture, and chandeliers where human figures are carved from ram's horns. The reception desk is on the first floor, above the heavy stone buttresses of the street level.

Famous guests included Goethe, the brother of Marie Antoinette (Joseph II, who arrived incognito in 1777), King Gustav III of Sweden (1783), the violinist Paganini, who cut his name into the windowpane of the room, and in 1573, Duke Albert V of Bavaria who arrived with his son and a retinue of 416 people.

Rooms are handsomely styled and furnished, costing from 700 AS ($37.24) to 900 AS ($47.88) in a single, and doubles range from 1,000 AS ($53.20) to 1,600 AS ($85.12). A buffet breakfast is included in the charges.

Hotel Central, Am Sparkassenplatz (tel. 24866), is one of the most unusual hotels in town. It's housed in a super-hi-tech format of textured concrete with windows whose edges are beveled into angular glass and steel rectangles. The lobby floor is covered with hand-set mosaics of colored paving blocks arranged into pastel-colored circles. Above your head, it looks as if the bubble-making machine on the Lawrence Welk show went crazy. Thousands of glass balls hang from the high ceiling on golden strands of metal wire.

The management is friendly and capable, and on the premises you'll find one of the most popular discos in town, along with an indoor pool, a sauna, and in total contrast to the rest of the hotel, a romantically baroque café with marble columns, sculptured ceilings, large gilt-and-crystal chandeliers, and a collection of international newspapers. The comfortable rooms evoke an almost Japanese sense of simplicity. Doubles range from 1,300 AS ($69.16) to 1,900 AS ($101.08), while singles cost 1,000 AS ($53.20) to 1,400 AS ($74.48), with breakfast included. Prices depend on the season.

Hotel Maria Theresa, 31 Maria-Theresien-Strasse (tel. 35616), is the best known hotel on this famous street a few blocks away from the winding alleys of the oldest parts of Innsbruck. A striking oil portrait of the empress herself hangs in the reception area. The friendly staff at this Best Western hotel will do everything possible to make you feel comfortable. Singles rent for 715 AS ($38.04) to 1,050 AS ($55.86), with doubles costing from 1,075 AS ($57.19) to 1,600 AS ($85.12), with breakfast included. All the rooms have been recently redecorated. Underground parking is available for guests.

Hotel Roter Adler, 4 Seilergasse (tel. 21069), is a dramatically renovated first-class hotel inside a 500-year-old house in the old part of town. In the lobby, modern orange banquettes curve around the antique stone arches that support the vaulted ceiling. The rest of the establishment has lots of exposed wood and cozy corners. Charges for the well-furnished rooms range from 550 AS ($29.26) to 830 AS ($44.17) per person, with breakfast included. The staff is attractive and friendly.

Hotel Grauer Bär, 5-7 Universitätsstrasse (tel. 34531), lies on a street lined with baroque buildings. Its lobby is big enough to park a bus in, with a high ceiling, Oriental rugs, and a small baroque statue of a cherub flying against one wall at eye level. To the side of the lobby is a large persimmon-colored dining room with an ornate ribbed and vaulted white ceiling supported by a central stone column. The bedrooms rent for 700 AS ($37.24) to 850 AS ($44.17) in a single and for 550 AS ($29.26) to 700 AS ($37.24) per person in a double, with breakfast included. Prices depend on the plumbing and the season. There is parking in back.

The Middle Bracket

Hotel Schwarzer Adler, 2 Kaiserjägerstrasse (tel. 27109), is one of Innsbruck's oldest hotels. Five minutes from the train station, it has an antique facade of beige-colored stucco, black shutters, and a big-windowed tower extending upward from the building's corner. Inside you'll find all the vaulted ceilings, aged paneling, and gemütlich clutter you'd expect from such a historic building. Singles cost from 700 AS ($37.24) to 900 AS ($47.88), and doubles range from 550 AS ($29.26) to 800 AS ($42.56) per person, with breakfast included. Half board is offered for 200 AS ($10.64) per person extra.

Hotel Maximilian, 7-9 Marktgraben (tel. 37577). Built in 1982, this inner-city hotel rates as one of the most attractive and up-to-date in Innsbruck. It sacrifices little of the antique charm of yesterday in its willingness to provide modern and convenient accommodations. The woodwork in the lobby is a beautifully crafted example of fine carpentry, while the reception desk is staffed with a bevy of helpful people.

The 40 rooms are modern and comfortable. The most desirable ones look out over the back, where you'll have a closeup view of the shingled onion dome of the oldest church in Innsbruck (now used as the headquarters of a company which makes keys). Each of the rooms has an attractive modern bath and comes with breakfast included. Compact singles range from 680 AS ($36.18) to 800 AS ($42.56), while doubles cost from 1,200 AS ($63.84) to 1,350 AS ($71.82).

Villa Blanka, 8 Weiherburggasse (tel. 37771), is a balconied contemporary hotel designed in a big-windowed rectangular format looking out over a well-planted park. It lies about 20 pedestrian minutes from the center of the city. The inside is filled with contoured leather chairs, big modern paintings, and a series of paneled rooms with coffered ceilings ranging from the dramatically contemporary to the rustically conservative. The long sun terrace is set on a balcony above the ground floor, with a view over the rare trees of the hotel's landscaping. Singles range from 620 AS ($32.98) to 650 AS ($34.58), while doubles cost around 550 AS ($29.26) per person, with breakfast included.

Hotel Mozart, 15 Müllerstrasse (tel. 23038), is a renovated hotel with a central location and a pleasant series of spacious bedrooms. Comfortably furnished singles rent for 560 AS ($29.79) to 630 AS ($33.52), while doubles cost from 820 AS ($43.62) to 1,000 AS ($53.20), with breakfast included. All units contain private bath.

The **Clima Hotel,** 7 Zeughausgasse (tel. 28361), although set in an uninspiring neighborhood, lies only a five-minute walk from the historic center of town. Its saffron-colored facade shelters the top-rated restaurant in town (see Belle Époque under dining selections), plus a preferred disco. The elegant lobby of the hotel is filled with alpine antiques, beautifully upholstered chairs, and a scattering of 19th-century oil paintings. Guests enjoy breakfast beside a tile stove in a wood-paneled re-creation of the interior of a chalet, or morning coffee in the cobblestone-covered courtyard ringed with vines and arbors. Many of the efficiently organized bedrooms provide a view of the mountains, and each contains a private bath, radio, and phone. Singles range from 600 AS ($31.92) to 700 AS ($37.24), with doubles costing from 950 AS ($50.54) to 1,150 AS ($61.18), with breakfast included. There is also a garage for motorists.

Hotel Greif, 3 Leopoldstrasse (tel. 27401), is a five-story building with a desirable location near Innsbruck's arch of triumph and a light-brown facade. The vertical neon sign bolted to the side of the building illuminates the neoclassic pediments above each of the big windows. The modernized interior is filled with comfortable furniture, warm colors of beige, white, and crimson, along with adaptations of chalet chairs. The carpeted bedrooms are partially paneled and rent for around 690 AS ($36.71) per person, based on double occupancy, with breakfast included. The supplement in a single is another 150 AS ($7.98) per day.

Hotel Mondschein, 6 Mariahilfstrasse (tel. 82784), is a peach-colored hotel with a double row of vertical bay windows running from the ground to the fifth floor. A wrought-iron bracket extending over the sidewalk announces that the hotel was built in 1473, although it was renovated in 1982. One of the best aspects of this place is its location on the banks of the river. On the premises is a restaurant with an old vaulted ceiling and lots of wrought iron, as well as a lobby area with tile floors and Oriental rugs. The colorful and comfortable bedrooms rent for 700 AS ($37.24) in a single and 1,080 AS ($57.46) in a double.

Hotel Royal, 16 Innrain (tel. 26385), is a modern hotel with a riverside location convenient to everything in the city. Of interest to motorists, it has enough parking to give you a free spot (usually). Each of the spacious and comfortable bedrooms is simply and attractively furnished, with its own private bath, small TV, phone, and radio. The sunny dining room is pleasingly filled with burnt-orange carpeting and sunflower-colored walls. Doubles cost around 1,050 AS ($55.86), and singles rent for 690 AS ($36.71), with breakfast included.

Tourotel Breinössl, 12 Maria-Theresien-Strasse (tel. 24165), lies behind an unusual blue-green facade on a major street of Innsbruck. It's covered with flowered loggias and gently protruding bay windows. The inside is tastefully woodsy, with lots of hanging cloth lamps in the paneled restaurant, welcome touches of wrought iron and regional sculpture in the rustic restaurant, and attractively modern furniture in the comfortable bedrooms. Singles range from 525 AS ($27.93) to 625 AS ($33.25), while doubles cost from 825 AS ($43.89) to 975 AS ($51.87) with breakfast included. All accommodations contain private bath, phone, radio, and color TV.

The Budget Range

Gasthof-Hotel Weisses Kreuz, 31 Herzog-Friedrich-Strasse (tel. 21890), lies on a street in the old town which has changed little since 13-year-old Wolfgang and his father, Leopold Mozart, stayed here in 1769. The hotel's old facade is relieved with an extended bay window which stretches from the second to the fourth floor. The ground floor is pierced with an arcade, while naïve stencils adorn the white stucco of the upper stories. A wrought-iron sign extending over the sidewalk holds the symbol of the hotel, a white cross.

You'll have to climb past two restaurants and a series of hand-painted ceramic plates set into the stucco of the stairway before arriving at the third-floor reception area. There you'll be pleasantly surprised by the carved stone columns, a TV room with an arched wood-covered ceiling, a collection of massive

Tyrolean chests, and a carved balustrade worn smooth by the palms of generations of visitors.

Depending on the plumbing, prices range from 360 AS ($19.15) to 550 AS ($29.26) in a single and from 600 AS ($31.92) to 950 AS ($50.54) in a double, with breakfast included in all the rates. The informal ground-floor restaurant has been renovated into a modern format of terracotta floors, hanging lamps, and a paneled wall covered with color photographs of food that are almost guaranteed to make you hungry.

Pension Stoi, 4 Südtirolerplatz (tel. 25434), is an unpretentious pension across from the train station. The modern masonry-trimmed ground floor contains a coffeeshop with reasonably priced food and drink. Charges for the simply furnished rooms are: single, 330 AS ($17.56); double, 460 AS ($24.47); triple, 590 AS ($31.39); and quad, 700 AS ($37.24). Breakfast, service, and taxes are included in the rates.

If the pension is full, they may place you in their annex at 7 Salurnerstrasse, also a comfortable place to stay, with the same prices and facilities as the Stoi.

Gasthof Goldener Löwe, 8 Seilergasse (tel. 22127). This place is centrally located in the old city and might be considered run-down by everyone except the adventurous. You climb a stairwell to what was probably used as a large private home, which has been converted into a warren of small rooms that haven't been painted in a while. The German-speaking management is friendly, and the prices are right: 240 AS ($12.77) in a single and 450 AS ($23.94) in a double. The facade is an elegant combination of gray and white baroque detailing. Closed in November.

Hotel Gasthof Goldene Krone, 46 Maria-Theresien-Strasse (tel. 26160), has a pastel green-and-white facade looking over the traffic on this baroque street. The bedrooms are modern and clean, with big windows and concealed reading lights above the built-in beds. On the premises are a Tyrolean-style paneled restaurant with an alpine atmosphere and a lighthearted café with a long narrow format stretching into a series of hideaway banquettes perfect for intimate talks. Singles range in price from 325 AS ($17.29) to 550 AS ($29.26), with doubles going for 260 AS ($13.83) to 450 AS ($23.94) per person. Garage space is available to guests.

Staying at Hungerburg

Hotel Bellevue, Hochinnsbruck/Hungerburg (tel. 36965), is a large and rambling white-walled building with a well-maintained series of flowered balconies and grassy lawns. My favorite room has a red and blue-black Persian carpet with a high ceiling of honey-colored beams and brass chandeliers. On the premises are an indoor pool, a sauna, a restaurant, café, and the kind of bar you'd like to spend time in. From the windows of the spacious modern bedrooms you'll have a view of the mountains and the city of Innsbruck. Doubles range from 1,080 AS ($57.46) to 1,320 AS ($70.22), while singles go for 600 AS ($31.92) to 780 AS ($41.50), with breakfast included. Rates depend on the location of the units, each of which contains a private bath. The hotel is closed in November.

Hotel Pension Zur Linde, Hungerburg (tel. 37103), is a Tyrolean-style hotel with a complicated hipped and gabled roof covered in red tiles, plus a central slate-covered tower capped with a weathervane which usually points to the nearby mountains. The house is furnished with many antiques and original paintings and sculptures by Tyrolean artists. All the rooms have private balconies which look down onto the pleasant sun terrace. Prices for bed and breakfast are from 330 AS ($17.56) to 450 AS ($23.94) per person, depending on the season and the plumbing. On the premises are big gardens, a café, and a wine restaurant. The Patscheider family are the agreeable hosts.

Café/Pension Alpina, Hungerburg (tel. 36989). Botanists will love naming the varieties of flowers that grow from the windowboxes attached to the three floors of balconies of this family-run hotel. Guests often choose to sit under the parasols on the pleasant lawn, sipping coffee and planning their next excursion to Innsbruck. The interior is paneled in light-grained pine, with alpine-style stools around the bar. The accommodating designer of this place surrounded the ceramic oven in the restaurant with a banquette. The Mair family prepares homemade pastries fresh every day in the café. The pleasant bedrooms rent for 375 AS ($19.95) in a single and 285 AS ($15.16) to 375 AS ($19.95) per person in a double, with breakfast included. Prices depend on the plumbing and the room assignment.

Lodging at Amras

Hotel Kapeller, 96 Philippine-Welser-Strasse (tel. 43106). You'll notice several pieces of polychrome church art scattered throughout the public rooms here, as well as a stone- and wood-trimmed decor of well-crafted rusticity. The in-house restaurant is comfortable, pleasant, and clean, while the rest of the hotel is totally satisfactory and above average in every way. The hotel has a cozy bar in the lobby and a garden. The Happ family charges 720 AS ($38.30) for singles and 1,050 AS ($55.86) for doubles in their pleasantly furnished rooms. Breakfast is included in the rates. You'll find this hotel near the church in the center of the village.

WHERE TO DINE: This is never a problem in Innsbruck, as this alpine town has more than 150 restaurants, inns, and cafés, some of which offer entertainment at night. I suggest that if you're only going to be in Austria for a short time, you should stick to original Tyrolean specialties. However, if that doesn't suit you, you'll find an array of international cookery as well.

The Leading Restaurants

Belle Époque, Clima Hotel, 7 Zeughausgasse (tel. 28361), my favorite restaurant in Innsbruck, is festooned with Edwardian-era palms, belle-époque chandeliers, and crisply ironed pink napery. It occupies most of the ground floor of the Clima Hotel (see "where to stay"). By the standards it sets, you'd never guess you were within a hotel dining room. You'll probably be greeted at the door by the charming co-owner, Gudrun Wolf, whose husband Friedrich concocts the establishment's excellent cuisine. In warm weather, you'll be offered a seat amid the vines of the garden, where strains of live piano music accompany meals on weekends.

Many of the sophisticated specialties are researched and invented during the Wolfs' annual visits to the culinary citadels of France. Your meal might include a "variation of gooseliver," a salad of Atlantic fish with fresh asparagus in a watercress-flavored vinaigrette, homemade tagliatelle with basil and paprika, medallions of pork, veal, and beef with an herb sauce and three kinds of vegetable purée, a roulade of wild salmon, ragoût of venison, and a tempting array of desserts. A skillfully arranged "menu gastronomique" costs 480 AS ($25.54) for four courses or 740 AS ($39.37) for seven courses. Many guests end an evening here with a visit to the Clima disco.

Domstuben, 3 Pfarrgassee (tel. 33353) is located, as its German name implies, near the cathedral of St. Jakob. You can choose between the ground-floor or the upper-level restaurants, both of them rustically and tastefully filled with lots of wood and handcrafted details. The lower level has a vaulted ceiling. Hors d'oeuvres come from a well-stocked buffet. They might be followed by such delectable dishes as Bohemian veal gulasch with homemade egg noodles, Ticino-style venison, or grilled scampi. Look for the daily specials as well. To follow, you face a full range of desserts, perhaps kiwi mango salad in Grand Marnier with vanilla cream. A la carte meals range from 300 AS ($15.96). The restaurant is open seven days a week, and reservations are suggested.

Weinhaus Jörgele, 13 Herzog-Friedrich-Strasse (tel. 26469), is an attractive, historic wine house brimming with atmosphere and a rustic Tyrolean decor. H. P. Cammerlander, the proprietor, and his friendly staff work hard to create a pleasant ambience—successfully so, if you judge by the repeat customers. On the ground floor, you can stop at the wine bar with the wine cellar in the background. Here you can taste some excellent Austrian and Italian wines. Upstairs you enter a gemütliches restaurant, where traditional foods of the winelands are served. Meals are priced at around 130 AS ($6.92). With the extensive menu and wine list found here, you're sure to enjoy your meal.

Restaurant Goldener Adler, 6 Herzog-Friedrich-Strasse (tel. 26334), is the kind of Teutonic establishment that has a firm reputation and a loyal following. Visitors from other Austrian cities often plan ahead to eat here, in the same way that Goethe did when he visited Innsbruck so long ago. The menu is attractively old-fashioned, specializing in such Tyrolean dishes as braised beef, veal Tyrolean style, noodles with sauerkraut, cabbage soup with bacon, and a superb tafelspitz. There's also fondue, and for dessert, try the Salzburger nockerl. A full meal will cost from 300 AS ($15.96). You can dine in the Andreas-Hofer Stube or the Kaiser-Josef Stube on the second floor or in the Batzenhäusl or Goethe Stube downstairs. The latter is an evening restaurant, where meals are accompanied by zither music. The same menu and prices apply to all the rooms.

Gourmet, 6 Mariahilf (tel. 87141). Diners lucky enough to get window seats in this second-floor restaurant enjoy a view of the river and the old city on the opposite bank. When you enter, you'll check your coat and perhaps enjoy a drink at the street-level bar before climbing up to the Tyrolean dining room. Beneath a wooden ceiling, you can sample such dishes as chicken fricassee with morels and wild rice, a changing array of fish dishes, chicken liver pâté with fresh berry jelly, rack of venison, and beaujolais-flavored noodles with crab sauce. Carlo Aichner translates each item on the menu into English, often suggesting appropriate wines or side dishes for his guests. Your dining companions might include such luminaries as the Lord Mayor of Innsbruck and his entourage. Set menus cost around 440 AS ($23.41) and 600 AS ($31.92). Reservations are suggested, and food is served every day of the week except Sunday.

Moderate to Budget Dining

Churrasco, 2 Innrain (tel. 26398), is an attractive, warmly decorated pizzeria housed in a pink stucco building at the riverside. Inside you'll see an airy and comfortable decor which includes a copper sculpture composed of vertical pipes of varying sizes welded together above the bar. You can sit in one of several rooms. You climb antique stairs to the second floor to reach the pizzeria, La Mamma. There you can enjoy such specialties as game alla carbonara, a mixed fish roast, and at least 16 pasta dishes and seven different meat specialties. In summer the management places tables outside at the edge of the river. Full meals range from 180 AS ($9.58) to 315 AS ($16.75), depending on what you order. Specialties on the ground floor are the same, except for the emphasis on grilled meats.

Moby Dick, Adamgasse (tel. 33580), near the train station, has a dimly lit ambience and a nautical theme, as its name would suggest. Although having little to do with historic Innsbruck, it's still a relaxing place to drop into for a drink, a snack, or a seafood dinner. The decor includes a horseshoe-shape bar and lots of ship's lanterns and polished brass. Menu items run to quick lunches and all the seafood dishes you'd expect. Full meals range from 180 AS ($9.58) to 315 AS ($16.75).

Stiftskeller, 31 Burggraben (tel. 23490). This unpretentious restaurant is housed in an 18th-century yellow-and-white palace, whose baroque detailing can be admired from the streetside beer garden. At night the garden is illuminated by lights attached to the verdant shade trees.

You can, of course, in cold weather dine inside. There, a crucifix of a tormented Christ hangs with other pieces of sculpture under a high wooden ceiling in one of the simple rooms. There are several other seating possibilities down some of the tiled corridors.

This place can get rowdy at night, but the management works hard cleaning up the next day to prepare for another onslaught. Simple meals are posted on a blackboard, and they usually include soup, a main course, and dessert for around 135 AS ($7.18). The cellar is open daily from 9 a.m. to midnight.

Stiegl-Bräu, 25 Wilhelm-Greil-Strasse (tel. 24338), is a likeable beer hall near the Holiday Inn in the center of town. Popular with locals because of its well-prepared homemade food, the restaurant offers three different wood-paneled rooms, plus copious amounts of wine and beer if you want that. Fixed-price meals range from 115 AS ($6.12) to 170 AS ($9.04).

Weisses Kreuz Restaurant, 31 Herzog-Friedrich-Strasse (tel. 21890), in the Gasthof-Hotel Weisses Kreuz, is a good place to find typical Tyrolean food served in a country atmosphere generated by the painted facade and the happily cluttered, rustic interior. The restaurant on the second floor is open from 11 a.m. to 2:30 p.m. and 5:30 p.m. to midnight. During the summer season, a zither player entertains guests in the evening. On the first floor, a bar and a snack restaurant are open all day, as is a beer garden just in front of the hotel in Innsbruck's pedestrian area. In all the facilities, you can stop in just for a beer, but if you're hungry, you'll find a good selection of simply prepared fare, including Wiener schnitzel, rumpsteak with french fries, and grilled chicken. A full meal costs from 250 AS ($13.30).

Restaurant Kaffee Ottoburg, 1 Herzog-Friedrich-Strasse (tel. 34652), dating from the 13th century, is almost completely covered in wood and has green and red brocaded chairs, pretty waitresses, and Tyrolean music playing softly from near the well-stocked bar area. Beer comes in tall clear glasses without handles.

Upstairs is a well-known restaurant, separated into four rooms on two different floors, each having the same menu. They have names such as Maximilian Stube and Herzogstube. Each room holds a maximum of five tables in a setting that might be called "19th-century Gothic." The decor includes paneling grown smoky with time, carefully notched ceiling beams, and irregular floor plans which create intimate nooks and out-of-the-way crannies for intimate dining.

A daily menu is offered for 110 AS ($5.85). Specialties include venison stew, a special mixed grill, pork chops with rice and carrots, and fried trout, the latter priced by the gram. The chef will also do a veal shank for two persons. The international menu emphasizes Tyrolean specialties, best seen in the dessert list, which offers two kinds of strudel and several other pastries. An average à la carte meal will cost around 180 AS ($9.58).

Altes Haus Delevo, 9 Maria-Theresien-Strasse (tel. 28088). You enter this 18th-century beer hall from the busiest street in the inner city, which helps to make this one of Innsbruck's most popular gathering places. The clientele is gemütlich. Two anterooms have arched ceilings and golden-grained paneling. Farther on, a high-ceilinged bar area is usually filled with lots of beer drinkers and is accented with blue tiles and medieval sculpture. What you'll see on the ground floor is only a fraction of the total area available to guests here.

Down a flight of steps is a dimly lit cellar with blue-checked tablecloths. Upstairs, an open gallery permits a view of the bar and opens into another drinking area, at the end of which is a round table under a conical ceiling. Even the beams of this place are painted with pithy sayings (one of them, translated, means "old wine makes old hearts young again").

The beer is priced from 25 AS ($1.33) and is served in ceramic mugs, while the food is classically Austrian and Tyrolean, including small cheese dumplings, pork roast with sauerkraut, and apple strudel. Meals are priced at around 180 AS ($9.58). An inexpensive selection of Austrian wines is available.

Hirschstuben, 5 Kiebachgasse (tel. 22979). The old-style decor of this Tyrolean restaurant encompasses two rooms, one with a beamed and one with a vaulted ceiling. You'll see hand-chiseled stone columns, brocade chairs, and a large stainless-steel bar dividing the two rooms. You'll have to go down a few steps from street level, but once you're there you can select an array of daily specials that might include fish soup, trout meunière, sliced veal in cream sauce Zurich style, veal steak with morels and cream sauce, beef Stroganoff, peppersteak, and for dessert, either Austrian crêpes or Salzburger nockerl. Fixed-price meals range from 115 AS ($6.12), while à la carte dinners average 200 AS ($10.64). Reservations are suggested.

Altstadtstüberl, 13 Riesengasse (tel. 22347), provides a pleasant destination point after a walk through the old town. In one of Innsbruck's most historic sections, the restaurant offers an uncomplicated decor well suited to the presentation of the simply prepared and generous portions of the Austrian and Tyrolean specialties. These include Tyrolean-style liver, meat-and-marrow soup, tafelspitz, grilled pork, beef, and chicken, along with potatoes smothered in cheese sauce. Fixed-price meals range from 75 AS ($3.99) to 210 AS ($11.17), while à la carte dinners average 300 AS ($15.96). The restaurant is closed on Sunday.

Basco, 12 Anichstrasse (tel. 20149). Set into a shop-lined street running into the busy Maria-Theresien-Strasse, this long and narrow restaurant stretches almost endlessly past an animated array of open kitchens and crowded bars. Many guests come here just for a drink, planting themselves with their friends and sometimes their dogs on one of the sun-flooded stools in front. A busy corridor leads past the open kitchens where teams of uniformed chefs prepare the establishment's medley of the cuisines of Italy, Mexico, and Spain. Dining tables are set in back amid a greenhouse decor of live plants, a bubbling fountain, and pinpointed lighting. Some of the menu items are meant for two persons, including paella and the fritto misto di mare. You can also try tortelloni tricolore, several kinds of enchiladas, a handful of fish dishes (including filet of sole), and an array of grills such as a juicy "Cattlemansteak." Full meals cost from 220 AS ($11.70).

Weisses Rössl, 8 Kiebachgasse (tel. 23057). You'll enter this time-honored place through a stone archway opening onto one of the most famous streets of the old town. At the end of a flight of stairs, with a crucifix at the top, you'll find two rooms with red-tile floors and about the most extensive set of stag horns (complete with the initials of the hunter and the date of the shooting) in Innsbruck. The simple menu offers daily specials and typical Tyrolean dishes usually served with pommes frites. Specials include saftgulasch with polenta, a grilled plate "alt insprugg" served for two persons, and a variety of schnitzels. Service is friendly, and meals range from 75 AS ($3.99) to 125 AS ($6.65). The restaurant is closed on Sunday and for all of November.

Wienerwald Breinössl, 12 Maria-Theresien-Strasse (tel. 24165). This chain might be called the Howard Johnson's of Austria. It offers chain-restaurant gemütlich, generous portions, and hours that are usually longer than those of many smaller restaurants, including on Sunday. This particular branch is on one of the main inner-city streets of town. It offers a cavernous beer hall with a high ceiling, plus several smaller rooms. The simple and wholesome food includes six kinds of soup, three kinds of salad, five kinds of chicken, and six kinds of schnitzel, along with a sampling of beef and pork dishes. A children's menu is also offered. Beer and wine are served by the glass. The menu is in both English and German, and a meal usually ranges from 100 AS ($5.32) to 175 AS ($9.31), depending on what you order.

Some Leading Cafés

Café Munding, 16 Keibachstrasse (tel. 24118), on a quiet corner in the old town, is a comfortable-looking house built in 1720 in a baroque format of frescoes, carved bay windows, and lots of Tyrolean detailing. The interior has been modernized, offering an interconnected series of simple rooms, one of which has an ornate plaster ceiling and an abstract mural. The first thing you'll see when you enter is a pastry and chocolate shop. Food is served in the inner rooms, which in addition to coffee priced from 18 AS (96¢), includes pizzas from 60 AS ($3.19), and toasts from 30 AS ($1.60), plus wine by the glass. The waitresses wear black dresses and frilly blue aprons.

Stadtcafé, 2 Rennweg (tel. 26869). Between sips of your coffee, priced from 18 AS (96¢), you can admire the attending nymphs and deities supporting the base of the equestrian statue in front of the elegantly modern café. It has a tall ceiling with starburst chandeliers, warmly tinted banquettes, and large photographs of theatrical scenes from the nearby Landestheater. It's open from 9 a.m. to midnight, with hot food served from 11 a.m. to 3 p.m. and from 5 to 11 p.m. In addition to just coffee and pastries, you can also order full meals here, including grilled pork, veal, rumpsteak with poppyseed noodles, pasta, Tyrolean soups, and ham and cheese sandwiches. A menu of the day costs 150 AS ($7.98).

Alte Teestube, 6 Riesengasse (tel. 22309). The music which will probably accompany your beverage at this old-fashioned tea room might have pleased Mozart or one of his contemporaries. You can order a surprisingly varied array of tea here, any of which would go well with the pastries glistening temptingly in the light from brass candlesticks. The location is one flight above a street-level restaurant in the center of the old town. Coffee or tea begins at 15 AS (80¢), while pastries average 19 AS ($1.01). The establishment is open every day except Saturday.

Dining in the Environs

Gasthof Wilder Mann (tel. 77387) at Lans. If you appreciate architecture, you'll enjoy studying the stucco tower attached to the corner of this elongated building with the half-timbered triangular section just under the sloping roofline. The interior is pleasantly spacious and rustic, with good service and a series of well-prepared traditional specialties such as wine soup, venison pâté with cumberland sauce, filet steak in a pepper cream sauce, and something called Wilde Mann Platte, which is an assorted collection of several kinds of savory meat with french fries and fresh vegetables for two persons. Dessert could be a Salzburger nockerl. Meals average about 275 AS ($14.63). The restaurant is open daily except from mid-January until the beginning of February. The Schatz and Schöpf families are the gracious owners of this place.

Restaurant Kapeller, 96 Philippine-Welser-Strasse (tel. 43106) at Amras, is set in a beautiful decor of modernized chalet chairs, Oriental rugs, and a tasteful and well-constructed combination of stone, stucco, and wood. Menu items are imaginatively light, including salads made with generous amounts of radicchio, avocados, mushrooms, and gorgonzola. If you like soup, try the cream of fennel, and if you're looking for fish, sample the John Dory in white wine sauce or the fresh trout. Meat courses include venison in season, tafelspitz, filet of roast hare, and many veal and pork specialties. Fixed-price meals range from 180 AS ($9.58) to 420 AS ($22.34), while à la carte dinners cost from 135 AS ($7.18) to 385 AS ($20.48). The restaurant is closed on Sunday and for all of January, and reservations are strongly suggested.

SHOPPING: On their home turf, you can purchase such Tyrolean specialties as lederhosen, dirndls, leather clothing, woodcarving, loden cloth, and all sorts of skiing and mountain-climbing equipment. You can stroll around such streets as the Maria-Theresien-Strasse, the Herzog-Friedrich-Strasse, and the Museumstrasse, ducking in and making discoveries of your own, perhaps finding some treasured gift or souvenir.

Here are a few of my recommendations if you're seeking something special:

Tiroler Heimatwerk, 2 Meraner Strasse (tel. 22320), is one of the best stores in Innsbruck for such handcrafted Tyrolean-style items as sculpture, pewter, textiles, woolen goods, hand-knitted sweaters, lace, and bolts of silk for do-it-yourselfers. You can purchase regionally inspired fabrics and dress patterns which you can whip into a dirndl (or whatever) as soon as you get home. Also for sale are carved chests, mirror frames, and furniture. The elegant decor includes ancient stone columns and old, well-maintained vaulted ceilings. The friendly saleswomen wear regional dresses.

Gmunder Keramik, 15 Wilhelm-Greil-Strasse (tel. 23152), is the Innsbruck outlet of this famous ceramic house whose headquarters are in Gmunden. Its merchandise includes lidded beer mugs in a variety of colorful, hand-worked patterns, plus complete dinner or coffee services.

Lanz, 15 Wilhelm-Greil-Strasse (tel. 23105), is a bright clothing store where the staff wear regional dresses and where the inventory includes everything you'd need to look authentically Tyrolean. Specific items include dresses, sweaters, dirndls, stockings, handkerchiefs, lederhosen, hand-knit sweaters, leather belts, sport coats, and overcoats. The store carries children's clothing and apparel for men too.

Handwerkskunst, 15 Wilhelm-Greil-Strasse (tel. 23152), also at the same address, stands near the Bozner-Platz. This shop sells an attractive selection of handmade objects, such as pewter tankards, vases, candlesticks, boxes of all shapes, silver and Tyrolean garnet jewelry, crystal, textiles, brass antique-style vessels, and porcelain hand-painted breakfast services.

Lodenbaur, 4 Brixner Strasse (tel. 20911). This is the closest address you'll find to a department store in Innsbruck devoted to regional Tyrolean dress. Most of the goods are made in Austria, including a full array of lederhosen, coats, dresses, dirndls, and accessories for men, women, and children. Be sure to check out the basement as well.

AFTER DARK: Innsbruck is more lighthearted about its nightlife than is Vienna. If you're in luck you'll get to attend a summer concert in the park or perhaps take in an operetta at the theater. You might retire to a beer hall to listen to brass bands and yodeling or be lulled by zither music at a restaurant.

Why not stroll through the Aldstadt and, if it's a summer night, meander through the Hofgarten, which is lit? Perhaps you'd enjoy taking the funicular to Hungerburg for an overview of the night lights of Innsbruck, where many of the historic buildings and fountains are illuminated. Best of all, you can attend a

Tyrolean folkloric evening or retreat to a typical local wine tavern offering entertainment.

The average drink here costs from 50 AS ($2.66) to 80 AS ($4.26), except in the strip clubs, which often charge far more. Likewise, you almost never have to pay a cover charge except in one of the "erotic" clubs.

It's wise to check with the Tourist Office as to current offerings, both theatrical presentations and folkloric ones. For example, in summer there's often a parade of a Tyrolean brass band in costumes, with a concert at the Goldenes Dachl. There are also likely to be concerts at Ambras Castle, ecclesiastical music at Wilten Basilica, organ concerts at the Igls parish church, and so on. Summer is the active season for this type of public entertainment.

If you want casino action, you have to drive to the resort of Seefeld (see attractions coming up), where the **Spiel-Casino** there offers roulette, baccarat, blackjack, or whatever from 5 p.m. There's also a restaurant, **Locanda,** on the premises.

Many of the restaurants, in addition to food, offer Tyrolean evenings. That way, your dining choice also becomes your nightclub for the evening, which is a lot cheaper than going to a restaurant, then a separate nightclub.

Typical among these is the **Stiftskeller,** 31 Burggraben (tel. 23490), already recommended as a restaurant. It presents a Tyrolean evening, beginning at 8. The folklore program offers an evening of country music, songs, yodeling, zither playing, hackbrett, xylophone, alphorn, singing saws, raffele, folk dancing, and schuhplatteln.

Tyrolean entertainment is also featured at the **Heuriger** at the Hotel Weisses Kreuz, 31 Herzog-Friedrich-Strasse (tel. 21890). In the wine tavern, open to midnight, you can order legs of pork and crisp chicken while enjoying the music.

Clima Disco, 7 Zeughausgasse (tel. 28-3-61). By anyone's standards, this is the most sophisticated, glamorous, and alluring disco in Innsbruck. Set in the basement of the Clima Hotel, its futuristic decor is light years away from the alpine ambience of the hotel's lobby or the belle-époque decor of the adjacent restaurant. Against a scarlet background of plushly upholstered banquettes and wraparound sound, columns of illuminated water bubble within plexiglas pipes. On a busy night, the bar is one of the most active in town. The club is open between 9 p.m. and 2 a.m. every night except Sunday and Monday.

Club Central, Hotel Central, Am Sparkassenplatz (tel. 20310), is the elegantly futuristic disco inside one of the most architecturally innovative hotels in town. An over-30 crowd gathers here under festive lights in a comfortably padded and upholstered room which occasionally offers live music. There's no dress code, although many of the clients tend to "dress up." Entrance is free, and it's open till 3 a.m. every day of the week except Tuesday.

Club Filou, 12 Stiftsgasse (tel. 21-54-12), in the heart of the old city, is my favorite bar and nightclub in Innsbruck. In summer, the tiny square in front of its facade blossoms with ivy-covered trellises, recorded music, and quadruplicate parasols which protect the copper-covered outdoor bar. If you venture inside, past the antique cash register (whose zinc-plated drawers contain candy), you'll find an intimate and sophisticated hangout filled with Victorian settees and pop art. The right-angled bar is usually patronized by visiting musicians, athletes, and attractively trendy local residents. Food is available until 3 a.m. every night which you can enjoy at the bar or at one of the tiny tables. The house specialty is spareribs, although salads, soups, schnitzels, scampi, smoked salmon, and desserts are also available. A main course begins at around 90 AS ($4.79), but no one will mind if you order only a snack or just a drink.

In a separate, very old room, the high ceiling of a disco is supported by medieval stone columns and ringed with a high-tech steel balcony. There's no cover charge. Long drinks in both the café (which opens at 6 p.m.) and the disco (which opens at 9 p.m.) begin at around 65 AS ($3.46). Both sections close at 4 a.m. Filou is open seven nights a week.

Casablanca Café Americain, 4 Adolf Pichlerplatz (tel. 28-55-92). Anyone over 25 might feel that they've stepped into alien territory, but if you're the right age, on the make, and into punk rock, you'll fit in here. A marble foyer leads into a high-ceilinged room filled with mirrors, lattices, Bogart/Bergman memorabilia, a prominent bar, and dozens of tiny tables. Drinks begin at 20 AS ($1.06) and are served between 4 p.m. and 1 a.m. on weekdays and between 5 p.m. and 1 a.m. on weekends.

Tiffany, Rhombergpassage (tel. 34927), is a popular dance bar which accepts credit cards and serves an international cuisine. It's open from 8:30 p.m. to 4 a.m. every night of the week. The clients range from the relatively conservative to a smattering of punk rockers, but Tiffany is generally acknowledged to be one of the city's more interesting clubs.

Highlife Club, 2 Seilergasse (tel. 22163), has a higher percentage of gay clients than any other nightclub in the city. It's small and often gets very crowded. If you decide to go, you'll notice flowers on the wood bar, a cramped gold and metallic dance floor, and a light show visible through branches and paper flowers. Drinks cost from 65 AS ($3.46), and on Saturday night there's a cover charge of 50 AS ($2.66). The club is open seven days a week from 8:30 p.m. to 4 a.m., but doesn't start to fill up until after 10 p.m.

Queen Anne Club, 6 Amraserstrasse (tel. 35155), has a high ceiling, lots of colored lights, and a stage for the musical acts that sometimes appear here. You'll find plenty of places to sit, plus a nearby pub under the same management (Paulis Pub), where a more sedate crowd talks quietly in a warmly masculine ambience of wood and olive-colored velvet.

Nightclub Lady-O, 2 Bruneckerstrasse (tel. 26432), near the train station, offers voyeuristic clients a collection of charming female artists. On one recent occasion they included Speedy Gonzales (erotic acrobatics), Brigitte Varga ("black magic"), and Willy Mexiko (trained pets and striptease). You might also have caught Carlos Nepopo and his Brazilian carnival collection of women's clothing. Entrance fee is 50 AS ($2.66), while the first drink costs 125 AS ($6.65). The club is open daily from 8 p.m. to 4 a.m., with shows beginning at 10:30 p.m.

Goethe Stube, Restaurant Goldener Adler, 6 Herzog-Friedrich-Strasse (tel. 26334). Aside from the good food (see my restaurant recommendation), this place offers a nightly program including the zither and "jodlers." No admission is charged, but at least one drink is obligatory. It's open from 7 p.m. to midnight.

Scotch Club, 5 Museumstrasse (tel. 25411), is open every day from 8:30 p.m. to 3:30 a.m. This nightclub, which has disco music for dancing, welcomes a wide range of clients of all persuasions. It accepts credit cards, and contains a restaurant serving an international cuisine.

Club Innsbruck

Visitors who stay in Innsbruck at least three days automatically become members of Club Innsbruck, which meets every Monday at 8 p.m. at the Hotel Grauer Bar, 5 Universitätsstrasse. You'll get a membership card at your accommodation when you check in for the necessary length of stay, assuring you of a surprising number of advantages. The card is also available at the Tourist Office (see under "Practical Facts").

Hotel and restaurant owners and the staff of the Tourist Office welcome you at the club meeting, give you a drink, and dispense information and advice to make your vacation better. You'll be shown slides by mountain guides. Hiking and mountaineering tours are arranged, and badges are awarded for participation.

Your membership card entitles you to free rides on the Innsbruck Mountain Bus daily from 9 a.m., leaving from the Kongresshaus (convention center), and participation in the Innsbruck mountaineering program, with free mountain guides. You get a 50% reduction in admission price at the Museum of Tyrolean Folk Art, the Hofkirche, the Ferdinandeum State Museum, and the Olympic Museum, plus a 20% reduction on fares on the Nordkette, Patscherfofel, and Mutterer Alm cable cars and lifts, and a 10% reduction on fees at some tennis courts and greens fees at golf courses.

For further information, ask at the Tourist Office (see above).

THE SIGHTS: As I mentioned above, **Maria-Theresien-Strasse,** which cuts through the heart of the city from north to south, is the main street of Innsbruck, a good place to begin your exploration. Often it's fascinating just to watch the passersby, especially when they're attired in the Tyrolean regional dress. Once this street was traversed by wayfarers heading over the Brenner Pass from Italy and on to Germany. Many 17th- and 18th-century houses line Maria-Theresien-Strasse.

On the south end of this wide street, a **Triumphpforte** (triumphal arch), modeled after those in Rome, spans the shopping street. Maria Theresa ordered it built in 1765 with a two-fold purpose: to honor the marriage of her son, the Duke of Tuscany (later Emperor Leopold II), to a Spanish princess, and to mourn the death of her beloved husband, Emperor Franz I. From this arch southward the street is called Leopoldstrasse.

Going north from the arch along Maria-Theresien-Strasse you'll see **St. Anna's Column** (Annasäule), which every visitor seems to photograph. It enjoys the same renown in Innsbruck as the Eros statue does in Piccadilly Circus. Standing in front of the 19th-century Rathaus (the present city hall), the column was erected in 1706 in thanksgiving for the withdrawal in 1703 of Bavarian invasion armies during the War of the Spanish Succession. On top of this Corinthian column a statue of the Virgin Mary stands on a crescent moon, with statues of the Saints Cassianus, Virgilius, George, and Anna surrounding the base.

Not far north of the Annasäule, the wide street narrows and becomes the Herzog-Friedrich-Strasse running through the heart of the **Altstadt** (old town), the medieval quarter. This street is arcaded and flanked by a number of well-maintained burgher's houses with a jumble of turrets and gables. Look for the multitude of dormer windows and oriels. Most of the buildings here are overhung with protective roofs to guard them against snowfalls.

Hofburg, 1 Rennweg, to the east of the Aldstadt, is the 15th-century imperial palace of Emperor Maximilian I, rebuilt in rococo style in the 18th century on orders of Maria Theresa. Later it was to hold sad memories for the empress, as it was here that her husband died in 1765. The palace, the exterior of which is colored Maria Theresa ochre (a yellow which the empress favored) and flanked by a set of domed towers, is a fine example of baroque secular architecture. The structure has four wings and a two-story Riesensaal (giant's hall), painted in white and gold and filled with portraits of the Habsburgs. The rooms recall the power and heyday of that ruling family.

You can visit the state rooms and the Riesensaal on guided tours, lasting about half an hour, daily from 9 a.m. to 4 p.m. It's closed Sunday from mid-October to mid-May. Admission is 20 AS ($1.06).

The **Hofkirche,** 2 Universitätsstrasse, is a Gothic-style church built in 1553 by Ferdinand I. Its most important treasure is the cenotaph of Maximilian I, although his remains, alas, are not in this elegant marble sarcophagus glorifying the Roman Empire. He was never brought here from Wiener Neustadt where he was entombed in 1519. The tomb, a great feat of the German Renaissance style of sculpture, has 28 bronze 16th-century statues of Maximilian's real and legendary ancestors and relatives surrounding the kneeling emperor on the cenotaph with 24 marble reliefs on the sides depicting scenes from his life. Three of the statues are based on designs by Dürer. Tyrol's national hero, Andreas Hofer, is entombed here.

The Hofkirche has a lovely Renaissance porch, plus a nave and a trio of aisles in the Gothic style. One gallery contains nearly two dozen small statues of the saint protectors of the house of Habsburg. The wooden organ, dating from 1560, is still operational.

Another chapel, the Silberne Kapell, or silver chapel, was constructed between the church and the palace in 1578 on orders of Archduke Ferdinand II of Tyrol as the final resting place for him and his wife, Philippine Welser. The chapel takes its name from a silver Madonna. Silver reliefs on the altar symbolize the Laurentanian Litany. Alexander Colin designed the sarcophagi of Ferdinand and Philippine.

The Hofkirche and chapel are open from the first of May until the end of September from 9 a.m. to 5 p.m.; otherwise from 9 a.m. to noon and from 2 to 5 p.m. Admission is 17 AS (90¢).

The **Hofgarten,** a public park containing lakes and many shade trees, including weeping willows, lies north of Rennweg. Concerts are often presented at the Kunstpavillon in the garden during the summer months.

The **Goldenes Dachl,** or Golden Roof, is perhaps Innsbruck's greatest tourist attraction, certainly its most characteristic landmark. It's a three-story balcony on a house in the old town, the late Gothic oriels capped with 2,657 gold-plated tiles. It was constructed for Emperor Maximilian I to serve as a royal box where he could sit in luxury and enjoy tournaments in the square below. Completed at the dawn of the 16th century, the Golden Roof was built in honor of Maximilian's second marriage, to Bianca Maria Sforza of Milan (Maximilian was a ruler who expanded his territory not by conquest but by marriage). Not wishing to alienate the allies gained by his first marriage, to Maria of Burgundy, which was ended by her death, he had himself painted on this balcony between the two women. But he is looking at the new wife, Bianca.

Inside the building you can visit the **Olympic Museum,** 15 Herzog-Friedrich-Strasse (tel. 20948), where video films are shown of Innsbruck and the most interesting scenes from the 1964 and 1976 Olympic Winter Games in English, plus exhibits from the Winter Olympics and an international Olympics stamp collection. The museum is open daily from 9:30 a.m. to noon and from 2 to 5 p.m.

Take a look at Helblinghaus, on Herzog-Friedrich-Strasse opposite the Goldenes Dachl. It's a Gothic structure to which a rococo facade was added.

Dom zu St. Jakob (the Cathedral of St. James), on the Domplatz, was rebuilt from 1717 to 1722 from designs by Johann Jakob Herkommer, a baroque architect. It has a lavishly embellished baroque interior, part of it done by the Asam brothers, and is roofed with domes. The church was heavily damaged in Allied bombing raids in World War II. One of the chief treasures of the cathedral is *Maria Hilf* by Lucas Cranach the Elder, on the main altar. In the north aisle, look for a 1620 monument honoring Archduke Maximilian II, who died in 1618. The church is open from 6 a.m. to noon and from 2 to 5 p.m. It's closed Friday morning.

The **Stadtturm,** or belfry, is seen at the old Rathaus (town hall) on the east side of Herzog-Friedrich-Strasse. It rises 190 feet high, and from it you'll have a good view of the city and its environs. Originally built as a watchtower in the 14th century, the Stadtturm has undergone many changes over the centuries. It's open daily from the first of April until the end of October from 9 a.m. to 6 p.m., to 7 p.m. in July and August. Admission is 20 AS ($1.06).

The **Tiroler Volkskunstmuseum** (Tyrol Museum of Popular Art), 2 Universitätsstrasse, houses one of the largest and most impressive collections extant of the artifacts of life in Tyrol, ranging from furniture, often painted, to regional garb.

The museum, adjoining the Hofkirche on its eastern side, is in the **Neues Stift,** or New Abbey, dating from the 16th and the 18th centuries. Rooms on three floors are filled with exhibits. A collection of Tyrolean mangers, or Christmas cribs, contains some from the 18th century. The Stuben (the finest rooms) are on the upper floors. Displays include a range of styles from Gothic to Renaissance to baroque, as well as a collection of models of typical Tyrolean houses. The museum is open from 9 a.m. to 5 p.m., to noon on Sunday. Admission is 20 AS ($1.06).

Ferdinandeum Tyrol Museum (Tiroler Landesmuseum Ferdinandeum), 15 Museumstrasse (tel. 22003), has a celebrated gallery of Flemish and Dutch masters. This museum also traces the development of popular art in the Tyrolean country, with highlights from the Gothic period. You'll also see the original bas-reliefs used in designing the Goldenes Dachl. The museum is open daily from the first of May until the end of September from 9 a.m. to 5 p.m. (also from 7 to 9 p.m. Thursday). The rest of the year, the hours are 10 a.m. to noon and 2 to 5 p.m.; closed on Sunday afternoon and all day Monday. Admission is 14 AS (75¢).

The **Alpenzoo Innsbruck-Tirol,** 37 Weiherburggasse (tel. 3-67-75), lies on the southern slope of the Nordkette below Hungerburg plateau, affording a striking view of Innsbruck and the surrounding mountains. It contains only those animals indigenous to the Alps, plus alpine birds, reptiles, and fish. The zoo is open daily from 9 a.m. to 6 p.m., to 5 p.m. in winter. Admission is 50 AS ($2.66).

EXPLORING IN THE ENVIRONS: Many of the satellite resorts such as Igls (coming up) can properly be considered day trips from Innsbruck. Therefore for the moment I'll highlight only those attractions on the most immediate outskirts of the city.

Hungerburg

Hungerburg mountain plateau (2,860 feet) is considered by many to be the most beautiful spot in Tyrol, affording the best view of Innsbruck, especially on a summer night when much of the city, including fountains and historic buildings, is floodlit. Some of the most scenic hotels in the Innsbruck environs are here, several of which I have recommended above.

You can drive to the plateau or else take the funicular, which departs about four times on the hour from 9 a.m. to 8 p.m., then about every 30 minutes until 10:30 p.m. There's an 11 p.m. funicular on Friday and Saturday night. Round-trip fare is 36 AS ($1.92).

From the plateau, the Nordkette cable railway quickly takes you up to the Seegrube and the Hafelekar (7,655 feet) for a sweeping view of alpine peaks and glaciers. This is the starting point of high mountain walks and climbing expeditions. In summer the cable railway runs every hour between 8 a.m. and 6 p.m. A round trip from Innsbruck to Hafelekar and back costs 208 AS ($11.07), while a trip between Hungerburg and Hafelekar is tabbed at 172 AS ($9.15).

Schloss Ambras

This medieval castle, two miles southeast of the heart of Innsbruck on the edge of the Mittelgebirgsterrace, is divided into a lower and an upper castle, the latter a fortress in the Middle Ages, subsequently much renovated. Archduke Ferdinand II, regent of Tyrol who died in 1595, had Schloss Ambras reconstructed as a Renaissance palace. It was his favorite residence and the center of the cultural life of his court.

The castle has a fine arms and armor collection, particularly jousting equipment, as well as an array of tapestries, antiques, frescoes, and a gallery of imperial portraits from the 15th to the 18th centuries. The Spanish Hall, built in 1570, is a highlight of Ambras, one of the first German Renaissance interiors. Visitors can see this as well as private rooms where Ferdinand lived with his beloved wife, Philippine Welser. Even her bathroom is shown on tours. Unfortunately, Vienna (the Kunsthistorischesmuseum, in particular) made off with most of Ferdinand's rich collections of objets d'art.

Schloss Ambras is open from the first of May until the end of September daily except Tuesday. Admission is 10 AS (53¢). To visit the upper castle costs another 10 AS.

After viewing the interior, you can take a leisurely stroll through the castle grounds.

The Wilten Basilica

The southern district of Innsbruck where the Sill River emerges from a gorge, Wilten is one of the most dramatic landscapes in the environs of the city. It's an ancient spot that was once the Roman town of Veldidena.

Its parish church, constructed from 1751 to 1755, became a basilica in 1957. Built in a rich rococo style with twin towers, this is considered one of the most splendid houses of worship in the Tyrolean country. It's noted for its stucco work by Franz Xaver Feichtmayr. Matthaus Gunther is responsible for the frescoes on the ceiling. A sandstone figure depicting "Our Lady of the Four Columns" has been the subject of pilgrimage since the Middle Ages.

Across from the basilica is a cluster of baroque buildings which are the outgrowth of an abbey founded there in 1138. The abbey church, dating from the 1650s, merits a visit. It has a porch guarded by two stone giants and a grille from 1707 found in the narthex. This church was damaged by World War II Allied bombing.

Bergisel

If you're driving, head out the Brenner road to Bergisel (2,450 feet), a lovely wooded section in the environs ideal for leisurely strolls in the warm months. It lies near the gorge of the Sill River on the southern outskirts of Innsbruck, about a 20-minute walk from the Wilten Basilica. Here you'll see the ski jumps built for the 1964 and 1976 Olympic Winter Games. You'll have splendid views from the jumps.

The hill here is a historic site, scene of the 1809 battles in which Andreas Hofer led some Tyrolean peasants against French and Bavarian forces. He was later shot to death in Mantua on orders of Napoleon. Below the ski jump, on the north side, is the Andreas Hofer monument erected in 1893 to commemorate the battle. Tyroleans speak of this as their "field of remembrance," and it's filled with memorials and visitors. However, heroic though the local deeds may be, they may not interest North Americans. I recommend that you visit here just for the views and the relaxing walks.

TOURS: Sightseeing tours of Innsbruck, lasting about an hour, leave by bus from the Hofburg at 10:15 a.m., noon, and 2 and 3 p.m.

A special two-hour bus tour leaves from Maria-Theresien-Strasse, the Central Railway Station, and Bozner Platz at 10 a.m. and 2 p.m.

Daily bus excursions from Innsbruck to the most beautiful part of Tyrol—Zillertal, Alpbach, and Kühtai—and to the favorite places in neighboring Italy and Germany and other parts of Austria, can be arranged at your hotel, a travel agency, or the Tourist Office.

2. Igls and the Environs

This section, site of many of the Olympic Winter Games of 1964 and 1976, might be called "Olympic Innsbruck." It consists of a cluster of resorts, the best known of which is Igls, all lying within easy reach of the Tyrol capital, often with a commuting time of only half an hour. Each of these resorts perched on the slopes where the Olympics took place could be an alternative to staying in Innsbruck, which is often crowded.

A complete system of lifts opens up alpine scenery to everybody, from the beginner to the most advanced skier—or to the sightseer in warm weather.

IGLS: Lying on a sunny plateau in the alpine foothills at an elevation of 2,875 feet, Igls is the resort choice of many people who prefer to stay here—in either winter or summer—and commute to Innsbruck, three miles north. Although its number swells greatly with winter and summer visitors, the town has a population of fewer than 2,000 souls. Because it's so popular, Igls is certainly not the cheapest resort in Tyrol.

A streetcar from the Berg Isel station in Innsbruck will deliver you to Igls, 1,000 feet higher than the capital, in about 30 minutes. Buses on route "J" leave every 30 minutes on the hour and half hour from Igls and the main railway station in Innsbruck. The local train on the no. 6 line leaves Innsbruck at a quarter past each hour and Igls at a quarter to.

The outdoor air at Igls, long known as the "sun terrace" of Innsbruck, is never likely to be too hot, even on the hottest day in Austria. In fact it feels air-conditioned outside even in summer. Although much of its world renown has been based on winter sports, this is a popular summer resort too, a place to rest or wander along alpine trails, to play golf on an 18-hole or a nine-hole course, to enjoy tennis, or whatever.

This is the favorite place for Innsbruckers to come to ski, and they're joined by throngs of visitors. Igls shared the Winter Olympics festivities and sporting competition with Innsbruck, and following the success of the 1976 event, this small resort town can boast a thrilling bobsled and toboggan run that enjoys great renown among the sporting crowd flocking here in winter—both Americans and Europeans.

The major excursion from here is to take a cable car up to **Patscherkofel,** at an elevation of 6,430 feet, a ride covering about 2½ miles and taking about 18 minutes. Patscherkofel is the mountain that gives Innsbruck its vista. Many long ski descents from the mountain are possible.

A small kindergarten for children is in a log cabin in the **Kurpark,** a natural wooded area near the center of the village.

The area code for Igls is 05222.

Food and Lodging

Schlosshotel (tel. 77217), the most glamorous hotel in town, sits on its own grass-covered plateau at the end of a narrow street running into the main artery of the resort. It rises above its surrounding conifers, jutting an elaborate roofline of slate-capped spires, intricate chimneys, and baroque curves toward the nearby farming hamlet of Vils. The wraparound veranda is graced with a pair of stone lions.

As the proportions of the outside imply, the bedrooms inside are high-ceilinged and spacious. They sometimes offer splendid views of the mountains, and always contain a private bath. Most clients check in here on the full-board plan, at a cost ranging between 1,500 AS ($79.80) to 2,000 AS ($106.40) per person daily. An excellent restaurant serves both traditional and international food in turn-of-the-century surroundings. The schloss is closed between November 1 and mid-December and during most of April, and it also offers both indoor and outdoor swimming pools.

Sporthotel Igls (tel. 77241) is a fancifully designed hotel built in a style that's a cross between a baroque castle and a mountain chalet. Some of the details include jutting bay windows, at least three hexagonal stone-trimmed towers with ornate detailing, and rows of flower-covered balconies. The spacious interior is dotted with antiques and conservative furniture, with plenty of gemütlich corners and sunny areas, both indoors and out.

The hotel has two restaurants, an à la carte grill room, two elevators, a bar, and a big indoor/outdoor swimming pool, plus a range of health and cure facilities. Horseback riding, golf, and tennis are close at hand. In winter the hotel offers a daily five o'clock tea dance. With half board included, rates in a double range from 950 AS ($50.54) to 1,450 AS ($77.14), depending on the room and the season. Singles pay a daily supplement of 150 AS ($7.98), and a nearby annex holds the overflow from the main hotel.

Hotel Alpenhof (tel. 77491) is a tastefully furnished chalet with a salon, while other facilities include a warmly inviting bar area and a sunny terrace where Victor and Tilly Kittler serve well-prepared buffets. The hotel was modernized in 1980. The carpeted and comfortable bedrooms rent for 600 AS ($31.92) to 770 AS ($40.96) per person in a double and from 700 AS ($37.24) to 850 AS ($45.22) for a single. All rates include full board and vary according to the room and the season. The hotel is open from December to March and May to September.

Aegidlhof (tel. 77108) is a rambling chalet near the Kurpark and the ski lifts. The interior has lots of hand-worked details, such as antique armoires set into niches designed especially for them, wrought-iron window bars and lighting fixtures, beamed ceilings, and Oriental rugs. The Skardarasy family, your hosts, charge from 360 AS ($19.15) to 750 AS ($39.90) for a single and 275 AS ($14.63) to 600 AS ($31.92) per person for a double, with breakfast included. Prices depend on the season, the accommodation, and the plumbing. Open December to October.

Hotel Bon Alpina (tel. 77219) is a tastefully designed chalet, with Tyrolean atmosphere. In the center of the village, a ten-minute walk from the ski lifts, the hotel has a cozy restaurant, a scattering of antiques in the public rooms, and comfortable, simple bedrooms which rent for 490 AS ($26.07) to 650 AS ($34.58) per person, based on double occupancy, with half board included. Singles pay a daily supplement of 150 AS ($7.98). The hotel has a sauna and solarium as well as a sunny terrace.

Hotel Astoria (tel. 77481) is a wood and white-painted chalet near the center of Igls. The interior is darkly furnished with heavy wooden ceilings, autumnal colors, and hanging brass lamps. On the premises are a padded bar and a small swimming pool. The light-colored bedrooms have private baths, southern balconies, telephone, and TV. The hotel is near the cable cars and a three-minute walk from the public tennis courts. Doubles range from 440 AS ($23.41) to 565 AS ($30.06) per person, with breakfast included.

Hotel Batzenhäusl (tel. 77104). The ornate paneling in the tavern is carved from what the locals call "stone pine," the glow from which beautifully complements the flowered carpets, leaded windows, and hand-worked lamps. The other sections of this comfortable hotel are crafted in a more modern style, still appealing and intimate, with ample use of heavy ceiling beams, flagstone floors, and Oriental rugs. The hotel is an antique chalet with a recently built addition more or less in the same style as the original intricately carved building. Dietrich Arnold and his attractive family, the owners, charge from 350 AS ($18.62) to 600 AS ($31.92) per person, with breakfast and taxes included. For half board, they ask a 150 AS ($7.98) supplement per person.

Waldhotel (tel. 77272) is a wood and stucco chalet with red shutters. It's in a flowering garden which members of the Maier family work hard to maintain throughout the summer. Facilities include an indoor swimming pool, a sauna, and a fitness room, as well as a sunny restaurant with immaculate napery, a cozy bar, and a flagstone-covered sun terrace. With full board included, doubles rent for 680 AS ($36.18) to 750 AS ($39.90) per person, while singles range from 750 AS ($39.90) to 825 AS ($43.89), depending on the season. Each of the comfortable rooms has its own bath. Open December to October.

Hotel Tirolerhof (tel. 77194) has one of the prettiest facades in Igls. Designed in a rambling format of Tudor-style half-timbers, gabled red tile roofs, and a long expanse of greenery rising on every side, the hotel offers apartment accommodations for between two and eight persons, as well as standard hotel rooms. In a wooded area four minutes from the center of town, the hotel charges 350 AS ($18.62) to 500 AS ($26.60) for a single with complete bath, only 280 AS ($14.90) to 340 AS ($18.09) for a bathless room. Couples pay 240 AS ($12.77) to 310 AS ($16.49) per person in a bathless room, 300 AS ($15.96) to 380 AS ($20.22) per person in a room with bath. Breakfast is included in the rates. Apartments, with living room, bedroom, kitchen, dishes, linen, bathroom, phone, radio, and balcony, rent for 600 AS ($31.92) to 750 AS ($39.90) for two persons and from 700 AS ($37.24) to 1,000 AS ($53.20) for four persons.

Restaurant Batzenhäusl, in the Hotel Batzenhäusl (tel. 77104). "Gemütlich" is a word to describe this carefully paneled antique-style dining room, where the chalet chairs are intricately carved and the service is relaxed and friendly. A specialty of the house is the flambé filet steak "Didi," a popular recipe which is prepared at your table. Other well-prepared dishes include Austrian specialties such as three kinds of meat on the same platter (covered in a mushroom cream sauce), apple strudel, and a series of savory meat-flavored soups. You might prefer the outdoor veranda or the garden in summer, although the dining room inside is most attractive. Fixed-price meals range from 110 AS ($5.85) to 325 AS ($17.29), while à la carte dinners cost from 120 AS ($6.38) to 445 AS ($23.67).

PATSCH: This small village above Igls stands on the sunny western slope of the Patscherkofel, with a panoramic view of the Stubai Glaciers. Lying on the old Roman road below the Patscherkofel peak, Patsch is only a short distance from the mountain's Olympics slopes.

In winter you'll find facilities here for skiing, including cross-country runs, and ice skating and curling. There's a ski school in the village. Horsedrawn sleighs take you along snow trails.

In summer you can go on hikes, swim, or play golf and tennis. Summer skiing is possible on the Stubai Glacier.

The Patsch area code is 05222.

Food and Lodging

Grünwalderhof (tel. 77304), once the private hunting lodge of the counts of Thurn and Taxis, is today operated by members of the same family. The hotel stands on the site of an ancient Roman road. Proudly housed in one of the prettiest chalets in town, it has a pleasant relief of natural-grained lattice under the slope of its gabled roof, striped shutters, and a modern extension stretching out the back toward the secluded outdoor swimming pool. Inside, the ceiling vaults are covered with an artist's rendition of regional wildflowers, while the decor includes a scattering of antiques, lots of paneling, and a spacious and comfortable dining room filled with leather upholstered chairs. On the premises are a small indoor pool, a sauna, and a tennis court. With half board included, rates range from 350 AS ($18.62) to 600 AS ($31.92) per person, while a supplement of 95 AS ($5.05) per day is charged for single occupancy. Prices depend on the season and the room.

Hotel Altwirt (tel. 77409) enjoys a quiet location and an excellent view of the Stubai Glaciers. It was built around a carefully planned design incorporating heavy timbers, lots of wood, terracotta floor tiles, and colorful accents of well-chosen textiles. The simple bedrooms have big baths, often tiled in attractively somber tones of grays and blues, plus secluded balconies. The large indoor pool has sweeping views over the snow-covered mountains which you can enjoy from the comfort of the heated water. Singles range from 480 AS ($25.54) to 575 AS ($30.59), while doubles cost from 400 AS ($21.28) to 500 AS ($26.60) per person, with half board included. Children under 6 stay free in their parents' room, while youngsters aged 6 to 11 pay 20% of the adult rates.

Hotel Bär (tel. 77504) is an amply proportioned hotel that towers five stories above the alpine meadow where it sits a few hundred yards from the center of the village. The inside is covered with paneling tinted the same brown color as the hide of the animal the hotel is named after (a bear). It includes lots of attractive touches, such as big panoramic windows looking over the mountains, a carefully prepared buffet, an antique-style ceramic stove surrounded by a warming bench, an indoor pool, warmly appealing restaurants, and a bar. The cozy and well-furnished bedrooms cost from 300 AS ($15.96) to 560 AS ($29.79) per person, with half board included. Prices depend on the plumbing and the season.

Hotel Eschenhof, 1-3 Dorfstrasse (tel. 77172). Ideal for sports enthusiasts, this modern chalet maintains its own tow lift a few steps away from its wood and stucco facade. The modern and comfortable bedrooms are contained in a rambling, big-windowed extension. On the premises are several sunny lawn areas, an indoor pool, a sauna, a tennis court, and a big sun terrace for mid-morning coffee. The bedrooms have private bath and wood detailing, renting for 390 AS ($20.75) to 530 AS ($28.20) per person, with full board included. The Ostermann family are the owners.

MUTTERS: On a sunny southern plateau above Innsbruck, Mutters is just 6½ miles from the Tyrolean capital. You can drive to the center of the city from here in about 15 minutes, or get there via the Stubaital railway in just 20 minutes. The village is separated from Innsbruck by a wide green forest belt which lies above the city and the Inn Valley.

Mutters is in the skiing and recreation area of the Mutterer Alm and the Axamer Lizum, which were the central base for the sites of the 1964 and 1976 Olympic Winter Games. Mutterer Alm is the place for easy-going skiers. It can be reached by cableway.

The area code for Mutters is 05222.

Food and Lodging

Hotel Sonnhof, 12 Burgstall (tel. 33747), is a recently constructed stucco chalet in a quiet country location a few minutes' walk from the center. The simple streamlined interior has big windows, colorful accessories, and includes an indoor pool, a sauna, and access to a flagstone-covered outdoor terrace. The Ullmann family maintains the rustically modern bedrooms in top-notch condition, making every effort to perfect the savory cuisine served in the airy and attractive restaurant. With half board included, singles cost 700 AS ($37.24) to 880 AS ($46.82), while doubles range from 625 AS ($33.25) to 825 AS ($43.89) per person, depending on the plumbing and the season.

Hotel Altenburg, 4 Kirchplatz (tel. 27053). The ground-floor entryway of this pretty flowered chalet is sheltered with a three-arched arcade, which serves as an attractive backdrop for the summertime café set up on the pavement outside. The interior is covered with horizontal planking, long ago sanded smooth and beautifully finished, while many of the ceilings are beamed and timbered and set with recessed pin lights. The elegant restaurant is filled with upholstered banquettes and conservative furniture, with big windows overlooking the mountains. Rates with half board included range from 400 AS ($21.28) to 450 AS ($23.94) per person. The hotel is closed from the end of September until Christmas. The Wishaber family are your genteel hosts.

Muttererhof (tel. 27491) has a gabled roof and a dignified chalet facade within a few minutes' walk of the village center. Its balconies are covered with flowers. On the premises are a covered swimming pool with sliding glass doors that remain open in summer, an elegantly carved and paneled restaurant filled with carved chairs, leaded windows, and antique artifacts, plus a big lawn area with summertime café tables. Charges range from 380 AS ($20.22) to 410 AS ($21.81) per person in a double, and singles pay a daily supplement of 40 AS ($2.13). Prices depend on the season. Open December to March and May to October.

AXAMER LIZUM: This resort was created for the 1964 Olympic Winter Games. It's about a half-hour drive, 11 miles southwest from Innsbruck. The highest station on the system of funicular and lifts is at Hoadl (7,665 feet). You can also take a chair lift to Birgitzköpfl (6,700 feet).

In summer you can take pleasure in hiking on alpine footpaths and attending folkloric evenings. Winter brings the opportunity to participate in sports for the whole family. A variety of tracks and ski runs, a natural ice rink, and ski-bob runs are here, plus the longest natural toboggan run in Tyrol. Three chair lifts and four ski tows serve the skiers who come here. Experts find some of the slopes at Axamer Lizum especially challenging.

The area code for Axamer Lizum is 05227.

Food and Lodging

Hotel/Sportpension Lizumerhof (tel. 8244) is an elongated, mountain building set on a forested hill within sight of the rocky bluffs around it. Near the ski lifts, the hotel is family-run, cozy, unpretentious, and an attractive destination for summertime and wintertime lovers of sports. The dining room has colorful napery, lots of sunshine, and what looks like an 18th-century group portrait. My favorite room has a sloped ceiling and an onion-shape brick-and-plaster fireplace in the center. The owners charge 600 AS ($31.92) to 650 AS ($34.58) per person, with full board included. The hotel is open from December to April and June to September.

3. The Stubai and Wipp Valleys

One of the most beautiful valleys in Tyrol is the Stubaital, a 25-mile-long area with an endless vista of glacier tops and alpine peaks, some 10 miles from Innsbruck. From the Brenner Road you can fork off at Schönberg into the Stubaital, where you'll find little villages such as Fulpmes and neighboring Neustift, which are both summer and winter playgrounds.

One of the first hamlets you'll encounter, and one of the most charming, is **Mieders** (3,120 feet). From here a chair lift goes up to Kopeneck at 5,350 feet.

If you decide to lodge in one of these little-known resorts, you'll find the prices favorable to your pocketbook. However, it's possible to stay in Innsbruck and drive through the valley, either by private car or on a bus, in a day. It's also possible to take a narrow-gauge electric train. If you travel by rail, you can only go as far as Fulpmes. After that, you must continue by bus.

The Wipp Valley, or Wipptal, is the valley of the Sill River, stretching from Innsbruck to the Brenner Pass. An autobahn—a great engineering feat—pierces the valley right on the outskirts of Innsbruck, going over **Europabrücke** (Europe Bridge), 625 feet high and 900 yards long. As you travel over it you'll literally feel that you're driving on a highway in the sky.

The **Brenner Pass,** known as the lowest gap in the major alpine chain, has been used since Roman times—and probably before. The pass marks the boundary between Italy and Austria.

Your first stopover in this section might be—

FULPMES: The major resort and the most ancient hamlet in the Stubai Valley is Fulpmes, surrounded by high mountains. Mention of a village here goes back to a document of 1344. The resort lies about halfway up the valley. Serles Mountain, to the south of Fulpmes, rises to a height of 8,900 feet. You might enjoy an excursion up to Telfes, slightly more than a mile by road above Fulpmes.

Most visitors see the Stubaital on day trips from Innsbruck, but the resort, a spot to visit in both summer and winter, offers a wide range of excellent hotels charging moderate prices, a winning combination. In summer there's an indoor, heated swimming pool between Fulpmes and Telfes. Chair lifts operate in both summer and winter, one going from Fulpmes to Froneben at 4,430 feet and one to Kreuzjoch, at 6,900 feet.

If you're here at the right time you might enjoy a historical play presented about Tyrol's hero, Andreas Hofer, who led Bavarian and Tyrolean peasants against Napoleon and freed Tyrol from the French emperor's domination.

The Fulpmes area code is 05225.

Food and Lodging

Hotel Alphof, Herrengasse (tel. 3163), is a four-story chalet on a quiet lane a short distance from the center of the village. Run by a family, it has an interior with lots of rustic details, such as a green ceramic stove, knotty-pine paneling in one of the dining rooms, and a restaurant with more formal chairs upholstered in mountaintop colors of evergreen and persimmon. On the premises is a sauna, and both indoor and outdoor tennis courts are close at hand. Doubles, with half board included, cost from 320 AS ($17.02) to 500 AS ($26.60) per person.

Hotel Pension Auenhof (tel. 2763). The lobby of this chalet has gently arched ceiling beams, lots of carved wood, and white plaster walls dotted with antique farm utensils. The salon has an unusual country baroque armoire with four different portraits painted on its double doors, and a wood-trimmed fireplace that curves toward one of the conversational areas. On the premises are a sauna and an attractive restaurant, and access is possible to lots of ski and hiking trails. A ski bus makes frequent stops at the hotel on its way to the slopes. With half board included, rates range from 390 AS ($20.75) to 525 AS ($27.93) per person, based on double occupancy. At Christmastime, the prices go up about 125 AS ($6.65) per person. Singles pay a daily supplement of 90 AS ($4.79).

Sporthotel Cristall (tel. 3424) is a big-windowed chalet with four floors of attractively furnished, wood-paneled bedrooms. The in-house restaurant has a green ceramic oven, turquoise curtains, and a wholesomely alpine decor of wooden walls and ceilings. An intimate bar on the premises provides an attractive place to meet people. A summertime outdoor café is cantilevered above the slope of the hill into which this hotel is built, with an outdoor swimming pool visible from many of the flowered balconies. There's a sauna on the premises, as well as access to a host of sporting facilities. With half board included, doubles rent for 520 AS ($27.66) to 790 AS ($42.03) per person, while singles range from 540 AS ($28.73) to 820 AS ($43.62). Prices depend on the accommodation and the season.

Alpenhotel Tirolerhof (tel. 2422). My favorite part of this beautifully embellished double chalet is the central fireplace near the reception desk. It looks like something that a witch in an enchanted forest used to lure Hansel and Gretel into her house on a cold night. Its design of roughly applied stucco is curved around a widely splayed grate and fanciful andirons, and in winter it's usually kept burning most of the day. The rest of the hotel has dozens of elegantly rustic touches, such as the rich carving on some of the ceilings and the many rural artifacts strewn tastefully around the intimately lit interior. On the premises are an indoor pool, a hot whirlpool, a sauna, and access to the many nearby sports facilities. The well-furnished bedrooms rent for 500 AS ($26.60) to 600 AS ($31.92) per person in a double, with full board. Singles pay a daily supplement of 40 AS ($2.13).

Hotel Holzmeister (tel. 2260) has dozens of architectural details which a team of craftsmen probably took months to complete. Many of the vaulted ceilings are embellished with painted regional designs, while the woodwork on the walls and ceilings is painstakingly polished and elegantly ornate. The balustrade on the stairwell leading to the upper floors is appropriate to the style of architecture, while each bedroom is a unique statement of comfort and rural charm. On the premises are a sauna and a solarium, and there's access to the many sports facilities of this alpine village. With full board included, rates range from 480 AS ($25.54) to 690 AS ($36.71) per person, depending on the season and the room assignment. Each of the accommodations has a private bath.

Sporthotel Brugger, 35 A Bahmstrasse (tel. 2870), is a traditionally maintained four-story chalet with a combination of wood balconies, stucco walls, and a cozy interior with all the modern conveniences. In one of the restaurants someone has arranged a colorfully embroidered collection of cowbells on the wall, while in the main dining room the wood of the upholstered chairs matches the amber-colored paneling on the walls. The spacious and comfortable bedrooms rent for 320 AS ($17.02) to 500 AS ($26.60) per person in a double, with half board included.

NEUSTIFT: The name of this village means "new monastery" or "new church," and in fact it's a few centuries more recent than, say, the 12th-century *New* Forest in England. But Neustift dates back to 1505, when Emperor Maximilian I did some hunting here and had a chapel built, called "das neue Stift."

This village and others in the Stubai Valley have been in the tourist business since the 19th century, when mountain climbers discovered the area and made it accessible.

Neustift, about 3,000 feet above sea level, is surrounded by extensive hiking trails for summer visitors, leading up to the glaciers of the Stubai Alps. The Stubai Glacier lift will take you to a dizzying 10,050-foot height, where year-round skiing is pursued.

There are baby slopes here, served by T-bars, or you can take a chair lift from Neustift to Elferberg, a favorite with advanced skiers. Elferberg is also known for its panoramic view and long toboggan runs.

Neustift's area code is 05226.

Food and Lodging

Alpenhof/Neustifterhof, Neder Neustift (tel. 2711), blends together a pair of Tyrolean chalets with an underground passage. They lie a few steps from the most modern indoor tennis courts in the region in an outlying hamlet (Neder Neustift), less than a mile east of the center of the resort. The sprawling interiors of these houses contain impressively crafted arrays of public rooms, each paneled in full-grained softwoods and filled with comfortable nooks and crannies. There is a pair of restaurants, along with an alpine bar with an adjacent cubbyhole of a firelit stüberl. Andreas Haas is the owner of this place, and his two sons do their best to make visitors feel at home. The hotel was built in 1961, and since then has undergone three complete renovations, making it one of the best maintained hotels at Neustift. Annual closing is from November 8 to December 18.

Each of the 60 balconied bedrooms is outfitted with a private bath and a modernized form of Tyrolean charm. Depending on the season and accommodation, half-board rates range between 430 AS ($22.88) and 760 AS ($40.43) per person, based on double occupancy. The buildings also contain a handful of apartments, which come with breakfast included in the price. Depending on the season, each apartment goes for between 740 AS ($39.37) and 1,270 AS ($67.56) per day based on double occupancy. The in-house swimming pool has a timbered ceiling, its own sauna, and a big-windowed view over the surrounding countryside.

Sporthotel Neustift (tel. 2509) is a pleasant wood and stucco chalet with ornamental eaves and painted country baroque patterns around the windows. The cozy interior has paneled rusticity, as well as wintertime fireplaces illuminating the well-prepared cuisine in the mountain dining room. The family owners of this engaging hotel charge 550 AS ($29.26) to 700 AS ($37.24) per person, with half board included. Prices depend on the season, and apartments are available for between two and four guests. Each room has a private bath, a minibar, radio, and TV (upon request). A tennis court, fitness room, and sauna are on the premises.

Hotel Edelweiss (tel. 2280). The grass-covered slope of an alpine hill separates this wood-trimmed chalet from an evergreen forest. Inside, a heavily timbered decor evokes mountain Austria. Guests congregate beside a roughly plastered fireplace, within sight of leaded windows exposing the surrounding countryside and nearby village. An indoor swimming pool with an adjacent sauna are a few steps from a decorative fountain ringed with chaise longues. You'll recognize this place at the edge of town by its country baroque window trim and jutting balconies. In summer the attractively furnished and comfortably appointed bedrooms rent for 500 AS ($26.60) to 580 AS ($30.87) per person daily, going up in winter to 580 AS ($30.87) to 690 AS ($36.71) per person on the same arrangement.

Restaurant Hoferwirt (tel. 2201) is housed in a tastefully up-to-date hotel of the same name which blends easily into the style of the structures around it. The interior has immaculate napery and white walls which act as a good foil for the cuisine served by a staff of efficient local residents. Specialties include baked lasagne, herb soup with shrimp, fondue bourguignonne for two, crab tails, and peppersteak. Meals range from 250 AS ($13.30). Reservations are suggested.

STEINACH IM WIPPTAL: This little resort lies at the head of the Gschnitztal, another lovely valley cutting through the Stubai massif. Gschnitztal is most often visited from Steinach. If you take a fast train out of Innsbruck, you can be in Steinach im Wipptal in about half an hour. Be specific as to where you want to go, as there's another Steinach in Austria.

With well-tended ski trails and excellent runs, Steinach is attractive to winter visitors, but it may be that summer tourists have the best of it here, with the beauties of two valleys to explore.

From here you can travel to **Gries am Brenner,** along the Sill River. Some 15 miles from Innsbruck and 8 miles from the Brenner Pass, Gries, at an altitude of 3,810 feet, sits at the foot of the Padauner Kogel. This village too is both a summer and a winter resort. In the vicinity is the Brennersee, a beautiful lake.

To reach Gries you must go up a steep road. Roman soldiers marched along this route in ancient times, as it was their road to the colonies of Rome in the north. The railway line from here cuts deep into dark tunnels, piercing the Alps until it reaches the border of Italy.

The area code for Steinach im Wipptal is 05272.

Food and Lodging

Hotel Steinacherhof (tel. 6241) is a big elegant hotel, a cross between a chalet and a private villa. The facade is assembled from weathered planking and white-painted stucco. Architectural details include a row of arched windows stretching toward the rear gardens, plus a large curved extension containing a sunny, attractive dining room which often has live music. The hotel has installed sun terraces on top of two of the building's low-lying extensions, although guests are free to roam through the gardens if they wish.

On the premises is a big indoor swimming pool, with a nearby café, an outdoor tennis court, a bar painted an eye-catching cerulean blue, and a Tyrolean restaurant with knotty paneling carved into neoclassical designs. With full board included, singles range from 700 AS ($37.24) to 900 AS ($47.88), while doubles cost 610 AS ($32.45) to 890 AS ($47.35) per person. Prices depend on the season and the room, and all accommodations contain private baths. The hotel is open from December to October.

Hotel Weisses Rössl (tel. 6206) is in many ways the center of social life in the village. From one side the hotel presents a lime-green neoclassical facade with white detailing and weatherproof windows. The older section has such antique details as vaulted ceilings, regional memorabilia, and a collection of weapons and hunting utensils from another era. In the chalet-style addition that stretches off the back, members of the Jakober family have installed cozy alpine bedrooms, with lots of custom-made carpentry. A stone-walled room on the premises contains an indoor pool with a nearby sauna and fitness room. The dining room is large and sunny, and welcomes passing visitors as well as hotel guests.

The price in a double for a room and full board goes from 525 AS ($27.93) to 575 AS ($30.59) per person. Singles on the same plan pay from 590 AS ($31.39) to 640 AS ($34.05). Prices depend on the season and the room, and all units contain a private bath. Open December to October.

4. Seefeld

Seefeld, 15 miles northwest of Innsbruck, is the third member of Austria's Big Three of international rendezvous points for winter sports crowds, the other two being Zell am See and Kitzbühel. This fashionable resort lies some 3,450 feet above sea level on a sunny plateau.

Seefeld was the site of the Nordic ski competitions in the 1964 and 1976 Olympic Winter Games, to which it owes much of its renown. Skiers are served with 16 cable cars and lifts, 50 miles of prepared *langlauf* (Nordic skiing) tracks, and other cross-country ski trails. The major ski areas are Seefelder Joch and the Härmelekopf, with runs for those of varying degrees of proficiency, from novice to expert.

Other winter activities offered here include curling, horse-drawn sleigh rides, indoor and outdoor skating, horseback riding, and indoor tennis.

Summer visitors can enjoy swimming in either a heated, open-air pool or the lake, fishing, tennis, golfing on the largest 18-hole course in Austria, or walking on the 25 miles of well-tended paths.

Whatever time of year it is, you can try your luck at the **casino,** where roulette, baccarat, blackjack, and slot machines are played.

While you're based in Seefeld, it's relatively easy to explore parts of Bavaria in West Germany. You may or may not get to see little **Wildmoos Lake.** It can and does sometimes vanish all in a day or so, and then there may be grass and grazing cows on what has become meadowland. However, it will suddenly come back again, and if conditions are right, it will become deep enough for swimmers. Wildmoos Lake comes and goes more frequently than Brigadoon.

The little German town of **Mittenwald,** one of the highlights of Bavaria, can easily be explored on a day trip from Seefeld.

Seefeld's area code is 05212.

THE RESORT HOTELS: Hotel **Klosterbräu** (tel. 2621) is the most unusual and most elegant hotel in town. Constructed around a 16th-century cloister, the hotel combines so many architectural features that it's sometimes hard to believe that the view from the different angles are actually of the same building. The dramatic entrance is under a thick stucco arch which is only slightly wider than the rest of the arches which run along the ground floor. The interior contains soaring vaults supported by massive columns of the same kind of porous stone that built Salzburg (you can still see prehistoric crustaceans embedded in the stone).

Someone has taken pains to add plush accessories such as thick carpeting, Oriental rugs, intimate lighting, a scattering of antiques, and acres of beautifully furnished paneling, some of it carved into intricate designs. The modern sections blend discreetly into the older ones and give the added allure of, for example, a dome-shaped fireplace that juts gracefully into one of the well-furnished public rooms, as well as sweeping staircases and an occasional piece of old sculpture.

The bedrooms are encased in a towering chalet behind the front entrance. The windows look out over the midsummer buffet set up near the outdoor sun terrace. The charge for staying at such a luxurious hotel is not cheap: Singles rent for 1,700 AS ($90.44) to 2,500 AS ($133), and doubles cost 1,500 AS ($79.80) to 2,300 AS ($122.36) per person. These tariffs include full board in the hotel's renowned restaurant, and the prices vary according to the season and the room assignment. The hotel is open from December to March and June to September.

Restaurants on the premises include a country-style Bräukeller with simple furniture and live music, a rustically elegant Tyrolean room with carved ceiling beams, pewter candelabrum on each table, and impeccable service, plus a more formal dining room where guests sit on wooden chairs upholstered in alpine patterns below ancient ceiling vaults. Dishes include cream of broccoli soup, duck in orange sauce, sumptuous salads dotted with breast of marinated chicken, and a host of international and Austrian specialties. The person at the next table might be a vacationing celebrity from Germany traveling incognito. Fixed-price meals range from 215 AS ($11.44), while à la carte dinners average 185 AS ($9.84) to 420 AS ($22.34). Reservations are suggested.

In the evening the chicly dressed patrons often drop in at Die Kanne nightclub, whose showgirls, comedians, and musical revues provide a high spot in the nightlife of the village. A daily afternoon tea dance in winter allows the hotel guests to meet one another. The big indoor swimming pool has a café area nearby, while an outdoor pool is visible from the sunny balconies of the well-furnished bedrooms, where you can enjoy breakfast if you want. Golf, tennis, mountain climbing, and skiing facilities are all within walking distance.

Hotel Wildsee-Schössl, 195 Innsbrucker Strasse (tel. 2390). What is today my favorite hotel in Seefeld was little more than a rundown pension until its owners rebuilt it in 1982. What emerged from their efforts was a radically reconstructed hostelry whose thick walls resemble those of a miniature, very ornate castle. A corner watchtower with a funnel-shape roof was added, along with jutting balconies, step-fronted gables, and red-and-white striped shutters. The location is across from the lake, along the side of the road leading into Seefeld from Innsbruck.

The beautifully appointed interior contains Austrian antiques, ticking grandfather clocks, alpine painted blanket chests, and dozens of comfortably upholstered cubbyholes to sink into with a drink. A blazing corner fireplace greets winter visitors near the reception desk. The in-house restaurant is reviewed separately. Accommodations lie at the top of a stairwell lined with hunting trophies. Furnishings are full-grained Tyrolean, with plush carpeting, timbered ceilings, and sunflooded windows. Depending on the season, rates for half-board range from 830 AS ($44.17) to 1,500 AS ($79.80) in a single and from 720 AS ($38.30) to 1,300 AS ($69.16) per person, based on double occupancy. In the basement is a sauna and steambath.

Hotel Astoria (tel. 2272) is a luxurious double chalet with a panoramic view of the Alps. Managed by Herman Schneeweiss, the hotel takes care to maintain the flowered terraces and the gardens in good condition, and offers its guests an array of conservatively furnished public rooms, an open fireplace in the hotel lounge, bars, and a well-known restaurant. An indoor swimming pool has tall windows looking out over the forest, with a sauna and exercise room nearby. An evening dance band complements the good international cuisine served in the dining room. Hotel guests have access to an 18-hole golf course, fishing, riding, tennis courts, and a wide selection of nearby mountain paths. The well-dressed patrons come from around the world, and pay from 900 AS ($47.88) to 1,200 AS ($63.84) per person. These prices, which vary according to the accommodation and the season, include half board.

Karwendelhof (tel. 2655) is one of the most elegant hotels in the Tyrol. It's constructed in a chalet format with two distinct sections, the exterior walls of which are painted in regional designs. The 100-year-old Tyrolean parlors have parquet floors, heavily beamed ceilings, and lots of antique accents. The bedrooms are elegantly simple, often with at least one of the walls constructed of massive natural-grained planks.

The K-Keller nightclub is one of the social centers of the village, while a casino in an adjoining building opens at 5 every night.

Fritz and Elisabeth Wilberger are the engaging owners. Per-person rates, with full board included, range from 1,300 AS ($69.16) to 2,100 AS ($111.72) in a double and 1,305 AS ($69.43) to 1,500 AS ($79.80) in a single. Prices vary according to the season and the accommodation.

The hotel restaurant, called Alte Stube, is completely covered in old paneling by now burnished to a rich mellow glow. Menu items include beef, veal, and pork dishes, accompanied by fresh vegetables, and followed by regional cheeses and home-baked pastries. Fixed-price meals cost around 175 AS ($9.31) to 500 AS ($26.60), while à la carte dinners average from 225 AS ($11.97) to 450 AS ($23.94). Reservations are suggested.

Grandhotel Hohe Munde (tel. 2191) is an inner-village chalet with six floors of big windows and flowered balconies. At night the lights from the café, bar, and graciously furnished restaurant shine through the big plate-glass windows onto the street outside. The rest of the hotel is conservatively and tastefully furnished with comfortable chairs and vivid colors. In winter the management hosts a five o'clock tea dance, and on the premises is a huge bar area, surrounded by dozens of upholstered stools. Prices for room and full board range from 1,080 AS ($57.46) to 1,280 AS ($68.10) in a single, from 880 AS ($46.82) to 980 AS ($52.14) per person in a double, the quotation depending on the season and the accommodation. Good food accompanied by live zither music is available in the Klause restaurant.

Hotel Lärchenhof (tel. 2383). The salons of this graciously appointed luxurious hotel are big and sunny, permitting a wide vista from almost any point within. Intimate conversational groupings are scattered throughout the paneled interior. The wood-trimmed bedrooms often have curtained dividers between the sleeping areas and the sitting areas, as well as private bath and all the modern comforts. Guests can enjoy quiet moments on the flowered sun terraces which stretch over wide expanses of the second floor as well as over the hotel's grassy lawns. An indoor pool is on the premises. Prices in either a single or double range from 1,080 AS ($57.46) to 1,660 AS ($88.31) per person, with full board included. The hotel is open from December to April and June to September.

Alpenhotel Lamm (tel. 2464). The overhanging eaves of this elaborate hotel are supported by heavy beams that extend at an angle from the second floor to the outer edge of the roofline. The corners are rounded into protruding towers decorated with regional illustrations and designs, many of which are clearly visible from the village church next door. The cozy interior has ceiling beams, as well as an intimate bar, a scattering of rural artifacts and baroque sculpture, a dance bar, a sauna, a steambath, and a hot whirlpool. The most expensive bedrooms are fairly elegant and spacious. The charge is from 650 AS ($34.58) to 1,500 AS ($79.80) per person for a bed and full board. Prices depend on the season and the accommodation.

Hotel Eden (tel. 2258) is a sprawling modern chalet with a facade covered with wooden balconies, a single painted illustration, and a wood and stucco extension jutting out from the front. An outdoor café contained within the natural windbreak of the hotel does a thriving business, both winter and summer. The interior has unadorned paneling, stone floors, big windows, and all the essential ingredients for the provision of comfort without excessive frills. You'll probably enjoy at least one drink at the curved wooden bar, or in one of its U-shaped banquettes, before retiring to one of the brightly colored bedrooms. These rent for 1,040 AS ($55.33) per person, with full board included. The hotel is open only from December until March.

Hotel Post (tel. 2201) is an imposingly tall chalet with two peaked roofs and evenly spaced rows of dark-toned balconies. You'll probably be greeted in the paneled reception area by a member of the Schneider family, each of whom contributes to keeping this hotel running smoothly. The public rooms contain upholstered furniture and soft lighting. On the premises are a hotel disco, a shaded garden, two restaurants, and comfortable and invitingly attractive bedrooms. These rent for from a low of 550 AS ($29.26) to a high of 1,900 AS ($101.08) in summer. In winter, these same tariffs include full board.

Strandhotel Seespitz (tel. 2218) has a large, welcoming design that usually reminds everyone who sees it of the perfect vacation house. Designed like an oversized chalet, with lots of interesting angles and corners, it's separated from the lake only by a well-maintained lawn and a barrier of water-loving plants. The inside is heavily beamed, airy, and filled with light from the big panoramic windows. Charges are from 400 AS ($21.28) to 825 AS ($43.89) per person for bed and breakfast. Half board costs an additional 90 AS ($4.79) per person. Prices vary according to the season and the accommodation.

Hotel Wetterstein (tel. 2283). There's a delicacy to the wraparound balconies of this unusual hotel that can't be found anywhere else in Seefeld. The hipped roofs of the original gray and white-trimmed core rise above a well-planned addition containing the oversize arched windows of the public rooms. The overall effect is appropriate to its location as the village's best viewpoint over the nearby tennis courts, which are transformed into a skating rink in winter. The sun terrace is popular in all seasons.

The interior of the hotel is outfitted with a kind of no-nonsense masculinity which is unpretentious and appealing. Parts of the bedrooms are usually covered with horizontal planking, while all of them contain a private bath. With half board included, prices range from 550 AS ($29.26) to 920 AS ($48.94), depending on the season and the room assignment.

Dreitorspitze (tel. 2951) is a six-story peak-roofed chalet whose comfortable bedrooms enjoy dramatic views of the mountains. The interior has a warmly appealing combination of honey-colored woods and subtle shades of red, which are contained both in the furniture's upholstery and in the vivid patterns of the dozens of Oriental rugs scattered throughout the public rooms. The hotel has an elevator, plus an indoor swimming pool, a sauna, a sun terrace, and a large garden with a putting green for outdoor golf practice. Rates range from 535 AS ($28.46) to 1,300 AS ($69.16) per person, depending on the season and the plumbing. Prices include full board, which is personally supervised by the hotel's owners, Inge and Ludwig Morasch.

Hotel Tyrol-Alpenhof (tel. 2221) is a modern adaptation of a chalet, with four floors of white concrete shielded by wooden shutters and balconies. The main dining room has Empire-style crystal chandeliers, black and gold patterned carpeting, and white and gold Louis XVI-style armchairs. A less formal restaurant is darkly paneled and rustically intimate, with cozy lighting and a woodsy kind of elegance. On the premises are both an indoor and outdoor pool, a hot whirlpool, a disco bar, and at least one wintertime fireplace throwing off welcome heat. Tariffs range from 700 AS ($37.24) to 1,500 AS ($79.80) per person, with half board included. Prices depend on the accommodations and the season.

Hotel Schönegg (tel. 2375) is a chalet hotel with an interior decor of conservatively modern furniture. A bar, restaurant, and a sauna are on the premises, as well as warmly contemporary paneling and furnishings. Close to the village center, the hotel is managed by the Schwenniger family, who charge from 425 AS ($22.61) to 860 AS ($45.75) per person, depending on the season, with half board included.

Sporthotel Stern (tel. 2235) is a simple chalet with green shutters, a red roof, and friendly management. On the premises you'll find a cozy bar area padded with leather, plus a paneled restaurant filled with rustic mementos. In winter there's disco dancing in the bar. With half board included, charges range from 580 AS ($30.87) to 840 AS ($44.69) per person, depending on the season and the plumbing.

Hotel Marthe (tel. 2505) is a generously sized chalet with golden-brown wooden balconies and shutters, plus a woodsy location a few minutes' walk from the center of the resort. Inside you'll find a heated indoor pool, a bar where you're likely to encounter a member of the friendly Hans Marthe family, an informal restaurant, and cozy bedrooms accented with lots of wood. Rates range from 520 AS ($27.66) to 880 AS ($46.82) per person daily, with half board included. Prices depend on the season and the room.

Hotel Diana, 97 Klosterstrasse (tel. 2061). At least some of the allure of this unpretentious hotel comes from the welcome extended by its owner, Helga Öfner, and her husband, Sigmund. Their balconied establishment lies at the center of town, along a pedestrian zone close to the nightlife and sporting facilities. Guests congregate in the paneled warmth of the plant-lined public rooms. The Tyrolean restaurant contains a tile stove, while a less formal Stüberl serves snacks and drinks. Each of the 22 comfortably furnished bedrooms has its own phone and bath. Depending on the season, a double or twin rents for between 650 AS ($34.58) to 925 AS ($49.21) per person, with singles offered for between 720 AS ($38.30) and 960 AS ($51.07), these tariffs including half board.

Hotel Christiana (tel. 2553) is a comfortable, contemporary chalet, with lots of exposed wood and a rustic, homey character. It has an indoor pool accessible through big glass doors in the cellar, thanks to the hotel's location on the slope of a hill. Five pedestrian minutes from the center, the hotel charges between 300 AS ($15.96) to 550 AS ($29.26) per person, based on double occupancy, the prices depending on the season. A buffet breakfast is included, and all units have a private bath (many of them contain a balcony as well).

WHERE TO DINE: Most guests book into a Seefeld hotel on the half- or full-board plan. But perhaps at least once you'll want to skip your hotel dining room to try one of the recommendations described below.

Restaurant Wildsee-Schössl, 195 Innsbrucker Strasse (tel. 2390), in the hotel previously recommended, emerges as one of the finest dining rooms in a region where competition is fierce. Contained within a re-creation of a Teutonic castle beside the lake, it consists of a trio of beautifully appointed rooms, lined with pieces of pewter and filled with rose-colored napery. The first room as you enter, my personal favorite, is ringed with burnished paneling and canopied with a vaulted ceiling. Menu specialties are likely to include filet of sole in a saffron-flavored cream sauce, julienne of chicken with a bouquet of salad, a heavenly version of smoked wild salmon with a cranberry parfait, filet of lamb in an herb sauce, fennel cream soup, and veal medallions with fresh asparagus and hollandaise. Full meals are priced from 500 AS ($26.60), and the restaurant is open all year, even when much of Seefeld is closed.

Restaurant Locanda (tel. 2655), in the cellar of the casino, is a wood-covered Tyrolean restaurant with handcrafted wooden banquettes and lots of mountain rusticity. Menu items include "seadevil" with chive sauce, fresh zucchini baked with cheese, several leafy salads, veal steak Parma with buttered noodles, and a wide range of Austrian and Italian cheeses, pastries, and wines. À la carte dinners cost from 300 AS ($15.96). The restaurant is closed on Monday through the spring, summer, and autumn.

Sir Richard (tel. 2093), on the outskirts of town, creates an elegant aura of year-round Christmastime because of its masses of flowers, dozens of burning candles, and the immaculately pressed linen that covers the wood tables. Whether the menu items prepared by the chefs are Italian or Austrian, they are presented on delicate china with attentive service. You might begin your meal with watercress soup, followed by one of a variety of lamb, veal, or fish dishes, often accompanied by masterful sauces. Even the fresh leafy salads have just the right degree of tartness. A fixed-price meal costs 585 AS ($31.12), while à la carte dinners can average 600 AS ($31.92). Your meal will probably be accompanied by live Tyrolean music in a style which Austrians appropriately call "evergreen." Reservations are suggested, and the restaurant is closed on Monday in November. It's also closed for all of May and from mid-November until December 1.

Birklstüberl (tel. 3322) is a straightforward restaurant serving Austrian specialties in a rustically traditional environment. Specialties are well prepared and include fresh meats and vegetables, soups, cheeses, and homemade desserts. À la carte meals range from 110 AS ($5.85) to 360 AS ($19.15). Reservations are suggested.

APRÈS-SKI: Seefeld in season bustles with typical wine and beer cellars, along with nightclubs and discos Drinks in most places range from 60 AS ($3.19) to 85 AS ($4.52).

However, the major nighttime attraction is the **Spiel-Casino Seefeld,** at the Hotel Karwendelhof, already recommended. It opens at 4 p.m., offering baccarat, blackjack, American and French roulette, and 65 slot machines. The casino is so popular that many visitors drive here from Innsbruck, 20 minutes away by auto. The Karwendelhof might be your entire stop for the evening, as it contains the Alte Stube, a good restaurant, and a nightclub, K-Keller, that often presents shows with international artists.

The **Hotel Klosterbräu,** also recommended previously, is the center of the most sophisticated nightlife on the après-ski circuit in Seefeld. Its nightclub, Die Kanne, presents an international orchestra and a floor show during its hours of 9 p.m. to 3 a.m. In winter the club also opens at 5 p.m. for a tanz-tee (tea dance). The hotel also features international specialties in its restaurant, Ritter Oswald Stube, and a gemütlich atmosphere in its Bräukeller, open from 10 a.m. to midnight, presenting Stimmung music after 8 p.m.

Bar Tenne, inside the Hohe Munde (tel. 2191), offers a huge rectangular bar, rustic country-style decor, and plaid carpeting for an après-ski crowd who usually meet and mingle easily.

LEUTASCH: If for some reason you don't wish to anchor for the night in Seefeld, you can drive northwest through the Valley of Leutasch (Leutaschtal), which is one of the most scenic valleys in northern Tyrol. It runs under the Wettersteingebirge to the border of Bavaria.

Among the villages in this valley, Leutasch has the best food and accommodations.

The area code for Leutasch is 05214.

Food and Lodging

Hotel Kristall (tel. 6441) has elegant two-toned designs embellishing the outside window frames and long rows of flowered balconies. The interior is outfitted with amber-colored paneling, stone detailing, and a combination of traditional and rustically contemporary furniture. The gemütlich restaurant usually has live music, while the hotel bar is a popular rendezvous spot. On the premises are an indoor pool, a sauna, an exercise room, a solarium, along with Ping-Pong and pool tables. The Bader family charges from 485 AS ($25.80) to 775 AS ($41.23) per person in a double and 535 AS ($28.46) to 820 AS ($43.62) in a single. Half board is included, and tariffs depend on the season.

Hotel Leutascherhof (tel. 6208) is a three-story chalet with a big extension stretching out the back, plus a rounded bay window jutting out from one of the corners. The paneled interior is intimately lit, especially in the cozy bar and the dining room, where small framed pictures are scattered around for visual interest. The hotel was almost completely rebuilt in 1976, with private bathrooms added to each of the comfortable bedrooms. The cost in a double is from 400 AS ($21.28) to 580 AS ($30.87) per person, while singles are charged from 350 AS ($18.62) to 580 AS ($30.87). Breakfast is included in all the tariffs. Prices depend on the room assignment.

5. Resorts Around the Zugspitze

The Zugspitze, part of the Wetterstein Alps, is a frontier mountain separating West Germany from Austria. The highest peak, almost 9,700 feet high, is in the neighbor country but can easily be seen from Tyrol. Its principal resorts are Garmisch-Partenkirchen in West Germany and Lermoos in Austria.

If you're exploring in this area, it's always wise to have your passport with you, as you'll cross the frontier if you follow my recommendations for this section of Tyrol.

Chances are, most readers of this guide will approach the Zugspitze from the Austrian side. If so, you can take a cableway, the Tiroler Zugspitzbahn, from Ehrwald-Obermoos, circling in a half moon through the Bavarian resort, Garmisch, and coming back to where you started. You can also take the trip by cog rail from Garmisch, perhaps departing from there, going up one side of the mountain and down the other, landing in Austria.

EHRWALD: With the most resort facilities of any place in the Tyrol section at the foot of the Wetterstein Alps, Ehrwald is popular in all seasons. It's one of a trio of resorts which includes Lermoos and Biberwier, sharing the same attractions (see below).

Bavaria, to the north, can easily be reached using Ehrwald as a base. Most visitors, however, just pass through Ehrwald to take the cable car for the ascent to the **Zugspitze**, one of the major attractions to be found in the west of Austria.

To reach the cable car, drive west from Ehrwald until you see a sign indicating Talstation Obermoos. Or you can take a bus from Ehrwald to that point. Here you board the Tiroler Zugspitzbahn, which will take you to the mittelstation at Gamskar (6,610 feet). From that point you go to the Zugspitzkamm station (9,203 feet), which had to be blasted out of the mountain rock. Your next stop is the summit of the Zugspitze, arriving at Zugspitzwestgipfel, 9,680 feet above sea level.

A busy restaurant at the summit has windows with one of the greatest panoramic views in all of Europe. From here you can see Grossglockner, the Dachstein, and the Bavarian Alps. To the north you're able to see as far as the Starnberger See, a lake in Bavaria.

This cable car is at its busiest during the summer months. Service is hourly from 8 to 11:30 a.m. and 1 to 5 p.m.

Ehrwald's area code is 05673.

Food and Lodging

Hotel Schönruh (tel. 2322). From the flagstone-covered terrace on one of the upper floors, guests have a sweeping view of the fertile valley. This well-run hotel looks almost like a Mediterranean villa because of its curved walls, bay windows, and ornamental tower. Once you're inside, however, you'll know you're in a Tyrolean country house because of the crossbeam timbering, the roughly finished plaster walls, the ceramic stoves, and the mountain decor. Peter Kotz takes special care with the cuisine, which is served on immaculate napery in one of the two dining rooms. Depending on the season, comfortable rooms rent for 520 AS ($27.66) to 620 AS ($32.98) per person in a double and from 600 AS ($31.92) to 700 AS ($37.24) in a single. These prices include full board. Open from January to March and May to September.

Hotel Alpenhof (tel. 2345). The big chimneys visible from the outside let you know that wintertime fires will probably be throwing off a welcome heat indoors. The main salon has a bar, a fireplace, a coffered ceiling, and a welcoming color scheme of ambers, beige, and white which are appealing. Throughout this hotel you'll find charmingly rustic touches, such as the ceramic stove in the alpine-style Stuben restaurant, the acres of paneling, and the thick walls sometimes set with leaded glass. There's also a more formal pink-upholstered dining room.

In winter the management hosts a five o'clock tea dance with disco music in the café. The facilities include an outdoor tennis court, a sauna, and access to the village swimming pool. Per-person rates range from 420 AS ($22.34) to 780 AS ($41.50), based on double occupancy, with half board included. Tariffs during Christmas and New Year's rise slightly more. Singles pay a daily supplement of 90 AS ($4.79).

Hotel Sonnenspitze, 14 Kirchplatz (tel. 2208). Viewed from the front this 19th-century hotel is charming enough to look almost like an oversize cuckoo clock. It has a symmetrical facade whose entrance you'll reach from a two-sided stairwell rising gracefully from the street-level outdoor café. The ornamental overhang of the eaves is crafted into a baroque curve which shelters the flowers on the wooden balconies.

There is a lot of decorative stonework inside, as well as big arched windows, a warmly inviting color scheme, and a scattering of old armoires and antique pewter. The Leitner family are the owners of this congenial place. They close from mid-October to mid-December every year, but the rest of the time they charge from 520 AS ($27.66) to 600 AS ($31.92) for a bathless single and from 520 AS ($27.66) to 840 AS ($44.69) per person for a double (many of these contain private bath). Full board is included in these tariffs.

Alpenhotel (tel. 2254) is a pleasantly designed chalet hotel which has the unusual added benefit of having the terminus for the Zugspitzbahn cable car attached to its side. If you stay here, you shouldn't miss riding to the top for a meal or a snack in what's considered an engineering marvel and a panoramic delight. Back at the bottom, your simply furnished room with full board included will cost 380 AS ($20.22) to 530 AS ($28.20) per person, depending on the season. All the accommodations contain private bath. The hotel is open from December to March and June to October.

LERMOOS: About a mile to the northwest of Ehrwald is Lermoos, a resort attracting visitors in both summer and winter—and it's not bad in spring and fall, either. It joins with Ehrwald and Biberwier to form a trio of resorts close enough together to allow you to take advantage of the facilities of all three. The threesome is linked by bus, with departures about every 30 minutes.

Warm-weather pursuits, besides going up the Zugspitze (see above), include hiking, mountain climbing, easy strolls through meadows and forests, swimming, mini-golf, boating, fishing, cycling, riding in horsedrawn carriages (fiacres), and more.

When the snow falls, this becomes a white sports arena with, of course, downhill and cross-country skiing, ice skating, curling, tobogganing, winter walks, swimming in covered pools, and sunbathing(!). The carriage ride of summer is exchanged for a horse-drawn sleigh ride along snowy roads. Both Lermoos and Ehrwald have sleigh ranks on their church squares. You can reserve a vehicle for your ride between 10 a.m. and 4 p.m. daily. For more information, phone 28-94 at Lermoos or 27-36 at Ehrwald.

Whatever the weather, after dark you can enjoy Tyrolean evenings, learn to dance Tyrolean style, or just relax in a wine cellar or beer tavern.

Lermoos is well situated, set against the backdrop of the Zugspitze. You can take a chair lift to the side of the Grubigstein station (6,500 feet), from which you'll have a magnificent view of the mountain peak. Via the chair lift, you can eventually reach the top station at 7,215 feet above sea level.

The area code for Lermoos is 05673.

Food and Lodging

Hotel Drei Mohren (tel. 2362) was built in 1806 and renovated in 1961. Its windows are crowned with regional embellishments, with a three-sided bay window extending toward the street from the white stucco facade. Management encourages its guests to go fishing for the region's trout, pike-perch, and carp. The hotel owns a small lake nearby, where guests can swim. Other facilities include an elegantly simple sitting room, with heavy ceiling beams and lots of exposed stone, a series of inviting public rooms with wintertime fireplaces, and two statues of Moorish attendants waiting in stylized poses beside the elevator doors.

Its 50 rooms rent for 385 AS ($20.48) to 700 AS ($37.24) per person, based on double occupancy, while singles cost 450 AS ($23.94) to 720 AS ($38.30), according to the season and the accommodation, with full board included. Freshwater fish is the specialty of the chef, and platters are served in a restaurant appropriately known as the trout room. The menu in season also includes wild game.

Sporthotel Zugspitze (tel. 2630) is a chalet hotel, with painted designs around the windows, heavy overhanging eaves, and masses of flowers hanging from the balconies. Guests usually decide to spend some time on the sun terrace, which offers a view of the nearby mountains. The interior has big plate-glass windows, lots of exposed wood, and a rustic, homey feeling enhanced by Oriental rugs and light-grained furniture. In a restfully isolated position a few minutes from the center of the village, the hotel charges from 590 AS ($31.39) to 680 AS ($36.18) per person for half board.

Hotel Post (tel. 2281). The lobby of this pleasant hotel is decorated with antiques, including a baroque chest-on-chest with unusual legs. The decor includes beamed and coffered ceilings, a scattering of hunting trophies, a working ceramic stove, and a collection of contemporary and alpine-style chairs. The ambience is relaxed and attractively informal. A bar area often features evening dancing with live folkloric music. With half board included, rates in a double are from 500 AS ($26.60) per person per day, with singles costing 550 AS ($29.26). An indoor swimming pool is on the premises.

Hotel Edelweiss (tel. 2214) is a modern chalet-style hotel with an annex that offers all the up-to-date comforts but also lots of rusticity. Both are near the Grubig chair lift. A large indoor pool is nearby, as well as a children's playroom. For a bed and full board, singles pay from 700 AS ($37.24) to 720 AS ($38.30), with the cost in a double going from 650 AS ($34.58) to 770 AS ($40.96) per person. The hotel is open from December to October.

Hotel Tyrol, 10 Oberdorf (tel. 2217), is a hillside chalet with a distinctive design that includes a big sun terrace set on top of a curved glass-walled extension. The warmly tinted decor includes multicolored flagstone floors, panoramic views over the village, and a convivial gathering place near the bar's hanging copper lamps. Situated a few minutes from the train station, near the nursery slopes, the hotel charges between 350 AS ($18.62) and 520 AS ($27.66) per person in a double room, half board included. Prices in the sunny, comfortable rooms depend on the season. Singles pay another 75 AS ($3.99) per day.

Hotel Bellevue (tel. 2151) includes an almost surrealistic illustration of a skier on its stucco facade and a host of balconies angle toward the sun. The place has much cozy comfort, including a rustic stuben restaurant, a convivial bar area with hanging lamps, and a convenient location near the ski lifts, one minute from the center of the village. Charges range from 500 AS ($26.60) to 600 AS ($31.92) per person in a double and from 600 AS ($31.92) to 700 AS ($37.24) in a single. These tariffs depend on the season, and all include half board. Open December to October.

Après-Ski

There's nothing fancy here in the way of nightlife, but Teutonic revelers seem to have a good, often rowdy time. If you like to dance, you might check out the already-recommended **Hotel Tyrol,** which often has a live group playing for your entertainment.

Live groups often play for dancing at the Taverna bar of the also-recommended **Hotel Post.** If there's no live action you're likely to get disco music. The Post is also known for its Tyrolean folkloric evenings in season. Likewise, the Kellerbar at the just-cited Hotel Tyrol also occasionally stages these Tyrolean evenings.

When I was last at the recommended **Hotel Drei Mohren** they were having a beer-drinking competition, and I understand this is a regular feature. Here the action might be more Bavarian than Tyrolean . . . and a lot of fun.

When you return from the slopes after a hard day of skiing, you can join the throngs at the **Simon Konditorei** which has the best and most mouthwatering pastries in town, along with Swiss hot chocolate wearing a "top hat" of whipped cream.

Drinks in most establishments range from 50 AS ($2.66) to 85 AS ($4.52).

BERWANG: In the far-northern reaches of the Tyrol country, very close to the West German border and encircled by mountains, is Berwang, an as-yet-unspoiled village with friendly innkeepers. The little resort, at an elevation of 4,400 feet, has both an upper and a lower village. In winter people enjoy skiing here with runs at varying stages of difficulty. The ski season usually ends in March.

You can reach Berwang by state road 189 from Innsbruck, or you may prefer to approach it by the main Bavarian highways heading south (for example, departing from Ulm via Kempten). From Garmisch in Bavaria, a good highway takes you here by way of Elbsee, crossing the border at Griessen and Lermoos. If you're traveling by train, the station to look for is Berwang-Bichlbach. Don't forget to bring your passport.

The Berwang area code is 05674.

Food and Lodging

Alpenhotel Berwangerhof (tel. 8288) is a large, five-story hotel built in two interconnected sections. The generous balconies look out over the nearby village, the center of which is a few minutes away. The decor of the cozily rustic public rooms ranges from vintage Tyrolean to an up-to-date ambience of red upholstered chairs and vividly patterned carpeting. Overall, the effect is enhanced with Oriental rugs, wide vistas of accommodating public rooms, massive wood detailing, and lots of alpine flavor. On the premises of the hotel is the largest indoor swimming pool in Austria. The manager invites guests to a daily five o'clock tea dance, often with live entertainment, after which they can move onto their choice of three bars and several restaurants.

Closed from mid-April to mid-May, and from mid-October to mid-December, the hotel charges from 420 AS ($22.34) to 790 AS ($42.03) per person, with half board included.

The main restaurant in this international hotel offers an intriguing combination of the designs of several different countries, with a tasteful emphasis on honey-colored woods, coffered ceilings, painted embellishments, and unusual accessories. Menu items include lasagne, gulasch, cold plates, and a variety of meats.

Sporthotel Singer (tel. 8181) is an elegant chalet with two interconnected sections, each with symmetrical peaked roofs. The interior has the kind of simple rusticity that gives the feeling that each object was carefully chosen by a skilled decorator. Many of the bedrooms have beamed ceilings, and the public salons are reinforced with massive timbers bolted and pegged into carefully finished paneling. There's also a darkly intimate bar. The Tyrolean-style bedrooms rent for 480 AS ($25.54) to 1,150 AS ($61.18) per person, based on double occupancy, with half board included. Singles cost from 550 AS ($29.26) to 750 AS ($39.90), also with half board. Prices depend on the season and the plumbing options. Günter Singer and his family are the sports-minded hosts of this congenial hotel.

Kaiserhof Sporthotel (tel. 8285). The Kuppelhuber family are your hosts in this prosperous-looking chalet whose twin roofs and flowered balconies rise from a slight knoll at the edge of town. The modernized interior offers plenty of Tyrolean touches, including expanses of glossy paneling, light-grained ceilings, and a helpful staff outfitted in alpine costumes. On the premises are two restaurants, a tavern, an indoor swimming pool with an adjacent paddle pool for children, a pool table, a beauty salon, tennis court, steambath, and covered parking garage. The place makes an effort to accommodate families with small children. Bedrooms offer much comfort, with several homelike touches. With half board included, per person rates range from 400 AS ($21.28) to 670 AS ($35.64).

Gasthof-Pension Edelweiss (tel. 8223) is one of the loveliest chalets in town, lying at the bottom of the village near the Mulden and Sonnen lifts. It's been run by members of the Sprenger family since 1924, and today offers the same attractive hospitality as it did when it was established. The facade is embellished with designs around each of the windows, while a slightly protruding extension has a tongue-in-cheek illustration of a hardy farmer and his coy companion. The paneling on the interior extends into the comfortable bedrooms. Motorists will find an underground garage at their disposal. Prices in a double range from 360 AS ($19.15) to 500 AS ($26.60) per person, with half board included. Singles pay a daily supplement of 25 AS ($1.33).

Après-Ski

The most popular place to go at night is the **Sporthotel Singer,** already recommended. Here a four-man band plays for dancing. Of course there's the usual round of kellers and stüberls. But what makes Berwang a bit exceptional is an array of varied entertainment staged weekly in season, ranging from torchlit processions on skis to beauty contests to amateur nights.

REUTTE: The capital of the Ausserfern district, Reutte lies in the Valley of the Lech, north of the Fernpass. Its location on the traffic route between Füssen in West Germany, the Fernpass, and the upper part of the Lech Valley brings a lot of summer traffic through the town. Reutte is also served by the same train as Lermoos and Ehrwald.

This is mostly a summer resort, with three nearby lakes popular for swimming in summer, although I find them too chilly for my personal comfort. The largest and most attractive of the three lakes is three-mile-long **Plansee**, a body of emerald-green water lying four miles to the east of Reutte. In the Tyrolean country only the Achensee surpasses this lake in size. A short canal links the Plansee to the Heitenwanter See, one of the most beautiful lakes in Tyrol. Included in the lake trio are the **Frauensee**, two miles northwest of Reutte, and the **Urisee**, about a mile to the northeast.

Many of the burghers' houses you'll see in Reutte are from the 18th century, most often with oriels and painted gables. The **pfarrkirche** (parish church) dates from 1691.

From Reutte you can explore the Lech Valley, which has developed a winter sports trade.

Reutte's area code is 05672.

Food and Lodging

Hotel Urisee (tel. 2301) is a lakeside chalet with wood-trimmed loggias and monochromatic decorations around some of the frontal windows. It's surrounded by a wraparound sun terrace, while the interior has overhead pin lights suspended from crisscrossed ceiling beams and rustically attractive furnishings. The bedrooms are woodsy and outfitted in shades of brown and beige. With half board included, overnight rates are around 460 AS ($24.47) per person. During the peak midwinter holiday season per-person prices are about 75 AS ($3.99) higher. The Turri family are your hosts.

Alpenhotel Ammerwald (tel. 8131) is big on local color. Outside the center, the hotel is composed of two symmetrical sections joined in the middle by a connecting series of public rooms. The facade has big windows, cutout shutters, and a long expanse of white stucco stretching toward the back. The cozy, warmly tinted interior has amber-colored paneling, lots of orange and brown fieldstone detailing, and attractive textiles in autumnal colors of subtle reds and greens. The quiet and sunny rooms rent for 325 AS ($17.29) to 575 AS ($30.59) in a single and from 375 AS ($19.95) to 500 AS ($26.60) per person in a double, with breakfast included. On the premises are a sauna, a swimming pool, a bowling alley, and a bar which has become a fashionable rendezvous point.

The Fraundorfer family, your hosts, seem to know every colorful character in the region, as well as dozens of international guests. Many of them enjoy the well-known restaurant, whose specialties include roasted hare in pepper sauce, wild venison (in season) with mushrooms, and an array of fresh salads. Fixed-price meals cost 130 AS ($6.92) and 200 AS ($10.64), while à la carte dinners cost from 125 AS ($6.65) to 500 AS ($26.60), depending on what you order. Reservations are suggested.

Hotel Tirolerhof (tel. 2557) seems to be one of the few hotels in the Tyrol not designed like a chalet. It rises five stories above the center of town in a simplified baroque style. The curved roofline is covered in red sheet metal rimmed with fragile ice catchers. The interior has a decor of exposed wood, wrought-iron lighting fixtures, and attractive furniture. The comfortable bedrooms rent for 400 AS ($21.28) to 480 AS ($25.54) per person, with half board included. Prices depend on the plumbing, the season, and the room assignment.

6. The Lower Inn Valley

The Valley of the Inn River, called Inntal in German, goes through Tyrol from the southwest to the northeast, a distance of some 150 miles, separating the Swiss frontier at the Finstermünz and the Bavarian border at Kufstein at the far side. For the purpose of convenience in touring I've divided the Inntal into the Upper Inn district (see below) and the Lower Inn Valley.

The heart of a popular tourist district of Austria is formed by the Lower Inn Valley, the Ziller Valley to the south, the Alpbach Valley, and the Achensee area in the north. The section abounds in villages and small towns with lifts and cableways taking visitors on panoramic trips high in the air with magnificent vistas spread out before them.

If you're planning to overnight or spend a longer time in the Lower Inn Valley, you'll find the widest range—at least the best choice—of accommodations in Kufstein, the last Austrian town on the Inn before it enters Bavaria.

Your first stopover in the lower portion of the Inntal might be—

HALL IN TIROL: This old salt-mining town at the foot of the Bettelwurf massif, five miles along the river valley from Innsbruck, was a prize possession of the princes of Tyrol. No longer enjoying the prosperity of other days, Hall is now trying to make a name for itself as a spa to attract a tourist industry. You'll sometimes see it referred to as "Solbad Hall."

Even if you don't choose to overnight here, you may want to stop off for a view of Hall's **Obere Stadt,** or upper town. You begin your exploration at the center of the lower town, the Untere Stadtplatz. The heart of the old town, the Obere Stadtplatz, has many colorful buildings, often with oriels and grilles. Narrow little medieval streets branch off from the upper town square, which still functions in its age-old role as a marketplace. Two of the most charming of streets to seek out, really no more than cobbled alleyways, are the Sparkassegasse and the Arbesgasse.

The **parish church** *(pfarrkirche),* much improved in the 15th century, is in the late Gothic style, although the interior is rococo. The 15th-century Rathaus (town hall) has an attic like a pavilion.

SCHWAZ: About 17 miles northeast of Innsbruck, the old mining town of Schwaz, on the south bank of the Inn River, is even older than Hall in Tirol, just visited, going back to the 12th century. It came into prominence, however, from the 15th to the 17th centuries when it grew fat and rich from copper and silver mines. Today it produces only mercury.

Many of the burghers' houses remain from the town's time of great prosperity. In the Stadtplatz (town square), you can see the much-photographed, Gothic-style **Fuggerhaus,** with oriels, turrets, and an arcaded courtyard.

A Franciscan church, **Franziskanerkirche,** completed in 1515, has both Gothic and rococo touches and three naves. You can visit the cloister, which is pure Gothic. Here the church's treasure, nearly two dozen wall paintings depicting scenes from the Passion of Christ, is displayed.

The 15th-century **pfarrkirche** (parish church) of Schwaz is considered the largest Gothic hall church in Tyrol. It has a roof of some 15,000 plates of copper, worth a vast fortune. Inside you'll see a quartet of aisles and two parallel chancels. Seek out the altar dedicated to St. Anne in the south side aisle.

KUFSTEIN: A settlement at this site on the Inn River has existed for many centuries. Kufstein was first mentioned in a document near the end of the eighth century, and a Bavarian fortress was established here in 1205. In 1393 the settlement was raised to the status of a town by its ruling duke, Stefan III of Lower Bavaria. Emperor Maximilian I wrested the fortress from the Bavarians in 1504 and added Kufstein to the Austrian domain of the Habsburgs.

The old frontier fortress town has often suffered the ravages of hostilities between Bavaria and Austria through the centuries. The town was put to the torch in 1703, losing most of its early medieval character but not its fortress, which, although much added to and altered since the 13th century, still dominates the town, the last outpost of Austria in the Inn Valley.

Today only the memories of its turbulent past linger in this peaceful little holiday resort town, about 1,650 feet above sea level, surrounded by woods and lakes with fields green in summer and snow-blanketed in winter. Much traffic between Bavaria and Tyrol passes through here, and it's a convenient touring point for the Kaisergebirge, the limestone range of the Alps.

A promenade runs along the waterfront in the lower part of Kufstein. An outstanding attraction of the town is the **Heldenorgel** (the organ of heroes) in the Burgerturm. This is the world's largest open-air organ, having 4,307 pipes, and honors the Austrian and German troops who died in the two World Wars. In summer at noon and again at 6 p.m. recitals are given on the organ, which can be heard some eight miles away.

The **Festung** (fortress) contains a Heimatmuseum (local museum) in which you can see artifacts from primeval life in the Inn Valley, rural implements, a wooden smoke kitchen (about 250 years old), a pleasant farmhouse room from 1638, a display of illustrations depicting the war-torn history of the castle and the town, many objects of ecclesiastical art, old national costumes worn by people of Kufstein from 1800 to 1850, a room of the old craftsmen, many stones and minerals from the surrounding area, a diorama of "Animals in the Mountains," and many examples of the birds and animals from this part of Austria, plus a museum-gallery of the arts.

Highlight of guided tours is the Kaiserturm, or emperor's tower, a massive edifice finished in 1522. You can visit cells in which prisoners were held captive. The fortress served as a state prison as late as 1865. The last part of the tour is the 230-foot-deep well going down to the groundwater of the River Inn.

Tours, each lasting more than an hour, are conducted through the apartments and cells of the castle from the first part of April until the end of October, starting at 9:30 and 11 a.m. and at 1:45, 3, and 4:45 p.m. (more frequently upon demand in peak season). The museum and the Kaiserturm are closed on Monday in April, May, June, September, and October and from November to the end of March. Admission is 20 AS ($1.06).

For the best view of Kufstein, visit either Pendling, a mountain across the Inn River, or else Heldenhügel (Mountain of Heroes), where you'll see a memorial dedicated to Andreas Hofer, the Austrian patriot who led a band of peasants made up of Bavarians and his fellow Tyroleans against the forces of Napoleon in 1809.

One of the most interesting excursions from Kufstein is to take the **Ursprungpass Road** which runs along for more than 15 miles, connecting Kufstein to Bayerischzell in West Germany (bring your passport). From Bayerischzell, you can begin your tour of the Bavarian Alps (see *Dollarwise Guide to Germany*).

Another excursion can be made to **Thiersee,** a tiny lake at the foot of a mountain. The lakeside village presents a Passion Play somewhat similar to the world-renowned one staged at Oberammergau in Bavaria.

Erl, another little town that merits a visit, lies about seven miles down the

Inn Valley from Kufstein, near the West German-Austrian border. A Passion Play is presented here every five years, the next one coming up in 1988. This play originated here in 1613, but its production was abandoned for many years until its revival in 1959.

The area code for Kufstein is 05372.

Food and Lodging

Hotel Andreas Hofer, 8 Pirmoserstrasse (tel. 3281), named after the famed Austrian patriot, is a modern building in the center of town. Its big auditorium is sometimes used for civic functions, but the hotel adjoining it is clean, comfortable, and contains features such as an informal café and beer hall with a wooden ceiling and a wall constructed from smooth river rocks, a four-lane bowling alley, a beamed restaurant loaded with charm dating from 1900, a separate café/bar upholstered in red, and comfortable, conservative air-conditioned bedrooms which have just a hint of the 1950s. With breakfast included, single rooms cost from 385 AS ($20.48), and doubles go for 325 AS ($17.29) per person. A covered parking garage fills the basement of the angular building, and a large open-air parking lot lies just behind it. The father-son combination of Thomas Sappl, Senior and Junior, are your hosts.

Berghotel Pfandl, Kaisertal (tel. 2460). A more outdoorsy place would be hard to find, especially since the only way you reach it is by hiking for around an hour along a well-marked mountain trail. The hotel will arrange for transportation of your luggage from the garage where you'll park your car (called the Pfandel Garage und Parkplatz, it's indicated on signs from the center of Kufstein). If you're coming by train, a taxi will take you from the station to the garage, from which point you'll begin your climb. Both the excursion and the hotel itself are worth the effort.

The hotel was initially constructed in the 13th century. It's been under the direction of the same family since 1788. It has a covered cupola for a stork's nest, natural-grained cutout wooden balconies, and an elegantly formal interior with polished paneling and lots of well-constructed furniture. On the premises is an indoor pool, plus two restaurants serving savory Tyrolean specialties. Members of the Schwaighofer family charge 520 AS ($27.66) to 640 AS ($34.05) per person, with full board included. It would be wise to phone before you begin your climb.

Hotel/Restaurant Goldener Hirsch, 19 Unterer Stadtplatz (tel. 4504), is a forest-green and white building with baroque trim and a prominent storefront on the ground floor. Leo Prister, the owner, has installed a streamlined modern decor under the high coffered ceiling of the formal dining room. The functional bedrooms are furnished with patterned wallpaper and comfortable beds. The charges per person, whether in a single or a double room, begin at 225 AS ($11.97), with breakfast included.

Hotel Post, 2 Unterer Stadtplatz (tel. 4524), offers simple rooms, friendly service, and what turns out to be a great bargain. At the edge of the lake, the hotel was once an elegant villa, now painted avocado green. The big-windowed restaurant extends in a modern addition on the ground floor. Monika Stecher, the owner, charges from 300 AS ($15.96) to 350 AS ($18.62) per person for half board.

Gasthof Alpenrose, 47 Weissachstrasse (tel. 2122), in the center of town, is a modern stucco building designed like a chalet without balconies. It was built in 1971 and renovated in 1985. It has a boxy extension partially trimmed with wooden planking, stretching off to one side. The alpine dining room is tastefully outfitted with a forest-green patterned carpet and a ceiling composed of wooden beams. Rates, based on double occupancy, range from 520 AS ($27.66) to 660

AS ($35.11) per person, and singles pay a daily surcharge of 90 AS ($4.79). Half board is included in the room price, which varies according to the season and the plumbing.

7. The Achen Valley

One of the most famous lakes in Austria and the largest in Tyrol—some say the most beautiful too—is the **Achensee.** This body of water, usually a light-green color, is 5½ miles long and about three-quarters of a mile wide, surrounded by coniferous forests with the majestic peaks of the Sonnwendgebirge and the Karwendelgebirge as a backdrop.

In summer the entire Achen Valley becomes virtually a holiday resort, with its little villages connected by a steamer which runs from one to another. This is of course the best way to see the lake. You'll notice lots of anglers trying their luck at fishing in the Achensee.

Although it's mainly known as a summer resort, the valley also attracts skiers in winter, with good snow conditions from December to April and five lifts with superb facilities for alpine skiing. More than 30 miles of well-tended cross-country courses take ski trekkers through woods and pastures into the Karwendel valleys. There are also cleared paths for long walks and rides in horse-drawn sleighs. Curling, skating, indoor tennis, bowling, and some minor après-ski activity make for a happy winter holiday.

How to get to the Achen Valley? It's not too difficult. At some point midway in your exploration of the Inn Valley you came to the town of **Jenbach,** on the north bank of the Inn. From there it's possible to take a cog railway up to the lake. If you're driving you can head north from Jenbach along a road that winds around a lot at first, until it reaches Achensee. A bus also follows this route. If you're traveling by train you will be deposited at Maurach, at the southern tip of the lake.

Should you be seeking food and lodging, you'll find the most desirable accommodations in—

PERTISAU: This little village on the west side of the lake lies about three miles northwest of Maurach. It's the most frequented resort on the lake in summer, also doing a minor business in winter, attracting those who prefer a holiday in the snow.

Pertisau's area code is 05243.

Food and Lodging

Hotel Kristall (tel. 5490). During high season this tastefully decorated chalet is almost like a village within the village. Its public rooms are filled with the kinds of ornamentation that give a rich, full look to the elegant room. Details include old polychrome sculpture, lots of paneling, gracefully curved wrought iron, and touches of brasswork and flickering candles. The richly decorated bedrooms rent for 650 AS ($34.58) to 750 AS ($39.90) per person, based on double occupancy, with full board included. Singles pay a daily surcharge of 95 AS ($5.05). Prices charged by the Adolf Rieser family vary according to the room and the season. There's also an outdoor swimming pool on the grounds.

Hotel/Pension Christina (tel. 5361) is a cozy hotel attached to one of the most attractive cafés in town. The paneled rooms are outfitted with all the modern comforts, renting for 500 AS ($26.60) to 610 AS ($32.45) per person, based on double occupancy, with full board included. Singles pay a daily surcharge of 40 AS ($2.13). The hotel arranges for guests to take breakfast at the nearby Kristall, under the same management, and if they wish, to use its swimming pool and sauna.

The **Café Christina** (tel. 5361), attached to the hotel, has Oriental rugs, green marble floors, upholstered bentwood chairs, and a rustically elegant decor of hanging potted flowers, well-polished wood, and pink napery. You can select a richly decorated pastry from the glass countertop, or order snacks and coffee at one of the tables.

Hotel Rieser (tel. 5251) is a big chalet hotel surrounded by low-lying buildings which contain a pool, a sauna, a two-lane bowling alley, a table-tennis room, and a solarium. The hotel also has two indoor and six outdoor tennis courts, a squash court, mini-golf, and a children's play area. The public rooms of the main building are richly filled with Oriental rugs, comfortable wood-framed chairs, heavy ceiling beams, and a scattering of carefully inlaid antique reproductions. Charges for full board range from 620 AS ($32.98) to 675 AS ($35.91) in a single, from 580 AS ($30.87) to 685 AS ($36.44) per person in a double. The color scheme throughout is woodsy and warmly tinted, especially in the dining room where the chef prepares generous portions of savory veal steak with pungent sauce, thick cuts of beef, and tasty regional specialties. Fixed-price meals range from 95 AS ($5.05) to 220 AS ($11.70), while à la carte dinners cost from 100 AS ($5.32) to 300 AS ($15.96), depending on what you order. Service is friendly and efficient.

Hotel Karlwirt (tel. 5206) is a five-story, antique-style chalet with sun-bleached wood balconies and an interior decor filled with high ceilings, heavy beams, and cozy sitting areas (some of them near a stone fireplace). Franz Joseph came here on a hunting trip about a year before he was crowned emperor. The comfortably rustic dining room has elegant combinations of white plaster and light-grained wood, immaculate napery, and efficient service.

The bedrooms have large areas of light-grained wood which usually cover at least one wall and part of the ceiling. In a nearby building, under ownership by the same family, is a popular restaurant, the Langlauf Stüberl, the tables of which are grouped around a central fireplace whose smoke rises through a metallic funnel.

With full board included, singles rent for 530 AS ($28.20) to 620 AS ($32.98) and doubles for 450 AS ($23.94) to 580 AS ($30.87) per person. The hotel, open from December to October, is a few minutes' walk from the center of town.

As an alternative to staying in Pertisau, you can drive north to—

ACHENKIRCH: A marvelously engineered road runs along the eastern shore of the Achensee, going through tunnels and affording delightful views of the lake which you might otherwise miss unless you get to take the lake steamer that runs in summer. If you take this road north you'll find the village of Achensee lying at the north end of the lake of the same name.

If you're seeking a good and inexpensive place for a lakeside holiday, go on northwest from the village of Achensee for about two miles, which will bring you to Achenkirch. This little resort has a number of moderately priced hotels serving good, hearty food.

If you continue north from here for about six miles, you'll be at the Achen Pass and the Bavarian border.

The area code for Achenkirch is 05246.

Food and Lodging

Sporthotel Achenseehof (tel. 6348). The facade of this hotel has an arched entrance, the shutters are painted in stripes of red and white, and many of the ground-floor windows are protected with decorative ironwork. The establishment sits in a park-like area whose edges form a gentle curve extending like a peninsula into the lake. The woodsy interior has lots of paneling, big windows, several fireplaces, and light-grained, heavily beamed ceilings. The owners charge from 560 AS ($29.79) to 600 AS ($31.92) per person for a bed and half board. Prices vary according to the plumbing and the season.

8. The Ziller Valley

Back at Jenbach in the Lower Inn Valley, from whence I suggested setting out northward to explore the Achensee Valley, I'll now take you south through the **Zillertal** (the German name for the celebrated Ziller Valley) east of Innsbruck, a resort mecca in summer and a playground for lovers of winter sports.

Some say this is the most beautiful valley with the most rewarding scenery in all the Tyrolean country. You may wonder about this claim as you go through the first stretches of the Zillertal, but don't turn back. It gets more impressive the deeper you penetrate into the valley.

When you first enter the Zillertal, you'll pass rich meadowlands where cows are grazing (if it's spring, summer, or autumn), looking as sleek and healthy as those in Switzerland. On your west will be the Tux Alps and on the east the Kitzbühel Alps, to which I'll devote space later on in this chapter. As tempting as it may be to head for these alpine areas, I advise continuing for the time being deeper into the Ziller Valley, which will suddenly grow narrower, the scenery becoming more dramatic.

The people of the Zillertal are said to be the finest singers in Austria, generation after generation of valley families having inherited magnificent voices and making use of their talent.

I always pass through the first of the little villages and resorts, since in my opinion better ones are ahead.

The first town that merits a stopover is—

ZELL AM ZILLER: Don't confuse this resort with Zell am See in Land Salzburg. Zell am Ziller is the major town of the lower section of the Ziller Valley.

Once it was a goldmining town, but those days are long gone. Today any gold mined here is from summer and winter visitors—but that's not meant to suggest that the resort is overpriced. Quite the contrary. Inns here are most reasonable in their prices, making Zell am Ziller a good choice for those seeking a budget holiday.

Like comparable Austrian villages, Zell has a **parish church** *(pfarrkirche)*, this one dating from 1782. Constructed on an octagonal design, it's surmounted by a huge dome.

The best possible time to be in Zell am Ziller is on the first Sunday in May, when the residents of the Zillertal come together for one of the great folk events of Europe, the **Gauderfest.** This heavily attended occasion is like some huge May Day bash, honoring the ushering in of spring.

The glorious voices mentioned above fill the valley with song. It's a very real *Sound of Music*, and you expect to see Julie Andrews come prancing over some hill or meadowland at any time. At this centuries-old Maytime festival you not only hear the people of the valley sing, you also get to watch and listen as they play their musical instruments, particularly harps and zithers.

Music isn't all that goes on at the Gauderfest. The beer drinking rivals that at the Oktoberfest in Munich. Just for this occasion, a powerful (I say lethal) malt drink, Gauderbier, is brewed and lavishly imbibed.

Once this village was known only as a summer holiday site, but in recent times it has become a winter sports resort as well. In 1978 the Kreuzjoch area was opened to skiers, and Zell am Ziller took its place on the tourist ski maps of

Europe. In season a free ski bus stops at the major hotels to transport guests to these slopes.

You can go by gondola to a restaurant with a view of the **Gründalm** (3,350 feet), and then continue by chair lift to **Rosenalm** (5,775 feet), where you'll find another restaurant, this one with a panoramic view. From Rosenalm, a drag lift can take you to a lofty citadel 7,430 feet above sea level.

Another ski area, the **Gerlosstein,** more than three miles from Zell am Ziller, also has bus service, but not as frequently. From the bottom station, a cableway will lift you to 5,400 feet where, if you wish to go on, you can take a chair lift up to 6,020 feet.

If you're coming directly to Zell am Ziller, you can fly to the nearest international airport, Munich, in West Germany, and arrange your further transportation there. A narrow-gauge railway runs from Jenbach in the Lower Inn Valley up the Zillertal to Zell.

The area code for Zell am Ziller is 05282.

Food and Lodging

Hotel Tirolerhof (tel. 2227) is a five-story chalet with prominent balconies and a desirable location in the center of the village. On the premises is a Tyrolean disco with thick wood walls and lots of rustic detailing, as well as an intimate country restaurant. Local residents are likely to gather in the evening for some serious beer drinking, and no one seems to mind if you join them.

The cozy bedrooms have concealed lighting, comfortable beds with thick blue-gray quilts, and all the modern comforts. The hotel is an attractive choice for a stopover. On one night at least you're likely to be entertained by the Schuhplätter. A member of the Waidhofer family will quote you a full-board price ranging from 450 AS ($23.94) to 520 AS ($27.66) per person, depending on the season and the accommodation. Singles pay a daily surcharge of 35 AS ($1.86). Open from December to October.

Hotel Bräu (tel. 2313) is a five-story chalet with no frontal balconies. Instead its buff-colored facade is embellished with baroque *trompe-l'oeil* corniches around some of the window frames and heraldic symbols under the eaves. The elegant bedrooms have plenty of exposed wood to reflect the sun streaming through the big windows and contain well-chosen alpine furniture. Facilities include some very old furniture against the carved paneling of the public rooms, a flowering sun terrace near the well-kept lawns, and a gemütlich restaurant with immaculate pink and white napery and well-prepared food. With full board included, rates range from 450 AS ($23.94) to 530 AS ($28.20) in a single and from 450 AS ($23.94) to 510 AS ($27.13) per person in a double, depending on the season and the plumbing. The hotel is open from January to October.

Berghotel Zellerhof (tel. 2614) looks like two or three chalets joined together into a balconied format of exposed wood and white-painted stucco. In the center of the village, the hotel has an attractively woodsy decor which includes a big-beamed ceiling, a scattering of rustic artifacts, and cozy bedrooms with parquet floors and patterned area rugs. All of them are equipped with private bath.

Members of the Kröll family often provide a dance band which performs in a big room adjoining the main dining room. They also host a weekly barbecue in the cellar. The cost, based on double occupancy, is from 490 AS ($26.07) to 540 AS ($28.73). Singles pay a daily surcharge of 65 AS ($3.46). Half board is included in these tariffs, which vary according to the season and the accommodation.

MAYRHOFEN: The road divides at Zell am Ziller, and to reach the next destination I've selected, you take the southwest route to the popular resort of Mayrhofen. After a visit there, I recommend that you return to Zell and then go southeast to Gerlos in the other direction.

But first, Mayrhofen.

This resort, standing at 2,075 feet, enclosed by towering alpine peaks and lying at the foot of the glaciers crowning the adjacent Alps, is a premier summer holiday spot and winter playground, the finest in the valley in terms of facilities and accommodations. Some of the best food you'll find in the area is served here.

For decades Mayrhofen has drawn summer holiday crowds with its endless opportunities for rambling and mountaineering, hang gliding, shooting, tennis, fishing, swimming in a heated outdoor pool, mini-golf, cycling, and even summer skiing in the Hinterlux glacier area at the top of the valley.

However, in recent years the resort village has come more and more into the picture as a ski center. Starting from scratch, you can learn to ski at the school run by Riki and Ernst Spiess. The children's ski training is especially good here, and there's also a kindergarten, making this an ideal family resort.

Skiing is possible in the Penkenjoch section to the west of Mayrhofen, with a cableway taking you to nearly 6,000 feet. Mayrhofen has always offered good skiing for beginners and intermediates, but now, with new Penken terrain, there's more for the experts. From the belvedere here you'll be rewarded with one of the most spectacular views you'll see of the Zillertal alpine range. There's a restaurant here too.

You can also ski in the Ahorn area, to whose 6,250-foot height you're lifted by cableway departing from the south of Mayrhofen. At the top, five drag lifts wait to serve you. Also at the top station you'll find—guess what?—a restaurant with a panoramic view.

A wealth of other winter activities is available, including sledging on a natural toboggan run, alpine curling, ice skating, horse-drawn sleigh rides, horseback riding, and sports in an indoor arena.

Mayrhofen is a mecca for mountain climbers during nonskiing seasons, and you can find enjoyable nighttime entertainment ranging from tea dances to fondue evenings all year. You can also hear some of that famous Ziller Valley singing at folk festivals in July and August. The dates are different each year, so check at the tourist office.

Mayrhofen is reached by the Zillertal railroad, and one of the most popular diversions in summer is to take a ride on the narrow-gauge steam train between Zell am Ziller and Mayrhofen.

From here you can also embark on some important excursions into the Alps around the Zillertal, where you'll be rewarded with some of the most spectacular scenery in Tyrol. By the time you reach Mayrhofen, the trail through the Zillertal which you've been following will have split up into four different parts, each one tempting. These valleys radiate off the Zillertal like blades of a big fan, reaching into the Alps. Three of them have the suffix *grund* (the German word for ground) on their names: the Stillupgrund, the Zemmgrund, and the Zillergrund. The latter takes its name from the alpine range.

You may not have time to explore all these valleys, but if you can make time for one, I suggest you make it the fourth of the quartet, the **Tuxertal,** or Tux Valley, the loftiest one, which cuts like a deep slash through the mountains. This valley comes to its terminus at several glaciers, including the Olperer, 11,400 feet high. You can take a bus from Mayrhofen to either the village of Lanersbach or on to Hintertux, both in the Tuxertal. The road runs west from Mayrhofen for some 13 miles to the end of the valley from which ski lifts branch off in several directions.

You come first to **Lanersbach,** the largest village in the Tuxertal, lying in a sunny, sheltered spot. From here you can take a chair lift to the Eggalm plateau where there's a restaurant at 6,560 feet. One of the most scenic panoramas of the Ziller Alps stretches before your eyes at this point.

Hintertux is at the top of the valley, which of course is your ultimate destination. Once in this village you're virtually on the doorstep of magnificent glaciers. There are views in every direction. Because of thermal springs, Hintertux also enjoys a reputation as a spa. You may want to buy some woodcarvings here, as the craftsmen in the valley are well known for their skill.

You can ski on the glaciers in summer. A chair lift or a gondola from Hintertux will transport you to Sommerbergalm (6,800 feet). Once there, you can take a drag lift west to Tuxer-Joch Hütte (8,300 feet).

Mayrhofen's area code is 05285.

Food and Lodging at Mayrhofen

Elisabethhotel (tel. 2929) is the most luxurious hostelry in town. The chalet facade has carefully detailed balconies, heavy overhanging eaves, a rounded stone entryway, painted designs, and a tower extending up from the center of the roof for whatever stork should built a nest there. The spacious and elegant interior is one of those tasteful places which only the right combination of money, taste, and skilled woodworkers can create. The bar area is a favorite rendezvous point, while the restaurant is outfitted in Zillertal decor which includes a gently arched wooden ceiling. On the premises are a marble-covered steamroom, a sauna, a solarium, a fitness center, and an indoor pool with half-timbered walls and a massively beamed ceiling.

Each of the rooms has a mini-safe as well as a private bath, TV, radio, and all the modern conveniences. High-season rates range from 995 AS ($52.93) per person in a double and from 1,045 AS ($55.59) in a single, with full board included. Open December to October.

Alpenhotel Kramerwirt (tel. 2216) is a well-run hotel built Tyrolean style in the heart of the village near the church. There's been a hotel on this spot for the past 300 years, although the building you'll see today dates from around 1900. Its facade has stone trim around some of the windows, green shutters, a painted illustration of a medieval figure, and a tower-like construction high above the roofline. The rustic interior is paneled with dozens of examples of good woodwork, along with a scattering of Oriental rugs and antique painted chests.

Some of the romantic bedrooms have four-poster beds and big marble-covered baths. On the premises is a small indoor pool, plus a sauna and a Turkish bath. A gemütlich nightclub, the Andreas Keller, is—obviously—in the cellar, containing exposed masonry, massive ceiling beams, checked table-cloths, and live musicians entertaining the drinkers and diners.

With full board included, rates in a double range from 625 AS ($33.25) to 875 AS ($46.55) per person, depending on the season and the plumbing. Singles pay a daily surcharge of 100 AS ($5.32).

Hotel Neuhaus (tel. 2203). Someone has lavished money and attention on the balconied exterior of this traditional hotel in the center of town. The forest-green shutters are well painted, while decorative talismans hang vertically from the slope of the slate-covered eaves. The hotel is actually a collection of large houses, all in the same style, connected together with passageways and walkways. The interior has both old and new sections, with a decor that includes both deep-relief carving in the 19th-century hardwoods and contemporary fireplaces built into the outside angle of a wall in the sitting room. The dining room has an arched wooden ceiling, while the bar area might be a relaxed place for a drink before dinner. The spacious bedrooms rent for 650 AS ($34.58) to 800 AS ($42.56) per person for full board. Josef Moigg is the proprietor.

Hotel Neue Post (tel. 2131). The older of the two buildings which form this hotel was built in 1626. It has a romantically paneled weinstube with an elaborately coffered ceiling and lots of atmosphere. The newer part contains comfortable bedrooms, lots of big, sunny windows, and much modern comfort. Skiers tend to gravitate to the bar, open from 5 p.m. to 12:30 a.m., where music provides lively entertainment. There is friendly, efficient service, against a rustically attractive decor. There's also an underground parking garage in the building. Depending on the plumbing and the season, half-board tariffs range from 420 AS ($22.34) to 540 AS ($28.73) per person.

Gasthof Zillergrund (tel. 2377) is near a clear spring-water stream about a five-minute drive (or a 30-minute walk) from the center of the village. The impressive entrance hall is accented with lots of wood and an intricate Oriental rug, while the dining room has a ceramic stove and lots of exposed fieldstone. Rudolf Pfister is the congenial owner of this chalet hotel. He charges around 450 AS ($23.94) per person in a double, with full board included. Singles pay a daily surcharge of 15 AS (80¢). A large outdoor café sometimes serves as a destination point for visitors who want to make the trek up from the village.

GERLOS: It's not for the St. Moritz crowd, but Gerlos, a tiny resort in the Alps offering year-round pleasure, has its own special brand of warmth, hospitality, and fun which brings repeat visitors, people who are not seeking the international limelight. Gerlos is in fact a secret which its devotees rather hope will stay that way. For majestic mountain scenery, Gerlos is hard to beat, set against a backdrop of the Kreuzjoch, looming over the resort from its 9,020-foot height.

To reach the resort, lying in a secluded, sunny valley at an elevation of 4,065 feet, you take a winding mountain road from Zell am Ziller. If you drive to here in winter you'll need snowchains on your tires, but remember—no chains on the autobahn. If you're coming from Innsbruck, 48 miles away, for instance, you can get your chains put on as soon as you reach Zell. There's also a bus service from Zell am Ziller, the ride taking about 45 minutes, depending on road conditions. You should proceed cautiously on a drive to Gerlos even in warm weather, as the steep, winding road may be crowded with motorists.

Gerlos is a good ski resort, with runs ranging from beginners' slopes to those which challenge experts. You can take the Isskogel double-chair lift up to 5,500 feet, where you can see a sweep of five valleys, glaciers, and peaks of the Alps.

Summer visitors find a broad choice of pleasures, from hiking on the mountain trails to sailing, windsurfing, and fishing in the waters of the mammoth Durlassboder reservoir just outside the village. Horseback riding is offered in summer or winter, and when trails are snowy you can take a sleigh ride.

If you continue along the road to the east you'll reach the Gerlos Pass and the Krimml waterfalls already visited in Chapter VIII on Land Salzburg. This Gerlos Pass road is one of the most scenic in Austria, linking the Ziller Valley with the upper Pinzgau region of Land Salzburg.

The area code for Gerlos is 05284.

Food and Lodging

Hotel Gaspinerhof (tel. 5216) consists of three large chalet-style buildings, each connected by underground passages and stairways. They're filled with antiques from the countryside, ranging from spinning wheels to grandfather clocks to just about the most beautiful painted armoires in the region. In one of the public rooms you might even stumble across a harp. On the premises you'll find an indoor pool, a sexually mixed sauna, and romantically rustic bedrooms. With full board included, rates in high season range from 550 AS ($29.26) to 950 AS ($50.54) per person in a double, with singles paying an additional 10%. An annex holds the overflow and costs less than the main building.

Hotel Glockenstuhl (tel. 5217). The Eberl family are the owners of this wood and stucco chalet with overhanging eaves and neobaroque painting around some of the windows. A big-windowed café on the ground floor is a good place for coffee and snacks, and there is also a rustic bar. The dining room is spacious and outfitted with a large crucifix against one wall. The big bedrooms have simple and attractive furniture along with comfortable beds. The charge in a double ranges from 330 AS ($17.56) to 390 AS ($20.75), with singles paying a daily surcharge of 60 AS ($3.19). Half board is included in these tariffs, which vary according to the season and the plumbing.

Gasthof Pension Hubertus (tel. 218) is a hillside chalet whose three upper floors are covered with aged wooden planks and relatively ornate balconies. The two bottom floors are made of white-painted stucco, with an arched entrance, big windows, and a wide veranda covered with a rustic porch. The interior has a yellow-and-white ceramic tile stove, vividly painted antique furniture, and country curtains and ceiling beams. The spacious bedrooms have lots of exposed light-grained wood, and they rent for 400 AS ($21.28) to 500 AS ($26.60) per person, with half board included.

Après-Ski

For such a small village the nightlife in Gerlos is surprisingly sophisticated, although it can be folkloric as well. Yodelers in lederhosen are likely to appear in any bar anytime, and chances are you'll definitely be entertained by a concert on an electric zither before you leave.

Gerlos has about eight clubs and dancing bars, each charging from 75 AS ($3.99) for a typical hard drink. Most of the nightlife activity takes place in the hotels, principally the already-recommended **Hotel Glockenstuhl** and the **Hotel Gaspingerhof.** Often you might find yourself dancing next to a visiting celebrity, including, on one occasion, Margaux Hemingway, traveling incognito of course.

9. The Alpbach Valley

To tour another alpine valley, this one much smaller than the Zillertal, you can take the road north again, branching off to the east north of Schlitters and heading east again to Reith. Once there you can cut southeast to one of the most delightful and undiscovered valleys in the Tyrolean country. Thomas Wolfe wrote home to his mother of the Alpbachtal that "the valley has some of the most beautiful mountains and villages" he'd ever seen.

ALPBACH: One of the smallest valleys branching off from the Inn set among rich meadows, dark woods, rivers, and mountains, this was a copper- and gold-mining area ruled by the Fuggers in medieval times. The little settlement of Alpbach developed during that time. The town now enjoys minor renown as a meeting place of intellectuals, being the headquarters of the European Forum, an organization founded in 1945. Under its auspices, scientists, politicians, artists, and economists meet here to discuss the problems of the world.

From the village you can wander through meadows and forests to centuries-old farmhouses, nestling near high mountains, and enjoy warm hospitality and folkloric evenings in this tradition-steeped valley.

From nearby Brixlegg, a cableway will take you to the Grosser Galtenberg, a mountain standing 7,960 feet high.

Alpbach's area code is 05336.

Food and Lodging

Hotel Böglerhof (tel. 5227) has a history almost as old as that of the town itself. Built in 1470 as the home of a bowmaker, it became a hostel, a courthouse, and later a prison for the errant miners of the region. In 1936 Thomas Wolfe stayed here in what was at the time a farmhouse. The owner between 1945 and 1979 was the mayor of Alpbach, and he did everything he could to restore it to its rustic glory.

Today what you'll see are two symmetrical chalets with sun-bleached wooden balconies and elegantly embellished ground-floor windows. In summer thousands of geraniums and petunias virtually seem to set the chalet on fire because of their vivid colors. The interior has lots of old detailing such as massive ceiling beams, exposed carved stone, shiny paneling, and in the bedrooms romantically carved and painted furniture. On the premises is a double-level disco, plus an outdoor sun terrace, several bar areas, an indoor pool, an outdoor pool, a sauna, and a solarium. Tennis players can use the nearby outdoor courts free. The hotel has cozy restaurants where fresh-baked bread is served at every meal.

The charge for a room and half board is 625 AS ($33.25) to 1,050 AS ($55.86) in a single and from 600 AS ($31.92) to 750 AS ($39.90) per person in a double. Prices depend on the season and the plumbing facilities. Guests here can enjoy such events as a weekly Romantic dinner and wine tastings.

Hotel Post (tel. 5203) is a Tyrolean chalet surrounded by two tennis courts, a big outdoor pool, and masses of flowers. The interior contains a pub area popular with the après-ski crowd. The public rooms are filled with painted doorways and antique-style chests, along with lots of paneling and invitingly rustic detailing. A sauna offers a place to relax after a cold day outside. The Silberberger family, your hosts, charge from 500 AS ($26.60) to 700 AS ($37.24) per person, based on double occupancy, with full board included. Singles pay a daily surcharge of 100 AS ($5.32). Open December to October.

Hotel Alpbacherhof (tel. 5237). There's something streamlined and elegant about the simple interior of this hotel, almost as if the decorator wanted a lighter effect than is usually found in chalet hotels. Nonetheless the design retains the rustic beauty of exposed wood. The main fireplace is flanked with red marble and built into a manorial-style format with a gently tapering plaster-covered chimney. The Andreas Bischofer family, the owners, have installed both an indoor and an outdoor pool, along with modern baths in all the comfortable bedrooms. For bed and full board, rates range from 850 AS ($45.22) to 1,100 AS ($58.52) per person, depending on the season. The hotel is open from December to March and May to September.

Haus Angelika (tel. 5339) is a super-bargain. Built in 1970, it's a comfortable alpine-style pension serving breakfast in a rustically paneled room with red and black accents. In the sitting room you'll often find a blazing fire. It's a comfortable and well-managed place; it's in the center of the village, not too far from the local church. The charge is from 365 AS ($19.42) to 425 AS ($22.61) per person, with full board included. The Steinlechner family are your hosts. Open December to March and May to October.

REITH IM ALPBACHTAL: If you're seeking something more luxurious than tiny Alpbach offers, you can drive back to Reith and stay at the four-star hostelry recommended below.

Hotel Kirchenwirt (tel. 2648) is a modern chalet with sunny windows and flowered balconies. The ceilings of the interior are elegantly geometrical and rather ornate, sometimes finished in attractive combinations of light and dark woods. Even the big indoor pool has a crossbeamed covering. The Rieser family are your hosts, charging from 540 AS ($28.73) to 820 AS ($43.62) per person in a double and from 660 AS ($35.11) to 850 AS ($45.22) in a single. All tariffs include full board. Prices depend on the season and the plumbing. On the premises are a sauna, a table-tennis and exercise room, and a children's playroom.

The area code for Reith im Alpbachtal is 05337.

The neighboring town to Reith is—

RATTENBERG: This small border town of some 2,000 residents, once part of Bavaria, merits a stop just to look around the old quarter. Rattenberg, annexed by Maximilian I to be part of the Habsburg imperial holdings, was once a mining town, but the industry died out in the 17th century.

The old quarter still looks very much a medieval and Renaissance town. Many of the burghers' houses are from the 15th and 16th centuries, their oriels supplying the householders with a view of the comings and goings on the streets (a pursuit which has been replaced by television). Many of the old houses are coated with stucco, and a lot of the doors and some windows are framed in pink marble.

The same pink marble was used for finish in construction of the *pfarrkirche* (parish church) which dates from 1473. The two naves were later given the baroque decorating treatment.

As you walk down Hauptstrasse (main street) to see the old houses, you might also like to go on a shopping expedition, to purchase some of the glassware and local handicrafts for which Rattenberg is known.

You may want to go to the **Burg,** the fortified castle built on orders of Maximilian I when he confiscated the town from the Bavarians. The castle is in ruins, and it's about a half-hour walk from the town, but visitors go for the panoramic view of the area. Sometimes dramas are presented at the castle in summer.

10. The Kitzbühel Alps

Hard-core skiers and what are euphemistically called "the colorful people of the international leisure set" are attracted to this ski region. The Kitzbühel Alps are covered with such a dense network of lifts that they now form the largest skiing area in the country, with a series of superlative runs. The action centers at the town of Kitzbühel, but there are many satellite resorts that are much less expensive, such as St. Johann in Tirol.

Kitzbühel is, in a sense, a neighbor of Munich, 81 miles away, whose municipal airport is used by most visitors who frequent the Kitzbühel Alps in wintertime.

KITZBÜHEL: Edward, Prince of Wales (you may remember him better as the Duke of Windsor), may have put Kitzbühel on the international map of fashionable ski resorts with his "discovery" in 1928 of what was then a town of modest guest houses. Certainly, his return a few years later with Mrs. Simpson caused the eyes of the world to focus on this town, and the "upper crust" of England and other countries began flocking here, placing a stamp of elegance and sophistication on Kitzbühel.

At the time of this 20th-century renaissance, however, Kitzbühel was already some eight centuries old by documented history, settlement having been here much, much longer than that. Archeological finds have shown that during the Bronze Age and until the ninth century B.C. copper was mined and traded in nearby mountains. The settlement "Chizbuhel" is first mentioned in docu-

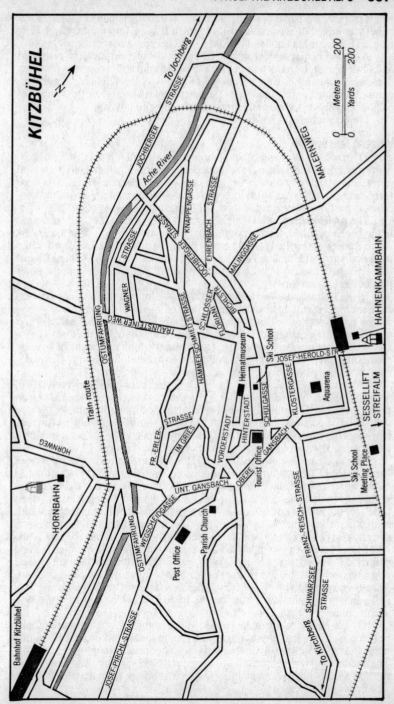

KITZBÜHEL

To Jochberg

JOCHBERGER STRASSE

Ache River

STRASSE

WAGNER

JOCHBERGER STRASSE

KNAPPENGASSE

EHRENBACH STRASSE

MALINGGASSE

MALERN WEG

SCHLOSSER STRASSE

FLORIAN GASSE

BICHL GASSE

TRAUNSTEINER WEG

HAMMERSCHMIED STRASSE

OSTUMFAHRUNG

Train route

Ski School

Heimatmuseum

JOSEF-HEROLD-STR.

HAHNENKAMMBAHN

Meters
Yards
0   200
0   200

HORNWEG

FR. ERLER STRASSE

IM GRIES

VORDERSTADT

HINTERSTADT

SCHULGASSE

KLOSTERGASSE

GANSBACH

Aquarena

SESSELLIFT STREIFALM

Ski School

Meeting Place

UNT. GANSBACH

OBERE GANSBACH

Tourist Office

HORNBAHN

OSTUMFAHRUNG

WEGSCHEIDGASSE

Parish Church

Post Office

FRANZ-REISCH-STRASSE

SCHWARZSEE STRASSE

To Kirchberg

JOSEF-PIRCHL-STRASSE

Bahnhof Kitzbühel

ments of 1165, the name being derived from the ruling family of Chizzo. Kitzbühel was a part of Bavaria until 1504, when it came into the hands of Holy Roman Emperor Maximilian I of Austria and became a part of Tyrol.

A second mining era began in Kitzbühel in the 15th century, this time gold and silver being the products, and the town became fat and prosperous for many decades. Numerous buildings from the mining days are still here, as are remnants of the town walls and three of the gates. In what used to be the suburbs of Kitzbühel you'll see some of the miners' cottages still standing.

The Kitzbühel area code is 05356.

What to See and Do

The town has two main streets, Vorderstadt and Hinterstadt, and unlike St. Moritz where all the buildings are of modern vintage, Kitzbühel has preserved its traditional style of structures, at least in its core along these streets. You'll see three-story stone houses with oriels and scrollwork around the doors and windows, heavy, overhanging eaves, and Gothic gables.

The **parish church** *(pfarrkirche)* was built from 1435 to 1506 and renovated in the baroque style in the 18th century, restored again in 1951. The lower part of the **Church of Our Lady** (Liebfrauenkirche) dates from the 13th century, the upper part from 1570. Between these two churches stands the **Ölberg Chapel** (Ölbergkapelle) with a 1450 "lantern of the dead" and frescoes from the latter part of the 16th century.

In the **Heimatmuseum** (local museum), 34 Hinterstadt, you'll see artifacts from prehistoric mining times in Europe and of the north alpine Bronze Age; a winter sports section with trophies of Kitzbüheler skiing greats and displays showing the development of skiing here; and exhibits detailing the town's history. At one time this building was the town granary, built on the site of an early medieval castle. The center of the building is from the 13th century. The museum is open daily from 9 a.m. to noon.

In winter the emphasis in Kitzbühel, 2,300 feet above sea level, is on skiing, and facilities are offered for everyone from novices to experts. The ski season starts just before Christmas and goes on until the beginning of April. With more than 50 lifts, gondolas, and mountain railroads on five different mountains, Kitzbühel has two main ski areas, the Hahnenkamm and the Kitzbüheler Horn. Cable cars are within easy walking distance, even in ski boots.

The linking of lift systems on the Hahnenkamm provides the celebrated **Kitzbühel Ski Circus**, which makes it possible to ski downhill for more than 50 miles, with runs that suit every stage of proficiency. Numerous championship ski events are held here, one being the World Cup event each January, when top-flight skiers pit their skills against the toughest downhill course in the world, a stretch of the Hahnenkamm especially designed and prepared for maximum speed. A ski pass entitles the holder to use of all the lifts that form the Ski Circus.

Skiing became a fact of life in Kitzbühel as long ago as 1892, when the first pair of skis was imported from Norway and intrepid daredevils began to slide down the snowy slopes at breakneck speeds. Many great names in skiing have since been associated with Kitzbühel, perhaps the most renowned being Toni Sailer, a native of the town, who was the triple Olympic champion in the 1956 winter games.

Of course there are many other winter activities offered: curling, skibobbing, ski jumping, ice skating, tobogganing, hiking on cleared trails, and hang-gliding, as well as such indoor activities as tennis, bowling, and swimming. The children's ski school provides training for the very young. And don't forget the après-ski, with bars, nightclubs, and discos rocking from tea time until the wee hours.

Kitzbühel has summer too, with activities including walking tours, visits to the Wild Life Park at Aurach (about two miles from Kitzbühel), tennis, horseback riding, golf, squash, brass band concerts in the town center, cycling, and swimming. For the latter, there's an indoor swimming pool, but I recommend going to the Schwarzsee (Black Lake). This *see*, about a 15-minute walk from the center of town, is a peat lake and has bathing establishments, boats to rent, fishing, a waterski school, and restaurants.

In either summer or winter, you can take the cable car which leaves for Kitzbüheler Horn (6,550 feet) every half hour.

Kitzbühel is not a cheap place to stay, but to make things easier on your pocketbook, the Tourist Office, 18 Hinterstadt (tel. 2155), has come out with a Guest Card for summer visitors. This card is valid after being stamped by your hotel or guest house and entitles you to reductions, some of them quite substantial, on the price of many activities, plus some freebies.

Where to Stay

Although there's a wide range of hotels in Kitzbühel, reservations are absolutely mandatory in the high-season months, particularly the peak ski times such as February. As for Christmas in Kitzbühel, someone once wrote, "It's best to make reservations at birth."

Deluxe Living: The core of **Hotel Schloss Lebenberg** (tel. 4301) is a medieval knight's castle whose simple walls and turrets have been covered with a smooth layer of unblemished stucco. A modern extension looking vaguely like a cross between a villa and a chalet has been added nearby. The entire complex sits on a hill looking over the village, with dozens of mountain paths originating at its door. Very little of the castle's original decor has survived the passage of the years, and the interior is filled with wall-to-wall carpeting and modern furniture. Nonetheless the hotel is comfortable and inviting, with a large indoor pool, a range of health and cosmetic facilities, a big sun terrace, and an energetic social program. The breakfast buffet in the elegant dining room is lavish. The hotel charges from 600 AS ($31.92) to 1,500 AS ($79.80) per person, based on double occupancy; singles pay a daily surcharge of 150 AS ($7.98). Half board is included in the price.

Parkhotel (tel. 4395) is an elegantly sprawling mountain-style villa with a half-timbered upper section and a solid lower section of thick gray stone. It stands in a large park slightly removed from the center of town, and has been known for years as one of the resort's most important hotels. The interior has an appealing combination of high beamed ceilings, wood floors, and thick plaster walls which virtually kill the noise between the rooms.

On the premises are outdoor tennis courts, an outdoor pool, an indoor fitness center with a hot whirlpool, a sauna, a solarium, and a café. The après-ski bar often has live music, especially during the winter, and an engaging crowd of chic habitués. Rooms cost from 750 AS ($39.90) to 1,400 AS ($74.48) per person, depending on the season and whether or not the accommodation has a private balcony. Half board is included in the room price. The hotel is open December to March and June to September.

Hotel Maria Theresia (tel. 4711) is a modern chalet with six stories of carefully applied decoration on its facade and an interior where much effort has been spent on creating a woodsy and quality-oriented decor. On the premises are a large bar area, a stone-trimmed lobby with an open fireplace, a sauna, a Turkish bath, a Viennese café, and dining facilities. Much of the paneling is darkly tinted, even in the comfortable bedrooms. Charges in a double, all of which contain a private bath, range from 600 AS ($31.92) to 1,250 AS ($66.50) per person, with half board included. Prices vary widely according to the season. Singles pay a daily surcharge of 60 AS ($3.19).

First-Class Choices: The ancestor of the **Hotel Goldener Greif** (tel. 4311) was built in 1271, and parts of it probably still remain buried within the massive walls of this well-known hotel. It was completely modernized in 1954, and the facade has a vivid series of trompe l'oeil baroque frescoes which give a realistic illusion of depth to the windows. From another angle the hotel is pure chalet style, with lots of balconies and red-and-white shutters. Owner Josef Harisch likes unpretentious charm with a good dose of luxury thrown in.

In the heart of the old town, next to the Spiel-Casino, this hotel is a traditional favorite for lots of vacationers who'd prefer never to stay anywhere else. The vaulted interior contains open fireplaces, comfortable furniture, and a free-form swimming pool. With half board included, rates range from 600 AS ($31.92) to 1,800 AS ($95.76) per person.

Romantikhotel Tennerhof (tel. 3181), in an elevated position on the outskirts of Kitzbühel, near the Hornbahn cable car and the golf course, is a comfortable hotel which has evolved from a centuries-old Tyrolean farmhouse. The whole house is beautifully furnished in alpine style with great care and taste, offering a touch of good living and complete relaxation in a lovely garden setting. Some of the public rooms have dramatic multicolored flagstone floors, ceramic-tile stoves, well-placed hunting trophies, and a collection of chalet chairs. The views from the outdoor café encompass the pool and the village. The restaurant offers wholesome food, with vegetables and herbs straight from the hotel garden. The owners, Mr. and Mrs. Pasquali, take a personal interest in their guests and see that a high standard of service is maintained. Full board costs from 1,150 AS ($61.18) to 1,600 AS ($85.12) in a single and from 1,000 AS ($53.20) to 1,350 AS ($71.82) per person in a double. Prices depend on the season and the plumbing. Open December to March and June to September.

The Moderate Range: The **Schlosshotel Münichau** (tel. 2962) is a 14th-century hunting lodge with red-and-white chevron shutters, at least three slate-roofed towers, and a severe medieval design. Lying four kilometers from the center of Kitzbühel, the hotel commands an impressive view of the mountains from its location in the center of lush alpine meadows. An outdoor pool and a few medieval buildings are visible from the windows of the individually decorated bedrooms. The public rooms are embellished with unusual engravings and covered with vaulted ceilings. You'll find at least three open fireplaces, as well as a rustically elegant restaurant. With half board, the cost in winter ranges from 600 AS ($31.92) to 1,300 AS ($69.16) per person, depending on the plumbing. The cheaper units are in a comfortable modern annex a few steps away from the main building. Summer rates are slightly cheaper.

Hotel Jägerwirt (tel. 4281). The name of this place means "Hunter's Inn," and even if you don't like to hunt wild animals, you should love the blazing fires and the mellow paneling of this rustically attractive hotel. In a design of three small chalets joined with a central section, the hotel has a bar area with hewn overhead beams and friendly service, as well as spacious bedrooms with lots of exposed wood. On the premises, a nightclub, the Halali, has an octagonal dance floor with dining tables set up around it and a timbered ceiling radiating out from the center like the spokes of a wheel. The restaurant is a member of the Chaîne des Rôtisseurs.

The Bartenstein family, the owners, charge from 400 AS ($21.28) to 1,200 AS ($63.84) per person in a double and from 520 AS ($27.66) to 1,250 AS ($66.50) in a single, with half board included. Prices vary widely according to the season. There are some apartments with hot whirlpool bath and color TV. The hotel has a special movie room with many English-language video films. Both indoor and outdoor tennis courts are near the hotel, and a nine-hole golf course is about a four-minute walk away.

Hotel Weisses Rössl (tel. 2541) is outside the town gate in an imposing L-shaped building with a flagstone-covered rooftop terrace that shelters a small swimming pool, a fountain, and swinging settees. Views from the balconies adjoining the well-furnished bedrooms encompass much of the surrounding countryside. The public rooms include a round dance floor with the hotel's insignia (a white horse) inlaid into its center, two dining rooms, and a sitting room with a formal fireplace and an Oriental rug. Winter rates range from 520 AS ($27.66) to 1,000 AS ($53.20) per person, based on double occupancy, with half board included. Singles pay a daily surcharge of 90 AS ($4.79). The overflow from the main building spills over into the nearby annex, whose rooms fall at the lower end of the price structure. Summer rates are slightly cheaper.

Hotel Zur Tenne (tel. 4444) is one of the most popular hotels in town, frequented by a jet-set clientele who seem to return year after year, often asking for the same rooms. The facade is painted terracotta and buttercup, with a glass extension stretching toward the street in the center of town. The interior contains Tyrolean artifacts, mellowed paneling, open fireplaces, and a rustic collection of furniture. On the premises is a hot whirlpool, plus a health center area, along with a big nightclub/restaurant combination where guests look down on the dancing from two levels of balconies. Well-furnished singles range from 670 AS ($35.64) to 1,300 AS ($69.16), while doubles go from 1,100 AS ($58.52) to 2,000 AS ($106.40), with breakfast included. Half board is available for an additional 280 AS ($14.90) per person daily.

Hotel Tyrol (tel. 2468) is an attractively scaled chalet with five balconied stories and an open-sided wooden tower which the owners hope will eventually contain a stork's nest. In the center of town, the hotel has a simple decor and functionally practical bedrooms. On the premises is a large, somewhat bare dining room with a wood-paneled bar area. Prices range from 300 AS ($15.96) to 460 AS ($24.47) per person, with breakfast included. Prices depend on the season and the plumbing.

Hotel Schweizerhof (tel. 2735) is a well-designed cross between a chalet and a mountain villa. It has a hipped tin roof, lots of balconies, and an exterior which looks like a different building from practically every direction you observe it. The interior has some attractive antiques, Oriental rugs, and lots of beamed and paneled ceilings. The hotel is close to the departure point for the Hahnenkamm cable car. Singles rent for 520 AS ($27.66) to 1,050 AS ($55.86), while doubles range anywhere from 580 AS ($30.87) to 950 AS ($50.54) per person, with half board included.

Hotel Klausner (tel. 2136), eight minutes from the center of town, is an ochre-colored twin-roofed building with a big parking lot and a quiet location. The interior has lots of stone detailing, both on its floors and in an occasional column supporting the wood and plaster ceilings. The attractively simple bedrooms have high ceilings and functional furniture. A big garden with a sun terrace is close to the rear entrance. Prices with half board included range from 590 AS ($31.39) to 830 AS ($44.17) per person. Tariffs depend on the accommodation and the season.

Hotel Die Postkutsche, 30 Ehrenbachgasse (tel. 3291), has the kind of quiet good taste and generous use of space that only an elegant hotel can provide. The 18th-century entrance hall has chiseled stone columns supporting the vaulted ceiling, red stone flooring, and a gracefully curved stairwell sweeping past wrought-iron balconies to the upper floors. You'll recognize this place by the yellow-and-black chevron shutters, the baroque painting around some of the windows, and the elaborate wrought-iron sign arching over the street. Guests will find a bar, a weinstube with old paneling, and a beamed dining room serving French specialties. Each of the charming bedrooms has its own individual decor and much comfort. Tariffs range from 500 AS ($26.60) to 620 AS ($32.98) per person; These prices, which vary according to the season, are for bed and breakfast only.

Sporthotel Bichlhof (tel. 4022). Slightly more than two miles south of the center of the resort, this hotel offers panoramic views over most of the valley. Its tasteful chalet format includes a big covered swimming pool in a separate building, as well as a decor of exposed paneling and patterned carpeting. The spacious bedrooms sometimes have geometric grid patterns of dark wood against white walls that look almost Japanese in their simplicity. The cost of bed and breakfast is 780 AS ($41.50) to 1,000 AS ($53.20) per person in a double, with singles paying a surcharge of 60 AS ($3.19). The hotel is open from December to March and May to September.

Mainly Pensions: About a mile from the center of town, close to the Schwarzsee, is **Bruggerhof** (tel. 2806), a countryside chalet with orange awnings covering its outdoor sun terrace. The interior has massively scaled ceiling beams, some of them carved into alpine patterns, and a warmly burning corner fireplace whose smooth stucco contrasts handsomely with the paneling around it. The dining room has geometrically patterned wooden ceilings and wrought-iron chandeliers, while another section has ornate stucco columns supporting the full-grained ceiling. Josef Reiter and his family are the owners, charging from 800 AS ($42.56) per person in a double, with full board included. Singles pay a daily surcharge of 100 AS ($5.32). Open December to March and May to September.

Hotel Hahnenhof (tel. 2582) is an old-fashioned villa at the foot of the Hahnenkamm. Its interior has fresh colors, lots of wall-to-wall carpeting, a scattering of antiques, and exposed ceiling struts composed of heavy beams. The hotel is a gracious place to stay, very quiet because of its isolation from the village, which is about ten minutes away. Prices for room and half board range from 470 AS ($25) to 610 AS ($32.45) per person, depending on the plumbing and the season.

Hotel Pension Alpina, 4a Hahnenkammstrasse (tel. 2731), is a graciously sprawling chalet with baroque ornamentation painted around the windows of its white facade. The interior is warmly furnished with lots of knotty pine and an assortment of autumnal colors. It has an indoor pool, modern bedrooms with only a few unnecessary frills, and an indoor pool. On the edge of a park, the hotel has a sweeping view of the valley. The Venlet family charges from 720 AS ($38.30) to 850 AS ($45.22) per person, based on double occupancy, with half board included. Prices vary according to the season, and singles pay a daily surcharge of 100 AS ($5.32). The hotel is open December to March and May to September.

Hotel Ehrenbachhöhe (tel. 2151) is an attractively isolated hotel at Hahnenkamm. Its chalet facade looks out over a wide vista of mountains, while in the warmth of the interior you can swim in the indoor pool, enjoy good cuisine in the paneled dining room, or a few beers under the massively cross-timbered ceiling of the bar area. The attractively detailed bedrooms rent for 700 AS ($37.24) per person, based on double occupancy, and singles pay a daily surcharge of 80 AS ($4.26). These prices include full board and vary according to the season. The hotel is open from December to April and July to August.

Gasthof Eggerwirt (tel. 2455) presents a beige-and-brown, traditionally designed facade. The borders of the windows are embellished with country baroque paintings, while the modernized bedrooms have chalet furniture and colorful accessories. The owners charge 700 AS ($37.24) per person for a bed and full board.

Where to Dine

Most guests stay at Kitzbühel on the half-board plan. It's also fashionable to dine around, checking out the action at the various hotels. With one or two exceptions, most notably the Unterberger Stuben, all the best restaurants are in hotels.

Wirtshaus Unterberger-Stuben (tel. 2101) is a preferred hangout for the rich and famous who come every year to Kitzbühel. In addition to an occasional German-speaking film star (or whatever), you'll also find a scattering of athletes, urbanites, entwined couples, and hunters. Overall, the ambience is authentically Tyrolean. The owner, Mr. Unterberger, is the son of the town's most appreciated cook. Having learned to cook at his mother's stove, he and his wife decided to open this country-style inn in what had been his old family home.

In a setting of old paintings and rustic paneling, you are likely to be served one of your finest meals in the Tyrol. Try, if you see it on the menu, a poppyseed soufflé, or any of the specialties of the many countries which once belonged to the Austrian Empire. The fresh fish and the game are well prepared and savory. Dessert will probably feature (in summer) the succulent mountain berries of the region, or you might order the poached apples filled with white chocolate mousse.

An average meal will cost around 420 AS ($22.34), although it could conceivably rise or fall 250 AS ($13.30), depending on what you order. Reserve ahead and please be on time. The restaurant is open from 9 a.m. to midnight, with warm meals served only between noon and 1:30 p.m. and between 6:30 and 10 p.m. The chef takes off during all of June and all of November and on Tuesday between March 15 and June 30 and from December 1 to 20.

Restaurant La Cave, Hinterstadt (tel. 3435). You'll recognize the building which contains this restaurant by its Tyrolean porch jutting out above the cobblestones of one of the two main streets of town. Don't confuse La Cave with the ground-floor pizzeria within the same building. Head for the stone steps which descend into the basement for one of the finest dining experiences in town.

In a vaulted room ringed with burnished wood of a local evergreen, you can enjoy such specialties as pike-perch with a watercress cream sauce, stuffed salmon en gelée with a cabbage-flavored cream sauce, salad of rabbit with a truffled vinaigrette sauce, Tyrolean wine cream soup, filet of sole with smoked bacon in a Reisling sauce, and medallions of pork in a beer sauce flavored with cumin. Full meals begin at 400 AS ($21.28), and reservations are suggested. The restaurant is open seven days a week between 11:30 a.m. and 2 p.m. and between 6 p.m. and midnight.

Tennerhof (tel. 3181). You'll walk a short distance from the center of town before reaching the restaurant in this well-run hotel that looks like a balconied hunting lodge. The restaurant has a multicolored flagstone floor, a heavy beamed ceiling, and fern-green walls and tablecloths. Your attention will probably be directed toward the huge windows, whose view might give you pause between courses.

Specialties of the house include pungent lamb medallions, trout dishes, and a range of Tyrolean specialties, plus vegetables from the hotel garden when available. You'd better phone ahead for a table, since many of the guests staying at the hotel tend to fill up the dining room. Fixed-price meals range from 275 AS

($14.63) to 400 AS ($21.80), while à la carte dinners go from 600 AS ($31.92). A gourmet meal costs 800 AS ($42.56).

Restaurant Zur Tenne (tel. 4444). Even if you don't stay at this fashionably sporty hotel attached to this three-tiered restaurant, you'll at least want to stop in for a drink or a meal. The ambience is improved by the attitude of the young waiters who do everything they can to be helpful. Scattered with antiques, the restaurant looks down on a floor that later in the evening is filled with dancers. Menu items include steaks (which are sometimes grilled right at your table on a hot slab of stone) and Tyrolean specialties. Don't forget to stop for a nightcap at the adjoining bar area. Meals range from 250 AS ($13.30). Reservations are important.

Schloss Lebenberg (tel. 4301). The royal family of Monaco has graced the dining room of this hotel. If the elegantly upholstered Louis XVI chairs and the striped wallpaper are not to your liking, you'll find three other dining areas nearby, all sharing the same menu. Fresh bread and butter are *de rigueur*, and specialties include cream of tomato soup with gin, calf liver Tyrolean style, and a tempting array of fresh desserts, many of them made (in summer only) with whatever mountain berries are in season. Fixed-price meals go for 225 AS ($11.97) and 330 AS ($17.56), while à la carte dinners cost from 165 AS ($8.79) to 410 AS ($21.81). The restaurant is closed from early April til mid-May and from early October until the beginning of December.

Goldener Greif (tel. 4311). The floor of this elegant restaurant is covered with a series of Oriental rugs, the white napery is spotless, and the ceiling is a webbed network of crossbeam panels. The effect is of the inside of a hunting lodge. Specialties include a fresh cream soup made with brains, an array of schnitzels, and simple desserts. The menu is rather limited, although the ambience is warm and inviting. Fixed-price meals cost 110 AS ($5.85) and 165 AS ($8.79), while à la carte dinners range from 110 AS ($5.85) to 325 AS ($17.29).

Stamperl (tel. 2555). Popular with the hardy locals who seem to survive in Kitzbühel even when the tourists leave for the season, this gemütlich restaurant is filled with old wood and lots of atmosphere. Marikka Lichter was a well-known popular singer in the German-speaking world before she came here to direct the honest and savory food coming from the kitchen. Dishes include Wiener schnitzel, beef gulasch with noodles, tafelspitz, and pork cutlet with buttered noodles, plus an array of what is said to be the best ice cream in Kitzbühel. À la carte meals range from 250 AS ($13.30). The house is done in a charming blue Tyrolean motif with baroque designs around the windows.

A Shopping Note

In a studio at 4 Franz-Reisch-Strasse, **Leni Kuborn-Grothe** produces exquisite embroidered jewelry items, such as spangled hearts. She also makes tiaras, featherweight but looking as rich as though they came from the treasury of the Habsburgs. You can get something different here in the line of souvenirs of your trip that you will enjoy showing and/or giving to family and friends when you return home.

Après-Ski

Kitzbühel has about the best après-ski life in the Tyrolean country. Even before the approach of night the activity has already begun in the mad dash for a seat at the **Praxmair,** Vorderstadt (tel. 2646). This is one of the most famous pastry shops in Austria, and it's known for its florentines. Later on the Praxmair Keller pulsates with life, especially if the owner, Toni Praxmair, stages one of his Tyrolean evenings, complete with zither music and yodelers. Inevitably, the woodcutter's folk dance will be presented. But if it's still five o'clock, the item to order is hot chocolate with a "top hat" of whipped cream. Coffee costs from 18 AS (96¢) to 30 AS ($1.60) and pastries from 30 AS ($1.60).

At the average place drinks cost from 50 AS ($2.66), rising to 80 AS ($4.26) in the more expensive establishments.

The biggest after-dark attraction is the **Spiel-Casino** (tel. 2300), in the already-recommended Hotel Goldener Greif. Opening at 7 p.m., it has a restaurant and a bar, in addition to offering roulette, blackjack, and baccarat. Its summer season is from July 1 to mid-September, and its winter season lasts from Christmas until the end of March.

One of the most popular places in town is **Zur Tenne,** Vorderstadt (tel. 4444). Usually the best live groups in town appear here, and dancers gyrate on the large floor. Every February "Miss Austria" is selected by a jury here. Eva Rueber-Steier went on to become "Miss World."

Currently the chicest disco is **Drop-In,** 22 Hinterstadt (tel. 2270), which stays open in season to 4 a.m. The **Alt Wien,** Vorderstadt (tel. 4746), also has a dance bar with a band.

Since most of the clubs of Kitzbühel are likely to be expensive, you might try the **Heurigenstadel Goldene Gams,** Vorderstadt (tel. 2611), in the center of town. The decor is neo-Grinzing, and you can order both hot and cold food until 2 a.m. You're even allowed to grill your own steak. A zither player is likely to be on hand to play *The Third Man* theme.

Try also the après-ski bar at the previously recommended **Park Hotel.** The ambience is atmospheric, and you're likely to be entertained by a singer accompanied on an electric organ.

If it's an English pub you seek, try **The Londoner,** Franz-Reisch-Strasse (tel. 3318), which lately has been very popular, drawing a chic crowd. There's another pub, also called **The Londoner,** Im Gries (tel. 4740), which is in the British pub style as well.

ST. JOHANN IN TIROL:
St. Johann does not have the chic reputation of Kitzbühel, but neither does it have the high prices. Many "dollarwise" visitors stay here, taking advantage of the lower tariffs, and go to Kitzbühel, six miles to the south, to enjoy the facilities there.

This village, lying between two mountains, the Wilder Kaiser and the Kitzbüheler Horn, is both a summer holiday center and a winter ski resort. In summer it has a busy, open-air swimming pool, and in winter, good ski runs appeal to both beginners and experts. A ski school and ski kindergarten, plus cross-country ski trails, add to the attractions. Bars in the snow are popular.

Many old-style Tyrolean houses fill the little town with charm, and some of the old inns have frescoed exteriors.

The Kaisergebirge, near St. Johann, draws many European mountain climbers.

The area code for St. Johann in Tirol is 05352.

Food and Lodging
Hotel Fischer, 3 Kaiserstrasse (tel. 2332), is a well-built chalet in the center of the village, with hanging vines flanking the sun terrace, plus evenly spaced rows of wooden balconies. The sunny bedrooms are comfortable (albeit somewhat small), and they have private baths and all the modern comforts. With half board included, prices range from 620 AS ($32.98) to 865 AS ($46.02) per person in a double. Singles pay a 50 AS ($2.66) daily surcharge. Prices vary according to the season.

The restaurant has a warmly intimate color scheme which is enhanced by the thick horizontal planks stretching across the walls. Dishes include North Sea salmon with dill sauce, cream of mushroom soup, schnitzels in cream sauce, and for dessert, a walnut parfait with marinated plums and kiwi.

Hotel Crystal, 5 Hornweg (tel. 2414), is a pleasant chalet, centrally located in the heart of the resort near the ski school. The interior is cozily outfitted with modern paneling and deep-seated chairs, with accents of wrought iron and modern textiles. The premises include a children's playroom and a sauna. The Lagler family, the hosts, charge winter rates ranging from 580 AS ($30.87) to 900 AS ($47.88) per person, based on double occupancy, with full board included. Singles cost 720 AS ($38.30) to 950 AS ($50.54) on the same plan. Rates are slightly lower in summer. The hotel is open from December to October.

Sporthotel Austria, 3 Winterstrasse-Weg (tel. 2507), is an oversize chalet with deeply recessed balconies and a rustically modern format of lots of exposed wood and contrasting white stucco. The elegant interior has carefully crafted paneling on many of its ceilings, stone and tile accents, and lots of brass chandeliers. The facilities include a big, attractive indoor pool with a bucolic mural covering one of the walls. Christine Mätzler, the hostess, charges winter prices of 920 AS ($48.94) to 1,050 AS ($55.86) in a single and 820 AS ($43.62) to 1,060 AS ($56.39) per person in a double, with full board. Rates are lower in summer. Open December to March and May to September.

Gasthof Post, 1 Speckbacherstrasse (tel. 2230), is about as solid a building as you'll find in the Tyrol. It was first constructed in 1224, and parts of its original hewn ceiling beams are still in place. The facade is an elaborately ornate stucco surface where *trompe-l'oeil* baroque frescoes have been painted around each of the windows. The hotel stands a few buildings away from the village church. Its interior is filled with stone and wood columns, a painted ceiling, and lots of bucolic charm. The paneled bedrooms range from large to intimately small. With full board included, high-season rates range from 650 AS ($34.58) to 820 AS ($43.62) per person.

Hotel Goldener Löwe, 23-27 Speckbacherstrasse (tel. 2251), is a seven-story flowered chalet whose many balconies barely conceal the oversize glass windows leading into the sunny bedrooms. In the center of town, the hotel offers well-furnished public rooms with tastefully modern furniture in conversational niches. The dining room has a futuristic design of rectangular solids hanging from the ceiling, cleanly angled structural supports, and contoured form-fitting chairs covered with red Chinese lacquer.

The hallways leading to the bedrooms have modern adaptations of baroque designs painted in pastel colors onto the ceilings and walls. Under the same management are an adjoining restaurant and a dance café with live music. With full board, the charges in a double range from 430 AS ($22.88) to 820 AS ($43.62), depending on the season, the accommodation, and the plumbing. Singles pay from 520 AS ($27.66) to 840 AS ($44.69), also with full board.

Hotel Park, 45 Speckbacherstrasse (tel. 2226), is a modern hotel that would look vaguely like a chalet except for its roofline, whose peak is broken into two distinct sections. My favorite feature in the contemporary sitting room is the copper-sheathed bonnet over the fireplace, which is built into a corner of two stucco walls. In winter the bedrooms rent for 700 AS ($37.24) to 890 AS ($47.35) per person, with half board included. Some of the accommodations with sloped ceilings up under the eaves cost less. Summer rates are slightly cheaper. In winter the congenial owner, Josef Grander, holds a weekly ski race whose winners are videotaped, followed by a Tyrolean buffet or fondue evening.

Hotel Europa, 18 Achenallee (tel. 2285), lies next to the village sports center. Its simple facade is a 1960s-style pastiche of black-and-white detailing with weatherproof windows and Tyrolean balconies. The interior has coffered ceilings, a hospitable bar area, and a big sundeck. Ernst Mechs, the owner, charges 650 AS ($34.58) to 770 AS ($40.96) per person in a double and 720 AS ($38.30) to 820 AS ($43.62) in a single, with full board included. Apartments are also available for between two and five guests. Prices depend on the season, and all units contain private bath, phone, and balcony. The hotel is open from December to September.

Speckbacherstuben, 31 Speckbacher Strasse (tel. 2843), is a local kind of restaurant popular with the residents of the village. It serves such items as bouillon with chives, warm cabbage salad with bacon bits, pork and lamb chops, and excellent salads using lots of fresh radiccio and leafy green lettuce. It's closed every Monday, and between mid-April and mid-May and for all of November. Meals cost between 110 AS ($5.85) and 275 AS ($14.63). Reservations are suggested.

FIEBERBRUNN: This spa and well-known winter sports resort lies in the Kitzbühel Alps in the Valley of the Pillersee-Ache, seven miles southeast of St. Johann in Tirol. It can be reached by car or bus from St. Johann, about a 20-minute ride, depending on road conditions.

From here you can take a chair lift to **Lärchfilzkogel** (5,440 feet). In summer a popular excursion is to 2,730-foot-high **Lake Piller,** six miles north on the road to Waidring (see below).

Fieberbrunn has an outstanding schloss hotel, recommended below.

The Fieberbrunn area code is 05354.

Food and Lodging

Schlosshotel Rosenegg (tel. 6201) was built in 1555. Its steeply sloping roof is studded with at least three rows of gables, as well as a collection of pointed towers. The weathered stucco facade is adorned with red-and-white striped shutters. The Eberhardt family maintains a rustic restaurant in an adjoining low-lying modern building, which also contains a popular bar and dancing pub, The Fox, and a wine bar, 's Weinfasse, with an open hearth, Viennese music, and candlelight, where the locals like to chat over a glass of wine. In the reception section, you'll find a cocktail bar and a hall sitting area. In the castle, there are 30 beautifully appointed bedrooms, with another 50 units in the new building joined to the hotel by a covered bridge. Rooms rent for 485 AS ($25.80) to 650 AS ($34.58) per person, including half board. Prices depend on the season and the accommodation.

Hotel Brunnhof, 15 Lindau (tel. 6452), is directed by the Leschhorn family. Its pleasant chalet format is surrounded by balconies and has a giant entrance archway. The warmly rustic interior is decorated with heavy timbers and lots of rustic artifacts. With half board included, high-season rates range from 580 AS ($30.87) to 790 AS ($42.03) per person. Prices depend on the plumbing and the season, and each of the accommodations has a private bath.

Restaurant La Pampa (tel. 6442). If you're in the mood for steaks and wouldn't mind taking a short excursion to a restaurant with a vaguely South American theme, this might be the place for you. It is run by the Erös family. The thick cuts of meat are grilled any way you prefer, and they're seasoned properly for maximum tenderness. Menu items include several kinds of soup (for instance, lobster bisque), roast beef Créole style, shrimp, frogs' legs, and a wide range of salads. À la carte meals range from 160 AS ($8.51) to 315 AS ($16.75). The restaurant is open from December to April and from July to September from 5:30 to 9:30 on weekdays, from 11:30 a.m. to 2:30 p.m. and 5:30 to 9:30 p.m. on Sunday. It's closed Wednesday.

WAIDRING: A Tyrolean village in the region where Tyrol, Bavaria, and Land Salzburg meet, Waidring is a popular holiday resort in summer and winter.

Summer visitors find 33 miles of well-tended walking paths, as well as high-altitude hiking trails on **Steinplatte** (6,000 feet). In winter, Steinplatte offers ideal skiing conditions from December to mid-April, with a good lift system. You can go up the local mountain on the Waidring-Steinplatte mountain road if you prefer, although that's probably a better summer pursuit.

A ski school, illuminated natural toboggan run, curling, cross-country skiing, Tyrolean folklore evenings, and moonlight tobogganing add to the attractiveness of Waidring.

Waidring's area code is 05353.

Food and Lodging

Sporthotel Tiroler Adler (tel. 5311) is a large balconied chalet in the middle of the village. Its balconies are covered in summer with masses of flowers, which contrast attractively with the weathered planking of parts of the facade. The interior has a woodsy contemporary decor that includes an elegant dining room and a slightly less formal restaurant with upholstered bar stools and light-grained paneling. Doubles range in price from 360 AS ($19.15) to 410 AS ($21.81) per person, with singles costing an additional 60 AS ($3.19) per day. Half board is included in these tariffs, which vary according to the season.

WESTENDORF: This charming, friendly Tyrolean village lies at an elevation of 2,575 feet on a sunny plateau in the Brizental (Brixen Valley) of the Kitzbühel Alps, undisturbed by through traffic. It's easily accessible by car, however, via the Inn Valley motorway to Wörgl and then the B70 Brixental road—but you'd better have heavy-tread tires on your car. You can also come here by train on the Innsbruck-Salzburg-Vienna railway.

Westendorf is surrounded by wooded mountains with walking and cycling trails, and summer visitors can ride the lifts up to the heights for views of the countryside.

For winter visitors the village has about 25 miles of prepared ski runs in use from the first of December until the middle of April, supervised by a well-organized mountain rescue service. Some 80 ski instructors are on hand to teach you how. Even tiny tots can learn to ski. The resort offers 15 chair lifts and T-bars, for which you need only one ski pass. There are good runs for both novice and intermediate skiers.

Other winter activities include sleigh rides, tobogganing, ice skating, curling, cross-country skiing, and after that, Tyrolean evenings complete with yodeling and whatever.

The area code for Westendorf is 05334.

Food and Lodging

Hotel Briem (tel. 6310) sits quietly in a sunny meadow a few minutes away from the village center. Run by the Briem family, it's designed in an attractively formal chalet format of recessed balconies, clean white stucco, and lots of painted ornamentation around the weatherproof windows. The interior is rustic, with a simple dining room and a lounge/bar area. Singles range 425 AS ($22.61) to 465 AS ($24.74), while doubles cost from 480 AS ($25.54) to 510 AS ($27.13) per person in high season, with half board included.

Sporthotel Jakobwirt (tel. 6245). The Ziepl family are the owners of this charmingly traditional alpine hotel. The decorated building angles itself around an arcaded outdoor sun terrace with café tables and waitress service. The public rooms have massive ceiling beams, some of them carved, a hospitably rustic bar area, a scattering of antiques, and geometrically patterned tile floors in natural colors. Partly because of its location in the center of the village, the hotel's restaurants are popular throughout the year. These include an attractively formal dining room with pink-upholstered chairs and a woodsy weinstube with green and white tablecloths. High-season prices range from 550 AS ($29.26) to 600 AS ($31.92) per person, based on double occupancy, and singles pay a daily surcharge of 75 AS ($3.99). Half board is included in these tariffs. The hotel has an indoor swimming pool, a sauna, and a solarium.

11. The Kaisergebirge

This nature reserve of Tyrol is known popularly by its nickname, "Kaiser." Lying to the north of the Kitzbühel alpine range (see above) and to the east of the Inn River, this is a land of coniferous forests and meadowlands filled in warm weather with contented-looking cows, a land of much beauty, ideal for hikers and climbers. It has towering mountain peaks and gorges of untamed beauty.

The Valley of the Kaiser connects with the Valley of the Inn at Kufstein. It divides the 6,560-foot-high Zahmer Kaiser (tame emperor) from the Wilder Kaiser (wild emperor), which has a jagged peak rising to 7,690 feet. Essentially, the Kaisergebirge is a limestone mountain range.

I will have two stopovers in this district, one in the southern part at Ellmau and another in the far-northern section, Walchsee, a lake-district retreat close to the Bavarian border. St. Johann in Tirol (see above) technically falls within this area, but because of its situation as a moderately priced resort near high-priced Kitzbühel, I included it in the district just visited.

ELLMAU: This holiday resort stands at 2,500 feet at the base of the Wilder Kaiser mountain and is considered the most beautiful spot in the valley. It lies in a triangle formed by Munich, Salzburg, and Innsbruck, within easy commuting distance of Kitzbühel. You can, of course, drive here. If you come by train, go to Kufstein, and from there a taxi will bring you to Ellmau.

In summer the little resort has an excellent hiking area and offers open-air concerts and Tyrolean evenings. It's also possible to take a cable car, the Hartkaiserbahn, for a panoramic sweep into the mountains.

Winter brings skiers to Ellmau, which has 10 lifts and well-maintained slopes. In addition, there are 52 more lift facilities in the surrounding area. In snow time you can participate in ice skating, curling, horse-drawn sleigh rides, cross-country skiing on well-kept courses, and of course, those Tyrolean evenings again.

Ellmau's area code is 05358.

Food and Lodging

Hotel Bär & Tyrol (tel. 2395) is a winning combination of at least six different buildings clustered together in an isolated position a few minutes' walk from the village church. The furnishings of the interior run the gamut from rustically modern (in the Hotel Bär) to 19th-century conservative (in the Hotel Tyrol), although the two styles compatibly merge with one another.

On the premises you'll find flagstone floors, Oriental rugs, comfortable settees, cafés, bar areas, and romantically furnished dining rooms. Everything is outfitted with taste and gemütlich comfort, with lots of visual stimuli to tease your aesthetic palate.

In a separate building is a pizzeria serving attractive food in an informal setting. An outdoor pool is a short distance away, as well as an array of both summer and winter activities. Hotel guests have access to the tennis courts and golf course in nearby Kitzbühel. Also on the premises is a wide range of massage, beauty, and physical therapy facilities. Management works hard to organize camping outings and social events.

Each of the upper-crust bedrooms is decorated individually, with ample use of rustic planking and unusual colors. Accommodations come in a wide variety of single or double rooms, including private outbuildings and apartments, some of them very luxurious. Charges range from 1,250 AS ($66.50) to 1,450 AS ($77.14) per person based on double occupancy and from 1,330 AS ($70.46) to 1,500 AS ($79.80) in a single, all tariffs including full board and depending on the season and the room assignment.

Some critics say that the best food in the province is served on the pink or green napery of this elegant restaurant. Americans will be flattered to see that the menu includes wines from California as well as Austria. Management invites guests to look into the kitchen, where an army of uniformed chefs prepares such dishes as cream of crayfish soup, delicate salads of watercress, crayfish meat, and morels, as well as salmon steaks in a mustard and cucumber sauce, or rack of veal in a marsala sauce with leafy spinach. Desserts could include such delicacies as walnut ice cream with honeyed sour cherries. Prices for elegant repasts served here range from 260 AS ($13.83) to 660 AS ($35.11). Reservations are important.

Hotel Hochfilzer (tel. 2501). The entrance to this lovely hotel is under an archway painted around its edges with intricate designs of vines and flowers. Above that is a depiction of a handsome peasant and his pretty wife flanked by flowered balconies and tastefully monochromatic paintings. The facade is only a hint of the kinds of personalized attention and detailing available in this rambling hotel. The friendly staff does everything it can to serve you at the thick-walled bar or in the cozy restaurant. The hotel has been owned by the Hochfilzer family since 1840. A modern chalet extension with lots of weathered wood and yellow shutters was added in 1973. Today the comfortable bedrooms rent for 425 AS ($22.61) per person for half board in a room with a private bath and a balcony in May, June, September, and October. In July and August, the high season, rent for the same arrangement is 500 AS ($26.60) per person per day.

Berghof Ellmau (tel. 2723) is a modern building with an unusual amount of big-windowed exposure toward the direct rays of the sun. Situated about ten minutes from the center of the village, this efficiently managed hotel charges from 400 AS ($21.28) to 600 AS ($31.92) per person, based on double occupancy, with singles paying a daily surcharge of 95 AS ($5.05). These tariffs include half board.

Alpenhof (tel. 2201) is a pleasant chalet a few minutes from the center of the village, close to the ski school and many of the chair lifts. Its facade looks like twin houses adjoining one another, with evenly spaced rows of balustrades set at the edge of the wooden balconies. The rustic interior contains comfortable bedrooms priced from 380 AS ($20.22) to 420 AS ($22.34) per person, with half board included. Tariffs depend on the season.

Hotel Kaiserblick (tel. 2230). *Blick* means "view" in German, and that's exactly what you'll get from the windows of this comfortable hotel. The sun terrace and the balconies are angled toward the village church, all of the Ellmau Valley, and the knife-edged mountains beyond. If you turn away from the scenery you'll see a hotel that is tastefully rustic, outfitted with pleasant autumnal colors and lots of well-polished paneling. An outdoor pool is set onto the lawn outside, maintained in good condition by the owners, the Howeg family. A curved staircase leads up to the cozy bedrooms. Per-person rates, based on double occupancy, with half board included, range from 290 AS ($15.34) to 420 AS ($22.34). Singles pay a surcharge of 35 AS ($1.86) per day, and tariffs depend on the plumbing and the season.

WALCHSEE: Both a lake and a village lying close to the West German-Austrian border bear the name Walchsee. This is one of the most remote corners of the Tyrolean country, and although known to Austrians and Bavarians, is little known to the average North American traveler. The lake, one of the largest and most beautiful in Tyrol, is set against a backdrop of alpine meadows and dark forests. In summer the Walchsee has many facilities for water sports. To reach the lake, you can drive or take a bus from St. Johann in Tirol or else from Kufstein.

The little resort village has excellent accommodations and food at moderate prices, which helps explain its popularity with European visitors.

If you develop "lake fever," you can also go to the smaller **Hintersteiner See,** facing the Wilder Kaiser at an elevation of 2,925 feet. However, the road to Lake Hinterstein is very poor.

The area code for Walchsee is 05374.

Food and Lodging

Hotel Panorama (tel. 5661) is one of the most pleasant hotels in the region. It sits on a hillside, affording good views from behind the flowers covering the dozens of balconies. A parasol-dotted sun terrace has been set up just outside the eight-foot arches of the ground floor. The inside is elegantly woodsy, with lots of exposed wood and much detail. On the premises is a hospitable bar area, plus an indoor pool which leads into a form of stone grotto. There are plenty of health facilities, as well as friendly, attractive personnel. High-season rates range from 500 AS ($26.60) to 700 AS ($37.24) per person, half board included. Tariffs vary according to the room assignment.

Hotel Schick (tel. 5331). The facade of this unusual hotel angles in a gentle curve toward an inner-village street. Sections of the white stucco are painted with soft shades of pink and blue into geometric regional designs. The interior has original uses of natural-grained pine, which acts both as a divider for the tables in one of the airy restaurants and as a warmly hospitable wall covering. Some of the decor includes half-timbered beams set into plaster walls, a round enclosure surrounding an open hearth, and lots of soft lighting. The hotel maintains an indoor swimming pool, a wide range of health and beauty treatments, and access to nearby tennis courts with professional instruction. Charges range from 600 AS ($31.92) to 900 AS ($47.88) per person, based on double occupancy, with singles paying from 655 AS ($34.85) to 950 AS ($50.54). All prices include full board. Each unit contains a private bath.

12. The Upper Inn District

I've already introduced you to the Inn Valley that lies to the east of Innsbruck. Now on a much different excursion we'll go west from the Tyrolean capital in the direction of the remote western province, Vorarlberg. Along the way will be many detours and offshoots through valleys. At Landeck we'll depart from the westward trek, swinging directly south along the Inn, stopping off at the summer and winter resorts of Serfaus and Nauders as we head for the Italian frontier. Along the way, large mountains such as the Ötztal Alps rise on either side.

Heading west from Innsbruck, your first stopover might be—

ZIRL: Although Zirl, eight miles to the west of Innsbruck, is usually visited as a luncheon stopover, the town does a busy tourist business, lying as it does at the crossing point of the main roads from Munich, the Brenner Pass, and Innsbruck.

The area code for Zirl is 05238.

Food and Lodging

Goldener Löwe (tel. 2330) is a small and high-quality hotel whose 200-year-old alpine format was renovated into a woodsy style of simple, comfortable rooms, each of which has a private bath. There's nightly Tyrolean dancing in the Löwengrube restaurant. If that doesn't appeal to you, there are also two rustic weinstubes. The Plattner family works hard supervising and preparing the specialties in the restaurant, which include freshly caught trout with chives and wild mushrooms, a host of regional dishes prepared with wild berries and natural ingredients, and excellent and imaginative desserts. Meals range from 120 AS ($6.38) to 375 AS ($19.95). Reservations are suggested.

Each of the comfortable rooms has a private bath. They rent for 950 AS ($50.54) in a double, and singles pay from 600 AS ($31.92) daily. The hotel also has some apartments available for up to four persons, and there's a garage on the premises.

KÜHTAI: From Zirl you can make an interesting scenic detour, leaving the Valley of the Inn for a while. Head first for Kematen, a village at the entrance of the Sellrain Valley and then west along the Melach Gorge. You'll pass through the valley villages of Sellrain and Gries, which I don't view as meriting a stopover, although Innsbruckers like to escape the city in winter and come here to enjoy the mountain air. After passing another village, St. Sigmund, you'll be on your ascent to the plateau at Kühtai, a high-up summer and winter holiday center.

This village, on the land register of the counts of Tyrol in the 13th century, was later a resort of emperors. Maximilian I acquired the shooting rights in Kühtai in 1497, and an imperial hunting seat was built beginning about 1622, by Archduke Leopold. The Jagdschloss, or hunting lodge, remains from that time and is now one of the most delightful accommodations in this section of the guide (see below).

Kühtai offers winter recreation, including ski slopes for all stages of expertise, cross-country tracks, and ski-bobbing, with snow "guaranteed" from November to May. A ski school and ski kindergarten add to the attractions, with après-ski enjoyment provided.

From Kühtai the road continues into the Ötz Valley, which I will treat separately in an upcoming division. For the purposes of this section, however, I'll take you northwest from the town of Ötz to Imst, another major stopover along the Upper Inn region.

The Kühtai area code is 05229.

Food and Lodging

Jagdschloss Kütai (tel. 201). The charming and aristocratically elegant grandson of Kaiser Joseph, Count Stolberg-Stolberg, is the owner of this former hunting lodge, parts of which date from 1450. Archduke Leopold ordered a more recent version built on this site, incorporating parts of an older building. What you see today is a solidly constructed chalet with red-and-white chevron shutters and a stunning view over the countryside. Many of the massively paneled and timbered public rooms contain vaulted ceilings and furnishings dating back to the 17th century. These include very old chests, glistening brass chandeliers, antique engravings, and carefully grouped hunting trophies. Rates range from 540 AS ($28.73) to 950 AS ($50.54) per person, with half board included.

The rooms at the cheaper end of the price scale are sometimes located in the comfortable annex nearby.

The cozily rustic restaurant radiates atmosphere and style. The chefs use the best quality meats to produce their specialties. The beef Stroganoff is heavenly. The leafy salads appear to have been picked minutes ago, and the desserts are richly satisfying combinations of chocolate, pastries, and fruit. The hotel is closed between May and November.

Hotel Mooshaus (tel. 207) is a homey, family-run hotel, Tyrolean style, which stands in the heart of the village not far from the ski lifts. Its public rooms include gently arched beamed ceilings, as well as wrought-iron accents dividing the congenial bar area from the rest of the establishment. The 48 rooms have all the conveniences, such as a private bath and phone. Some of the units also contain private balconies. On the premises you'll find a sauna, a solarium, and a sun terrace. In the Zirbenholzbar you'll be entertained by once-a-week dancing and special dinners. High-season rates range from 460 AS ($24.47) to 815 AS ($43.36) per person, based on double occupancy, and from 600 AS ($31.92) to 860 AS ($45.75) in a single, with half board included. If you visit at Christmas, however, there's a surcharge.

Specialties in the rustically appointed restaurant are perfect for appetites sharpened by a day outdoors. They include pork medallions in a mushroom cream sauce with spätzle, veal steak with mushrooms, and an unusual collection of ice creams, crème caramels, and special coffees (some of them mildly intoxicating). Meals range from 120 AS ($6.38) to 350 AS ($18.62). Reservations are suggested.

IMST: An old market town on a terrace above the river, Imst, at the mouth of the Gurgl Valley, is used as an overnight stop for many motorists as it lies at the junction of the Innsbruck-Landeck route. This is a good center for exploring the Pitz Valley and the Ötz Valley.

Imst is divided into an upper town (Oberstadt) and a lower town. If you're rushed, skip the lower one and visit Oberstadt. Its 15th-century **pfarrkirche** (parish church) was reconstructed after being swept by fire in 1822. The steeple of this large edifice is the highest in Tyrol, 300 feet. A large statue of St. Christopher stands outside the church. St. Michael's Chapel, next to the parish church, is a war memorial, with monumental frescoes by local artists inside.

Imst is especially known for its **Schemenlaufen** (Ghost Walk), a festival presented every few years (next time is in 1988). Schemenlaufen is a masked Fasching (carnival) procession held two Sundays before Shrovetide. On Shrove Tuesday, the day before Ash Wednesday, the Auskehren, a masked carnival procession which symbolizes the last fight between good and bad ghosts, takes place. Revelers wear carved masks, such as those of witches looking like the opening act of *Macbeth*, many of which are more than a century old. If you're not around at carnival time, you can see a collection of these masks in the local museum (**Heimatmuseum**) at 1 Ballgasse.

The area code for Imst is 05412.

Food and Lodging

Hotel Post (tel. 2554) is an enormous hotel composed of a 15th-century core and a more recent addition. The two main buildings are angled at 90 degrees from one another and are set in the midst of a pleasant park. The older of the two has an onion-dome tower and a steeply sloping gabled roof, as well as elegantly painted monochromatic embellishments. The Singer family maintains a full-fledged array of sporting activities around the hotel, including a covered swimming pool whose sliding glass doors open onto a view of the valley. The interior has an impressive collection of country antiques, wrought-iron doors, and carved paneling. With full board included, rates range from 580 AS ($30.87) to 780 AS ($41.50) in a single and from 520 AS ($27.66) to 760 AS ($40.43) per person in a double. Tariffs depend on the season.

Alpenhotel Linserhof (tel. 2415) is composed of two alpine chalets set in a meadow between a forested hillside and a small lake. The interior is rustically outfitted with wrought-iron accents and lots of exposed wood. On the premises is an indoor pool, plus a friendly staff and a pleasant restaurant with a mellow patina covering its paneled walls. This is a hospitable place to spend the night. Hermann Linser, the owner, charges from 420 AS ($22.34) to 700 AS ($37.24) per person, with full board included. These tariffs include accommodations in apartments as well as in hotel rooms.

Hotel Stern (tel. 3342) is a well-run chalet with a sunny location on a grassy lawn and a rustically woodsy interior. The public rooms are dotted with an informally cluttered collection of hunting trophies, cooking utensils, and rustic artifacts. The pleasant bedrooms cost from 530 AS ($28.20) to 590 AS ($31.39) per person, with full board.

Terrassenhotel Linser (tel. 2860) has an up-to-date exterior which includes flat roofs and big windows. The interior is attractively rustic, most of it covered with horizontal planking and regional accessories. From the grassy front lawn guests can look out over the mountains. On the premises is a sauna, plus a big indoor pool, a well-managed restaurant, and a bar. The hotel sits in the middle of a meadow somewhat removed from the center of the village. The charges for bed and breakfast are from 385 AS ($20.48) to 425 AS ($22.61) per person in a double, from 435 AS ($23.14) in a single. Open from December to October.

Hotel Eggerbräu (tel. 2460) is a large, severely designed modern building with an abstract multicolored mural decorating one side. The interior is more rustic than you'd guess by looking at the outside. In addition to its tastefully decorated restaurant, it has a hospitable bar area and cozy, well-furnished bedrooms. The cost in a double, with full board, is 560 AS ($29.79) to 610 AS ($32.45) per person. Singles on the same plan pay from 615 AS ($32.72) to 675 AS ($35.91).

ARZL: The Pitz Valley is certainly not the most spectacular in Tyrol, but it's quite suitable if you're seeking a tranquil mountain valley like that which so delighted Thomas Wolfe decades ago. Arzl lies a short drive southeast of Imst on the south bank of the Inn River. From here you can continue your exploration by taking a curvy road that pierces the Pitztal (Pitz Valley), which runs south into the Ötztal Alps, lying between two other valleys—Ötztal on its eastern side and Kaumertal in the west.

If you take the road all the way to the end of the valley, passing through the hamlets of Trenkwald and Plangeross, you'll arrive at **Mittelberg** at the head of the valley. For your effort and time you'll be rewarded with a splendid view of the Mittelberg Glacier. The main town in the Pitztal through which you'll pass is St. Leonhard.

Arzl's area code is 05412.

Food and Lodging

Hotel Post (tel. 3111), a pleasant chalet, is filled with all the accoutrements you'd probably want in an alpine hotel, including a green ceramic stove, lots of paneling, and an open fireplace. Renovated in 1972, the hotel charges 430 AS ($22.88) to 460 AS ($24.47) per person in a double, with half board included. Singles pay a daily surcharge of 40 AS ($2.13).

LANDECK: Back on the main road after a detour into the Pitz Valley, continue your westward journey through the Upper Inn district, coming to a stop at Landeck, 15 miles west of Imst, lying at an elevation of 2,675 feet. Landeck is an industrial town, and hardly the most attractive one in the Inn Valley, but it's a convenient stopover choice.

The old town was built at the junction of the Inn and Sanna Rivers, and also the junction of the roads from the Reschen Pass and from Arlberg. It's on the rail line that leaves Innsbruck going toward the far western Austrian province of Vorarlberg and points in eastern Switzerland. Landeck lies south of the Lechtal alpine range.

Burg Landeck, a 13th-century castle, dominates the town and houses a local museum. However, its most striking feature is the view that unfolds from here. The 1471 **pfarrkirche** (parish church) stands on a terrace almost as if it were at the foot of the schloss. It's one of the best-known Gothic-style buildings in the province. Inside, note the altarpiece from the 16th century. The winged altarpiece is in the late Gothic style.

In season, some of the hotels in Landeck present Tyrolean folkloric evenings.

The Landeck area code is 05442.

Food and Lodging

Hotel Schrofenstein (tel. 2395) contains an elegantly antique entrance area, complete with an old beamed ceiling, marble floors, and Oriental carpets. The bedrooms are more modern, possessing all the comforts. On the premises is a rustic wine cellar plus an attractive restaurant. With breakfast included, singles cost 420 AS ($22.34), while doubles rent for 650 AS ($34.58). The hotel is open from December to October.

Hotel Schwarzer Adler Landeck (tel. 2316) is a typical Tyrolean hostelry. The sunny interior gives off a feeling of solid tradition and security. With half-board included, this family-run hotel charges 375 AS ($19.95) per person daily. There are also eight apartments, accommodating two to four persons each, which are cozy, rustic, and quiet, overlooking the town. Rental for these costs 550 AS ($29.26) per day.

FISS: Fiss and its neighboring hamlet, Ladis, on the east side of the Inn River, may be reached by car or by taking the train to Landeck and going on by bus. Secure snow conditions, long ski runs, and concomitant winter activities are available here without the hustle and bustle of larger ski centers. Fiss has retained much of the originality of a Tyrolean mountain village.

The area code for Fiss is 05476.

Food and Lodging

Schlosshotel Fiss (tel. 6397) looks like an updated version of a medieval fortress. Part of this effect is because of the square tower whose ground floor is pierced by an arched passageway, allowing cars to pass below it. The rest of the establishment stretches into the slope of a hill, which a guest can climb thanks to a series of flagstone steps flanked with carriage lamps. The rustic interior has massive ceiling beams, a scattering of antiques, and a pleasant dining room. The cozy bedrooms are outfitted with autumnal colors and lots of horizontal planking. Rooms rent for 400 AS ($21.28) to 440 AS ($23.41) per person in a double and 420 AS ($22.34) to 460 AS ($24.47) in a single, all tariffs being quoted on the full board plan. The hotel is open from December to April and June to September.

SERFAUS: Lying on the west bank of the Inn River, Serfaus is a convenient stopover between Landeck (see above) and Nauders (see below), if you're touring. This was once a farm village, but has been turned in recent years into a colorful summer holiday retreat and winter sports resort set against a backdrop of peaks crowned with icy white hoods. It has an exceptional range of good hotels at moderate prices.

Sunny slopes in an extensive skiing area span three mountain valleys and have cable car, chair lift, and surface lift transport. You'll find intermediate and beginner ski runs, cross-country trails, and other winter sports facilities.

Summer visitors can walk to centuries-old mountain farms, listen to brass bands, swim, and find perfect relaxation in this hospitable spot.

The town is known for its two churches from the Middle Ages—one from the 14th century and the other from the dawn of the 16th century. Many buildings here still bear testimony to the ancient Rhaeto-Romanic cultural traditions of the area.

The Serfaus area code is 05476.

Food and Lodging

The **Hotel Cervosa** (tel. 6211) stands on the periphery of Serfaus. It's a large double chalet with lots of balconies and contains many facilities for the amusement of both summer and winter guests, including a typical Tyrolean restaurant, a sun terrace with chaises longues and waitress service, a hospitable bar, and a host of well-furnished public rooms. On the premises is a big indoor swimming pool, plus two saunas, and a wide choice of massage and beauty facilities. The Westreicher family, the hosts, charge from 520 AS ($27.66) to 1,400 AS ($74.48) per person per day for a room and half board. Tariffs vary widely according to the season. The most expensive accommodations are apartments suitable for up to four persons.

Hotel Alpenhof (tel. 6228) is an alpine chalet a four-minute walk from the center of the village. The interior has some of the most charming detailing around, much of it finished from light-grained knotty pine, well sanded, with a mellow glow. On the premises are dozens of charming extra touches, along with an indoor pool, plus accommodating and friendly service performed by the Karl Schuler family. High-season rates range from 850 AS ($45.22) to 1,100 AS ($58.52) in a single and from 785 AS ($41.76) to 1,250 AS ($66.50) per person in a double, including half board.

Hotel Furgler (tel. 6201) is a large modern chalet in the center of the village. Its public rooms contain lots of heavy ceiling beams, horizontal planking, and a blazing fireplace within a tapering plaster chimney. On the premises is a well-maintained dining room filled with thick stucco walls and lots of light, plus an indoor swimming pool with table tennis, chaise longues, and big windows. The rustically comfortable bedrooms rent for 780 AS ($41.50) to 1,050 AS ($55.86) per person. Full board is included in these prices, which vary according to the season and the accommodation. There's a garage on the premises.

Hotel Löwen (tel. 6204) is an attractively painted stone-trimmed chalet with gray and terracotta designs around its wood-framed windows. Inside, the hotel has lots of horizontal planking, a beamed dining room, a bar, a swimming pool, a sauna, and a billiard room, plus a flowered sun terrace. Charges for bed and full board range from 450 AS ($23.94) to 1,300 AS ($69.16) per person. Rates vary widely according to the season and the accommodation. The Tschiderer family are your hosts. The hotel is open from December to April and June to September.

Hotel Schwarzer Adler (tel. 6491) is a five-story, square-based chalet with wood and regional designs accenting its facade. The interior has rustic touches, including heavy timbers and lots of light-grained paneling. On the premises is a health center containing a sauna, a whirlpool, a Turkish steambath, and a fitness center. The Lugger family take special care of the cuisine they serve. Rates range from 385 AS ($20.48) to 700 AS ($37.24) per person, depending on the season. In addition to the dining room, there's also a pleasant wine cellar.

Après-Ski

The hotels already recommended dominate this form of activity. The kellers and taverns of the hotels charge from 65 AS ($3.46) for hard drinks in most cases. In the peak season the **Hotel Cervosa** brings in live groups that entertain while patrons dance. The **Hotel Furgler** is also likely to provide the same type of nighttime diversion.

NAUDERS: This village of narrow streets, at an elevation of 4,585 feet, is known for its location near the Swiss, Austrian, and Italian frontiers, which has made it an international gathering place with some excellent hotels, charging reasonable prices.

About 12 minutes from the heart of Nauders you can take a drag lift to Stables (6,400 feet), then on to Stableschochboden (7,352 feet). There's also a chair lift to the west of the resort, called the Mutzkopf lift, going up to Rialsch at more than 6,000 feet. A restaurant with a panoramic terrace and a good view lies here on a belvedere.

For the most exalted view of all, you can take a trip by a gondola to **Bergkastel,** which rises some 2,625 feet from its point of origin at the Reschen area to the east of Nauders. From there drag lifts go to the Bergkastel summit at 8,530 feet.

Some four miles from Nauders you come to the Reschen Pass at 4,955 feet and the Italian border.

The area code for Nauders is 05473.

Food and Lodging

Hotel Astoria (tel. 310) is a pleasant balconied chalet set in the middle of town. On the premises, directed by the Ernst Wiestner family, is a cozy collection of public rooms embellished with brass chandeliers, well-finished wood paneling, and an attractively formal dining room and a slightly less formal weinstube. Everywhere here the colors are reminiscent of a woodsy mountaintop house, even though the establishment is set in the middle of the village. On the premises is an indoor pool, plus a sauna, a solarium, and a dancing bar where the management sometimes presents live musical entertainment. The price in a double ranges from 560 AS ($29.79) to 750 AS ($39.90) per person, with half board included. Rates depend on the room and the season, and all the accommodations contain a private bath.

Hotel Almhof (tel. 222). Herr Kröll turns out to be a delightful host at this tastefully rustic chalet with an arched entryway and generously proportioned balconies. The interior is a winning combination of plush Oriental rugs, massive ceiling beams, attractive lighting, and elegantly chosen accessories. Taking great pride in their establishment, the Kröll family have even had its name carved into one of the well-finished ceiling beams in the dining room. You'll find a country weinstube, a hospitable bar, an indoor pool with a sauna, and a choice of health facilities, along with a children's playroom.

Although the hotel is in the center, the ski run comes almost to its doorstep. In high season the comfortable bedrooms rent for 700 AS ($37.24) to 1,250 AS ($66.50) per person in a double or an apartment, and from 800 AS ($42.56) to 1,050 AS ($55.86) in a single. These prices vary according to the time of year and include half board.

Hotel Margarete Maultasch (tel. 235) is a rustic hotel with lots of innate charm. Its stucco and shingle facade is composed of a pleasing series of curves and angled lines. The interior is a tasteful collection of mellow paneling and massive ceiling beams, some of which are arranged like spokes of a wheel around the top of a circular fireplace in one of the cozy sitting rooms. The facilities include an indoor swimming pool, a sauna, a solarium, and a table-tennis room. The Senn family are the owners, charging winter rates of 750 AS ($39.90) per person, based on double occupancy, with full board. Singles pay a daily surcharge of 35 AS ($1.86). Prices are slightly lower in summer and vary according to the room assignment.

Hotel Schwarzer Adler (tel. 254) is a well-constructed chalet with a prominent restaurant on the ground floor. The real appeal is on the inside, where some of the heavily timbered ceilings and walls are reinforced with angled cross-beams and accented with a happily cluttered ambience of contrasting fabrics and rustic details. You'll find an occasional antique blanket chest, as well as a blazing fireplace. The Tschiggfrey family are your hosts, charging 600 AS ($31.92) to 640 AS ($34.05) per person in a double and from 660 AS ($35.11) in a single. Prices vary widely according to the season and include full board. Breakfast is lavish enough to be called brunch.

Hotel Erika (tel. 240) is capably managed by Essat and Ilse Mangalify, who make guests feel at home in their attractively rustic modern chalet. The public rooms have benefited from the lavish attention of carpenters, who added built-in cabinets and wooden accents throughout the hotel. The bedrooms have lightly finished wooden planks covering the ceilings, as well as comfortable beds and private baths. Well-prepared Austrian specialties are served in the elegantly woodsy dining room. Charges in a double range from 400 AS ($21.28) to 620 AS ($32.98), including half board. Singles pay a daily surcharge of 55 AS ($2.93).

Sporthotel Tirolerhof (tel. 256) is a six-story chalet which is a little taller than the other inner-village buildings surrounding it. From the upper-floor sun terrace and from the balconies guests can look down on the outdoor swimming pool. A brick-and-plaster exposed chimney provides winter heat to the comfortable chairs clustered around it. The furnishings of the tasteful public rooms include attractive woodsy pieces and lots of autumn-colored Oriental rugs. An indoor swimming pool is on the premises, and other features include a hospitable bar, an attractively paneled weinstube, and a big sun terrace. Much of the clientele tends to be mildly athletic and sports loving. The Senn family are your hosts, charging from 400 AS ($21.28) to 480 AS ($25.54) per person in high season, based on double occupancy, with breakfast. Singles pay a daily surcharge of 85 AS ($4.52).

Après-Ski

It's not especially organized but relaxed and casual, the way most skiers prefer it.

Guests of the previously recommended **Hotel Almhof** are likely to be entertained by zither music in the late afternoon when they return from the slopes. A feature of the establishment is a grill room where you can cook your own meats to your desired perfection, just as you do back home.

One of your most elegant evenings with chic, convivial company is likely to be spent at the four-star **Hotel Astoria**, also recommended previously. It draws a fun-loving crowd to its bar, and later on guests can arrange to go on horse-drawn sleigh rides in the winter's night, returning in time for a body-warming glass of kirsch.

The **Hotel Margarete Maultasch,** also recommended before, has a night-club, Lady M, with music for dancing, and on occasion it also has fondue evenings.

Drinks at all of the establishments recommended above begin at 65 AS ($3.46).

13. The Ötz Valley

This next excursion into the Ötz Valley is actually an offshoot detour that can be made before you reach the midpoint of your tour of the Upper Inn district. Following the Valley of the Inn, you head west from Innsbruck, but before reaching Imst you can take a good but winding road (no. 186) south toward the Italian border. Along the way you'll find many worthy stopovers, each town or village offering good food and hotels, again at reasonable prices.

The Ötztaler Ache flows through the valley which extends for about 35 miles from the south bank of the Upper Inn. The mouth of the valley is at Ötz (spelled *Oetz* on some maps). Along the road you'll see many waterfalls as you ascend. I hope you'll be there on a sunny day, to marvel at the glaciers and peaks of the Ötztal Alps spreading before you. The valley cuts deep into the heart of some of the highest peaks in the eastern alpine range and leads into the midst of what has been called the "Tyrolean arctic," a glacier region of ethereal beauty. The mountain villages have glacier lifts for extensive skiing. Glacier skiing is possible from spring through fall on the gigantic Rettenbachferner.

This long valley has good skiing in its lower and outer reaches, but if it's summer and you're here just for the sightseeing, the inner or mid part is the most spectacular.

Our first stopover is at—

ÖTZ: Ötz (also spelled Oetz) is reached by going three miles south from the junction of the Inn River and the Ötztaler. A holiday center in both winter and summer, the resort, noted for its mild climate, is perched 2,695 feet high on a sunny slope. Ötz has many old buildings, often with traditional oriels and painted facades. A Gothic **pfarrkirche** (parish church) dates from the 14th century, although it was enlarged centuries later.

Just two miles southwest of the town is a warm body of water, **Piburger Lake** (3,000 feet), which is popular in summer.

From Ötz, you can also make a 5½-mile trek south to the hamlet of **Umhausen,** the oldest village in the valley, now a holiday resort.

The area code for Ötz is 05252.

Food and Lodging

Sporthotel Habicherhof (tel. 6248) has a strikingly modern design based on an alpine chalet. A six-story central section rises above rambling extensions containing the public rooms and a sun terrace, as well as a woodsily futuristic building with large windows and an indoor pool. The building blends attractively into the slopes of the hillside. The high-ceilinged interior contains lots of smooth planking and coffered ceiling panels, as well as a bar area with alpine stools, cozy restaurants, and sitting rooms. The multilingual staff, directed by the Haslwanter family, creates a homey, informal atmosphere. The hotel sits on the main road leading into town, in the heart of the valley, surrounded by abundant snowfields. With full board included, rates per person range from 485 AS ($25.80) to 625 AS ($33.25).

Alpenhotel Oetz (tel. 6232), in the center of the village, is built on a stone foundation pierced with big arched windows. Visitors enjoying the view from the raised sun terrace are sheltered from the wind by the balconied hotel facade behind them. The interior has softly shining wood and parquet floors, paneled ceilings, and sunny colors—lots of homey comfort. Solid, traditional cookery, usually well prepared, is available in the dining room. The Falkner family charges from 350 AS ($18.62) to 465 AS ($24.74) per person for lodging in a single, double, or triple room, with half board included. Prices depend on the season, and each of the comfortable units contains a private bath.

Hotel Drei Mohren (tel. 6301) is one of the most distinctive structures in the village. Dating from the turn of the century, the building is a baroque fantasy of onion domes, medieval towers, and hipped roofs, with dozens of arched windows piercing through the thick white walls. Most of the grandly paneled bedrooms have private balconies and carved headboards. The chalet restaurant is done with old engravings and beautifully finished paneling. With half board included, the price is 500 AS ($26.60) per person. The management is friendly, providing a light-hearted touch. On the premises are an outdoor tennis court and a covered garage.

Gasthof zum Stern, 6 Kirchweg (tel. 6323). Parts of this pleasant inn date from 1611. Today the facade is opulently covered with bay windows painted with country baroque designs. You'll recognize the hotel by the gilt and wrought-iron bracket hanging over the sidewalk, just below the cascades of summertime geraniums. The paneled interior is filled with charm and rustic details, including a ceramic stove. The Griesser family, the accommodating owners, charge around 290 AS ($15.34) per person, based on double occupancy, with singles paying a daily surcharge of 25 AS ($1.33). These prices include half board and vary according to the season.

Heiner (tel. 6309). In high season this café and pastry shop has an avid collection of last year's fans waiting for a table. The family who runs this place is so well known that some of the locals simply call the establishment by the family name, Haid. Aside from a wide collection of coffees and teas, the establishment sells eight combinations of yogurt, six kinds of refreshingly flavored milk, eight kinds of milkshakes (one of them with red wine), at least ten kinds of flavored eggnog, and about 40 different concoctions that include ice cream in some way.

If you don't like sweets, you'll find about 15 kinds of carafe or bottled wine, as well as cognac. If dinner or lunch is on your mind, you can enjoy oxtail soup flavored with sherry, a crab cocktail, a host of omelets, and there are also children's platters. More filling are the various kinds of veal, beef, and pork dishes (wild game in season), served with tasty salads. The price for meals varies widely. However, some specials are offered ranging in price from 120 AS ($6.38) to 230 AS ($12.24), while à la carte meals begin at 150 AS ($7.98), going up to 295 AS ($15.69). It's open daily except from mid-November to mid-December.

Continuing up the valley, your next stopover might be—

LÄNGENFELD: This major tourist resort, attracting both winter and summer visitors, is in the heart of the Ötz Valley, at the mouth of the Sulz Valley. The Fischbach torrent splits Längenfeld into two distinct parts. For miles around you can see the 240-foot high spire of the **pfarrkirche** (parish church) in upper Längenfeld.

If you base here, you might enjoy an excursion north to the **Stuibenfälle,** or Stuiben Falls, about two miles southeast of Umhausen. Perhaps the single most outstanding natural attraction of the Ötz Valley, the falls plunge down some 500 feet under a natural rock bridge. Wear your hiking shoes, as it's about a 20-minute walk from the road.

Langenfeld's area code is 05253.

Food and Lodging

Gasthof zum Hirschen (tel. 5201) has been under the direction of the Gstrein family since 1860. Its chalet facade is embellished with stone detailing and a painted depiction of a jousting tournament. The interior is especially attractive. There's more paneling than you could literally shake a stick of knotty pine at. Nestled under some of the well-maintained plaster vaults, an alpine chest or a weathered crucifix appears. This is a pleasant place from which to explore the local foot trails. Charges, with half board included, range from 500 AS ($26.60) per person, based on double occupancy. Singles pay a daily surcharge of 60 AS ($1.60), and tariffs vary according to the season.

Hotel Edelweiss (tel. 5206) has a large L-shaped floor plan that was created when a modern wing was added to an existing chalet. The simple interior is a combination of authentically rustic decor (as reflected by the weinstube) and a slightly more contemporary format of painted panels set between areas of natural-grain wood. The Engelbert Kuen family, the owners, charge from 300 AS ($15.96) to 380 AS ($20.22) per person, with full board included, for their comfortable but simple bedrooms.

SÖLDEN: The capital of the inner Ötz Valley, Sölden, about 4,400 feet above sea level, draws visitors to this valley in summer, to the woods in spring and autumn, and to the heights in winter.

Sölden is the best known village in the valley, linked by road, cable car, and ski lift to its higher sister village, **Hochsölden** (6,800 feet), a much more compact resort. Often winter visitors to Sölden on the half-board arrangement take lunch in Hochsölden when they visit it for the day. There's a ski kindergarten at Sölden.

You can take a cable car from Sölden, passing over glacial fields to some 10,000 feet on the **Geislacherkogel,** where from the upper station you'll be rewarded with a panoramic sweep of the Ötztal Alps. The Geislacherkogel from Sölden is the highest in Austria. A tunnel through the glacier connects the summer glacier resort of Rettenbachferner with the Tiefenbachferner, a large summer ski resort.

Sölden is also the beginning of the **Ötztal Glacier Road** (Ötztaler Gletscherstrasse), one of the loftiest roads in the Alps, rising to some 9,250 feet.

The area code for Sölden is 05254.

Food and Lodging

Hotel Central (tel. 2260). This riverside chalet is designed around two big interconnected sections. The interior is constructed from high-quality building materials which include large quantities of beautifully grained timbers, big stucco arches, glowing wooden floors, and regional monochromatic detailing on some of the walls. The comfortable furnishings include leather-covered settees, Oriental rugs, and woodcarvings prominently displayed on some of the vertical supporting beams. The spacious bedrooms are tasteful, opulent, and spacious, all of them containing a private bath.

On the premises is a bar with live Tyrolean music and a rustically intimate restaurant with excellent service and specialties. They include an array of light-textured international dishes such as calves' liver in a chanterelle cream sauce. Garnishes for some of the main courses are unusual and tasty. They include ginger crêpes, for example, or a sweet chestnut parfait in a Calvados and grape sauce. Prices in the restaurant range from 210 AS ($11.17) to 695 AS ($36.97).

Guests of the hotel in high season pay from 1,300 AS ($69.20) to 1,800 AS

($95.76) for a single and from 1,200 AS ($63.84) to 1,700 AS ($90.44) per person, based on double occupancy, with prices rising higher at Christmas.

Hotel Sölderhof (tel. 2317) is a contemporary chalet whose facade has maintained the rustic painted detailing of the region. The main salon contains a big curved bar, an attractively coffered ceiling, comfortable chairs and banquettes, and a collection of Oriental rugs covering the tile floor. On the premises is an informal stube as well as a more formal, elegantly appointed dining room. A hot whirlpool and sauna are part of the health facilities. Rates range from 600 AS ($31.92) to 780 AS ($41.50) per person. These prices include half board and vary according to the season.

Hotel Bergland (tel. 2234). The architect of this striking hotel incorporated a chalet format with steep rooflines over an assembly of trapezoids, rectangles, and cubes. The result is a pleasing hotel where guests are pampered. The upper-level sun terrace with its dozens of parasols is one of the most popular places in town on a sunny day. Set just at the edge of the village, this family-run hotel has an elegant interior covered with paneling below heavy ceiling beams. The public rooms contain a scattering of antique alpine chests, as well as beautifully appointed restaurants and bars (two of each). On the premises is a dancing bar with live music, an indoor pool, a sauna, and an engaging, friendly staff. The bedrooms are warmly intimate and are usually accented with well-finished planking. Charges range from 800 AS ($42.56) to 950 AS ($50.54) per person, with half board included. Prices vary according to the season.

Hotel Sonne (tel. 2203) is an attractive, modernized chalet with an attentive management by members of the Gurschler family. Situated next to the chair lift to Hochsölden, the hotel has a rustically mellow interior filled with paneling, regional accessories, and modern comfort. On the premises are an attractive restaurant, an intimately lit bar area, and cozy paneled bedrooms. High-season rates are 660 AS ($35.11) per person in a double and around 720 AS ($38.30) in a single. Prices depend on the season, and all accommodations contain private bath. Full board is included in the price, which rises over Christmas.

Hotel Alpina (tel. 2202). Built into the slope of a hill and flanked by towering conifers, this pleasant hotel rises five stories above the alpine path running alongside it. Its windows are embellished with painted borders, and its attractively simple interior has lots of paneling and modern conveniences. High-season rates range from 620 AS ($32.98) to 700 AS ($37.24) per person, based on double occupancy, and from 620 AS ($32.98) to 730 AS ($38.84) in a single. Full board is included in these rates. A sauna, a Turkish steambath, and a hot whirlpool are on the premises.

Gasthof Waldcafé (tel. 2319) is a pleasant chalet on the side of the mountain practically in the path of most of the major ski runs. On the premises is a congenial restaurant, as well as simple bedrooms. The owner charges from 420 AS ($22.34) to 550 AS ($29.26) per person. Half board is included in these tariffs.

Café/Restaurant Hermann (tel. 2326). An alpine stream runs nearby, and the air couldn't be fresher than it is from the balconies of this pleasant chalet. Set some distance above the village, the hotel is capably directed. The interior is accented with big windows looking out over the forest, paneling, and regionally inspired detailing. The bedrooms have attractively wood-trimmed formats and modern comfort. Prices range from 450 AS ($23.94) to 580 AS ($30.87), with half board included.

Après-Ski

There's quite a lot of nightlife, centering customarily around the major hotels. If you get bored, you can take the cableway up to **Hochsölden** and check out the more casual nightlife there.

You can drink at one of three bars and listen and dance to a live band at the already-recommended **Hotel Central,** the best spot for nightlife in Sölden. Chances are, you'll get to hear lederhosen-clad music-makers. At times, if the house count is right, the place takes on a carnival-like atmosphere.

The **Hotel Sonne** brings in live bands to play for dancing, and once a week the staff here stages a Tyrolean evening.

The other leading hotel for nightlife is the recommended **Hotel Bergland,** which on my last visit had the best band in Sölden.

Young people are fond of the Alm Bar in the **Hotel Tyrolerhof** (tel. 2288), a modern hotel in the center of the resort.

Hard drinks in most places begin at 65 AS ($3.46).

HOCHSÖLDEN: This upper-level resort (6,800 feet), towering over just-visited Sölden, lies on a sunny alpine plateau and attracts visitors in both summer and winter. At first Hochsölden may not seem like a village at all, being more a cluster of modern hotels. It's connected to its lower sister by road, cable car, and ski lift. Because of the easy communication between the two resorts, the much larger facilities of Sölden, including the après-ski life, are available to guests at the Hochsölden hotels.

Its higher elevation makes it possible to ski at Hochsölden longer than at Sölden. Rettenbachferner and Tiefenbachferner, summer glacier skiing areas, are easily accessible to both resorts (see above).

Hochsölden's area code is 05254.

Food and Lodging

Hotel Edelweiss (tel. 2298) is an impressively designed hotel among a handful of other hostelries on the bleak alpine meadows near the top of the mountain ridge. Except for a curving glass-walled extension and a low-lying building containing a swimming pool, the structure looks like an oversize chalet. The paneled interior has lots of heavy beams and comfortable couches. On the premises are a bar and a restaurant, usually filled with an enthusiastic crowd of skiers. The woodsy bedrooms are accented with exposed planking. They rent for 600 AS ($31.92) to 1,000 AS ($53.20) per person. These prices vary widely according to the season and include half board. Visitors who are not hotel guests have access to the timbered nightclub through a separate door on the ground floor.

Sporthotel Schöne Aussicht (tel. 2403) is one of the handful of chalet hotels in this ski village. This one has a popular day bar, a scattering of blazing fireplaces, a big health and fitness area with a sauna and solarium, a hairdressing salon, and simple, comfortable bedrooms. Overnight rates range from 420 AS ($22.34) to 900 AS ($47.88) in a single and from 360 AS ($19.15) to 850 AS ($45.22) per person, based on double occupancy. Half board is included.

Alpenhotel Enzian (tel. 2252). On sunny days in late winter you're likely to see dozens of visitors stretched out on chaise longues on the big sun terrace of this elegant alpine hotel. Designed with curved corners, gables, and honey-colored exterior planking, the Enzian contains a modern interior with lots of exposed wood. On the premises are a billiard room, a bar and restaurant, a sauna, and simple, modern bedrooms. The Riml family charges from 810 AS ($43.09) to 910 AS ($48.41) per person in a double, with singles paying from 860 AS ($45.75) to 930 AS ($49.48), all with full board. The hotel is open from December to April and June to October.

Hotel Alpenfriede (tel. 2227) is a six-story wooded chalet with angled bay windows extending out from the ground floor. The interior has a sunny, airy decor that's attractively uncluttered. On the premises is a paneled sitting room and a warmly tinted bar area with heavy ceiling timbers, plus a sun terrace, TV room, and table-tennis room. With half board included, high-season rates range from 500 AS ($26.60) to 720 AS ($38.30) per person, based on double occupancy, with singles paying a daily surcharge of 75 AS ($3.99). The Lengler family are your hosts.

Après-Ski

As mentioned, you can avail yourself of the more active nighttime diversions of Sölden, down below, but you'll also find plenty of informal nightlife on your doorstep if you're based in a hotel in Hochsölden. Naturally, most of the après-ski nightlife centers around the major hotels, which charge from 65 AS ($3.46) for a hard drink in most places.

Even if you have your ski boots on, you can join the dancing throngs at the **Hotel Hochsölden** (tel. 2229), which comes alive just as soon as skiers return from the slopes for the day and darkness falls. That means that this tea dance is going strong by 4:30 p.m.

The **Hotel Edelweiss,** previously recommended, is one of the liveliest places on the after-dark circuit, with a live band playing for dancing.

More disco unfolds live at the also-recommended **Schöne Aussicht.** The dress here is wide-ranging—some men dress up in jackets and ties, others preferring sweaters.

OBERGURGL: This village with the funny-sounding name is part of a three-resort complex which includes Hochgurgl (see below) and Untergurgl. Obergurgl, lying less than two miles upstream from Untergurgl, is one of the loftiest villages in Austria, 6,322 feet, and the second-highest parish in Europe. This is where the Swiss physicist and aeronaut, Dr. Auguste Piccard, landed in his celebrated balloon.

This district is one of the major ski centers of the Tyrolean country. It's not well known among American skiers, although if you stay here you'll be virtually on the doorstep of the Ötztal Alps, surrounded by towering peaks and glistening glaciers. Some of the ski runs end right in the village. A two-stage chair lift, leaving from the center of Obergurgl, services the principal ski area, the Gaisberg-Hohe-Mutt.

The area code for Obergurgl is 05256.

Food and Lodging

Hotel Austria (tel. 314). Hans Steiner and his family are the congenial hosts of this pleasantly balconied chalet whose angled facade—located a short distance above the resort—provides lots of sunny terrace space. The tasteful interior is covered with beautifully grained panels and carved timbers, along with coffered ceilings, thick Oriental rugs, and lots of well-crafted architectural extras. On the premises are a sauna, a solarium, a hot whirlpool, and a Turkish steambath, as well as a bar area, a nightclub, and a baronial fireplace giving off wintertime heat. There's also an elegant restaurant with a subdued color scheme of pink, blue, and knotty pine. The comfortably rustic bedrooms rent for 1,000 AS ($53.20) to 1,400 AS ($74.48) for a single and for 900 AS ($47.88) to 1,300 AS ($69.16) per person, based on double occupancy. These tariffs vary widely according to the season, and full board is included. Open November to April and June to September.

Hotel Edelweiss & Gurgl (tel. 224) has been owned for many years by members of the Scheiber family. Designed like a contemporary chalet, with lots of balconies angled toward the sun, the hotel is close to the center of the village, but has lots of space around it for a peacefully secluded feeling. The public rooms have much paneling and rustic comfort. On the premises are a big conference room, a day bar, and a farmer-style restaurant. Prices range from 700 AS ($37.24) to 950 AS ($50.54) per person. Full board is included in the rates, which vary according to the season.

Fitnesshotel Gotthard (tel. 335) is an attractive chalet sitting a five-minute walk above the center of the resort. The interior has carefully crafted wooden walls and ceilings, some of them rather elaborate, a Tyrolean-style collection of architectural extras such as a ceramic stove surrounded by a warming bench, a well-rated restaurant with panoramic views over the countryside, a bar, a fitness room, and a big indoor pool covered with an impressive set of timbers. The rustically cozy bedrooms—each with a modern bath—rent for 850 AS ($45.22) to 1,080 AS ($57.46) per person. Here, as in every other hotel in the village, prices vary widely according to the season. Full board is included.

Hotel Hochfirst (tel. 232), near the Festkogel chair lift, is one of the biggest hotels in town. Designed like an enormous slope-roofed chalet whose facade is tastefully divided into several different planes, the establishment benefits from a raised sun terrace and a jutting extension containing the indoor swimming pool. The pleasant interior has furniture upholstered in soft colors, half-timbered walls, heavy ceiling beams, and lots of paneling. On the premises is a restaurant and a bar, plus all the comforts you'd expect. Rates range from 500 AS ($26.60) to 1,350 AS ($71.82) in a single, while doubles go from 480 AS ($25.54) to 1,250 AS ($66.50) per person, with half board included. The wide price ranges are because of seasonal differences, the winter being the more expensive season.

Hotel Josl (tel. 205) is a pleasant chalet with a big sun terrace and a gently sloping alpine roof. A minute's walk from the center of the village, its simple and rustic interior welcomes guests in both summer and winter. The Sport Café inside is popular with skiers and outdoors lovers. The hotel charges from 500 AS ($26.60) to 600 AS ($31.92) per person for a bed and half board. Tariffs depend on the season.

Hotel Alpina (tel. 295), run by the Platzer family, is a six-story chalet with lots of wooden balconies angled toward the sunlight. The paneled interior has much regional detailing, including a green ceramic stove in the rustic knotty-pine-covered restaurant. A cozy bar and a formal dining room are also on the premises. In high season, with half board included, rates range from 600 AS ($31.92) to 1,050 AS ($55.86) per person, based on double occupancy. Singles pay a daily surcharge of 110 AS ($5.85). Rates are slightly lower in summer, and special wintertime tariffs are available for clients staying a week or more.

Berg Gasthof Gamper (tel. 238), owned and managed by Anna Gamper, is a tastefully designed chalet lightly embellished with regionally inspired painted illustrations. Near the Gaisberg lift, slightly away from the center of the village, the hotel has public rooms containing a crackling fireplace constructed from large gray stones, along with comfortable banquettes and a well-finished collection of ceiling panels which give the establishment a cozily rustic feeling of well-being. The simple bedrooms have various kinds of wood, including light-grained knotty pine covering some of the walls. With full board, rates range from 380 AS ($20.22) to 420 AS ($22.34) per person.

Hotel Burger (tel. 228) has a stone foundation and a pleasant chalet design. In a quiet open meadow on a hillside above the village church, the hotel offers good views of the glacier and the nearby mountains. The interior is simple, rustic, and comfortable, with lots of country-style accessories mingling happily with the streamlined design. Prices with full board range from 700 AS ($37.24) to 800 AS ($42.56) in a single and from 650 AS ($34.58) to 750 AS ($39.90) per person in a double. Prices vary according to the season. The hotel is open from November to September.

Après-Ski

There's quite a bit of après-ski life in Obergurgl, most of it relaxed and casual, with hard drinks costing from 65 AS ($3.46) in most places.

After you return from the slopes you might want to join your fellow skiers for drinks in the Sport Café at the already-recommended **Hotel Josl.** This is a popular rendezvous spot, at least to begin your evening festivities.

The disco at the also-recommended **Hotel Austria** is one of the most sophisticated and expensive places for nighttime diversions.

There are not only two bars but frenetic dancing to disco music at the recommended **Hotel Hochfirst.** Often Tyrolean evenings are presented at this hotel, and if so, you should reserve a table, as they're very popular.

Local folk music evenings are also presented at the **Hotel Josl,** but with no particular regularity. You'll have to inquire locally.

HOCHGURGL: If Hochgurgl (7,050 feet) were actually a village, it would take the "loftiest village in Austria" title away from other claimants. However, Hochgurgl is really little more than a cluster of hotels, whose owners anxiously await the first snowfall each year. You can approach Hochgurgl from the Timmelsjoch Alpine Road. A ski bus runs back and forth between Hochgurgl and Obergurgl.

This is an area for dedicated skiers who want access to some of the highest peaks of Europe. A three-section chair lift, leaving from Untergurgl, just outside Obergurgl, will transport you to Wurmkogl at some 10,000 feet. At this lofty elevation skiing is possible all year. From a restaurant at Wurmkogl you have a magnificent view of the Italian Alps.

Hochgurgl's area code is 05256.

Food and Lodging

Hochgurgl Hotel (tel. 266) is an elegant chalet which glows at night from the many lights illuminating its rustically contemporary facade. The interior contains handsomely appointed apartments and private rooms, many of them filled with hand-worked paneling and comfortable furniture. The Tyrolean weinstube inside is filled with old paneling and rustic accessories, and has about the coziest ambience in town. The house specialty here is a savory roasted leg of venison, stuffed with bacon, onions, mushrooms, and lots of spices. This is served with a cream sauce made from apple schnappes, juniper berries, and raspberries.

The other facilities at this accommodating hotel include a fitness center, a sauna, a massage room, a hairdresser, a dance bar, an elevator, and a big indoor pool. You'll also find a ski boutique on the ground floor. Rates range from 1,000 AS ($53.20) to 1,250 AS ($66.50), per person, with half board included. The luxurious apartments are even more expensive.

Hotel Alpenrose (tel. 249) is a tastefully designed chalet with white walls and darkly contrasting wood trim. Riders on the nearby chair lift can clearly see the regional designs painted around the windows on part of the facade. The pleasant interior has much modern comfort, with paneled and simply furnished rooms. The Egger family charges from 550 AS ($29.26) to 760 AS ($40.43) per person. These prices include half board.

Sporthotel Ideal (tel. 290) is a chalet set in a slightly isolated, sunny position just outside the village. On the premises is a well-stocked ski store and a pleasantly woodsy decor of horizontal planking, paneled and coffered ceilings, tastefully vivid colors, and comfortable furniture. Facilities include a sauna, a bar, a dining room, a weinstube, and a reading room. Rates range from 520 AS ($38.30) to 750 AS ($39.90), with half board included. Prices vary widely with the seasons.

Hotel Riml (tel. 261) might have the most contemporary design in town. With its gently sloping roof and an emphasis on restful horizontal lines, the hotel has big windows that open into pleasantly woodsy bedrooms. The public rooms are covered with large amounts of light-grained paneling in an airy, sunny format. A restaurant, a bar, a sauna, and a bowling alley are on the premises. The Riml family are your hosts, charging 740 AS ($39.37) to 910 AS ($48.41) per person for a bed and full board. Prices depend on the plumbing and the season, and children under 14 receive a discount.

Berghotel Angerer Alm (tel. 241) is an attractive wood-trimmed chalet built into the side of a sloping meadow. It required a team of careful craftspeople to complete the richly paneled interior, which was embellished with such details as a masonry fireplace that funnels its smoke through a beaker-shaped copper canopy built into the wall. Some of the furnishings of the public rooms include rustic alpine chests scattered among comfortable armchairs. On the premises are a bar area, a chalet restaurant, an indoor swimming pool, a popular sun terrace, and a Ping-Pong room. The comfortably rustic bedrooms rent for 740 AS ($39.37) to 1,050 AS ($55.86) per person, with half board included. Room prices vary according to the season.

Alpenhotel Laurin (tel. 227) has an attractive boxy design with most of the elements of a traditional chalet. Built into a hillside, the hotel does a thriving business on its raised sun terrace and in its comfortable, tastefully decorated restaurant. Menu items include all the regional and Austrian specialties, such as a collection of imaginative salads, schnitzels, well-prepared vegetables, and fruited desserts. Rates for bed and full board range from 750 AS ($39.90) to 950 AS ($50.54) per person, depending on the season and the exposure. Open from November to April and July to September.

VENT: This is the end of the valley—the end of the road, so to speak. Vent is small and unspoiled, and many discriminating visitors prefer it to Obergurgl and Sölden, which are likely to be overrun at the height of the ski season.

Driving south from Sölden, you go first to the hamlet of Zwieselstein. There you fork in a southwesterly direction, proceeding for about eight miles, passing through the Venter Tal, or Valley of Venter, with its magnificent alpine scenery, until you reach this mountain village (about 6,200 feet above sea level). If you don't want to drive, you can take a bus from Zwieselstein to Vent in summer, a favorite season for mountain climbers. Vent has not only a weather station but also a glacier observatory.

A wickedly steep mountain road, with gradients up to 30%—more suitable for mountain goats than for vehicles—will take you to **Rofenhöhe,** which at 6,606 feet is one of the loftiest villages in Austria with year-round residents. To the north is the **Wildspitze,** the tallest peak in the north Tyrolean country, at 12,375 feet. **Kreuzspitze,** 11,340 feet, looms on the right, and to the south is **Thalleitspitze,** 11,175 feet.

If you come to Vent to ski, a drag lift will transport you to the top station (8,850 feet).

The area code for Vent is 05254.

Food and Lodging

Hotel Similaun (tel. 8104) presents a simplified chalet design—with many concessions to late 20th-century building techniques—to a panoramic view of the Alps. This is the most contemporary hotel at the resort. It has an interior decoration that is light and airy, with ample use of exposed wood. Horbert Gstrein, the owner, charges 440 AS ($23.41) to 450 AS ($23.94) per person for a bed and full board. The most expensive seasons, whose figures are included in these rates, are Christmas, Easter, and spring carnival. Mr. Gstrein is the headmaster of the local ski school and speaks English.

Hotel Post (tel. 8119). Directed by the Pirpamer family, this white-painted, wood chalet has a big-windowed restaurant visible from the ground floor. Near the chair lift, the hotel contains a covered swimming pool, sauna, solarium, and elevator. Each of the pleasant bedrooms has a private bath, and rents for 250 AS ($13.30) to 450 AS ($23.94) per person, depending on the season, with breakfast included.

14. The Paznaun Valley

In this snowy valley 56 miles from Innsbruck, the postcard-pretty views are a dime a dozen, the snowland being a valley about 22½ miles long lying between Landeck and Galtür. The Trisanna River is its waterway. To reach the Paznaun, head west from Innsbruck, then take a southwesterly route as signposted. At the head of the valley at Galtür is the impressive Fluchthorn mountain peak.

Only a limited number of Americans have discovered the Paznaun Valley so far, yet it offers superb skiing. The main village is Ischgl, which has put together a ski circus spilling over with runs and lifts across the border into Switzerland. Galtür, the second most important village, has lots of terrain on Ballunspitze and Seinisjoch. The valley is a choice starting point for ski mountaineering tours in the Silvretta glacier region and among the peaks of the Samnaun Alps.

You can even get a touch of the "winter wonderland" experience in summer by taking a highly recommended excursion deep into the Blue Silvretta mountain range, with towering peaks and glaciers as a backdrop.

ISCHGL: The major town of the Paznauntal is both a summer resort and a winter ski center, near the border of Switzerland. A most attractive village, Ischgl lies about halfway along the valley where the Trisanna Valley branches off. The resort, built on terraces at 4,600 feet, is about a half-hour drive from Landeck. It can also be reached by bus from Landeck.

West of town, you can take the Silvrettabahn cableway up to **Idalpe** (7,600 feet). The panoramic view from the lofty station is among the most impressive in the Austrian Alps. From the east part of Ischgl you can take yet another cableway to the Pardatschgrat station at 8,600 feet.

The Ischgl area code is 05444.

Food and Lodging

Hotel Elisabeth (tel. 5411), one of the most elegant hotels in the region, has a monumental curved facade covered with balconies, all of which face south. The well-appointed interior contains an attractively somber color scheme which is brightened with flashes of color from the many Oriental rugs and well-chosen upholstery fabrics. In the center of it all, masons have installed an open fireplace, with a conical chimney tapering gracefully up toward the ceiling.

On the premises are a rustic nightclub with live music, a café and pastry shop, a bar, a pizzeria, a covered pool and fitness center, and spacious, luxuriously equipped bedrooms. These have all the modern comforts, including a big color TV, a mini-bar, balconies with southern exposure, and a host of extras. In high season they rent for 950 AS ($50.54) to 1,800 AS ($95.76) per person, with half board included. Singles pay a daily surcharge of 200 AS ($10.64).

The Marend restaurant has lots of space between its beautifully decorated tables and a soft color scheme of dusty rose, muted grays, and wood tones. Specialties are well prepared and ideal for an appetite whetted by mountain air (the roast beef is very tasty). À la carte meals range from 150 AS ($7.98) to 400 AS ($21.28).

Hotel Madlein (tel. 5226). If you look at it from a certain angle you can count three wood-covered chalets which interconnect to form this well-situated hotel. Near the center of town, convenient to the cable cars, the hotel contains a swimming pool, lots of fitness facilities, and a cozy series of public rooms. These include a nightclub (which sometimes attracts well-known musical groups), two attractive restaurants, and a sitting room with an open fireplace built into a wall composed of massive gray rocks. High-season rates range from 1,080 AS ($57.46) to 1,340 AS ($71.29) per person in a double, from 1,170 AS ($62.24) in a single, with full board included. A wide range of apartments suitable for up to four persons is also available. Open January to April and June to September.

Hotel Post (tel. 5233) is an imposingly sized chalet hotel in several different sections. The interior has rustic accents which include lots of paneling, geometrically ornate ceilings, a central fireplace whose smoke rises through a stucco funnel, and a well-appointed dining room. The cozy bedrooms rent for 550 AS ($29.26) to 1,050 AS ($55.86) per person. These tariffs include half board and vary with the time of year and the plumbing assigned.

Hotel Christine (tel. 5346) is a pleasant chalet with a rustic interior which includes a bar, a pool, and a central fireplace surrounded by banquettes. Rates in high season, with breakfast included, range from 440 AS ($23.41) to 700 AS ($37.24) per person. Prices vary according to the time of year, and all accommodations contain private bath.

Gasthof Goldener Adler (tel. 5402). No one knows exactly when this inn was built, but it was mentioned in a legal document in 1640. Later it served as the region's courthouse in the 17th and 18th centuries. Today it sits behind a six-story pastel-colored facade, with white trim and a solidly prosperous kind of ambience. The carved entrance is set with stained glass, while the panels of the interior range from full-grained natural wood to those painted in light colors with regional designs. You'll find lots of rustic details and modern comfort. Johann Kurz and his family are the owners. They charge from 740 AS ($39.37) to 1,120 AS ($59.58) per person, with half board included. The higher price is for apartments available for two to four persons. The gasthof is closed between early October and the end of November. It contains a Tyrolean restaurant serving well-prepared local specialties.

Alpenhotel Ischglerhof (tel. 5331) is a comfortable hotel owned and managed by the Ludwig Kurz family. Its combination of different alpine styles includes a conical tower whose windows are surrounded with pink borders. The rambling surfaces of the rest of the hotel are covered for the most part with wooden balconies. The public rooms are elegantly decorated. A rustic and comfortable bar area has darkly intimate lighting and dance music, while one of the sitting rooms contains a hospitably inviting open fireplace. Rooms rent for 600 AS ($31.92) to 900 AS ($47.88) per person, including half board. Prices vary according to the time of year.

Après-Ski

The après-ski lift begins early with a "tea dance" at the already-recommended **Hotel and Café Christine.** Here the owners, Rudolf and Anna Wolf, welcome not only their own guests but visitors from the other hotels to a lively atmosphere.

The **Hotel Elisabeth,** also recommended previously, has one of the most intimate and romantic candlelit atmospheres on the après-ski circuit. In season a live band is brought in to play music for dancing and your entertainment.

One of the most elegant places to gather at night is the **Hotel Madlein,** also recommended, which has dancing and music. Head for the Almbar with its wooden beams, whitewashed brick, and attractive young patrons.

Hard drinks at all the establishments in town begin at 65 AS ($3.46).

GALTÜR: At the head of the Paznauntal and at the foot of the Silvretta Pass (closed to winter traffic) is Galtür, near the Swiss border and about an 18-minute drive from Ischgl, just visited. This relatively unspoiled resort, perched at a rather exalted 5,800 feet, has been well known for decades as a ski mountaineering center and a popular summer resort, attracting mountain climbers.

It has become better known in recent years for its downhill and its Nordic, or *langlauf*, skiing. You can purchase the Silvretta ski pass which entitles you to use the lifts at Ischgl as well as chair and drag lifts to take you from Galtür to the highest station at 7,260 feet. The Silvretta ski pass, incidentally, opens up a total of nearly 50 lifts. Snow is good here from December to April.

There's a bus link between Galtür and Landeck, some 25 miles away. Gältur's area code is 05443.

Food and Lodging

Hotel Ballunspitze (tel. 214). The creative architect who designed this attractive hotel began with a clapboard house to which he added a modern balconied extension that ended up being about four times as big as the original house. The family who direct it, the Leo Walters, make guests feel at home. Their public rooms have been carefully paneled and filled with comfortably rustic furniture. The hotel sits at the edge of the village, within walking distance of most everything. Charges, with half board included, range from 320 AS ($17.02) to 340 AS ($18.09) per person, based on double occupancy, and singles pay from 360 AS ($19.15) to 380 AS ($20.22) daily.

Hotel Fluchthorn (tel. 300) is a tall alpine-style chalet whose form is slightly more streamlined than the others around it. It has monochromatic paintings and a warmly rustic interior. Fixtures include heavy ceiling beams, along with brass chandeliers, ceramic stoves, and comfortable easy chairs. On the premises are a dancing bar, a Tyrolean-style restaurant, and a sauna, as well as covered tennis courts and an indoor pool just a few steps down the street. The hotel is closed between the first of October and mid-December. High-season rates range from 700 AS ($37.24) to 920 AS ($48.94) in a single and from 540 AS ($28.73) to 890 AS ($47.35) per person, based on double occupancy. Half board is included, and tariffs are considerably cheaper in summer.

Hotel Pazmaunerhof (tel. 333) has been owned and directed by members of the Lorenz family for the past century. Designed in a typical Tyrolean style with lots of balconies, this attractively unpretentious hotel has been expanded to include a collection of rustically paneled rooms with chalet furniture and lots of cozy comfort. The big-windowed dining room serves tasty, well-prepared Austrian specialties. High-season prices range from 620 AS ($32.98) to 660 AS ($35.11) per person, with full board included. Open December to April and June to October.

Almhof (tel. 253) is a modern hotel with big windows and lots of balconies. It's built into the side of a hill, with a collection of tastefully rustic bedrooms (often with Tyrolean furniture) and paneled public rooms that include a hot whirlpool, a sauna, and a restaurant. The hotel was built by the Huber family. High-season rates range from 625 AS ($33.25) to 900 AS ($47.88), with half board included.

The same management runs the **Hotel Wirlerhof** (tel. 346), a recently expanded chalet, with a decor that includes an updated kind of rusticity. On the premises is a curved bar with intimate lighting, along with two restaurants and a café dance bar. With half board included, per-person rates range from 625 AS ($33.25) to 1,050 AS ($55.86) in high season.

Gasthof Landle (tel. 213) is set between an alpine creek and a treeless mountain. The unusual design of this hotel includes a conservative chalet joined at its side to a larger, more innovative addition. The Zangerle family, the owners, prepare tasty specialties for the cozy restaurant and make their guests feel welcome. The simple bedrooms are attractive and clean. Prices range from 380 AS ($20.22) to 540 AS ($28.73) per person, with half board.

Hotel Alpenrose (tel. 201) is an attractive modern chalet whose simplified exterior sits against a backdrop of craggy mountains. The streamlined interior has taste and all the modern comforts, one of them being a well-recommended restaurant where the old-fashioned cookery honors butter, cream, and rich dishes as dietary staples. After a day in the mountains this might be exactly what you want. You'll enjoy the braised beef with onions or the chef's special brochette. Meals range from 125 AS ($6.65) to 350 AS ($18.62).

Per-person rates in the hotel in high season go from 350 AS ($18.62) to 600 AS ($31.92), with half board included. The location is a few minutes' walk from the center of the village.

Alpenhotel Tirol (tel. 328) is a modern luxury chalet hotel a few minutes' walk from the center. Run by its owners, the Franz Lorenz family, the hotel has a welcoming, roomy hall with an open fireplace, a Spielerstübe, and a large Zirbenstube paneled in knotty pine. All are furnished in traditional Tyrolean style. Such facilities as a whirlpool bath, sauna, solarium, and fitness room are available. The bedrooms, which radiate coziness and warmth, rent for 600 AS ($31.92) to 900 AS ($47.88) per person for half board in high season, based on double occupancy. Singles pay a surcharge of 90 AS ($4.79) per day. The hotel serves generous and well-prepared meals, including a buffet breakfast.

Après-Ski

For such a small ski village the nightlife is more extensive and sophisticated than one might imagine.

The early evening begins with a tea dance at the already-recommended **Hotel Wirlerhof-Almhof.** The ski crowd here—still wearing their boots—arrive right from the slopes. Coffee, hot chocolate, beer, and tempting pastries are downed in a lively atmosphere of smoke, drink, and good times.

More in the center of town, the place to go is the also-recommended **Hotel Fluchthorn,** where there's a lively dance bar in the cellar that at some point seems to draw every skier in town.

Hard drinks in most places begin at 65 AS ($3.46).

15. The Arlberg

There's no such thing as a sacred ski mountain—so far as I've ever heard—but if there were it would have to be the Arlberg, the mecca of the serious skier. Alpine skiing went out from here to conquer the world. On the east side of the Arlberg, 71 miles west of Innsbruck, is what's known as the cradle of alpine skiing. Here were born the names and the legends known to all dedicated skiers: the Ski Club Arlberg, the early Kandahar races, Hannes Schneider and his Arlberg method.

The Arlberg, with peaks that top the 9,000-foot mark, lures skiers with its vast network of cableways, lifts, runs stretching for miles, a world-renowned ski school, and numerous sporting amenities. Runs begin at the intermediate level, reaching all the way to the "nearly impossible."

The Arlberg, the loftiest mountain in the Lechtal range, marks the boundary between the settlers of the Tyrolean country and the Vorarlbergers who live in the extreme western province of Austria. One of the Arlberg's most celebrated peaks is the Valluga, at 9,220 feet.

In 1825 a road was opened allowing vehicular traffic to travel to the Arlberg Pass. A six-mile-long rail runnel was opened in 1884, linking Tyrol and Vorarlberg, and finally in 1978 a new road tunnel linked the two provinces. Toll for the highway tunnel is 160 AS ($8.51). The road tunnel is the third longest in Europe. If you're not driving, you'll find the area serviced by the well-known Arlberg Express rail link.

ST. ANTON AM ARLBERG: Alpine skiing is no longer in the cradle, having come of age to the point where St. Anton is now more the citadel of this winter sport, for a modern resort has grown out of the old village on the Arlberg Pass which was the scene of ski history in the making. This is a center for a ski area that is considered among the finest in the Alps.

It was at St. Anton (4,225 feet) that Hannes Schneider, born here in 1890, evolved modern skiing techniques as a very young man and started teaching tourists how to ski in 1907. The Ski Club Arlberg was born here in 1901. In 1911 the Arlberg-Kandahar Cup competition came into being with donation of a valuable trophy to be awarded annually to the best alpine skier. Before his death in 1955 Schneider saw his ski school rated as the world's finest. Today the ski school, still at St. Anton, is one of the world's largest and best, with about 300 instructors, the majority of whom speak English.

The little town is on the main railway line at the end of the six-mile Arlberg tunnel. It's a compact resort village, with a five-story cap on building. No cars are allowed in the business area, but sleds and skis are plentiful.

The snow in this area is considered perfect for skiers, and the total lack of trees on the slopes makes the situation ideal. The ski fields of St. Anton stretch over a distance of some six square miles. Beginners stick to the nursery slopes down below, and for the more experienced skiers there are the runs from the Galzig and Valluga peaks. A cableway will take you to **Galzig** (6,860 feet), where there's a self-service restaurant. You go from here to **Ballugagrat** (8,685 feet), the highest station reached. The peak of the **Valluga** at 9,220 feet commands a sweeping panoramic view. St. Christoph (see below) is the mountain annex of St. Anton.

In addition to the major ski areas I just mentioned, there are two other important sites attracting followers of the sport: the **Gampen/Kapall** and the **Rendl.**

St. Anton am Arlberg in winter is quite fashionable, popular with the wealthy and occasional royalty, a more conservative segment of the jet set than you'll see at other posh ski resorts. There are many other cold-weather pursuits than just skiing, including ski jumping, mountain tours, curling, skating, tobaganing, and sleigh rides, plus après-ski on the quiet side.

There's so much emphasis on skiing here that few seem to talk of the summertime attractions. In warm weather you'll find St. Anton tranquil and bucolic, surrounded by meadowland. A riot of wildflowers blooming in the fields announces the beginning of spring.

The area code for St. Anton am Arlberg is 05446.

Food and Lodging

Hotel St. Antoner Hof (tel. 2910). What's considered one of the best hotels in town is the domain of the Raffl family. Their balconied property sits at the edge of the main road running through St. Anton about a block from the historic center. Each accommodation contains a wood-ringed balcony, expanses of beautifully grained paneling, ceiling timbers, plush upholstery, and efficient modern bath. Most guests take advantage of this establishment's cheaper rates for extended stays by checking in here for a week or more. In winter, rates in a single, with half board included, range from between 8,000 AS ($425.60) and 8,300 AS ($441.56) per week. Per-person weekly rates for a double, also with half board, range from 6,200 AS ($329.84) to 7,250 AS ($385.70). Some full apartments, with whirlpools and open fireplaces, are available as well.

Guests enjoy an array of public rooms, each of which seems awash with Tyrolean accessories, thick timbers, and collections of rustic implements guaranteed to dazzle the eye and warm the spirit. The staff seem good-natured here, doing their best to ensure a guest's comfort. A rock-ringed indoor pool, a Jacuzzi, sauna, solarium, arrays of blazing fireplaces, and good cuisine are all part of an experience here. A handful of indoor tennis and squash courts lie adjacent to the hotel.

Hotel Schwarzer Adler (tel. 2245), in the center of the village, has been owned and operated as a hotel by the Tschol family since 1885. The building which houses it, however, was built as an inn (or hospice) in 1570, using stones taken from the ruins of nearby Arlen Castle. The hospice became known for its hospitality to travelers crossing the Arlberg mountain, and today the hotel maintains the same time-honored tradition. Its painted facade is striking, especially the ornate sundial. The furnishings include some antique armoires painted in regional designs, an occasional ceramic stove, and comfortable chairs. On the premises is a well-liked café, the Tschol, as well as a disco bar reached through a ground-floor door leading into a modern addition.

The hotel charges high-season prices ranging from 950 AS ($50.54) to 1,500 AS ($79.80) in a single and from 900 AS ($47.88) to 1,450 AS ($77.14) per person, based on double occupancy, for a room and half board. Rates drop about 30% in summer. The in-house restaurant is a friendly and well-run establishment, with many of the specialties coming from the region. The schnitzels and Sacher torte taste as good as they do in Vienna. Meals range from 175 AS ($9.31) to 350 AS ($18.62). Both the hotel and restaurant are closed in October and November.

Hotel Alte Post (tel. 58265). The reception area's antique Tyrolean chest which fills a specially made niche is only one of the dozens of charming touches put into place by the attractive owners, Claudia and Michael Zanner. Designed long ago in a rambling, four-story format of ochre-colored walls, green shutters, and jutting gables, the hotel can easily be reached from the town's rail station. It was originally built in the 17th century as a postal station. The renovations of 1984 retained most of the thick-timbered beauty and added yard upon yard of plush upholstery and full-grained paneling.

Since it became a hotel in the 1920s, some prominent skiers and show business personalities have relaxed with lesser known clients in the hotel's dozen of cozy niches, some of which are warmed with crackling fires. The hotel contains an excellent restaurant, a sauna, whirlpool, and fitness center. Its bar is covered separately under après-ski. Depending on their size, accessories, and the season, singles cost between 875 AS ($46.55) and 1,800 AS ($95.76), and doubles go between 1,750 AS ($93.10) and 3,700 AS ($196.84), with half board included. Rooms combine old-fashioned paneling with modern comforts such as tiled and timbered private bath, phone, TV, and sometimes very elegant accessories.

Hotel Arlberg (tel. 2248), owned by the Ennemoser family, is a big, attractively styled hotel with dramatic sweeping lines in the construction of its wood and stucco facade. The richly paneled interior gives off a warmly hospitable tinge to the clients who appreciate the bar and restaurants. There's a wintertime disco, as well as comfortable bedrooms with plenty of exposed wood tones. A tennis court, covered swimming pool, Turkish bath, and sauna all belong to the hotel. Winter rates range from 1,020 AS ($54.26) to 1,320 AS ($70.22) per person, with reductions granted off-season. Some of the accommodations are small suites. Half board is included in the tariffs quoted.

Hotel Mooserkreuz (tel. 2730) is a generously sized mountain inn on the sunniest part of the slopes above the village. This hotel stands on the road to the Arlberg Pass. The Rahofer family will help to make your stay pleasant. Guests have free use of the indoor pool as well as the sauna, and the hotel bus makes frequent runs to the center of town and to the ski lifts. High-season prices are from 900 AS ($47.88) to 1,180 AS ($62.78) per person, with reductions granted in the off-season. Half board is included.

Hotel Tyrol (tel. 2340). When you enter the reception area of this attractive chalet you'll see a sweeping staircase rising from the lobby to the upper floors. Near the edge of the village, the hotel has an attractively decorated series of cozy public rooms, a restaurant, and comfortable bedrooms. Rates in high season range from 960 AS ($51.07) per person, with half board included. The public tennis courts are a three-minute walk from the hotel.

Sport Hotel (tel. 3111) is just three pedestrian minutes from the beginning of the chair lifts. On the premises of this hotel are a café, a steakhouse, a tavern, and a formal restaurant, as well as a cocktail bar and nightclub with dancing. There's also an ozone-enriched swimming pool with a water cascade, a fitness center with a sauna, and intimately cozy bedrooms with TV, radio, phone, and private bath. The hotel is pleasantly paneled and well furnished throughout. The cost for a bed and half board goes from 1,350 AS ($71.82) per person in high season.

Gasthof Montjola (tel. 2302) is a rustically appealing Tyrolean guest house with green-and-white striped shutters, lots of exposed wood, and an interior that has much charm. Throughout, you'll see heavy ceiling beams, a stone-rimmed fireplace, rustic knickknacks, and immaculately set dining room tables. Fondue is a specialty, and it's usually prepared by a member of the Nohl family. In summer rates are 350 AS ($18.62) per person daily, with breakfast included. In winter guests book in here mainly on the half-board plan, costing from 725 AS ($27.93) to 880 AS ($46.82) per person, based on double occupancy. Singles pay a daily surcharge ranging from 60 AS ($3.19) to 90 AS ($4.79).

Hotel Rosanna Stüberl (tel. 2011) is an attractively designed chalet with long rows of balconies and big windows. The interior has well-finished paneling, as well as a gently arched ceiling over one of the restaurants. The reception area has intricate beams, carved into geometric patterns. A rustic bar area is a relaxing place for a drink. Food served in the restaurant includes raclette, fondue, homemade specialties, and a wide assortment of tortes. Your meal will usually be accompanied by live music, sometimes on a zither. Overnight rates, with half board included, range from 1,000 AS ($53.20) to 1,130 AS ($60.12) per person in high season.

Après-Ski

St. Anton's after-dark lights are among the most glittering in the Tyrol. However, it's likely to be expensive, with beer beginning at 50 AS ($2.66), and hard drinks costing from 85 AS ($4.52). Hopefully you'll like your fellow skiers, as in season it's likely to be elbow-to-elbow (or whatever) in most places.

The chic rendezvous of the resort is the already-recommended **Hotel Arlberg**. Its Kellerbar is one of the liveliest in St. Anton.

One of the most alluring spots in town for a drink lies within the thick walls of the already recommended **Hotel Alte Post.** Off the lobby is a spacious and beautifully rustic room awash with alpine paneling, ceiling beams, comfortable banquettes, and some of the most attractive people at the resort. A pair of brass lions struggling with serpents flanks the blazing fire set near the entrance. An eight-sided bar offers roundabout seating near an intimate dance floor. Disco music makes the place animated later in the evening. The bar is open only between November and Easter.

The **Hotel Tyrol,** also recommended previously, enlivens the nightlife scene with its nightclub and live band.

At the **Hotel Rosanna Stüberl,** also recommended, the Stüberl offers live music after dark.

One of the most popular discos in St. Anton is at the **Hotel Schwarzer Adler,** also recommended previously.

Yet another center is the **Sport Hotel,** also recommended before. Its Taverna offers live music, and if disco is still your scene, then there is "Drop-In."

ST. CHRISTOPH: The mountain annex of St. Anton, St. Christoph (5,850 feet), is linked to the St. Anton terrain by a cableway at Galzig. It's on the road to the Arlberg Pass and has essentially the same ski facilities available at St. Anton, only here you're closer to the action than at that village. However, St. Anton is the place to go for après-ski activity if you're staying at St. Christoph.

If you're not driving your own car, take the train to St. Anton, then go either by bus or taxi to St. Christoph.

A hospice, long ago destroyed by fire, was built on this spot in the 15th century, serving stranded travelers rescued from avalanches or caught in snowdrifts.

The area code for St. Christoph is 05446.

Food and Lodging

Arlberg Hospiz (tel. 2611) is a prosperous-looking, white-walled building whose steep gabled roof looks strong enough to support even the heaviest blanket of snow. This establishment was built on the site of the medieval hospice that burned down. A chapel still stands next door, commemorating the lives of those who died crossing the pass. Memories of that historic inn live on through the service offered by the Werner family.

The interior is loaded with rustic comfort, including beautifully finished paneling, gently vaulted ceilings, a scattering of wintertime fireplaces, and a big bar area in an even larger sitting room.

Rates range from 1,500 AS ($79.80) to 2,050 AS ($109.06) per person. These tariffs include an excellent half board in a restaurant classified as a Relais de Campagne.

Food served is a far cry from what was offered to the wandering monks of the Middle Ages. Dishes include tempting salads, wine soup, marinated herring hausfrau style, a range of Austrian specialties (often with an unusual twist), game with spätzle, and an array of desserts, many of which in summer make use of the fresh berries grown in the surrounding mountains. Meals range from 280 AS ($14.90) to 700 AS ($37.24). It's closed during all of May and for most of October and November.

16. Lienz and East Tyrol

East Tyrol is like an afterthought—of but not actually in Land Tyrol. When Italy won South Tyrol in 1919 in the aftermath of World War I, East Tyrol was like a refugee child separated from its mother and not reunited with her. This part of Tyrol was cut off from the rest of the province by a narrow projection of Italian land which connects to Land Salzburg.

Italy, including what used to be South Tyrol, lies to the south and west of

East Tyrol, with Land Salzburg to the north and Carinthia to the east. The little subprovince, of which Lienz is the capital, is cut off from its neighbors on the north by seemingly impenetrable Alps. East Tyrol is known as Osttirol in German.

Because of its isolated position, East Tyrol tends to be neglected by the average North American tourist, which is a shame. The grandeur of its scenery and the warm hospitality of its people make it worth visiting. It's crowned by the magnificent peaks of the Hohe Tauern, the Grossvenediger, and the Grossglockner, and to the south lie the Lienz Dolomites, which invite exploration. The scenery along the Drau and the Isel Valleys is spectacular. These two main valleys have many little side hollows worth exploring, especially the Virgental. You'll see a lot of alpine pastureland, meadows, relatively undiscovered valleys, and beautiful lakes.

The Romans occupied East Tyrol in ancient times. Later, the Slavs moved into the area as settlers and made it a section of Carinthia. It has known many rulers, from the Bavarians to the French. Even Great Britain had a hand in running things here, when the Allies made East Tyrol a part of the British-occupied sector of Austria from 1945 to 1955.

Since 1967 it's been possible to reach East Tyrol by taking the three-mile-long Felbertauern Tunnel, a western route through the Alps. If you're driving, you can come from the east or the west. From the Grossglockner Road, you take the Felbertauern Road and the tunnel. If you're driving from the north to Lienz, the East Tyrol capital, you can take the Falbertauern Road from Land Salzburg, passing through the tunnel. In summer you may want to take the Grossglockner Road and the Iselberg Pass. This road runs along the boundary between East Tyrol and Carinthia.

It's also possible to take a train from Italy to East Tyrol. Corridor trains also operate between Innsbruck and Lienz. As you pass through Italy on this trip, the trains are locked and you don't have to show your passport or clear Italian Customs.

Woodcarving, long a pursuit in East Tyrol, is still practiced in tranquil chalets during the long winter months. You might like to shop for some pieces while you're here.

LIENZ: Don't confuse this city with *Linz*, the capital of Upper Austria. Lienz with an *e* serves as the capital of East Tyrol. It lies at the junction of three valleys —the Isel to the northwest, the Puster to the west, and the Drau to the east. The old town of Lienz stretches along the banks of the Isel River, with **Lieburg Palace,** a 16th-century building now the seat of local government, overshadowing the Hauptplatz (main square).

The sights of Lienz are easy to see, taking no more than about 1½ hours. One of the main attractions is **Schloss Bruck** (Bruck Castle) with its **Osttiroler Heimatmuseum** (Museum of East Tyrol). This was the fortress of the counts of Görz, who held sway over vast estates until they fell prey to the Habsburgs at the beginning of the 16th century. The castle stands at the head of the entrance to the Valley of Isel, less than a mile from the center of Lienz.

In the museum, much has been preserved of the life and times of the people of East Tyrol, including handicrafts and peasant dress. The Rittersaal (knight's hall) shows how the castle looked in the Middle Ages. The most important feature of the museum is the Albin Egger-Lienz gallery, containing a magnificent collection of the art of this outstanding native painter, who died in 1926. Most often, he took the Tyrolean country and its people as his subjects. Another section displays artifacts unearthed at the archeological site of the Roman town of Aguntum (see below).

The museum is open daily from around Easter until the end of October from 10 a.m. to 5 p.m. Off-season it's closed Monday. Admission is 30 AS ($1.60), and there's a restaurant at the schloss.

If you have time, visit **St. Andrä** (Church of St. Andrew), the outstanding feature of which is the collection of 16th-century tombstones carved of marble quarried outside Salzburg. The last of the counts of Görz is buried here. The church, consecrated in 1457, was restored in 1968, having fallen into a sad state of disrepair. During the restoration workmen uncovered murals, some dating from the 14th century. The nave is in the late Gothic style, and the church is considered the finest example of Gothic architecture in East Tyrol. A memorial chapel honors Lienz war dead. The renowned painter, Albin Egger-Lienz, mentioned above, is entombed here.

In winter Lienz, at an elevation of 2,850 feet, attracts skiers to its two major ski areas: the **Hochstein** and the **Zertersfeld,** serviced by chair and drag lifts. The height of the top station is 7,225 feet.

In summer the town fills up with mountain climbers, mainly Austrians, who come to scale the Dolomites. This is a good base for many excursions in the area. For example, from Schlossberg, you can take a chair lift up to **Venediger-warte** (3,335 feet). You can also explore the excavations of **Aguntum,** the Roman settlement, three miles east of Lienz. You can bathe in **Lake Tristacher,** three miles south of the city.

The **Dolomites,** actually the northwestern part of the Gailtal alpine range, lie between the Gail Valley and the Drau Valley. Their highest peak is the Grosse Sandspitze at more than 9,000 feet.

The Lienz area code is 04852.

A Range of Hotels

Romantikhotel Traube (tel. 2552). The location couldn't be more ideal, in the very center of town on a street lined with decorative trees. The distinctive facade is painted a vivid red, with forest-green shutters and a striped canopy covering part of the ground-level café. The interior reflects the general sophistication of the staff. Furnishings in both the public rooms and the bedrooms are elegant and comfortable. On the roof is a covered swimming pool, while in the cellar a vaulted disco (often with live music) provides evening entertainment.

This hotel has been owned for many generations by members of the Vergeiner family and is run now by Günther Wimmer and his wife. Prices are from 620 AS ($32.98) to 820 AS ($43.62) for a single room and from 550 AS ($29.26) to 850 AS ($45.22) per person in a double, with a buffet breakfast included in all rates. A special half-board price of an additional 125 AS ($6.65) to the regular rates is offered for stays of more than one week and includes not only breakfast and a four-course meal but also a choice of different entertainment, ranging from a wine tasting to a romantic dinner with harp music.

The decor of the pleasant and spacious bedrooms is conservatively modern, often with views opening onto the nearby mountains. The hotel is open all year.

Hotel Sonne (tel. 3311). Its modernized mansard roof and uncluttered windows rise from one end of the Sudtirolerplatz. The hotel was originally built in the late 1960s, but almost completely renovated in 1978. Today, in addition to a charming staff, it contains terracotta floors, Oriental rugs, a sauna, and a very large bar with a timbered ceiling and fireplace, as well as a wood-trimmed and sun-flooded restaurant. The reservations system is tied in to the Best Western network.

The cozy bedrooms are conservatively outfitted with modern furniture and occasional expanses of knotty pine paneling. Each unit has a private bath, phone, radio alarm, and TV/video connection. Depending on the season, and with breakfast included, singles rent for between 600 AS ($31.92) and 650 AS ($34.58), while doubles cost between 510 AS ($27.13) and 670 AS ($35.64) per person. The hotel has a roof garden and sun terrace, as well as an underground garage.

Hotel Post, 7 Sudtirolerplatz (tel. 2505). Most of the ground floor of this severe-looking hotel is filled with the wooden banquettes of the most popular café/bar in town. Under vaulted ceilings, in the light of a pair of small-shaded chandeliers, most of the active socializers of Lienz gather every evening after work.

However, if you're interested in a hotel room, the reception area opens with its own entrance onto the square. A small lobby contains baronial settees heavily carved with cherubs and mythical beasts. There's a garden set up with café tables in back. Each of the 30 comfortably and well-maintained bedrooms contains a private bath, phone, and conservative furniture. The Lederer family charge from 650 AS ($34.58) in a single and from 600 AS ($31.92) per person in a double, with full board included.

Gasthof Pension Haidenhof (tel. 2440) looks like an appealing cross between an alpine chalet and a Mediterranean villa. The windows of the hotel's central section are bordered with painted Tyrolean designs, while on either side symmetrical wings with strong horizontal lines stretch toward the surrounding forest. Views from the balconies of the bedrooms encompass most of Lienz. On the premises is a sun terrace, along with a series of pastel-colored vaulted ceilings, plus a paneled restaurant. Prices range from 430 AS ($22.88) to 465 AS ($24.74) per person for a bed and full board. The hotel is open from December to October. It's about 20 minutes from the center of town.

Hotel Glöckturm, 2 Pfarrgasse (tel. 04852), is a sprawling old-fashioned hotel set in a wooded area beside the river. The facade looks as though three different buildings were welded into a single unit, all of them painted a baroque yellow with red and sea-green trim. The interior is simple and attractive. Christian Gasser, the owner, charges around 290 AS ($15.34) per person in a double and 325 AS ($17.29) in a single, with breakfast included.

Gasthof Goldener Fisch (tel. 2132), about two minutes by car from the center of town, offers views of different mountains from practically every room in the house. The prosperous-looking facade is painted beige with brown shutters, which tends to accent the jutting bay windows festooned in summer with flowers. The interior has lots of exposed paneling, a ceramic stove, and a hospitable bar and restaurant. The Egon Vergeiner family, the hosts, charge 300 AS ($15.96) for a single and 500 AS ($26.60) for a double, with breakfast included.

Where to Dine

Romantikhotel Traube (tel. 2552). Amid Tyrolean accents of flowered banquettes, gilded wall sconces, and big arched windows, this airy restaurant offers elegant meals in comfortably paneled surroundings. Uniformed waiters present such well-prepared specialties as paprika-flavored chicken with sour cream sauce and buttered noodles, piccata of hare with ham-flavored spaghetti, Tyrolean calves' liver with tomatoes, bacon, and roast potatoes, along with peppersteak in a cognac-flavored cream sauce, and at least seven wild game dishes. Try, if featured, the venison schnitzel, breast of pheasant, or medallions of goose. Fixed-price dinners cost from 160 AS ($8.51), while à la carte meals begin at 400 AS ($21.28). Food is served every day; reservations are recommended. The restaurant, classified as a Relais et Château, is closed in November and for part of December and during the last two weeks of April.

MATREI IN OSTTIROL: A winter sports resort and summer holiday retreat, Matrei in East Tyrol has much charm. From its location, winter visitors can avail themselves of two ski regions with well-prepared descents from above the 7,500-foot mark as well as interesting tracks for cross-country skiing and ski hiking. There are reliable snow conditions in the Goldried ski area (more than 6,500 feet) and at the runs near Matrei Tauernhaus and the Venedigerblich mountain railway.

In summer this is a choice spot for mountain climbing, walking, horseback riding, and tennis.

To reach Matrei by train, you can go to Lienz via Spittal or Innsbruck. From Lienz there's a Postal Bus connection. Of course you can also come here by car. Just don't confuse Matrei in East Tyrol with another Matrei which you may have passed through in your exploration of the Wipp Valley.

The area code for Matrei in Osttirol is 04875.

Food and Lodging

Hotel Goldried (tel. 6113), with its regularly spaced towers and alpine setting, looks much like a modernized version of a Teutonic fortress. Its dozens of balconies look out over a valley, combining access to good skiing with a pleasant, comfortable format. All of the accommodations within the main hotel and its annex, the Dependance Goldriedpark, are well-equipped apartments which contain a fireplace, private sauna, children's room, kitchen, clothes washer and dryer, and up to three bedrooms, sometimes on two different levels.

Apartments vary in size and can accommodate up to eight persons. Most visitors check in here for a week at a time. Depending on its size, an apartment in high season begins at 5,700 AS ($303.24) per week for up to four persons, and from 8,600 AS ($457.52) per week for up to six persons. Low season prices run about 25% less than those stated above. A one-time cleaning charge, beginning at 550 AS ($29.26), is levied at the end of your stay.

There's an outdoor terrace with a pool, plus a Tyrolean bar, a kindergarten with child-sitting facilities, and an indoor pool. The hotel is only a few yards from a double chair-lift, the Hohe Tauern Süd, and the beginning of a network of almost endless cross-country ski tracks. Partly because the hotel is owned by a group of Swedish investors, it serves as the winter training ground for the Swedish National Ski team.

Hotel Rauter (tel. 6611) has an attractive modern facade. It looks like a combination of a beach resort house and an alpine chalet. The most distinctive feature is the huge simplified adaptation of an arched window from a Gothic church set into a curved area above the front entrance. The bedrooms have lighthearted elements that might be Japanese, art deco, or modified Gothic, depending on your whim.

This is definitely a year-round hotel, containing facilities geared to sports of all seasons. These include a big indoor pool and a summer outdoor pool, as well as both in- and outdoor tennis courts. Horseback riding is nearby, and the hotel bus makes frequent winter runs to the ski slopes. Anglers will find rich fishing areas close to the hotel.

The Obwexer family charges from 600 AS ($31.92) to 900 AS ($47.88) per person in a wide variety of accommodations, with half board included. A comfortable annex holds the overflow from the main hotel. The restaurant, considered one of the finest in Austria, is tastefully outfitted with accessories. Specialties include medallions of spring lamb with a calvados cream sauce and parsley apples and sweet corn. Meals range from 150 AS ($7.98) to 500 AS ($26.60).

Pension Alpengasthof Tauernhaus (tel. 8811) is a rustic complex of at least three buildings clustered in an alpine meadow about nine miles from the center of Matrei. Technically it's up in the Tauerntal at about 5,000 feet. You can reach it by bus from Matrei if you want to spend some time in this isolated place. The accommodations house anywhere from one to six persons in simple bedrooms accented with lots of wood. Otto Brugger, the owner, along with his family, charges around 350 AS ($18.62) per person in a single or double, with full board included.

Gasthof Panzlwirt, 4 Tauerntalstrasse (tel. 6518), offers Tyrolean-style hospitality in an enlarged and modernized chalet. The house is one of the most decorative in the village, accented with regional designs around many of the windows and weathered wooden balconies. The hotel is owned and managed by members of the Panzl family, who are descendants of Johann Panzl, a fierce soldier and noted eccentric who fought for the freedom of the Tyrol in the wars against the French in the early 19th century. The Panzlwirt contains a bowling alley, a café, a restaurant, an underground garage, and a series of pleasantly furnished public rooms. With breakfast included, per-person rates range from 320 AS ($17.02) to 365 AS ($19.42). Each of the rooms has a private bath, and many of them contain balconies.

VIRGEN: This village in the Virgental (Valley of the Virgin) lies to the west of Matrei in Osttirol, visited above. The road through the valley is stunning, stretching for slightly less than 12 miles. Along it you pass through gorges and tunnels. Eventually you can see the 11,480-foot-high Dreiherrenspitze.

Virgen's area code is 04874.

Food and Lodging

Gasthof Sonne (tel. 5204) is a comfortable hotel built up on a terrace on the side of a hill in the center of the village. The main section has a hipped roof over white walls and a restaurant filling most of the big glass-walled extension on the first two floors. The interior has lots of rustic detailing and well-finished paneling. The Duregger family, your hosts, charge rates ranging from 325 AS ($17.29) to 440 AS ($23.41) per person for full board and an overnight stay.

SILLIAN: The highest village in the Valley of Puster (Pustertal), Sillian lies in the Dolomites a short distance from the Italian border. It's sunny and fog-free, even in winter, and has good snow conditions from December to March. Skiers will find the area serviced by chair and drag lifts. This unique landscape attracts nonskiers and summer visitors with its many beautiful walks.

On the outskirts of Sillian are the ruins of the 13th-century **Heimfels Castle,** once occupied by the powerful counts of Görz.

The Sillian area code is 04856.

Food and Lodging

Pension Adelheid (tel. 6286) is a white-walled house with a prominently hipped and gabled red tile roof. A modern extension shoots out from the side of the main building, which has an interior decor of light-grained paneling and simple furnishings. Prices, with full board included, range from 325 AS ($17.29) to 350 AS ($18.62) per person.

OBERTILLIACH: A short distance from Sillian, this little hamlet near the Italian frontier might be an ideal stopping place in summer if you're gulping down all the beautiful scenery in the area, or in winter if you'd like to ski in the Lienz Dolomites.

The area code for Obertilliach is 04857.

Food and Lodging

Gasthof Weiler (tel. 5202) has attractive proportions and simple lines. You'll reach it by climbing a curved stone staircase which ends at a stone-flanked sun terrace. The well-furnished interior is filled with warmly tinted colors and lots of exposed paneling, while the cozy contemporary bedrooms are outfitted with comfortable furniture and different shades of various earth colors. On the premises are a bar and restaurant, serving regional cooking. Rates in singles range from 325 AS ($17.29) to 420 AS ($22.34), while per-person charges in a double go from 345 AS ($18.35) to 410 AS ($21.81), with half board included. Prices depend on the season.

Chapter XI

VORARLBERG

THE WESTERNMOST PROVINCE of Austria, and the smallest one other than Vienna, is Vorarlberg, a land of mountain villages and lakes, of deep valleys and meadowlands. This province is known for its natural beauty and scenery. In autumn, for example, one of the most beautiful spots on the European continent is the plain of the Rhine Valley near Dornbirn.

This is where Central Europe meets Western Europe, the Arlberg massif separating Vorarlberg from Tyrol. Essentially this province lies between Lake Constance and the Arlberg mountains. Local legend has it that this—not Mount Ararat in the Middle East—is where Noah landed with the ark after the flood waters had receded.

Of all the provinces of Austria, Vorarlberg is the most like Switzerland. In fact at the end of World War I it almost became part of that neighbor country. Vorarlbergers speak the Alemannic dialect of German, which is more closely related to the language of the Swiss just across the border to the west than it is to that spoken elsewhere in Austria.

Bregenz, the province's capital, opens onto Lake Constance, which Austria shares with both West Germany and Switzerland.

Vorarlberg is supported by tourism and industry, mostly textiles. Outside its best known tourist centers, such as Zürs and Lech, prices in the province are quite reasonable, especially in gasthof-type accommodations.

This is the most highly industrialized province of Austria—after Vienna, of course—but industry rarely pollutes the air and somehow seems to blend in with nature for the most part. For instance, one of its major industries is hydroelectric installations in the mountains.

If you're traveling by train from Innsbruck, (Chapter X), you can reach Bregenz in Vorarlberg in about 3½ hours.

1. Bregenz

The capital of Vorarlberg province, Bregenz, once the Roman town of Brigantium, sits on terraces rising above the water at the eastern end of Lake

Constance (Bodensee, in German). One of the major tourist goals in the province, Bregenz is really a small, "two-in-one" place—a modern town along the shore of the lake with a traffic-free old town towering over it. In summer the promenade along the shoreline is popular.

On lake vessels, you can travel the Bodensee district, venturing into West Germany and Switzerland, which share Lake Constance with Austria. For a panoramic view of the lake and the town, with Switzerland looming in the background, take the cable-car ride to Pfänder (see below).

Bregenz is at its liveliest in July at the time of its celebrated **music festival,** an event that rivals the festival at Salzburg. Many concerts are given, some open-air and some at the Festspiel-und-Kongresshaus. Most exciting are the elaborate productions of operas, operettas, and musical comedies presented on a large stage floating on the lake, with the audience watching from an amphitheater which seats 6,500 persons. You'll see ornate barges arriving with elaborately dressed actors and singers. The stage is on a series of islands anchored by pillars driven into the lake bottom.

The Unterstadt, or the **Lower Town,** is the shopping district, with traffic-free malls along the lake shore. In spring the quays of the Unterstadt blaze with color from flowerbeds as in some lakeside Swiss towns.

The **Vorarlberger Landesmuseum** (Vorarlberg Regional Museum) on the Kornmarkt is a rich repository of the artifacts and culture of the province. Exhibits are to be seen from the prehistoric days of the province, as well as Roman artifacts. You'll see a storybook of history with Romanesque and Gothic ecclesiastical works of art which come from churches in the district. See, in particular, a portrait of the Duke of Wellington by Angelica Kauffmann, who died in 1807. The museum is open from 9 a.m. to noon and from 2 to 5 p.m. daily except Monday, charging 10 AS (53¢) for admission.

The **Upper Town** is called both Oberstadt and Altstadt. Once the stronghold of the counts of Bregenz and Montford, it's of interest to the lover of antiquity. If you're driving, head up the Kirchestrasse, the Thalbachgasse, and the Amstorstrasse. Park and stroll back into the Middle Ages as you go along the quiet squares and narrow streets of the old quarter. Before the Upper Town was Roman Brigantium, this was the site of a Celtic settlement.

Among Oberstadt's attractions is **Martinsturm,** or the Tower of St. Martin, from the 13th century. A museum with local artifacts is on the upper floor of the tower. **St. Martin's Chapel,** founded in 1363, at the base of the tower, contains some murals from the 14th century. Far more interesting than any art, however, is the view of the surrounding area to be seen from the top of the tower.

The **Pfarrkirche** (parish church) is dedicated to St. Gall. This 15th-century sandstone structure has a sunken nave from the 18th century.

The most important excursion in the environs is to **Pfänder,** to the east of Bregenz, reached by traveling 7½ miles by a narrow little twisting road through the mountains. To get there, head out of Bregenz along the road to Lindau, in West Germany, turning right in the direction of Lochau, where you pass a parish church. Make a right turn onto a secondary road leading to Pfänder. You'll come to a car park from which you go by foot to the Schwedenschanze belvedere, at nearly 3,500 feet. From the terrace you'll have a fine view of the town and the lake.

If you don't go by car, you can get to Pfänder from Bregenz by cableway. Go to the lower station, which is about 500 yards east of the Kornmarkt. It takes about seven minutes to reach the summit. The cableway usually runs from 8:30 a.m. to 8 p.m., but in peak season, July and August, the run continues until 10 p.m. while the sky is still pierced with light. Allow about an hour and 45 minutes for this excursion.

If you're in Bregenz the second half of June any year, you might drive south of the town to the hamlet of **Hohenems,** which is about 11 miles from Lake Constance. The little town has a well-attended music festival, but don't count on staying at a hotel here. Accommodations for festival time are fully booked a year in advance. However, you might call the Hohenems Tourist Office (tel. 23-01), where a member of the staff will try to get you an accommodation in a private home.

The festival consists of compositions by Franz Schubert, although Schubert, who died at the age of 31, had no connection with Hohenems. It was selected as the site for the festival, called the Schubertiade Hohenems, by the noted German baritone Hermann Prey when he launched the event in 1976. The festival is presented in two rather small concert halls, the larger one seating only 475 persons.

For tickets to the festival, you can write to the **Schubertiade Hohenems,** Postfach 100, A-6845 Hohenems, Austria. Tickets for most performances range from $8 to $40.

The area code for Bregenz is 05574.

WHERE TO STAY: Schwärzler Hotel, 9 Landstrasse (tel. 22422), lies within two minutes by car from the center of town and is by all accounts the best hotel in Bregenz. Such noted visitors as Arthur Ashe, Leonard Bernstein, José Carreras, Richard Claydermann, and Birgitt Nilsson have all stayed at this elegant hotel. The hotel offers well-furnished bedrooms with private balcony and a view of the mountains. On the premises are a restaurant, a covered swimming pool, a flowered sun garden, a bowling alley, and a host of extras. Rates in a single range from 600 AS ($31.92) to 820 AS ($43.62), while prices in a double go from 520 AS ($27.66) to 640 AS ($34.05) per person, with breakfast included.

Hotel Weisses Kreuz, 5 Römerstrasse (tel. 22489), is a graciously proportioned baroque building with a green-and-white facade and a steeply pitched roof with three tiers of gables. Completely renovated in 1983, the interior is filled with painted armoires, elegant antiques, and conservative furniture. In the center of town, the hotel is a popular gathering place for local residents. There's an à la carte restaurant on the premises. In comfortably furnished bedrooms, rates for bed and breakfast range from 480 AS ($25.54) to 750 AS ($39.90) in a single and from 820 AS ($43.62) to 1,800 AS ($95.76) in a double. Prices depend on the season.

Berghof Fluh, 7 Fluherstrasse, Bregenz-Fluh (tel. 24213), is a comfortable modern hotel designed almost like a spacious private home. Lying in Fluh, a small village just outside town, the hotel has a long flowered sun terrace with a view of the Swiss Alps. You'll also find a series of rustic public rooms, many of which are paneled, and a German-style tavern with a beamed ceiling, a handsome wooden bar, and an occasional visit by a local rock band. The sunny and cheerful bedrooms rent for 400 AS ($21.28) to 450 AS ($23.94) in a single and from 800 AS ($42.56) in a double for bed and breakfast. Half board is available for 150 AS ($7.98) per person extra. The in-house restaurant is often visited by German, Swiss, and Austrian urbanites. A friendly waiter will present you with a small handwritten menu which will usually have an assortment of fish, game, and crispy salads from both the Austrian and international repertoire of fine cuisine. A la carte meals range from 90 AS ($4.79) to 130 AS ($6.92). It's closed Monday.

Gasthof Adler, Mehrerauerstrasse (tel. 31788), is a long horizontal structure with a steeply pitched red tile roof set above two floors of red-shuttered windows. Part of the facade has been covered with modern planking, although the rest of the hotel looks much older. The cozy interior contains a restaurant, a bar, and a coffeeshop, as well as a sauna. The bedrooms are furnished with painted furniture and lots of exposed wood. Per-person rates range from 220 AS ($11.70), with breakfast included. None of the rooms has a private bath, but the facilities in the hallways are adequate.

Hotel Heidelberger Fass, 30 Kirchstrasse (tel. 22463), is an unusual baroque hotel in the center of town. Its facade is crowned with a big rococo gable with elaborately curved sides. The interior has lots of well-finished paneling, crisscrossed ceiling beams, and country-style accessories. The attractive restaurant serves well-prepared Austrian specialties. Singles cost 450 AS ($23.94), while doubles go for 375 AS ($19.95) per person, with breakfast included.

WHERE TO DINE: **Zoll,** 118 Arlbergstrasse (tel. 31705), is a discreetly elegant restaurant which has become one of the stars of Austrian nouvelle cuisine. Ingredients are ultra fresh and perfectly attuned to the seasons. The handwritten menu lists imaginative recipes made from hare, quail, and fresh fish from the lake. Specific dishes include venison schnitzel with spinach spätzle, cheese ravioli made in house, zander filet with optional seaweed garnish, a savory tafelspitz with homemade horseradish, and an excellent wine list (the steward will make an honest selection for you if the names are a bit confusing). The restaurant is closed for two weeks in January and June, and on Thursday during the rest of the year. À la carte meals range from 250 AS ($13.30) to 600 AS ($31.92), while fixed-price meals cost from 350 AS ($18.62) to 900 AS ($47.88).

Berghaus Pfänder (tel. 21184). From your panoramic eyrie in this lofty place, you'll be able to see into both Germany and Switzerland. In an environment filled with exposed wood, you'll enjoy such specialties as roast calves' liver, fish or meat ragoûts, and delectable desserts. À la carte meals cost between 150 AS ($7.98) and 335 AS ($17.82). Reservations are suggested.

AFTER DARK: If you're in Bregenz on a summer night you don't need nightlife, for few smoke-filled clubs could compete with a walk along the lakeshore and a visit to a café. However, if you seek richer divertissements, you can visit the **Spiel-Casino Bregenz,** 2 Römerstrasse (tel. 25127), where roulette, baccarat, and blackjack are played from 4 p.m. daily. The parking garage at the casino is free.

2. The Bregenz Forest

From Bregenz you can make one of the most interesting scenic excursions in Vorarlberg—or in Austria, for that matter—deep into the Bregenzerwald, or Bregenz Forest. It's not as well known as the Black Forest of West Germany, but in my opinion it has just as much charm and character as its sister *wald* to the north.

The forest takes up the northern part of the Vorarlberg alpine range. A state highway splits the valley of the Bregenzer Ache River, making motoring easy, but the true charm of the forest lies off the beaten path in the little undiscovered valleys cut by tiny tributaries of the river. In spring the beautiful alpine meadows burgeon with wildflowers. In the background you can see the towering Alps.

Don't expect a proliferation of trees in the Bregenz Forest. The Austrians have cleared a lot of the woodlands to make meadows, where you'll see contented cows grazing, reminiscent of Switzerland.

One of the most frequented areas for sports and recreation is the **Bödele,** lying between the Valley of the Ache (don't you love that name?) and the Valley of the Rhine. Skiers are drawn to the highlands in winter.

The people who live in the forest are strong on keeping the old customs alive. If you're passing through the valley on a Sunday, you'll probably see Vorarlbergers going to church in their traditional garb. The headdress of the women is often striking, ranging from small crowns to wide-brimmed black straw hats. Unlike most of the rest of Europe the people of this area wear white for mourning rather than black.

BEZAU: The best known village of the Bregenz Forest, Bezau is surrounded by a landscape that's beautiful in both winter and summer. In the spring, summer, and autumn, you can hike, go mountaineering, swim, fish for trout, and play tennis or mini-golf.

In winter there's alpine skiing with the Hinterbregenzerwald ski ticket covering a range of more than 50 lifts and cable railways. There are some 25 miles of cross-country ski trails. You can also go tobogganing or play tennis at one of the three courts inside a hall.

A cableway from here will take you to the Baumgartenhöhe at 5,350 feet. Bezau's area code is 05514.

Food and Lodging

Kur Sporthotel Post (tel. 2207) is one of the loveliest hotels in the region. It's composed of two tin-roof chalets covered with cedar shingles and flowery balconies. An elaborate wrought-iron sign extends over the driveway leading up to the hotel's location between a collection of houses and a big open field. This establishment was founded in 1850 as a link in the Austrian postal services. Renovated in 1976, the hotel contains a blazing fireplace open to view on four sides, lots of rustic beams, tastefully discreet lighting, and a collection of alpine antiques.

The bedrooms are country-style luxurious, and have many rustic details as well as modern bath and up-to-date comforts. On the premises is a heated indoor pool whose ceiling is a crafted wood-beamed marvel. Prices for bed and full board range from 700 AS ($37.24) to 850 AS ($45.22) per person, based on double occupancy, and from 750 AS ($39.90) to 820 AS ($43.62) in a single.

Gasthof Gams (tel. 2220) is a dignified-looking hotel which rambles across a big lawn a few buildings away from the village church. The facade is an appealing combination of cedar shingles, white stucco, steeply pitched gables, and recessed balconies. Although the core of the hotel was built in 1648, guests find all the modern comforts, particularly the well-heated outdoor pool whose entrance is through a low opening on the inside of the hotel. It is heated from May to October. Also on the premises are two outdoor tennis courts, a hot whirlpool, a sauna, a big garden, and several rustically antique-style sitting rooms. The wood-paneled bedrooms range from 500 AS ($26.60) to 640 AS ($34.05) per person, with half board included. Prices depend on the season, the accommodation, and the plumbing.

The restaurant is outfitted in an appealing style which originated years ago in the region, and specializes in game, particularly venison. You'll also be offered seafood, such as a well-prepared filet of sole, along with filet steak, curry dishes, and desserts which include a variety of fresh mountain berries. Full meals cost from 145 AS ($7.71) to 345 AS ($18.35).

DAMÜLS: This is one of the leading ski centers for winter sports in the Bregenz Forest, at an elevation of 4,680 feet. One skier who goes here every year describes it as being for connoisseurs. Hotels organize weekly après-ski programs, so check to see what the action is during your stay here. The village is small, so it's easy to get to know your fellow visitors well.

Damüls is an area of great scenic beauty, making a summer visit pleasant. This is the loftiest village in the forest.

The Damüls area code is 05510.

Food and Lodging

Hotel Damülser Hof (tel. 210) is a peacefully isolated collection of modern chalets interconnected with covered passageways. All of them sit in a sloping alpine meadow a short walk from the village church. The elegant interior has enough variety in its decor to please most guests. Each of the cozy public rooms is crafted from such top-quality materials as exposed bricks, carved and painted wooden ceilings, and intricately crafted wrought iron. There are intimate niches, soft lighting, and several fireplaces. On the premises are a bar area, an indoor pool, a sauna, a good restaurant, a bierstube/café, a dance bar, a sporting goods store, a bowling alley, and a big sun terrace. The paneled bedrooms rent for 530 AS ($28.20) to 820 AS ($43.62) per person in high season, with full board. The Klauser family are the accommodating hosts.

Hotel Mittagspitze (tel. 211), a short distance away from the village church, is a pleasingly designed chalet with an angled facade of alternate areas of white walls and weathered planking. The attractive decor emphasizes lots of amber-colored paneling, simple furniture, and tasteful accessories. Many of the rooms have private balconies, renting for 520 AS ($27.66) per person in units holding from one to three persons. Apartments for four or more cost around 590 AS ($31.31) per person. These prices include full board. The in-house restaurant serves tasty and well-prepared food accompanied by excellent service.

MELLAU: One of the most charming and relatively unknown resorts in the Bregenz Forest is Mellau, a hamlet set against gently rolling mountains with plenty of woodland for walking. Trout fishermen find excitement and rewards in the Bregenzer Ache with its fast-flowing waters. Canoeing from here in the river's rapids is a thrilling sport. The village has a large, heated outdoor swimming pool.

Many folkloric evenings give visitors the chance to be entertained by groups wearing the traditional dress of the valley.

The area code for Mellau is 05518.

Food and Lodging

Hotel Pension Kreuz (tel. 2208) is a modern, five-story hotel with two distinct sections, each with a symmetrically peaked roof and lots of big-windowed balconies. The pleasant interior is dotted with rustic accessories, such as a stone-rimmed fireplace, heavy beams, hunting trophies, and brass chandeliers, and includes an attractive, up-to-date dining room. On the premises is an ozone-enriched swimming pool, plus a sauna, a collection of bar areas, a bowling alley, a dance hall, a reading room, and a daytime café with its own bakery. Hedwig Metzler, the owner, rents her woodsy bedrooms for 550 AS ($29.26) to 720 AS ($38.30) in a single and 520 AS ($27.66) to 950 AS ($50.54) per person in a double. All tariffs include full board. Prices vary according to the season and the accommodation.

Hotel Engel (tel. 2246). The oldest members of the Rogelböck family remember when their hotel was housed in a much older building whose picture you can see inside the modern chalet that replaced it. The cozy interior is accented with warmly designed textiles, blazing fireplaces, sunny and well-decorated restaurants, and a big indoor pool. Rooms, with full board included, rent for 400 AS ($21.28) to 500 AS ($26.60) per person in a double. Singles pay a daily supplement of 50 AS ($2.66). The hotel is open from December to October.

3. Feldkirch and Dornbirn

Up to now I've assumed that you might enter Austria from Lake Constance if you're coming from either Switzerland or West Germany or directly from the Bavarian section of the latter country. However, you might also approach from another part of Switzerland, coming into Feldkirch. After visiting Feldkirch, I'll introduce you to the largest city of Vorarlberg, Dornbirn, which is even bigger than the provincial capital, Bregenz.

FELDKIRCH: This old town, considered "the gateway to Austria," lies on the road through the Arlberg. If you're traveling by rail from Switzerland, Feldkirch will be your first town in Austria. Unfortunately, many people rush on to other destinations, but it will be worth your time to get off the train and explore this town that goes back to medieval days.

Feldkirch was once a fortified town which grew up at the "heel" of Schattenburg Castle on a tributary of the Ill River, becoming known for its classical Latin school. The old town, which can be explored in about an hour, is the tourist attraction, the new town lying to the northeast.

The heart of the old town is **Marktgasse** (market street), a rectangle with arcades. Many of the old houses are graced with oriels and frescoed facades. A popular wine festival is held here in July, with the town filling up with revelers.

Among the curiosities of the old town is the **Katzenturm,** or tower of the cats. The cats in this case were actually lions. The tower was named for a defense cannon here adorned with lion heads. The **Churertor,** or Chur Gate, is another Feldkirch landmark. Sights include the **Domkirche** (cathedral church), known for its 15th-century double nave. See the *Descent from the Cross*, a 1521 painting by Wolf Huber of the Danube school.

Schattenburg Castle, once a defense fortress and now a museum and restaurant, can be reached by car by heading up Burggasse, or you can climb the steps by the Schloss-steig. Parts of the castle were built at the turn of the 16th century. From the castle precincts you have a view of the Valley of the Rhine.

The **Heimatmuseum** (local museum) in the castle exhibits a wealth of furnishings of the region, ranging from those that filled a farmer's shack to pieces that graced the hall of a nobleman. Also displayed are a large collection of art and an armor collection. The museum is open from 9 a.m. to noon and from 1 to 5 p.m. daily except Wednesday. Admission is 10 AS (53¢). There is also a restaurant in the castle.

The area code for Feldkirch is 05522.

Food and Lodging

Hotel Illpark, 2 Leonhardsplatz (tel. 24600), has the most strikingly contemporary facade in town. The drama of its format is enhanced by its location on a brick-covered square at the edge of the old quarter. The 92 tastefully decorated bedrooms have private bath, mini-bar, TV, and radio. On the premises is a cafeteria, plus a beer cellar with an adjoining bowling alley (the perspective of which looks like a time tunnel from some space war), a dance bar, and an indoor swimming pool. Except for the rustic beer hall the decor is contemporary, with pin lighting and lots of attractively muted colors.

With breakfast included, doubles cost 950 AS ($50.54) while singles rent for 500 AS ($26.60). The international menu in the restaurant features week-long specials from many different countries. When I was last there the emphasis was on Provence, and the food items included a well-prepared Mediterranean fish soup. Meals range from 170 AS ($9.04) to 380 AS ($20.22). Reservations are suggested.

Central Hotel Löwen, 15-19 Neustadt (tel. 22070), has an ochre facade with an entrance beneath an arched street-level arcade. The interior is outfitted with a collection of rococo-framed mirrors, eclectically grouped chairs, and accessories, including what look like family portraits. The owners charge from 440 AS ($23.41) to 540 AS ($28.73) for a single and 420 AS ($22.34) to 435 AS ($23.14) per person in a double, with full board included.

Hotel Hochhaus, 177 Reichsstrasse (tel. 22479), a minute's walk from the train station, is in two separate balconied sections, one of which rises almost twice as high as the other. The hotel is painted a pastel yellow with neutral-toned balconies. On the premises is a ground-level sun terrace, and the comfortable bedrooms have big windows and contemporary furniture. Rates range from 230 AS ($12.24) to 350 AS ($18.62) for a single and from 200 AS ($10.64) to 320 AS ($17.02) per person in a double, with breakfast included.

Restaurant Lingg, 10 Kreuzgasse (tel. 22062), has a good local reputation, and many of the town's lunches take place here. The dining section is one floor above ground level in an old structure on the main square, whose medieval buildings are visible from the windows. You could begin your meal with melon with shrimp, served in a homemade mayonnaise sauce, and then follow with one of several well-prepared meat, fish, or game specialties from the Austrian kitchen. Full meals range from 100 AS ($5.32) to 300 AS ($15.96). It's closed Monday, and reservations are suggested.

DORNBIRN: The "city of textiles," Dornbirn lies in the heart of Vorarlberg province, of which it is the largest town and the commercial center. A trade fair in mid-July ties in with the Bregenz Festival. Dornbirn, only seven miles from the provincial capital, is at the outskirts of the Bregenz Forest on the edge of a broad Rhineland valley.

The city center is the Marktplatz (market square), graced by a 19th-century parish church in neoclassical style and by the **Rotes Haus** (Red House), a 1639 building which is now a restaurant.

The most exciting excursion in the environs is to **Karren** (3,200 feet), about 1½ miles from the heart of town. The sturdy of foot and shank will make the climb in about two hours, but you can take a cable car and get there in five minutes. For your trouble, you'll be rewarded with a magnificent view. From here you can hike down to the Rappen Gorge, with the Ache River flowing through it.

Dornbirn's area code is 05572.

Food and Lodging

Parkhotel, 6 Goethestrasse (tel. 62692), is an elegant modern hotel in a park area in the heart of town. A hotel of international standards in both comfort and cuisine, it serves as the preferred rendezvous point for the area's political and industrial leaders. The rather grand decor is conservative and contemporary, with lots of wood accents and big windows looking out over the lawns. On the premises are tennis courts, a sauna, and an indoor pool. Rates in one of the comfortably furnished bedrooms range from 380 AS ($20.22) to 420 AS ($22.34) per person in a double and from 480 AS ($25.54) to 510 AS ($27.13) in a single. Breakfast is included in all the tariffs.

Hotel Zum Verwalter, 1 Schlossgasse (tel. 62579), belongs to a family that has run the hotel for the last two centuries. The hotel is composed of a beautiful ochre house with green shutters and a steeply pitched roof, plus an attractive balconied addition stretching out into the well-maintained lawn. The interior provides the kind of high-quality decor which many will find loaded with charm. The comfortable bedrooms have paneled ceilings, gracefully curved headboards, and warm colors. They rent for around 290 AS ($15.34) to 420 AS ($22.34) for a single and 210 AS ($11.17) to 340 AS ($18.09) per person in a double, with breakfast included. These prices vary according to the season, the exposure, and the accommodation. The Herburger family are the friendly owners.

Sport & Tagungshotel Rickatschwende, Bödelestrasse (tel. 65350), is a sprawling modern hotel built onto an older shingle-sided house. Tennis courts, an indoor swimming pool, and a sauna are on the premises, as well as a series of paneled public rooms. The hotel sits at the edge of a grassy field at the edge of town. The cozy bedrooms have warm colors, lots of exposed wood, and big sunny windows. They rent for 750 AS ($39.90) to 800 AS ($42.56) in a single and 640 AS ($34.05) to 690 AS ($36.71) per person in a double, with full board included. A garage is on the premises.

Katharinenhof, 2 Felder-Strasse (tel. 62577), is a flat-roofed contemporary hotel with turquoise and white designs painted below some of the windows and a ground-floor extension stretching toward the street. The hotel has both a covered swimming pool and a sauna on the premises. Rates range from 450 AS ($23.94) to 515 AS ($27.40) in a single and from 330 AS ($17.56) to 350 AS ($18.62) per person in a double, with breakfast included. The Zumtobel family are your hosts.

Krone (tel. 62720). The solidly constructed dining room is large enough to hold many hungry diners. The chef is skillful at his craft. Choices from the kitchen include avocado with crabmeat, which might be followed by a ragoût of venison with fresh spätzle. Your dessert might be an array of fresh sorbets or a praline soufflé with ice cream. Set meals range from 105 AS ($5.59) to 400 AS ($21.28); à la carte from 110 AS ($5.85) to 320 AS ($17.02). The Krone is closed Wednesday and for part of Saturday.

Rotes Haus (tel. 62306) was constructed in 1639 and has today one of the best decorated facades in town. It's been known for many years as a bastion of conservative, high-quality traditional cookery. A glance at the menu will reveal a modified nouvelle cuisine. Items on the menu—designed like a page from an old-fashioned newspaper—include lamb with mint sauce, blue trout in butter sauce, osso buco, and a salad buffet that's crispy and well stocked. Full meals range in price from 150 AS ($7.98) to 420 AS ($22.34). Reservations are suggested, and it's closed during most of November.

4. Bludenz and Its Valleys

This little alpine town, at an elevation of about 2,000 feet, is at exactly the halfway point between Paris and Vienna on the main highway connecting the capital of the province, Bregenz, with the capital of the country, Vienna. Some of the houses in the town were here in the Middle Ages.

Bludenz is the gateway to five major mountain valleys: the **Klostertal,** the **Montafon,** the **Brandnertal** (Brand Valley), the **Grosswalsertal,** and the **Walgau.**

The Klostertal goes toward the east where lies the internationally renowned skiing territory of the Arlberg. The Montafon leads southward to the Silvretta alpine road, power stations, dams, artificial lakes, and the Silvretta-Nova ski center. The beautiful Brand Valley to the southwest has as a highlight the Lünersee, the largest lake in the eastern Alps. These three valleys are visited below.

Motorists pass through here, traveling the route from Lake Constance to the Arlberg and the Montafon Valley. Because of the valley's attractions, a variety of excursions are offered originating in Bludenz, including trips to some of Austria's finest skiing centers.

Besides the heavy tourist business engendered here, Bludenz also has an industrial side, with chocolate factories rivaling those of Switzerland, plus textile plants.

The town is surrounded by mountains, some of which reach a height of about 9,800 feet. Directly north of the town you can take a cableway to **Muttersberg** (4,635 feet), called the sun terrace of Bludenz.

The area code for Bludenz is 05552.

FOOD AND LODGING: Schlosshotel, 5 Schlossplatz (tel. 63016), in the center of town, is built high up on the same rocky bluff as the castle and the baroque church. The hotel design is solidly conservative, with recessed balconies, red shutters, and a sprawling L-shaped format. The establishment encompasses well-maintained bedrooms in both the main building and the rambling annex a few steps away.

The interior decor has massive timbers, ornate chandeliers, and warmly textured colors. You might enjoy at least one meal on the sun terrace, or under the gently arched ceiling of the dining room. A bowling alley is on the premises, as well as a children's playroom and a putting green. The in-house café serves ice creams and pastries, while the restaurant offers well-prepared Austrian specialties. The Dörflinger family charge from 550 AS ($29.26) to 650 AS ($34.58) per person in a double and 650 AS ($34.58) to 700 AS ($37.24) in a single, with half board included.

5. The Brand Valley

Often visited from Bludenz (see above), the Brand Valley (Brandnertal in German) is one of the most scenic valleys in Austria, a place of rare beauty surrounded by glaciers, with many side valleys. Romantic little villages and lush pastureland are set against a panoramic alpine backdrop. This is a valley with a wealth of inns and hotels, especially at Brand (coming up).

Skiers are attracted to the mountain ranges here, namely Niggenkopf and Palüd. The valley runs for almost ten miles before reaching Brand.

BRAND: A few centuries ago exiles from the Valais in Switzerland settled this village at the mouth of the Zalimtal near the Swiss border. At an elevation of 3,400 feet, Brand has long been a popular mountain health resort spread out along a mile stretch at the base of the Scesaplana mountain range. It's now a much-visited winter sports center, the main resort of the Rätikon district of Vorarlberg.

You can take a cableway to the top of the Tschengla at 4,095 feet, as well as a chair lift to Eggen at 4,165 feet. From there, you can make connections to Niggenkopf at 5,235 feet.

A cable car also goes to the glacial **Lünersee** (Lake Lüner), a rather austere body of water which is the largest lake in the eastern Alps. It has been dammed and a reservoir created. The trip to Lünersee takes about two hours, 12 minutes of which is by cable car which runs from June until mid-October. If you're at the lower station by 8 a.m. you can catch the first car, but you must leave by 5 p.m.

Brand's area code is 05559.

Food and Lodging

Hotel Scesaplana (tel. 221) has a tasteful chalet-inspired design of wood accents, accommodating sun terraces, and balconied extensions angling out from the peak-roofed core. The hotel, skillfully managed by Ruth and Helmut

Schwärzler, is in the center of the resort and has an attractively paneled interior. On the terrace is an indoor swimming pool, and there are indoor and outdoor tennis courts, a sauna, a solarium, a steam bath, whirlpool, massage, two restaurants, a bar, and a disco. A range of other sports is within easy access, including riding, fishing, skiing, and carriage drives (many of them cost an additional fee). Clients on the half-board plan receive a wide choice of specialties included with the evening meal. The tariffs are from 775 AS ($41.23) to 1,300 AS ($69.16) per person, double occupancy, for half board. Singles pay a daily supplement of 75 AS ($3.99) daily.

Hotel Walliserhof (tel. 241) is a solidly built hotel with rows of recessed balconies and big windows looking out over the village church on one side and a long expanse of fields on the other. The public rooms are rustic, dotted with heavy timbers. On the premises is a covered pool, plus a sporting goods store and a sauna. Both indoor and outdoor tennis courts are nearby. The Meyer family, your hosts, charge from 810 AS ($43.09) to 1,000 AS ($53.20) per person in a double and from 890 AS ($47.35) to 1,050 AS ($55.86) in a single, with full board included. Prices depend on the season and the room assignment.

Hotel Colrosa (tel. 225) is a popular stopover point for families and athletes, set in a quiet location on a forested hillside, not far from the center of town. Designed like a chalet, the hotel contains rustically pleasant rooms capped with beamed and paneled ceilings and accented with fireplaces. Capably managed by the Heinz Beck family, the hotel charges from 520 AS ($27.66) to 620 AS ($32.98) per person daily, with full board included.

Hotel Hämmerle (tel. 213), owned by a family of the same name, is a woodtrimmed chalet with a modern extension added on to a much older core. In the center of town, the hotel offers a big sun terrace, lots of grass-covered lawns for children's games or for playing, and a pleasantly paneled interior illuminated by brass chandeliers sometimes accented by a depiction of a double-headed eagle. Many of the cozy bedrooms have private balconies and views over the mountains. With full board included, rates in a double range from 500 AS ($26.60) to 600 AS ($31.92) per person in high season. Singles pay a daily supplement of 25 AS ($1.33).

Hotel Lagant (tel. 285) is a chalet hotel at the edge of the village, near the Niggenkopf chair lift. Built in 1970, the establishment contains an indoor swimming pool, an elevator, a big sun terrace, and cozily attractive public rooms. On the premises is a hospitable bar and a restaurant serving well-prepared Austrian specialties. Charges for a bed and full board range from 430 AS ($22.88) to 490 AS ($26.07) per person in a double in high season, with singles paying from 540 AS ($28.73) to 600 AS ($31.92).

Après Ski

Nightlife is very casual but fun at Brand, especially in the peak of the season. Drinks begin at 50 AS ($2.66) in most places.

The Scesa Taverna nightclub at the already-recommended **Hotel Scesaplana** is the major rendezvous point in town and has the most sophisticated entertainment. Tea dances usually get under way here at 4:30 p.m., and the Irish coffee is said to be the best in town. You'll also want to sample their fine draft beer later in the evening.

Special folkloric Vorarlberg evenings are also organized in season (ask at the tourist office to see what's featured at the time of your visit).

6. Little Walser Valley

The Kleinwalsertal (Little Walser Valley) is not to be confused with the Grosswalsertal (Big Walser Valley), mentioned above. Both take their name from the exiles who settled here from the Valais section of Switzerland. Little Walser lies in Vorarlberg, but is separated from the rest of the towns and hamlets of the province. The Allgäu Alps cut it off completely from the rest of Austria, so that although it's technically a part of this country, it's governed by West German customs and uses the West German mark instead of the Austrian schilling as the coin of its realm. As German appearing as this valley may seem, however, you're reminded that you're still in Austria when you mail a letter, as Austrian stamps are necessary.

To say "completely" cut off isn't quite accurate, since Little Walser Valley *can* be reached directly from the rest of Austria, but you'd have to take a mountain goat trail to make the journey. Otherwise, to enter the valley you start at Oberstdorf at the border between West Germany and Austria.

The Breitach River runs through this broad valley, which is surrounded by limestone mountains. The valley is rich in tradition, and most of the old folk customs and dress are still kept alive by its people.

Little Walser Valley is both a summer and a winter resort. People come in summer to enjoy the pure mountain air, and they retreat here in winter for the snow.

RIEZLERN: This is the biggest hamlet in the valley, at the head of the Schwarzwassertal, or Black Water Valley. One of its most popular attractions is its **Spiel-Casino Kleinwalsertal.** Germans flock over the border to play roulette, baccarat, and blackjack from 5 p.m. The casino also has a restaurant and a bar. It's open from Christmas until the end of January and from April to December 23.

South of the hamlet, you can take a cableway, called the Kanzelwandbahn, to a mountain perch at 6,555 feet.

The area code for Riezlern is 05517.

Food and Lodging

Berghotel Stern (tel. 5208) is an attractive chalet, with heavy eaves and regional decorations painted around the borders of the windows. Built in 1936, the hotel has dozens of handcrafted extras you'll only find in an older building, including thick wall paneling, oversize beams, and a scattering of fireplaces. On the premises is a Swiss-style restaurant, plus a gemütlich bierstube, a dancing bar, a bowling alley, a sauna with massage facilities, a children's play area, and a covered swimming pool. Per-person rates range from $23 to $52 in a single and from $20 to $43 in a double, with half board included. Prices depend on the season and the plumbing. Meals in the sympathetic dining room are often accompanied by zither music.

Gasthof Traube, 56 Walserstrasse (tel. 5177), is a contemporary chalet with an attractively simplified facade which still retains such oldtime accents as overhanging eaves and long wood-trimmed balconies. The hospitable interior includes dozens of ceiling beams and lots of rustic paneling. The hotel charges between $25 and $32 per person in summer and between $32 and $36 per person in winter, with half board included. The Hugo and Christl Fischer family, your sports-loving hosts, do much to make your stay comfortable.

HIRSCHEGG: If you blink you'll have passed through this hamlet. You can take a chair lift from here to the top station of the Heuberg at 4,500 feet, but the main reason for stopping in Hirschegg is the excellent accommodation described below.

Hirschegg's area code is 05517.

Ifen-Hotel (tel. 5071). Built in 1936, this hotel is approved by at least five European hotel associations, including the prestigious Relais et Châteaux. Seen from a distance, the place looks like a pleasing marriage between a Mediterranean villa and a Teutonic piece of art deco. Architectural features include gently curving walls and distinctive struts extending at an angle from the exterior walls to the edge of the overhanging eaves. Views from the dozens of balconies encompass most of the village and the valley it sits in.

The elegant public rooms are filled with heavy beams, big windows, and rustic accessories, all in the framework of luxurious comfort. On the premises are four outdoor tennis courts, three indoor tennis courts, a covered swimming pool, and a wide range of sports and fitness facilities. A team of chefs prepare elegant meals for the restaurants, which often feature live folkloric music. Otto and Renate Simon, the sophisticated hoteliers, welcome an assortment of guests from around the world. They charge between $27 and $70 in a single and between $27 and $80 per person in a double, with half board included. Prices are based on the season and the plumbing.

7. The Montafon Valley

Montafon is a high alpine valley known for its powdery snow and sun. It stretches some 26 miles at the southern tip of Vorarlberg, with the Ill River flowing through on its way to join the Rhine. The valley, filled with mountain villages and major winter recreation areas, is encircled by the mountain ranges of Rätikon, Silvretta, and Verwall.

Montafon has been called a "ski stadium," so designated because it's a vastly integrated ski region. One ski pass covers unlimited use of 70 cable cars, chair lifts, and T-bars in all four main ski areas of the valley, as well as transportation between the resorts.

Hochjoch-Zamang has fine skiing in the back bowls and down the front, and is the main mountain at Schruns of Hemingway fame (see below). Tschagguns has Grabs-Golm for some easier runs. Silvretta-Nova at Gaschurn and St. Gallenkirch is a superb ski circus on several mountains, and the Schafberg of Gargellen is secluded in a side valley.

SCHRUNS/TSCHAGGUNS: These hamlets are so close together that they can be treated as one, being only about three-quarters of a mile apart. Schruns is the major town of the Montafon, lying on the right bank of the Ill River. Tschagguns, a smaller resort than Schruns, is on the left bank. Although known for winter sports, both are also popular in summer.

At Schruns you can go by cableway to the already-mentioned Hochjoch-Zamang. First, you go to Kapell at 6,025 feet, where you'll find its renowned restaurant. On the sun terrace here, people do everything from making love to getting an alpine suntan. A chair lift will take you from Kapell up to Sennigrat at 7,550 feet. It's finally possible to take a so-called Hochjoch taxi (really a lift) from Sennigrat to Kreuzjoch.

From Tschagguns you can take a chair lift to Grabs-Golm at 4,550 feet. You'll also find a restaurant here. After that, you can go by drag lift to Hochegga at 5,202 feet.

About Schruns, where he spent winters while he worked on *The Sun Also Rises,* Hemingway said that he preferred to go where the rain became snow.

The area code for both Schruns and Tschagguns is 05556.

Food and Lodging at Schruns

Hotel Alpenhof Messmer (tel. 2664) presents a view of the valley and the mountains. Dieter and Charlotte Messmer have taken care to landscape this pleasant hotel into the hillside on which it sits, a short distance from the center of town. The interior has rustic accessories as well as an indoor pool (whose ceiling is supported by massive timbers), a hot whirlpool, and several open fireplaces. The bedrooms, a monochromatic delight of textiles, usually contain color TV, private bath, and phone. Rates in doubles range from 575 AS ($30.59) to 1,100 AS ($58.52) per person, depending on the season and the accommodation, with full board included. Occupants of singles pay an additional from 80 AS ($4.26) per day.

Sport-Hotel Alpenrose (tel. 2655) is a contemporary chalet, with lots of wood-accented balconies, stone retaining walls, and big windows. From the downhill side you'll notice a streamlined wood-and-glass extension looking out over the valley. The interior is loaded with rustic accessories, knotty paneling, and leather armchairs. On the premises are an indoor pool, a sauna, massage facilities, a children's playroom, a hospitable bar area, a reading lounge with an open fireplace, and a ceramic tile oven with its own warming bench. Ten minutes from the center, the hotel charges 550 AS ($29.26) to 900 AS ($47.88) per person for a room and full board. Prices vary according to the time of year and the accommodation. The hotel is open from December to October.

Löwen-Hotel Schruns, Silverttastrasse (tel. 3141). The creative designers of this hotel decided to give guests the best of both worlds. They set a pleasantly rambling chalet on top of a big lawn area in the center of town. The shrub-dotted lawn in front is actually poised on the top of the roof of an ultramodern steel, glass, and concrete construction which contains an Olympic-size swimming pool.

This is in many ways a social center of the town, and except for outdoor recreation, it provides almost everything you need for a vacation. On the premises are five restaurants, a bar accented with flowered patterns which contrast nicely with the exposed wood, and a popular disco with live acts. Among the restaurants, the most appealing are the French restaurant and the Montafoner Stübe, where meals range from 140 AS ($7.45) to 600 AS ($31.92).

The imaginatively designed bedrooms attract an international clientele who frequently return every year. With full board, rates in a double range from 1,170 AS ($62.24) to 1,280 AS ($68.10) per person, with singles paying 1,365 AS ($72.62) to 1,475 AS ($78.47). The hotel is closed from mid-October until a few days before Christmas.

Hotel Krone (tel. 2255) is a peach-colored baroque building with white trim, black shutters, stone edging, and a hipped roof with at least one pointed tower. Owned by members of the Mayer family since 1847, the hotel has a shaded beer garden, a collection of rustic artifacts, and ornate paneling whose rich glow is reflected in the leaded windows. Management takes special care of its cuisine, which is well prepared and beautifully served. For a bed and full board, the charges are from 480 AS ($25.54) to 540 AS ($28.73) per person in a double or single. Prices vary according to the season. Each of the pleasant bedrooms has a private bath.

Feuerstein (tel. 2192) is the best-known place in town for ice cream and pastries. Housed in an antique-style building above the town, the establishment provides a breathtaking view in addition to its attractively decorated pastries. Some of them are miniature works of art. Coffee costs from 20 AS ($1.06) and pastries from 23 AS ($1.22).

Food and Lodging at Tschagguns

Cresta Hotel (tel. 2395) looks like a skillfully blended collection of modern additions gradually added on to an older architectural core. The entrance is under a soaring concrete arch supported at one end by a masonry column. You can have a drink at the bar or a meal near the green tile stove in the Taverne. Here, daily specials include grilled veal steak, asparagus in season, a whole array of fresh salads, and desserts such as Viennese strudel. Meals range from 100 AS ($5.32) to 300 AS ($15.96) and include both fixed-price and à la carte selections. The bedrooms are often paneled with light-grained wood, and all are comfortable. High-season rates, with half board included, range from 420 AS ($22.34) to 650 AS ($34.58), based on double occupancy. Singles pay a daily surcharge of 60 AS ($3.19). Prices depend on the season, the plumbing, and the accommodation.

Sporthotel Sonne (tel. 2333) is an attractive chalet, half of whose facade is decorated with gray-green shutters and the other half with wood-trimmed balconies. An older building, for some visitors even more charming, is connected to the new one with a covered passageway. The interiors are filled with pleasing variations of soft reds, russets, and wood-grained colors, with big windows that flood the public rooms with sunlight. The bedrooms have lots of space and rustic furnishings, some of them painted with floral designs. A covered swimming pool and a sauna are both on the premises. In high season, Heidi and Hubert Schöpf, the pleasant owners, charge 400 AS ($21.28) to 685 AS ($36.44) for a single and 410 AS ($21.81) to 660 AS ($35.11) per person in a double. These prices include full board. Tariffs vary depending on the season and the room assignment. The cheaper units are usually in the older section. Open December to April and June to September.

Alpenparkhotel (tel. 2557). Warm and intimate are the first impressions visitors have when they enter this family-run hotel on a hillside above the village. A few minute's walk from the center, the hotel is designed like a chalet with wood-trimmed balconies, big panoramic windows, and a raised sun terrace. The furnishings complement the paneling and the autumnal colors, while the well-equipped bedrooms are most comfortable. On the premises are a hospitable bar and an attractive restaurant. In high season, the Pobitzer family charges from 675 AS ($35.91) in a single and from 595 AS ($31.65) to 675 AS ($35.91) per person in a double, all prices including full board. The hotel is open from December to September.

Après Ski

You can resort-hop, going back and forth between Schruns and Tschagguns, checking out whatever action appeals to you. Hard drinks begin at 75 AS ($3.99) in most establishments.

At Schruns, the already-recommended **Hotel Alpenrose** brings in a band every Saturday night in season to play for dancing. It also sponsors *schuhplättler* nights about twice a week.

The **Kurhotel Montafon** (tel. 2791), which is the leading spa hotel of this resort, also presents a one-man band in its Taverne where music is played until after midnight.

The **Löwen Hotel,** also recommended, had the liveliest band on my last visit. Disco action is in the Löwen-Grube. Occasionally you can see folkloric shows here, as well as international shows. It's probably your best bet in town.

Tschagguns also is lively after dark in season. The moment they return from the slopes, skiers pile into the previously recommended **Cresta Hotel** and the **Sporthotel Sonne** for drinks, either hot chocolate or beer. Later, as the evening progresses, both of these places have dancing.

If you'd like a stube for some gemütlich fun and reasonable meals, try the **Gasthof Löwe** (tel. 2247), run by the Tschohl family.

GASCHURN: This resort, reached by bus from either Bludenz or Schruns, lies at an elevation of 3,230 feet and is the starting point for the Silvretta-Nova winter sports arena. Gaschurn and the smaller resort, **Partenon,** are similar in position to Schruns and Tschagguns. In summer, visitors can fish for trout in the Ill River (not to be confused with the Ache River—or its source).

A chair lift from Gaschurn takes you into one of the most beautiful ski regions in Austria, the **Silvretta-Nova.** Visitors can ride on the world's largest gondola lift, carrying six persons. In addition there are seven chair lifts and 20 T-bar lifts. This extensive lift system enables you to use the 50 miles of well-kept slopes, ranging from nursery runs to the most sophisticated slopes and touring routes. The ski school offers single and group lessons as well as cross-country skiing, and there's a ski kindergarten.

From the Silvretta-Nova section, a drag lift will take you to the Gampabinger Berg at 7,210 feet.

Not only is the Silvretta-Nova a major ski area, the **Versettla** is as well. It's reached by a two-stage chair lift. The top station is at 6,590 feet. In about 18 minutes you can rise 3,310 feet.

The Gaschurn area code is 05558.

Food and Lodging

Sporthotel Epple (tel. 251) is a first-class vacation hotel in the center of town, designed in a contemporary format. The decor is luxurious, conservatively modern, and rustic, with lots of exposed wood and comfortable furniture. A covered swimming pool, a sauna, and tennis courts are on the premises. The hotel charges from 950 AS ($50.54) to 1,300 AS ($69.16) in a single and from 1,100 AS ($58.52) to 1,300 AS ($69.16) per person in a double, with full board included. Prices depend on the season and the accommodation.

Zum Fässle, the adjoining restaurant, offers a friendly welcome to visitors, as well as a varied menu specializing in Swabian specialties. These include a juicy roast beef with onions, an array of crispy salads, homemade spätzle, and desserts such as tasty strudels. Full meals range in price from 185 AS ($9.84) to 390 AS ($20.75). Both the hotel and the restaurant are closed from mid-April to mid-December.

Posthotel Rössle (tel. 331). The older section of this 100-year-old hotel has a weathered shingle facade, green shutters, and a gently sloping gabled roof. In 1966 the Kessler family added a bigger chalet section with modern comforts. These include both an indoor and outdoor pool, whose waters flow into one another, and a massive structure with soaring lintels and curved walls whose roof supports a sun terrace.

The public rooms inside are universally rustic, accented with well-finished paneling, although the older section contains more colorful units. Also on the premises are a sauna, a bowling alley, and an open fireplace. The 85 beds rent for 700 AS ($37.24) to 970 AS ($51.60) per person, with full board included. The hotel is open from December to April and June to September.

Hotel-Pension Sonnblick (tel. 212) is a contemporary chalet set at the edge of the village near a steeply rising hill. The accommodating sun terrace is flanked with stone retaining walls, while the interior is outfitted in alpine modern, with an open fireplace, brass chandeliers, and rustic accessories. The bedrooms are somewhat on the small side, but are sunny and comfortable, sometimes giving a view of the village church and the hills beyond it. On the premises are an indoor pool, a sauna, a café, a day-bar, and an elevator. An older section is connected to the new part by a passage. For a room and full board, doubles are charged from 580 AS ($30.87) to 920 AS ($48.94) per person, with singles paying from 630 AS ($33.52) to 1,000 AS ($53.20). Prices depend on the season and the plumbing.

Restaurant Alt Montafon (tel. 232), covered throughout its two dining areas with thick panels and 19th-century farm implements, offers about as much local flavor as you're likely to find in the region. The owner of this restaurant is an avid hunter, and the menu understandably includes the "antlered fruits" of the region. In addition the homemade noodles are sometimes laced with pungent cheese, the garden vegetables are fresh and crispy, and the house specialty is roasted veal. Be sure to reserve a table because in winter this is one of the most popular places around. Meals cost from 115 AS ($6.12) to 550 AS ($29.26), and it's closed on Monday.

Après Ski

Once a week the tourist office issues an information sheet to keep guests informed about what's going on in and around Gaschurn. That way you won't miss out on any of the folkloric evenings, with traditional song and dance, along with special dinners, picture and slide evenings, and lots more. Hard drinks in most places begin at 75 AS ($3.99). Occasionally the town sponsors a dual slalom in the evening, which is floodlit.

The best place for après-ski life is the Taverne of the already-recommended **Sporthotel Epple,** where in chic, snug surroundings you can enjoy zither music and dancing on most nights every week in season.

The **Hotel Versettla,** also recommended, has disco action twice a week.

At the **Hotel Verwall** (tel. 206), run by the hospitable Durig family, you can dance to live music in the "Design Bar."

GARGELLEN: This is a charming mountain village at the end of the valley, with no through traffic. To reach the hamlet of Gargellen, you turn to the southwest —the road is marked—before you approach St. Gallenkirch. Gargellen lies between the Silvretta alpine range and the Rätikon. If you don't have a car, you can reach this resort by taking a bus from Schruns, after leaving St. Gallenkirch. You go five miles southwest through the Valley of the Gargellen to the village of Gargellen (4,675 feet).

Mountaineers flock to this well-patronized summer holiday resort. Trout fishing in the many fast-flowing mountain streams in the environs is another lure. You might enjoy a dip in the heated open-air swimming pool or taking a horseback ride.

In winter this is a ski place, with an extended ski area. Lifts link well-prepared runs for both beginners and experienced skiers. You'll also find a well-known ski school, a ski kindergarten, and cross-country slopes.

You can be transported to the resort's highest station, at 7,600 feet.

The area code for Gargellen is 05557.

Food and Lodging

Sporthotel Bachmann (tel. 6316) has an attractive chalet format constructed on top of a modern swimming pool set into the hillside. The interior is intimately cozy, combining lots of polished knotty paneling, ceramic tile stoves, open fireplaces, and rustically comfortable furniture. The dining room has massive beams supporting the ceiling and soft red upholstery. Also on the premises are an outdoor pool, a sauna, and tennis courts with a teacher. You have access to a host of wholesome alpine activities. High-season rates range from 600 AS ($31.92) to 900 AS ($47.88) per person, with full board. Prices vary according to the season and the room assignment. Singles pay a daily surcharge of 25 AS ($1.33). Open December to April and June to September.

Hotel Silvretta (tel. 4088) is built on a hillside amid scattered farms and houses. The interior is accented with decorative stone walls, blazing fireplaces, weathered timbers, and thick plank-covered walls. On the premises are a double-lane bowling alley. a sun terrace, a restaurant, and a sauna with massage facilities, plus a music bar from which you can watch the activities in the indoor pool. The Schaper family, your hosts, charge 550 AS ($29.26) to 700 AS ($37.24) per person for a bed and full board. Prices depend on the season. The hotel is open from December to April and June to September.

Alpenhotel Heimspitze (tel. 6319) is a chalet filled with a kind of heavy grace and dozens of handcrafted extras. Some of the ceiling beams look hand hewn, and the knotty paneling attractively complements the autumnal colors of the finely patterned carpeting. You'll notice a scattering of carved alpine chests and polychrome statues, as well as soft lighting and a big fireplace trimmed with river rocks.

The bedrooms sometimes contain flowered upholstery with white backgrounds, lace-trimmed tablecloths, and big sunny windows. The hotel is popular for both its rooms and its restaurant. Rates in high season range from 650 AS ($34.58) to 720 AS ($38.30) for a single and from 650 AS ($34.58) to 920 AS ($48.94) per person in a double, with half board included.

Skiers and hikers will be glad to know that lunch on this plan can be taken either in the main hotel or in the Schafberg restaurant at the top of one of the chair lifts. The Thöny family are your hosts. A children's playroom is on the premises, as well as a country restaurant whose tables are often decked with alpine roses. Specialties include fresh salads, tafelspitz, pork filet with buttered spätzle, and a wide choice of pastries. Full meals range from 165 AS ($8.79) to 335 AS ($17.82). The restaurant is closed on Monday, and both the hotel and the restaurant are closed between early May and mid-June and between early October and mid-December.

Hotel Feriengut Gargellenhof (tel. 6274). The oldest sections of this weathered chalet are built almost completely of different kinds of wood, both inside and out. Even the newer sections offer old-fashioned comfort in a tastefully designed format of rustic detailing and polished paneling. On the premises you'll find blazing fireplaces, leaded windows set with dozens of rounded panes of glass, cascading flowerboxes, and a scattering of painted regional antiques. The town's outdoor pool, tennis courts, and the Schafberg's ski lifts are a short distance away.

The mountain-style bedrooms offer lots of comfort, costing from 620 AS ($32.98) to 900 AS ($47.88) per person in high season, based on double occupancy. Singles pay a daily surcharge of 70 AS ($3.72). All tariffs include full board. The hotel is open December to April and June to September.

Many visitors to this area make an excursion to one of the two in-house restaurants, both of which offer impressive mountain views. Specialties include homemade liver spätzle soup, Vorarlberg-style sauerbraten, a savory array of juicy meats, and heavenly desserts, all served in big portions to an enthusiastic crowd of regular customers. Whether you eat in the dining room or on the sun terrace, the establishment serves the kind of hearty, well-prepared food that goes well with the mountain air. Meals range from 165 AS ($8.79) to 445 AS ($23.67). Both the hotel and the restaurant are closed in May, October, and November.

Hotel Edelweiss (tel. 6317) is a well-maintained chalet with a gabled roof and four floors of comfortable bedrooms. A few steps from the village church, in a cluster of other chalets, the hotel is administered by the Drexel family. The hotel has only 30 beds, renting for 630 AS ($33.52) to 700 AS ($37.24) per person in a double, with full board. Singles pay a daily surcharge of 55 AS ($2.93). The hotel, open from December to April and June to September, is about a three-minute walk from the ski lifts.

Hotel Alpenrose (tel. 6314) is a tastefully symmetrical chalet built into the side of an alpine meadow. Its facade is appealingly covered with weathered planking, and its interior provides rustic comforts, including a panoramic dining room with a woodsy decor, an agreeable bar area, a sauna, a whirlpool, a children's playroom, and physical fitness facilities. In high season, the charge for a bed and full board is 800 AS ($42.56) to 860 AS ($45.75) per person. Open December to April and June to October.

Après Ski

It's a tiny village, but there are some nocturnal stirrings, with hard drinks priced from 85 AS ($4.52).

British skiers, in particular, like to drop in at the already-recommended **Hotel Edelweiss** for one of the best teas in town, with delicious pastries.

The four-star **Hotel Madrisa** (tel. 6331) is probably the most popular spot for nightlife. Its band plays for dancing couples every night, and it's also been known to present fondue evenings and to stage fashion shows.

The **Hotel/Café Dörflinger** (tel. 6386) is a modest, family-run place, but its bar is a major rendezvous point for the skiing crowd.

At the **Hotel Silvretta,** just recommended, you can enjoy drinks at the bar beside the swimming pool.

Perched high on a mountain terrace, the **Hotel Vergalden** (tel. 6321), run by the Braunger family, brings in a local band once a week for dancing and rowdy fun in general. After a night's festivities here many guests take a thrilling toboggan ride back to their own domicile.

8. Arlberg—the West Side

The east side of Arlberg was visited in Chapter X on Innsbruck and Tyrol, so it's time for me to tell you the "west side story" of this massif which separates Vorarlberg from Tyrol.

This part of Austria is one of the major meccas for winter sports in Europe. Leading resorts on the celebrated Arlberg massif, the highest mountain range in the Lechtal Alps, include Lech and Zürs, and there's also rustic, tiny Stuben, with its own north-facing snow-catcher, the mighty Albona. An Arlberg ski pass allows the holder to use the 70 ski tows, chair lifts, and cable cars in the entire Arlberg region.

Up through the Flexen Pass, you come to Zürs, a chic, elegant, refined resort with skiing at Trittkopf and Mahdloch. Lech is larger, with easier skiing on Kriegerhorn and Mohnenfluh.

LECH: Founded in the 14th century by emigrés from the Valais district of Switzerland, Lech, on the northwestern flank of the Arlberg mountain range, still has its original **pfarrkirche** (parish church) from that era. This archetype of a snug alpine ski village is practically joined to Oberlech, a satellite resort a little farther up the mountain. Lech stands at 4,730 feet; Oberlech, at 5,600 feet.

Zürs, a sister village to Lech, is considered slightly more fashionable, but Lech has its own claim to fame: it has played host to Prince Charles and Princess Diana.

Lech is 8½ miles from Landen, and you can reach it and Oberlech by bus from St. Anton am Arlberg. Lech also lies on a major rail route.

In summer, visitors like to come here to tour the Upper Lech Valley, which stretches for about 35 miles to a lovely vale lying between the Lechtal and the Allgäu Alps.

Lech, Oberlech, and Zürs are linked by about 70 lifts, making for a magnificent ski circus. Snow is advertised as guaranteed from the end of November until the end of April. Oberlech has a pedestrian zone with frequent cable-car connections. Lifts and runs are close together. It's possible to ski between Lech and Zürs. A cable car, whose last run is at 1 a.m., connects Oberlech to the heart of Lech. You can take the Rüfikopf cable car from the heart of the resort to Rüfikopf (7,635 feet).

Regardless of which resort you stay in, I suggest you go to Oberlech if the day is sunny and find yourself a spot in one of the big sun-terrace restaurants there.

The Lech area code is 05583.

Food and Lodging at Lech

Hotel Arlberg (tel. 2134) is a sprawling chalet well equipped for an alpine vacation. In addition to a well-maintained lawn area, the grounds contain an outdoor pool, tennis courts, and a flowered sun terrace where waiters serve meals on well-ironed tablecloths. The interior contains beautiful regional antiques, some of them painted, carefully crafted paneling, and elegant accessories. Guests appreciate the intimate lighting in the bar after a day in the brilliant sunshine and also enjoy the warmth from the sitting room's baronial fireplace.

The food served in the richly outfitted dining room is as generous as the decor itself. The Schneider family directs a team of chefs who prepare a daily specialty from one of three or four European culinary traditions, as well as a consistently available array of Austrian-inspired foods which includes a wide array of game and fish dishes, cream-flavored gulasch, and cream schnitzels. Meals range from 200 AS ($10.64) to 450 AS ($23.94). Hotel tariffs go from 850 AS ($45.22) to 2,350 AS ($125.02) per person, with full board. Prices vary throughout the course of the year. The hotel is open from December to April and June to September. The restaurant is closed from mid-April to the end of July and from mid-September to the end of November.

Hotel Schneider Almhof (tel. 3500) is a huge building designed like several chalets clustered together. The interior is luxuriously outfitted with blazing fireplaces (including one beside the indoor pool), painted alpine cupboards, richly tinted fabrics, and polished stone. The international clientele who come here spend lots of time on the sun terrace and value the hotel's location near the ski lifts.

The well-furnished bedrooms rent for 2,500 AS ($133) to 3,400 AS ($180.88) in season for a single with full board included. In a double, on the same plan, the charge is 2,800 AS ($148.96) to 2,900 AS ($154.28) per person. Small apartments cost more.

Specialties in the elegant Walliser Stuben are written on a limited menu, whose every item uses impeccably fresh ingredients. It emphasizes unusual recipes, some strongly influenced by nouvelle cuisine. Suggestions include medallions of venison in an orange pepper sauce, exotic salads, and an international array of fish and meats. Dinners range in price from 320 AS ($17.02) to 650 AS ($34.58). The hotel is closed in summer.

Hotel Jagdhaus Monzabon (tel. 2104) is a tastefully decorated four-star hotel in the center of town. Designed like a chalet, it has public rooms that are outfitted with heavy beams, hunting trophies, comfortable chairs, and accents of wrought iron. On the premises are a beauty salon, an indoor swimming pool, a sauna, billiard tables, a bar, a café, and a restaurant. Willy Schneider and his family are the owners, charging from 1,200 AS ($63.84) to 1,500 AS ($79.80) per person in a single or double and 1,550 AS ($82.46) to 2,100 AS ($111.72) per person in apartments sleeping up to four. Half board is included in these high-season rates.

Gasthof Post (tel. 22060). Queen Beatrix of the Netherlands is a frequent visitor to this establishment. But even without royal clientele it's still called the noblest hotel in town. Designed as a Romantik-Hotel, the chalet facade is ornamented with trompe-l'oeil murals. This hotel long ago served as a postal station, and displays many of the accessories that might have been used a century ago, including alpine painted chests, furniture that could have come from a wealthy farmer's house, and a scattering of baroque sculpture.

Clients fortunately get the best of the 20th century during their use of the indoor pool, the nearby tennis courts, the massage facilities, or any of the convivial gathering places, which include a popular sun terrace and several bars. Special summer arrangements are offered for fitness weeks and cooking courses.

The Moosbrugger family has installed all the modern conveniences in the bedrooms, which sometimes have elaborately painted headboards and refrigerators concealed in old chests. Accommodations include some units which are vast. Depending on the time of the year, singles range from 1,000 AS ($53.20) to 2,400 AS ($127.68), while doubles cost from 800 AS ($42.56) per person, and suites go for 3,400 AS ($180.88). Half board is included in the rates.

The restaurant is a member of Relais et Châteaux, and serves food worthy of that designation. The menu includes dozens of Austrian classics, especially game dishes, while the tafelspitz served here will help you understand why it was Franz Joseph's favorite dish. Other delicacies include lamb, fresh fish, rabbit pâté, and an impressive dessert list. Fixed-price lunches range from 200 AS ($10.64) to a peak 1,000 AS ($53.20) if you really shoot the works. À la carte meals go from 230 AS ($12.24) to 550 AS ($29.26). Reservations are advisable.

Hotel Krone (tel. 2551). This building became a hotel when it was acquired by a member of the Pfefferkorn family in 1865. The ceiling in the bar dates from about a century earlier (1741, to be exact). Today the hotel sits in a favored position between the village church and the river, with an expanded contemporary format containing 100 beds. The interior is attractively woodsy, containing ceramic tile stoves, beamed ceilings, paneled accents, and comfortable fireside chairs.

On the premises is an ultramodern fitness center containing a sauna, a solarium, massage facilities, a hot whirlpool, and a Turkish steambath. The big-windowed restaurant has a panoramic view and a well-prepared menu with big portions. Specialties include fish soup Provence style, roast veal in a chicken liver sauce, and several regional recipes. Meals range from 145 AS ($7.71) to 390 AS ($20.75). Occupants of the hotel enjoy the evening dance bar, which is in an adjoining wing to avoid disturbing sleepers in the pleasant bedrooms. Per-person rates in a double range from 625 AS ($33.25) to 1,700 AS ($90.44), depending on the season. Half board is included.

Tannbergerhof (tel. 202) is an attractive shingled chalet with green shutters and lots of interior space. The atmosphere is conducive to helping both athletes and nonathletes appreciate sports and outdoor activities, although there's certainly enough inside to distract even the most ardent sportsperson. The public rooms are accented with well-finished paneling, a ceramic tile stove with a warming bench, soft lighting, and a blazing fireplace. On the premises is a popular evening disco, plus a lounge bar, and a restaurant serving specialties such as paprika gulasch and an array of veal dishes. With full board included, per-person rates range from 750 AS ($39.90) to 1,700 AS ($90.44), depending on the season. Meals in the restaurant cost from 200 AS ($10.64) to 550 AS ($29.26), and reservations are suggested. In a separate chalet, a three-minute walk from the hotel, the management maintains a covered swimming pool, a hot whirlpool, and a sauna.

Hotel Pension Lech (tel. 289). The Grabher family are the owners of this pleasant hotel comprised of two chalets, five minutes away from the ski lifts. The interiors are handsomely paneled and accented with soft lighting. On the premises are a sauna and a bowling alley. In high season, the comfortable bedrooms rent for 900 AS ($47.88) to 1,050 AS ($55.86), with half board included.

Hotel Pension Solaria (tel. 2214) is a partially shingled green-shuttered chalet set on a hillside at the edge of the village, a few minutes' walk from the center. The interior has attractively finished wood accents and lots of cozy comforts. There is easy access to the village's sporting facilities, including the nearby ski lifts which you can reach by skiing a short distance downhill from the front door. The pleasant bedrooms rent for 450 AS ($23.94) to 1,200 AS ($63.84) per person, based on double occupancy, and singles pay a daily surcharge of 50 AS ($2.66). Half board is included in these prices, which vary according to the season. The Ender family, your hosts, will arrange to have breakfast served in your room if you wish.

Hinterwies (tel. 2531) is a white-walled chalet with wood-grained shutters and baroque-style embellishments. The interior is tastefully outfitted with lots of exposed wood, country-style furniture, and light colors. One of my favorite parts is the flagstone-covered back terrace which leads up to the tapering chimney of a brick fireplace protected by the overhang of the upper floors. The uncluttered bedrooms have lots of personalized and appealing touches. They cost from 1,180 AS ($62.78) to 1,570 AS ($83.82) per person in high season, based on double occupancy. Singles pay from 1,370 AS ($72.88) to 1,600 AS ($85.12) during the same period. These tariffs include full board. Open only from December to April.

Food and Lodging at Oberlech

Sonnenburg (tel. 2147) is a large double chalet with symmetrically peaked rooflines and alternating areas of white walls and wood-trimmed balconies covering the modern facade. In front the management has constructed a sun terrace looking down the hillside, while indoors the decor is warm, intimate, and woodsy. Many of the walls are accented either with brick or horizontal planking, with a scattering of regional antiques to augment the mellow glow from the paneling.

On the premises is an indoor pool with a panoramic view, plus a kindergarten, two restaurants, and a collection of well-maintained bedrooms with modern comfort. A short distance away an annex (called Hohe Welt) charges slightly less than the main building for the pleasantly furnished rooms. Within the two buildings the charges in high season range from 750 AS ($39.90) to 1,760 AS ($93.63) per person. Prices depend on the room assignment.

Hotel Montana (tel. 2460), above the village, has a large sun terrace looking out over Lech. It's designed like a light-grained chalet and has a stylish interior, making ample use of fuschia and pink as the appealing colors, which contrast well with the ruddy paneling. The in-house swimming pool is backed by an abstract mural, while the café/bar area is an attractive place for a midafternoon drink. The owner, Guy Ortlieb, an expatriate Frenchman, organizes weekly farmer buffets and cocktail parties, and does what he can to make his guests feel at ease in the sporty ambience of this pleasant hotel. Full-board rates in high season range from 975 AS ($51.87) to 1,625 AS ($86.45) per person, based on double occupancy. Singles pay a daily surcharge of 100 AS ($5.32).

The hotel's Zur Kanne has been elected to several prestigious rankings, including the Chaine des Rôtisseurs. It's known for serving the best fish in the valley, including salmon in saffron sauce, frogs' legs Provençale, and Alsatian wine soup. At the tables the waiter will present a woman (if accompanied by a man) a menu with no prices indicated. In case she wonders, a full meal ranges from 250 AS ($13.30) to 500 AS ($26.60). In high season, with full board included, rates range from 1,000 AS ($53.20) to 1,600 AS ($85.12) per person in a double, with singles paying a daily surcharge of 100 AS ($5.32).

Après Ski

Lech has perhaps the finest après-ski life in Vorarlberg, and if you ever get bored here, you can also check out the action at the satellite resorts or go over to Zürs.

Dedicated skiers always head for the Scotch Bar of the **Hotel Kristberg** (tel. 2488), which is owned and run by Egon Zimmermann, a former Olympic racer.

The evening begins even earlier, however, with a tea dance at the **Hotel Tannbergerhof** (tel. 2202), where Hilde Jochum welcomes you for a good time. Later in the evening you can dance to disco music.

The Stüberl of the **Hotel Berghof** (tel. 2635) is deserving of its popularity. The Burger family make you feel most welcome, and you can stick around enjoying their fine cuisine later on if you wish.

The **Hotel Krone** (tel. 2551) has disco dancing to a resident band in the evening. Run by the Pfefferkorn family, this hotel is centrally located and has two bars and a hot whirlpool bath if you're interested.

Hard drinks at most places begin at 85 AS ($4.52).

Dining at Zug

Rote Wand (tel. 2758). If you decide to try this appealing restaurant, you can feel safe in knowing that both Prince Rainier of Monaco and King Hussein of Jordan have tried it also. A specialty of the house is spätzle with cheese, which many diners enjoy almost as much as the roast veal and pork, the warm cabbage salad, or the tafelspitz. Some diners say that the real attraction, however, is the fondue bourguignonne or chinoise, which you could precede with a soup made from a purée of venison. If you're up for dessert, the hot curd strudel is heavenly.

Reservations are suggested for meals which range from 275 AS ($14.63) to 600 AS ($31.92). The interior includes massive ceiling beams over a rustically attractive alpine-style decor. The restaurant is next to the onion dome of the village church. In winter the owners will arrange for a horse-drawn sleigh to pick you up in Lech, if you telephone. They're open from December 1 until around April 20 and again from July 1 until the end of September.

Auerhahn (tel. 2754) is an old room in a building at the edge of the village. The furnishings are vintage farmer's style, and the ambience is friendly, warm, and woodsy, with a likeable kind of hubbub coming from the crowded tables inside. Specialties include fondue, liver noodle soup, Provence-style lamb, and an array of pork dishes. Dessert might be a traditional strudel smothered in vanilla sauce. À la carte meals range from 250 AS ($13.30) to 400 AS ($21.28). Reservations are suggested, and the restaurant is closed in May and October.

ZÜRS: An immaculate resort lying about 2½ miles from Lech in a sunny valley, Zürs (about 5,600 feet) consists of half a mile of typical white stucco Vorarlberger buildings, with carved wood balconies. The resort, really a collection of hotels, is reached via the magnificent Flexen Road.

Unlike most of the places we've visited, Zürs is strictly a winter resort, and nearly all the hotels close in summer. This mountain village has an abundance of "guaranteed" snow. In fact, once Pierre Trudeau, then prime minister of Canada, was snowed in and missed a summit meeting. Because of its location Zürs is avalanche prone, but these potential snowslides do not deter the loyal habitués of Zürs. The snow here has been compared to talcum powder.

Zürs (pronounced "Seurs") is a favorite of monarchs and film stars. More formal than Lech, it's considered one of the most elegant resorts in the world, far more select than St. Moritz or Gstaad, although lacking their ostentation. The resort has 130 ski instructors. Many of the wealthy guests, often from South America, have their own personal teachers.

A drag lift east of Zürs takes you to **Hexenboden** (7,700 feet). From there a cable lift goes to **Trittkopf** (7,875 feet), where you'll find a mountain restaurant and a sun terrace.

In the west, a chair lift will take you to **Seekopf** (7,175 feet). From the windows and terrace of the restaurant here, you can see the frozen Zurser Lake. From Seekopf a chair lift goes to the top station at 8,035 feet.

The area code for Zürs is 05583.

Food and Lodging

Hotel Zürserhof (tel. 2513). Five separate chalets combine forces in the shelter of an alpine valley to create this most luxurious of mountain refuges. This is the establishment that put Zürs on the tourist map, and is the preferred choice of King Hussein and his American-born queen, as well as the playground of VIPs from around the world. It grew from a house erected by the Count and Countess Vallay Tattenbach in 1927, when they began to accept paying guests. When Hitler took over Austria, the Tattenbachs sold it and emigrated to Costa Rica. In 1955 the establishment was taken over by Ernst Skardarasy.

The accommodations usually consist of private apartments, many of which have stone fireplaces, lots of space, and opulent comforts. The public rooms are decked out with old panels, antiques, and Persian carpets. There's music almost every night in the cellar bar, and a wide assortment of even the most esoteric sports (an indoor driving range for golfers, for example). A tennis player's admirers can watch him or her volley on the indoor courts from the security of a café area and relax later in the sauna or whirlpool.

Specialties in the elegant restaurant are a lighter version of the traditional Austrian cuisine, with the freshest ingredients used. There's an emphasis on buffets. À la carte meals range from 350 AS ($18.62) to 700 AS ($37.24). Singles and apartments for one person go for 2,200 AS ($117.04) to 2,300 AS ($122.36), while doubles and apartments cost 2,200 AS ($117.04) to 3,800 AS ($202.16) per person, with full board included.

Sporthotel Lorunser (tel. 22540). The late Princess Grace of Monaco used to send her children here, and today you're likely to spot two or three Princess Caroline look-alikes at the hospitable bar of this luxurious hotel. Rustically designed with cedar shingles and regional paintings around the windows, the hotel has intricately carved ceiling beams, open fireplaces, well-finished paneling, and dozens of elegant accessories and furnishings, as well as comfortable wood-trimmed bedrooms. For bed and full board, the rate in a double ranges from 1,500 AS ($79.80) to 1,800 AS ($95.76) per person, with suites peaking at 2,500 AS ($133). Regular singles are charged from 1,610 AS ($85.65) to 2,020 AS ($107.46), also with full board. The Lorunser is open only from December to April.

Central Sporthotel & Villa Edelweiss (tel. 2662). The imposing facade of this large hotel, which is open only in winter, incorporates white walls, cedar shingles, and painted embellishments. This is the oldest hotel in Zürs, although you'll find it hard to believe after looking at the brightly painted bedrooms which seem to come in a rainbow assortment of vivid colors. The public rooms include open fireplaces, a small bar, a popular disco, a white dining room with occasional gilt accents, and a French restaurant painted an eye-catching forest green.

Specialties include a roast pork filet stuffed with ham and cheese and covered with a thick mushroom cream sauce. Meals range from 175 AS ($9.31) to 500 AS ($26.60), whereas accommodations cost from 1,400 AS ($74.48) to 1,900 AS ($101.08) in a single and from 1,250 AS ($66.50) to 1,750 AS ($93.10) per person in a double. These prices include full board. Tariffs vary according to the accommodations, and rooms in the annex are slightly cheaper.

Thurnher's Alpenhof Sporthotel (tel. 2191). This distinctive-looking chalet has vertical timbers running in uninterrupted lines from near the ground floor to the eaves. The attractive effect is almost like looking at a weathered gridwork stretched across the white facade. The interior is a tasteful collection of carved panels, polished wood, and warmly textured fabrics. The dining room is crowned with timbers almost big enough to be railroad ties, and is furnished with elegant upholstered chairs.

On the premises are an indoor swimming pool, a fitness room, a sauna, a solarium, a sun terrace on the fourth floor, cinema with video, table tennis, billiards, a children's playroom, and one of the best kitchens in the Arlberg area. Each of the bedrooms has a private bath and modern comfort. They range in price from 1,450 AS ($77.14) to 2,500 AS ($133) per person in a double, with full board included. Apartments are available for up to 2,800 AS ($148.96) per person daily. Singles pay daily surcharges ranging from 200 AS ($10.64) to 250 AS ($13.30). Elfi and Oskar Thurnher, your hard-working hosts, do everything they can to make your vacation pleasant.

Hotel Hirlanda (tel. 2262) is a pleasant chalet with a rustically cozy interior containing an open fireplace, a farmer-style restaurant, a bar, and a collection of livable bedrooms. These usually have dark wood accents, chalet furniture, and white walls. They rent for 1,250 AS ($66.50) to 1,400 AS ($74.48) per person, with full board included. A sauna and a covered garage are on the premises. Oswald Wille and his family are your hosts. Open only from December to April.

Hotel Enzan (tel. 22420) is a pleasantly symmetrical chalet with lots of wood accents and muted orange shutters. The interior is a tasteful combination of wood walls, coffered ceilings, warmly tinted upholsteries, and open fireplaces. On the premises are two dining rooms, a bar, a sun terrace with waiter service, and a sauna. The Elsensohn family, your sports-loving hosts, do everything they can to create a relaxed ambience. The hotel is at the edge of the village near the cable-car station. Prices, with full board included, range from 1,250 AS ($66.50) to 1,800 AS ($95.76), depending on the accommodation, the season, and the plumbing.

Hotel Mara (tel. 2644). The Hartinger family are your hosts at this simple chalet with its wood-paneled interior. Accents inside include lots of wrought iron, vertical planking on the walls of the intimate bar, and soft lighting. Tariffs during the summer are from 300 AS ($15.96) to 340 AS ($18.09) per person for bed and breakfast, with half board costing 430 AS ($22.88) per person. In winter, when half board is required, the rates are 910 AS ($48.41) to 1,050 AS ($55.86) per person, depending on the part of the season involved. The food served here is excellent. Each of the pleasant accommodations has a private bath, mini-safe, phone, TV, and refrigerator.

Hotel Albona (tel. 2341) is a contemporary chalet with big panoramic windows and a dramatic contrast between the light and dark areas of its facade. The interior is comfortably filled with velvet banquettes pulled around an open fireplace, rustic ceiling beams, and polished wood. On the premises are a range of health facilities (sauna, steambath, massage, and jet shower), indoor golf equipment, a cozy series of sitting rooms, a carefully decorated restaurant which exudes warmth, a popular farmer's-style bar and disco, and dozens of charming accents. With full board, rates in a single range from 1,970 AS ($104.80) to 2,050 AS ($109.06), while doubles go from 1,710 AS ($90.97) to 2,190 AS ($116.51) per person, depending on the season and the accommodation. Open only from December to April.

Après Ski

With its newly opened **Casino,** Zürs has a very fashionable nightlife, what there is of it. Naturally the hotels dominate the action. Hard drinks begin at 85 AS ($4.52).

The most luxurious and elegant place to be seen at night is the already-recommended **Hotel Zürserhof** where there's dancing to a live band.

However, if you like more informal action, you'll gravitate to the also-recommended **Hotel Edelweiss** in the heart of the resort, where there's also dancing at night.

For discos, check out those at the **Hotel Albona** and the **Hotel Mara,** both previously recommended.

STUBEN: This little hamlet and winter resort is almost a suburb of Lech, lying on the northern fringes of the larger village, on the west side of the Arlberg Pass. Stuben can be reached by bus, but the most romantic way to go from Lech is by horse-drawn sleigh.

The tiny hamlet has been a way station for alpine travelers for many centuries, but in recent years it has become a modern ski area, with its own lift station on Albona. Stuben does not enjoy the chicdom that Zürs does, but its prices are much more reasonable, and it's in a fine location for skiers, having links with St. Anton in the Tyrol as well as with Lech and Zürs in the Arlberg region. In fact the Arlberg ski pass mentioned above is valid for lifts and cars linking Stuben, St. Christoph, St. Anton, Zürs, and Lech.

Stuben is especially geared for family enjoyment, with children's ski courses, special meals, and hosts who help the small fry feel at home.

This was the birthplace of Hannes Schneider, the great ski instructor.

Stuben's area code is 05582.

Food and Lodging

Hotel Mondschein (tel. 511) is a 250-year-old country house with cascading window boxes and forest green shutters. The interior is more contemporary, although the hospitality inside is pure old-fashioned Austrian. The hotel offers much comfort, and facilities include a pleasant restaurant, a bar, and an indoor swimming pool. Charges range from 800 AS ($42.56) to 890 AS ($47.35) per person in winter, with half board included. Summer rates are from 450 AS ($23.94) to 500 AS ($26.60) per person for half board. Werner Walch is the friendly host.

Hotel Post (tel. 761). When it was built in 1608 this hotel served as a shelter for tired mail-coach travelers. Today it welcomes more up-to-date visitors in its rustically attractive public rooms, most of which have been designed in an attractively contemporary format of comfort and include open fireplaces and deep-seated chairs. On the premises are a restaurant and bar, both of which offer welcome refreshment after a day outdoors. Just at the edge of the village, the hotel charges from 680 AS ($36.18) to 820 AS ($43.62) for a single and from 630 AS ($33.52) to 780 AS ($41.50) per person in a double, with half board included. Prices vary according to the season and the accommodation. Rooms at the nearby "Hunting Lodge Post" cost about 20% less than units in the main hotel.

Hotel Albona (tel. 712) is an attractive chalet with wooden shutters. On a narrow street in the center of the village, the hotel is outfitted with lots of exposed wood, alpine furniture, and sunny colors. On the premises are a hot whirlpool, a dancing bar, a restaurant, and a collection of comfortable wood-trimmed bedrooms. The prices in a double in high season range from 620 AS ($32.98) to 810 AS ($43.09) per person, while singles cost from 750 AS ($39.90). All tariffs include full board. Open December to October.

Chapter XII

CARINTHIA

THE SOUTHERNMOST PROVINCE of Austria, Carinthia (Kärnten, in German) has been generously endowed by nature. Encircled by high mountains which give it fairly well-defined borders, it has been compared to a gigantic amphitheater, cut across by the Drau River (which becomes the Drava when it enters Yugoslavia). This province consists of mountainous Upper Carinthia in the west and the Lower Carinthian basin region in the east. Because of its warm and sunny weather and lakes, which attract bathers and water sports enthusiasts who don't go to ocean shores, a section of Carinthia is known as the Riviera of Austria. The Carinthian climate is the country's mildest.

Villach, to be previewed later, is the biggest road and rail junction in the eastern Alps, and Klagenfurt is the capital of Carinthia.

This is an ancient province, archeological discoveries in the area showing that it was known to the human race far back in unrecorded time. The Romans did not overlook it, their legions marching in to conquer alpine Celtic tribes of the kingdom of Noricum and establishing it as a Roman province.

For centuries this home of ethnic groups from Slovenia belonged variously to the kingdom of Germany and Avar-dominated Slavs from the east. Eventually the populace, hoping to fend off invasions, invited Bavaria to become Carinthia's protector. Thus it came to be ruled by Bavarians and was a part of the Holy Roman Empire. Bavarian settlers gradually assimilated with the Slav population.

When the Habsburgs took Kärnten as a part of their rapidly expanding empire, it was a duchy of the Holy Roman Empire under the Bohemian aegis, a situation resolved finally when Ferdinand I of Habsburg, soon to become emperor, married the heiress to Bohemia and made Carinthia an imperial duchy, later to be designated a province of Austria.

Yugoslavia claimed southern Carinthia after World War I, and in that confused time some of the territory was ceded to that country and more to Italy. All this land was later restored, and in 1920, after the collapse of the Habsburg Empire, a plebiscite was taken and a Slovenian minority in the south, along the Yugoslav border, voted to remain with Austria. A sizable minority of Carinthia's population of 600,000 today is Slovenian, but the majority of it is German.

The sunny weather and numerous idyllic lakes that are scattered among gentle hills and steep mountains make Carinthia mostly a summer tourist center. If you like water sports or just lazing in the sun, then a summer visit to this province might be in order. It's little known to or visited by North Americans, yet it's an ideal stopover point if you're heading south to Yugoslavia or Italy. The scenery is varied, and there is much beautiful countryside to be explored.

If you're athletic you can climb the gentle *Nocks* or else seek out the more demanding steep mountains. Fishing is a popular sport in this province, both in the lakes and the colder mountain streams. The region boasts more than 200 warm, clean lakes of varying sizes.

The "Carinthian Riviera" is the name given to the main lake area, including Wörther See, not far from Klagenfurt, the provincial capital. There are also Lake Ossiacher and Lake Millstätter. Weissensee, the fourth big lake, is less well known than the other three, but there are those who consider it the most beautiful. The best way to see the lakes in summer is to take one of the boats operating from April until the middle of October.

The best season to visit Carinthia if you want to enjoy the beauty and pleasure of the lakes is from the middle of May until the end of September, although the first two weeks in October are also ideal most years. In July and August tourists flock in, so if you plan to visit then, be sure you have reservations.

Although the warm lakes are the main drawing card for Carinthia, the province is making an increasing attempt to attract skiers to its mountains in winter. Skiing lasts from December until March, not April as in some parts of Austria farther north. As a ski center this province is much less expensive than Tyrol or Land Salzburg.

1. Klagenfurt

The provincial capital of Carinthia, Klagenfurt is a university town dating from 1161. Its charter was granted in 1252. The city lies only 38 miles from Italy and less than 19 miles from Yugoslavia. It is the cultural center of Carinthia.

Klagenfurt was destroyed by fire in 1514, but it was rebuilt and designated as the capital of the duchy in 1518. It was then a walled city, but the walls were torn down during the Napoleonic invasions in 1809. The center of the city is in quadrangular shape with four so-called rings, which are streets laid out along the former city walls. The center of this quadrangle and of the modern city is **Neuer Platz,** presided over by a fountain in the shape of a ferocious dragon called *Lindwurm,* the city's symbol.

It can get very hot in Klagenfurt in the peak of summer, but if you're there, do as the Klagenfurters do—retreat to nearby Wörther See (Lake Wörther) in the western sector of the city and linked to it by a man-made canal.

The Klagenfurt area code is 04222.

THE SIGHTS: A major sight is the **Landesmuseum,** or provincial museum, 2 Museumgasse (tel. 30552). On the grounds you can see Roman artifacts, including votive stones, gleaned from the excavations in Carinthia. The museum exhibits art and artifacts of the province from prehistoric times to the present. The most outstanding feature is a display of ecclesiastical art. Also on view is a scale model of Klagenfurt as it was at the dawn of the 19th century. See the skull of a rhinoceros which is said to have been a model for the renowned Dragon Fountain in the Neuer Platz.

The museum is open from 9 a.m. to 4 p.m., from 10 a.m. to noon on Sunday and holidays. It's closed on Monday. Admission is 15 AS (80¢).

The **Alter Platz,** both a broad thoroughfare and a square, is lined with many baroque mansions, some from the 16th century. It is the center of the Altstadt (old town) and is a pedestrian zone. Many crooked, narrow little streets and alleys open off the square.

The **Landhaus,** originally an arsenal, later Carinthian state headquarters, and now the offices of the provincial government, stands on the Alter Platz. The building was begun in 1574 and completed in 1590. A moated castle once stood on this site. The courtyard of the present building has two-story arcades. A set of staircase towers has bulbous caps. Its Grosser Wappensaal, or Great Blazon Hall, dating from 1739, was handsomely decorated by Joseph Ferdinand Fromiller, who died in 1760. The ceiling painting of the hall is in trompe l'oeil. It has 665 heraldic shields.

The state hall may be visited from April until the end of September from 9 a.m. to 5 p.m. It's closed on Sunday and Monday. Admission is 6 AS (32¢).

The **Trinity Column** in the Alter Platz is from 1681. One of the most interesting buildings on the square is the **Altes Rathaus** (old city hall) from the 17th century. It has a three-story arcaded courtyard. The **House of the Golden Goose** (Haus zur Goldenen Gans) on the Alter Platz is from the final year of the 16th century.

The **Domkirche** (cathedral) of Klagenfurt lies to the southeast of the Neuer Platz. Construction on this building began in 1578. The interior is richly adorned in stucco and has ceiling paintings from the 18th century.

If you have children with you, take them by the **Minimundus,** a world in miniature, lying 2½ miles from Klagenfurt on Lake Wörther (see below). This mini-town has building models which are 1/25th of their actual size, including not only castles but also the Eiffel Tower.

Here you'll also find boat landing stages for trips on the lake in summer. There's a mini-golf course in nearby Europa-Park.

WHERE TO STAY: The **Romantik-Hotel Musil,** 14 Oktoberstrasse (tel. 511660). By all accounts, this is one of the most unusual commercial buildings in Klagenfurt, probably the only one of its kind in Austria. It was originally built in 1550 around an oval-shaped courtyard whose ascending balconies are vaulted from the side walls like the skylights in a baroque dome. From the street-level café, visitors can peer upward through three tiers of brickwork, whose counterbalancing stresses are carefully concealed beneath chiseled stonework and thick coats of plaster.

The engaging owners of this historic spot are Bernhard and Uta Musil. The facade which you'll see from the street was rebuilt in what might be called a Biedermeier style in 1860. From the shop-lined street outside, you'll enter an understated lobby and register at a desk midway between a bustling pastry shop, a coffeehouse, and a restaurant. The true beauty of the hotel, however, grows stronger with each of the winding stone steps leading upstairs. Each room opens onto one of the tiers of oval balconies, whose pinnacle is capped with a glass skylight. This is the best and most prestigious hotel in town, even though it contains only 16 rooms. The Musil family sometimes refer guests to their other two well-maintained hotels a short walk away (see below).

The bedrooms are outfitted in an appealingly Austrian style, incorporating periods ranging from formal baroque to Biedermeier to farmer's baroque. Each contains a mini-bar, TV with a hookup to the "Skychannel" network of BBC news, and phone. Even the fuseboxes of this unusual hotel are concealed behind polychrome baroque statues. Room number 8, my favorite, contains an ornate four-poster bed and parquet floors. With breakfast included, per person rates range from between 850 AS ($45.22) and 950 AS ($50.54) in a double and from 1,140 AS ($60.65) to 1,300 AS ($69.16) in a single. The in-house restaurant, Musil-Stuben, is covered separately in the where to dine section.

Hotel Moser Verdino, 2 Domgasse (tel. 57878). The jutting tower of its elaborate pink and white facade was built in 1890 in a rich design of ornate cornices and trim. An insurance company occupies its top two floors, but the others are devoted to 78 well-scrubbed hotel rooms. Their furnishings vary widely, mingling a handful of modern pieces with groupings of antiques which the owners have collected throughout Austria. Each accommodation contains a tiled and renovated bathroom, TV with BBC "skysatellite" news, and a mini-bar. A buffet breakfast is included in prices ranging from between 780 AS ($41.50) and 1,150 AS ($61.18) in a single and between 500 AS ($26.60) and 750 AS ($39.90) per person in a double. The most popular café in town, the Café Moser Verdino, is near the oak-trimmed reception lobby.

Hotel Porcia, 13 Neuer Platz (tel. 51-15-90). Its yellow and white baroque facade is one of the highlights of the most memorable square in town. Visitors enter a street-level vestibule sheathed with reddish marble, then take an elevator to the second-floor reception area. There, Victorian armchairs mingle with Nubian lampbearers reflected in the arabesques of Moorish-style mirrors.

Luckily for motorists, a huge underground parking garage is beneath the Neuer Platz. Each of the comfortable bedrooms contains its own private bath, TV, and phone. Singles cost between 635 AS ($33.78) and 950 AS ($50.54), with doubles renting for between 500 AS ($26.60) and 600 AS ($31.92) per person, with breakfast included. This hotel is owned by those Klagenfurt entrepreneurs, Bernhard and Uta Musil, who manage the two other quality hotels in town just recommended.

Hotel Europapark, 222 Villacher Strasse (tel. 21137), is designed in a low horizontal format that blends pleasingly into the landscaped garden around it. The sunny interior is filled with simple imaginative furniture, with a warmly appealing collection of abstractly patterned fabrics. The Meschnig family, your congenial hosts, charge from 540 AS ($28.73) to 600 AS ($31.92) for a single and 750 AS ($39.90) to 800 AS ($42.56) for a double, with breakfast included.

Hotel Goldener Brunnen, 14 Karfreitstrasse (tel. 57380), on the cathedral square in the heart of the city, is a peach-colored building with an arcaded courtyard filled with burgeoning plants. The management sets café tables there in summer. The comfortable bedrooms rent for 500 AS ($26.60) to 700 AS ($37.24) for a single and 820 AS ($43.62) to 980 AS ($52.14) for a double.

Hotel Sandwirt, Pernhartgasse (tel. 56209). The neoclassical building which contains this historic hotel was originally built in the 1650s as a private house. Each of the Austrian presidents elected since 1945 has stayed here, enjoying the hospitality of Paul Jamek, whose ancestors bought the centrally located structure in 1899. You'll find portraits of those ancestors in the pine-paneled ground-floor stuberl, a few steps from the warmly decorated lobby. A series of wide steps leads to the 55 bedrooms. These vary widely in style, but they are usually high-ceilinged and comfortably old-fashioned. Room 40 is especially spacious, probably as big as four of the other rooms combined. All but a few of the units contain private bath and mini-bar. Depending on the plumbing, singles range from 450 AS ($23.94) to 780 AS ($41.50), while doubles rent for between 720 AS ($38.30) and 1,300 AS ($69.16). Half board is another 200 AS ($10.64) per person daily. The hotel is part of the Best Western reservations system.

Kurhotel Carinthia, 41 8-Mai-Strasse (tel. 511645), is a severely modern hotel with six floors of two-tone concrete facing and big glass windows. The conservatively furnished bedrooms include flowered fabrics and an occasional 19th-century antique. Centrally located, and very quiet, the premises contain a sauna, a hairdresser, a café, and a full range of health and massage facilities. Each of the pleasant bedrooms has a private bath. The charges are from 600 AS ($31.92) to 960 AS ($51.07) in a single and from 750 AS ($39.90) to 1,300 AS ($69.16) in a double.

Hotel Garni Blumenstöckl, 11 Oktoberstrasse (tel. 57793), is a very old hotel whose best feature might be the arcaded central courtyard. There you can sip drinks or coffee and admire the ornate wrought-iron balconies supported by the chiseled stone columns. Centrally located, the hotel offers peaceful and calm rooms, each of which has a private bath and shower. Per-person prices are around 400 AS ($21.28), with breakfast included. The hotel is closed during part of September and October.

Hotel Wörthersee, 338 Villacher Strasse (tel. 21-1-58). Set across the road from the lake, a few miles west of the center of town, this sprawling hotel looks like a cross between an Edwardian villa and a Teutonic castle. Its core was built by an Austrian nobleman as his lakeside house in 1840, then greatly enlarged in the ornate and timbered style of the day in 1892. A tunnel beneath the road leads to the hotel's grass-covered swimming area and a lakeside walkway stretching for several miles. The hotel is frankly at its best in summer when lakeside breezes ventilate the balconied rooms. Each of the wood-trimmed bedrooms contains a radio, alarm, phone, and private bath, and many also have a mini-bar and balcony. Depending on the season, the accommodation, and the exposure, singles range between 630 AS ($33.52) and 700 AS ($37.24), with doubles costing between 540 AS ($28.73) and 610 AS ($32.45) per person. These tariffs include half board.

Hildtraud Strohschein is the handsome owner and chef, who prepares a cuisine widely sought after in the area. His elegant repertoire includes such specialties as cream of broccoli soup with quail eggs, crayfish cream soup, home-made pâté de foie gras, salads of smoked venison with marinated wild mushrooms, rack of baby lamb cooked in a shell of sea salt and egg yolks, and a white and dark chocolate mousse with a cocoa cream sauce. À la carte meals range in price from 110 AS ($5.85) to 375 AS ($19.95).

WHERE TO DINE: Rôtisserie Ascot, 9 Kramergasse (tel. 57171), is one of the best restaurants in the entire province. You'll find this elegant dining establishment in a pedestrians-only zone near the center of town, housed in a sienna-colored building and entered via a covered passageway. The restaurant is on the second floor. The French-oriented menu includes such specialties as snail soup, fish soup, lamb consommé with truffled dumplings, entrecôte with fresh cabbage, fresh salmon, blini with salmon caviar, and succulent calves' liver with white pepper sauce. Lamb dishes are also a specialty, and they're most often prepared à la Provençale with plenty of herbs. Dessert might be a kiwi sherbet or a choice of more filling and richer concoctions. Meals range from 180 AS ($9.58) to 380 AS ($20.22). It's closed on Sunday and four weeks in June.

Musil Stuben, Hotel Musil, 14 Oktoberstrasse (tel. 511660). Within its two intimately proportioned rooms, some of the most intensive restorations in town have reverted the decor to its 17th-century origins. One wall contains plaster casts of each of the building's owners, going back to 1660. Other accessories include hunting trophies and photocopies of historical documents, including bills of sale, affecting the hotel. If you decide to dine here, be sure to request a table in the stuben, as it is more charming. Remember to reserve a table. The entrepreneurial owners have translated the regional menu into English. You can begin with Westphalian ham with cumberland sauce, or else gulasch soup, following with three kinds of veal scallops, four kinds of filet steak, sole, trout, or game dishes. A serve-yourself salad bar offers arrays of seasonally adjusted produce. Full meals cost from 325 AS ($17.29).

Weinstube Kanzian, 2 Kardinalplatz (tel. 512283) attracts a collection of amiable citizens who gather near the potted palms, chattering at tables separated from one another by screens. Specialties include Wiener schnitzels that are so big they hang over the edge of the plate, and an array of juicy meats with french fries. Your first course could be one of several kinds of soup, while the meal might not be complete without a piece of homemade torte for dessert. There's a wide selection of beer and wine as well. À la carte meals cost from 150 AS ($7.98) to 225 AS ($11.97) and set menus from 65 AS ($3.46) to 175 AS ($9.31).

Knödelstube, 11 Villacher Strasse (tel. 511774), is a likeable weinstube in the center of town. The ambience is that of an inner-city heurige, while the food is solidly wholesome and traditional. Of the many recipes on the menu, the most popular are the noodles, which are prepared with meats, cheeses, vegetables (such as sauerkraut), or as the base of several kinds of soup. Dessert might be apple-flavored noodles with cider sauce (which is appropriate to the name of the restaurant, "The Noodle Room"). À la carte meals range from 65 AS ($3.46) to 180 AS ($9.58).

Wiery, 106 Tessendorfer Strasse (tel. 43239), is a popular restaurant accommodating all kinds of local citizens, who appreciate the rich beer and savory food. Dishes include roast pork in a pungent sauce, soups, salads, and tortes. Full meals cost from 80 AS ($4.26) to 230 AS ($12.24). It's closed in October and every Saturday.

Restaurant Gourmet, 10 Villacher Strasse (tel. 51-20-59). Photographs from the great days of Hollywood fill the large windows, and your fellow diners are likely to be local university students. The entrance lies off a busy boulevard. You can sit at the corner bar near the door or venture toward one of the tiny tables where counterculture "gourmets" enjoy vegetarian specialties, wine, and beer. Main dishes are likely to include potato puffs with vegetables and salads, rice platters with salad, yogurt, and fruit, nine different yogurt-based dishes, banana curry rice, or polenta with vegetables. A dish named after the Rothschilds is concocted from mushrooms, tofu, corn, and mixed grains. Wiener schnitzels are also offered to diehard meat-eaters. Fixed-price meals begin at 55 AS ($2.93), with à la carte dinners costing from 100 AS ($5.32). The establishment is open only at night between 8 and 10 seven days a week.

Bierjokl Pri Joklnu, 21 10-Oktober-Strasse (tel. 51-45-61). You'll find everyone from Yugoslav students to Franz-Joseph look-alikes enjoying the original graphics covering the walls, as well as the beer, wine, and special teas. Among the latter, these brews include one scented with mango, another flavored with cabbage, and a caffeine-loaded variety known as "Gunpowder Temple of Heaven." The location of the café is a short walk from the center, lying on a street running into Neuer Platz. If you're hungry for light and flavorful dishes, you can sample a four-cheese tortellini, spaghetti with tomato sauce, lamb cutlets, ratatouille, and a selection of soups, including borscht. The menu is written in German and Serbian, with meals costing from 100 AS ($5.32). The establishment is open from 7 a.m. to midnight every day except Sunday. (On Friday and Saturday, it closes at 2 a.m.) Sunday hours are between 5 p.m. and midnight.

THE CAFÉ LIFE: The **Café Moser Verdino,** Hotel Moser Verdino, 2 Domgasse (tel. 83434). Other cafés in town might be older and more historic, but there's no question that this is the most popular and lighthearted gathering place. It seems to be constantly crowded with clients of all ages. In a decor ringed with Austrian marble, brass trim, and plush upholstery, you can gaze at rows of lithographs by artist Ernst Fuchs. Snacks, light meals, elegant pastries, wine by the glass, and beer are served seven days a week between 6:30 a.m. and midnight.

Café Musil, 10 Oktoberstrasse (tel. 511660), inside the well-known hotel of the same name, is the best café in town. Patterned after a Viennese coffeehouse, the establishment serves a filling breakfast and an array of tortes and pastries which usually come fresh from the oven. Coffee and pastries cost 18 AS (96¢) to 30 AS ($1.60).

A SHOPPING NOTE: **Kärntner Heimatwerk,** 2 Herrengasse (tel. 55575), housed on the street level of a pink-and-white baroque building in the center of town, offers the best collection in Klagenfurt of locally made handcrafts. You'll find a selection of embroideries, ceramics, wrought iron, glassware, and textiles sold by the meter.

EXCURSIONS FROM KLAGENFURT: St. **Veit an der Glan** was the capital of Carinthia from 1170 until yielding the honor to Klagenfurt in 1518, the dukes of Carinthia holding power when the province was an imperial duchy before the Habsburg takeover. The town was surrounded by high walls in the 15th century.

In the rectangular Hauptplatz (main square) at the center of town is a Trinity Column, dating from 1715, erected to mark the town's deliverance from the plague. Also on this square is the fountain called Schüsselbrunnen. The bottom part of this fountain is believed to have been excavated at the old Roman city of Virunum. A bronze statue crowning the fountain is a depiction of a miner from the 16th century, which St. Veit has adopted as its symbol.

The Rathaus (town hall) has a baroque exterior, but the building is from 1468. It has a lovely arcaded courtyard. Guided tours are conducted through the great hall of the Rathaus from 8 a.m. to noon and from 1 to 4 p.m., except Wednesday afternoon. It's also closed Saturday and Sunday from November to April.

The pfarrkirche (parish church) is Romanesque with a Gothic choir. A circular *karner* (charnel house) is nearby. The baronial castle here served as an arsenal in the 16th century but has now been turned into a regional museum displaying artifacts of the area.

St. Veit an der Glan stands at the center of the most castle-rich section of Austria, with more than a dozen of the fortress complexes lying within a 6½-mile radius of St. Veit.

The best known and most visited is **Hochosterwitz Castle,** (tel. 2020), about six miles to the east of St. Veit, first mentioned in documents of 860. In 1209 the ruling Spanheims made the Osterwitz family hereditary royal cupbearers, owners and occupants of Hochosterwitz as a fiefdom. When the last of that line was a victim of a Turkish invasion, the castle reverted to Emperor Frederick III and was subsequently passed by him to the governor of the area, Chrishof Khevenhüller. In 1570 Baron George Khevenhüller, also the governor, purchased the citadel and fortified it against the Turks, providing it with an armory and adding the gates, a task completed in 1586. Since that time the castle has been the property of the Khevenhüller family, left to them by Baron George, as shown on a marble plate in the yard dated 1576.

The castle, standing in a spectacular spot on a lonely, isolated hilltop 530 feet above the valley, gives an eagle's-eye view of the area around. It's considered the most striking castle in the country. To reach it, you go up a 16th-century approach ramp and through a total of 14 fortified gates. You can visit a number of rooms that have been opened to the public by the Khevenhüller family to show off the armor collection. In the private rooms you can also see a portrait gallery of the ancestors of the present owners.

Visits are possible from Easter until the end of September from 9 a.m. to 6 p.m. for an admission of 35 AS ($1.86). There's a regional-style café and restaurant in the inner courtyard open to the public.

You can also strike out from St. Veit heading south again on the main road back to Klagenfurt. If you turn left after four miles and travel east, you'll reach the Ausgragungen, or **excavations at Magdalensberg,** at a distance of about nine miles from St. Veit. Magdalensberg was a Celto-Roman settlement site and is considered the oldest Roman habitation north of the Alps. It is known that the Romans built a town here when they came this way to trade in the final century before the birth of Christ. In 1502 a farmer made the first discovery of a settlement here when he found a bronze statue, now called the *Magdalensberg Youth* (on display in Vienna).

However, it was not until the late 19th century that excavation work began. Even then collectors were mainly interested in discovering valuable Roman art objects. Serious archeologists began to work the site during the Allied occupation of Austria. As you explore the ruins, you can see the foundations of a temple as well as public baths and some mosaics. Tours lasting about 1½ hours are conducted through the site May to October from 8 a.m. to dusk, costing 20 AS ($1.06).

A celebrated pilgrimage, known as the "Four Hills Pilgrimage," starts from here every April. Complete with burning torches, the pilgrims race over four hills, and the run must be completed within 24 hours. This event is pagan in origin.

At the summit of the mountain the Austrians have erected a pilgrimage shrine honoring two saints: Mary Magdalene and Helen. From it a beautiful panoramic view of the encircling mountain range, including the Klagenfurt basin, unfolds before you.

Returning once more to St. Veit, you can head northeast along Route 83, which becomes the E7. When you reach the junction with 93, turn west along the upper Gurk Valley road, passing through the hamlet of **Strassburg,** which was a walled town in the Middle Ages. Here there is a pfarrkirche (parish church) in the Gothic style, which you might want to visit if you have time. The Heilig-Geist-Spital Church, dating from the 13th century, has some lovely frescoes. Dominating the village is a castle built in 1147 but much changed over the centuries. Once this was the headquarters of the powerful prince-bishops of Gurk. It has been turned into a Heimatmuseum (local museum).

The major goal of every pilgrim, however, lies two miles to the west—the **Cathedral of Gurk,** principal feature of the little market town in which it stands. From 1072 until 1787 this was the see of a bishop. The dom (cathedral) is a three-sided basilica erected from the mid-12th century to the beginning of the 13th, considered one of the most splendid examples of Romanesque ecclesiastical architecture in the country. A set of towers with onion-shape domes rises nearly 140 feet.

The cathedral is rich in artwork, including the Samson doorway, an excellent example of Romanesque sculpture dating from 1180; some 16th-century carved panels which tell the story of St. Emma, an 11th-century countess who was canonized in 1938; the main 17th-century altar with dozens of statues; and a 1740 baroque pulpit. In the bishop's chapel you can see Romanesque murals which, other than the main altar, are the most important art objects in the cathedral.

The dom can be visited from the first of April until the first of November from 7:30 a.m. to noon and 1 to 5 p.m. On Saturday and Sunday it opens for visits at 11 a.m. In the off-season it's open from 7:30 a.m. to noon and 1 to 4:40 p.m., opening at 10 a.m. on Saturday and Sunday.

After visiting the Cathedral of Gurk, you can take the same road going east and back through Strassburg. Back on the E7, and depending on your time and interest, you can either turn north to visit the town of **Friesach** or else go south again, passing through St. Veit en route to Klagenfurt.

If you opt for the Friesach detour, you'll find an interesting old town worth exploring. Friesach may have been your gateway to Carinthia if you came here from Vienna. You enter Friesach after going through Styria. This is an ancient town, whose first mention in historic annals occurred in the mid-ninth century. It was once a property of the prince-archbishops of Salzburg, who held onto it until the beginning of the 19th century. Lying in the broad Valley of Metnitz, this was once a major stopover for traders between Venice and the capital of Austria.

Some of medieval Friesach survives, including part of the town walls which date from the early 12th century. In one section of town you can see the remains of a moat. The Romanesque Stadtpfarrkirche (town parish church) building, noted for its stained glass in the choir, was constructed in the 13th century. The town has a number of other interesting buildings, including a Dominican monastery from 1673, built on the site of a much older structure and containing a 14th-century church. In summer, open-air plays are performed at the monastery. You can also visit the 13th-century Heiligblutkirche (Church of the Holy Blood) south of the Hauptplatz, the main square of the town.

West of Friesach, a mile-long road or footpath takes you to the hill, **Petersberg,** on which is the Church of St. Peter, dating from the 10th century. Here you can visit a watchtower to see 12th-century frescoes. You can also see the ruins of a castle that belonged to those prince-archbishops of Salzburg. North of the town on another hill is a second castle, partially reconstructed but still much in ruins. Standing on Geiersberg, this schloss is from the 12th century.

I have no accommodations to recommend in Friesach, but you can travel up the Valley of the Melnitz some 24 miles to the mountain summer resort and winter ski area of **Flattnitz** (4,560 feet). It has a circular church in the Gothic style, dating from 1330, built on the site of an earlier Romanesque house of worship.

Flattnitz has some fine hotels with good rooms and excellent food, everything at moderate cost.

The Flattnitz area code is 04265.

Food and Lodging at Flattnitz

Hotel Eisenhut (tel. 32119) is a sprawling chalet set at the base of a forested hillside. On the premises are a small indoor pool, a sauna, a bar, and a friendly staff directed by the Rothenpieler family. The simple bedrooms rent for 300 AS ($15.96) to 450 AS ($23.94) for a single and 300 AS ($15.69) to 425 AS ($22.61) per person in a double. These tariffs include full board. The hotel is open from December to March and June to September.

Alpenhotel Ladinig (tel. 316) is a generously sized country baroque hotel next to a 12th-century church in an isolated alpine meadow. The renovated interior contains wide hallways with massively handcrafted stairwells and a scattering of sturdy furniture and paneled walls and ceilings. The Ladinig family, who acquired this building from the diocese in 1917, charge from 350 AS ($18.62) to 400 AS ($21.28) per person, depending on the room assignment and the plumbing, with full board included.

A Side Trip to Maria Saal

In the immediate vicinity of Klagenfurt you can visit the pilgrimage church of **Maria Saal,** standing on a hill overlooking the Zollfeld plain, some 6½ miles north of the provincial capital near what was once the Roman city of Virunum, capital of Noricum province.

Maria Saal is a major pilgrimage church of the province. A house of worship was first built here by Bishop Modestus around the mid-8th century. The present church, with its twin towers made of volcanic stone dominating the valley, dates from the early part of the 15th century, when a defensive wall was constructed to ward off attacks from the east. In the latter part of that century the Magyars had a try at taking the fortress-church but were not able to conquer it, nor were the Turks in later years.

One of the church's most outstanding features is a "lantern of the dead" in the late Gothic style at the south doorway. There are some marble Gothic tombstones on the church grounds. See also the *karner* (charnel house), which is octagonal in shape and Romanesque in style, with two tiers of galleries. The church has many objets d'art, but it is the 1425 image of the Virgin inside that has made it the subject of pilgrimage.

An interesting excursion to take from Maria Saal is to the **Herzogstuhl,** or Carinthian ducal throne, one mile to the north. A double throne on this ancient site was constructed from Roman stones found at Virunum. The dukes of Carinthia used it as a location from which to grant fiefs in medieval days.

2. Lake Wörther

The biggest alpine lake in the province is Wörther See, or Lake Wörther, ten miles long, lying to the west of Klagenfurt and linked to the city by a man-made channel, mentioned above. In summer it's a mecca for devotees of water sports. In spite of its being an alpine lake, the waters of Wörther See are amazingly warm, its temperature often going above 80° Fahrenheit in midsummer. Beginning in May, Austrians go swimming here, a most unlikely occurrence in most other alpine lakes of other provinces.

The little villages around Wörther See are flourishing summer resorts, especially such centers as Maria Wörth and Velden. Leaving Klagenfurt, we'll go first along the northern perimeter of Lake Wörther, stopping off in the little village of—

KRUMPENDORF: This is just a small stopover along the road, but it contains some moderately priced hotels serving good food. It's also well equipped for water sports. A city bus from Klagenfurt will deliver you to Krumpendorf. This safe, pleasant resort does a thriving family business. Its hotels are spread out, vying for choice spots along the Wörther See.

Krumpendorf's area code is 04229.

Food and Lodging

Seehotel Koch (tel. 3674) is one of the most appealing hotels on the lake. In a small park area, its central building contains a rustically paneled weinstube originally built in 1496. A newer building, constructed in 1972, accommodates the overflow from the older section. The public rooms are tastefully decorated with lots of hewn wood, sunny colors, and well-upholstered furniture. Facilities include a lakeside pier, a beachside bar, a hotel bar, a breakfast terrace, a swimming pool, tennis courts, and a mini-golf course. The sunny bedrooms, each of which has a private bath, rent for 250 AS ($13.30) to 300 AS ($15.96) per person, with breakfast included.

Strandhotel Habich (tel. 607), set in a park-like garden at the edge of the lake, is administered by members of the Habich family. The exterior looks like a well-appointed private house, and the homey atmosphere inside contributes to that feeling. On the premises are five outdoor tennis courts, a lakeside swimming area with piers for boating, a covered swimming pool, a flowered breakfast terrace, a children's play area, and a rustically paneled interior with woodsy appeal. Per-person rates, with full board included, range from 550 AS ($29.26) to 615 AS ($32.72), depending on the season and the room assignment. The hotel is open from the first of May until the middle of October.

Ganymed, 1 Halleggerstrasse (tel. 8631). The recipes and cuisine of this excellent restaurant are the product of the hard work of head chef Ernst Sander. Your meal might include salmon in a mustard sauce, roast breast of pheasant with truffle juice, filet of beef in a mushroom cream sauce, roast breast of pheasant with truffle juice, filet of beef in a mushroom cream sauce with green spätzle, and many more specialties which change with the availability of ingredients. The nougat terrine with liqueur and fresh fruit is worth the extra calories. A gourmet fixed-price extravaganza is available at 500 AS ($26.60), while à la carte meals cost between 170 AS ($9.04) and 400 AS ($21.28).

PÖRTSCHACH: Known for its promenade along the lakeside, Pörtschach, where many lavish villas have been constructed, is the major resort along the north shore of Lake Wörther and one of the premier resorts in Carinthia. A section of the town juts out on a tiny peninsula, and in summer the promenade is a blaze of flowerbeds. Pörtschach is a sports-oriented resort, with waterskiing, sailing, riding, and golf available.

To the southwest of the resort stands Leonstein Schloss, and in the surrounding area you can take many nature walks or go on scenic drives.

The area code for Portschach is 04272.

Food and Lodging

Hotel Schloss Leonstein (tel. 2816). A century ago Johannes Brahms composed one of his violin concertos here. What you'll see today is a 14th-century, once-fortified castle whose public rooms are tastefully filled with well-chosen furniture. Throughout the establishment are wrought-iron accents, old terracotta tiles, stone detailing, and vaulted ceilings. On the premises are tennis courts, massage and beauty facilities, an assortment of water sports, and cozily elegant bedrooms, some of them duplexes. Prices for a room and full board are from 670 AS ($35.64) to 900 AS ($47.88) in a single, from 620 AS ($32.98) to 1,080 AS ($57.46) per person in a double.

The restaurant offers a candlelit ambience which many Austrians travel a long way to find. Either served in the courtyard or inside, the food is consistently good, including filet of trout, Valencian fish soup, veal cutlet with cream sauce, and zander filet. The imaginative salads complement the homemade desserts, which are often accompanied by live music. Full meals range from 190 AS ($10.11) to 380 AS ($20.22). Reservations are suggested.

Hotel Schloss Seefels (tel. 2377) is a lakeside collection of elegantly ornate buildings that curve along the shoreline just behind a screen of trees. On the premises are quays sheltering a small flotilla of motorboats, as well as facilities for tennis (four outdoor courts), swimming (both indoor and outdoor pools whose waters interconnect), and fitness. The elegant and cozy bedrooms are freshly outfitted with decorator colors, discreetly flowered fabrics, and well-polished antiques. My favorite of the luxurious sitting rooms contains a massively ornate ceramic stove with laurel garlands, an ornate chandelier, and comfortable chairs upholstered in light-colored fabrics.

You'll find dozens of sporting locales, including a sauna with a built-in TV, as well as a handful of bars and an à la carte restaurant where an unusual dessert might be a pistachio parfait. Full meals range from 285 AS ($15.16) to 500 AS ($26.60). Room prices go from 790 AS ($42.03) to 1,420 AS ($75.54) for a single and from 645 AS ($34.31) to 1,650 AS ($87.78) per person for a double, with half board included. Prices vary widely with the season and the accommodation.

Parkhotel (tel. 2621)is a modern concrete-and-glass cube jutting up from a peninsula extending into the lake. The hotel is surrounded with a large tree-dotted park, which makes the area quiet and peaceful. The spacious public rooms are streamlined of any excess flamboyance, yet maintain a kind of restrained contemporary dignity, especially with their high ceilings and big windows. Facilities include a supervised kindergarten, a private beach with an outdoor pool for children, a host of water sports, an indoor swimming pool, and a range of massage and beauty facilities. Open from May until September, the hotel charges 700 AS ($37.24) to 1,600 AS ($85.12) per person, with half board included. Prices depend on the accommodation.

Seehotel Werzer-Astoria (tel. 2231) is a resort hotel scattering into several buildings of varying ages. One of the most unusual is the 19th-century bathhouse, which extends into the lake, crowned with a latticed tower. On a peninsula jutting out into the lake, the hotel offers big lawns, a private beach, sauna and massage facilities, a host of boat-oriented water sports, and eight outdoor tennis courts. On the premises are spacious public rooms, with big windows and lots of sunlight. These include a wine tavern, a lakeview restaurant, and a terrace with waiter service. Management plays host at Carinthian buffets and dinner dances. With full board included, prices range from 920 AS ($48.94) to 1,050 AS ($55.86) per person in a single or double.

Hotel Rainer (tel. 2300) is scattered among four houses set at the edge of the lake. The older buildings have lots of architectural embellishments including towers, gables, and porches, from the 19th century. Set on a big, well-maintained lawn, the houses look out over the hotel piers and the private beaches. On the premises are two outdoor tennis courts, water sports facilities (often with instruction), and a range of accommodating public rooms. Per-person rates range from 440 AS ($23.41) to 1,600 AS ($85.12) per day, with half board included. The hotel is closed from mid-October until the end of April.

You'll walk through a dramatic black entryway before reaching the Lucullus restaurant, which might be the main reason for staying here. The walls are ornamented with dozens of such elegant knickknacks as antique keys and hand-hammered pieces of ironwork. Your meal might include salmon, mussel soup, fresh shrimp, and kiwi sherbet. Fixed-price meals cost from 455 AS ($24.21). The Lucullus is closed on Sunday and Monday. Barbara and Gerhard Rainer are the hard-working owners.

Gasthof Joainig, 4 Kochwirtplatz (tel. 2319), is a graceful country house with a hipped and gabled roof, louvered wooden shutters, and masses of summertime flowers in flowerboxes. On the premises is a big sun terrace, while the interior contains a pleasant collection of wooden furniture and a large bar/café/pastry shop. The smallish bedrooms are trimmed with wood and are comfortable. Per-person rates range from 390 AS ($20.75) to 500 AS ($26.60), based on double occupancy, with full board included. Singles cost another 35 AS ($1.86) per day.

La Bohème (tel. 3191) is a popular and elegant restaurant with a Paris-inspired decor where specialties include seafish soup, braised stuffed mushrooms, filet steak La Bohème in a delicate cabbage and mushroom sauce, and an array of desserts such as raspberry or lemon sorbets. À la carte meals range from 240 AS ($12.77) to 480 AS ($25.54). Reservations are suggested.

VELDEN: Considered the most sophisticated resort in Carinthia, at the western end of the Wörther See, Velden is called the heart of the Austrian Riviera. The resort has many beautiful parks sweeping down to the lakeside, and from most of the hotel bedrooms you'll have views of the sparkling blue lake with the peaks of Karawanken in the background, marking the Yugoslav and Italian borders.

Naturally, the big attraction here is water sports, ranging from bathing in the warm alpine lake to waterskiing and surfing. Instruction is available in water activities. The long swimming season begins the first of May and continues until the end of October. You can also play golf at a course 2¼ miles from Velden on the south bank of the lake, and many of the resort hotels have tennis courts.

Most guests spend their days bathing in the lake and later enjoy dancing. Five o'clock tea dances are popular, and you can also trip the light fantastic to the music of orchestras on lake terraces. Summer festivals are often staged in Velden, and balls and beauty contests keep the patrons of the resort amused. Also, this is a fine center for motoring, with good roads taking you on many scenic routes.

In addition, Velden has a well-patronized **casino,** with a restaurant and bar. The casino, offering blackjack, baccarat, and roulette, opens at 7 p.m.

The Velden area code is 04274.

Food and Lodging

Parkhotel, Südufer (tel. 22980). You'll find this comfortable hotel uphill from the center of town, commanding an impressive view into the valley below. The renovated interior contains cozy niches to relax in, along with tastefully appointed bedrooms filled with the modern conveniences. Per person rates for full board range from 1,100 AS ($58.52) to 1,900 AS ($101.08).

The heart and soul of the place lie within the well-recommended restaurant which is open to non-residents who make a reservation. A verdant terrace opens through glass doors in warm weather. Chef Hans Senekowitsch concocts a sophisticated array of specialties which change frequently, but might include a mousse of smoked trout with caviar in a champagne-flavored gelatin, river crayfish in a dill-flavored yogurt, a strudel of calves' brains with baby spinach and a mushroom ragoût, cabbage with a truffled cream sauce, and a suprême of freshwater char with tarragon and fresh asparagus. Full meals begin at 150 AS ($7.98) but could go much higher.

Hotel Schloss Velden (tel. 2655) was built as a home for one of the local aristocrats in 1603. The owner, of course, is long dead, but the ornate towers at each of the building's four corners and the neoclassical extension stretching toward the lake are still painted an ochred yellow, much the way he built them originally. A Renaissance archway capped with no fewer than three obelisks flanks the entrance to the gardens, while a long L-shaped extension with steeply pitched roofs sweeps off to one side.

On the premises is a modern annex connected to the main building, built roughly in the same style (although vastly simplified), as well as outdoor tennis courts, a musical bar with live music, an elegant red-walled restaurant, a cozy weinstube, and several terraces, some of them with outdoor bars. Water sports are available at the lakeside. The well-furnished rooms are equipped with modern comforts, while the public rooms are filled with luxurious old furniture and elegant accessories. Prices are from 750 AS ($39.90) to 1,080 AS ($57.46) per person for a bed and full board included. The hotel closes for the winter at the end of September, opening again at the beginning of May.

Hubertus Hof (tel. 2676) is a symmetrically designed, three-story house with a dignified, restrained facade that emphasizes the curved wrought-iron balconies and its gracefully hipped roof. The simple and dignified interior contains comfortable furniture and lots of cozy niches. An equally pleasant second building in the gardens accommodates the overflow from the lakeside house and also contains a café and a big sun terrace. On the premises are a swimming beach, a restaurant, an array of sporting activities, and a small library. Rates in both singles and doubles range from 420 AS ($22.34) to 950 AS ($50.54) per person, with half board included. Prices depend on the season and the plumbing. The Kenney family are your hosts.

Seehotel Europa (tel. 2770) is a white-walled hotel built in a contemporary format in a tree-dotted area at the edge of the lake. Its pier area contains water sports, plus a private bar. The nearby tennis courts are floodlit at night for round-the-clock volleying. On the premises are a dancing bar, a big sun terrace covered by an awning, and a modern dining room with angular chairs. A comfortable annex nearby holds the overflow from the main hotel. Per-person rates, in a single or double, range from 525 AS ($27.93) to 895 AS ($47.61), with half board included. Prices depend on the plumbing and the season.

Hotel Alte Post-Wrann (tel. 2141) is a friendly hotel partially concealed behind well-positioned plantings in the center of town, close to the casino. Its facade is pierced with stone-trimmed arched windows leading into the pleasant bedrooms. A private beach maintained by the hotel is a two-minute walk from the front door. On the premises is a rustic wine tavern called the Reblaus, whose outdoor entrance is marked by massive beams that probably came from a wine press. There's also a paneled restaurant dotted with hunting trophies, a ceramic tile stove, and chandeliers fashioned from deer antlers. Rates range from 460 AS ($24.47) to 650 AS ($34.58) in a single, while doubles cost from 325 AS ($17.29) to 620 AS ($32.98) per person, with half board included. Tennis courts are nearby. Prices depend on the season and the plumbing.

The hotel also has the Wrann restaurant (same phone), in a verdant summertime location in a garden, whose entrance is also marked by those massive beams. Under a canopy of trees you can order schnitzels, curried rice, veal in cream sauce, and a range of traditional Austrian and regional recipes, many of them served with homemade spätzle. Open all year, the restaurant suggests that reservations be made. Full meals range from 150 AS ($7.98) to 300 AS ($15.96).

MARIA WÖRTH: Part of this village, on the southern side of the lake across from Pörtschach, juts out into the Wörther See on a rocky peninsula, providing a good view of the surroundings. From Maria Wörth you can patronize the golf courses in the nearby hamlet of Dellach.

The village's pfarrkirche (parish church) is Gothic with a baroque interior and, to confuse its styles even more, a Romanesque crypt. It's noted for its main altar, dating from the 15th century. The circular *karner* (charnel house) in the yard, with a round tower, was built in 1278. The church is a pilgrimage sanctuary.

Nearby is another noted church, the Rosenkranzkirche, from the 12th century, often referred to as "the winter church." It has some 11th-century Romanesque frescoes of the apostles.

The area code for María Wörth is 04273.

Food and Lodging

Hotel Astoria (tel. 2279) is an attractively designed hotel built in several interconnected sections with a pointed tower jutting upward from the center. It sits at the neck of a peninsula extending into the lake, with its own marina and bathing beach as well as two big piers, one of which is covered with deck chairs. The elegant public rooms have lots of sunny space and a scattering of Oriental rugs. On the premises are an indoor pool, a sauna, a masseur, a garage, a bierstube, and two restaurants. Per-person rates in summer range from 450 AS ($23.94) to 950 AS ($50.54) double occupancy, with singles paying a daily surcharge of 75 AS ($3.99). These prices include half board.

Hotel Wörth (tel. 2276) is a balconied chalet set on a hillside sloping steeply down to the lake. Guests enjoy the sun terrace, the rustically beamed dining and sitting rooms, and the attractively streamlined bedrooms, many of which provide private balconies and a view of the village church a short distance away across the blue waters of a small inlet. The hotel has an attractive beach area and a convenient location in the center. Summer rates range from 620 AS ($32.98) to 810 AS ($43.09) per person. Full board is included in these tariffs. Open May to September.

Strandhotel Harrich (tel. 2228) is a lakeside hotel whose wood-trimmed balconies stretch across a generous expanse of shoreline. The building sits amid a well-planned garden, with an abstractly shaped sun terrace cantilevered above the slope of the hillside. There's also a lakeside grassy area with a scattering of deck chairs. On the premises are an indoor pool, a sauna, a fitness room, and conscientious management. The accommodations include apartments and bungalows. Singles range in price from 750 AS ($39.90) to 820 AS ($43.62), with doubles costing from 680 AS ($36.18) to 730 AS ($38.84) per person, including full board. The hotel is open only from March to October.

3. Lake Ossiacher

For the next journey, we'll head west from Klagenfurt, passing through Moosberg and going on to Feldkirchen. Before long I'll introduce you to Lake Ossiacher (Ossiacher See, in German), third-largest lake in the province, some seven miles long. Its water temperature in summer is only minutely cooler than that of Lake Wörther—a comfortable 79° Fahrenheit.

The lake is ringed with little villages that have been turned into resorts attracting summer visitors, mainly Austrians, who come here to bathe and enjoy water sports.

FELDKIRCHEN: Our first stopover, Feldkirchen, is an old town that was once the property of the Bamberg bishops. At a major crossroads, Feldkirchen grew and prospered from traders passing through the area. (It is not to be confused with Feldkirch in Vorarlberg.)

Segments of the Middle Ages live on in Feldkirchen, especially in its patrician houses and narrow streets. Visit the old quarter to see the Biedermeier facades added in the first part of the 19th century. The village has a pfarrkirche (parish church) in the Romanesque style but with a Gothic choir. If you go inside you'll be rewarded by a look at some frescoes from the 13th century.

In the vicinity of the town are some small lakes worth a visit if time permits.

OSSIACH: This resort on the south side of the lake is small (pop. of 650) but it's still the biggest settlement on the Ossiacher See. It has a Benedictine abbey originally built in the 11th century but reconstructed in the 1500s. The monastery was dissolved a century or so ago. Now special events of the Carinthian Summer Festival take place here. On several occasions Leonard Bernstein has conducted the orchestra.

SATTENDORF: On the north shore of the lake, Sattendorf, both a summer and a winter resort, is well equipped with good hotels to receive guests. In summer you can breathe the pure mountain air and wander across alpine meadows and deep into the forest. There's bathing both in indoor pools and in Lake Ossiacher.

From the lake you can go on several easy excursions, including one on the Kanzelbahn cable car, 10 minutes away, and a 20-minute run by car to either Italy or Yugoslavia (if you have a visa). You can also make day shopping trips to either Klagenfurt, already visited, or Villach (see below).

Food and Lodging

Sonnenhotel Zaubek (tel. 2713) is a contemporary hotel with wide balconies and a flat roof. The interior is filled with wood detailing, heavy ceiling beams, wrought-iron touches, and lots of sports and health facilities. On the premises are a small indoor pool, a sauna, a pleasantly airy restaurant, and a bar with evening dancing. The Zaubek family, your conscientious hosts, charge from 425 AS ($22.61) to 850 AS ($45.22) per person, with half board included. Prices depend on the size of the accommodation and the season.

ANNENHEIM: This little lakeside resort is on the north side of Ossiacher See, near the end of the lake. From here a cable car, the Kanzelbahn, will take you to Kanzelhöhe at 4,880 feet. You will find an observatory tower from which you can view the surrounding country.

4. Villach

In the center of the Carinthian lake district, Villach is the gateway to the south. If you get bored, you can always drive over into Yugoslavia (visa required) or Italy for the day. Or if you're heading south already, this would make a good stopover.

An industrial town, Villach, the second-largest town in Carinthia, lies in a broad basin of the Drau River. There was a settlement here in Roman times, and later Villach was the property of the bishops of Bamberg, a distant see near Nürnberg, Germany, from the 11th century until Maria Theresa acquired it for the Habsburgs.

At the center of the **Aldstadt** is the Hauptplatz (main square) at the north end of which is a bridge over the Drau. On the southern part is a **pfarrkirche** (parish church) dedicated to St. Jacob. It has three aisles and a mixture of styles, with a baroque altar and Gothic choir stalls. Like most towns of its size, Villach has a **Trinity Column** dating from 1739, commemorating deliverance from the plague.

Theophrastus Bombastus von Hohenheim, Swiss-born chemist and physician better known as Paracelsus, lived here as a youth while his father practiced medicine.

From the heart of the old town it's a 2½-mile drive to **Warmbad-Villach,** known for its thermal swimming pools and mineral springs. This spa, on the southern fringe of Villach, whose waters are said to counteract the aging process, is the only such place where visitors can swim at the source of thermal waters.

In the **Schillerpark,** on Peraustrasse in Villach, you can see a large panoramic relief of the province which might be helpful before you set out on a tour.

It is called *Relief von Karnten*. You can see the relief from the first of May to October 31 except Friday, Sunday, and holidays from 10 a.m. to 4:30 p.m. Admission is 5 AS (27¢).

Villach is a good center from which to explore the Carinthian lake district, including the Villacher Alpe, an 11-mile journey via a toll road. There are panoramic views in many directions, the best spots for viewing being marked.

At the end of the road it's possible to travel up to the summit of Dobratsch (7,100 feet), going partway by chair lift and then by foot. This is one of the most celebrated views in Austria. Allow about 2¾ hours for this excursion.

The area code for Villach is 25501; for Warmbad-Villach, 04242.

FOOD AND LODGING: **Romantik Hotel Post** (tel. 26101) was built in 1500, incorporating many of the rich vaulted ceilings that you'll still see today. The facade is a Teutonic fantasy of carved stone detailing, Ionic columns, and intricately patterned wrought iron. Between 1548 and 1629 this was the town palace of one of the richest families in Carinthia. During that period the building hosted an emperor, a king, an archduke, and later an empress (Maria Theresa). Later the nephew of Napoleon I dropped in and signed a registration slip which still belongs to the hotel. On the premises of this historic place are a baronial fireplace, plus an arcaded courtyard shielded from the sun with an ancient collection of chestnut trees, and a host of elegantly furnished bedrooms. Singles rent for 630 AS ($33.52), while doubles go for 345 AS ($18.35) to 490 AS ($26.07) per person, with breakfast included.

The establishment pays special attention to its cuisine, much of which is heavily laced with cheese, butter, and cream, following recipes similar to those used in aristocratic homes 200 years ago. These include tafelspitz, schnitzels (sometimes stuffed with cheese and ham), and recipes made from local venison, including soups, pâtés, and stews. Fixed-price dinners in the vaulted restaurant range 280 AS ($14.90) to 420 AS ($22.34).

Hotel Europa (tel. 26766) is an elegantly detailed corner building in the center of town. The three-story hotel is painted a pale yellow and is accented with white trim and restrained neoclassical detailing. The renovated interior is filled with conservative furniture and pleasing tones of grays, reds, and browns. A Viennese-style coffeehouse is on the premises. Singles range from 515 AS ($27.40) to 610 AS ($32.45), while doubles cost 760 AS ($40.43) to 920 AS ($48.94) including a buffet breakfast.

Ebner, Heiligengeist (tel. 3910). Many of this establishment's residents return year after year for the bucolic relaxation that this large house offers. Outfitted in Carinthian style, the place is a few steps from the many footpaths which wind through the nearby forests. There's a swimming pool and a thermally heated spa on the premises, along with comfortable bedrooms. With full board included, the cost ranges between 430 AS ($22.88) and 565 AS ($30.06) per person. Much of the allure, however, derives from the excellent dining room. Many of the dishes are worth the special trip there, as testified by hundreds of Austrian families on a holiday. They include rack of baby lamb, sweetbreads, several kinds of hearty soup, crisply fresh salads, and temptingly caloric desserts. Fixed-price meals begin at 110 AS ($5.85).

Food and Lodging at Warmbad-Villach

Kurhotel Karawankenhof (tel. 25503) is a large modern hotel with a flat roof and long rows of symmetrical balconies. It maintains a battery of health facilities on the premises, as well as being connected by underground passageway to the spa facilities. These lie just on the other side of the huge outdoor pool, whose waters, heated by underground springs, are warm enough even for wintertime bathing. Set in the midst of a flowering garden, the hotel offers modern comfort to a conservative clientele who appreciate the bar, the open fireplaces, and the in-house restaurant. Rates in singles range from 640 AS ($34.05) to 830 AS ($44.17), while doubles cost from 600 AS ($31.92) to 780 AS ($41.50) per person, with half board included.

Kurhotel Josefinenhof (tel. 25531) is a sprawling contemporary hotel with evenly spaced rows of big windows and metal balconies. A sun terrace stretches toward the well-maintained lawn area, while a comfortably simple collection of public rooms offers warmly tinted resting places. On the premises are an open fireplace, an indoor pool, a bar, several restaurants, and a host of health and beauty regimes, including facilities for hydrotherapy. Singles range from 520 AS ($27.66) to 930 AS ($49.48), while doubles cost 610 AS ($32.45) to 1,050 AS ($55.86) per person, with full board included.

Warmbaderhof (tel. 25501) is a large and elegant hotel closely linked to the town's cure facilities. On the premises is a large heated pool with a ceiling shaped like a continuous barrel vault covered with wood strips and an abstract mural at the far end. The lush gardens are visible from the streamlined balconies leading into the comfortable rooms. An angular outdoor pool connects with the waters of the indoor pool. A wide range of sporting activities, many of them organized, are close at hand, including tennis, horseback riding, and walking tours. The management sometimes has evening dances on the big sun terrace. Two restaurants on the premises serve well-prepared food. Prices range from 820 AS ($43.62) to 1,050 AS ($55.86) in a single and from 600 AS ($31.92) to 1,450 AS ($77.14) per person in a double, with half board included.

LAKE FAAKER: If you're in Villach in summer, you may want to drive over to Lake Faaker (Faaker See, in German), a small body of water that is nonetheless popular with swimmers and devotees of sports such as waterskiing. This is quite a warm lake, with water temperatures in July and August reaching 79° Fahrenheit. Campers like to come here.

The area code for Faak am See is 04254.

If you'd like to stay at the lake, you'll find—

Food and Lodging at Faak am See

Inselhotel (tel. 2145) is a summertime hotel at the edge of the lake. Its attractive facade has evenly spaced rows of recessed balconies, masses of flowers, and oversize windows. The decor inside is tastefully contemporary, with stone-flanked open fireplaces, accents of wrought iron, a simple restaurant serving well-prepared food, and a bar. The hotel is set on an island in the middle of the lake. A motorboat will pick you up at the mainland pier and redeposit you if you want a break on shore. Closed from the end of September until the third week of May, the hotel charges from 730 AS ($38.84) to 1,450 AS ($77.14) per person, according to the season and the plumbing, with full board included.

Strandhotel Fürst (tel. 2115) is a simple and attractive modern hotel at the edge of the water near a sandy beach. A flagstone-covered path stretches past a collection of lawn chairs on its way to the lake. The public rooms are airy, spacious, and filled with comfortable contemporary chairs. Rooms rent for 250 AS ($13.30) to 520 AS ($27.66) per person.

Da Luciano Unteraichwald (tel. 3122) is an Italian restaurant decorated with hanging fish nets and Mediterranean memorabilia vaguely reminiscent of Naples. Menu items include sardines marinated in cabbage and olive oil (guaranteed to appeal to both Austrian and Italian tastes), minestrone, an array of pasta dishes, and a savory veal schnitzel in Madeira sauce. You can also try the grilled lobster, which goes well with the crispy array of salads. Desserts might be marinated in Grand Marnier. Meals range from 125 AS ($6.65) to 650 AS ($34.58) and up. Closed Monday and October, November, and March.

5. Spittal an der Drau

Lying west of Lake Millstater, Spittal, like Friesach in the east, is another "gateway" to Carinthia. It is not to be confused with Spital in Tyrol or Spital am Pyhrn in Upper Austria. This city on the Drau River is one of the leading centers of Upper Carinthia. It's at the foot of the Goldeck, which rises more than 7,000 feet and is reached by cableway.

Spittal an der Drau's area code is 04762.

THE SIGHTS: Spittal is noted for the **Porcia Schloss,** really an Italian palazzo rather than an Austrian castle. It sits next to a park. It was constructed between 1533 and 1597 and is considered the most impressive Italian Renaissance building in the country. Its most striking architectural feature is the courtyard designed in the Italianate style with three-story galleries enclosing three sides.

The **Bezirksheimatmuseum** (regional museum) is on the second floor of the castle. Exhibited here are artifacts of the Drau region, local handcrafts, and regional costumes. It is open mid-May until the end of September from 9 a.m. to 5:30 p.m., charging an admission of 25 AS ($1.33).

In the environs, you can visit Teurnia-Ausgrabungen, the **excavations at Teurnia,** three miles northwest of Spittal at the village of St. Peter im Holz. The village grew up on the site of a Celtic settlement and, later, Romans lived here, as evidenced by excavation of a forum tha was destroyed by the Slavs in the seventh century.

A museum here displays artifacts dug up right before World War I, from the cemetery of a fifth-century church, including mosaics bearing early Christian symbols. The museum is open May to October from 9 a.m. to noon and 1 to 5 p.m. Admission is 15 AS (80¢).

Food and Lodging:

Hotel Ertl (tel. 2048) is designed in a long, three-story format of cream-colored stucco with detailed trim around the windows. The hotel sits almost on the street, although there's a verdant garden with a sun terrace stretching off to the back, as well as a few café tables set up on the side. The dining room inside is attractively set up with pink napery, coffered ceilings, and brass chandeliers, while the warmly tinted bedrooms are cozy and appealing. An outdoor pool and a mini-golf area are on the premises. With full board included, singles go from 440 AS ($23.41) to 530 AS ($28.20) and doubles from 420 AS ($22.34) to 510 AS ($27.13) per person.

Hotel Alte Post (tel. 2217) is a traditionally decorated hotel with a streamlined collection of furniture. In the center of town, the hotel has rooms which are comfortably furnished and spacious. With breakfast included, rates range from 275 AS ($14.63) to 500 AS ($26.60) per person, depending on the season.

6. Lake Millstätter

The second-largest lake in the province, the blue Millstätter See to the east of Spittal is eight miles long, one mile wide, and 460 feet deep. This beautiful lake is set against a backdrop of the forested Seerücken (2,840 feet) to the south and Nockberge to the north. Reflected in the lake are the peaks of the Reisseck and Kreuzeck in the far distance.

MILLSTATT AM SEE: Lying about midway along the northern rim of the lake, Millstatt rivals Seeboden as the principal Lake Millstätter resort.

The average hotel here is open only during the warm months. The highest prices are charged in July and August, when reservations are mandatory at this popular resort. Prices are often reduced in late spring and early autumn, and it's usually easy to find a room at those times. An organ music festival is held here in August.

Millstatt's main sight, other than the lakeside location, is the **Stift** (abbey), founded in 1080 as a Benedictine monastery but taken over by the Jesuits near the end of the 16th century. Part of its buildings has been used as a hotel since 1773—Hotel Lindenhof, once the mansion of the Grand Master of the Knights of St. George.

In the abbey courtyard stands a 1,000-year-old "Judgment" lime tree. The cloister, which has Gothic vaulting and Romanesque arches, is reached from the east side of the court. The abbey contains a fresco of the Last Judgment, considered a masterpiece of Austrian Renaissance art. The abbey church (Stiftskirche) has a Romanesque doorway that is the major architectural attraction of the complex.

The area code for Millstatt am See is 04766.

Food and Lodging

Hotel am See Die Forelle (tel. 2050) is an attractive yellow hotel with a simple facade which includes clean lines and black shutters. The lakeside terrace is sheltered with chestnut trees, while the interior contains bright, light-colored rooms, attractively uncluttered public areas, a bar, and a sunny restaurant. The conservatively furnished bedrooms are filled with tasteful objects and comfortable furniture. On the premises is an outdoor pool plus a big, well-maintained lawn area. The Aniwanter family are the owners of this streamlined hotel. They charge from 650 AS ($34.58) to 1,250 AS ($66.50) per person, with full board included. Open May to October.

Hotel Post (tel. 2108), constructed around 1900, looks much older. Designed like a baroque country villa, it has ochre walls, black shutters, and neoclassical trim around the windows. The interior is a pleasing mixture of Victorian and contemporary furniture. There's an open fireplace plus a restaurant with well-polished knotty-pine paneling and massive chandeliers. The renovated bedrooms are simple and comfortable. New rooms, built in 1985, offer great comfort and have private bathroom, phone, radio, and a balcony facing either south or west. In each of the south-facing rooms, there is a separate recess to sleep one or two children, as well as a stove and a refrigerator. Prices in the Post are 400 AS ($21.28) to 660 AS ($35.11) per person for half board in a double.

The owners of the Post, the Sichrowsky family, also have the **Hotel Postillion,** with a large lawn near the lake which is for the use of guests of both hotels. Rates at the Postillion are from 500 AS ($26.60) to 1,000 AS ($53.20) per person, also for half board in a double room. If you prefer, you can arrange for full board at either of the hotels or simply for bed and breakfast.

Strandhotel Marchetti (tel. 2075) is an elongated yellow-walled hotel with dark shutters and a lakeside position. Flanked by well-trimmed chestnut trees, the establishment has a lakeside terrace sheltered with sun parasols and a collection of simply furnished public rooms bathed in vivid sunlight. A range of sporting activities are within walking distance. The Marchetti family charge from 520 AS ($27.66) to 700 AS ($37.24) per person in a double and from 500 AS ($26.60) to 535 AS ($28.46) in a single. Full board is included in the tariffs. Also on the premises are a small library and an elevator. The hotel is open from December to February and April to October.

Hotel Gasthof Seewirt (tel. 2110) is a modern hotel with recessed balconies, big windows, and an asymmetrical design. The sunny interior is rustically up to date and includes a simple restaurant. Per-person rates, based on double occupancy, range from 580 AS ($30.87) to 640 AS ($34.05), with singles paying a daily surcharge of 50 AS ($2.66). These tariffs include half board.

Pension Silberhof (tel. 2171) is an elegant 19th-century house with dozens of interesting architectural details, including a vertical row of bay windows and half-timbering across the upper floors. The renovated interior is graced with enormous picture windows which offer a view of the nearby village and the lake. Set a short distance above Millstatt, the hotel is managed and directed by the conscientious Maria Silbernagl. The charge, with breakfast, in a room with private bath, is 275 AS ($14.63) per person daily.

SEEBODEN: Many prominent Austrian families have summer villas at this resort on the western side of Millstätter See, using it the way some French families do the Côte d'Azur. Seeboden is quite popular in summer with water sports enthusiasts who enjoy skiing and boating on the lake.

The most popular excursion to take from here is along a narrow road for about six miles to the Hansbaueralm at 5,635 feet. This is the lower station from which a cable car will take you to the Tschiernock mountain (6,850 feet).

The Seeboden area code is 04762.

Food and Lodging

Sporthotel Royal Seehof (tel. 81714) is composed of two modern buildings set in a grassy park at the edge of the lake. A few steps away, guests enjoy access to six outdoor tennis courts, a sandy beach area, a glass-walled indoor pool that looks somewhat like a big greenhouse, and three indoor tennis courts, each with a sliding roof for ventilation on hot days. The simple and well-furnished interior contains a bar and a restaurant. The Santner family are your hosts, charging 1,050 AS ($55.86) to 1,250 AS ($66.50) per person in a double, with singles paying 1,170 AS ($62.24) to 1,400 AS ($74.48). Full board is included in the rates, which vary according to the season and the plumbing. The hotel is open from May to September.

Strandhotel Koller (tel. 81245) is a lakefront hotel constructed in two interconnected sections on a well-maintained lawn. Many of the comfortable rooms have balconies looking over the water, and within view of the old-fashioned cabana and bathing pier. The woodsy interior has plenty of rustic accents, including open fireplaces, comfortable wooden furniture, and a pleasing combination of warm colors. On the premises are a big-windowed restaurant, an indoor pool, a sauna, and a cafe/weinstube. A range of sporting facilities is within walking distance. The hotel is open only from Easter until mid-October. It charges 580 AS ($30.87) to 640 AS ($34.05) per person, with full board included.

Hotel Pension Klein (tel. 81218) is a modern chalet construction with a few regional designs painted across its wood-trimmed, big-windowed facade. Set on a grassy lawn, the hotel charges from 400 AS ($21.28) to 525 AS ($27.93) per person, with half board included. Rooms are clean and comfortable.

RADENTHEIN: You reach this village three miles east of the lake by taking the road to Turracher Höhe (refer to Bad Kleinkirchheim, below). If you stay here you can head west to Lake Millstätter or east to Bad Kleinkirchheim, and you'll enjoy a reasonably priced accommodation at either place.

The area code for Radenthein is 04246.

Hotel Metzgerwirt (tel. 2052) is designed like a concrete cube pierced with modern windows. This pleasant hotel is unpretentiously filled with wood accents, open fireplaces, and home-style decor. On the premises is a rustic restaurant serving well-prepared dishes, along with cozy sunny bedrooms renting for 420 AS ($22.34) to 490 AS ($26.07) per person in a double and 450 AS ($23.94) to 530 AS ($28.20) for a single, with full board included. Prices vary widely with the season and the plumbing.

TREBESING: Going north from Seeboden on the way to Gmünd you find this hamlet, which is off the beaten path but lies in an area of great scenic beauty. It attracts both summer and winter visitors.

Trebesing's area code is 04732.

Hotel Trebesinger Hof (tel. 2350) is a pleasantly designed contemporary chalet set on top of a covered swimming pool whose waters are visible through the plate-glass windows on the ground floor. Sunk into the lawn area in front of the hotel, a reflecting pool contains a roughly hewn sculpture looking vaguely like some pagan emperor's crown magnified to hundreds of times its original size. The Neuschitzer family are the accommodating hosts, keeping their pleasantly rustic public rooms in tip-top condition. On the premises are a sauna, a bar, massage facilities staffed by the owner himself, and a woodsy restaurant serving well-prepared food made from fresh ingredients. Rooms with full board rent for 480 AS ($25.54) to 550 AS ($29.26) per person. Prices depend on the season and the accommodation.

GMÜND: This small town is in the lower region of the Lieser Valley, at the start of the Malta Valley. It's not on the lake but lies northwest of Seeboden on the road to Salzburg, an easy commute to the Millstätter See. Austrians use it as headquarters for exploring the Nock sector of Carinthia, which lies to the southeast of the town and is visited by mountain climbers in summer and skiers in winter.

The **Altstadt** (old town) of Gmünd still has defensive walls pierced by gates erected in the 16th century. Its Old Castle from the 15th century is now mainly in ruins.

A popular excursion from Gmünd is through the **Malta Valley,** taking a toll road beginning to the northwest of the town. This is one of the most enchanting valleys in the country and considered the loveliest in Carinthia. The scenery consists of waterfalls and newly developed artificial lakes along with a nature reserve.

The area code for Gmünd is 04732.

Food and Lodging

Gasthof Kohlmayr, 7 Hauptplatz (tel. 2149), presents a light-brown facade with restrained white trim to the main square of town. The decor inside is conservative and pleasant, with lots of rustic accessories and exposed wood. Charges in a single or double, with half board included, are 350 AS ($18.62) per person per day.

Gasthaus-Pension Alte Mühle (tel. 2257) is a beautifully detailed chalet with elegant balconies and charmingly old-fashioned embellishments standing out in monochromatic low relief. The interior contains lots of rustic accessories and an open fireplace. Open year round, the pleasant hotel offers rooms priced at 245 AS ($13.03) per person, based on double occupancy, with singles paying a daily surcharge of 45 AS ($2.39). All units contain private bath and come with breakfast included.

Pension Platzer, 26 Vorstadt (tel. 2745), is a low-lying hotel set at the edge of a small freshwater lake. A garden with well-maintained roses stretches off to the back, while the interior is pleasantly decorated with lots of exposed wood, coffered ceilings, and conservative furniture. The pleasant bedrooms range from 280 AS ($14.90) to 310 AS ($16.49) per person, based on double occupancy, with full board included. Singles pay a daily surcharge of 35 AS ($1.86).

7. Bad Kleinkirchheim

A seven-mile drive to the east of Lake Millstätter you'll come upon Bad Kleinkirchheim, once just a popular summer spa but now a thriving winter ski area as well. Since World War II this resort in the Carinthian Nock mountains has become a mecca for skiers of the not-too-demanding variety. It's about fourth in popularity among Austrian ski resorts, with Tyrol, Land Salzburg, and Vorarlberg centers in the lead. Its winter season is also shorter than those of loftier alpine areas.

Cross-country skiing and winter hiking are popular here, with long runs and even gradients. The Kaiserburg chair lift takes skiers to the upper station at 6,250 feet. The satellite resort of St. Oswald, 2½ miles north of the spa, has some good hotels.

Visit the hot springs of Bad Kleinkirchheim, Katharinenquelle, and the pilgrimage church of St. Katharina, which is known for its carvings.

The area code for Bad Kleinkircheim is 04240.

FOOD AND LODGING: The **Kurhotel Ronacher** (tel. 282), built in 1908 as an elegant way station for clients who came for the cure at the adjacent spa, offers a thermal indoor swimming pool, a log-cabin sauna, many physical therapy techniques, a first-class restaurant, and a café. The interior is luxuriously furnished with pine paneling, ceramic stoves, and open fireplaces, along with comfortably rustic furniture. The bar area affords a rendezvous point, while frequent buffets provide a lavish spread of delicacies. Helga and Günther Ronacher do everything they can to provide a restful environment for their guests. A range of both organized and freely scheduled sporting events is available. Rates, with full board included, range from 920 AS ($48.94) to 990 AS ($52.67) per person in a double and from 990 AS ($52.67) to 1,060 AS ($56.39) in a single. Prices vary with the season and the room assignment.

Hotel Römerbad (tel. 8234) is a well-designed chalet with prominent balconies and attractive contrasts of light and dark detailing. The interior reflects its forested hillside location. It has an open fireplace, wrought-iron appointments, lots of exposed wood, a friendly bar, and big panoramic windows looking out over the forest. A range of sporting facilities is within easy walking distance of this pleasant hotel, which is efficiently directed by its owner, Ingrid Putz. Singles rent for 730 AS ($38.84) to 800 AS ($42.56) and doubles for 700 AS ($37.24) to 760 AS ($40.43) per person, these tariffs all including full board. Prices depend on the season and the room assignment.

The dining room here is considered one of the best in town. The cuisine specializes in imaginative recipes based on fresh ingredients, many of which come from the region. A typical meal might include a marinated salad, medallions of venison with green noodles and cabbage, and honeyed dessert parfait with blackberries. Fixed-price or à la carte meals range from 180 AS ($6.38) to 450 AS ($23.94). Restaurant patrons who are not guests of the hotel are welcome if they make reservations.

Hotel St. Oswald (tel. 591) is an imaginatively designed alpine chalet with an unusual roofline. The interior is luxuriously furnished with wooden ceilings, a scattering of open fireplaces, antique pewter, hand-painted antiques, and brass chandeliers. On the premises are a sunny indoor swimming pool, an accommodating bar with a hand-painted wooden ceiling, dozens of intimate nooks, and a full range of indoor and outdoor sporting facilities. The Scheriau family, the attractive owners, along with their children, do everything they can to make a vacation pleasant. They often stage dances with Carinthian music, as well as activities for children, including painting, handcrafts, and short trips. Charges range from 630 AS ($33.52) to 1,050 AS ($55.86) per person, with full board included. Prices depend on the season and the accommodation.

Hotel Pulverer (tel. 288), is a carefully designed collection of several chalet buildings arranged into a hotel and athletic complex near the ski lifts. Guests have a wide choice of elegantly decorated public rooms, some of which have gently vaulted wood ceilings, big windows, plaid carpeting, and ceramic tile stoves (the chimney of one of these rises more than two stories under a cathedral ceiling in the reception area). There's also a scattering of open fireplaces, along with cozy dining nooks, alpine style, with hunting trophies and antique art objects. Elegance and comfort, all with a woodsy rusticity, are trademarks here. On the premises are an indoor pool and a range of health and beauty regimes. There's also access to lots of sporting facilities. Rates range from 880 AS ($46.82) to 1,050 AS ($55.86) for a single and from 800 AS ($42.56) to 960 AS ($51.07) per person in a double, with full board included. Prices vary according to the season and the accommodation.

Hotel Alte Post (tel. 212) is a rambling hotel which makes a gentle curve around a manicured lawn with an outdoor pool set at the far end. Nearby are several outdoor tennis courts, while indoor courts are a few steps away. The interior is rustically filled with heavy beams, stippled plaster, and open fireplaces. The in-house bar is a warmly decorated hideaway, while the dancing bar is a rendezvous point for dozens of vacationers. The facade is a fancifully detailed ensemble of blue and white paint around arched entrances and rounded windows. Singles go from 860 AS ($45.75), while doubles run from 730 AS ($38.84) to 960 AS ($51.07) per person, with full board. Prices vary with the season and the room. Open December to October.

Hotel Kirchheimerhof (tel. 278) is a hillside chalet with recessed latticework balconies and a low-lying extension cantilevered above the sloping lawn. The view from the sun terrace takes in most of the village, while on a sunny day you might see farm animals grazing not far from the foundations. On the premises is an indoor pool, plus a dancing bar with a high ceiling, along with a cozy series of public rooms (some with open fireplaces) outfitted with rustic paneling and plenty of well-chosen accessories. The Hinteregger family charge from 700 AS ($37.24) in a single and from 640 AS ($34.05) to 780 AS ($41.50) per person in a double, with full board included.

Sonnalm (tel. 507) is a pleasant chalet with strong horizontal lines and regionally inspired painted illustrations bordering the outside of the panoramic windows. The sunny interior, which looks out over verdant lawns, has a beamed and paneled interior with lots of carved detailing. An open fireplace is outlined by a rounded travertine arch and capped by an abstractly shaped plaster dome. The emphasis throughout this hospitable place is on comfort. The spacious bedrooms have private balconies. They rent for 570 AS ($30.32) to 640 AS ($34.05) per person on the full board plan. The owners, the Burgstaller family, keep the hotel open from December to October.

NEARBY RESORTS: From Bad Kleinkirchheim you can either stay at or just visit two satellite resorts in the area.

Feld Am See

This tiny resort lies on the shores of Lake Feld (Feldsee, in German), a diminutive lake that's one of the most idyllically situated in Carinthia.

To reach it, drive east from Döbriach, passing through Radenthein (see above). At that village, turn on a secondary road which will take you to Feld am See, where you can enjoy a lakeside holiday or else explore either Brennsee or Afritzersee, two lakes immediately south of Feldsee. The road skirts the shores of both these little lakes. The area is one of the most charming and undiscovered spots in the province.

The Feld am See area code is 04246.

Hotel Lindenhof (tel. 2274) is the attractive establishment belonging to the Nindler family. One of the entrances is below a rectangular plaque set with regional designs in colors of terracotta and white, while another is set into an old-fashioned facade with country baroque detailing around the shuttered windows. The interior is warmly outfitted with high ceilings, tartan-patterned carpeting in autumnal colors, wrought-iron detailing, and lots of cozy comfort. On the premises is a wood-covered bar area illuminated with forgiving light, as well as a restaurant and sauna. Rooms, with half board, rent for 560 AS ($29.79) to 640 AS ($34.05) per person in a double and from 620 AS ($32.98) to 640 AS ($34.05) in a single. Prices vary with the season. Open December to October.

Turracher Höhe

From Bad Kleinkirchheim, take a road northeast to reach this popular spot at an elevation of 5,785 feet, at the pass leading over the Gurktal alpine range into Carinthia. This is sought out as a ski resort in winter and is much visited in summer for its scenic views. You'll be in the vicinity of two lakes, the Schwarzee (black lake) and the Turracher See.

A chair lift will transport you to Kornock (6,560 feet). Mountain climbers are drawn here in summer to scale the peaks in the Nock area. Turracher Höhe is on the border of the province of Styria.

The area code for Turracher Höhe is 04275.

Hotel Hochschober (tel. 8213). Barbara and Peter Leeb set the tone of this lakeside resort, where casual clothes are the order of the day and where the sporting facilities include an indoor pool, a sauna, massage, bowling, indoor shooting, and where activities feature musical programs in the music room and a disco in the basement. Three mountain lakes in the immediate vicinity provide destination points if you want to go walking. Built in 1929, the hotel looks like the ideal kind of place for a country vacation. The interior is rustically paneled, containing woodsy accessories and open fireplaces, along with plenty of comfortable lounge areas, a bar, and a supervised children's play area. The warmly decorated restaurant serves good food priced from 120 AS ($6.38) to 300 AS ($15.96) for a full meal. Charges in the hotel range from 600 AS ($31.92) to 750 AS ($39.90) per person, with full board. The hotel is open from December to April and June to October.

8. Lake Weissen

The fourth-largest lake in Carinthia, Lake Weissen (Weissensee, in German), is also one of the loveliest and least known. On its shores are a few hamlet-size resorts, and more hotels are being built, but tourism is in the infancy stage here. The lake's major resort is Techendorf (see below). Neusach is another small holiday hamlet.

Of the major lakes visited so far, the Weissensee, southwest of Spittal an der Drau (see above) is the highest. It's about seven miles long and rather narrow, about 550 yards across. Its waters are warm in summer more than 75° Fahrenheit.

It's not possible to drive around Lake Weissen. Visitors usually walk to it, although you could get there by boat.

TECHENDORF: As mentioned above, this is the major resort on Lake Weissen, perched on the northwest shore. A bridge spans the lake from here. If you take the bridge you'll find a chair lift to take you up to the Naggler Alm (4,382 feet), which is gaining popularity as a ski area.

Techendorf's area code is 04713.

Food and Lodging

Sporthotel Alpenhof (tel. 2107) is a contemporary chalet with wood-trimmed balconies and low-lying wings stretching off to one side. Built in 1976, with special emphasis on the view available from the panoramic windows, the hotel contains a simplified rusticity, with warm colors and exposed wood detailing. An adjoining building houses massage and health facilities, which you may not have time for because of the many sporting possibilities within easy reach. The Zöhrer family maintain the pleasant bedrooms, charging 510 AS ($27.13) to 900 AS ($47.88) per person in a double and 520 AS ($27.66) to 1,100 AS ($58.52) in a single, with half board included. Prices vary according to the season and the plumbing.

Strandhotel Weissensee (tel. 2219) is a lakeside chalet whose wood-and-stucco facade is accented with green shutters, patterened balconies, and masses of summertime flowers. Set in the midst of a well-maintained garden, the hotel has a pleasant sun terrace, a range of nearby water and land sports, a sauna, a bar, an appealing restaurant with a ceramic tile stove and heavy beams, and elegantly simple bedrooms. These often have decorative arches separating the sleeping from the sitting areas, big windows with balconies, and attractively contemporary furniture. Per-person rates, in a single or double, range from 560 AS ($29.79) to 950 AS ($50.54), with full board included. Prices vary with the season and the room. Open May to October.

Hotel Enzian (tel. 2221) is an imposingly old-fashioned chalet behind a set of stone columns flanking the path to the main street. Designed with weathered balconies and an attractively hipped roof, the hotel contains simple and attractive accommodations outfitted with warm colors and modern comfort. On the premises are an outdoor tennis court, a big lawn leading up to the lake, a rustic bar, and a restaurant serving well-prepared Austrian specialties. Rates range from 550 AS ($29.26) to 620 AS ($32.98) for a single and from 520 AS ($27.66) to 650 AS ($34.58) per person in a double, with half board. Open June to September.

9. The Möll Valley and Mallnitz

Called Mölltal in German, this valley was known in the days of the Romans, with legions passing through it often during their long reign in Carinthia. This is still a much frequented route, as it is now the southern gateway to the Grossglockner Road described in the Land Salzburg section (see Chapter VIII). The valley contains the remains of several castles from the Middle Ages.

The resorts of Heiligenblut and Döllach, described below, lie roughly between Zell am See in Land Salzburg and Lienz, the capital of East Tyrol. Also in this section, I'll take you on a detour north of Obervellach to visit the ski resort of Mallnitz, which lies directly to the south of Badgastein in Land Salzburg, although there's no road to there through the towering alpine ranges.

KOLBNITZ: The first stopover I recommend in the Möll Valley, Kolbnitz, is a sunny hamlet set against a mountain backdrop. To reach it, drive northwest from Spittal. This can be the center for many day excursions, either into the Carinthian lake district or to the Grossglockner area. You can even have your car loaded on the train at Mallnitz to go through the tunnel to Badgastein. But the main reason for stopping here is the hotel recommended below.

The Kolbnitz area code is 04783.

Hotel Marhof (tel. 243) played an important role in the feudal politics of the region when it was built in 1150. The founding fathers of this hotel proudly called themselves "free peasants" (as opposed to the masses of serfs in the region), in exchange for which they paid annual revenues to the ruling aristocrat. Much later, when Franz Joseph tried to bestow a title upon a former owner, Joseph Walter, the "free farmer" proudly refused, saying that he preferred the title of his ancestors.

Today the family seat of all this is a prosperous-looking hip-roofed building with a stucco facade and green-and-white chevron shutters. Transformed into a hotel in 1967, the building has a wood-accented interior, unpretentious furniture, an outdoor pool, and a big lawn area for sunbathing. Heinz Walter, the owner, will welcome you into the cozy dining room, where dishes include tafelspitz, beef soups, and Viennese-style food which, of course, means schnitzels. The cost of a bed and full board is 320 AS ($17.02) to 490 AS ($26.07) per person. The hotel is open from December to March and May to October.

OBERVELLACH: Most of the castles in the Möll Valley are centered around this little village, which also has a late Gothic church known for its 1520 altarpiece by Jan van Scorel, one of the Dutch masters. The artist was a great admirer of Dürer, as evidenced by his works. In the Middle Ages, Obervellach was a gold-mining town.

Among the medieval castles near this village are Oberfalkenstein from the 15th century and Groppenstein from the 12th and 15th centuries.

MALLNITZ: Before you continue your exploration of the Möll Valley, I recommend a detour to Mallnitz, which is both a summer and a winter ski resort. Lying directly north of Obervellach, a five-mile drive up a steep road, this is a great bargain resort at any time of year, the prices being quite reasonable since Mallnitz is neither fashionable nor well known.

At an elevation of 3,900 feet, it's so high up that the mountains around it wear permanent ice caps. In summer hikers go on mountain expeditions from this resort, a cable car taking passengers to Elschesattel (8,600 feet). There are several ski lifts and horse-drawn sleigh rides are popular in winter.

Mallnitz lies at the southern end of the Tauern railroad tunnel. Since you can't drive directly from here to Land Salzburg, why not have your car loaded on the train? Otherwise, if you want to go north to that province you'll have to take a long and circuitous highway route.

The area code for Mallnitz is 04784.

Food and Lodging

Alpenhotel Mallnitz (tel. 262) is an attractive chalet hotel set in the hollow of a rocky valley. The service is relaxed and friendly, thanks almost entirely to the tone set by the Alber-Berlinger family, who do everything they can to be helpful. Built in 1905, the hotel has richly textured paneling, big windows, lots of rustic accessories, and an impressive collection of hunting trophies. Meals in one of the warmly appealing restaurants could include an array of veal or beef dishes, many of them grilled and covered with savory sauces, tasty soups, cold marinated herring, and homemade desserts. The pleasant bedrooms rent for 500 AS ($26.60) to 620 AS ($32.98) for a single and for 460 AS ($24.47) to 600 AS ($31.92) per person in a double, with full board included. Prices vary with the season. Open December to April and June to September.

Hotel 3 Gemsen (tel. 396) is a pleasant chalet building with two floors of shutters, balconies, wood trim, and regionally inspired designs. Just to the left of the front entrance someone has stenciled three deer between the painted dates of both the year of founding and the year of renovation, which are 1758 and 1979 respectively. Inside, the decor is covered with vaulted or beamed ceilings, rustically home-style furnishings, and lots of warm colors. On the premises are an alpine bar, a simple restaurant, and lots of cozy comforts. The Peter Sterz family, the hosts, charge 420 AS ($22.34) per person in a single or double, with half board included. Fly-fishing for trout in a mountain lake and high alpine shooting (chamoix and deer) can be arranged.

WINKLERN: This little resort, 19 miles to the west of our stop in Obervellach, stands at an elevation of 3,100 feet. It's north of Lienz, the capital of East Tyrol, and Iselberg. From here you can enjoy a view of some of the highest mountains in Austria.

Winklern has a **pfarrkirche** (parish church) with a watchtower from the Middle Ages.

The Winklern area code is 04822.

Hotel Defreggerhof (tel. 252) is an attractively embellished four-story house with gables, balconies, and sunflower-colored illustrations around the borders of its windows. The hotel is a convenient starting point for walks through the surrounding hills. On the premises are a heated indoor pool and a sauna. There is easy access to the village's sporting facilities. Rates range from 380 AS ($20.22) to 440 AS ($23.41) per person, based on double occupancy, with singles paying a surcharge of 70 AS ($3.72) per day. Half board is included in these tariffs.

DÖLLACH: A gold- and silver-mining center in the Middle Ages, Döllach is now a small Möll Valley resort, its reasonable prices attracting visitors in both summer and winter. Lying six miles from Heiligenblut, our next destination, Döllach is at a 3,360-foot elevation, set in an area of some beautiful waterfalls.

The **Grosskirchheim Castle** has artifacts from the town's mining days preserved in a regional museum.

The area code for Döllach is 04825.

Food and Lodging

Hotel Schlosswirt (tel. 411), one of my favorite hotels in the region, is a well-proportioned chalet with flowered balconies, weathered siding, and a desirable location at the edge of the forest. The castle is just behind the hotel. All the outdoor sports are available within a few minutes' walk. The interior has a kind of unpretentious elegance that comes mainly from fine woods and careful craftsmanship. The spacious bedrooms have comfortable furniture and lots of horizontal parking. The Sauper family, hotel owners, charge 580 AS ($30.87) to 780 AS ($41.50) per person for half board. Activities provided for guests include tennis, a sauna, swimming in the pool, horseback riding, and fishing.

On the premises are an attractive bar area and one of the best restaurants in the region. Your meal might begin with cream of trout soup and fresh chives, followed by a juicy pork filet stuffed with gorgonzola. Dinners range from 95 AS ($5.05) to 275 AS ($14.63). Reservations are suggested. On Sunday, dinner is served in the 500-year-old castle, where you can also have cocktails and enjoy wine-tasting gatherings.

Hotel Post (tel. 205) is the traditional spot in town, offering lots of rustic detailing and a choice of comfortable rooms. The English-speaking staff is friendly and accommodating, preparing a savory cuisine served in a woodsy dining room. The per-person rate in a single or double is 280 AS ($14.90) to 320 AS ($17.02), with full board included.

HEILIGENBLUT: If you enter the Möll Valley from the north, coming from Zell am See along the Grossglockner Road, this is the first important little resort you'll reach. It lies at the foot of the southern slope of the Grossglockner. Because of its location there's a lot of traffic through here in summer.

The steeple of the 15th-century **Pfarrkirche** (parish church), backgrounded by the lofty mountain, is a much-used subject for illustrations and photographs.

In summer Heiligenblut is the headquarters for a well-known mountain climbing school. In winter skiers take over.

Heiligenblut's area code is 04824.

Food and Lodging

Hotel Glocknerhof (tel. 2244) is built dramatically on a sloping hillside a stone's throw from the beautifully severe lines of the village church. The hotel's exterior walls are covered with weathered balconies. The interior is rustic, warm, cozy, elegant, and alluring, all at the same time. On the premises are a covered swimming pool, with big windows looking out at a sweeping panorama, an inviting bar, a sauna, a sun terrace, a children's playroom, an open fireplace, a dancing bar, and a host of organized activities which include *schuhplatter* evenings, dinner dances, and buffet cookouts.

Prices range from 500 AS ($26.60) to 1,160 AS ($61.71) per person in a double and from 630 AS ($33.52) to 1,090 AS ($57.99) in a single, with half board included. Prices vary according to the season. The most expensive accommodations within this price range are small, tastefully furnished apartments. The overflow from the main hotel is housed in one of three annexes operated by the owners, the Pichler family.

Hotel Post (tel. 2245) is a pleasant chalet with wrap-around balconies. A wide sun terrace offers a sunny resting place. The paneled interior is accented with wrought-iron chandeliers, warmly tinted fabrics, big windows, and alpine colors of red and forest green. On the premises are a bar area with lots of massive timbers and a restaurant serving well-prepared local specialties. Each of the comfortable bedrooms has a private bath, as well as a private balcony, radio, and phone. Doubles range from 520 AS ($27.66) to 540 AS ($28.73) per person, while singles go for 560 AS ($29.79) to 580 AS ($30.87), with full board. The hosts, the Eder family, keep the hotel open from December to September.

Haus Senger (tel. 2243) is a weathered double chalet, with recessed balconies and a covering almost completely fashioned from wood planks. The cozily rustic interior has massively hewn vertical supports, open fireplaces whose plaster chimneys are crafted into abstract shapes, stone detailing, and lots of cozy niches. The comfortable bedrooms rent for 340 AS ($18.09) to 400 AS ($21.28) per person, with half board included. Prices depend on the plumbing and the season.

10. The Gail Valley

A lovely valley running parallel to the Valley of the Drau, the Gailtal, as the German-speaking people call it, lies between the Carnic alpine range and the Gail Valley Alps. A trip here will take you into the deepest southern fringes of Carinthia along the Italian border. You'll find the resorts here to be largely undiscovered, unpretentious, and modestly priced.

HERMAGOR: This is the major town in the Gail Valley, lying to the west of Lake Presseger which gives it some claim to being a summer resort. Its **Pfarrkirche** (parish church) is from the 15th century. In summer Hermagor is popular with hikers and climbers who head for the hills.

The Hermagor area code is 04282.

Food and Lodging

Hotel Wulfenia and **Hotel Sonnenalpe** (tel. 421 and 425) are two sprawling chalets connected to one another by a raised tunnel stretching over the parking area between them. These massive hotels have many facilities, including all the usual sporting equipment, as well as comfortable public rooms outfitted with softly glowing paneling, open fireplaces, stone detailing, panoramic windows, and rustically contemporary furnishings.

On the premises are a full range of health and beauty facilities, as well as an indoor pool, whirlpool, sauna, and Turkish steambath. A bowling alley and outdoor tennis courts are also available. Clients appreciate the bars, disco, restaurants, and the organized entertainment arranged by the vivacious hosts, the Pucher family.

With full board included, prices range from 590 AS ($31.39) to 920 AS ($48.94) per person in a double and from 680 AS ($36.18) to 950 AS ($50.54) in a single. These prices vary with the accommodation and the season.

KOTSCHACH-MAUTHEN: With a name like that for your vacation site, no one will know where you're going if you tell them, but you'll know that this resort is in the upper part of the Gail Valley. *Mauthen* refers to the toll that was once collected here. The town has a 16th-century **Pfarrkirche** (parish church), known as the "cathedral of the valley."

This little resort is at a major road junction through which you go heading south to the Plöcken Pass, with Italy as your ultimate destination. From Kötschach-Mauthen you can go south to the pass for a distance of just under nine miles, but it's a narrow, twisting road with gradients of 14%. I consider it suitable only for skilled alpine drivers who don't mind the numerous hairpin curves. The Italian motorists coming north don't seem to mind!

The area code for Kotschach-Mauthen is 04715.

Food and Lodging

Kürschner Gesundheits-Hotel (tel. 259), painted a pale yellow with white trim, contains an elegant vaulted reception area, comfortable bedrooms, and virtually every kind of massage, acupuncture, and nutritional care available in Austria. On the premises are a big garden with a heated swimming pool, a tennis court, and a friendly management who frequently organize walking tours, garden parties, and group activities. Singles range from 520 AS ($27.66) to 765 AS ($40.70), while doubles go for 480 AS ($25.54) to 785 AS ($41.76) per person, with full board included. Prices vary with the season, the accommodation, and the plumbing.

Kellerwand, at Mauthen (tel. 269), is one of the most elegant restaurants in the region. You'll be greeted by the sounds of classical music as soon as you enter. You'll probably want a drink at the small, well-appointed bar area before you're led to a beautifully set table where fresh flowers, silver candlesticks, and painted porcelain along with fresh bread are de rigueur. Menu items include strips of sautéed calves' liver with leaf spinach, trout dumplings, chicken in burgundy sauce, cream of mushroom soup, and veal in a sherry sauce. If you're interested in a dessert after all that, it could be a vanilla ice cream confection with a Grand Marnier sauce. Closed between mid-October and mid-December, the restaurant requests reservations and charges from 125 AS ($6.65) to 475 AS ($25.27) for full meals.

11. Lake Klopeiner

The waters of Klopeiner, the warmest lake in Carinthia, can reach 82° Fahrenheit in summer. The lake, surrounded by woodlands and shaped like an amphitheater, lies to the south of the market town of Völkermarkt. Lake Klopeiner is fairly small—only 1⅛ miles long and less than half a mile wide at its broadest point. In summer it's thronged with fun-loving Austrians. The government does not permit motor-powered craft on the lake, endeavoring to keep its sky-blue waters free of pollution. The resorts that ring the lake are part of the commune of St. Kanzian.

St. Kanzian's area code is 04239.

Strandhotel Marolt (tel. 2321) is an imposing-looking hotel whose different sections are joined together like a series of balconied cubes stretching along the lakeshore. The wood-trimmed facade contains big sliding windows that open into the well-furnished bedrooms, each of which has a private bath. On the premises are a covered swimming pool, several outdoor tennis courts, a bathing pier, a dancing terrace for outdoor parties, and a pleasant restaurant. On the spacious grounds around the hotel are a series of at least three annexes which hold the overflow from the main building. Singles cost from 405 AS ($21.55) to 645 AS ($34.31), while doubles go for 355 AS ($18.87) to 645 AS ($34.31) per person, with full board included. Prices vary according to the room and the season.

12. The Vellach Valley

Southeast of Klagenfurt, the Carinthian capital, the Vellach Valley leads to the Yugoslav border. It's a place well known in history. Your fellow visitors to this area are likely to be Yugoslavians.

The major stopover in the valley is—

EISENKAPPEL: This town is also known by its Yugoslav name, Selezna Kapla. It lies at the foot of Karawanken, 24 miles from Klagenfurt, or Celovec, as you're likely to hear it called in this valley, the home of a Slovenian ethnic group. Eisenkappel is only 10 miles from the Jezersko Pass, at the Austro-Yugoslav border.

The town is surrounded by centuries-old forests and mineral springs, and it has many cultural and historical curiosities, owing to its position as a frontier town. The southernmost of all the market villages of Austria, Eisenkappel is known both as a summer tourist center and a winter ski resort.

There are many sky-blue lakes and white mountain peaks nearby. Lake Klopeiner, to the north of this town, is the warmest lake in Carinthia, as described above. Five miles to the southwest you'll see Trögerner Gorge.

The Eisenkappel area code is 04238.

Food and Lodging

Hotel Obir (tel. 381) is a strikingly dramatic hotel constructed of red brick with black-framed windows set into its many outside angles. In the center of town close to the thermal baths, the hotel has a big airy format and a simplified interior decor much in keeping with the modern exterior. The bedrooms rent for 730 AS ($38.84) to 780 AS ($41.50) in a double, from 440 AS ($23.41) to 480 AS ($25.54) in a single. All tariffs include full board.

STYRIA

THE "GREEN HEART OF AUSTRIA," Styria (Steiermark, in German) is so called because forests cover about half the land mass, with grassland and vineyards blanketing yet another quarter. The second-largest province in the country after Lower Austria, Styria has many neighbors. It borders not only Yugoslavia and Hungary but also the Austrian provinces of Burgenland, Lower Austria, Upper Austria, Land Salzburg, and Carinthia. Part of Styria takes in the alpine ranges of the Salzkammergut, and some of it (the eastern part) resembles the steppe country of the great Hungarian plain.

This land of valleys and rivers, mountain peaks and glaciers, was long an area bitterly fought over, being greedily attacked through the ages by Huns, Hungarians, and Turks, among others. But not all of its suffering from the depredations of battle were in previous centuries. Great damage was inflicted in World War II, particularly in East Styria.

Even in Celtic times the mountains of Upper Styria were known as a prime source of the iron ore on which the tribes depended for their weapons and other valuable implements. The Romans exploited the rich deposits, and the Crusaders used armor made from Styrian iron to fight the "infidel" in the east. Iron resources shaped the economy of Styria, and today it is Austria's leading mining province. Nine-tenths of all the iron ore produced in Austria comes from Erzberg, which means "ore mountain."

Styria is steeped in tradition, more so than any other Austrian province. The distinguishing costume often worn by Styrian men is a case in point. Derived from an original peasant costume, it's made of stout greenish-gray cloth with Styrian green material being used for the lapels and as a stripe down the outside of the pant legs.

Styria is one of the bargain provinces of Austria. Even its top hotels charge prices that would be in the moderate range in most of the major cities of Europe. You can take the train here from either Salzburg or Vienna, and state bus service links all the towns and villages of the province. I think, however, that the ideal way to travel here is by car, since you'll want to be adventurous and head up an unknown valley or drive right up to some castle-fortress.

You'll find good hunting country in Styria. In fact a lot of the game you see on those hunter's menus throughout Austria ran wild in Styrian woodlands during its lifetime. In summer you can fish for trout in the Enns and other rivers. Mountain climbing is another popular summer activity.

In the last decade or so Styria has been entering the winter holiday scene as a ski area, but it still has a long way to go before it will have the facilities of Land Salzburg or Tyrol. Likewise, its après-ski life is not yet nearly on a par with that of already-flourishing Austrian ski centers.

Graz, the capital of Styria, is the second-largest city in the country. In imperial times it was best known as the place to which state officials retired. It even acquired the nickname "Pensionopolis" (City of the Retired) from this fact.

1. Graz

Graz, capital of the iron-rich province of Styria, combines a modern way of life with historical architecture to achieve a harmonious blend of past and present. Its history as a settlement probably dates back to prehistoric times, brought about by its location at the base of a hill at a ford across the Mur River, an important facet of transportation in the beginning of civilization. Romans, Slavs, and Bavarians all took their turn in the development of a town on the northern edge of a plain where the Mur leaves the wooded mountains of central Styria.

Early settlers, fearing flooding, established fortifications on the steep dolomite hill overlooking the river's ford site. The name of the city is derived from the Slavic word *gradec*, meaning "little fortress." This little castle was built on the hill which is now the Schlossberg in Graz. The town is first mentioned in historical documents from early in the 12th century. Graz has come under many governments, among them those of Germany, Bohemia, Hungary, the Babenbergs, the Habsburgs—you name it.

The medieval town developed at the foot of the Schlossberg, and some buildings of the late Gothic period remain, constructed when Emperor Frederick III used Graz as a capital after being forced out of Vienna by the Hungarians. The Burg (castle) and the cathedral of that era, houses that seem to huddle together, narrow-gable roofs, and arcaded courtyards contribute to the city's charm today.

Life wasn't always kind to the people of Graz. In 1480 they must have felt that fate was being extra cruel. In that year of the "Plagues of God," the little town was afflicted by locusts, the Black Death, the Turks, and a threat from the Hungarians.

When the Habsburg inheritance was divided in 1564 into Austrian and Spanish branches, Graz became the capital of "Inner Austria," the residence of Archduke Carl, who ruled Styria, Carinthia, and Italian Habsburg patrimonial lands. Graz was again prosperous. Carl had the town's fortifications strengthened on Italian designs, with bastions and moats.

A Jesuit College and Lutheran foundation school were both active by the end of the 16th century. Johannes Kepler, who gained renown for his mathematical and astronomical knowledge, began his teaching career at the Lutheran school. Fine arts and commerce flourished in Graz, bringing honor and riches to the city, as reflected in palaces and mansions of that period, although when Ferdinand II became emperor, he moved his court to Vienna in 1619. The influence of Italian baroque architects made its impact during this period.

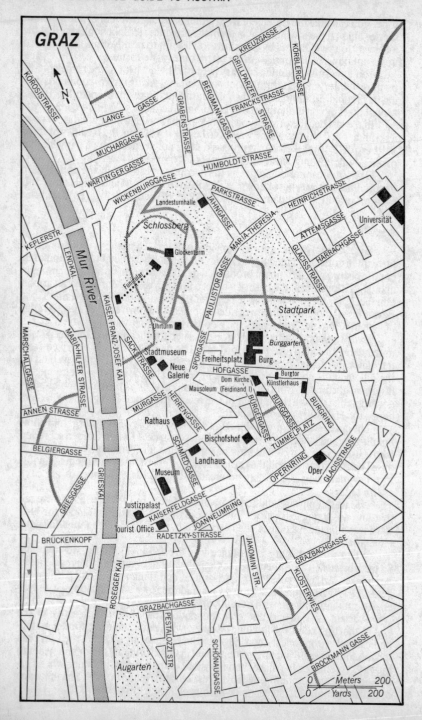

The city walls were demolished in 1784, and the area they occupied, the *glacis* (slopes), was planted with trees. Napoleon's armies made three appearances here when he was trying to take over all of Europe, and the defeat of Austria at the Battle of Wagram in 1809 resulted in a treaty which forced Graz to level the battlements of the Schlossberg, in retaliation for the failure of the French troops to seize the citadel earlier that year. Only the Uhrturm (clock tower) and the bell tower were saved, rescued by payment of a high ransom by the citizens of Graz. Schlossberg was transformed into the beautiful park on that site today.

World War II saw much destruction by bombers, and the early entry of Russian troops into the city continued the devastation. However, during the occupation Graz was allotted in 1945 to the British and reconstruction began, so that today you can enjoy warm hospitality in the "Garden City" of Austria.

Graz is a city of some quarter of a million inhabitants at present, with such thriving industrial enterprises as breweries, machine factories, trading companies, and service industries. The Graz Fair is a commercial and industrial event of great importance in southeast Europe. Three universities, an opera house, a theater, museums, concert halls, and art galleries are the center of cultural life for Lower Styria.

If you're in the vicinity in the fall of the year, you might want to attend the Steierischer Herbst (Styrian Autumn) festival, which features contemporary art, music, and literature.

The area code for Graz is 00316.

TRANSPORTATION IN GRAZ: Graz City Transport operates streetcar and bus service throughout the city. Jakomini Square in the city center is the point of intersection of all streetcar lines. To use the network of bus lines, starting points are at Jakomini Square or from terminals of the streetcar lines. For information on any phase of the transport system, telephone 78931.

Radio **taxi** service is available by phoning 983 or 2801.

PRACTICAL FACTS: For information, check with the **Graz Tourist Office,** 16 Herrengasse (tel. 705241).

Emergency services are available by telephoning as follows: **police,** 133; **fire,** 122; **ambulance,** 144; **medical,** 1900-4566; **drugstore,** 18.

To find out about the **weather,** phone 16.

Lost and found: In an emergency, you can ask at any police station (wachzimmer). Otherwise, try the Lost and Found office, 56 Grabenstrasse (tel. 76531, ext. 4157). In criminal cases, apply to the Duty Officer at Police Headquarters, 8 Paulustorgasse (tel. 76531, ext. 2121).

The main **post and telegraph office** is at 46 Neutorgasse (tel. 9800). There's also a post office next to the main railroad station (Bahnhof).

For information on **air travel,** call Thalerhof Airport, south of the city (tel. 291541), or the AUA (Austrian Airlines) city office, 16 Herrengasse, Landhaus (tel. 79641). Lufthansa also has a city office, at 6 Herrengasse (tel. 72583).

If you're traveling by **car,** Graz is connected to the European superhighway system, via roads to the southbound and the Pyhrn autobahns as well as to the main road through the Mur and Mürz Valleys. The city offers all necessary services to motorists. Ask about this courtesy at the Tourist Office (see above).

Postal Bus information is available at Postverkehrsbüro Graz, 19 Andreas-Hofer-Platz (tel. 71525), if you want to travel to outlying areas by this means.

WHERE TO STAY: Accommodations range from first-class hotels to camping sites. There are many reasonably priced family hotels and inexpensive lodgings, and even the top hotels will strike many as being easy on the pocketbook. I'll lead off with the more expensive choices, and then preview a selection in the middle and budget range.

Hotel Steirerhof, 12 Jakominiplatz (tel. 76350), one of the best hotels in Graz, is the traditional, conservative favorite, lying near the Opera on a large inner-city square. It's been severely modernized into a contemporary decor. On the premises are a piano bar and a restaurant, plus a courtyard with café tables. Singles range from 1,000 AS ($53.20) to 1,500 AS ($79.80), while doubles cost 1,200 AS ($63.84) to 1,850 AS ($98.42), with breakfast included.

Hotel Daniel, 1 Europaplatz (tel. 911080), has a boxy urban look with a flat roof and a sprawling design of concrete and glass. The contemporary interior is filled with upholstered banquettes and modern accessories, and is often frequented by business people from other cities. On the premises are a popular bar area and an elegantly efficient restaurant. A short walk from the old city at the station plaza, the hotel charges from 720 AS ($38.30) to 900 AS ($47.88) in a single and from 1,050 AS ($55.86) to 1,300 AS ($69.16) in a double or suite. All units contain private baths and modern comfort, and breakfast is included in the tariffs.

City Hotel Erzherzog Johann, 3-5 Sackstrasse (tel. 76551), stands near the pedestrian zone in the old city. This elegant hotel arranges some of its rooms around a skylit atrium surrounded by gracefully curving wrought-iron balconies and verdant plants. There's an array of attractive facilities on the premises, including a contemporary bar area with vivid accents of black and brass, along with a formal restaurant and spacious high-ceilinged bedrooms. Reached from the street through a chiseled stone archway, the hotel charges from 720 AS ($38.30) to 790 AS ($42.03) for a single and from 920 AS ($48.94) to 1,200 AS ($63.84) for a double, including a breakfast buffet. Prices vary according to the plumbing.

Alba Hotel Wiesler, 4 Grieskai (tel. 91-32-41). The quayside foundations of this historic hotel date back to 1603. Recent renovations have transformed it into the most desirable hotel in town. The view from the neoclassical windows encompasses many of the medieval city's baroque spires, which soar toward the mountains on the opposite side of the river. During the upgrading of the hotel in 1985–1986, its architects completely reconstructed the lobby with marble and fine detailing in an updated interpretation of art nouveau.

Wiesler's restaurant is a sophisticated blend of good food, crystal chandeliers, paneling, and uniformed waiters. There's a less formal snack bar for sit-down or takeaway food, plus the Café Jugendstil where an array of international newspapers supplements the fresh pastries and rich coffee. In the bar, piano music and special drinks tempt residents and non-residents alike. Many of the 97 rooms and most of the suites contain unusual artwork and sweeping views. After you register, an employee brings fruit and tea to your room. With breakfast included, singles cost 1,300 AS ($69.16), with doubles renting for 1,600 AS ($85.12).

Hotel Weitzer/Goldener Ochs, 15 Griesgasse (tel. 913801), has been in the same family for four generations. (It's not to be confused with the previously recommended Hotel Wiesler.) Standing on the river, it consists of two buildings connected by a glass overhead tunnel. The Weitzer itself is the more formal of the two, with large, old-fashioned, and spacious rooms; whereas accommodations in the Goldener Ochs tend to be small and boxy. However, the whole complex is well run and modernized with much contemporary comfort. Depending on the plumbing, singles range from 665 AS ($35.38) to 1,110 AS ($59.05) and doubles cost from 940 AS ($50.01) to 1,720 AS ($91.50). The Restaurant Kasserolle on the ground floor is considered by some residents to be among the best in town. Furnished in a modern, warmly tinted style, with formally dressed waiters even at lunchtime, the establishment offers an elegant salad bar with an array of greens, cold marinated vegetables, and varieties of lettuce including the deluxe mache. The chef's tafelspitz is especially good. Meals range from 115 AS ($6.12) to 350 AS ($18.62).

Schlossberg Hotel, 30 Kaiser-Franz-Josef-Kai (tel. 702577). Housed behind a beautifully embellished cerulean-blue facade, this 15th-century country baroque inn is my favorite hotel in Graz. Renovated from a decrepit rooming house in 1982 by a former race-car driver, Helmuth Marko, the hotel is now one of the most unusual and most charming hostelries in town. It was personally decorated by the owner's wife, with choice 19th-century furniture (she has her own antique business as well as excellent taste). The hotel offers 43 individually designed rooms, each of which combines the thick original walls with dozens of modern comforts. There's an early Biedermeier ceramic stove in the bar area and several pieces of baroque sculpture are set into well-placed niches. There's also a courtyard with a lion's head fountain. Prices range from 620 AS ($32.98) to 920 AS ($48.94) in a single and from 1,050 AS ($55.86) to 1,700 AS ($90.44) per person in a double. The hotel has a swimming pool, and guests can enjoy drinks on a terrace with a superb view of Graz.

Hotel Europa, 89 Bahnhofgürtel (tel. 91-66-01). Opened in 1986, this downtown hotel offers easy access from the nearby railway station. The building's mansard roof shelters 120 comfortably modern bedrooms, each of which contains a phone, radio, eight-channel color TV, mini-bar, and private bathroom. Singles cost between 850 AS ($45.22) and 1,000 AS ($53.20), with doubles renting for between 1,300 AS ($69.16) and 1,500 AS ($79.80). After their arrival guests relax in the sauna, whose plunge pool is the chilliest in town, the solarium, or at the intimate bar. Snacks and drinks are served in the Bistronette restaurant, while more formal meals are available in the plant-festooned restaurant, the Four Seasons (Vier Jahreszeiten). Motorists appreciate the 400-place parking garage and the covered shopping center, both of which are connected to the hotel.

Parkhotel, 8 Leonhardstrasse (tel. 33511), is a large hotel rambling across a gently angled corner of a street near the Opera, the City Park, and the university. The interior is a pleasing combination of baronial accessories (suits of armor and hanging tapestries in the beamed dining room) and modern comforts. An in-house garage will solve your parking problems. For rooms with bath, radio, and TV, the Florian family charge 775 AS ($41.23) for a single and 1,100 AS ($58.52) for a double, with breakfast included.

Hotel Gollner, 14 Schlögelgasse (tel. 72521), the preferred choice of the city's visiting opera stars, is across the street from the Opera House. Its renovated interior has a kind of 1950s simplicity, with a no-nonsense contemporary decor and spacious bedrooms. On the premises is a restaurant serving wholesome food. Singles cost from 390 AS ($20.75) to 950 AS ($50.54), while doubles range from 660 AS ($35.11) to 1,400 AS ($74.48), with breakfast included.

Hotel Mariahilfe, 9 Mariahilferstrasse (tel. 913163), is a four-story stucco building with a red tile roof, prominent gables, and modified neoclassic detailings around the windows. Centrally located, the hotel has comfortable public rooms with an elevator, red leather chairs, brass chandeliers, and a display of tiny flags from most of the major countries of Europe. The cozy weinstube offers Styrian specialties. With breakfast included, rooms with bath cost 680 AS ($36.18) for a single and 920 AS ($48.94) for a double. Bathless rooms go for 350 AS ($18.62) in a single and 625 AS ($33.25) in a double.

Hotel Drei Raben, 43 Annenstrasse (tel. 912686), near the train station, not far from the old city, is a contemporary hotel, offering all the modern comforts. Well-furnished bedrooms rent for 480 AS ($25.54) in a single and from 720 AS ($38.30) in a double, with breakfast included.

Pension Süd, 10 Stemmerweg (tel. 281860). Ten minutes by car from the center of town, heading south, this simple white-walled pension offers a kind of no-frills accommodation with lots of peace and quiet. On the premises are an indoor pool and a sauna. Singles cost from 510 AS ($27.13) to 530 AS ($28.20), while doubles range from 610 AS ($32.45) to 630 AS ($33.52), with breakfast included.

Hotel Grazerhof, 10 Stubenberggasse (tel. 79824), is centrally located on a relatively quiet street in the center of town. The marble-floored lobby offers a group of leather-backed swivel chairs near the reception desk. A popular and unpretentious restaurant offers meals to hotel residents, outside shopkeepers, and shoppers in general. Most of the 26 comfortable bedrooms contain private baths and phones. Depending on the plumbing, singles rent for between 160 AS ($8.51) and 550 AS ($29.26), while doubles cost between 480 AS ($25.54) and 720 AS ($38.30).

On the Outskirts

Gastehaus/Café Zum Kreuz, 451 Kärntnerstrasse (tel. 29-2436) at Strass-gang, is an ochre-colored guesthouse which has been run by the same family for more than a century. In a suburb south of Graz, the establishment contains only a dozen rooms, as well as a popular restaurant that's often the destination for people from the city who come here for the Styrian wines and the gutbürgerlich cookery. Homemade sausages are a specialty in September and March. Singles cost 360 AS ($19.15) while doubles go for 515 AS ($27.40), with breakfast included. A four-lane bowling alley is close by.

Hotel/Restaurant Pfeifer Zum Kirchenwirt, Graz-Mariatrost (tel. 391112), in an agricultural suburb seven kilometers from the center of Graz, is an ochre-colored hotel which has comfortable rooms—some of them very modern—and a gutbürgerlich restaurant with lots of wood trim. On the premises are a sauna and lots of thoughtful details. The hotel's exterior is an appealingly old-fashioned combination of country baroque detailing, hipped roofs, and exposed stone. All the bedrooms have complete bath, phone, and radio. Some of the large ones have mini-bar and TV. The Pfeifer family charges from 430 AS ($22.88) to 480 AS ($25.54) in a single and from 640 AS ($34.05) to 750 AS ($39.90) in a double, with breakfast and taxes included in the rates.

WHERE TO DINE: The variety of restaurants is enormous, ranging from first-class establishments to beer halls to student hangouts. Prices in even the top restaurants are moderate. You can dine in the hotels (which have some of the best food in town) or in cozy pubs and intimate bistros.

My recommendation, for the most part, is to skip the typical international cuisine when possible and concentrate on genuine Styrian specialties. These include wurzelfleisch, a kind of stew, or the different kinds of sterz, a dish made of buckwheat or corn. The homemade sausages in all their infinite varieties are generally excellent. Vienna is noted for its hendl (chicken) dishes, but Graz chefs also do chicken extremely well.

The art of beer brewing is particularly cultivated in Graz. For the local Puntigam or Reininghaus beers, as well as for the Gösser beer, which is brewed in Upper Styria, the people of Graz have a special predilection.

Or you may want to try Styrian wine which grows on steep slopes exposed to the sun. Important varieties such as Welschriesling, Muskat-Sylvaner, Traminer, but also the Schilcher, which grows only in a limited area in West Styria, have received international recognition.

Many of the wine restaurants of Graz provide background music in the evening.

Hofkeller, 8 Hofgasse (tel. 702439), has a gilt-edged reputation in town as a haven for gourmets who appreciate well-cooked traditional foods. The restaurant, which was formerly a simple wine and beer tavern, has been transformed into an elegant room with refreshing touches of vivid green. The tables are covered with fine napery, good silverware, and beautiful porcelain. The limited menu is augmented by a list of daily specials, whose appearance is heavily dependent on the availability of the ingredients. Your meal might include seafood salad in walnut oil, artichoke hearts stuffed with goose liver and mushrooms, a wide selection of fish, or a savory lamb cut flavored with thyme. Full meals range from 90 AS ($4.79) to 350 AS ($18.62). Reservations are suggested. Closed Sunday.

Weincomptoir Stündl, 55 Heinrichstrasse (tel. 33413). With its lace-covered windows, rows of plants, and geometric patterns, it looks more like a tea room than a restaurant. However, the evening crowd is likely to be among the most sophisticated in Graz. Its cerulean facade is found on a commercial street which requires a taxi ride from the center of town. Owner Wolfgang Stündl offers such dishes with nouvelle cuisine flair as noodle salad with shrimps and mussels; spaghetti with bacon, mushrooms, and zucchini in a garlic-flavored cream sauce; lamb-stuffed ravioli with thyme butter; trout grilled with a fennel-flavored cream sauce; and chicken with rosemary and creamed cabbage. Full meals begin at 300 AS ($15.96). The establishment is open only for dinner between 6 p.m. and 2 a.m. daily except Friday and Sunday.

Isola di Giorgio, 58 Kaiser-Franz-Josef (tel. 78771). The best Italian food in Graz is served within this series of warmly decorated rooms at the edge of the river. A battery of uniformed waiters will address you in Italian, German, or English. A bubbling aquarium and a refrigerated display case tempt visitors with rows of seafood. If you request a table in the room to the left, you'll be able to observe the well-rehearsed culinary theatrics of the busy kitchen staff. Menu specialties include melon with port, selections of antipasti, scampi cocktails, penne alla Giorgio, lasagne verde, tagliatelle with cream, zuppa di pesce, grilled calamari, gamberoni al cognac, and an array of fresh fish which is on display. Full meals begin at 500 AS ($26.60).

Victorian Steakhouse, 15 Burggasse (tel. 79139). Aside from its restaurant, this place also shelters one of the hottest bars in town, frequented by an attractive crowd of young people. The bar area is a dimly lit, horseshoe-shaped rendez-vous point where you'll be lucky to get a seat. You can eat at the bar if you wish, although the Victorian-style steakhouse might be more appealing.

The decor includes depictions of everybody from voluptuous nudes to the Queen of England, as well as John Bull flanked by two Union Jacks, cut red-velvet wallpaper, impeccably dressed waiters, and a pianist playing classical music or American jazz.

When I was last there they were having a British week, with a special menu featuring steak-and-kidney pie, beef Wellington, and grilled lamb cutlets. However, they always have an array of steaks, chops, and cutlets, along with fish dishes, cooked the way you want them. Mixed drinks are available, and the wine list contains a brief history of the building. Steaks cost from 120 AS ($6.38), and full meals go for around 350 AS ($18.62). There's a popular disco in the basement, called "Downstairs."

Gambrinuskeller, 6-8 Färbergasse (tel. 700243). The decor, like the menu, combines elements from rustically conservative Austria with overtones of the Middle East and the Balkans. In addition to lots of exposed wood, the dining rooms contain Oriental rugs which cushion the unyielding surfaces of the banquettes. A large oil painting of a Balkan peasant girl in native headdress dominates one end of the room, while a stainless-steel deli-style case separates the busy kitchens from the dining areas. The unusual menu offers Brazilian, Persian, and Italian foods as well. You might enjoy cevapcici, churrasco of pork, Iranian-style kebabs, Italian pasta dishes, and grilled steaks. Dessert could be anything from baklava to apple strudel. Full meals average around 150 AS ($7.98), with a wide variation of possibilities on either end.

Restaurant Goldene Pastete, 28 Sporgasse (tel. 73416), is housed inside the oldest inn in Graz, constructed in 1571. It's owned by Walther Patterer and his family, who have run it for more than a quarter of a century. The restaurant is housed in a five-story Renaissance building of pink stucco with green shutters and lots of windowboxes. The waiters, each dressed in regional garb, are kept busy running from the kitchens to the three dining rooms on three different floors. In addition to 140 places inside, the summer garden holds an additional 60 diners. Open from 10 a.m. to midnight every day but Saturday and Sunday, the restaurant serves gutbürgerlich food to all walks of life. The international menu contains an occasional Yugoslav dish, such as cevapcici, but mainly it offers Austrian specialties, including zander (a fish), several noodle dishes, grilled veal, steaks, pork roast in a pepper cream sauce, and schnitzel Cordon Bleu. Full meals range from 115 AS ($6.12) to 240 AS ($12.77). It's closed for the last two weeks in August.

Landhaus-Keller, 9 Schmiedgasse (tel. 700-276). A dimly lit corridor extends past at least three rustic and authentically Teutonic dining areas (there are six if you count the nooks and crannies). It eventually opens onto a series of outdoor tables behind the restaurant. This outdoor area, surprisingly, opens onto a neighboring courtyard with flowers and a view of the arcade of a baroque church. A sign in the window advertises "delicacies from lakes, rivers, and streams," as well as a wide selection of veal, beef, pork, and both roast and fried chicken dishes.

Specialties are usually from Styria, based on old recipes. You might begin with sour cream soup with burnt polenta, meatballs with sauerkraut, Styrian cheese dumplings in beef broth, and browned omelets with blueberries. It's open from 10 a.m. till 1 a.m. every day but Sunday and holidays. Meals average around 135 AS ($7.18). The original building was constructed in the early 16th century, and hosted such famous guests as Metternich, Franz and Eduard Sacher, Field Marshal Esterhazy, and the Duke of Wellington.

Kepler Keller, 6 Stempfergasse (tel. 72449), is probably the best known evening wine tavern in Graz. Named after the Renaissance mathematician and astrologer Johannes Kepler, who used to live there, the establishment has during its lifetime served a glass of wine or beer to practically everyone in Graz. The interior is cozily welcoming, done up in a pleasingly authentic decor of thick paneling and rustic accessories, but my favorite area is the candlelit courtyard, whose outdoor tables are flanked with a three-story arcade whose repeating arches are supported by chiseled Doric columns accented with cascading flowerboxes.

Live music is usually part of the evening's entertainment. In addition to traditional meals, such as schnitzels, pork, steaks, omelets, cheeses, and salads, the establishment serves carafes of the local wine. The specialty of the house is a Styrian rosé called Schilcher, whose grape only grows south of Graz. The restaurant also serves copious quantities of the Styrian beer called Gösser. It's open from 5 p.m. till 2 a.m. every day, with live music after 9 p.m. (the last meal is served at 1 a.m.). The restaurant is closed on Sunday. Full meals average between 100 AS ($5.32) and 225 AS ($11.97), although simple platters can be had for less.

Krebsenkeller, 12 Sachsstrasse (tel. 79377), near the Hauptplatz, is about the closest establishment to a total entertainment complex available in Graz. You enter a covered passage which ends in an enclosed courtyard, one side of which has a beflowered loggia. Café tables are usually set up under a grape arbor, although you can choose between an underground "keller," a ground-level stüberl, or a gemütlich restaurant, each of which has different entrances from the courtyard. This labyrinthine arrangement of rooms was built in 1538 by a local official and his wife. Simple fixed-price meals are a real bargain. They cost from 80 AS ($4.26) to 110 AS ($5.85), although the more expensive à la carte items can go much higher. Menu items include grilled dishes of varying degrees of spiciness, a full range of soups, salads, fish, and game.

Restaurant Stadtkeller, 3 Andreas Hofer Platz (tel. 73354). Housed in a stucco building with primitive flying buttresses, this gutbürgerlich restaurant can be found on a busy traffic circle near the river. Inside, hanging glass lamps, timbered ceilings, and stenciled wall murals combine with an unpretentious menu to create a typical Styrian ambience. Fixed-price meals range from 115 AS ($6.12), although you can eat here at virtually any price level, from economy to upper bracket. Menu items come from both the Austrian and the international kitchen, and include a wide variety of pizzas, the most interesting of which is made from "fruits of the sea." There are also Italian pastas, Hungarian dishes, and typically Styrian platters. The terrace overlooks the river and often accommodates a wide variety of local residents, a good sign.

Stadtheuriger, 8 Hans-Sachs-Gasse (tel. 71588). You'll walk down a dark tunnel before reaching the vaulted ceilings of this 400-year-old wine restaurant. Although a bit stark, the locale is clean and bright, ringed with fresh layers of plaster and cream-colored paint. Cold meats, salads, and seafood come from a glass display case, while the Styrian dishes listed on the menu include filet of peppersteak, strudels, pork medallions, and filet steak with mushrooms. Full meals cost from 350 AS ($18.62) and are served daily except Sunday from 11 a.m. to 1 a.m.

THE CAFÉS OF GRAZ: Café Glockenspiel, 4 Glockenspielplatz (tel. 80291). On a quiet baroque square, this ground-floor café is housed in a lime-colored, ornately embellished building with blue and white café tables set up in front. A formally attired waiter will take your order for coffee, light snacks, and sandwiches. The interior is comfortably upholstered with serpentine banquettes, blue-flecked upholstery, and mahogany paneling and tables. Original paintings and lithographs are displayed amid a crowd of people who can be either jet set or vintage dowager, depending on the time of day. Coffee and pastries cost from 20 AS ($1.06) to 30 AS ($1.60) each. It's closed on Sunday.

Café Am Tummelplatz, 8 Hans-Sachs-Gasse (tel. 71588), connected to the previously recommended Stadtheuriger, is elegant, manicured, well-carpeted, and filled with marble tables and well-stocked pastry displays. Waitresses in frilly aprons serve hot chocolate "mit Schlag" (whipped cream). A special coffee, Maria Theresia, costs 50 AS ($2.66), and pastries begin at 20 AS ($1.06). Closing day is Sunday.

Café Leinich, 4 Kaiser-Josef-Platz (tel. 80586). Perfect on a summer day, with a view looking over the activity in the open-air market, this popular institution serves good coffee and homemade pastries. Devotees of the rich concoctions, where fresh fruit and berries are used in abundance, include students, workers, and retired people (some of whom plan their afternoon around the time spent here). Coffee and pastries each range from around 15 AS (80¢) to 28 AS ($1.49). It's closed in August and on Sunday.

THE SIGHTS: The **Old Quarter** of Graz is, in great part, preserved in its original state, and a tour through it is a must for visitors (see "Tours," below). Major sights include the **Hauptplatz** (main square) in the heart of the city, surrounded by ancient houses with characteristic brown-tile roofs with narrow gables. The most notable is the House of Luegg at the corner of Sporgasse, known for its arcades and facade dating back to the 17th century.

A few steps down Herrengasse, the wide shopping and business street, is the **Landhaus,** seat of the provincial government, a Renaissance masterpiece completed in 1565 by an Italian architect, Domenico dell'Allio. Above the main gate a window is especially highlighted, intensifying the effect of the gate. The courtyard is bounded on the south by an arched arcade traversing the court. The arched Renaissance-style well was poured in bronze near the end of the 16th century.

After that, the next major site is the **Landeszeughaus,** or armory, next to the Landhaus. Being the capital and main city of the province, Graz was militarily important in earlier times, and for more than two centuries it was a bulwark against the ever-invading Turks. The armory, built from 1642 to 1645 by Anton Solar, dates from the time of the Turkish wars. Its early baroque gate is flanked by statues of the war deities, Mars and Bellona, the work of Giovanni Mamolo. The four floors of the building are separated by the original strong wood-beamed ceilings.

Now a museum displaying three centuries of weaponry, the Zeughaus contains some 30,000 harnesses, coats of mail, helmets, swords, pikes, muskets of various kinds, pistols, arquebuses, and other implements of war. In 1749 Empress Maria Theresa, in recognition of Styrian military service and strategic significance, allowed this arsenal to remain when others in her empire were destroyed.

You can visit the armory, April to October, Monday to Friday from 9 a.m. to 5 p.m. It closes at 1 p.m. on Saturday and Sunday. Admission is 15 AS (80¢).

Paulustor, or Paul's Gate, between the remnants of the former rampart of Graz, dates from the time of the fortification of the city by Italian architects. The side of the gate facing the city is plain, the exterior being decorated with large coats-of-arms of Archduke Ferdinand and his first wife, Anne of Bavaria.

Another major attraction is the **Landesmuseum Joanneum,** which has departments at different locations. The natural history displays are at the old Joanneum building, 10 Raubergasse. The collections of the Old Gallery and of the arts and crafts department are in the new Joanneum building at 45 Neutorgasse. Here you'll see stained glass, altarpieces, and important art from the Middle Ages, some going back to the 12th century.

The New Gallery on the third floor of the former Herberstein town house, 16 Sachsstrasse, shows art from the 19th century to the present. The Styrian Museum of Folklore is at 13 Paulustorgasse. At the Eggenberg Palace (see below) you'll find the department of prehistory and early history, including an extensive collection of Roman stones in an open-air pavilion in the park, the Münzenkabinett, a coin collection, and the Styrian Hunting Museum.

Most Joanneum exhibits are open Tuesday to Friday from 9 a.m. to 4 p.m., to noon on Saturday and Sunday. Admission is 15 AS (80¢).

The **Domkirche** (cathedral), between Burgergasse and Burggasse, was originally the Romanesque Church of St. Aegydius, a fortified church outside the town walls, first mentioned in a document in 1174. In the 15th century Frederick III had it converted into a spacious three-bayed city parish church in the late Gothic style, although instead of a Gothic spire the structure later acquired a wooden turret. Archduke Carl of Inner Austria attached the church to his residence, the Burg (castle), and later entrusted it to the Jesuits. After the dissolution of that order it became the cathedral church of the bishops of Seckau. Inside you'll see two shrines, circa 1475, made in Mantua, and a baroque high altar, the 18th-century creation of Father Georg Kraxner.

Next door on Burggasse is the **Mausoleum of Emperor Ferdinand I,** one of the most remarkable buildings of Graz. Started in 1614 and completed in 1638, it was intended as the tomb of the emperor and his first wife. The church, crowned by a crossing cupola with the tomb chapel also vaulted, is regarded as the best example of mannerism in Austria. The high altar is an early work of J.B. Fischer von Erlach, done from 1695 to 1697. The central sarcophagus of the tomb intended for Ferdinand's parents contains only the remains of his mother. His father, Archduke Carl of Inner Austria, was interred elsewhere.

Other than the cathedral, the most important church in Graz is **Mariahilferkirche** (Church of Our Lady of Succor), 3 Mariahilferplatz; built for the Minorite brothers on the right bank of the Mur River. Pietro de Pomis carried out reconstruction of the church in the early 17th century and painted the celebrated altarpiece depicting St. Elizabeth interceding with the Virgin Mary. This painting made the church a place of pilgrimage.

Overlooking Graz, **Schlossberg,** the formerly fortified hill, rising to a height of 1,550 feet above sea level, is an island of quiet. As I mentioned above, the fortifications were leveled in 1809 by terms of a treaty Napoleon dictated to a defeated Austria. You can take a cable railway to the restaurant on top or climb the winding stairs. From the top you'll be able to look down on the city and its environs. Guided tours of the citadel are given daily (except in the winter) on the hour from 8 a.m. to 5 p.m., starting from the bell tower opposite the upper station of the cable railway.

The **Clock Tower** (Uhrturm) on the citadel is a curiosity above the walls of the former Citizens' Bastion. It acquired its present appearance in 1555-1556, when the original Gothic tower was given Renaissance treatment, resulting in a circular wooden gallery with oriels and four huge clock faces.

The **Burg** (castle) northeast of the Hauptplatz in the Old Quarter is distinguished by its unique double-spiral staircase constructed in 1499 for Emperor Maximilian I.

About two miles from the city, you can visit **Schloss Eggenberg** (Eggenberg Palace), a square 17th-century building with towers on its four corners and an accentuated facade over the main gate. The palace sits in a large park now used as a game preserve. The four wings of the baroque-style structure surround a large court with arched arcades and two smaller courts separated by the palace church. You can take guided tours of the baroque state apartments on the second floor from the first of April until the end of October from 9 a.m. to 1 p.m. and 2 to 4 p.m. (time of last tour departure). Admission is 15 AS (80¢).

The ground floor of the south wing houses the Landesmuseum Joanneum's department of prehistory and early history mentioned above, with a good collection of Styrian antiquities. Visits are possible from the first of February until the end of November from 9 a.m. to 5 p.m. for 15 AS (80¢) admission.

The Styrian Hunting Museum, another part of the Landesmuseum Joanneum collections, is on the first floor of the palace, with the same visiting hours and admission charge.

A major attraction in the environs is about ten miles north of Graz, at Stübing, the **Austrian Open-Air Museum** (Osterreichisches Freilichtmuseum), (tel. 22431), set in a wooded valley branching off from the Valley of the Mur. Here you'll see rustic buildings from all the Austrian provinces, some as much as 300 years old. The 70 authentic structures include a smokeroom house (Rauchstubenhaus) from East Styria of a type also seen in Land Salzburg, and circular, triangular, and rectangular houses. The museum is open from the first of April to the end of October daily except Monday from 9 a.m. to 4 p.m. Admission is 35 AS ($1.86).

TOURS: Guided **walking tours** are offered all year long on Saturday at 3 p.m. and also on Friday at 11 a.m. and Sunday at 3 p.m. from May to October, costing 30 AS ($1.60) per person. From the meeting place at the City Tourist Office, Graz-Steiermark-Haus, 16 Herrengasse, you are taken through the old city (see description under "Sights" above) to the Landhaus (the seat of the provincial government), Stempfergasse, Glockenspielplatz, Bürgergasse, the Dom (cathedral), the mausoleum, the Burg (castle), the Schauspielhaus (theater), Freiheitsplatz, Hofgasse, Sporgasse, Franziskanerplatz, and the Hauptplatz (main square).

Bus Sightseeing tours are available Monday through Friday from the end of April to the beginning of October, departing at 3 p.m. from the Grazer Congress (convention center), Landhausgasse, and costing 100 AS ($5.32). The guide points out such landmarks as the main Post Office, the Stadtkeller, the underpass of the main bridge, the electric cable railway to the Schlossberg, Feidorfplatz, Leechkirche (the Leech Church), Elisabethstrasse, Landeskrankenhaus (Hospital of the Land Steiermark), Hilm Pond, the university, Heinrichstrasse, Paulustor (Paul's Gate), and the opera house, among other sights. The tour ends at Eggenburg Palace where you can visit the state rooms and the park, after which you're taken at about 5:15 p.m. to the Renaissance courtyard of the Landhaus, concluding the tour.

Other **guided bus tours** are available at any time through the City Tourist Office at the above address. These require a minimum of five persons, who are taken on a 2½-hour sightseeing trip at a cost of 180 AS ($9.58) (less if the party is larger), which includes the guide, bus, and entrance fees for the various places visited.

Every Friday at 2 p.m., the tourist office offers trips to **Piber,** 15 miles west of Graz, where visitors see the stud farm where the white Lippizaner stallions are bred and receive their initial training before appearing at the Spanish Riding School in Vienna. The tour to Piber costs around 170 AS ($9.04) per person.

Back in the city, an **electric cable railway** will take you in 3 minutes some 1,550 feet up from the lower station at 38 Kaiser-Franz-Josef-Kai to the upper station at the Schlossberg Restaurant. This run is made about every 15 minutes. The fare is around 8 AS (43¢) to ride up, 5 AS (27¢) to ride down, or 10 AS (53¢) for a round trip for adults. Children under 6 ride free, while those over 6 pay half the adult fare.

Many other tours are offered, by foot, bus, streetcar, car, cable, and even swimming in Graz and its environs. Ask at the tourist office.

SHOPPING: You might begin your shopping expedition at the Hauptplatz, which is the main square in the center of town. The major shopping streets, including Herrengasse, branch off from here. Of course the major item to buy, if it appeals to you, is Styrian clothing in the famous Styrian grays and greens, a style of dress that has spread all over Austria. You'll find a good selection of dirndls and hats in particular, as well as local handcrafts and leather clothing.

Steirisches Heimatwerk, 4 Paulustorgasse (tel. 77106), is a large, many-roomed store selling cookbooks, shoes, dirndls, a big selection of regional blouses, dresses, coats, silk, wool, and cotton fabrics, as well as objects made from glass, ceramics, and wood. Every item is made in Austria. Some of the more unusual items include hand-painted depictions of the local saints in small wooden frames. The sales personnel are helpful. The store is part of the local folklore museum.

Brühl and Söhne, 8 Stubenberggasse (tel. 71048), sells Styrian clothing for men, women, and children. The antique cash register here is a minor work of art, and the personnel are helpful and friendly. Their inventory includes dirndls, coats, skirts, hats, vests, suits, and accessories.

Anton Pichler, 28 Herrengasse (tel. 79562), sells hats of all kinds. The varieties range from Tyrolean and Styrian traditional designs to more updated versions, including golfing and hunting hats. The elegant chrome- and marble-trimmed exterior opens to reveal a wood-paneled rectangle with hundreds of hats covering the paneled walls.

GRAZ AFTER DARK: Sometimes restaurants combine dancing with disco action and nightclub shows, so at one address you might make an evening of it. The cafés often have music as well. Because of the university in Graz, many of the after-dark haunts are heavily frequented by young people.

The **Opernhaus** (opera house) at the Opernring presents both opera and ballet (phone 76451 for information about programs and tickets). The building was built "in the style of Fischer von Erlach" at the end of the 19th century.

In summer you can often hear concerts in the **Stadtpark,** or city park, which adjoins the northeast side of the citadel.

The **Styrian Autumn,** an arts festival, takes place during parts of September and October. It has a reputation for being avant-garde, presenting everything from jazz to mime.

Haus Gottinger, Strassgang (tel. 281850), is a formal disco for the over-30 crowd. You'll need a car to get here because it's about a 20-minute ride from the center of Graz. When rock groups come for special appearances the cover charge is slightly more than the regular entrance fee of 50 AS ($2.66). There's a restaurant as well. It gets popular on weekends, and is open from 7 p.m. to 4 a.m.

"Downstairs," Victorian Steakhouse, 15 Burggasse (tel. 79139), is the basement addition to one of the most popular bars and restaurants in town (see my dining recommendations). You reach it by descending a worn flight of stone steps from the bar area upstairs, where you might want to stop first for a drink. Covered with brick vaulting, the disco contains slot machines, a small dance floor, a long rectangular bar area, and a vaguely Dickensian decor of dark banquettes and old English beer ads. There's no cover charge, and drinks cost from 50 AS ($2.66) to 60 AS ($3.19). The disco is open from 8:30 p.m. to 2 a.m. every night.

Una, 28 Kaiser Franz Josef-Kai (tel. 70-27-27). One of the city's trendiest hangouts lies beside the river next door to the Schlossberg Hotel. Its interior is a new-world combination of hi-tech accessories set against a jet-black backdrop and lots of exposed chrome. The place is popular throughout the early evening, but becomes especially crowded later at night when disco and new wave music fill its cramped but comfortable interior. The place serves two-fisted drinks, whose prices begin at 65 AS ($3.46), every day of the week. Simple food and snacks are offered at night between 9 and midnight.

2. Bad Gleichenberg

The most important summer spa in South Styria, Bad Gleichenberg, lies southeast of Graz near the border of Yugoslavia, in a setting of rolling hills and vineyards. This is one of the most interesting—but little known—parts of Austria to explore. Untersteiermark, or Lower Styria, where this spa is located, was a lot larger in the days of the Habsburgs. Much of its territory was lost to Yugoslavia following the breakup of the empire after World War I.

Bad Gleichenberg's setting is a lovely valley opening to the south. In the area's magnificent parks, you'll see exotic plants, including the giant sequoia. You can partake of the mineral waters of the Emma, Konstantin, and Johannisbrunnen springs and even take a bottle home with you. The spa has an interesting entertainment program, plus special tours in the environs.

You can drive to Bad Gleichenberg, take an express train from Vienna, or a bus from Graz or Vienna.

Bad Gleichenberg's area code is 03159

FOOD AND LODGING: Hotel Austria (tel. 2205) is a prosperous-looking white-walled villa with gray shutters and a raised sun terrace. The light coming in from the big old-fashioned windows floods the interior. On the premises is an informal bar area covered with a brick vaulted ceiling, and a collection of public rooms is filled with comfortable furniture in distinguished combinations of white and dark colors. The cost of a bed and full board ranges from 550 AS ($29.26) to 600 AS ($31.92) per person.

Hotel Gleichenbergerhof (tel. 2424) is a pleasant contemporary chalet set in a forested area with a masonry sun terrace stretching below the white and dark-colored facade. The interior has lots of rustically modern accessories, including a piano bar and an open fireplace. The Kaulfersch family charges 450 AS ($23.94) to 495 AS ($26.33) per person, based on double occupancy, including full board. Singles pay a daily surcharge of 35 AS ($1.86), also on the full board plan. All units contain private bath, balcony, and phone. The hotel is open from February to December.

KAPENSTEIN: As an alternative to staying in Bad Gleichenberg, you can drive east to this little hamlet and its schloss hotel near the Yugoslav border.

The area code for Kapenstein is 03157.

Schloss Kapfenstein (tel. 2202) is a solidly built castle with a hipped roof and a curving extension that's almost as old as the main building itself. Set in the middle of verdant forests and rich fields, the castle accepts paying guests in rooms filled with antique furniture and all the modern comforts. Singles cost 385 AS ($20.48), and doubles rent for 800 AS ($42.56), with breakfast included. A bed and full board goes for 500 AS ($26.60) per person daily.

The hotel is closed between mid-December and early March. You can eat on the castle's terrace if you wish, as it offers a view of the village below. Every Thursday the Winkler-Hermaden family presents a Styrian buffet; otherwise specialties are based on regional recipes such as roast hen, homemade blutwurst and sausages, and apple strudel. A la carte meals cost from 80 AS ($4.26) to 240 AS ($12.77), while fixed-price meals run from 85 AS ($4.52) to 140 AS ($7.45).

3. Leoben

In 1797 Napoleon signed a peace treaty in Leoben in Upper Styria, a town built on a loop of the Mur River northwest of Graz and known for its ironworking industries and lignite mining. In fact it's the seat of a mining college. But because it's industrial, don't assume that the town is without attractions.

The **Altes Rathaus** (old city hall) stands on the Hauptplatz (main square) of Leoben. The **pfarrkirche** (parish church) of the town has two towers dating from the latter 17th century. The **Mautturm**, or toll tower, called the "mushroom tower," is Leoben's most distinguishing landmark, dating from 1615.

If possible, visit the 14th-century **Church of Maria Waasen,** which has some excellent stained glass in the choir. One of its windows depicts the Passion of Christ. This church is west of the town, near the bridge spanning the Mur.

A popular excursion is to **Göss,** 1¼ miles south of Leoben, where the celebrated Göss beer is produced. The brewery took over what had once been a nunnery, dating from the 11th century. It's considered the oldest nunnery in Styria and still has a Gothic church and a Romanesque crypt.

Leoben's area code is 03842.

FOOD AND LODGING: **Hotel Kindler,** 7-11 Straussgasse (tel. 43202), incorporates a richly decorated older building with a strikingly contemporary big-windowed building just next to it. A few doors away from the antique civic buildings in the center of town, the hotel is comfortably decorated with modern furniture and tasteful colors. Singles range from 190 AS ($10.11) to 340 AS ($18.09), while doubles cost 180 AS ($9.58) to 280 AS ($14.90) per person, depending on the season and the plumbing.

Bauman's (tel. 42565), in the center of town, is housed in a French-style mansion rising three ornate floors across the street from a beautiful little park. On the premises are a coffee shop, a pub, and a restaurant, s' Reinderl. Styrian specialties as well as international cuisine are served in a rustically decorated dining room. Lines of copper pots as well as a series of spoked wheels decorate the plaster walls of this wood-trimmed restaurant. Specialties ordered from the menu will cost from 65 AS ($3.46) to 190 AS ($10.11). This establishment is open all year except on Saturday evening, Sunday, and bank holidays.

The Iron Road, no. 115, northwest from Leoben leads to the old market town and ski area of—

VORDERNBERG/PRÄBICHL: The market town of Vordernberg lies at the foot of the Präbichl Pass in the heart of Upper Styria. On its east is the Hochschwab mountain range and on the west the Eisenerz (iron ore) Alps with the romantic Gesäuse canyon. Its alpine location makes this area attractive either as a summer resort or a winter holiday center. Vordernberg is the oldest center of the Styrian iron industry. Iron mining here is ancient, having been a pursuit of the Celts and the Romans.

On the town's Hauptplatz (main square), you can visit the **Iron Works Museum** (wheel works no. 4). The 17th-century **Pfarrkirche** (parish church) has in its graveyard tombs of former hammermill and wheel works owners. The town's **Laurentius Church** is from the 15th century. The **Rathaus** (town hall) still has its original tower and stucco ceiling. A richly decorated wrought-iron fountain dates from 1668. There are many splendid burghers' houses in Vordernberg.

The Präbichl, with its Polster and Grubl skiing areas, is well known as a ski center in Styria. A number of ski lifts lead up to the skiing grounds, with their well-prepared, avalanche-free slopes which allow skiing until April. A ski school, cross-country tracks, toboggan runs, curling and ice-skating rinks, and cleared footpaths are all part of the winter holiday scene.

Summer visitors can take mountain walks and climbs in the Hochschwab area and the Alps, to see the rich alpine flora. From May to October, guests can visit the Styrian Erzberg (ore mountain) on guided inspection tours.

Hotel Hubertushof, 36 Hauptstrasse (tel. 03849/214), is a contemporary chalet built into a gently sloping meadow. The cozy interior is comfortably filled with conservative modern furniture, lots of paneling, and rustic accessories. Per-person rates, with breakfast included, range from 250 AS ($13.30) to 300

AS ($15.96), depending on the season. All accommodations have private baths. Every Saturday and Sunday the management provides live music at a late afternoon "tea dance."

4. Murau

Lying on both sides of the Mur River at the foot of the Stolzalpe, which rises to nearly 6,000 feet, the old town of Murau is a winter ski region and also the center of many a summer excursion. It's easily reached from Salzburg via the Tauern motorway, as well as from Carinthia, Vienna, and the rest of Styria.

Murau's **pfarrkirche** (parish church) of St. Matthew dates from the 13th century. Note the "lanterns of the dead," a late Gothic sculpture in front of the church. Remnants of the medieval walls of the town can be seen.

Summer visitors enjoy high alpine tours. Two chair lifts will take you through the Murau recreation area. Skiers come here in winter especially for the fine cross-country tracks. The Murau center is a good place for rest and relaxation at any time of the year. It advertises itself as "not intended for the masses." It's a good family vacation spot.

In summer you can take a ride on an old steam-engine train on the narrow-gauge Murtal railway which goes through the Mur Valley on its run to Tamsweg in the neighboring province of Land Salzburg.

The 900-year-old **Stift St. Lambrecht** (convent of St. Lambrecht) with fine collections of ecclesiastical art and artifacts is nearby, as is the little romantic village of **Oberwölz**. Both are worth a visit. You can go also a short distance to **Wildbad Einöd** for thermal baths.

Murau's area code is 03532.

FOOD AND LODGING: Hotel Brauhaus (tel. 2437) is a solid-looking building set in front of a reflecting pool surrounded by seasonal flowers. Comfortable bedrooms rent for 250 AS ($13.30) in a single and for 200 AS ($10.64) to 310 AS ($16.49) per person in a double. These prices include a breakfast buffet. The establishment is better known for its restaurant, serving well-prepared meals on a flagstone-covered terrace or inside in a vaulted dining room. Directed by the Lercher family, the hotel includes a sauna. The location is within an easy walk of the village's sporting facilities.

Gasthof Lercher (tel. 2431) is a pleasantly designed, sunflower-colored building with white trim and a generously rambling design that includes several different sections. In the center of town, the hotel is directed by the Lercher family, who carefully maintain the flagstone-covered entrance hall and the rustically accommodating bar area. Singles cost 350 AS ($18.62) per day, while doubles rent for from 320 AS ($17.02) per person, with breakfast included.

5. Turracher Höhe

A section of Turracher Höhe was previewed above in the chapter on Carinthia (Chapter XII), but part of it is also in Styria, at the western end of the province on the pass over the Gurktal alpine range that leads into Carinthia. This is both a summer tourist center and a winter ski area.

The mountains surrounding the plateau (5,785 feet) on which Turracher Höhe is situated are excellent for hiking. The Turrachersee (Lake Turrach) is ideal for fishing, windsurfing, sailing, and rowing.

The Nock mountain range (7,875 feet) has wide, carefully prepared ski slopes, cross-country tracks, and marked winter hiking trails. T-bars and chair lifts are available, as is a ski school.

The area code for Turracher Höhe is 03533.

Seehotel Jägerwirt (tel. 8257) looks like a collection of lakeside chalets carefully joined together with low-lying reception areas and public rooms. The interior is filled with recreational facilities such as a sauna, a children's play area, tennis courts, bars, and restaurants, all of them mixed with a scattering of open fireplaces and rustic furniture. A lakeside terrace covered with flagstones provides a place for pleasant outdoor dinners in summer. The Brandstätter family are the accommodating hosts, charging from 590 AS ($31.39) to 840 AS ($44.69) per person in a double, with singles paying from 590 AS ($31.39) to 740 AS ($39.37). These prices include full board and use of the sauna, whirlpool, and indoor swimming pool. The hotel is open from June 10 until October 15 and from December 20 until April 25.

6. Dachstein-Tauern

In northwest Styria you'll find the major ski area in the province. The Dachstein, in the Salzkammergut, is a gigantic alpine mountain range cutting across Land Salzburg, Upper Austria, and Styria, with mammoth glaciers lying between its peaks. The Enns River separates the Dachstein and the Tauern massifs. This is the site of championship ski races and also the place for powder skiing.

The principal Styrian ski resorts, Schladming and Ramsau, are previewed below.

RAMSAU: At the foot of the mighty Dachstein massif, which reaches a height of nearly 10,000 feet, Ramsau is an emerging ski resort, rivaling but not yet surpassing Schladming (see below). The prices here are, in general, lower than those at Schladming. Ramsau lies on a high plateau to the north of Schladming.

The Ramsau area code is 03687.

Food and Lodging

Sporthotel Matschner (tel. 81721) is a double chalet whose identical wings are separated by a collection of flowered balconies. On the premises are an indoor swimming pool and supervised tennis courts with a resident coach. The hotel provides easy access to the many nearby sporting facilities. Rates range from 580 AS ($30.87) to 950 AS ($50.54) per person, with full board included, depending on the season and the accommodation. All rooms have private bath, radio, and balcony, and rates include participation in the organized sporting activities.

Alpengasthof Peter Rosegger (tel. 81223) is a pleasant chalet surrounded by larches and a grassy field, with a cozy interior of rustic furniture, country chintz, and exposed paneling. Fritz and Barbara Walcher are the young and attractive owners of this place, charging from 560 AS ($29.79) to 590 AS ($31.39) per person in high season, with a Styrian half board included. On the premises are a sauna, a fitness room, table tennis, and a paneled gaststube with a ceramic stove dating from 1667. There's also a summertime terrace.

Almfrieden Hotel (tel. 81753) is a contemporary chalet with two symmetrical wings joined by an interconnecting section. Set at the base of a rock-strewn mountain, the hotel looks out over a grassy meadow and a nearby sun terrace covered with parasols. The interior is rustically paneled with pine boards and dotted with open fireplaces and mountain-style chairs. Guests can use the sauna, solarium, TV room, fitness room, play table tennis and chess, or try marksmanship on the indoor rifle range, all on the premises. With full board included, rates per person range from 500 AS ($26.60) to 750 AS ($39.90) in rooms with private bath. Prices depend on the season and the accommodation.

Hotel Post (tel. 81708) is an attractively detailed chalet with summertime flowerboxes, heavy overhanging eaves, and an interior decor of rustic accessories and lots of paneling. On the premises are an indoor pool, a sauna, an elevator, a nearby cinema, and a restaurant and bar with an open fireplace. The Lackner family are your hosts, charging from 410 AS ($21.81) to 550 AS ($29.26) per person in a double and from 485 AS ($25.80) to 585 AS ($31.12) for a single, with full board included. Prices vary according to the season and the plumbing. Open December to October.

Pension Ennstalerhof (tel. 81080) is an attractive chalet with flowered balconies, a pleasant garden, and a warmly rustic interior with autumnal colors, Oriental rugs, big windows, and open fireplaces. In high season the pleasant and practical rooms with bath rent for 475 AS ($25.27) per person, with half board included.

Hotel Restaurant Pehab Kirchenwirt (tel. 81732) is a rambling balconied building in the shadow of the village church in the center of the resort. The pleasantly furnished interior is filled with warm colors, open fireplaces, and wrought-iron accents. On the premises are a bar, two restaurants, and a sauna. There is easy access to the nearby public indoor swimming pool and the ski facilities. The comfortable well-furnished rooms rent for 430 AS ($22.88) to 630 AS ($33.52) per person, with full board included.

Hotel Alpenkrone (tel. 81414) is a pleasantly balconied chalet in a sunny meadow, with a comfortably rustic interior filled with wood paneling and regional flowered fabrics. Alfred Pilz and his family are your congenial hosts, charging from 440 AS ($23.41) to 500 AS ($26.60) per person, with half board included. Prices are 125 AS ($6.65) lower off-season.

SCHLADMING/ROHRMOOS:
This skiing center is in the Dachstein-Tauern recreation and winter sports area on highway no. 308 and the Vienna-Bruck/Mur-Graz rail line, making it easy to reach. The Planai (6,235 feet) and the Hochwurzen (6,070 feet) have fast downhill runs and ski slopes, equipped with a cableway, five double-chair lifts, a connectable three-seat chair lift, ski buses, and 15 ski hoists, at all altitudes. Some 22,000 persons per hour can be transported.

The Dachstein-Südward cableway makes skiing at 8,865 feet possible in summer. There are ski schools, and you can leave small children at the kindergarten, which has a children's ski hoist.

Miles of winter footpaths make for good, invigorating walking. You can also enjoy horse sleighing, tobogganing, ski-bobbing, curling, game feeding trips, and many other winter activities. Cafés and bars offer lively après-ski, as do the hotels. In summer you'll enjoy mountaineering, swimming, tennis, bowling, and a lot of top-quality entertainment, along with warm Styrian hospitality.

Schladming is an ancient town lying in the upper valley of the Enns River between Dachstein to the north and Schladminger Tauern to the south. It was a silver- and copper-mining town in medieval times. Old miners' houses can still be seen in the town. The pfarrkirche (parish church) is late Gothic. An 1862 church in town is the largest Protestant church in Styria.

The area code for both resorts is 03687.

Food and Lodging at Schladming

Sporthotel Royer (tel. 23240), opened in 1975, offers a gracious and contemporary place to stay, with a large collection of sporting facilities. Conceived in a daringly modern design of recessed balconies and dramatically angled rooflines, the hotel has a big indoor as well as a heated outdoor swimming pool, two outdoor and three indoor tennis courts, two squash courts, three bowling alleys, pony riding for children up to 14 years old, and children's play facilities. There's easy access to the many outdoor ski and hiking trails in the vicinity. On the premises are a comfortably appointed bar area, a grill, and a rustic restaurant, as well as a more formal dining room. The warmly furnished bedrooms rent for 900 AS ($47.88) per person in high season, based on double occupancy, with half board included. Singles pay a daily surcharge of 175 AS ($9.31).

Romantik Hotel Alte Post, 10 Hauptplatz (tel. 22571). The first records of this historic restaurant in the center of town date from 1618. The facade is the kind of symmetrical chalet you'd expect in the hills nearby, with a round arched door and dark shutters. The renovated interior, in addition to being a popular restaurant, offers rooms priced from 465 AS ($24.74) per person, based on double occupancy, with half board costing another 150 AS ($7.98). Singles pay a daily surcharge of 100 AS ($5.32) per night.

In the high-ceilinged formal dining room, a sophisticated menu of nouvelle cuisine awaits gastronomes who make a meal here a special event. You might enjoy a mousse of chicken livers with leaf lettuce or a combination of wild salmon and fresh asparagus baked in an orange sauce, perhaps a ragoût of snails or aiguillettes of venison in a creamy sauce. Even if you're staying at the hotel, reservations are advised for full à la carte meals which average 225 AS ($11.97) or fixed-price menus ranging from between 140 AS ($7.45) and 375 AS ($19.95). The establishment is closed for most of November. Less formal meals are served in the rustic Knappenstube.

Haus Barbara, 553 Coburgstrasse (tel. 22077), is an attractively decorated three-story chalet with a picture of a female saint wielding a sword and carrying a chalice painted onto the facade. A short walk from the village, just opposite the Planai cable car, the hotel includes a bar with an open fireplace and a collection of pleasant rooms, each of which has a private bath, phone, and radio. Many of them also contain balconies. No meals are served other than breakfast, which is included in the price of 235 AS ($12.50) to 365 AS ($19.42) per person in a double and 275 AS ($14.63) to 400 AS ($21.28) for a single. Prices depend on the season.

Food and Lodging at Rohrmoos

Gasthof Waldfrieden (tel. 61487). Built by the Stocker family in 1964 and renovated in 1976, this hotel is a pleasantly sprawling chalet with festoons of summertime flowers hanging from its wooden balconies and painted decorations around many of its windows. Each of the 40 rooms has its own private bath, balcony, and phone. The in-house restaurant is pleasantly beamed, with lots of wooden accents. A flagstone-covered terrace provides a mountain vista in summer, while sports lovers will appreciate the many skiing and hiking facilities in the vicinity. High-season rates, with full board, range from 410 AS ($21.81) to 510 AS ($27.13) per person, double occupancy. Singles pay from 440 AS ($23.41) to 560 AS ($29.79) for a room and full board. The hotel is open from December to March and May to October.

Gasthof Sonneck (tel. 61232) is a simple balconied chalet with white walls, big windows, and wooden balconies. A flagstone-covered terrace provides a relaxing place for a midafternoon cup of coffee. The interior is pleasantly paneled and rustically outfitted with glowing pine and tasteful furniture. The rooms, which look out over the mountains, cost from 410 AS ($21.81) to 520 AS ($27.66) per person in high season for double occupancy, on the full-board plan. Open December to September.

Hotel Rohrmooserhof (tel. 61455) is an attractively proportioned chalet with long rows of wrap-around balconies and big windows to let sunlight stream into the simply furnished bedrooms. Set into the slope of an alpine hillside, the hotel has an outdoor pool, a pastry and confectionary shop, and a collection of public rooms accented with lots of wood paneling. Tennis courts and a wide range of sporting activities are close at hand. Depending on the season, rooms rent for 610 AS ($32.45) to 680 AS ($36.18), with full board. Open December to September.

Schwaigerhof (tel. 61422) is an attractively embellished five-story chalet with a prominent eyrie for a stork's nest jutting above the gently sloping roof and a hillside location with a view of the mountains. The interior contains an indoor swimming pool, lots of pine paneling, a bar, and two restaurants. Each of the bedrooms has its own bath, and a host of sporting facilities are available nearby. The Stocker family charge from 490 AS ($26.07) to 550 AS ($29.26) for a room and full board, based on double occupancy. Singles pay from 540 AS ($28.73) to 600 AS ($31.92), also on the full board plan. The hotel is open from December to October.

PICHL-MANDLING: Another well-known winter sports center is comprised of Pichl and its neighboring villages of Mandling, Gleiming, Preunegg, and Vorberg. In the Enns Valley, the center has the same accessibility by car, bus, or train as does Schladming/Rohrmoos (see above).

Pichl has avalanche-proof, prepared skiing grounds for users from beginners to experts, a cabin cableway, two double-chair lifts, and nine ski hoists. You'll find natural toboggan runs, curling rinks, a ski school, and a ski kindergarten. Nonskiers will enjoy walks along the cleared footpaths, folkloric events, and sleigh rides. The area is also a lure for summer visitors, who can explore the mountains on foot, swim, and make trips to surrounding attractions.

Pichl-Mandling's area code is 06454.

Alpengasthof-Hotel Pichlmayrgut (tel. 305) is one of the most distinctively styled hotels in the region. It stretches over a sprawling expanse of alpine hillside in various wings, one of which looks like a medieval castle with chevron shutters. A more recent addition is built in roughly the same style, with big windows, a rounded watchtower, and lots of stone masonry. On the premises are an indoor pool, 130 beds, a sauna, a bar, a café, two restaurants, and a host of additional facilities. Singles range from 575 AS ($30.59) to 640 AS ($34.05), while doubles cost from 610 AS ($32.45) to 660 AS ($35.11) with full board included. Open December to October.

7. From Tauplitz to Altaussee

The Styrian Salzkammergut, a section the province shares with both Upper Austria and Land Salzburg, is one of the most beautiful regions of Styria. In the northwest part of the province and long a summer holiday center, this is rapidly developing as a winter ski resort area as well. This area is just to the southwest of the Land Salzburg lake district.

TAUPLITZ/TAUPLITZALM: Ranking among the most popular winter sports centers and recreation areas in Austria, Tauplitz and its pasture and lake district, Tauplitzalm, are also good for summer holidays.

The Tauplitzalm can be approached from Tauplitz by chair lift, and the scenic mountain area is a fine country for hiking You can enjoy swimming, tennis, mini-golf, folkloric entertainment, and dancing, plus 5 p.m. tea. The Tauplitzalm can also be reached from Bad Mitterndorf (see below) on the Tauplitzalm alpine road.

In winter the flying ski jump on the Kulm near Tauplitz is a constant attraction. The two places account for more than a dozen ski lifts, ski schools with special children's courses, and long-distance running schools for walking on skis. This is a training center for domestic and foreign national ski teams.

The area code for Tauplitz/Tauplitzalm is 03688.

Food and Lodging at Tauplitz

Gasthof/Pension Horst Hechl (tel. 268) is an imposingly Teutonic-looking building set in front of an outdoor tennis court, with an outdoor swimming pool in back. The gabled and hipped roof contains a series of attractively decorated bedrooms, which cost from 380 AS ($20.22) per person, with half board included. On the premises are a sauna, a bar, and salons with wintertime fireplaces and lots of paneling.

Pension/Café Sonnenuhr (tel. 2256) is a generously proportioned alpine-style house with a gabled roof, four stories of wood-framed windows, and lots of encircling balconies. A low-lying extension off to one side has a big terrace on top. The interior is filled with contrasting patterns and colors and big-windowed views of the surrounding mountains. Rates range from 365 AS ($19.42) to 400 AS ($21.28) per person daily, double occupancy, with full board included. Singles pay a daily surcharge of 30 AS ($1.60). Open December to September.

Food and Lodging at Tauplitzalm

Sporthotel Kirchenwirt (tel. 306) is a sprawling balconied chalet built into the side of a mountain. Many of the walls are covered with cedar shingles, while the interior is a cozy combination of knotty-pine paneling, freshly imaginative colors, and rustic accents. On the premises are a covered swimming pool, a sauna, a day bar, a sun terrace, and tasteful rooms costing 475 AS ($25.27) to 650 AS ($34.58) per person daily in high season, with half board included. Prices vary with the plumbing and the season.

BAD MITTERNDORF: Long renowned as a health spa in the Salzkammergut, Bad Mitterndorf's proximity to Tauplitz has made it a ski center as well. Lying in the southern foothills of the Totes Gebirge, Bad Heilbrunn, 1¼ miles to the south, is a satellite of Bad Mitterndorf. Salza-Stausee, a lake, is south of the village.

The area code for Bad Mitterndorf is 06153.

Food and Lodging

Kur und Sporthotel Bad Heilbrunn (tel. 2486) is a striking modern hotel complex that rises abruptly from the forested hillside into which it was built. On the premises are both an indoor and an outdoor swimming pool, plus a wide range of physical therapy and spa facilities. Many of the contemporary bedrooms have private balconies and baths, along with all the modern conveniences. Singles range from 610 AS ($32.45) to 890 AS ($47.35), while doubles run from 800 AS ($42.56) to 940 AS ($50.01) per person, depending on the exposure, the accommodation, and the season. These prices include full board.

Hubertushof (tel. 2595) is a well-designed chalet with four floors of balconies, big windows, and wood trim. The tasteful interior is outfitted with rustic furniture, wood ceilings, and earth colors. Charges for bed and full board range from 395 AS ($21.01) to 420 AS ($22.34) per person. The hotel is open from December to October.

Hotel Kogler (tel. 2325) has a chalet facade and a T-shaped floor plan. Its balconies are usually draped with summertime flowers, while a verdant garden stretches away from the big windows of the ground-floor reception area. The cost of a bed and full board ranges from 420 AS ($22.34) to 600 AS ($31.92) per person, depending on the season.

Pension Lord (tel. 2553) is an attractively simple chalet whose uncomplicated design includes wooden balconies stretching across part of the facade and a big picture window piercing through a section of the ground floor. Five minutes on foot from the center of the village, the hotel offers an indoor pool, lots of mountain views, and a rustically modern interior filled with comfortable furniture. Gertrude Praesoll is your accommodating host, charging from 330 AS ($17.56) to 350 AS ($18.62) per person in a single or double, with full board. The hotel is open from December to March and May to September.

Grimmingwurz'n (tel. 3132) is an elegantly rustic restaurant which draws a steady stream of loyal local diners. The menu ranges from regionally inspired to international. Food items include cream of snail soup, plus an array of fish, ragoûts, and meat, particularly veal. Desserts feature a range of seasonally adjusted fruited pastries and sorbets. À la carte meals range from 150 AS ($7.98) to 400 AS ($21.28), while fixed-price menus cost from 225 AS ($11.97) to 650 AS ($34.58). It's closed from mid-November to mid-December.

IRDNING: Instead of staying at Tauplitz or Bad Mitterndorf, you might want to take a secondary road leading to one of the most beautiful hotels in Europe, where guests can find facilities for rest and recreation.

Hotel Schloss Pichlarn (tel. 03682/2841). Some parts of this sprawling castle are more than 800 years old. Other sections are undeniably modern, including the up-to-date amenities in the comfortable rooms. The entrance is through an arched door covered with chevron designs. The interior is accented with soaring arches, ornate chandeliers, and thick Oriental carpets. The bedrooms are filled with fine antiques and tasteful colors, while on the premises are an elegant dining room, an accommodating bar area, an outdoor terrace, and a range of sporting facilities including an indoor and outdoor pool, a sauna, massage facilities, and a beauty salon. Many other attractions lie a short distance away. Prices range from 1,250 AS ($66.50) to 1,850 AS ($98.42) in a single and from 1,180 AS ($62.78) to 1,660 AS ($88.31) per person in a double, depending on the accommodation and the season. Full board is included in these tariffs.

BAD AUSSEE: Surrounded by lake, mountains, and woods, Bad Aussee is an old market town and spa in the "green heart" of the Salzkammergut. It lies in the Valley of Traun, with the Totes Gebirge and the Dachstein massif visible in the distance. The ideal time to visit this salt- and mineral-spring spa is in June, when fields of narcissus burst into bloom, one of the most spectacular signs of spring coming to Europe.

Bad Aussee, at the confluence of a pair of upper branches of the Traun River, is considered the capital of the Styrian section of the Salzkammergut. Only three miles to the north is Lake Altaussee, with the spa town of Altaussee (see below) on its shore.

In summer this is a good center for walking and climbing in one of the most beautiful sections of Austria. Although Bad Aussee has long been known as a summer spa resort, it has also developed into a winter ski center, with the location of several ski lifts nearby making it attractive to ski enthusiasts.

Bad Aussee's best-known association is with Archduke Johann of the House of Habsburg. In 1827 he married the daughter of a local postmaster, an occurrence that in that era and within the empire was a *cause célèbre* that rivaled the romance of the Duke and Duchess of Windsor. A statue of the "Prince of Styria," Johann, can be seen in the Kurpark.

Incidentally, the Bad Aussee Glaubersalt spring is said to be particularly effective for losing weight, but I can't vouch for the truth of that claim.

The area code for Bad Aussee is 06152.

Food and Lodging

Eurotel Erzherzog Johann, 62 Kurhausplatz (tel. 2507), is a conservatively designed, lemon-colored building with stone detailing, forest-green trim, and an arched entranceway in the center of town. The rustic interior offers a handful of wintertime fireplaces, beamed ceilings, and comfortably up-to-date furniture, as well as easy access to the area's sporting facilities. The spa facilities are connected to the hotel by a covered passageway. Twin-bedded rooms rent for 620 AS ($32.98) to 740 AS ($39.37) per person, while singles go for 720 AS ($38.30) to 840 AS ($44.69). These prices include half board and vary according to the season.

Pension/Villa Kristina (tel. 2017) is a regionally styled villa about five minutes on foot from the center of town. The steep-roofed, wood-trimmed house is loaded inside and out with dozens of handcrafted details, a scattering of antiques, and all the modern amenities. Surrounded by a flowering park, the hotel offers shaded terraces as well as balconies adjoining some of the pleasantly furnished rooms. The Raudaschl family, your obliging hosts, charge from 500 AS ($26.60) to 575 AS ($30.59) in a single and from 475 AS ($25.27) to 525 AS ($27.93) per person in a double. The supplement for an apartment is 150 AS ($7.98) daily. All prices quoted are for half board. The rates vary slightly according to the season.

Hotel Wasnerin (tel. 2108) was established in 1860 as a hotel for visiting nature lovers, although the building you see today was constructed in 1934. Built with generously rambling proportions, in a gabled and hip-roofed style with lots of exposed wood and elegantly arched windows looking out on a raised sun terrace, the hotel offers simply decorated bedrooms for 280 AS ($14.90) to 360 AS ($19.15) per person, double occupancy, with full board. Singles pay 380 AS ($20.22) to 420 AS ($22.34) for a room and full board. Prices depend on the season and the plumbing. Open December to September.

Lewandofsky (tel. 2571) welcomes a loyal crowd of clients into its old-fashioned dining room which serves a wide range of strictly Austrian pastries along with coffee. The summertime garden area adjoins the city park and offers a view over the central square of town, as well as of the people flocking to the spa facilities for "the cure." Coffee costs from 18 AS (96¢) to 25 AS ($1.33), and pastries average 22 AS ($1.17).

ALTAUSSEE: This is a more tranquil spot for a stopover than Bad Aussee nearby. It also lies in the Styrian section of the Salzkammergut. Lake Altaussee, facing the Totes Gebirge, is one of the most beautiful bodies of water in Styria. It's about two miles long, with rowboats for rent so that you can explore its area. For many decades Altaussee was only a lakeside summer resort, but because of the nearby ski region of Mount Loser (4,995 feet), it now does a winter ski trade as well. From Altaussee you can see the Dachstein glacier.

From Altaussee trips can be arranged in summer to the **Aussee Salt Mines,** two miles to the northwest. Conducted tours, lasting about an hour and 25 minutes, are offered from 10 a.m. to 4 p.m. daily, except Sunday, costing 70 AS ($3.72). The mines, called Salzbergwerk, were used by the Nazis to store valuable art to prevent its destruction by Allied bombing raids.

The Altaussee area code is 06152.

Food and Lodging

Hotel Seevilla, 60 Fischerndorf (tel. 71302), is a romantic villa with arched windows, hipped roofs, and lots of exterior detailing. The interior contains deeply coffered ceilings, exposed wood, and a curving stone staircase leading to the tasteful bedrooms. On the premises are a bathing beach and an indoor pool, as well as a restaurant and café at the lake, and there is access to a wide range of nearby sporting facilities. Each of the units has a private bath, balcony, minibar, radio, and TV hookup. The Maislinger family charges from 565 AS

($30.06) to 735 AS ($39.10) per person in a double and from 625 AS ($33.25) to 1,020 AS ($54.26) in a single, with half board included.

Hotel Kitzer (tel. 71227) is a beautifully detailed chalet with a Viennese-style restaurant on the ground floor. Visitors will find a popular sun terrace dotted with parasols in summer, as well as a tastefully paneled interior with lots of accessories, including a dome-topped ceramic stove. The Berndl family are the conscientious owners, charging from 440 AS ($23.41) to 510 AS ($27.13) per person, with full board included. Prices vary slightly with the season.

Gasthof zum Loser, 80 Fischerndorf (tel. 71373), is one of the best restaurants in the region, with a body of local folklore to fill a volume and a loyal clientele that includes actors and poets from as far away as Vienna and California. Many of the fish served here are caught in the nearby lake, and some of the best ones are smoked in the restaurant's own smokehouse nearby. Every Thursday owner Hans Glaser hosts a musical evening, which is the most fun event in town. Glaser himself plays the bass-fiddle. His wife Heidi and their children are a visible presence at the restaurant. Framed on the walls of the restaurant are signed photographs of satisfied clients.

In addition to the smoked fish, specialties include wild game dishes, saddle of venison, wild mushroom soup, Styrian-style pork in cabbage, and homemade spätzle. The restaurant is closed the last week in March until mid-April and between the first of October and December 20. À la carte meals cost from 125 AS ($6.65) to 375 AS ($19.95). You can stay here on full-board terms, ranging from 525 AS ($27.93) to 530 AS ($28.20) per person daily. The hotel is open from December to September.

8. Bruck an der Mur

A while back, at Leoben we headed west to take in the resorts and attractions of West Styria. If we had continued north along the Mur River instead, I would have brought you to Bruck an der Mur, at the point in the Styrian alpine range where the Mur and the Mürz flow together. The ruined fortress of Lanskron looks down on the bustling industrial town of Bruck, where factories process iron ore.

The area code of Bruck an der Mur is 03862.

THE SIGHTS: The main attraction of the principal plaza (Hauptplatz) of the town is the **Eiserner Brunne,** a lacy wrought-iron well, done in 1626, one of the finest existing examples of Styrian ironwork.

Also on the Hauptplatz stands the most impressive building in Bruck, the 15th-century **Kornmesserhaus.** Some of it is in the flamboyant Gothic style, while other architectural parts are based on designs of the Renaissance. It has a splendid loggia and arcades.

The **Pfarrkirche** (parish church) is on the Kirchplatz (church square). Its major treasure is a sacristy door which, like the fountain just visited on the Hauptplatz, is of wrought iron, circa 16th century.

FOOD AND LODGING: Hotel Bauer (Zum Schwarzen Adler) (tel. 51331), dating from 1683, is better known as the inner-village restaurant than as a hotel, although it does offer a limited number of rooms to guests who willingly choose to eat in the restaurant as well. The smallish but well-furnished double rooms usually have modern bath and much comfort. Doubles cost 625 AS ($33.25), while singles rent for 395 AS ($21.01), with breakfast included. The restaurant is host to a swelling crowd of local diners, who sit either in the main dining room or in the rustically decorated stüberl. Dishes include venison pâté with cumberland sauce, an array of roast meats with noodles, and homemade pastries, some of them richly covered with whipped cream. À la carte meals range from 115 AS ($6.12) to 270 AS ($14.36).

Hotel/Restaurant Bayer, Hauptplatz (tel. 51218), next door to the Rathaus, offers friendly service, comfortable rooms, and good food, right in the heart of town. The bathrooms and many of the furnishings have recently been remodeled or replaced, under the direction of the owners, Sepp and Helga Bayer. Doubles range from 420 AS ($22.34) to 700 AS ($37.24), with singles going for 225 AS ($11.97) to 500 AS ($26.60), breakfast included. Half board in the family-style restaurant is another 125 AS ($6.65) per person daily.

FROHNLEITEN: South of Bruck an der Mur you'll come to an Austrian golfing center with an 18-hole international championship course. Long before it discovered golf, however, Frohnleiten was already an ancient town. It has a pfarrkirche (parish church) with rococo embellishments, and to the southwest of town stands a castle from the Middle Ages, **Rabenstein Castle.** It was constructed on the foundations of a Roman fort, and when the baroque craze swept Austria, the castle was not spared.

The town also has an **alpine garden** stretching across 22 acres and exhibiting more than 10,000 species from nearly all the continents of the world where plants grow.

You may want to dine at **Weissenbacher** (tel. 03126/2334), on the road to Graz, which serves well-prepared and traditional Austrian food such as fresh asparagus in season, and ham, cheese, beef, and chicken dishes to a loyal crowd of clients who appreciate the large portions and the rich desserts. À la carte meals range from 110 AS ($5.85) to 215 AS ($11.44).

WEIZ: If you're seeking reasonable accommodations in the area, you can drive east from Frohnleiten along a twisting secondary road until you reach Weiz. This is a typical Styrian town—clean and neat, the new blending harmoniously with the old, and mountains forming a backdrop.

Weiz is often visited by Austrians who like to ride on its narrow-gauge railway, running on Saturday from July to September. The twin-towered church here was built in the 1600s as a fortress against Turkish invaders from the east.

Romantik-Hotel Modersnhof (tel. 03172/3747) looks like an enlarged private house with big arched windows on the ground floor and a long row of cutout wooden balconies. It actually has a history of at least 250 years, and the well-furnished public rooms offer dozens of cozy seating areas with views over the quiet landscape around it. A curving iron staircase leads up to the bedrooms, all with bathroom, color TV, radio, and hair-dryers. Units rent for 550 AS ($29.26) to 820 AS ($43.62) per person in a double, from 725 AS ($38.57) to 980 AS ($52.14) in a single for the room and half board.

The pleasant dining room offers a menu which is considered one of the finest in this part of Austria. There is a small but well-chosen selection of specialties which include cream of tomato soup, trout filet, veal filet "house style" (with rosemary, mushrooms, and hollandaise sauce), and an array of fresh salads and homemade desserts. À la carte meals range from 195 AS ($10.37) to 400 AS ($21.28), while fixed-price meals cost 325 AS ($17.29) and 500 AS ($26.60). The restaurant is closed Monday, and reservations are suggested.

9. Aflenz Kurort

This is one of the best bases you can find if you want to go mountain climbing in the Hochschwab. It has a reputation as both a summer resort and a winter sports site. Aflenz Kurort (5,095 feet) can be reached from Kapfenberg in about half an hour.

In winter the attraction is the chair lift to Bürgeralm, which has a ski tow. In summer the chair lift is used by climbers exploring the Hochschwab mountains.

The Aflenz Kurort area code is 03861.

FOOD AND LODGING: Aflenzerhof (tel. 2245). The oldest part of this hip-roofed stucco house was built in the 15th century, although since then it has been considerably modernized to include 1960s-style accessories and vivid colors which complement the thick walls and the vaulted ceilings. Guests who prefer more up-to-date accommodations can stay in the nearby annex, built in a big-windowed modern style with lots of wood trim and pleasant landscaping in a flowered garden. The Schaffenberger family charges from 345 AS ($18.35) to 450 AS ($23.94) per person in a single or double with private bath, including full board. Open December to October.

Hubertushof (tel. 31310) is a dignified stucco house with flowerboxes and green shutters at the windows, as well as a gabled roofline looking out over stately shade trees. The interior is a colorful assemblage of furniture covered with contrasting patterns and country-style accessories. The charge for bed and full board range from 330 AS ($17.56) to 385 AS ($20.48) per person, based on double occupancy. Singles pay a daily surcharge of 30 AS ($1.60) on the same full-board plan. Open December to October.

Specialties in the restaurant include all kinds of Austrian-style sausages, served with black bread, and the kinds of caloric desserts that will send you jogging the next morning. A la carte meals cost between 80 AS ($4.26) and 200 AS ($10.64).

Alpengasthof Gollner (Bürgeralm) (tel. 2426). In winter this attractive alpine hotel can only be reached by chair lift, although if you don't have a car you'll enjoy the ride up even in summer. The interior is pleasantly furnished with unpretentious taste by the Gollner family, who do everything they can to make guests feel at home. None of the rooms has a private bath, but toilets and showers are easily accessible. Per-person rates, with half board included, are 275 AS ($14.63) daily.

10. Mariazell

Mariazell is the most celebrated pilgrimage center in Austria, in addition to being a winter playground and a summer resort. It is the national shrine of Austria, Hungary, and Bohemia.

The object of pilgrimage is a church dating from the dawn of the 13th century, with three prominent towers. It was originally constructed in the Romanesque style then fashionable, and a Gothic choir was built on in the latter 14th century. The bulbous domes are baroque, a style laid on most of Austria's churches in the 17th century. Fischer von Erlach, both senior and junior, baroque architects by now familiar to readers of this guide, aided in the Mariazell transformation. In the church is the grave of the world-famous Hungarian, Cardinal Mindszenty, and the Mindszenty Museum. In 1983, Pope John Paul II visited Mariazell and the cardinal's burial place.

In the treasury are votive offerings accrued over some 600 years. The Chapel of Grace is considered the national shrine of Austria. Miracles are attributed to its statue of the Virgin, giving rise to fame that spread all over Europe. The statue is mounted on an altar designed by the younger von Erlach. In summer large groups gather on Saturday night for torchlit processions to the church.

The treasury is open from the first of May until the end of October from 10 a.m. to noon. Admission is 15 AS (80¢).

Over the years Mariazell has attracted much royalty, some of the Habsburgs, in particular, being fond of this village.

Many fathers take their children to Mariazell to teach them how to ski, a generations-old tradition. Here are all the appurtenances of a modern winter sports and recreation center: avalanche-proof grounds for skiers of all skills, a cableway, a chair lift, numerous ski hoists, a natural toboggan run, a skating rink, a ski school, and a ski kindergarten. Mariazell is a winter holiday center for the whole family.

Its high altitude and good, brisk climate make this a favored summer vacation site, with a multitude of recreational pursuits to choose among. You can go walking on about 125 miles of footpaths, mountaineering, swimming, rowing, sailing, windsurfing, canoeing, fishing, horseback riding, glider flying, and camping, or you can play tennis or golf.

For the most dramatic views in the area, take a chair lift to Gemeindealpe (5,335 feet) or a cableway to Bürgeralpe (4,170 feet), leaving from the center of town. The round-trip fare for the chair lift is 90 AS ($4.79) and for the cableway 70 AS ($3.72). Both the modes of transportation operate daily from 9 to 11:30 a.m. and 1 to 4:30 p.m. They are closed in November.

The area code for Mariazell is 03882.

FOOD AND LODGING: Hotel Feichtegger (tel. 2416) is a centrally located, flat-roofed, five-story hotel with evenly spaced rows of recessed balconies. The angularity of the facade is relieved with masses of flowers in the window boxes. Inside you'll find a rustically modern bar area, a restaurant, a paneled tavern, and sunny, comfortably decorated bedrooms. With breakfast included, rates range from 205 AS ($10.91) to 350 AS ($18.62) in a single and from 240 AS ($12.77) to 325 AS ($17.29) per person in a double.

Scherfler's Hotel Goldenes Kreuz (tel. 2309). The ground-floor facade of this hotel near the basilica has been severely modernized, but the upper stories still retain the rococo detailing and white trim of the year they were built. The interior has lots of elegant accessories, two restaurants (one modern and one regionally paneled), and attractively furnished rooms filled with provincial designs painted on the comfortable furniture. With half board included, the per-person rate in a double is 475 AS ($25.27), with singles paying a daily surcharge of 35 AS ($1.86).

Hotel Goldene Krone (tel. 2583) is an old Styrian house with substantial proportions, stone trim, and a steeply pitched gabled roof next to the basilica. Most of the solidly constructed furniture was added when the hotel was remodeled. On the premises is a contemporary bar area with decorative masonry accents, plus a simple restaurant and comfortable bedrooms. These rent for 325 AS ($17.29) to 380 AS ($20.22) per person in a double, with half board included. Singles pay a daily surcharge of 45 AS ($2.39). The Moser family are the helpful managers.

PRENTICE HALL PRESS   Date_____

ONE GULF + WESTERN PLAZA, NEW YORK, NY 10023

Friends, please send me the books checked below:

$-A-DAY GUIDES

(In-depth guides to low-cost tourist accommodations and facilities.)

☐ Europe on $25 a Day $12.95
☐ Australia on $25 a Day $10.95
☐ Eastern Europe on $25 a Day (avail.
   Oct. '86) $10.95
☐ England on $35 a Day............. $10.95
☐ Greece on $25 a Day.............. $10.95
☐ Hawaii on $45 a Day $10.95
☐ India on $15 & $25 a Day $9.95
☐ Ireland on $35 a Day.............. $10.95
☐ Israel on $30 & $35 a Day $10.95

☐ Mexico on $20 a Day $10.95
☐ New Zealand on $35 a Day $10.95
☐ New York on $45 a Day $9.95
☐ Scandinavia on $40 a Day.......... $10.95
☐ Scotland and Wales on $35 a Day..... $10.95
☐ South America on $25 a Day $9.95
☐ Spain and Morocco (plus the Canary
   Is.) on $40 a Day $10.95
☐ Washington, D.C., on $40 a Day $10.95

DOLLARWISE GUIDES

(Guides to accommodations and facilities from budget to deluxe, with emphasis on the medium-priced.)

☐ Austria & Hungary $11.95
☐ Egypt............................ $11.95
☐ England & Scotland $11.95
☐ France $11.95
☐ Germany......................... $11.95
☐ Italy $11.95
☐ Japan & Hong Kong $11.95
☐ Portugal (incl. Madeira & the Azores) . $11.95
☐ Switzerland & Liechtenstein $11.95
☐ Bermuda & The Bahamas........... $10.95
☐ Canada $12.95
☐ Caribbean $12.95

☐ Cruises (incl. Alaska, Carib, Mex,
   Hawaii, Panama, Canada, & US) $12.95
☐ California & Las Vegas $11.95
☐ Florida.......................... $10.95
☐ New England $11.95
☐ Northwest $11.95
☐ Skiing in Europe (avail. Oct. '86) ... $12.95
☐ Skiing USA—East $10.95
☐ Skiing USA—West $10.95
☐ Southeast & New Orleans $11.95
☐ Southwest $11.95
☐ Texas (avail. Oct. '86).............. $11.95

THE ARTHUR FROMMER GUIDES

(Pocket-size guides to tourist accommodations and facilities in all price ranges.)

☐ Amsterdam/Holland $5.95
☐ Athens........................... $5.95
☐ Atlantic City/Cape May $5.95
☐ Boston........................... $5.95
☐ Cancún/Cozumel/Yucatán $5.95
☐ Dublin/Ireland $5.95
☐ Hawaii $5.95
☐ Las Vegas $5.95
☐ Lisbon/Madrid/Costa del Sol $5.95
☐ London $5.95
☐ Los Angeles $5.95

☐ Mexico City/Acapulco $5.95
☐ Montreal/Quebec City $5.95
☐ New Orleans $5.95
☐ New York........................ $5.95
☐ Orlando/Disney World/EPCOT $5.95
☐ Paris $5.95
☐ Philadelphia...................... $5.95
☐ Rome $5.95
☐ San Francisco $5.95
☐ Washington, D.C................... $5.95

SPECIAL EDITIONS

☐ Bed & Breakfast—N. America $7.95
☐ Fast 'n' Easy Phrase Book
   (Fr/Ger/Ital/Sp in one vol.) $6.95
☐ Guide for the Disabled Traveler....... $10.95
☐ How to Beat the High Cost of Travel ... $4.95
☐ Marilyn Wood's Wonderful Weekends
   (NY, Conn, Mass, RI, Vt, NJ, Del, Pa). $9.95
☐ Motorist's Phrase Book (Fr/Ger/Sp) ... $4.95
☐ Museums in New York $8.95

☐ Shopper's Guide to the Caribbean
   (avail. Oct. '86) $11.95
☐ Shopper's Guide to the Best Buys in
   England, Scotland & Wales......... $10.95
☐ Swap and Go (Home Exchanging) $10.95
☐ Travel Diary and Record Book........ $5.95
☐ Where to Stay USA (Lodging from $3
   to $30 a night) $9.95

In U.S. include $1 post. & hdlg. for 1st book; 25¢ ea. add'l. book. Outside U.S. $2 and 50¢ respectively.

Enclosed is my check or money order for $_____

NAME_____

ADDRESS_____

CITY_____ STATE_____ ZIP_____